PLACES OF THE UNDERGROUND RAILROAD

PLACES OF THE UNDERGROUND RAILROAD

A Geographical Guide

Tom Calarco, with Cynthia Vogel, Kathryn Grover, Rae Hallstrom, Sharron L Pope, and Melissa Waddy-Thibodeaux

AN IMPRINT OF ABC-CLIO, LLC
Santa Barbara, California • Denver, Colorado • Oxford, England

Library of Congress Cataloging-in-Publication Data

Calarco, Tom, 1947–
   Places of the Underground Railroad : a geographical guide / Tom Calarco ; with Cynthia Vogel [et al.].
       p. cm.
   Includes bibliographical references and index.
       ISBN 978–0–313–38146–1 (hard copy : alk. paper) — ISBN 978–0–313–38147–8 (ebook)
1. Underground Railroad—Guidebooks. 2. Historic sites—United States—Guidebooks.
3. Historic sites—Canada—Guidebooks. 4. Fugitive slaves—United States—History—19th
century. 5. Fugitive slaves—Canada—History—19th century. 6. Abolitionists—United States—
History—19th century. 7. Abolitionists—Canada—History—19th century. 8. Antislavery
movements—United States—History—19th century. 9. Antislavery movements—Canada—
History—19th century. I. Vogel, Cynthia. II. Title.
E450.C39   2011
973.7'115—dc22   2010025116

ISBN: 978–0–313–38146–1
EISBN: 978–0–313–38147–8

15 14 13 12 11   1 2 3 4 5

This book is also available on the World Wide Web as an eBook.
Visit www.abc-clio.com for details.

Greenwood
An Imprint of ABC-CLIO, LLC

ABC-CLIO, LLC
130 Cremona Drive, P.O. Box 1911
Santa Barbara, California 93116-1911

This book is printed on acid-free paper ∞

Manufactured in the United States of America

CONTENTS

LIST OF ENTRIES

GUIDE TO RELATED TOPICS

Border Towns
Amherstburg, Ontario
Cincinnati, Ohio
Clermont County, Ohio
    (Bethel, Moscow, New Richmond,
    Felicity, Williamsburg)
Louisville, Kentucky
Madison, Indiana
Marietta, Ohio
Maysville/Augusta, Kentucky
New Albany, Indiana
Niagara Falls, New York/Ontario
Quincy, Illinois
Ripley, Ohio
Wheeling, (West) Virginia
Wilmington, Delaware

**Renditions/Recoveries of Fugitive
    Slaves in Behalf of Slaveowners**
Albany, New York
Baltimore, Maryland
Boston, Massachusetts
Cassopolis, Michigan
Cincinnati, Ohio
Chicago, Illinois
Chillicothe, Ohio
Cleveland, Ohio
Columbus, Ohio
Detroit, Michigan

Harrisburg, Pennsylvania
Indianapolis, Indiana
Madison, Indiana
New Albany, Indiana
New York, New York
Philadelphia, Pennsylvania
Pittsburgh, Pennsylvania
Quincy, Illinois
Ripley, Ohio
Rocky Fork/Alton, Illinois
Sandusky, Ohio
Wilmington, Delaware

**Rescues of Fugitive Slaves from
    Attempted Renditions**
Boston, Massachusetts
Cincinnati, Ohio
Detroit, Michigan
Mechanicsburg, Ohio
New York, New York
Oberlin, Ohio
Philadelphia, Pennsylvania
Princeton, Illinois
Sandusky, Ohio
Southeastern Pennsylvania
Syracuse, New York
Tabor, Iowa
Troy, New York
Washington, D.C.

Schools for Blacks
Adrian, Lenawee County, Michigan
Buxton, Ontario
Chillicothe, Ohio
Cincinnati, Ohio
Columbus, Ohio
Eleutherian College/Lancaster,
    Indiana
Erie, Pennsylvania
Farmington, Connecticut
Oberlin, Ohio
Pittsburgh, Pennsylvania
Ripley, Ohio
Washington, D.C.
Wilmington, Delaware

Terminals
Burlington, Vermont
Chicago, Illinois

Cleveland, Ohio
Detroit, Michigan
Erie, Pennsylvania
Niagara Falls, New York/Ontario
Oswego, New York
Rochester, New York
St. Albans, Vermont
Sandusky, Ohio

Vigilance Committees
Albany, New York
Boston, Massachusetts
Chicago, Illinois
Cincinnati, Ohio
Detroit, Michigan
New York, New York
Philadelphia, Pennsylvania
Syracuse, New York
Troy, New York

LIST OF ILLUSTRATIONS

Maps

LIST OF SIDEBARS

PREFACE

Places of the Underground Railroad: A Geographical Guide presents a geographic overview of the Underground Railroad. Entries were chosen in part to reflect representation from all regions of the United States and Canada. Efforts, when applicable, were made to link the locations and show that a network existed, though often decentralized and variable over time and place. It is not meant to be comprehensive. Any such survey would require numerous volumes, but care has been taken not to exclude any of the most significant locations.

This book supplies researchers, students, and academics with a broad picture of the Underground Railroad, using up-to-date information. It covers the beginnings of organized aid to fugitive slaves during the period following the American Revolution up to the Civil War, and does this through the stories of various locations, primarily north of the Mason-Dixon Line. It also delineates the routes fugitive slaves may have taken, with three entries that identify the rivers, canals, seaports, and railroads that were sometimes used, as well as showing in the entries the relationships that were developed among conductors in various locations—features that make this a truly unique reference work on the Underground Railroad.

In addition to the listing of the entries in the front of the book, there are listings by geography and category. The latter includes entries in the book that fit the following: Border Towns, which were important places on crossing points between the North and the South, or the United States and Canada; Renditions, which includes places where fugitive slaves were apprehended and returned to slavery; Rescues, which lists places where notable rescues of fugitive slaves from slave-catchers or law enforcement authorities were made; Schools for Blacks, which lists places with early schools for blacks and fugitive slaves; Terminals, which were gateways to Canada; and Vigilance Committees, which lists places with notable, organized Underground Railroad committees.

"In dealing with history rather than legend," Larry Gara wrote in *Liberty Line*, "each local story should be investigated, the basis for the tradition examined, and the sources evaluated."[1] The objective of this book has been to do just, and to encourage the continued investigation of the Underground Railroad and the unraveling of its mysteries. We have only begun to bring to light the many neglected stories that are among our nation's most dramatic moments.

Tom Calarco
2010

NOTE

1. Larry Gara, *Liberty Line,* Lexington: University of Kentucky Press, 1961: 192.

ACKNOWLEDGMENTS

The authors would like to thank those who contributed to our presentation of the most accurate picture of the Underground Railroad currently possible. These include Friends of Dr. Richard Eells House in Quincy, Illinois; the Allen County Library in Fort Wayne, Indiana; the Levi Coffin House in Fountain City, Indiana; Jae Breitweiser and Historic Eleutherian College in Lancaster, Indiana; the Randolph County Historical Society in Winchester, Indiana; the Lenawee County Historical Society in Adrian, Michigan; Gwendolyn Mayer of the Hudson, Ohio, Library; the Hanby House in Westerville, Ohio; Sherry Sawchuck, of the Mount Pleasant, Ohio, Historical Society; the Westfield Washington (Indiana) Historical Society; the Ohio Historical Society in Columbus; the Muskingum, Ohio, County Public Library in Zanesville; the Worch Memorial Library in Versailles, Ohio; the Mechanicsburg Public Library in Mechanicsburg, Ohio; and Gary Knepp. We also would like to thank those who have continually supported our work, including the North Country Underground Railroad Historical Association, Bryan and Shannon Prince, Chris Densmore, Kate Larson, Owen Muelder, Diane Coon, Judith Wellman, Fergus Bordewich, Scott Christianson, Randy Mills, Graham Hodges, Steve Strimer, and Peter Michael, editor of the *Underground Railroad Free Press*.

INTRODUCTION

The Underground Railroad is primarily a story of good Samaritans helping their fellow brothers and sisters along various routes to freedom. To say that it was merely the good guys (abolitionists) against the bad guys (slaveholders), however, is oversimplifying a very complex situation. Racism was pervasive in the North as well as the South, and even among many abolitionists. This racism was institutionalized because of the profit motive of slavery, and it took nearly a century of superhuman effort by thousands of individuals to finally end it. It is another version of the classic story of the struggle of humanity to overcome greed that has plagued its efforts to create the perfect society since the beginning of civilization, and it has important lessons for us today.

The Underground Railroad took shape as it became apparent that reasoned, dispassionate discourse could not end slavery and that those enslaved had no hope of becoming free unless they forcibly and illegally threw off their chains by escaping. And those who aided them were lawbreakers as well. So the movement's mantra became the higher law and the concept of civil disobedience developed as its underlying principle. The situation that those in the Underground Railroad faced shows us why we must remain vigilant even in a democracy to prevent the tyranny of the majority from stealing our human rights. This is even more important today when small segments of society have much greater means to influence the great majority of us.

The Underground Railroad started slowly at the local level, developing networks that expanded regionally, and eventually reached out across states and into Canada. Beginning with individualized efforts to aid fugitive slaves around the time of the American Revolution, it came to involve generations of some families and made continual progress that led to the Civil War. It reached to Montreal in the north, Mexico in the south, Nova Scotia in the east, and Kansas in the west, and included people from all segments of society, though most were evangelical whites, free blacks, and Quakers.

Underground Railroad Beginnings

The first documented group to help slaves seeking their freedom was the Pennsylvania Abolition Society, organized in Philadelphia mainly by Quakers around the time of the American Revolution. Gradually, increasing numbers of fugitive slaves from the eastern shore of Maryland began fleeing up through Delaware and New Jersey where considerable numbers of sympathetic Quakers and free blacks were ready to help. Other early gateways were the Susquehanna River into York County, Pennsylvania, where fugitive slave aid was reported as early as 1804, and the footpaths through the Allegheny Mountains into Adams County, Pennsylvania.[1]

Fugitive slaves began fleeing across the Ohio River after the War of 1812, which brought slaves greater awareness of freedom north of the Mason-Dixon Line.[2] On ships bound for New England and New York City, docked in the harbors of the Carolinas and Virginia, slaves also began stowing away, often with the complicity of seaman, many of whom were black and sympathetic.[3] Inland, in the South, some of the earliest manifestations occurred in Guilford County and the New Garden Quaker Meeting of Levi Coffin's youth, where slaves were being assisted before 1815.[4]

Regional Collaboration

Many of the entries in the book show closely knit networks in their regions. However, these routes changed over time for various reasons, sometimes because of relocation, death, or the opening of more efficient thoroughfares like the ubiquitous upperground railroads that began to appear after 1850. As Wilbur Siebert wrote, "guides had almost always a choice between two or more routes . . . the underground paths . . . formed a great and intricate network, and it was in no small measure because the lines . . . converged and branched again at so many stations that it was almost an impossibility for slave-hunters to trace their negroes."[5] Naturally, the closer slaves lived to the Mason-Dixon Line, the more likely they were to attempt an escape. Slaves also were provided with opportunities to escape while traveling in coffle gangs on foot, often from Virginia, which had an overabundance of slaves, to the Kentucky auctions in Lexington and Louisville. Motivation for escape also was much greater during these forced migrations because many of the slaves faced separation from their families.[6]

Thoroughfares and Gateways

Fugitive slaves often made their getaways on foot, especially in the South, and conductors more often used wagons and carriages to take them short distances to nearby collaborators. However, the use of rivers, canals, and as it developed, the railroad became major arteries for escape. The Saltwater Underground

Railroad also was a significant thoroughfare. Not only were slaves often boat pilots in the South, but in the North as many as 20 percent of the seaman were free blacks.[7]

Organization

One of the most vehement contentions of revisionist historians that has gained currency among many mainstream historians is that the Underground Railroad had little if any organization. However, the truth is that there was plenty of organization and there is mountains of evidence to support this.

The first formally organized Underground Railroad association was the New York Committee of Vigilance, formed in 1835 under the leadership of David Ruggles. A lengthy 1837 report enumerates aid to fugitive slaves and details the committee's struggles with slavecatchers. Though predominantly a black organization in the early years, it invited whites like Gerrit Smith, Isaac Hopper, and Lewis Tappan to attend its meetings. As a result of the Committee's success, the New York State Antislavery Society in 1838 appealed to cities around the state in their weekly, *Friend of Man*, to organize similar vigilance committees. A month later, the American Anti-Slavery Society made this request nationwide in the *Emancipator*. Based on various reports, up to 1856, the New York Committee, which became the New York State Vigilance Committee in 1848, aided about 3,200 fugitive slaves.[8]

The Philadelphia Vigilance Committee, originally formed in 1837 under the leadership of Robert Purvis was another important Underground Railroad organization. It aided more than 100 fugitive slaves per year until 1842, when it suspended operations and passed on this duty to the Pennsylvania Anti-Slavery Society. A predominantly Quaker organization, the Pennsylvania society was coordinated by Miller McKim and relied strongly on collaboration with free blacks. A second Philadelphia Vigilance Committee formed in 1852, from which William Still emerged as the leader. During Still's tenure, it aided more than 800 fugitive slaves, most about whom Still recorded detailed records.

Other records of organized activity were kept by Francis Jackson, treasurer of the Boston Vigilance Committee. From 1851 to 1861, his Records Book recorded the names of fugitive slaves, the amount of money spent on them, and their destinations. It also included a list of the committee members, as well as unofficial associates, mainly blacks, whose homes were used to harbor fugitive slaves. In all, the committee aided 430 fugitive slaves.[9]

Evidence of collaboration between the Boston, New York, and Philadelphia committees, as well as with agents in Washington, D.C., is well documented.[10] One prominent collaboration involved Still, Charles Ray of the New York Committee, and Jacob Bigelow, coordinator of the Road's activities in DC, in the year 1855 rescue of Ann Maria Weems. Fugitive slaves, like Frederick Douglass in 1838, were regularly sent by both the New York and Philadelphia committees to New Bedford, which had connections with the Boston Committee.

Although detailed record books do not exist of Underground Railroad efforts in the Midwest, it was the real heart of the Underground Railroad. The activities of Levi Coffin and John Rankin have been preserved in numerous accounts, including those by Coffin and members of the Rankin family, as well as thousands of stories testifying to its operation there, many dutifully recorded and preserved by Wilbur Siebert during the 1890s.[11]

Another important point of revisionist historians that has gained currency, and rightly so, was the underemphasis of the contributions of blacks in the Underground Railroad. The failure to tell the story of black participation occurred because of a number of circumstances related to black demographics and culture, which Cheryl LaRoche discusses in her recent dissertation, *On the Edge of Freedom.* Historians like Larry Gara, Benjamin Quarles, Charles Blockson, and Keith Griffler have tried to rectify this.

Overall, what I think emerges, is interracial cooperation. You see this in the operation of most of the major urban vigilance committees like New York, Philadelphia, and Boston, and lesser groups like those in Cincinnati; Wilmington, Delaware; New Bedford, Massachusetts; Chester County, Pennsylvania; and Albany, Syracuse, and Rochester, New York. Much was dependent on time and place, and who lived where and when. In New York and Cincinnati, it began solely black and grew more interracial; in Detroit, it was directed by blacks, with some white associates. But in some places, the Underground Railroad was run solely by blacks. This should not suggest that blacks and whites worked together in perfect harmony. Racial prejudice was prevalent even among abolitionists and diehard agents of the Underground Railroad. Nevertheless, some white and black individuals had close, personal relationships, like Miller McKim and William Still.

The connections that made up the Underground Railroad were complex and multifaceted. It was not some large centralized network, but an evolving pastiche of relationships and routes through which freedom never was guaranteed.

NOTES

1. Robert C. Smedley, *History of the Underground Railroad in Chester and Neighboring Counties of Pennsylvania.* Lancaster PA, 1883: 27–28; 37.

2. Wilbur H. Siebert, "Beginnings of the Underground Railroad in Ohio," *Ohio History*, January 1947: 71–76.

3. Gary L. Collison, *Shadrach Minkins: From Fugitive Slave to Citizen.* Boston: Harvard University Press, 1997: 54–56, 190; Charles Emery Stevens, *Anthony Burns A History.* Boston: John P. Jewett & Company, 1856: 176–180; Horatio Strother, *The Underground Railroad in Connecticut*, Middletown, CT: Wesleyan University Press, 1962: 42–44.

4. Levi Coffin, *Reminiscences.* Cincinnati, OH: Robert Clarke & Co, 1880: 15–31.

5. Wilbur Siebert, *The Underground Railroad: From Slavery to Freedom.* New York: Macmillan, 1898: 62.

6. Coffin, *Reminiscences*, 398.

7. W. Jeffrey Bolster, *Black Jacks: African American Seamen*. Cambridge: Harvard University Press, 1997: 2.

8. *Mirror of Liberty*, August 1838: 4; *The Colored American*, August 20, 1840; *The Liberator*, January 6, 1843; Charles Ray, *New York Evangelist*, May 24, 1849; Benjamin Quarles, *Black Abolitionists*. New York: Oxford University Press, 1969: 154.

9. Collison, *Shadrach Minkins*, 83.

10. See entries for Boston, New York, Philadelphia, and Washington, D.C.

11. See Siebert Collection, Ohio Historical Society, http://www.ohiomemory.org/cdm4/index_siebert.php?CISOROOT=/siebert.

TIMELINE

1775	Organization of the Society for the Relief of Free Negroes Unlawfully Held in Bondage, later called the Pennsylvania Abolition Society, the first organization to aid fugitive slaves, in Philadelphia
1780	Gradual emancipation law in Pennsylvania, first of its kind in the United States, sets the stage for the development of the Underground Railroad in Philadelphia
1793	Passage of the first federal Fugitive Slave Law, making it illegal to aid slaves fleeing from slavery
1796	Isaac Hopper, noted Quaker abolitionist, joins the Philadelphia Abolition Society
1803	Judicial decision by Chief Justice of Lower Canada (today known as Ontario), William Osgoode, declares slavery inconsistent with British law, setting a precedent that leads to the end of slavery in Canada
1808	Outlawing of International Slave Trade puts more emphasis on America's domestic slave trade, which becomes the major cause of slaves seeking freedom
1814	Charles Osborn, a Presbyterian minister from Tennessee, makes first public declaration in favor of immediate emancipation, with the formation of the Tennessee Manumission Society at the home of Quaker Elihu Swain, near the Holston River and present location of New Market, Tennessee
1816	Organization of American Colonization Society, which sought to send American blacks to Africa because in the final analysis they believe blacks cannot coexist in the United States on equal terms with whites, in Washington, D.C.
1817	Meeting of blacks in Philadelphia to protest the African Colonization. They insist as Americans that they should have the same rights and opportunities as whites

1822	John Rankin, Presbyterian minister, moves from Kentucky to Ripley, Ohio, and enlarges the Underground Railroad already in existence there
1822	Thomas Garrett, Quaker businessman, moves to Wilmington, Delaware, and puts his Abolitionist principles into action by aiding fugitive slaves
1826	Levi Coffin, a Quaker from North Carolina, moves to Newport, Indiana (today known as Fountain City), and begins operating his legendary station on the Underground Railroad
1827	*Freedom's Journal,* first black newspaper, begins publication in New York City, opposes African Colonization and calls for immediate emancipation
1829	David Walker, black used clothes dealer from Boston, publishes his manifesto, *Appeal,* calling on slaves to revolt
1829	Cincinnati race riot causes some black citizens to flee and form the Wilberforce Colony, the first colony of expatriate American blacks in Canada
1831	*The Liberator* begins publication in Boston, calls for immediate emancipation
1831	Nat Turner Revolt in Southampton County, Virginia, massacres 60 whites in an attempt to bring an end to slavery; it terrorizes the South, and harshly repressive measures are instituted to control the future behavior in the South of not only slaves but also free blacks
1832	Rankin's "Letters on Slavery," which illustrate the moral shortcomings of slavery, are serialized in *The Liberator*
1833	England outlaws slavery in the British Commonwealth, ending the last vestiges of slavery in Canada
1833	American Anti-Slavery Society forms in Philadelphia
1834	Lane Debates at Lane Seminary in Cincinnati led by abolitionist Theodore Weld galvanizes attention of the nation on the issue of immediate emancipation
1835	Ohio Anti-Slavery Society forms at the Stone Academy in Putnam, Ohio, strengthening the connections of that state's Underground Railroad
1835	New York Committee of Vigilance forms in Manhattan, the organizational model for later Underground Railroad organizations upon which the traditional view of the Underground Railroad was based
1835	Charles C. Burleigh abolitionizes Chester County, Pennsylvania, an area from which spring more Underground Railroad agents per capita than anywhere in the United States

1835	Gerrit Smith, Peterboro, New York multimillionaire, converts to immediate emancipation and begins his one-man war on slavery, which includes numerous activities in support of the Underground Railroad
1835–1837	Theodore Weld and his band of 70 abolitionize the North and recruit thousands who become part of the Underground Railroad
1837	Murder of Elijah Lovejoy, religious editor in Alton, Illinois, because he refused to abandon the discussion of slavery in his newspaper, causes outrage in the North and converts thousands to abolitionism
1838	William L. Chaplin, secretary of the New York State Anti-Slavery Society based in Utica, New York, calls for the organization of the Underground Railroad in upstate New York
1838	"Eliza," real life model for Eliza Harris in *Uncle Tom's Cabin*, escapes to freedom in Ripley, Ohio
1838	Frederick Bailey escapes from slavery in Maryland; shortly after, he changes his name to Frederick Douglass
1841	Founding of the British and American Institute, industrial school for fugitive slaves, in Dawn, Ontario, by Hiram Wilson
1842	Prigg Decision by the Supreme Court, relating to a case involving Margaret Morgan, a fugitive slave who had been living in York, Pennsylvania, rules that states had no jurisdiction in fugitive slave cases, causing some fugitive slaves in the North to flee to Canada, and resulting in the passage of laws by northern states to undermine its ruling
1842	Charles Torrey, radical abolitionist minister living in Albany, New York, organizes the Underground Railroad in Washington, D.C.; dies in prison four years later after being convicted of aiding fugitive slaves
1843	Henry Highland Garnet calls for slaves to revolt in his "Address to the Slaves" at National Negro Convention in Buffalo, New York
1843	John Cross, Congregational minister living in La Moille, Illinois, organizes the western Underground Railroad leading from Quincy, Illinois to Detroit, Michigan; the route expands across the state of Iowa by 1854
1843	Calvin Fairbank and Delia Webster, former Oberlin students, rescue Kentucky slave Lewis Hayden and his family from Lexington, but are captured and sent to prison
1845	Captain Jonathan Walker, seaman, arrested for aiding fugitive slaves in the Florida Keys has his hand branded with the initials "SS," for slave stealer, and Whittier writes a poem commemorating it

1846	Race riots in Madison, Indiana, remove black abolitionist George DeBaptiste to Detroit, where he joins with William Lambert and William Munroe in organizing the Detroit Vigilance Committee
1846	Gerrit Smith and John Brown, peripatetic, evangelical abolitionist, meet in Peterboro, New York
1847	Levi Coffin moves to Cincinnati to open free produce store and reorganizes the city's Underground Railroad
1847	Frederick Douglass begins publication of the *North Star* in Rochester, New York, becomes a leading spokesman for black America, and joins the Underground Railroad in Rochester
1848	Thomas Garrett found guilty of aiding fugitive slaves in Wilmington, Delaware, pays fine of $5,400, but vows to continue aiding fugitive slaves
1848	Seventy-seven fugitive slaves attempt to flee in a schooner named the Pearl from the harbor of Washington, D.C., by way of the Potomac River, but are captured at the entrance to Chesapeake Bay
1848	William and Ellen Craft escape to freedom, traveling from Savannah Georgia, to Philadelphia, Pennsylvania by train
1849	Henry "Box" Brown escapes to freedom from Richmond, Virginia, to Philadelphia, Pennsylvania, traveling in a box by train and boat
1849	Harriet Tubman escapes to freedom from Maryland
1849	Founding of the Elgin Association by Rev. William King in Buxton, Ontario, a settlement seeking to advance the moral and educational improvement of blacks in Canada
1850	Chance meeting of long lost brothers, former slave Peter Friedman and abolitionist William Still, in Philadelphia, Pennsylvania, prompts the latter to begin keeping records of fugitive slaves aided during his work for the Philadelphia Vigilance Committee
1850	Second federal Fugitive Slave Law is passed, effectively turning all American citizens into slavecatchers
1850	Harriet Tubman conducts first rescue mission in Maryland
1851	*National Era*, Washington, D.C., begins serialization of *Uncle Tom's Cabin* by Harriet Beecher Stowe
1851	Henry Bibb begins publication of the *Voice of the Fugitive* in Toronto
1851	Christiana Riot, in Lancaster County, Pennsylvania, led by former fugitive slave William Parker, prevents slavecatchers from apprehending their slaves and results in the death of Maryland slaveholder, Edward Gorsuch
1851	Jerry Rescue, led by citizens of Syracuse, New York, prevents federal authorities from returning Jerry Henry to slavery
1851	Fugitive slave Shadrach Minkins, rescued from federal authorities in Boston by Lewis Hayden and unofficial black members

	of the Boston Vigilance Committee, is forwarded to Montreal, Canada
1852	Philadelphia Vigilance Committee reorganizes under the leadership of William Still
1852	Anti-Slavery League, as reported by Indiana abolitionist William Cockrum, of Oakland City, organizes in the Ohio River Valley to bring slaves out of the South
1853	Mary Shadd and Samuel Ringgold Ward begin publication of the *Provincial Freeman* in Windsor, Canada
1854	Federal authorities successfully apprehend fugitive slave Anthony Burns in Boston, Massachusetts, despite rescue efforts of the Boston Vigilance Committee under the leadership of Lewis Hayden and Thomas Wentworth Higginson
1854	Kansas-Nebraska Act nullifies the Missouri Compromise and makes all future states north of Missouri subject to slavery to be determined by state referendum
1855–1856	Detroit Vigilance Committee reports aiding upwards of 1,600 fugitive slaves
1856	John Brown goes to Kansas and becomes nationally known exponent of using force to end slavery
1858	Oberlin-Wellington Rescue by Oberlin, Ohio, citizens and students prevents authorities from returning fugitive slave John Price of Oberlin to slavery
1859	John Brown, captured at Harpers Ferry, Virginia, and hanged at Charlestown, Virginia, galvanizes the attention of the Union
1860	Harriet Tubman leads rescue of fugitive slave Charles Nalle from federal authorities in Troy, New York
1872	William Still publishes *The Underground Railroad: A Record . . .* based on records he made as chairman of the acting committee of the Philadelphia Vigilance Committee
1875	Levi Coffin publishes his *Reminiscences*, in Cincinnati, Ohio
1883	Robert C. Smedley publishes the *Underground Railroad in Chester County, Pennsylvania*
1898	Wilbur Siebert publishes *The Underground Railroad: From Slavery to Freedom*

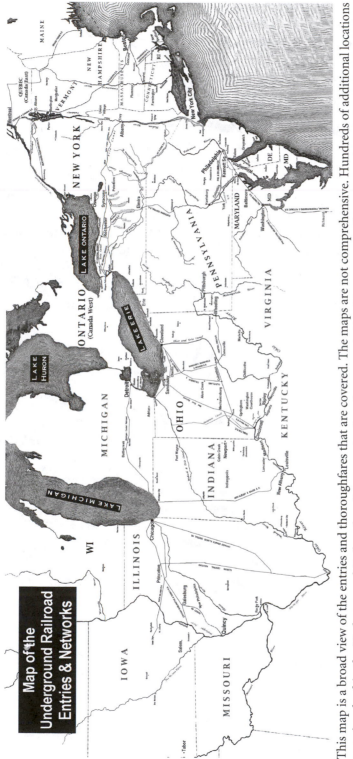

This map is a broad view of the entries and thoroughfares that are covered. The maps are not comprehensive. Hundreds of additional locations were involved in the Underground Railroad and some active locations are missing. However, an effort was made to list the most important communities. For greater detail, consult the five regional maps. (Courtesy of Tom Calarco)

A

ADRIAN, LENAWEE COUNTY, MICHIGAN

Adrian was the site of the first Underground Railroad station established in the state of Michigan. Its stationmaster was a woman, Laura Smith Haviland, who along with her husband, Charles, established the Adrian stop in the 1830s. However, her activities increased considerably after his premature death. A statue of Haviland, known to locals as Aunt Laura, was dedicated in front of the city hall in June 1909 as "A Tribute to a Life Consecrated to the Betterment of Humanity." It remained there for more than a century, until the old city hall was demolished in the summer of 2010 and the statue was put in storage for safekeeping. By spring of 2011, the statue is expected to be back on display at a nearby location.

An Abolitionized Community

Although Haviland is memorialized in Adrian's antislavery history, she did not act alone. The abolitionist cause attracted other, unsung heroes. After a failed attempt to capture George Branegan in Adrian in 1839, five Kentucky slave catchers seized him in nearby Jonesville, Michigan. A northern sensibility was all that stood between Branegan and bondage. When the claimant failed to prove ownership on a technicality in *Poynts vs. Branegan*, the court set Branegan free. At the annual Michigan Anti-Slavery Society Convention in 1844, A. M. Baker, of Adrian, testified that at least 20 fugitive slaves lived in Lenawee County. In 1854, the executive committee of the Michigan Anti-Slavery Society reimbursed an Adrian resident three dollars, a large amount in those days, for expenses in helping a fugitive slave. Although documented reports of aid to fugitive slaves in the Adrian area are scarce, the reputation of Haviland and other local abolitionists, and its proximity to the major terminal of Detroit, suggests that the community saw significant fugitive slave traffic.

Haviland had been inspired by another female abolitionist in Lenawee County. In the mid-1820s, Elizabeth Margaret Chandler began writing

The Fugitive Slave Law of 1793

The Fugitive Slave Law of 1793 was the first major legislation invoked by the federal government in support of the institution of slavery.

It imposed a fine of $500—equal to $20,000 today—and up to one year in prison for those convicted of helping fugitive slaves. Testimony of a slave owner or his representative before any legally appointed judge was enough to commit the alleged fugitive to slavery. However, because of the logistics involved, slave owners became dependent on slavecatchers. The law also facilitated slavecatchers in kidnapping free blacks and selling them into slavery, a practice that was common even before its passage. Among its provisions was the suspension of the alleged fugitive slaves' right to testify on their own behalf.

Ironically, the Fugitive Slave Law of 1793 did not originate from a case involving a fugitive slave. In 1791, a free black man was seized from Pennsylvania and taken to Virginia. When the governor of Pennsylvania demanded his return, Virginia's governor refused, claiming that no law compelled this. It prompted a congressional committee to prepare the 1793 law, which provided for the extradition from one state to another of those accused of a crime, which included fugitive slaves.

To combat it, abolitionists often used the writ of habeas corpus. The purpose of the writ was to challenge the claimants' legal right to the slave and permit their release in the custody of their legal representative. It allows the judicial authority to reflect on the merits of a case after thoughtful consideration of the evidence, which the defendant's counsel and the claimant are given the opportunity to present. Sometimes slavecatchers had nothing but their word as proof, and even slaveholders did not always bring sufficient evidence to support their claim.

antislavery poetry, and her work appeared in Benjamin Lundy's *Genius of Universal Emancipation* and William Lloyd Garrison's *The Liberator*. Chandler's inspirational words about the plight of slaves motivated others, especially women. One of them was Haviland. When Chandler established the Logan Female Antislavery Society in 1832, it was the first women's antislavery society in what had been called the Old Northwest Territory, and Haviland became a member. Two years after organizing the society, Chandler died of a fever at the age of 27. When Garrison visited Adrian in 1853 to help revive the Michigan Anti-Slavery Society that grew from her efforts, he paid his respects at Chandler's grave.

After the Logan society, more antislavery societies followed in Lenawee County. By 1838, the Raisin Anti-Slavery Society, in the Lenawee County town of Raisin, had 56 members. But they were not without opposition, even in their own county. On July 4, 1839, racists in the nearby Rome-Cambridge township area fired their guns first in the air and later into a blackened wooden doll to disrupt a patriotic celebration held by an antislavery group.

Haviland's Underground Railroad Participation

Haviland was far from a childless spinster with time on her hands. In 1829, when she and her husband, Charles, moved into a 16-by-18-foot log cabin near

Adrian, the 20-year-old Haviland was already the mother of two. In time, her family would grow to eight children. In addition to raising a family, and working for the Adrian station and Chandler's antislavery society, Haviland founded the first school for blacks in Michigan with help from her husband and brother. Haviland's brother, Harvey Smith, sold his 150-acre farm to raise capital for the school's construction, and the Raisin Institute opened in 1839. It admitted students regardless of race, religion, or gender.

It was a sign of Haviland's commitment that she did not abandon her abolitionist activities after the great tragedy of her life in 1845 when she lost five family members in a span of six weeks. The family had contracted erysipelas, a bacterial infection that resembles poison ivy. Haviland came down with it, too, but managed to fight it off. Erysipelas claimed the lives of her sister, both of her parents, her husband, and their youngest child, a baby.

At the age of 36, Haviland had become a widow with seven children and a $700 debt, an amount comparable to $20,000 today. Haviland gathered her strength, took over her husband's business, and expanded her efforts on behalf of the Underground Railroad. Two years later, she was targeted by proslavery individuals after helping the Hamiltons, a fugitive family.

Willis Hamilton was a freed slave, but his wife, Elsie, was a runaway. The couple had been living peacefully in Michigan when they arranged for someone to write to inquire about two daughters left behind. The letter, or news of it, reached Elsie's owner, Dr. John Chester of Tennessee, and he surmised that he could find her near Adrian. He and his son, Thomas, came to Michigan for Elsie, and when they failed to capture her, they blamed it on Laura Haviland. In 1847, the Chesters put a bounty of $3,000 on her head, dead or alive. A comparable amount in today's dollars would be roughly $80,000. After the close call, the Hamiltons took greater precautions. In 1850, when Thomas Chester tried to capture Elsie again, the Hamiltons had long since moved to Canada.

Dr. Chester was not the only slave owner thwarted by Haviland in 1847. John White, known as Felix White when he was a slave, had been attending the Raisin Institute. His owner, George Brazier, visited Haviland on the pretext of being a teacher. He must have mentioned Felix White to her, or perhaps she recognized his name from something White had told her. Regardless, Haviland suspected the man's true intent. Because White was working on a farm near Brooklyn, Michigan, Haviland allowed Brazier to visit the school. Meanwhile, a student volunteered to warn White, and Haviland loaned him one of her horses. White escaped to Canada the next day.

Michigan Women Contributed to Antislavery Movement

In the nineteenth century, when most political groups excluded women, Lenawee County was the exception. There, groups that wanted to reach the hearts and minds of the general public welcomed women as officers and members. These antislavery groups not only worked to liberate the slaves, they also hoped to expand the role of women in public life. Though most of their names are lost to history, we should remember that Laura Haviland was not the only Michigan woman active in antislavery efforts.

In mid-October 1852, delegates gathered at Adrian to establish a State Central Anti-Slavery Committee. In tribute to the town's importance, the group decided that at least seven of the sixteen or more committee members would have to live in or near Adrian. A year later, the group held a statewide convention at the Odd Fellows' Hall in Adrian, and that meeting drew William Lloyd Garrison. Thomas Chandler, Elizabeth's brother, served as President of the convention.

By 1860, a new group, calling themselves the Wide Awakes, had emerged. More than 900 Wide Awakes and 20,000 others converged on the fairgrounds in Adrian for a Republican rally in late October. Cassius Clay, the noted antislavery orator from Kentucky, was the featured speaker. Eleven days later, the nation elected Abraham Lincoln.

Although most abolitionists would have cited morality as the reason for their work, not all of them subscribed to a particular religion. For example, abolitionists James and Betsy Parker, from Rome township in Lenawee County, were Free Thinkers. An early Republican, Parker was elected to the state legislature on an antislavery platform in 1855.

Throughout her long life, Laura Haviland, keeper of the Adrian station on the Underground Railroad, followed the religious admonition to be her brother's keeper. In her autobiography, she summed up her feelings about slavery and her life's work: "Is it not the duty of every Christian to bring his or her religion into every line of life work, and act as conscientiously in politics as in church work?" (Haviland 454).

Despite the mercenaries who hunted her, Laura Haviland continued her humanitarian work up through and after the Civil War, traveling extensively to do so. As a result, the towns of Haviland, Kansas and Haviland, Ohio were named in her honor, and she was inducted as a charter member into the Michigan Women's Hall of Fame.

—Rae Hallstrom

Further Reading

Tom Calarco, *People of the Underground Railroad* (Westport, CT: Greenwood Press, 2008).

Lee M. Haines, *Laura Smith Haviland: A Woman's Life Work* (Marion, IN: Wesleyan Publishing House, 1977).

Laura Haviland, *A Woman's Life-Work: Labors and Experiences of Laura S. Haviland* (Cincinnati: Walden & Stowe, 1882).

Charles Lindquist, *The Antislavery-Underground Railroad Movement: In Lenawee County, Michigan, 1830–1860* (Adrian, MI: Lenawee County Historical Society, 1999).

ALBANY, NEW YORK

Albany was a major terminal connecting New York City with points north and west on the Underground Railroad. Organized efforts in the black community to aid fugitive slaves began here at least as early as 1831; based on reports covering various periods during the antebellum period, it is clear that thousands of fugitive slaves were aided.

Stephen Myers

The most important figure in Albany's Underground Railroad was the black stationmaster, Stephen Myers, whose involvement covered a period of about 30 years. Born a slave in the town of Hoosick in Rensselaer County, New York in 1803 (some sources say 1800), he was emancipated from the family of Dr. Eights in 1818. At least as early as 1838, Myers had begun working as a boatman, listing his occupation as a steward that year on the steamboat, *Diamond*. It was in boats traveling up the Hudson River that fugitive slaves were most often transported from

Stephen Myers house, Albany, New York, home of the prolific conductor, which was also the site of the city's vigilance committee office. (Courtesy of the Underground Railroad Workshop, Albany, New York)

New York City to Albany. As New York Committee of Vigilance member Charles Ray wrote: "we would alternate in sending between Albany and Troy, and when we had a large party we would divide between the two cities. We had on one occasion, a party of twenty-eight persons of all ages.... We destined them for Canada. I secured passage for them in a barge." (Ray, Florence T., *Sketch of the Life of Rev. Charles B. Ray*. New York: Press of J. J. Little & Co., 1887: 35).

Albany's Underground Railroad Network

An important convention that linked regional abolitionists met in Albany from February 28 to March 2, 1838 at the Presbyterian Church. Nearly 200 individuals attended, including Myers and many others, who would be linked to the Underground Railroad: Hiram Corliss, Union Village, New York stationmaster, who chaired the convention; Gerrit Smith, one of the major figures in the Underground Railroad; William Goodell, editor of *Friend of Man*; Beriah Green, president of the Oneida Institute, the state's only institution of higher education that enrolled blacks; Hiram Wilson, who would become advocate for fugitive slaves in Canada throughout the antebellum period; RPG Wright, the Schenectady barber and father of New York Committee of Vigilance president, Theodore Wright; Erastus Culver of Union Village, who later became a judge in Brooklyn and a legal advocate for fugitive slaves; and William L. Chaplin, secretary of the state antislavery society and future slave rescuer.

Among the resolutions passed was one that referred to aiding fugitive slaves: "we deeply sympathize with our colored brethren on their way from the great prison house of slavery; and also with those who have made good their escape from it and are now located in the province of Canada." ("Albany Anti-Slavery Convention." *Friend of Man*, March 14, 1838).

In April of that year, Chaplin called for the organization of vigilance committees in the larger communities of New York State. So it is likely that such a committee was organized in Albany that year, if not earlier.

Abel Brown and Charles Torrey

In 1839 and 1840, national abolition conventions assembled there, the latter to organize the Liberty Party; shortly thereafter a militant core of abolitionists and Underground Railroad operatives moved to the city. The radical abolitionist Rev. Charles T. Torrey joined forces with Rev. Abel Brown in Albany to establish the Eastern New York Anti-Slavery Society (ENYASS), which supported the Liberty Party. This society included members from all New York counties that bordered the Hudson River, the primary thoroughfare for the transport of runaway slaves from New York City. Apparently, based on reports in the ENYASS's newspaper, *Tocsin of Liberty* (later the *Albany Patriot*), and Stephen Myers's *Northern Star* and *Freeman's Advocate*, two vigilance committees were operating in Albany during the early 1840s: one a formal collaboration of the Liberty Party and the Albany Anti-Slavery Society members; the other, an informal group that was primarily associates of Myers and Albany's black community. During 1842, one report states, the former aided 350 runaway slaves (Brown 142).

The level of ENYASS's activity in the Underground Railroad is reflected in the following copy taken from the June 20, 1842, issue of the *Tocsin of Liberty* and signed Forwarding Merchants, Albany, N.Y.

> The vigilance committee are up to their elbows in work, and are desirous to have you inform a few of those men who have lately lost property consisting of articles of merchandize (falsely so called) in the shape, and having the minds and sympathies of human beings, that we are always on hand, and ready to ship cargoes on the shortest notice, and ensure a safe passage over the "Great Ontario." (Brown 111–112)

Succeeding issues of the *Tocsin* included reports from Brown with the following: "The forwarding business is still good, and a little more ready cash would place us upon a sure footing . . . Tell kidnappers to take notice, that we have such an amount of business on hand, that we have no time to report progress."

Characteristic of Brown and Torrey was their brazen attitude, which they expressed in flaunting their successes in their Underground Railroad work. An example of this was the following announcement Brown advertised in the *Tocsin* and *Vermont Freeman*, addressing a slaveholder, whose slave the ENYASS had helped:

> Mr. Fernandis:—This is to inform you that the noble Robert Hill reached this city in safety and was safely sent on his way rejoicing. We charge you $25 for money paid him and services rendered, and 56 cents for the letter containing the advertisement. Please send a draft for the same. (*Vermont Freeman*, July 1, 1843: 3)

A ruse was sometimes employed by the ENYASS to confuse slavecatchers. Coordinating with Torrey, who used his position as a newspaper correspondent in Washington, D.C., to cover his work in aiding fugitive slaves, the *Tocsin* would publish accounts of fugitive slaves arriving safely in Canada who were actually still being hidden in the South. When it appeared that the slavecatchers had taken the bait and abandoned the hunt for the fugitive slaves, agents sent the runaways North with little worry of being pursued. Letters and accounts from such Underground Railroad coordinators as William Still in Philadelphia, Charles Ray and Sidney Howard Gay in New York City, Francis Jackson in Boston, Eber Pettit in western New York, and Frederick Douglass in Rochester all testify to the heavy Underground Railroad traffic that passed through Albany.

Late in 1844 Brown died of an illness and Torrey was arrested and put in a Maryland prison for aiding runaway slaves where he died in 1846. These events effectively caused a collapse of the Eastern New York Anti-Slavery Society, though Chaplin, also a member of the ENYASS leadership attempted but failed to maintain its former level of activities. He took over as editor of the *Albany Patriot*, successor to the *Tocsin of Liberty*, but it ceased publication in 1848. Thereafter, he moved to Washington, D.C., to coordinate Underground Railroad efforts that Torrey had originated, being the primary instigator of the unsuccessful Pearl escape. Then in 1850 he was apprehended while leading several fugitive slaves from Maryland in a carriage and put in prison.

Though Brown, Torrey, and Chaplin were no longer part of the Albany effort, there were numerous other agents in the Albany area who shouldered the responsibilities. Among them were women, including the Albany Female Anti-Slavery Society, whose formation in 1843 was inspired by Brown and Torrey; and the Quaker sisters Lydia and Abigail Mott, who operated a clothing store on Maiden Lane in downtown Albany.

Albany Female Anti-Slavery Society

The Albany Female Anti-Slavery Society reported the continuous passage of fugitive slaves during the mid-to-late 1840s. Its annual report in 1845 stated that "We have sustained a monthly meeting for prayer and the execution of plans for the assistance of fugitives on their way to Canada" ("Report of the

Ladies' A.S. Society of Albany," *Albany Patriot*, July 2, 1845), noting that they had furnished them with clothing and other necessities. Their reports the following year mentioned support of a mission to Canada by Rev. Cyrus Prindle to minister to fugitive slaves, where he met Hiram Wilson at his manual labor school and renowned fugitive slave, Josiah Henson.

In 1847, the Mott sisters harbored George Lewis, a fugitive slave from Virginia, whose whereabouts had been discovered. Fortunately, Boston minister Leonard Grimes had learned of the situation during a visit to Albany and dispatched Boston Vigilance Committee member Austin Bearse, who sailed up the Hudson River to Albany on his yacht the *Moby Dick* to rescue Lewis. Bearse not only took Lewis out of a dangerous situation but brought him to live with his daughter in Boston.

Myers, the Stationmaster

It was Myers who took over leadership of Albany's Underground Railroad thereafter. In 1842, he was one of the three publishers of *The Northern Star and Freeman's Advocate*, which was introduced on January 20. It replaced *The Colored American* of New York City, which closed its offices at the end of 1841, as the nation's foremost black newspaper. In the *Northern Star*, Myers revealed that Albany blacks had been giving organized aid to fugitive slaves as early as 1831. Like the *Tocsin of Liberty*, Myers printed reports of aid to fugitive slaves, though his reports were not inflammatory. In the December 8, 1842 issue, he wrote:

> I will say a few words in relation to slaves who have passed through this city. There was one sent to our office by Mr. Morrell of Newark. We put him on board of a canal boat, paid his passage to Oswego, and furnished him with money to go into Canada. . . . We assisted two slaves that were sent to our office by William Garner of Elizabethtown [N.J.]; we furnished them with money for Canada by way of Lake Champlain.

Another even more intriguing story involving Myers was published in an 1848 issue of the *Albany Patriot*. It told of a steamboat, *The Armenia*, a "neat, swift, little day-boat from New York to Troy," could make the trip from New York-to-Albany in nine hours," which "nothing on the river" could outrace. The boat's design was marked by a novel "improvement" for such ships that allowed fugitive slaves to be more easily hidden because "the table [was] set on the first deck instead of below, as is usual. . . . A light, airy saloon, of a hot or a dark day, is altogether more comfortable than a close and dungeon-like place" ("Comfort and Economy for the Traveller," *Albany Patriot*, May 10, 1848). Its steward was Myers.

By 1855, Myers was devoting full-time to his efforts at aiding fugitive slaves. He was an exceptional organizer and could depend on many important individuals for assistance: editors Thurlow Weed, of the *Albany Evening Journal*, and

Horace Greeley, of the *New York Tribune*; New York governors William H. Seward, John Alsop King, and Edward D. Morgan; New York City merchants Moses Grinnell, Simeon Draper, and Robert B. Minturn; philanthropist James W. Beekman; Livingston County, New York patrician, General James Wadsworth; New York City contractor John P. Cummings; Albany stone manufacturer, William Newton; and John Jay, of Westchester County, the grandson of the Founding Father.

Myers also made the rounds at the state and national Negro conventions, and as a temperance lecturer. A colored temperance society in Lee, Massachusetts with 36 members was named after him. In addition, his letters show that he was lobbying the New York State legislature to remove the state's property qualification for blacks to vote and to defeat a bill there to provide funding to the American Colonization Society. His activities cast a wide network.

Among those in the Underground Railroad he worked with were Francis Jackson, secretary of the Boston Vigilance Committee, who forwarded fugitive slaves to him through Thomas Harley in Springfield, Massachusetts. Sidney Howard Gay was forwarding fugitive slaves from New York City, and there is also an account of Lewis Tappan forwarding one as well. It is likely he also had close contact with William Still in Philadelphia, as a number of fugitive slaves came to him by way of Philadelphia, including Harriet Tubman. Another noteworthy contact was abolitionist Judge Erastus Culver of Brooklyn, who employed Chester Arthur, the future president and whose law firm was involved in several noteworthy cases in which it defended fugitive slaves. Coincidentally, Arthur's father was the pastor of a church near Myers's vigilance committee office.

Strong documentary evidence exists of the large-scale movement of fugitive slaves through Albany in the mid-1850s. An 1856 broadside revealed that during one nine-month period between September 12, 1855 and July 15, 1856, he coordinated the movement of 287 fugitive slaves, and paid $542.36 for their passage and $76.60 for their board. He also listed the names of the members of his vigilance committee, in all twelve men including himself: Rev. John Sands, pastor of the African Wesleyan Church; C. Brooks, a maker of melodeons; Thomas Elkins, a pharmacist; Rev. J. J. Kelley, a Roman Catholic priest; William H. Topp, a prominent tailor and long-time black abolitionist leader and personal friend of William Lloyd Garrison; Captain Abram Johnson, a boatman, who was Myers's father-in-law; William Gardner and William Matthews, barbers; Minos McGowan, a lumber merchant; Richard Wright, a shoemaker; and James S. Wood (*Vigilance Committee Office*, Broadside, Albany, N.Y., July 1856; Calarco, 2004: 162).

The broadside also revealed the location of Myers's vigilance committee office during this time at 198 Lumber Street, now 200 Livingston Avenue. The building has been identified as still extant by researchers and has been undergoing preservation for use as a museum. It is an important discovery, for it was one of New York State's most important Underground Railroad stations.

In a later circular from 1858, Myers stated that 121 fugitive slaves were helped during a five-month period with $242 being paid for their passage [to Syracuse]. Myers also wrote in the circular that "hundreds of fugitives have fallen to my care during the last twelve years" (*Circular to the Friends of Freedom*, 1858; Calarco, 2004: 192), and that he is in need of funds to continue his efforts. He added that his financial books and accounts were open for anyone to inspect if they were concerned about the use of their contributions. He also appealed for clothing to be donated, and added that to save expenses, many fugitive slaves were sent into the country to work on farms, which was considered to be safe.

In a letter to Francis Jackson, six weeks later, he wrote that 67 more runaways have passed through and that he was accommodating "three different branches of the underground road" (Stephen Myers to Francis Jackson, Albany, May 22, 1858). Another letter later that year to John Jay identified a number of his benefactors, and explained that he collected 10 cents on every dollar received for his livelihood because he was devoting all his time to the "Underground business..." He also contrasted the way he ran his Underground with that in New York and Philadelphia, explaining that he had to collect and manage every dollar himself while they raised their funds through antislavery societies and fairs. He also mentioned nine fugitive slaves that Jay's father had sent him.

Myers's Network

Many businesses and groups were involved in Albany's Underground Railroad. Among those who bear closer scrutiny, all of whom were vigilance committee members, are lumber and shipping merchant Chauncey P. Williams; canal towboat operator Linnaeus P. Noble, who later moved to Syracuse and participated in the Jerry Rescue, and also became involved in the Underground Railroad in Washington, D.C. as publisher of the *National Era*; lumber merchant and temperance house proprietor Nathaniel Safford; and two men who were members of both the Albany and New York committees of vigilance and had residences for a time in both cities, George R. Barker and Andrew Lester. The presence of Barker and Lester in Albany shows the closeness of the connection between Albany and New York, and suggests more widespread organization than some historians have given credit to the Underground Railroad.

—Tom Calarco

Further Reading

African Americans in Albany, Ruth Roberts Collection, Albany Institute of History and Art, Albany, NY.

C. S. Brown, *Memoir of Rev. Abel Brown*, Worcester, 1849 (reprint with introduction and annotations by Tom Calarco; Jefferson, NC: McFarland, 2006).

Tom Calarco, *The Underground Railroad in the Adirondack Region* (Jefferson, NC: McFarland, 2004).

Stanley Harrold, *Subversives: Antislavery Community in Washington, D.C.* (Baton Rouge: Louisiana State University Press, 2003).

C. Peter Ripley, editor, *The Black Abolitionist Papers*, The United States, vol. 4, 1847–1859 (Chapel Hill: University of North Carolina Press, 1991).

ALUM CREEK QUAKER SETTLEMENT

Alum Creek, a Quaker settlement located 30 miles north of Columbus in the Morrow County, Ohio town of Marengo, was one of the state's most active Underground Railroad stops. Directly in line with several routes that started at gateways along the Ohio River, including Ripley, it harbored hundreds of fugitive slaves in various safe houses on their way to freedom.

The Benedict Family

Cyrus Benedict moved to Marengo and founded the Alum Creek Quaker Settlement in 1811. At least nine members of the Benedict family, covering three generations, became conductors; two of them began driving fugitive slaves when they were boys. The Sycamore Trail, whose sycamore trees with their white bark served as guideposts, ran along Alum Creek. Fugitive slaves waded in the water of the creek as they left safe houses to the south like the Hanby House in nearby Westerville, attempting to elude pursuing slave hunters while on their way to find another safe house in the Alum Creek Settlement.

Routes to Alum Creek

Many of the routes that started in Ripley zigzagged into several routes. One of them from Ripley passed through Sardinia then northeastward to New Market and Hillsboro. Another Quaker settlement, Samantha, was the next stop. It continued directly east to stations at New Petersburg and on to Paint Creek and Greenfield. One of the branches at this crossroads continued north toward Alum Creek. As early as 1820, Mahlon Pickrell and his associate Mahlon Stanton hauled fugitive slaves on the last leg of this route from Pickrelltown in Logan County. They drove their passengers at night by horse and wagon over a rough road through a swampy area, a distance of 35 miles. The route continued to Delaware and then to Alum Creek.

The first recorded Underground Railroad incident in Alum Creek occurred in 1836 when four slaves, a mother and her children, were rescued from their slave owner. They were on their way to Missouri and were camped on the banks of the Scioto River in Columbus, Ohio. After the family was rescued from their owner, they were transported to Ozem Gardner's farm near Worthington, and then to the Alum Creek residence of Daniel Benedict. The slave owner and two hired slavecatchers traced the family to the residence. They spotted two children on the property and attempted to abduct them. Their attempt was halted by Daniel Benedict and others. The local Justice of the Peace, Barton Whipple, charged the men with kidnapping. The charges were dropped when the accused men left town.

Black Bill

An 1839 Underground Railroad incident occurred that involved the Benedicts and other Alum Creek Quakers. A fugitive slave from Virginia known as "Black Bill," also known as Mitchell or Anderson, had come to neighboring Marion County in the fall of 1838. He worked as a butcher, barber, and laborer. He was also talented as a fiddle and banjo player, making him popular at dances in Marion. In July 1839, someone recognized him and informed his former master. Eight representatives of his hometown of Kanawha Salt Works, Virginia, arrived in Marion to claim him as the runaway slave of Adnah Van Bibber. He was arrested as a fugitive according to the Ohio state law.

Bill's wife asked the Quakers at Alum Creek to help her husband. Aaron L. Benedict and William Cratty were two of the nine men who intervened at Bill's trial. They had a plan to help Bill escape at the end of the trial; but to their surprise, the judge ruled in Bill's favor. The Virginians were outraged; armed with pistols and knives, they seized Bill and ordered the crowd to stay back. Bill was dragged from the courthouse and through the streets. Being pursued by the locals, the slaveholders took shelter in the office of a local judge. Bill managed to escape, running to the edge of a field where Aaron L. Benedict had a horse waiting for him. They were able to escape to the home of Reuben Benedict. Meanwhile, the Virginians were jailed and could not pursue Bill and his helpers. After resting for several days, Aaron L. Benedict and his brother-in-law Griffith Levering first took Bill to the Owl Creek Friends Settlement near Fredericktown, then to Greenwich, and on to Oberlin. From there, he was sent to Canada.

Delaware County Ohio's, Africa

In Delaware County, a small, unincorporated area once had the name of Africa. It was located at the edge of what is now the Alum Creek State Park. How the community got the name Africa involves the Underground Railroad. Before 1840, the tiny hamlet then known as East Orange was a rural crossroads north of Westerville. As the community grew, some citizens built small cabins as temporary housing while their larger homes were being built. The cabins were uninhabited until 1859. At this time, a slave owner in North Carolina died and his widow freed the slaves. This group of 35 free men, women, and children found their way across the Ohio River and safely to the town of Westerville. The group was invited to stay in the cabins. They lived there and worked for local farmers. These black residents became involved in the Underground Railroad and their community received the nickname, "Africa." The cabins are now gone, but the history of the community of Africa in Delaware County remains.

Other Conductors

Starting in 1844, Daniel Osborn, a local abolitionist and railroad conductor, kept a diary of the fugitive slaves who traveled through the Alum Creek neighborhood from April 14 to September 10, 1844. During that period of time, he aided 45 fugitives from Virginia and Kentucky. Among them was a former slave who went from Ohio back to Kentucky and returned with his wife, child, and sister-in-law. Another woman came from Canada and brought back four of her children and one grandchild from Kentucky.

Many fugitive slaves came to Alum Creek from Delaware, Ohio, 15 miles southeast of Alum Creek. The main conductor on this route was William Cratty, owner of a farm in Delaware County that became a historical landmark as a station. Cratty's activities, which began as early as 1836, became so well known by slavecatchers that a bounty of $3,000 (more than $60,000 today) was offered to any person who could deliver him, dead or alive, south of the Mason-Dixon line. Nevertheless, he continued his activities of hiding and transporting fugitive slaves for many years, perhaps more inspired by the threat of being captured than deterred by it. Due to his persistence and the geographical location of his farm, Cratty was a major contributor to the Underground Railroad and claimed to have helped 3,000 fugitive slaves. From Cratty's house, fugitive slaves were often delivered to the Benedict family members.

Udney Hyde, from Mechanicsburg, located 45 miles to the southwest, was another important conductor who made regular trips to Alum Creek. Other routes that led here were from Columbus, Worthington, Mount Gilead, and Shaw Creek. From the Alum Creek Settlement, fugitives walked or were transported by wagon north to stations at Mt. Gilead, Mansfield, and a Quaker Settlement in Greenwich, then on to Sandusky or Huron on Lake Erie. Another route took them to Oberlin, Berea, and then Cleveland. From the ports, the fugitives were put on board Lake Erie vessels bound for Canada.

Green and Dillingham

Not all fugitive slave stories ended happily. An incident involved a man who came to Alum Creek in 1837 without his wife and children. His name was Elisha Young, which he later changed to John Green. Aaron Benedict gave him a job and promised to help him rescue his family. In early autumn 1837, Benedict and Green drove a two-horse carriage to Ripley, Ohio, where they met with John Rankin. Green was taken across the Ohio River to Kentucky in a rowboat. The Rankin people explained to Green how to signal them when he returned to the river with his family. He traveled 60 miles into the slave state and was gone for two weeks. He was successful in rescuing his family and returning them to Alum Creek. About six weeks later, while Green was hunting, several men in a wagon arrived in Alum Creek at night. They entered his cabin and abducted his wife and children. Green and Aaron

Benedict chased them on horseback to Delaware, Ohio. Being a fugitive slave, Green was afraid to travel any farther. They returned to Alum Creek and Green was left without his family. Following this incident, Green traveled along the Underground Railroad to Canada. After the Civil War he went back to Kentucky, found his daughter, and brought her and her husband back to Ohio where they settled in Van Wert County.

Another sad story involved Alum Creek Underground Railroad conductor, Richard Dillingham. In 1849, he went to Tennessee to try to rescue a slave family from a cruel master. Before they reached their destination, they were discovered, and he was arrested and sent to prison in Nashville. A few months later, he died there during a cholera epidemic.

Three Generations of Benedicts

After the signing of the Fugitive Slave Law of 1850, activity on the Underground Railroad increased. In 1851, Mordecai Benedict, the youngest conductor at the age of six, began driving fugitives by the wagonload from the Benedict residence to the home of conductor Joseph Morris at the Shaw Creek Quaker Settlement—a distance of nine miles. By 1854 and 1855, the lines through Alum Creek and surrounding stations were very busy. During one month in 1854 (or 1855), 60 fugitive slaves were at the home of Aaron L. Benedict, the son of Aaron Benedict, and as many as 20 sat down for a meal served by his wife.

In 1857 Aaron L. Benedict built a second, larger brick house where he continued to hide fugitive slaves, this time in a cellar beneath the kitchen, accessed by a trapdoor. A reward of $1,000 had been placed on his head.

The Benedicts and other stationkeepers from Alum Creek and the surrounding area continued to aid fugitive slaves until the Emancipation Proclamation in 1863. At least six and as many as ten Alum Creek residents served as Underground Railroad stationkeepers. Stops in the settlement included the Alum Creek Friends Meeting Church and the residences of Cyrus Benedict, William Benedict, Reuben Benedict, Aaron L. Benedict, Daniel Benedict, Daniel Osborn, and Aaron Osborn. Of these structures, only the Aaron L. Benedict house is still standing.

—Cynthia Vogel

Further Reading

Levi Coffin, *The Reminiscences of Levi Coffin* (Cincinnati: Robert Clark & Co., 1880).

E. Delorus Preston, Jr., "The Underground Railroad In Northwest Ohio," *Journal of Negro History*, 17, No. 4, (October 1932).

Wilbur Siebert, "A Quaker Section of the Underground Railroad in Northern Ohio," *Ohio History*, 39, No. 3 (July 1930).

Wilbur H. Siebert, *The Mysteries of Ohio's Underground Railroad* (Columbus, OH: Long's College Book Company, 1951).

Wilbur H. Siebert, *The Underground Railroad from Slavery to Freedom* (New York: Arno Press and *The New York Times*, 1968).

Ralph M. Watts, "History of the Underground Railroad in Mechanicsburg" (*Ohio History*, 34, 1934).

AMHERSTBURG, ONTARIO

Known as the last stop or terminus of the Underground Railroad, Amherstburg, once known as Fort Malden, or simply Malden, is located on the east bank of the Detroit River in the former Canada West, about 15 miles south of Detroit. From the busy ports of Toledo, Sandusky and Cleveland, so many fugitive slaves crossed Lake Erie to Malden that it was appropriate to call it the chief place of entry. After 1850, as many as 30 fugitive slaves a day would arrive by steamboat.

"Wooding Up"

The community was a good place for "wooding up," an expression for restocking firewood, and this proved fortunate for two fugitive slaves from Kentucky. Underground Railroad conductors disguised George and his sister, Clara, as sailors and smuggled them onto a Lake Erie steamer at the first stop en route from Buffalo to Detroit. In Cleveland, their master boarded the ship with his slave hunter, expecting to head home empty-handed, but soon thanked Providence for leading them straight to his slaves.

It would have been unwise to disembark with slaves in Detroit, where many free blacks sympathetic to fugitive slaves lived and where a militant Underground Railroad organization existed. To avoid trouble, the slaveholder requested stopping on the Michigan side before arriving in Detroit. Believing they had the captain's cooperation, they relaxed their vigilance and went off to play cards. They had no way of knowing that they had misjudged the captain's sympathies when enlisting help. Captain Titus told his crew that not all the money in Kentucky was enough to make him stop before getting to Detroit and put them ashore.

The need for fuel could not be disputed and served as cover for what might otherwise be called open defiance of Southern interests. So, the ship docked in fugitive-friendly Malden, ostensibly to wood up. As soon as the plank was thrown from the gangway, George and Clara fled and the hunters gave chase. Locals intervened, however, protecting their newfound freedom.

Before the Underground Railroad

Canada was not always a safe haven. An early version of the Underground Railroad ran in the opposite direction, with Canadian slaves fleeing for the

United States. This was the result of a 1793 law governing Upper Canada, now Ontario, that decreed resident slaves would remain slaves, while granting freedom to new slaves entering the country. In 10 years, Lower Canada, including Quebec and the Maritimes, adopted a similar measure.

In those days, Amherstburg shouldered its own slaveholders. At the turn of the nineteenth century, Captain Matthew Elliot owned about 50 slaves. To keep them in line, he employed a whipping post. Troublemakers were tied to it, to immobilize them for the lash. Several of Elliot's slaves were among those who escaped to the Michigan Territory of the United States, and some made their way south to Indiana, where the law protected them. At this time, the North Star was not the guiding light. But by 1803, through the efforts of Upper Canada Governor John Graves Simcoe and Lower Canada Chief Justice William Osgoode, slavery was declared inconsistent with British law, effectively ending slavery in the Canadian provinces and making it a refuge for fugitive slaves.

Gateway to Freedom

Many U.S. refugees from slavery passed through Amherstburg rather than setting down roots in the town. Moving inland meant less risk of kidnapping and forcible return to the United States. Still, by one count, 800 blacks called Amherstburg home at the start of the U.S. Civil War, comprising 40 percent of the population.

As a gateway to other Canadian destinations, Amherstburg became the accidental host of happy reunions. Reverend William Mitchell in his book about the Underground Railroad recounted the story of a man named Hedgman, who relocated to Amherstburg after escaping from Kentucky. Slavery had separated him from his wife and children. Twelve years after arriving in Canada, Hedgman's melodious voice carried from a chapel to warm the heart of a new arrival. She opened the door to see who was singing and found her husband.

Yet difficulties abounded. Isaac Rice, assigned to Amherstburg by the American Missionary Association, lost popular support and funding, in part because he maintained that blacks could learn to manage their own affairs. He shared his personal possessions with fugitive slaves, practicing charity to such a degree that he personally lacked a sufficient change of clothing, and even sold his watch and bed to buy them food. In November 1843, he lamented this predicament in a letter to the newspaper, *The Liberator*:

> Whole families reach us, needing clothing, provisions, a home for a few days . . . They are driven from schools in the States, they are no better here. If they go in schools by themselves, their portion of public money is allowed; but Canadians will not teach them, so that your teachers from the States must do it and aid them also about getting land and various other ways. (Landon 2–3)

The black anti-slavery activist and Buffalo resident, William Wells Brown, had the pleasure of reuniting in Amherstburg with 17 people he had aided.

In his autobiography, Brown credited his own freedom and his name to a conductor for the Underground Railroad in Ohio. Thirteen years later, he wrote: "Even a name by which to be known among men, slavery had denied me. You bestowed upon me your own. Base, indeed, should I be, if I ever forget what I owe to you, or do anything to disgrace that honored name!" (Prince 66).

As a free man employed on a steamship, Brown could hide four or five fugitives at a time. In what may have been his best year, he helped 69 slaves reach Canada in 7 months in 1842.

The True Band

Fugitive slaves in Amherstburg established the first True Band in 1854, a self-help organization copied elsewhere by former slaves in Canada. Membership in the Amherstburg True Band grew to 600 men and women. The group collected monthly dues to fund good works: serving the poor, promoting school attendance and church harmony, solving disagreements without litigation, discouraging fraudulent charity collections in their name, and preparing members to participate in politics. Their efforts went a long way toward refuting the prevalent belief that black immigrants couldn't look after themselves.

—Rae Hallstrom

Further Reading

Fred Landon, Amherstburg, Terminus of the Underground Railroad, *Journal of Negro History*, 10, No. 1, Association for the Study of African-American Life: January 1925.

Eber M. Pettit, *Sketches in the History of the Underground Railroad* (Fredonia, NY: W. McKinstry & Son, 1879).

Bryan Prince, *I Came as a Stranger* (Toronto: Tundra Books, 2004).

Benjamin Quarles, *Black Abolitionists* (New York: Oxford University Press, 1969).

B

BALTIMORE, MARYLAND

During most of the antebellum period, Baltimore was the largest and most commercially successful city in the upper South. It was the processing and shipping point for tobacco grown in the areas south of it and for the cereals grown in northern and western Maryland. It was a shipbuilding center and the transportation hub for a vast region as well. The Baltimore and Ohio, Baltimore and Susquehanna, and Philadelphia, Wilmington, and Baltimore railroads connected the city to points south, north, and west; the Delaware and Chesapeake Canal ran from Baltimore to the Delaware River; the National Road, the nation's first turnpike, ran west from it; and the Patapsco River, on which the city is sited, opened it to the Chesapeake Bay and tied it to ports in North and South America.

Antebellum Period's Largest Free Black Population

Agricultural shifts, rural-to-urban migration, and an atmosphere that was generally unrestricted before about 1840 also made Baltimore home to the largest free black population of any city in the nation before the Civil War. When grains replaced tobacco as the principal crop of northern and western Maryland, the practicality of the slave labor system diminished. Because grain cultivation was intensive only at certain times of year and required far less labor overall, farmers in these areas found the occasional employment of paid labor cheaper than maintaining slaves. As a consequence, they either manumitted their slaves or sold them to the cotton states of the South. Many formerly enslaved people moved from rural areas into Baltimore, whose robust economy offered many jobs. And for many decades the necessity to have and carry freedom papers, a requirement in many Southern places, was largely overlooked. Thus the population of free blacks in Maryland swelled, and in Baltimore it rose in even greater measure. In 1800, 2,843 slaves and 2,771 free blacks lived in

Baltimore; by 1850 only 2,946 Baltimoreans were still enslaved and 25,442 blacks were free.

Center of Slave Trade

Nevertheless, Baltimore was a major center of the slave trade, an activity that raised the ire of many abolitionists. Quaker abolitionist Benjamin Lundy, who had moved to Baltimore in 1824 with his antislavery newspaper, *Genius of Universal Emancipation*, published an attack on slave auctioneer Austin Woolfolk in an 1825 issue of the newspaper; Woolfolk as a consequence sought out Lundy and beat him severely. In 1829, during his brief time in Baltimore as coeditor of the *Genius*, William Lloyd Garrison challenged Woolfolk to inflict the same punishment on him. When Woolfolk did not respond, Garrison publicly labeled Francis Todd, one of the captains of Woolfolk's slave ships, a robber and murderer. Todd sued Garrison for libel. Convicted and unable to pay the fine, Garrison was imprisoned in a Baltimore jail for 49 days.

Abolitionism

Despite its reputation as an infamous slave-trading center, Baltimore included what appears to have been a small cadre of abolitionists. Among the earliest known was the flour miller Elisha Tyson (1749–1824). Though scholars disagree on the scope of his activity—for example, historian Stanley Harrold has asserted that Tyson, a Quaker, only aided those who were illegally being deprived of freedom and was not strongly committed to abolitionism—Tyson's efforts to secure the freedom of free people who had been kidnapped and enslaved were numerous. Although his belief in the rule of law kept him from purchasing the freedom of enslaved people, and presumably would have inhibited him from violating the Fugitive Slave Law by helping fugitives escape, Underground Railroad historian R. C. Smedley alleges otherwise. Writing in 1883, Smedley based his work on first-hand accounts of participants in antebellum fugitive assistance and asserted that Tyson's home had been the beginning of a "line" of assistants between Baltimore and Chester County, Pennsylvania, from as early as 1801. He cited two instances of Tyson assisting the movement of fugitives north, in and after 1810.

Fugitives found Baltimore attractive because work was available, escape farther north was possible by numerous means, and its large population of African Americans made it possible to live in relative anonymity. Enslaved people in nearby areas and those from farther south who accompanied masters to Baltimore learned about these urban features from the many African Americans—both free people and enslaved people whose masters hired them out—who worked in maritime trades or carried goods to and from Baltimore markets, docks, and depots. Over time a network of free and enslaved people linked the city and rural areas and contributed to the flow of fugitives to the city. Historian Christopher Phillips has cited the case of the runaway Phil Carter, whose master advertised the likelihood "that he is gone to Baltimore, as his father is living there on Howard's hill, and is a dray man"; in another instance, the master of the enslaved Adnah Pierce stated his belief that she was "lurking in or about Baltimore," where her free husband then lived (66–67).

Escapes of Fugitive Slaves

Between 1773 and 1819, according to one local historian, almost 20 percent of all fugitive slaves in the region escaped to Baltimore, with a peak of nearly 30 percent in the 1810s, in contrast with only 7 percent who fled to Pennsylvania. With Nat Turner's revolt in 1830 and the quickening of antislavery organization and activity in the 1830s, city and state officials enacted measures to constrict freedom of movement, information, and assembly among people of color. Thomas Smallwood, whose collaboration with the Rev. Charles T. Torrey endangered his life in Washington, D.C., found it difficult to obtain the documents required to move his family from Baltimore to Canada. Philadelphia Vigilance Committee secretary William Still related the case of six people who escaped Baltimore and reached his office in April 1853:

> Baltimore used to be in the days of Slavery one of the most difficult places in the South for even free colored people to get away from, much more for slaves. The rule forbade any colored person leaving there by rail road or steamboat, without such applicant had been weighed, measured, and then given a bond signed by unquestionable signatures. . . . But, notwithstanding all this weighing, measuring and requiring of bonds, many travelers by the Underground Rail Road, took passage from Baltimore. (Still 136)

As Still indicated, escapes from Baltimore were frequent enough that slaveholders hired one Charles Taylor, who drove a stage between Baltimore and York and Columbia in Pennsylvania, to notify them of suspected fugitive slaves. Of the 664 fugitives Still documented in his 1871 *Underground Railroad*, more than 60 were from Baltimore City and County, the largest number escaping from any single place he described. In general terms fugitives traveled to Philadelphia, where they were directed either inland to New York State or by water to New York City and beyond, or they traveled as stowaways or crew on those vessels bound for New York and New England ports. For decades many enslaved people—including Frederick Douglass, who escaped from Baltimore in 1838—were hired out to work in the shipyards and on the wharves and vessels at Fell's Point, the city's shipbuilding center and an enclave of black settlement. By 1850, according to Christopher Phillips, two-thirds of all black males in Baltimore's second ward, in which

Fell's Point stood, worked in maritime shoreside trades or on vessels, many of which carried black crew into and out of the city. These men and women were critical in determining the vessels most likely to carry fugitives and in assisting their passage.

One of the best-known fugitive flights from Baltimore is that of Lear Green, who escaped from butter dealer James Noble by having herself crated in a chest in 1854. Green's mother and fiancé, the black barber William Adams, packed her and had her stowed on a steamer for an 18-hour passage to Philadelphia; Adams's mother, a free woman, accompanied her on the steamer as a passenger. Despite Noble's detailed runaway advertisement in the *Baltimore Sun*, Green escaped successfully, and Still forwarded her to Elmira, New York, where she married Adams. In his 1871 *Underground Railroad*, Still wrote that runaway advertisements in the *Sun* made the paper "quite famous for this kind of UGRR literature, and on that account alone the Committee subscribed for it daily" (72).

However, most of the agents living in Baltimore who took part in fugitive escapes have so far not been identified. In an 1895 letter Pennsylvania Underground Railroad activist Robert Purvis told Smedley, "The most efficient helpers, or agents we had, were two market women, who lived in Baltimore, one of whom was white, the other 'colored.' By some means, they obtained a number of genuine certificates of freedom or passports, which they gave to slaves who wished to escape. These passports were afterwards returned to them, and used again by other fugitives. The generally received opinion, that 'all negroes look alike,' prevented too close a scrutiny by the officials" (Smedley 355).

In 1857 fugitive assistant Thomas Garrett in Wilmington, Delaware, wrote of "an abolitionist in Baltimore" unknown even to him who had unwittingly told an informer about the escape of a group of people from Cambridge on Maryland's Eastern Shore. And in 1859, five years after Lear Green's escape, an unidentified "near relative" wrapped the fugitive William Peel in straw, boxed him, and sent him to Philadelphia as freight on the same steamer line Green had used.

Added to the escapes of black Baltimoreans were the numerous fugitives who passed through the city on their way north. Perry Wilkinson, whose master hired him out as a boatman running between Anne Arundel County and Baltimore, used the vessel on which he worked to escape to Baltimore upon learning of his impending sale; he went from there to York, Pennsylvania. William and Ellen Craft, she disguised as a white planter and he as the planter's servant, passed through Baltimore in their escape from Georgia in 1851. "They knew that they must pass through Baltimore, but they did not know the obstacles that they would have to surmount in the Monumental City," Still wrote. The ticket master at the rail depot readily sold a ticket to Ellen Craft but demanded a bond from a "gentlemen of well-known responsibility" before selling one to him. William responded that he was ignorant of the regulation and was "simply traveling with his young master to take care of him—he being in a very delicate state of health, so much so, that fears were entertained that he might not be able to hold out to reach Philadelphia, where he was hastening for medical treatment." The ticketer "waived the old 'rule,'" Still noted, and the Crafts boarded the train (Still 369). Benjamin Drew, who interviewed onetime fugitives in Canada in the 1850s related the story of Isaac Williams, who with another enslaved man escaped by foot from Virginia to Baltimore. There they lay "in the bush," watching the trains to find out where the depot was; the two men then followed one train to Havre de Grace and ultimately escaped to St. Catharines in Canada.

Several fugitive assistants also put themselves at great risk by traveling to Baltimore to retrieve enslaved people and send them north, a practice that few agents attempted. Urged by free people of Detroit to travel east to retrieve enslaved relatives, John Fairfield met the group in Baltimore, disguised them as white with face powder and wigs, and accompanied them by rail to Harrisburg, Pennsylvania. Harriet Tubman's first effort to aid enslaved people occurred in Baltimore in December 1850. She had come from Pennsylvania upon learning that her niece, Kessiah Bowley, was about to be sold in Cambridge, Maryland. Bowley's husband, a free ship's carpenter, had managed to remove her during the auction and brought her by boat to Baltimore. After bringing Bowley and her family out of the city, Tubman went back to Baltimore to retrieve her brother Moses and two other men.

Less successful were Underground Railroad activists Daniel Gibbons and Charles T. Torrey. Gibbons, a Pennsylvania Quaker abolitionist who over more than half a century is believed to have helped some 1,000 fugitives escape, went to Baltimore to find Abraham Boston, who had once lived with him but was taken by kidnappers. Boston, according to Smedley, was "the only person for whom he [Gibbons] ever went to Maryland," but Boston was nowhere to be found (Smedley 56). And Torrey, a Massachusetts cleric who had moved to Washington in 1841, went to Baltimore in 1844, helped several fugitives escape the city, and was then arrested on his return there to help others. Torrey was tried, found guilty, and jailed for six years; he died at a Baltimore jail in 1846.

Finally, many escaping slavery probably remained in Baltimore. As historian Barbara Jean Fields has noted, "Some fugitives found Baltimore, whether they chose it or not, the end of the line, since it was a much easier city to disappear into than to escape from" (34). Philadelphia John Robinson, a free man from Norfolk, came to Baltimore to work as a stonecutter and, during his time there, was arrested and tried for helping one enslaved person's escape attempt. Emeline Chapman escaped to Baltimore from Washington, D.C., in 1856 with her two infant children, and she may have remained there even though her master published a runaway notice seeking her apprehension in the *Baltimore Sun*.

—Kathryn Grover

Further Reading

Barbara Jean Fields, *Slavery and Freedom on the Middle Ground: Maryland during the Nineteenth Century* (New Haven: Yale University Press, 1985).

Cheryl Janifer LaRoche, "Resistance to Slavery in Maryland: Strategies for Freedom" (Special History Study, National Park Service for the Organization of American Historians, March 2007).

Christopher Phillips, *Freedom's Port: The African American Community of Baltimore, 1790–1860* (Urbana and Chicago: University of Illinois Press, 1997).

R. C. Smedley, *History of the Underground Railroad in Chester and the Neighboring Counties of Pennsylvania* (1883; reprint, Lancaster, PA: Stackpole Books, 2005).

William Still, *The Underground Railroad* (1871; reprint, Chicago: Johnson Publishing Co., 1970).

William J. Switala, *The Underground Railroad in Delaware, Maryland, and West Virginia* (Mechanicsburg, PA: Stackpole Books, 2002).

BATTLE CREEK, MICHIGAN

Long before Battle Creek became known for its breakfast cereal, the town served a far less mercenary cause, acting as a secret haven for runaway slaves. By 1844, Battle Creek, located in Calhoun County in southeastern Michigan, was a regular stop on the Underground Railroad. The Battle Creek stop followed Climax, and after Battle Creek, the route passed through Marshall, followed by Albion, and Parma.

Erastus Hussey

Erastus Hussey had never heard of the Underground Railroad when the Reverend John Cross asked him to serve as Battle Creek's conductor, but he learned fast. Once, he had 500 handbills printed to warn a posse of 30 armed kidnappers that Battle Creek abolitionists would put up a fight. The slave hunters turned back.

Another time, the people of Battle Creek hosted a group of 45 fugitive slaves for the night. Many of them had made homes in Michigan but sought greater safety in Canada after learning that Southerners had come to Michigan to attempt their rendition. The year was 1847, and the attack that prompted the exodus became known as the Kentucky Raid. Earlier, the Kentuckians had arrived in Battle Creek to plan the raid, where they were discovered by abolitionists and driven out. But they carried out their plan until stopped by a mob from Cassopolis. Realizing that they were no longer safe in the free state of Michigan, slaves began the journey north. The refugees reached Battle Creek and crossed the West Main Street Bridge by moonlight, accompanied by nine white men who traveled with them on horseback as guards.

Zachariah Shugart, a leader in the Quaker abolitionist movement in Cassopolis, was one of the guards, and he arrived wearing a white hat. By the light of the moon, the broad brim of his hat would have been impossible to miss. Atop a horse, Shugart would have been an easy target. But he showed defiance, not fear; and based on the turnout that night, he was not alone. Battle Creek's conductor, Erastus Hussey, recalled that "every man, woman, and child was upon the street and it looked as if a circus was coming to town" (Michigan Historical Commission, Historical Collections 280).

When Richard Dillingham, the Alum Creek Quaker, delivered advance news of the arrival, Hussey had just two hours to prepare. His wife, Sarah, was sick in bed, a hardship that meant he needed more help than usual. Three abolitionists supplied food: Elijah T. Mott, who owned the mill, donated 60 pounds of flour; Silas Dodge bought the potatoes; and Samuel Strauther bought the pork. Hussey himself supplied wood for the stove, and Lester Buckley supplied the shelter—an unoccupied house that he owned.

In later years, Hussey would recall that Buckley had sympathized with the abolitionist movement, despite being a Whig. At the time, more members of the Whig party stood for slavery than against, but over time the antislavery coalition grew. Nine years after the large fugitive group came through Battle Creek, disagreements over slavery caused the Whig Party to fold.

Without Mrs. Hussey to help on that August night, the fugitives, tired and hungry from their long march, cooked for themselves. Sarah Hussey recovered; but in three years, Dillingham, their 24-year-old messenger, would die in a Kentucky prison after being caught aiding fugitive slaves in Tennessee.

Fugitive Slaves Who Settled in Battle Creek

Most of the runaways who visited Battle Creek on that moonlit night in 1847 left for Canada in the morning, but a few stayed behind to make Battle Creek their home. One of them was William Casey, who joined the Underground Railroad. Perhaps Casey was encouraged by the apparent affluence and generosity of Samuel Strauther, the lone black abolitionist, and the one who supplied the travelers with meat. When the station at Battle Creek was established, there were only six known antislavery men in all of Battle Creek. Strauther was there from the beginning, serving the cause. He was already prominent in the community and the "colored Masonic lodge was named after him—Strauther lodge No. 3" (ibid. 280).

In addition to Casey, another fugitive slave called Battle Creek home. Perry Sanford, who may have been among the group of 45 fugitives on the West Main Street Bridge, spoke with the *Sunday Morning Call* in August 1884. He recalled that he and his fellow Kentucky field hands risked escape after learning they'd been sold to a Mississippi cotton planter. No slave wanted to pick cotton in the Deep South, where the conditions of slavery were far more severe and greatly shortened their life expectancy. The group crossed the Ohio River the night of Easter Monday, because they could move about with less suspicion on a holiday. After landing in Ohio, they traveled at night by covered wagon and hid in Quaker barns or the woods during the day. It took a month to reach Cass County, Michigan, and Sanford settled there until the night of the raid. He held the Quakers in great esteem for their help. When the Fugitive Slave Law passed, every black but Sanford and William Casey abandoned Battle Creek for Canada.

Free Soil Party

In 1848, a year after the Kentucky Raid, Michigan abolitionists chose Erastus Hussey to be one of three state representatives at the Buffalo convention where the Free Soil Party was born. Members of the new political party hoped to end slavery, but sought first to stop its spread. In part, the party's platform read: "*no more* slave states, and *no more* slave territory" (ibid. 264). Members of the Buffalo Convention resolved to proclaim on their banner "Free Soil, Free Speech, Free Labor and Free Men" and pledged to fight as long as necessary for victory.

The Free Soil Party appealed to Democrats, mostly in the North, who agreed with the Wilmot Proviso. In 1846, U.S. Representative David Wilmot drafted the Wilmot Proviso, which would have tied additional funding for the Mexican-American War to antislavery conditions. The legislation proposed outlawing the expansion of slavery into territories acquired as a result of the war. Though it passed the House, the Wilmot Proviso failed each time it reached the conservative, Southern-dominated Senate.

Crosswhite Affair

In nearby Marshall, the Crosswhite affair turned Wilmot Proviso Democrats against their party's presidential candidate, Michigan's Lewis Cass, who had sided with the South. One source hinted that the Crosswhite family might have been related to their owner, Francis Giltner, because their name described the color of their skin. Regardless, the court found that Michigan abolitionists broke the law when they helped Adam Crosswhite, his wife, and their four children escape to Canada. In December 1848, Giltner was awarded $1,926 in damages plus the cost of a suit, worth more than $54,000 in today's dollars.

While the Crosswhite case was a huge financial setback for Michigan abolitionists, it had national repercussions, too—handing proslavery forces a new president. In the presidential election of 1848, disgruntled Wilmot Proviso Democrats voted outside party lines to defeat Cass, who had abandoned the antislavery contingency in his own state. When Cass secured the proslavery votes he needed for the party's nomination, the change in allegiance must have seemed politically wise. But in the general election, it siphoned antislavery votes to the fledgling Free Soil Party, and threw the election to the Whigs. In 1849, the man who was sworn in as the twelfth president of the United States was not Cass, but Zachary Taylor, a slave-owning, war hero.

The verdict against the Marshall men in the Crosswhite case helped arouse Erastus Hussey's interest in politics. In 1847, he began publication of an anti-slavery newspaper called the *Michigan Liberty Press*; in 1848, he helped found the Free Soil Party; and in 1849, he won election to the Michigan House of Representatives. By 1850, when he and other abolitionists were seated, Calhoun County could claim a solid antislavery delegation in the legislature. In 1854, he presided over the Jackson, Michigan, Under the Oaks convention that dissolved the Free Soil Party and founded the Republican Party. Later that year, he became a member of the Michigan State Senate. After 1855, when more fugitives chose a more easterly route up through Ohio to Michigan, Hussey's workload on the Underground Railroad lightened. In 1860, he became a delegate to the Chicago convention that nominated Abraham Lincoln. Over the years he served Battle Creek as county clerk, alderman, and mayor.

Charles Barnes interviewed Hussey in 1885 for the Michigan Pioneer and Historical Collections, and asked how much he'd been paid for his work on the Underground Railroad. But there was no pay, not in the traditional sense; Hussey told Barnes: "We were working for humanity." Today, a plaque at the headquarters of the Kellogg Foundation in Battle Creek bears these words from Erastus Hussey: "I have fed and given protection to over 1,000 fugitives, and assisted them on to Canada."

—Rae Hallstrom

Further Reading

Anti-Slavery Activities, Medical History of Michigan (Minneapolis, MN: Bruce Publishing Company, 1930).

Michigan Historical Commission, Historical Collections, *Collections and Researches made by the Michigan Pioneer and Historical Society*, Volume 38 (Lansing, MI: Wynkoop Hallenbeck Crawford Co., State Printers, 1912).

Out of Bondage: Perry Sanford's Account, Sunday Morning Call newspaper (Battle Creek, MI, August 1884).

Working for Humanity, Sunday Morning Call (Battle Creek, MI, May 1885).

BEAVER, PENNSYLVANIA

Beaver, a borough in Beaver County, Pennsylvania, is located where the Beaver River flows into the Ohio River. Located on the Ohio border, the county was the site of considerable antislavery and Underground Railroad activity. Beaver is located about 30 miles northwest of Pittsburgh.

Fugitive slaves generally came to Beaver County from Uniontown, Pennsylvania, where they had fled, often from Morgantown (West) Virginia and Cumberland, Maryland.

Conductors in Beaver Area

In New Brighton, a few miles south of Beaver, were the homes of many Quakers who were active in the antislavery movement. In addition, Reverend Arthur B. Bradford, pastor of the Free Presbyterian Church, influenced fugitive slaves to come to this area. The Free Presbyterians' willingness to help slaves seeking freedom was widely known among the slaves still living in the South—in Kentucky, Maryland, Virginia, and even Huntsville, Alabama. Residents of Beaver County who helped the fugitive slaves included: Edward Townsend, who hid the fugitive slaves in a cellar that could be accessed by a trap door; Benjamin Townsend, who hid them in a cave located at Penn Avenue and Allegheny Road; and David Townsend, with his safe island in the Beaver River. Other operators included Milo Talbot, James Irvin, Lewis Townsend, E. Ellwood, Timothy B. White, Joshua Gilbert, a man known only as Rakestraw, and Rev. Abel Brown.

Another worker on the Underground Railroad was Jonathan Morris of New Brighton, whose home was near Little Beaver Creek. From here, the fugitives often were sent to a station in Salem, Ohio.

Other Underground stations in Beaver County included the Presbyterian Church, with its Covenanter Congregation; Geneva College in Beaver Falls; and the communities of Hookstown, Bridgewater, and Rochester.

The Fugitive Slave Law, passed in September 1850, got special attention in New Brighton. On December 5, 1850, local antislavery workers set up a meeting and adopted resolutions against it. The reasons they cited were that the law was anti-Christian and they vowed that they would reject it.

Rev. Abel Brown

Reverend Abel Brown, a Baptist Church reformer and a renowned abolitionist, was active in the Underground Railroad during the brief period he lived in the county. His home in Beaver became a frequent stop for fugitive slaves from 1837 to 1839; he also traveled into the South while living there to rescue slaves. In one case he went to Baltimore, Maryland, and aided the escape of a Virginia woman, crossing the Mason-Dixon Line near York, Pennsylvania. After forwarding the woman to another conductor, he was arrested and brought before the court. However, when sufficient evidence could not be found, the charges were dropped. In another trip into the South, he successfully aided the escape of a fugitive slave from Louisville to Cincinnati.

Richard Gardner was a fugitive slave previously owned by Rhoda B. Byers of Louisville, Kentucky. In 1849, he escaped with his wife and children from Kentucky and settled in Beaver. Shortly after his arrival, he was able to build a new house, and began preaching in a local Methodist church. On March 14, 1851, Gardner was arrested and transported to Pittsburgh by riverboat. At his trial, he was found guilty of being a fugitive slave and returned to Byers.

The people of Beaver were able to pay Byers $600 and Gardner was freed. On April 9, 1851, he returned to Beaver where he lived until his death about the year 1876.

McKeever Brothers

Thomas McKeever sheltered fugitive slaves in the barn on his farm in Beaver County, and his brother William McKeever hid fugitive slaves in the attic of his house located in West Middletown, Washington County, Pennsylvania. Often when the McKeevers could not safely transport fugitive slaves, they hid them in "Penitentiary Woods," a thick wooded area with a cabin about one mile from West Middletown. Fugitive slaves could live in this place for an extended period of time, if necessary. From here neighboring free blacks led them to Beaver County. John Jordan, a black hired hand, sometimes aided the McKeevers.

Many fugitive slave stories do not have happy endings. Three fugitive slaves had been hiding in a coal mine in the little village of Cannelton near Darlington. The mine, located in the northwest corner of Beaver County, belonged to William Welsh. Slavecatchers discovered them and ordered them to come out, but they refused. The slavecatchers then filled the mine entrance with brush and set it on fire. The fugitives could not escape and died in the cave.

The citizens of Beaver County formed two active antislavery societies, one on January 28, 1826, at the Greersburg Academy, and another during the early 1840s, under the leadership of prominent abolitionist William Scott in Chippewa Township.

Beaver County's Underground Railroad activities were closely connected to the Underground Railroad activities of Pittsburgh and Washington, Pennsylvania; Wheeling (West) Virginia; and Steubenville and Salem, Ohio.

—Cynthia Vogel

Further Reading

John Henderson Bausman, *History of Beaver County, Pennsylvania* (New York: Knickerbocker Press, 1904).

C. S. Brown, *Memoir of Rev. Abel Brown* (1849; reprint with introduction and annotations by Tom Calarco, *Abel Brown Abolitionist*, Jefferson, NC: McFarland, 2006).

Levi Coffin, *The Reminiscences of Levi Coffin* (Cincinnati: Robert Clark & Co., 1880).

Randolph County, Indiana, 1818—1990, compiled by the Randolph County Historical Society, 1990.

Wilbur H. Siebert, *The Mysteries of Ohio's Underground Railroads* (Columbus, OH: Long's College Book Company, 1951).

Wilbur H. Siebert, *The Underground Railroad from Slavery to Freedom* (New York: Arno Press and *The New York Times*, 1968).

The New England entries covered along with associated locations. (Courtesy of Tom Calarco)

BOSTON, MASSACHUSETTS

Boston was the intellectual center of abolitionism and an important stop on the Underground Railroad. There were a number of reasons for this: intellectual leaders of the abolition movement, including William Lloyd Garrison and David Walker, lived and worked in Boston; Massachusetts had a tradition that placed a high value on self-determination and was the second state to abolish slavery in 1783; and finally, having an economy fueled by the shipping and fishing industries, New England was a source of ready employment for black sailors, who were physically equipped for handling the rigorous life on the sea. As a result, cargo ships from the area in Southern harbors provided friendly refuges for slaves seeking freedom. In this way, many fugitive slaves gained their freedom and began coming to New England by sea as early as 1791.

David Walker and His *Appeal*

Most traditional histories have credited whites as the prime movers of the abolitionist movement and downplayed the contributions of blacks. However, much of the impetus for the movement came from blacks protesting their conditions. David Walker's revolutionary *Appeal*, for example, was a black message that resonated until the Civil War.

Born free in North Carolina prior to 1800, Walker moved to Boston after a life of travel, living in the Beacon Hill area during the 1820s. He opened a used-clothing shop near the waterfront where most of his customers were black seamen and became relatively prosperous. But his pride and intelligence compelled him to protest the inferior conditions of blacks in America. First, he organized meetings, and then began submitting articles to *Freedom's Journal* in New York. In 1829, he compiled his thoughts in the *Appeal to the Coloured Citizens of the World*, which he published and distributed in the South through the many contacts he had made among seamen.

The extent of the *Appeal*'s influence on the abolition movement is uncertain, but judging by the events that occurred after its publication, it had a lasting impact. Walker condemned colonization, excoriated Thomas Jefferson and Henry Clay, attacked the hypocrisy of the nation's so-called Christians, blasted Southern laws that prohibited slaves from being taught to read, and admonished all blacks whether free or slave for their submissiveness.

Although not universally embraced, even among the other abolitionists of his time, Walker's words probably had more influence on American blacks, especially the slaves in the South, than has been credited.

As many as 50 percent of New England seaman during this time were blacks and they are believed to have distributed copies of the Appeal to slaves, sometimes concealing copies of it, by having them sewn into the lining of their clothing. With their help the pamphlet was widely distributed. It wasn't long before a $3,000 reward was made for his life and a $10,000 reward to anyone who could bring him to the South alive. Walker's friends urged him to flee to Canada, but he ignored their warning.

Two months after the *Appeal*'s formal publication, Walker was found dead in his home. The cause was never determined.

William Lloyd Garrison

William Lloyd Garrison, founder of *The Liberator*, published the antislavery publication in Boston for 35 years from 1831 to 1866. Though the early subscribers of the paper were largely black, its reputation for advocating emancipation grew quickly across the nation. Garrison was also a founder of the New England Anti-Slavery Society, the American Anti-Slavery Society, and the Friends of Universal Reform. Garrison's influence was widespread, particularly among those fighting for women's suffrage along with the abolition of slavery, but he was scorned as well. Fines were levied against distributors of *The Liberator*, and one state even offered a bounty for his arrest and imprisonment.

TO THE FRIENDS OF THE FUGITIVE.

Alarmed at the operation of the new Fugitive Slave Law, the Fugitives from slavery are pressing Northward. Many have been obliged to flee precipitately, leaving behind them all the little they have acquired since they escaped from slavery. They are coming to us in increasing numbers, and they look to us for aid. Oppressed by the tyranny of a heartless and God-defying government, who will help them? Their first and most earnest desire is for *employment.* That is the greatest charity which finds it for them. Help us, then, all you who are friends of the fugitive, to extend to them this charity, this simple justice. Let all, who know, or can learn of places which may be filled by these men, women and youths, give information by letter or otherwise, to ROBERT F. WALLCUT, or SAMUEL MAY, Jr., 21 Cornhill, Boston.

Friend, whoever you are that reads these lines, this appeal is made to *you.* Cannot you find, or procure, one or more places where the hunted slave may abide securely, and work through the winter? We want you to attend to this AT ONCE.

N. B. Many of the fugitives come very poorly provided with clothing; and those who have garments of any kind to spare, will be sure to confer them on the suffering and needy by sending them, marked For fugitives, at 21 Cornhill, as above.

Ad in *The Liberator*, October 25, 1850, asking that contributions to aid fugitives be sent to the address of the offices of *The Liberator* in Boston. (Courtesy of Tom Calarco)

Boston's Vigilance Committees

Although not an official member of the Boston Vigilance Committee, Garrison opened up *The Liberator*'s offices for their meetings. The later most well known of the committees had more than 200 members, many of them from the Boston upper class. Among the most prominent were Francis Jackson, Henry and William Bowditch, Theodore Parker, Wendell Phillips, Samuel Gridley Howe, Samuel E. Sewell, Richard Henry Dana, Austin Bearse, Lewis Hayden, William Nell, Leonard Grimes, and Thomas Wentworth Higginson. The latter two were not listed on the official roster but played important roles in major incidents involving the committee. Hayden, Nell, and Grimes were the committee's most prominent black members.

The first documented action of organized vigilance in Boston occurred in 1836 when two women, Polly Ann Bates and Eliza Small, were claimed by a slavecatcher while traveling aboard a ship headed to Boston. Somehow word of the situation circulated after the boat docked in the harbor. A writ of habeas corpus was served by a black man, and Samuel Sewall, later an attorney for the Boston Vigilance Committee, was secured as counsel. The judge who heard the case decided the captain had no right to hold them and ordered the women released, but the agent declared his intention to re-arrest them under authority of the Fugitive Slave Law of 1793. In response, a mob of blacks forcibly took control of the women and led them away in a carriage. They were not recaptured, nor were the rescuers prosecuted. The Massachusetts Anti-Slavery Society pleaded innocent in the matter, only saying it did not condone violence.

Though the better known Boston Vigilance Committee was still some years in the future, in the spring of 1841 Charles Turner Torrey, one of the most celebrated abolitionists of his day, organized the earliest incarnation of the Boston Vigilance Committee. In June of that year he had the captain and mate of the schooner *Wellington* arrested for kidnapping the fugitive slave John Torrance, who had stowed away aboard their ship and who had been confined against his will after arriving in Boston Harbor.

Six years later, the Polly Ann Bates and Eliza Small affair, another incident occurred that brought Bostonians closer to the realization that a more formal vigilance committee to protect fugitive slaves might be needed. It involved a husband and wife from Norfolk, Virginia, George and Rebecca Latimer. Less than two weeks after their successful escape to freedom in the fall of 1842, George's owner came to Boston and had him arrested.

This created a stir in the Boston black community, which coincidentally had formed the New England Freedom Association (NEFA) on July 4, 1842, to protect fugitive slaves who were living in Boston and aid those who were fleeing slavery. Many white abolitionists like William Lloyd Garrison and Wendell Phillips quickly came to their support, and once again Samuel Sewall was enlisted to be counsel. Following a huge rally at Fanueil Hall, future Boston Vigilance Committee members Dr. Henry Bowditch, William Francis Channing, and Frederick Cabot published a weekly newspaper, the *Latimer Journal and North Star*, to protest this "enslavement." The result was that Latimer's owner agreed to sell him for only $400. It was a great victory for the Boston abolitionists. The *Latimer Journal* continued to publish until May 16, 1843, leading the effort that resulted in the state legislature passing a personal liberty law that forbid state authorities from participating in the prosecution of the first Fugitive Slave Law of 1793.

The NEFA continued its efforts until 1846, publishing advertisements in the *Emancipator* and *The Liberator* entitled, "Aid the Fugitive." It asked that food, clothing, and money be sent to 25 Cornhill Street in Boston, the address of *The Liberator* from 1837 to 1846, in care of William Nell, another clue to Garrison's actual ties to the Underground Railroad. There are others; in fact, Garrison is known to have forwarded fugitive slaves to prominent conductors like Sidney Howard Gay in New York, so apparently he was a member of the Road.

The NEFA became defunct after a few years, however, and apparently subsumed itself under an organization formed by a group of 40 individuals called the Boston Vigilance Committee. This group, the third to antedate the more famous later committee, was organized at the home of Henry Bowditch in Brookline after an incident that involved a runaway who had stowed away aboard a ship in Boston harbor but who failed to gain his freedom. In 1846, however, the sense of urgency provoked by the Latimer case no longer existed. Nevertheless, Theodore Parker, one of its organizers, wrote fellow committee member Samuel Gridley Howe that they should make it better known that they were ready to aid fugitive slaves as soon as they arrived in Boston, helping them to find jobs and sending them to Canada if they desired. Most fugitive slaves stayed in Boston rather than go to Canada at that time because the large and supportive black community helped them find work and start a new life. Perhaps even more important was that slavecatchers were seldom seen there. In fact, about this time, William Lloyd Garrison had boasted that there was no need for fugitive slaves to leave Boston for they would never be captured there.

All this changed, however, in 1850 with the passage of the second Fugitive Slave Law and the federal government's pledge to enforce it. This law created special federal commissioners to judge cases involving fugitive slaves and included other provisions that facilitated its prosecution. Two weeks after its passage, a widely advertised meeting was called at Fanueil Hall, among whose guest speakers was Frederick Douglass. A huge crowd turned out and resolutions were passed to aid and protect all fugitive slaves using any and all means to resist the new law. Former slaves who had settled in Boston were urged to stay.

At this time, the final, well-known incarnation of the Boston Vigilance Committee was organized. It started with 50 men, grew to 80, and eventually reached 209, the number of names listed in Austin Bearse's book, *Fugitive Slave Days in Boston*. Its president was Deacon Timothy Gilbert, founder of the legendary antislavery church, Tremont Temple; its secretary was Charles List, and its treasurer was Francis Jackson, wealthy attorney and civic leader. It had four subcommittees of eight members each: executive, legal, special vigilance and alarm, and finance. Its confidential agent and doorkeeper was Bearse.

William and Ellen Craft

Despite efforts by the local abolitionists, the estimated 600 fugitive slaves who had settled in Boston no longer felt secure. Organized groups with members in both the North and the South were making efforts to aid in the rendition of fugitive slaves. The celebrated William and Ellen Craft, the couple who had become famous following their escape from Georgia when Ellen disguised herself as a man and William acted the part of her slave, were among those who had reason to be wary. The Crafts had settled in Boston and had become active in the local black community. Both were gainfully employed: William, who had been a carpenter in the South, opened a used furniture shop, and Ellen took on sewing jobs out of her home. But owing to their prominence, it was not surprising when two slavecatchers, John Knight and Willis Hughes, showed up in

Boston after the passage of the new law with the intentions of claiming them under its jurisdiction.

Knight had worked with William when he was a carpenter in the South, and Hughes was a Georgia law enforcement officer. Knight approached William feigning friendship in an effort to entrap him, but when this failed they moved to have warrants served. However, they found difficulty finding a law enforcement officer to serve them. The committee immediately put Ellen in hiding but William was more defiant and remained at home, armed with a gun, and daring the authorities to confront him. The committee urged him to move and he went to the home of their most militant member, Lewis Hayden, on Southac Street, who rigged up explosives in case of an assault on his residence. He was well equipped with arms and had many associates ready to use them. In retaliation against slavecatchers, the committee issued a series of warrants against Knight and Hughes for attempted kidnapping and other charges. Each arrest required bail of $10,000, an enormous amount in those days, but local Southern sympathizers put up the funds. However, after their lives were threatened by a mob, and Theodore Parker personally warned them that this was only the beginning of their troubles, they decided to leave town.

The Crafts were reunited and formally married by Parker (in the South they had been married in an informal slave rite). Using a Bible and a sword for the pledge of their vows, Parker prayed that William would have the courage to use the sword if their freedom was threatened. They were then hustled out of Boston northward through Maine and overland through New Brunswick to Nova Scotia, fearing the federal authorities might be watching the boats. Finally, after two weeks, they set sail from Halifax for England, their $250 fare paid for by the vigilance committee.

It was another great victory for the committee, which continued to work diligently to protect its local black citizens by posting hundreds of advertisements and distributing thousands of handbills warning the public about slavecatchers; making plans for sudden and secret escapes by train, boat, and coach; considering legal challenges to the fugitive slave law; and compiling secret lists of associates, white and black, who might be called upon to do whatever was necessary to stop slavecatchers.

Shadrach Minkins and Lewis Hayden

In February 1851, the committee's boldest success occurred. Shadrach Minkins, also known as the slave Frederic Wilkins in Virginia, and who worked at the Cornhill Coffeehouse just a few doors down from the office of *The Liberator*, was seized by a U.S. marshal. Counsel was secured by the committee, and while a hearing was in progress, Lewis Hayden led 20 black men into the courthouse. In a matter of moments, the black men forced their way into the room where Shadrach was waiting during a recess, overpowered a few constables, and rushed him outside on their shoulders "like a black squall." As many as 200 men raced through the streets with Shadrach in what seemed like a random pattern that led them to the attic apartment of a black woman who lived near Hayden. There he was kept until a cab could be arranged to taken him and Hayden outside the city. Hayden then shifted to a smaller buggy and moved between Cambridge and Watertown, before hiring a wagon with two horses that took Minkins to Concord, where he stayed a couple days before being given passage on the railroad to Montreal, Canada.

Three days after Shadrach's rescue President Fillmore issued a special proclamation calling for the prosecution of all involved in the rescue. But by the time Hayden and his confederates were in court, Shadrach was safe and secure in Montreal, Canada. The vigilance committee raised funds for legal costs and its able defense team was able to avoid any convictions.

Thomas Sims

The committee was becoming a thorn in the federal government's plan to enforce the fugitive slave law and further efforts were focused on exercising its authority in Boston. On April 4, 1851, Thomas Sims was arrested in Boston on the pretense of a charge of theft. Sims, a skinny lad only 17 years old, had come from Savannah, Georgia, after stowing away on the M & H Gilmore, without any knowledge of the ship's crew. He was discovered just before reaching Boston and put in confinement until he could be turned over to the authorities but escaped in a small boat to the south of Boston Harbor. Sims put up a struggle during his arrest and wounded one of the officers with a knife before being subdued.

To guard against another rescue similar to that of the Shadrach rescue, the U.S. Marshal took extra precaution. He had a heavy chain installed around the perimeter of the court house and enlisted a force of more than 100 Boston policemen to surround it in addition to stationing a force of bodyguards within. Legal efforts were made by the committee to prevent Sims's rendition and meetings were held but to no avail. The government acted swiftly. They were determined to take revenge for the Shadrach rescue, and military units were called to ensure that their wishes were followed. Sims was ordered back to slavery by Commissioner G. T. Curtis, and was taken from the courthouse in Boston accompanied by 15 armed guards early on the morning of April 11, 1851 to the rig *Acorn*, which returned him to Savannah, Georgia.

Anthony Burns

The attempted rescue of Anthony Burns in 1854, though ultimately a failure, proved to be the Boston Vigilance Committee's most memorable action, in that it galvanized the nation and further polarized the North and South, leading to the inevitable conflict of the Civil War.

Burns had stowed away on a merchant ship in Richmond, Virginia, with the help of a sailor in February of that year. On May 24, 1854 Burns was leaving his job at a clothing store on Brattle Street when he was surrounded by slavecatchers who literally picked him up and carried him to the courthouse. He was immediately confronted by his master, Colonel Suttle, who personally came to Massachusetts for the rendition.

The vigilance committee held a secret meeting. Two sides formed: one that wanted to break in the courthouse and rescue Burns; the other that called for peaceful efforts and legal means. In the end, it was decided to call a public meeting at Fanueil Hall the following night to rally the public. This was well publicized and was used as a cover for an assault on the courthouse that would take place during the meeting at nearby Fanueil Hall, though this action was not taken with the full consent or knowledge of the majority of the committee. The rescue attempt would then be announced at the meeting according to the plan, and a large group of impassioned supporters would then be available to aid in the rescue.

At the Faneuil Hall rally, Wendell Phillips assured the audience that the city was opposed to the removal of Burns but that the public's support was needed to help them oppose the power of the federal government. He urged a strong showing at the courthouse the next morning when the hearing was to begin. Theodore Parker spewed out vitriol against the authorities in Virginia, whose citizens were demanding the return of Burns. But before he concluded, he was interrupted by a designated messenger that an attempt was being made to break into the courthouse.

The crowd turned into a frenzied mob as it rushed to the courthouse. On signal, the assault began with about 25 men, both black and white. Thomas Wentworth Higginson and Martin Stowell, a leader of the successful Jerry Rescue who had been brought in from Syracuse, led the way. The men were armed with guns, axes, and butcher knives and about 10 of them were using a battering ram in an attempt break down the door on the west side. Others used axes and some fired their pistols at the windows. The crowd closed in, some throwing stones at the windows, and a few rescuers forced open the door. Suddenly, one of the police guard was shot and there was a brief pause and retreat. The guard, a truckman named Batchelder, had been sworn in by the federal marshal for temporary duty. He was carried to a room, but an artery had been severed and he bled to death on the spot.

Police who had been stationed outside the courthouse restored order and arrested 13 of the attackers, including Stowell and Higginson, who was one of the rescuers who got inside and was cut on the chin by a cutlass wielded by a guard, managed to escape. No one was charged in the death of Batchelder because it was believed his injury was accidentally caused during the melee by one of his fellow guards; 40 years later, however, Higginson revealed that Batchelder had been the victim of a bullet from a pistol fired by Stowell.

The rescue attempt had failed and now a legal effort was their only resort. Despite some reluctance on his part, feeling that his case was hopeless, Burns was provided with counsel by the committee. They did their part, even eliciting false testimony from the prosecution that buoyed their hopes of a favorable decision. But it became clear after hearing Commissioner Edward Loring's decision that he had made up his mind at the outset and that the hearing was little more than a show to satisfy the abolitionists. His only decision, he said, was to determine if Burns was the Burns who ran away, and Burn had admitted this when he was arrested. During the trial, Colonel Suttle made it known that he was interested in selling Burns, but after frantic efforts by Rev. Grimes to raise the funds, the negotiations fell through—mainly on account of the resistance of U.S. Attorney Benjamin F. Hallett, who wanted Burns sent back to Virginia to show that the violations of the Fugitive Slave Law would not be tolerated by the federal government.

More than 50,000 people lined the streets of Boston the next day to watch Burns as he was paraded along with hundreds of soldiers and more than a hundred deputized marshals. The show of force and authority by the federal government was costly, equal to the value of many slaves—the cost to bring in federal troops alone being $14,000 ($500,000 today). Other expenses, including legal costs, marshals, courthouse damages, and the transport of Burns brought the government tally to nearly $4 million in today's currency (Shapiro 50).

While the federal government had won their case, it certainly was nothing more than a pyrrhic victory, and the defeated efforts of the Boston Vigilance Committee were in the end one of its greatest triumphs.

Francis Jackson's Account Book

A report by the committee later that year showed that they had aided 230 fugitive slaves since the passage four years earlier of the second Fugitive Slave Law in September 1850. By the time of the Civil War, more than 430 were accounted for (Collison 83), and a detailed accounting of the committee's financial expenditures until January 1, 1861, was preserved for posterity in an account book by its treasurer, Francis Jackson. The book also names many of the fugitive slaves who were aided and provides the destinations of some. About two-thirds were men. It also revealed the names of blacks paid to care for the fugitive slaves. Most of them lived on Southac Street or the neighboring streets on the north side of Beacon Hill.

The account book showed that the busiest year was 1851, during which 69 fugitive slaves were assisted; the slowest year was 1858 when nine were assisted. Nevertheless, because of the secretive nature of Underground Railroad and the specific circumstances pertaining to fugitive slaves, these numbers probably do not account for all the fugitive slaves aided in the Boston area during those years.

William Jackson house, Newton, Massachusetts, is now a museum that was home to a leading member of the Boston Vigilance Committee. (Courtesy of Tom Calarco)

Important Underground Railroad sites still extant in Boston include the homes of Lewis Hayden and William Cooper Nell. The latter was perhaps the most significant black integrationist of the era. He was a prolific writer, leaving several books and an extensive correspondence to document the antislavery activities of his day. Lewis Hayden was an escaped slave who went on to help with or lead numerous challenges to the Fugitive Slave Law in Boston. He later served as state senator and devoted his life to public service.

—Tom Calarco

Further Reading

Austin Bearse, *Reminiscences of Fugitive Slave Days in Boston* (Boston: Warren Richardson, 1880).

Vincent Y. Bowditch, *Life and Correspondence of Henry Ingersoll Bowditch* (Boston: Houghton, Mifflin & Company, 1902).

Gary L. Collison, *Shadrach Minkins: From Fugitive Slave to Citizen* (Boston: Harvard University Press, 1997).

Thomas Wentworth Higginson, "Cheerful Yesterdays," *Atlantic Monthly*, March, 1897.

Francis Jackson, "Boston Vigilance Committee Treasurer's Accounts."

Edward J. Renehan, *The Secret Six: The True Tale of the Men Who Conspired with John Brown* (New York: Crown Publishers, 1995).

Samuel Shapiro, "The Rendition of Anthony Burns," *Journal of Negro History*, January 1959: 34–51.

Wilbur H. Siebert, *The Underground Railroad in Massachusetts* (Worcester, MA: American Antiquarian Society, 1936).

BUXTON, ONTARIO

Buxton, founded by Reverend William King, was perhaps the most successful fugitive slave community in Canada. Among its noted residents were the celebrated fugitive slaves, William Parker, the leader of the Christiana Riot, and Ann Maria Weems, who escaped with the help of William Still in Philadelphia, and Charles Ray in New York City.

> ### William I. Bowditch Recalls His Efforts Aiding Fugitive Slaves
>
> William Bowditch was one of the leading members of the Boston Vigilance Committee that aided more than 400 fugitive slaves following the passage of the second Fugitive Slave Law. His house in Brookline, Massachusetts, remains today on a small dead-end street. In this letter to Wilbur Siebert, written on April 5, 1893, he describes the operation of the Underground Railroad in what was then the western fringes of Boston:
>
> > Dear Sir: In reply to the question contained in your letter of Mar. 28, last, I would say: We had no regular route and no regular station in Massachusetts. I have had several fugitives in my house. Generally I passed them on Wm. Jackson at Newton. His house being on the Worcester Railroad, he could easily forward any one. One person, I (with others) drove to Concord in a two horse carry-all, and deposited him with Mrs. Brooks, the mother of Judge Geo. M. Brooks. Sometimes we rescued them from the ships in the harbor.
> >
> > I have had in my house Wm. and Ellen Craft, John Brown, Jr., Henry (Box) Brown, and others . . .
> >
> > Respectfully yours, Wm. I. Bowditch
>
> *Source:* Wilbur H. Siebert Collection, Ohio Historical Society.

Rev. William King

King was a 35-year-old Presbyterian minister in the antislavery Toronto Synod when he inherited 14 slaves from the Louisiana estate of his late wife's father. Asked to resign his post until the problem was resolved, he could have renounced his inheritance. Instead, he claimed them with the intention of securing their freedom. From Louisiana, the group traveled by steamboat to Ohio, and then continued upland to Delta, Fulton County, Ohio, where King's family owned a farm that was an Underground Railroad stop.

Earlier, King had attended Glasgow University and emigrated from Scotland, living with his parents on their farm in Ohio, and then moving to Louisiana, where he became rector of a private school. There he spoke out against slavery, yet married a wealthy slave owner's daughter. They had two children. In 1844 he returned to Scotland to study theology at Edinburgh; but during this time, both his wife and children died. By 1846 the Presbyterian Church of Scotland had assigned the widowed minister to Canada, and within a year slavery came unbidden into his life. Later, he said:

> I believed it was necessary to provide them with homes where the parents could support themselves by their own industry and their children with the blessings of a Christian education. Three things were necessary for that end: land to place the families upon; a church where they could assemble on Sabbath and hear the gospel; and a day school where the children could receive a good Christian education. (Hill 77)

On November 28, 1849, he entered Canada with the slaves he had freed in the hope of establishing a settlement with his own former slaves as the first settlers. It had taken him more than a year to persuade his denomination to support his mission, which also faced much local opposition. However, his confidence never faltered, and on a 9,000-acre section between East Tilbury and Chatham in Raleigh township, Kent County, he founded the settlement he named for the British abolitionist, Sir Thomas Foxwell Buxton, one of his mentors. Buxton was located in the southwestern portion of the western peninsula of Ontario.

A Land of Milk and Honey

The land was flush with oak, elm, hickory, beech, and walnut, many with trunks two to four feet in diameter. In addition to the natural resources, the peninsula's geography made it a popular destination for fugitive slaves, who escaped from such port cities as Detroit, Cleveland, and Niagara Falls, many crossing the Detroit River at Fort Malden to "shake the lion's paw." The Buxton settlement flourished under the oversight of the Elgin Association, named in honor of the man who was governor-general of Canada in 1850.

The land was divided into 50-acre farms, each one with a road running past. Despite the poverty of the ex-slaves, some arriving without a single cent, there were no handouts. Settlers maintained their dignity, and earned good reputations, by purchasing the land for $2.50 an acre. The money was loaned on condition that they pay it back in 10 equal annual installments at 6 percent interest. In addition, each man agreed to build a house that conformed to certain minimum requirements, similar to zoning restrictions today. Log houses had to sit 33 feet from the road and face the street. Dwellings could be no smaller than 18 feet by 24 feet, and 12 feet in height. A picket fence was required.

By autumn 1852, 75 families had settled on Elgin Association land, with a population of about 400. An additional 100 black families purchased land nearby, bringing the total number of inhabitants to 500. On the Elgin grounds, 350 acres had been cleared, and 204 were farmed that season. Typical crops included wheat, corn, tobacco, and hemp. In 1853, another 150 acres had been cleared, and the settlement boasted 15 horses, 30 sheep, 128 head of cattle, and 250 hogs. By 1854, 726 acres had been cleared and fenced, and settlers raised

334 acres of corn, 95 acres of wheat, 48 acres of oats, and 100 acres of other crops. Their industrious nature was viewed with respect, and contrary to the predictions of opponents, the industry of the former slaves raised the value of the adjacent properties.

Fugitive Slaves Who Settled in Buxton

Settler Henry Johnson talked about what the Buxton settlement meant to him:

> I have lived in Canada four years—in Buxton one year. I came originally from Pennsylvania. The situation and circumstances of the colored people in Canada are better than in the United States. I have a large family—ten persons—and now I have bought, paid for, and have a deed of one hundred acres of land. The people here are very prosperous—they came into the woods without means, depending on their own hands; they never begged a meal here—nor have any goods nor old clothing been distributed. If any were sent, I should want it sent back . . . where money and clothes have been given, the tendency is to make men lazy . . . I wouldn't receive any of their help. I didn't want it. I felt it would do more injury than good. (Drew 306)

The enterprising settlers built a brickyard, gristmill, and pearl-ash factory. A blacksmith's shop, a cobbler's shop and a carpenter's shop also sprang up to serve the community. But use their timber to full advantage, they needed a sawmill. They got to work, and on July 4, 1855, their steam-powered sawmill was ready for operation. Soon, the mill was planing wood for an eight-mile plank road to connect the Great Western Railway to the Lake. The settlers wanted access to markets on both the Lake and the railroad.

The colony followed the rule of temperance and settlers abstained from the production, sale, and consumption of alcohol. Sobriety was considered a virtue and touted as evidence that the experiment was succeeding. In addition to hard work and temperance, worship played an important role in the Buxton settlement. Settlers kept the Sabbath as a day of rest, and many attended the Presbyterian church, which was built in 1850 and seated 200, where the Reverend King preached. But King understood that others preferred their own sects, and he welcomed the First Baptist Church of Buxton, established in 1853 by George Hatton, Alfred West, William H. Jackson, and Isaac Washington.

Education also was held in high regard. By April 1850, King had opened the Mission School and 16 children enrolled, two of them white, the children of Mr. and Mrs. Joshua Shepley. The Shepleys thought the Mission School would be better than the district common school, and they were not disappointed. By 1854, the Buxton school became fashionable, attracting as many whites as blacks. By 1855, 150 children were going to the school. Two more schools were built by 1857 to keep up with demand. In 1857 a correspondent from the *New York Tribune* visited Buxton and reported that the 14-year-old son of a former slave was attending school and reading Virgil:

Wilberforce, Ontario

In 1829, Cincinnati officials began strict enforcement of Ohio's Black Laws that had been passed in 1804. According to these laws, free blacks were required to have Ohio certified papers affirming their status as free persons. In addition, newly arriving blacks were required to post a $500 bond, as insurance against becoming wards of the state. In 1829, this would be equal to $11,000 in year 2007 dollars. The laws had been loosely enforced before this and when some free blacks refused to comply, mobs of white citizens began assaulting them. This prompted some of its black citizens to move to Canada, where they formed the first important black colony there, naming it Wilberforce, after the noted British abolitionist.

They purchased 800 acres in Upper Canada with donations from Quaker friends, and five or six families relocated in 1829. Food was scarce the first year, and the need to clear the forest for farming also delayed planting and minimized the harvest.

After three years, under the leadership of Austin Steward, a successful former slave from Rochester, New York, Wilberforce had grown to 32 families with a general store, sawmill, school, and inn. Unfortunately, Israel Lewis, whom they had sent on a fund-raising tour through the Northern states, had exaggerated their hardships and pocketed the donations he had collected. Humiliated, the community vowed to pay back the donors.

Although Wilberforce escaped a deadly cholera outbreak in nearby London, the town's prosperity suffered. Steward left in January 1837; and by 1856, the Baptist Church was forced to close its doors. Wilberforce was located north of London, near the modern community of Lucan Biddulph. Despite its failure, Wilberforce was important because it was the first major black American expatriate colony in Canada and heralded the founding of many more.

Isaac Riley, a fugitive slave from Missouri, recalled how much it meant to get an education: After I had a son, it grieved me to see some small boys in the neighborhood, who were hired out to work twenty miles from home. I looked at my boy, and thought if he remained, he would have to leave us in the same way, and grow up in ignorance. It appeared to me cruel to keep him ignorant. I escaped with my wife and child to Canada. . . . My children can get good learning here. (ibid. 298)

Henry Johnson echoed his sentiments:

I came to Buxton to educate my children. I lived twenty-three years in Massillon, Ohio, and was doing well at draying and carting—wanted for nothing—had money when I wanted it, and provisions plenty. But my children were thrust out of the schools, as were all the colored children—one must know how I would feel about it My daughter was doing well—advancing rapidly. She began to climb up into the higher classes, among the ladies, and the noblemen of the town thought it wouldn't do. The teacher liked her, but she was thrust out . . . nothing was the matter only she was black. (ibid. 307)

R. Van Branken had strong opinions about the schools:

We have good schools here. The separate schools and churches work badly for the colored people in the States and in Canada. In Rochester, N.Y., it injured them very much, although the separate school was petitioned for by a portion of the colored people themselves. In Cleveland, Ohio, they have separate churches, but no separate school. In Chatham [Canada], the separate school was by request of themselves. I never was in favor of such a thing. (ibid. 306)

The settlement supported the efforts of John Brown at Harpers Ferry, at least in spirit. In an August 27, 1859 letter, abolitionist John Brown informed his friend John Henri Kagi that he had found suitable men in Hamilton, Chatham, and Buxton for an unnamed enterprise that almost certainly was the raid on the federal armory. However, despite Brown's optimism for their participation in the raid, no fugitive slaves who had escaped to Canada participated in his ill-fated raid at Harpers Ferry. However, one white native Canadian, Stewart Taylor, and one free black Canadian resident, Osborne Perry Anderson, were among Brown's raiders at Harpers Ferry.

After President Lincoln issued the Emancipation Proclamation, some Buxton settlers chose to return to the United States, but others were still arriving. In the 1860s, during the War Between the States, a slave named Harrison Webb found a home in Buxton. Yet by 1873, the Elgin Association was no longer needed and the group disbanded. How many remained of the former fugitive slaves after the end of slavery is not known, but the Buxton settlement had transformed their lives. In January 1895, Reverend King died of malaria at the age of 82, leaving as his legacy the path, which led so many slaves to freedom and that gave them the opportunity to forge their own destiny by their industrious, upstanding example, and invalidating the premise of slavery—that they were not equal human beings.

—Rae Hallstrom

Further Reading

Benjamin Drew, *North Side View of Slavery* (Boston: John Jewett and Company, 1856).

Daniel G. Hill, *The Freedom Seekers: Blacks in Early Canada* (Toronto: The Book Society of Canada Limited, 1981).

Fred Landon, "The Buxton Settlement in Canada," (*Journal of Negro History*, 3 (October 1918): 360–367.

Bryan Prince, *I Came as a Stranger* (Toronto: Tundra Books, 2004).

C

CABIN CREEK, INDIANA

Cabin Creek was a black settlement in Randolph County, Indiana, located about 15 miles northwest of Newport (Fountain City). It was a prime destination for fugitive slaves because they could "blend in" with the settlement's free blacks. The area was seven miles long and two miles wide and had a dense population of free blacks. They came from North Carolina and Virginia, cleared the land and dredged the swamps by hand. Many of them purchased government land in 40- and 80-acre lots and became prosperous farmers. Others were squatters or rented their homes. They built churches and schools. During the 1840s, much of the land north of Modoc and south of Farmland was owned by blacks.

Cabin Creek's Underground Network

Cabin Creek was one of three communities in the southern Randolph County, Indiana, area with large concentrations of free blacks that were established in the early 1820s. The Greenville Settlement, which extended into Darke County, Ohio, was the first, established in 1822; Cabin Creek, the second in 1825; and Snow Hill Settlement, the third in 1838. Residents of these communities were very active in providing safe houses for the fugitive slaves and in transporting them from Newport, Indiana, a main station, run by Levi Coffin, to stations farther north. Fugitive slaves were sometimes housed for weeks or even months if they were too lame or too ill to travel. The names of most of the Underground Railroad conductors in these communities have not been recorded.

Most of the fugitive slaves that went to Cabin Creek came from Newport, Indiana. Lines from Newport usually went north to Winchester, Camden, and Fort Wayne and then in various directions to Canada. Another line went east to Darke and Mercer counties in Ohio and on to Toledo or Sandusky. A third line went northwest to Marion, Wabash, and Warsaw and into Michigan before going into Canada, either through Detroit or west around Chicago. Passage along this line began in the 1830s. Conductors included Daniel Sayre and Fred

Kindley of New Holland, August A. Peabody of Lagro, and Maurice Place of North Manchester, all in Wabash County.

Nathan Coggeshall, of Grant County, was a conductor who transported fugitives to and from Cabin Creek from 1840 until 1855. One of his usual routes was from Cabin Creek to locations in Grant County. Charles Baldwin, Aaron Hill, John Shugart, and Moses Bradford, all from Grant County, assisted him. Another destination was the home of Maurice Place in North Manchester in Wabash County, Indiana. Place lived on Maple Street in North Manchester and was a member of the Progressive Friends Meeting. From here fugitive slaves went on to Thomas Mason of Leesburg in Kosciusko County, and then to Stephen Bogue of Young's Prairie in Cass County, Michigan. From here they continued to Detroit, and then crossed the river into Canada.

George Shugart, who worked closely with Nathan Coggeshall, lived in Wayne County and later in Grant County, Indiana. He was a member of the Mississinewa Friends Meeting but was "read out" of the group for assisting fugitive slaves. In the 1840s, he built a house that was designed with hiding spaces for runaways. It had spaces between the walls, secret passages, and fallout doors, as well as a log cabin for their lodging. On one occasion George, assisted by his son John, was able to sneak two teenage female runaways out of his house, saying that they were his daughters.

William Hough and his son Daniel, who lived near the Greenville Settlement and were friends of Levi Coffin, often transported fugitive slaves to Winchester and to Cabin Creek Quakers John and Levi Bond, whose homes and barns were frequently used.

The Wilkerson Girls

During the winter of 1839, two fugitive slave girls, Susan and Margaret Wilkerson, ages 10 and 11, fled from Tennessee. They traveled over 200 miles to Cabin Creek with the North Star their only guide. They hid in woods and caves during the day, and crossed rivers and waded through swamps during the night. They also rode in wagons, on steamboats, and walked through the countryside. They eventually reached the home of their grandparents, Thomas and Milly Wilkerson.

Meanwhile, their owner was on their trail and traced them to the Wilkerson cabin. Milly, armed with a large corn knife, chased him away. But he came back with 17 armed men. Millie had summoned help from black neighbors, some of whom were present when the slavecatchers arrived. While Milly confronted the slavecatchers outside, her neighbors dressed Susan and Margaret as boys in oversized rolled up pants and slouch hats. When the slavecatchers entered the cabin, the black neighbors surrounded the girls who were unrecognizable to the slavecatchers and escorted them outside the cabin. They were then brought to the house of John Bond. He forwarded them to Levi Coffin in Newport. After staying with the Coffins for several weeks, the girls were transported to Canada via the Greenville and Sandusky, Ohio route.

At the time the Underground Railroad was active in eastern Indiana, many blacks lived in Randolph County. After the Fugitive Act of 1850 passed, many of the blacks there, fearing that they would be hunted, killed, or sent back to slavery, sold their property and moved to Canada. Some also went to larger cities, such as Richmond and Muncie, to find work. At the present time, only a few black families live in Randolph County.

—Cynthia Vogel

Further Reading

Levi Coffin, *The Reminiscences of Levi Coffin* (Cincinnati: Robert Clark & Co., 1880).

Randolph County, Indiana, 1818–1990, compiled by the Randolph County Historical Society, 1990.

Wilbur H. Siebert, *The Mysteries of Ohio's Underground Railroads* (Columbus, OH: Long's College Book Company, 1951).

Wilbur H. Siebert, *The Underground Railroad from Slavery to Freedom* (New York: Arno Press and *The New York Times*, 1968).

Ebenezer Tucker, *History of Randolph County, Indiana* (1882; reprint, Winchester, IN: Turner Publishing Co., 2003).

CASSOPOLIS, MICHIGAN

In the 1840s two of the Underground Railroad's major escape routes, the Quaker line and the Illinois line, led to Cassopolis, Michigan, where many Quakers and fugitive slaves had settled, near the southwestern corner of the state. The Illinois line followed the Mississippi River north, scuttled east from Illinois to Indiana, then resumed northwest. The Quaker line, named for the Quakers who supplied hospitality along its stops, followed the Ohio River, the largest eastern tributary of the Mississippi, until diverting north through Indiana.

The Kentucky Raid

Slave hunters targeted the area, including Kentuckians who raided southern Michigan in 1847. Although this invasion, known as the Kentucky Raid, was only one of several forays into Michigan by Kentuckians, it was the one that caused a national uproar. Many of the fugitive slaves who settled in Michigan's Cass and Calhoun counties had fled from bondage in Bourbon County, Kentucky. On or about August 1, 1847, 13 Kentuckians tried to steal them back.

Preceding the attack, throughout 1846 and most of 1847, slaveholders funded spies in Ohio, Indiana, and Michigan. One of them, named Carpenter, posed as a Massachusetts abolitionist. He is believed to have created maps that guided the Kentuckians to the fugitive slaves in Cass County. At the time, the county was home to about 50 former slaves.

Michigan abolitionists took reasonable precautions to protect the fugitive slaves, and one of these was to speak in code whenever new fugitives arrived.

The standard appeal was, "Can you furnish entertainment for myself and another person?" (Citizens and Settlers of Cass County 110) was unlikely to raise suspicion. For members of the Underground Railroad, it signaled that freedom was at stake. As an additional safeguard, agents were privy only to the information they needed to perform their tasks, which included the identity of the next conductor along the route, but not the one who had sent the fugitives into his hands.

The night of the Kentucky Raid, the Southerners split up, and one group invaded the Vandalia neighborhood of Zachariah Shugart, whose home was a station on the Underground Railroad. He also had leased property to a fugitive slave family. Under cover of darkness, slave hunters broke into the fugitive slaves' cabin and captured a black man, but not his wife. She slipped out a window and ran to Shugart's house unobserved. Shugart then mounted a horse and rode two miles west to Stephen Bogue's house. On hearing the news, Bogue saddled a fleet horse and rode at full speed to Cassopolis. Meanwhile, the kidnappers battered down the door of fugitives who were neighbors of Bogue, and subdued one of the men with the butt end of a riding whip. With two successful captures, the raiders turned south, hoping to cross into Indiana. But south of Vandalia, they encountered an angry mob from Cassopolis, led by a large blacksmith named Moses Brown.

The white abolitionist known as Nigger Bill was also there. Anyone who traveled south to the Ohio River, or onto Kentucky soil to help runaways come north, could be called a nigger runner. It is unclear whether this was considered an insult, a badge of honor, or a simple statement of fact. What we do know is that William Jones of Calvin earned his Nigger Bill nickname by guiding more fugitive slaves than most.

On that August night in 1847 near Vandalia, a crowd from Cassopolis brandished clubs. Although outnumbered, the Kentuckians flashed pistols and bowie knives. Violence seemed imminent until Quakers persuaded the kidnappers to abide by the law. The crowd accompanied the Kentucky men, and their nine shackled captives, to the county seat at Cassopolis.

Among the Kentucky raiders was a Baptist minister, the Reverend A. Stevens, forced by the crowd to carry the two-year-old he had ripped out of bed. The child's mother had almost escaped, when the good minister made the toddler cry. "The voice of the infant reached the mother, as was intended, and emerging from her hiding place she was made a captive" (*History of Cass County, Michigan* 112). Although the baby had been born on free land, under slave law the offspring of a slave automatically became chattel, and the Reverend, who owned the baby's mother, intended to press his claim.

By the time they arrived in Cassopolis at nine the next morning, the crowd had grown to 300, most of them sympathetic to the slaves. While the Kentuckians prepared to prove their claims, the Cassopolis sheriff arrested four of them on a charge of trespassing, one on a charge of assault and battery, and eight of the nine on charges of kidnapping. The ninth, the sheriff of Bourbon

County, escaped the charge while hidden by his defense counsel. The charges were finally dropped and the Kentuckians were released, but by this time their former slaves had fled, most of them going to Canada.

Later, the Detroit court overturned the Cassopolis judge's ruling, and granted the Kentuckians their property. In time, the Michigan abolitionists were fined and forced to pay court costs. But the outcome of the 1847 raid into Michigan, and the freeing two years later of Boone County fugitive slaves, David and Lucy Powell, who had escaped to Cass County and were captured by slave hunters, helped to catapult the concerns of slave owners into national politics, and may have influenced passage of the Fugitive Slave Act of 1850.

—Rae Hallstrom

Further Reading

Martin DeAgostino, "Tracks of freedom crisscrossed Michiana, but truths about the Underground Railroad are not ironclad," *South Bend Tribune*, February 28, 1999, sec. A, p. 1.

Charles E. Barnes, "Battle Creek as a station on the Underground Railroad," *Historical Collections and Researches made by the Michigan Pioneer and Historical Society* 38, 1912.

The History of Cass County, Michigan (Chicago, IL: Waterman, Watkins & Co., 1882: 109–115).

Tom Calarco, *People of the Underground Railroad* (Westport, CT: Greenwood Press, 2008).

CHATHAM, ONTARIO

Chatham, Ontario may be best known for hosting John Brown's secret antislavery convention on May 8, 1858. The town had long been a welcome refuge for fugitive slaves. They became, according to John Little, "as thick as blackbirds in a cornfield" (Drew 234), and their presence made it impossible to deny the exodus from the United States or the need for action.

In 1837 two steamboats connected Chatham, situated along the Thames River in southwestern Ontario, to Detroit and Buffalo, sometimes bringing over fugitive slaves. When Chatham became accessible by railway in the early 1850s, former slaves began to arrive in greater numbers.

In Chatham the skill and industry exploited previously without pay now flourished in home construction, millwork, and the cultivation of gardens and farms. In Tennessee, William Street's master took his wages, doling out nothing but "victuals and clothes." In Chatham the former slave opened a blacksmith shop and kept what he earned. Refugees from slavery succeeded in every handicraft, with colored shopkeepers and clerks occupying an entire street. A gentleman who had been one of the town's first settlers observed: "They are as good a body of people as you can find anywhere" (ibid.).

Nevertheless, there were some who held the notion that a Negro must behave in a humble and subservient manner toward white neighbors. Failing this, he could be labeled saucy. When asked what that meant, a white man admitted he would not permit a black man to treat him as his equal.

The True Band

By the mid-1850s, Chatham was home to a chapter of the True Band consisting of 375 members. The True Band was a self-improvement organization in which black men and women gathered for the purpose of educating themselves and enhancing their community. Members of True Bands took a general interest in the welfare of each other, engaged in various improvement projects, encouraged the pursuit of education, attempted to resolve differences without litigation, opposed the begging system, and raised money to help the poor and the sick.

Collections that had been taken up in the United States to help fugitive slaves in Canada were a source of shame for members of the True Band. They called it the begging system. The practice played on the sympathy of good-hearted white folk, inflamed in part by the 1852 publication of *Uncle Tom's Cabin*. Begging on behalf of escaped slaves reinforced the stereotype of the helpless Negro, a false impression promulgated by slaveholders. Worse, little money actually reached Canada. More often than not, those who begged in the name of so-called destitute fugitives were charlatans who kept the money for themselves. True Bands worked to put an end to the begging system.

Blacks Who Settled in Chatham

The former slave J. C. Brown moved from Dawn to Chatham in 1849. He had been a resident of Cincinnati when Ohio began to enforce the state's Black Law in 1829. The law demanded that every black pay $500 to secure their independence at a time when Brown earned no more than $600 in an entire year. In addition, the law made it illegal to hire a black person in preference to a white person, on penalty of $100, throwing about 3,000 blacks out of work. When Brown learned that Canada would grant them every privilege without regard to color, he formed a Colonization Society. On his arrival in Chatham, he found a little village of frame buildings and log cabins where blacks owned the property. Word of favorable conditions spread, doubling their number in Chatham in two years.

Henry Blue learned the trade of blacksmith while enslaved in Kentucky. Even though he called his master a kind and honorable man, he purchased his freedom and made his way to Chatham: "I should have been perfectly miserable," he said, "to have had to work all my life for another man for nothing" (ibid. 270).

Isaac Griffin had been a slave in Trimble County, Kentucky, for 46 years before he reached Chatham, where the law treated each man the same. He explained his decision to flee to Canada:

> A slave in the South suffers death many times before he does die. I felt, when free, as light as a feather—a burden was off of me. I could get up and go to my work without being bruised and beaten. The worst thought was for my children,—what they might have to go through. I cannot hear from them. (ibid. 285)

Dawn, Ontario

The founder of the settlement of Dawn, Ontario, was Josiah Henson, a former slave and Methodist minister who gained fame as the most well-known model for Uncle Tom in Harriet Beecher Stowe's *Uncle Tom's Cabin*. Stowe had read Henson's autobiography, and his life helped to inspire her creation of the character, Uncle Tom.

Henson and his first wife, Charlotte, already had four of their twelve children when Henson discovered that he was to be sold and separated from his family. He had tried to buy his freedom, but his master reneged on a promise to allow it. To keep their family together, the Hensons had no choice but to try to escape. They traveled from Kentucky through Indiana and Ohio, and then sailed to Buffalo, New York, where they crossed the Niagara River into Canada.

The family was living in Colchester in 1836 when Henson met the Reverend Hiram Wilson, a missionary sent by the American Anti-Slavery Society to minister to fugitive slaves, who joined him in establishing Dawn. Another supporter, the Quaker James Canning Fuller, raised funds in England, and this allowed Henson to purchase 300 acres for a school called the Dawn Institute, later the British American Institute. Managed in its early years by Wilson, it was a manual labor school where boys learned farming and the mechanical arts, and girls learned the domestic arts.

In 1855, the community numbered 100 whites and 70 blacks. Nine miles east of Dresden along the Sydenham River, Dawn thrived until the railways bypassed the settlement in the 1860s, forcing businesses to relocate. By 1918, so few people remained that the post office was closed, and today Dawn is a ghost town.

John Brown and the Chatham Convention

One of the most august members of African American history, Frederick Douglass, though not a delegate at John Brown's secret convention in Chatham, was well aware of it because John Brown wrote his provisional constitution while staying at Douglass's home. The constitution declared all blacks, free and slave, entitled to all the rights that were similarly guaranteed to whites under the U.S. Constitution. In Douglass's autobiography of 1881, he recalled Brown's obsession with ending slavery while visiting at Douglass's home:

> His whole time and thought were given to this subject. It was the first thing in the morning and the last thing at night, till I confess it began to be something of a bore to me. Once in a while he would say he could, with a few resolute men, capture Harper's Ferry, and supply himself with arms belonging to the government at that place, but he never announced his intention to do so. (320)

And so it was that 17 months before the raid on Harper's

Ferry, John Brown chose Chatham, Ontario for his secret convention. Although Chatham played no direct role in the raid on Harper's Ferry, there may not have been a Harper's Ferry without the meeting at Chatham. It may be said of Chatham that it welcomed those who wanted freedom and provided its civilized warmth as a gracious host to help provide the means, the way, and the fortitude to attack the yoke of slavery.

—Rae Hallstrom

Further Reading

Frederick Douglass, *Life and Times of Frederick Douglass His Early Life as a Slave, His Escape from Bondage, and His Complete History to the Present Time, 1881* (Electronic First Edition 1999, University of North Carolina at Chapel Hill).

Benjamin Drew, *North Side View of Slavery* (Boston: John Jewett and Company, 1856; Electronic First Edition, 2000, University of North Carolina at Chapel Hill).

Jean Libby, *Delegates to John Brown's Constitutional Convention of May 8, 1858, in Chatham, Canada, with Corresponding Black Conventions and Organizations*, originally published in John Brown Mysteries (Missoula, MT: Pictorial Histories Publishing, 1999), www.alliesforfreedom.org.

Jesse Macy, *The Anti-Slavery Crusade* (New Haven: Yale University Press, 1919).

CHICAGO, ILLINOIS

Chicago, located at the southwestern tip of Lake Michigan in Cook County, was an ideally situated terminus for the Illinois Underground Railroad. Routes by land, rail, and water converged in Chicago. At this port, the fugitives could board a steamer and sail for Canada, or be taken to Detroit, which was just a boat ride from Canada. Great Lakes ships regularly transported people and produce to and from Chicago.

Fugitives often crossed the Mississippi River at the Illinois towns of Chester, Alton, or Quincy before traveling to Chicago. Once past these towns the routes branched out and crisscrossed the state. Perhaps the fugitives took the Illinois-Michigan Canal, hiked along the towpath of the canal, or followed roads northward toward the lake. The Illinois Central and Michigan Central railroads were also used, but this method of travel for the fugitives was not as safe.

Another route started at Davenport, Iowa, where fugitives crossed the Mississippi River to Rock Island, Illinois, and from there they traveled eastward through safe and friendly territory to Chicago.

DuPage County, just 15 miles west of downtown Chicago, played a significant role in the history of the Underground Railroad in Illinois. From the mid-1840s, Wheaton, Glen Ellyn, Glendale Heights, Wayne Center, Warrenville, West Chicago, Lombard, Naperville, Downers Grove, Hinsdale, Lyons, and Oak Brook had stations on the Underground Railroad. Fugitives coming from the south, southwest, and western parts of the state passed through this area. Wheaton College, the Filer House (Glen Ellyn), the Peck House

(Lombard), and the Blodgett Home (Downers Grove) are examples of remaining structures in DuPage County that provided safe houses for fugitives seeking their freedom.

Stops in the Chicago Area

The Graue Mill and Museum in Oak Brook is one of the few remaining authenticated stations. Frederick Graue, a miller by occupation, housed fugitives in the basement of his gristmill. The Graue Mill's location on Salt Creek, a tributary of the Des Plaines River, made it an ideal location for harboring fugitives. Some research indicates that Mr. Graue built tunnels linking the basement of his mill with other hiding places.

In Will County, southwest of Chicago, Samuel Cushing and Peter Stewart were conductors. The Stewart home, located at the junction of the Kankakee and Forked creeks, welcomed fugitives.

Many of the fugitives who traveled Illinois routes had been enslaved in Missouri; others started their journeys in Kentucky or Tennessee. All wanted to find a place where they could be free and where their family members could no longer be sold away from them. Their efforts to find assistance became much more difficult after Congress enacted the Fugitive Slave Act of 1850. Slavecatchers could then enter Free States and detain any black person under the claim that he or she was a fugitive slave. The judges evaluating such cases would be paid twice as much if they returned, rather than freed, the detained black men or women. Abolitionists, and even casual humanitarians, could be punished with fines ($1,000) or imprisonment (six months) for assisting a fugitive slave. Black abolitionists faced the danger of these punishments as well as being sold into slavery. Despite the increased danger, the abolition movement actually grew after the passage of the law, although it had to be more secretive.

The Fugitive Slave Law ironically gave it more vitality, more activity, more passengers, and more opposition, which invariably accelerated the process rather than detaining it. The majority of the Chicago population and political and judicial leaders strongly opposed this new law. The Common Council of Chicago officially defied the Fugitive Slave Act of 1850, passing resolutions requesting the citizens and police of Chicago to abstain from any and all interference in the harboring and deliverance of the fugitive (Mann 70).

South of Chester, in southern Illinois, was a landing called "Liberty." Here, the Mississippi River was narrow, making it easier for the fugitives to cross. Nearby was a cave on James Clindon's farm, which provided a natural shelter. Many locals belonged to a religious denomination known as the Covenanters. These antislavery advocates had come to Illinois from Pennsylvania and established a series of Underground Railroad stations along a route that passed through Coulterville and Oakdale, down to a point near Nashville, Illinois. B. G. Roots, a surveyor for the Illinois Central Railroad, lived nearby in Tamaroa.

He arranged for the tracks to pass through his front yard at Kinsey Crossing Farm, just south of town. It is believed that he hid fugitives in sealed, Chicago-bound freight cars.

Fugitives who escaped from St. Louis traveled twenty miles north to Alton. The Rocky Fork New Bethel African Methodist Episcopal Church was an important Underground Railroad station in the Alton area. From there, passengers often went north to Jacksonville, where the black abolitionist Ben Henderson was active; or they might have traveled on a northeast route, essentially heading along what is today's Interstate 55, through Springfield and Bloomington to Chicago.

John Hossack

Among other important stations that helped fugitive slaves reach Chicago were those in New Philadelphia, Quincy, Galesburg, Princeton, and Ottawa. On the Illinois River, southwest of Chicago, Ottawa was the locus of several routes. In 1838, John Hossack moved to Chicago to become a contractor on the Illinois and Michigan Canal. When funding for the canal dried up, however, Hossack, having all of his capital tied up in the canal, was forced to seek other work and started a prairie farm, known as *Hossack's Grove*, in Cook County. It was during this time that Hossack first became involved in the abolitionist cause, and *Hossack's Grove* became a refuge for fugitive slaves. In 1849, Hossack moved to Ottawa and was involved in the lumber trade. He also bought and shipped grain to Chicago. In 1854 he built a mansion on the banks of the Illinois River and as many as 13 fugitives were housed there at one time.

In 1860, Hossack was one of several Ottawans charged and convicted in Federal Court in Chicago for violating the Fugitive Slave Law. This case involved Jim Gray, a slave who had reached Ottawa after fleeing slavery in Missouri. During the trial Gray was abducted from the Ottawa courtroom and helped to freedom in Canada. Hossack was subsequently indicted for violation of the Fugitive Slave Law and tried in Chicago before Judge Thomas Drummond of the U.S. District Court for the Northern District of Illinois. The jury convicted Hossack, but recommended mercy, and Judge Drummond sentenced Hossack to only 10 days in the Cook County jail and fined him $100. During his 10 days in prison, Hossack was taken out for rides and banquets by John Wentworth, the mayor of Chicago. He was treated like a hero by the citizens of Chicago.

The *Western Citizen*

Downtown Chicago was a hub of antislavery activity. Zebina Eastman first established the *Free Press* in Vermont before moving to Illinois and joining Benjamin Lundy in publishing the last issues of the *Genius of Universal*

Chicago, Illinois

LIBERTY LINE.
NEW ARRANGEMENT---NIGHT AND DAY.

The improved and splendid Locomotives, Clarkson and Lundy, with their trains fitted up in the best style of accommodation for passengers, will run their regular trips during the present season, between the borders of the Patriarchal Dominion and Libertyville, Upper Canada. Gentlemen and Ladies, who may wish to improve their health or circumstances, by a northern tour, are respectfully invited to give us their patronage.

SEATS FREE, *irrespective of color.*

Necessary Clothing furnished gratuitously to such as have *"fallen among thieves."*

"Hide the outcasts—let the oppressed go free."—*Bible.*

☞For seats apply at any of the trap doors, or to the conductor of the train.

J. CROSS, *Proprietor.*

N. B. For the special benefit of Pro-Slavery Police Officers, an extra heavy wagon for Texas, will be furnished, whenever it may be necessary, in which they will be forwarded as dead freight, to the "Valley of Rascals," always at the risk of the owners.

☞Extra Overcoats provided for such of them as are afflicted with protracted *chilly-phobia.*

Underground Railroad Advertisement
From the *Western Citizen*, July 13, 1844

Ad written by Rev. John Cross for the *Western Citizen* abolitionist newspaper published in Chicago promoting the Underground Railroad. (Illinois Newspaper Project)

Emancipation. In 1842, Eastman and Warren Hooper began publication of the antislavery newspaper, *Western Citizen*, on Lake Street in Chicago. The newspaper, which changed its name to the *Free West* in 1854, became notorious for its promotion of the Underground Railroad.

Chicago Conductors

The greatest strength of Chicago's Underground Railroad resided in its committed black population. It organized to thwart all attempts to capture or kidnap a fugitive. On September 30, 1850, many black Chicagoans met at the Quinn Chapel African Methodist Church on Wells Street to plan their actions in case attempts would be made to arrest fugitives. The purpose of these committee members was to be on the lookout for slavecatchers. According to a local newspaper, as a result of the meeting, they organized a black police force, the Liberty Association Vigilance Committee, consisting of seven divisions that regularly patrolled the city.

Dr. Charles V. Dyer, president of the Chicago, Burlington and Quincy Railroad, maintained a large boarding house in Chicago where fugitives received meals and were sent to the homes of free blacks who lived in the city. Black barber Louis Isbell, whose business was in a popular hotel, used his perfectly located shop to assist fugitives. Reverend Richard DeBaptiste, the brother of noted Detroit conductor, George DeBaptiste, often collaborated with his brother, who owned boats, in helping fugitives reach Canada. If in danger from slave catchers, fugitives could easily hide within Chicago's black community.

Philo Carpenter, Chicago's first pharmacist and one of the founding members of the Presbyterian Church there, was a very active member of the Underground Railroad and helped about 200 fugitives escape to Canada. One should remember that opposition to slavery was a religious issue before it became a political one. In 1851, Carpenter and the majority of the Third Presbyterian Church voted to abstain from participating in the meetings of the regional Presbytery because they believed that the church failed to discipline those guilty of holding their fellow man in bondage. When the Presbytery of Chicago removed them, they founded the First Congregational Church of Chicago.

John Jones

John Jones was born a free man in North Carolina, in 1816, the son of a black mother and white father. He moved to Memphis, Tennessee, then to Alton, Illinois, and finally to Chicago in 1845. It was here that Jones started his well-known tailoring shop on Dearborn Street. He became wealthy, and he and his wife, Mary, purchased a very large home on Dearborn Street. His house and his shop were stops on the Underground Railroad. Jones and his wife were friends with other black abolitionists like Frederick Douglass and also with Dr. Dyer and detective Allan Pinkerton, who also was involved in the Underground Railroad. Jones's home also served as a meeting place for abolitionist leaders, including Pinkerton, Douglass, and John Brown.

A self-educated man, Jones decided something had to be done about not only slavery but the black codes that were passed in many Northern states. Jones not only housed fugitive slaves in protest of slavery, but he also fought slavery by using the law to his advantage. Eventually, he led the fight to repeal the Illinois Black Laws by speaking, writing, organizing blacks and whites, and lobbying the state legislature. His efforts were successful in 1865 when the Illinois legislature repealed the Black Laws that restricted civil rights. Five years later, in 1870, after ratification of the 15th Amendment, Jones and other Illinois black men also voted for the first time. In 1871, in the aftermath of the Great Chicago Fire, Jones was elected to the Cook County Commission on the Union Fire Proof ticket, serving two terms. He was the first black officeholder in the state's history. While holding this post, he helped enact the local law that abolished segregated schools.

The Fugitive Slave Law of 1850

On September 18, 1850, the second Fugitive Slave Law was passed. It was a provision of the Compromise of 1850 that outlawed the slave trade in Washington D.C., and slavery in California, but extended slavery into the territories of Utah and New Mexico.

The new law put the handling of fugitive slave cases solely under federal jurisdiction. It included some of the same provisions as the earlier act and increased the fine for its violation to $1,000—equal to $41,000 today—and six months in prison for each fugitive slave assisted. It also established a system in which individuals were appointed to act as judges to hear cases involving the law. All that was required for the conviction of alleged fugitive slaves was their identification by two witnesses under oath that the individual was a fugitive from slavery.

The judges' decisions were prejudiced by a stipulation that paid them $10 for every fugitive slave convicted and $5 for those set free. Adding force was a $1,000 fine imposed on federal marshals who failed to follow an order arrest of a fugitive slave. Marshals also were liable for the value of any slave who escaped from them.

The law escalated tensions between the North and the South, and most Northern states followed with Personal Liberty laws to combat it. These generally prevented the use of state authorities or facilities in the agency of the law. However, some Northern states like Indiana and Illinois had black codes that acted to reinforce the law.

Perhaps the most noxious clause of the new law was its requirement of citizens to assist in renditions or face the same penalties as those who aided fugitive slaves. As many protested, this turned every citizen into a slavecatcher.

Because of Jones and his contribution to end the black codes, men with African ancestors gained the right to vote, testify in court, and serve on juries. Today where his tailoring shop once stood, now stand the state offices of Illinois.

Chicago was the last U.S. port for many fugitives from Missouri, Kentucky, and Tennessee. Access was by way of roads, the canal and its towpath, and rail. It developed a reputation for helping fugitives, from both the black and white population, and from people of all classes. Religious leaders, successful businessmen, doctors, lawyers, and others, all helped the fugitive on his flight to freedom. Many counties in northeastern Illinois also contributed to the success of the Underground Railroad.

—Cynthia Vogel

Further Reading

A. T. Andreas, *History of Chicago*, transcribed from the original by Walter Lewis (Halton Hills, Canada: Maritime History of the Great Lakes, 2003).

Lerone Bennett, Jr., *The Shaping of Black America* (New York: Penguin Group Incorporated, 1993).

Charles L. Blockson, *The Underground Railroad* (New York: Prentice-Hall Press, 1987).

Verna Cooley, *Illinois and the Underground Railroad to Canada* (Illinois State Historical Library, 1917): 76–98.

Robert P. Howard, *Illinois*, Illinois Issues (Springfield, IL: Sangamon State University and Illinois State Historical Society, 1988).

Charles W. Mann, *The Chicago Common Council and the Fugitive Slave Act of 1850, an Address Read before The Chicago Historical Society at a Special Meeting Held January,* 2007.

Owen Muelder, *The Underground Railroad in Western Illinois* (Jefferson, NC: McFarland & Co. Publishers, 2009).

C. H. Rammelkamp, *Illinois College and the Anti-Slavery Movement* (Illinois Historical Society Proceedings, 1908).

Wilbur Seibert, *The Underground Railroad from Slavery to Freedom* (1898; reprint, New York: Arno Press and *The New York Times*, 1968).

Harrison Anthony Trexler, *Slavery in Missouri, 1804–1865* (Baltimore, MD: The Johns Hopkins Press, 1914).

Glennette Tilley Turner, *The Underground Railroad in Illinois* (Glen Ellyn, IL: Newman Educational Publishing Co., 2002).

CHILLICOTHE, OHIO

Located in Ross County, halfway between Columbus and the Ohio River port of Portsmouth, Chillicothe served as the capital of Ohio from 1803 to 1810 and again from 1812 to 1816. The hilly terrain of southern Ohio was both challenging and beneficial for travelers during the nineteenth century. The steep hills and the narrow valleys made travel difficult, but the caves and large boulders often provided a safe place of refuge for the fugitive slaves. Once they had traveled far enough north, reaching Ross County and Chillicothe, they found flatter terrain and an easier path.

Four Underground Railroad routes went through Chillicothe. Two originated on the Ohio River at Portsmouth, Ohio, and followed the Scioto River on both sides of the river. These routes followed trails cut through the wilderness by Native Americans. The other two originated at Ripley and Gallipolis on the Ohio River.

The operators in Ross County included Presbyterians, Quakers, and free blacks. The free black community began assisting fugitive slaves as early as 1815. Churches that assisted in this endeavor were the First Baptist Church, an antislavery church, the Quinn Chapel African Methodist Episcopal Church, and the First Presbyterian Church.

Organized in 1798 by Reverend William Speer, the First Presbyterian Church is the oldest congregation in Chillicothe. Members of the church, led by Reverend Hugh S. Fullerton, hired a teacher to educate African American children in Chillicothe. Fullerton, an avowed abolitionist, encouraged his congregation to aid fugitive slaves as they made their way to Canada. The First Presbyterian Church was part of the Chillicothe Presbytery. In 1836 the Chillicothe Presbytery wrote to a sister church in Mississippi expressing a strong stand against slavery, thus making the Chillicothe Presbytery a leader in the abolitionist cause in southern Ohio. Many local Presbyterians were Underground Railroad operators.

Nearby Settlements That Were Stops

Stillguest Settlement, located about six miles northwest of Chillicothe in Ross County, also was a safe haven for fugitive slaves. Joseph Stillguest was a fugitive slave adopted by Tobias Hicks, whose family had originally founded the settlement. After the death of Hicks, Stillguest continued to aid fugitive slaves at the Hicks house, and the settlement thereafter took his name. Stillguest later moved to Urbana, Ohio, where he continued his Underground Railroad operations.

Paint Hill Farm was another stop for fugitive slaves near Chillicothe. It was built in 1804 by George Renick, who had moved from Hardy County, Virginia in 1797 to a location in the Scioto River valley near Chillicothe. He first ran a general dry goods store in 1802. By 1804 he began devoting all of his time to raising and breeding shorthorn cattle at Paint Hill while aiding fugitive slaves. Today, a flag at Paint Hill Farm commemorates his Underground Railroad participation.

Besides the Renick family at Paint Hill, others in the area who risked their lives harboring fugitive slaves were John R. Alston of the Carriage House; Albert Douglas of Tanglewood; Rev. William H. Beecher; the brother of Harriet Beecher Stowe; the Steel family; and Thomas Silvey.

Another nearby settlement that aided fugitive slaves was the Grassy Prairies, located five miles northeast of Chillicothe. It consisted of Quakers who had originally moved from Virginia and then to Redstone, Pennsylvania before settling in Ross County in 1799.

In Franklin, a village about 10 miles northwest of Chillicothe, an Ohio Historical Marker located next to a church states:

> The Concord Presbyterian Church congregation organized in 1805. The Concord Church was an integral part of the antislavery movement and was a station on the Underground Railroad. Reverend James H. Dickey, the congregation's second pastor, was known to be "an avowed anti-slavery man" and an "active Ohio abolitionist." The Anderson and Galbraith families, who were members of the congregation, were Underground Railroad conductors. Fugitives hid in the loft of the church until they could be taken to the next station in either Frankfort or Chillicothe. (*Ohio Historical Marker*, The Ohio Bicentennial Commission, The Ohio Historical Society, 2003)

The church is still standing and holds regular services.

Black Agents

Charles Langston, a free black originally from Louisa County, Virginia, established a school in Chillicothe for black children in 1836. He was a member of the Liberty Party and the Ohio Anti-Slavery Society and edited the civil rights journal, *The Palladium of Liberty*, from 1842 to 1843.

Many other free blacks in Ross County were Underground Railroad operators, including Jesse Fiddler, John Jackson, Reverend William M. Mitchell, Andrew Redman, Jessie Hamilton, James Leach, Lewis Leach, Harrison

Valentine, and Lewis Woodson. In Chillicothe, there were Langston, Richard and Robert Chancellor, members of the Hubbard family, John and Jesse Redman, and Tucker Issacs. Generally, their mode of operation was to hide the fugitive slaves in wagons and take them about 45 miles north to Columbus.

However, not all residents of Ross County were antislavery. Strong disagreement about the issue of slavery existed. Their views ranged from radical antislavery beliefs to conservative, strong "Copperhead" or proslavery beliefs. Because of these two opposing philosophies, the operation of the Underground Railroad was extremely dangerous. Fugitive slaves often had to take "doubleback" trails. These trails are evident when looking at Wilbert Siebert's trail map, which shows the zigzagging of routes through this part of the state. Fugitive slaves often were sent in the opposite direction of the next destination to confuse slavecatchers who sometimes did surveillance in Chillicothe, South Salem, Lattaville, Frankfort, Richmondale, and other towns in this part of Ohio.

—Cynthia Vogel

Further Reading

Blockson, Charles L., *Hippocrene Guide to the Underground Railroad* (New York: Hippocrene Books, 1994).

Blockson, Charles L., *The Underground Railroad: Dramatic Firsthand Accounts of Daring Escapes to Freedom* (New York: Berkley Books, 1994).

Coffin, Levi, *The Reminiscences of Levi Coffin* (Cincinnati: Robert Clark & Co., 1880).

Wilbur H. Siebert, "A Quaker Section of the Underground Railroad in Northern Ohio," *Ohio History*, 39, No. 3 (July 1930).

Wilbur H. Siebert, *The Mysteries of Ohio's Underground Railroads* (Columbus, OH: Long's College Book Company, 1951).

Wilbur H. Siebert, *The Underground Railroad from Slavery to Freedom* (1898; reprint, NY: Arno Press and *The New York Times*, 1968).

Ralph M. Watts, "History of the Underground Railroad in Mechanicsburg," *Ohio History*, 34 (1934).

CINCINNATI, OHIO

Cincinnati was one of the nation's busiest cities in the Underground Railroad. Fugitive slave activity was reported in the local newspapers as early as 1815, and English travel writer, E. S. Abdy, reported in 1834 that between 200 and 300 slaves were escaping into the city every year. One of the earliest crossing points along the Ohio River for fugitive slaves was near Cincinnati, according to D. H. Howard, whose family was involved in the Underground Railroad during its early period in northwest Ohio: "I think the main and principal route crossed the Ohio river near North Bend (about 10 miles west of Cincinnati)," he wrote to historian Wilbur Siebert (D. W. H Howard to Wilbur Siebert, Wauseon, Ohio, August 22, 1894).

Beginnings of Cincinnati's Underground Network

As with many urban areas involved in the Underground Railroad, Cincinnati's large black population drew fugitive slaves who felt safer with other fellow blacks. In the early years of the city's Underground Railroad most fugitive slaves who came to Cincinnati vanished into the "colored quarters," located primarily by the river. One such area on the eastern edge of the river basin, just below the hillsides near slaughterhouses, became known as Bucktown. Home to many black churches, schools, and civic organizations, Bucktown became the center of black life in Cincinnati. It also became the backbone of much of the local Underground Railroad efforts.

Churches were among the first places in Cincinnati to harbor fugitive slaves, especially the black churches. Allen Temple, the oldest of Cincinnati's black churches, dates back to 1808, when it organized as the Mill Creek Church. Because its members helped fugitive slaves, proslavery gangs burned the church three times between 1812 and 1815. In 1824, it joined with the African Methodist Episcopal denomination, and during the mid-to-late antebellum period it operated a chapel called Bethel on Sixth Street, whose pastor, Augustus R. Green, was actively involved in aiding fugitive slaves. The members of another black church, the Union Baptist Church, founded in 1831, harbored many fugitive slaves. A third black church, Zion Baptist, located on Third Street between Race and Elm streets and founded in 1842 by former members of the Union Baptist Church, regularly hid fugitive slaves in its basement.

Many white religious denominations also contributed to the city's Underground Railroad, including Quakers; Baptists; Methodists, notably the First Wesleyan Church, known as the antislavery church, founded in 1827 at Sixth Street and Vine; and Presbyterians, which had a strong "New School" presence, also sometimes referred to as Covenanters throughout the region.

Up through the early 1840s, the Underground Railroad in Cincinnati was primarily a black enterprise. Among its leaders were the city's most successful blacks including Henry Boyd, who amassed a fortune as a bed frame manufacturer and whose house had a secret room big enough to hide five persons, and William Watson, one of the city's most prosperous barbers. Another active black group was the Iron Chest Society, a benevolent organization that owned a real estate company. The Dumas Boarding House on MacAllister Street also was a sanctuary for fugitive slaves, especially after the 1841 Ohio court ruling that declared slaves brought into Ohio by their masters were automatically free. Prior to the ruling, it was a common location for slaveowners to board their slaves while on business in Cincinnati. Other active black agents were riverboat worker, William Casey, and riverboat barber, John Hatfield, both members of the Zion Baptist Church, and Thomas and Kitty Doram, owners of several boarding houses in the black community. As white slave rescuer Calvin Fairbank, who worked out of Cincinnati during the early 1840s, said, "Once in

Cincinnati there were as many places of safety as the number of fugitives demanded" (Fairbank 25).

Nevertheless, the Cincinnati Underground Railroad during this period was often a haphazard operation. A typical incident involved Anthony Bingey and his family, who escaped from Newport, Kentucky in 1836. According to Bingey, he came into possession of $500. Fearing sale to the Deep South, he contacted a Cincinnati man, James Williams, who agreed to take Bingey and all 15 members of his family to Canada for $400. After concocting a story for their master that they were going to a camp meeting in order to get a pass, they took a boat to Cincinnati, where they met Williams waiting with a wagon. He took them directly to Sandusky and a boat to Canada. The journey took six days.

Lane Seminary

A religious institution, Lane Seminary, galvanized the community to take notice of the antislavery movement and begin the integration of blacks and whites in the Underground Railroad. Founded in the Walnut Hills section of Cincinnati in 1829 to educate Presbyterian ministers, it was sponsored by New York merchant and evangelical supporter, Arthur Tappan. Recruiting the noted New England scholar and evangelical preacher, Lyman Beecher, to be the school's president in 1832, Tappan planned for the school to become the nation's first theological institution to enroll blacks. To further the latter ends, Tappan sponsored the enrollment of Theodore Weld, a charismatic speaker, whom he already had employed to further his manual labor school program on a speaking tour through the South. Weld had become an increasingly outspoken advocate of "immediate emancipation."

In 1834 Weld arranged a series of debates about slavery that were to become instrumental in promoting the abolitionist movement. The merits of immediate emancipation and colonization as solutions to slavery were debated over 18 days at the seminary in February of that year. Thirty-one debaters participated. What added to the drama was that the students were opposing the school's administrators, many of whom were members of the colonization society and opposed to immediate emancipation.

At the end of the debates, many concluded that not only was slavery a sin, but that the policy of the American Colonization Society to send blacks back to Africa was wrong. The students formed an antislavery society and, led by Weld, they reached out to Cincinnati's black community of about 2,000, many of them former slaves who had purchased their freedom. They opened a school in the Hall of Free Discussion in Cumminsville, teaching reading, writing, arithmetic, and geography, along with Sunday school and bible classes, and began participating in the Underground Railroad.

Cincinnati businessmen feared the effects of this radical band of students. During the summer of 1834, while President Beecher was out of town, the executive committee of the trustees issued a report that recommended banning the student antislavery society. Within a week, 51 students and one of the trustees, Asa Mahan, requested dismissal from the school. They were labeled the "Lane Rebels," and many accepted the invitation to matriculate to Oberlin College, which had already become a racially integrated school under the sponsorship of Tappan.

Many of the Lane Rebels became ministers, abolitionists, and social reformers in states throughout the North, as well as conductors of the Underground Railroad. They also converted many white Cincinnatians to abolitionism, including Gamaliel Bailey, the future proprietor of the *Philanthropist* and the *National Era*. Among those who would be indirectly affected was Harriet Beecher, the daughter of Lyman Beecher. A couple of years after the debates, she married Calvin Ellis Stowe, a Lane Seminary professor of biblical literature and a clergyman.

Harriet Beecher Stowe

During Harriet Beecher Stowe's 17 years in Cincinnati, she began collecting ideas for her famous novel, *Uncle Tom's Cabin*, which she began after moving to Maine in 1850. Many of the characters and events in the book were based on people she met and the experiences she had while living in Cincinnati. First printed as a serial in the abolitionist paper, *The National Era*, as a result of her acquaintance with Gamaliel Bailey in Cincinnati, the complete book was published in 1852. It was one of the most influential books ever written, fueling the fever pitch emotions that brought about the American Civil War.

Stowe later revealed that she and her husband had aided fugitive slaves while there. One of them was a servant hired by the Stowes. When it was learned that her master had been making inquiries about her, it was decided to move her along the Underground Railroad:

> [It] was recommended to carry her to some place of security till the inquiry for her was over. Accordingly, that night, a brother of the author [likely Henry Ward Beecher], with Professor Stowe . . . drove [with their servant] about ten miles on a solitary road, crossed the creek at a very dangerous fording, and presented themselves, at midnight, at the house of John Van Zandt, a noble minded Kentuckian, who had performed the good deed which the author, in [Uncle Tom's cabin], ascribes to Van Tromp. (Stowe 36)

During the latter 1830s, Adam Lowry Rankin, the son of noted Underground Railroad conductor from Ripley, was a student at Lane. In his memoirs, he said that he aided more than 300 fugitive slaves while at Lane and once enlisted the help of Harriet's husband, Calvin. In later years, Harriet admitted that: "Time would fail me to tell you all that I learnt incidentally of the working of the slave system, in the history of various slaves, who came into my family and of the underground railroad, which I may say ran through our barn" (Harriet Beecher Stowe to Elizabeth Follen, Andover, Massachusetts, December 16, 1852).

The *Philanthropist*

Another galvanizing event in Cincinnati during this decade was the publication of the antislavery newspaper, the *Philanthropist*. It was started by a former slaveholder from Kentucky, James Gillespie Birney. A former officer in the American Colonization Society, Birney decided to come to Ohio after strong opposition from fellow Kentuckians when he announced his intention to publish his antislavery newspaper there.

However, opposition in Cincinnati was nearly as strong. Local newspapers denounced Birney and his ideas; so instead of publishing in Cincinnati, he started the newspaper in the village of New Richmond, about 15 miles up the Ohio River from Cincinnati. After three months during which he showed his views not to be as radical as had been feared, he moved it to Cincinnati. However, his office was attacked several times in Cincinnati and his press destroyed. The most notable incident occurred on July 30, 1836 when a mob came to his house to tar and feather him, only to find that he was out of town. According to Clarissa Gist, who wrote about the events in a letter to her brother, "A considerable number collected and tore out the abolition printing press, and after destroying every part they could, they left it in the street" (to Erasmus Gist, Cincinnati, August 2, 1836). The mob also visited several other homes of abolitionists and blacks, which they vandalized. Finally, they took the press and threw it in the river.

On another occasion, Birney was fined for attempting to help one of his servants, an escaped slave, obtain her freedom. This was the first case in which Salmon P. Chase defended a fugitive slave. His argument, which failed to impress the court, was that when a slave owner voluntarily brought a slave into a free slave state, that slave automatically became free, an argument that later would become state law in 1841. Birney moved to New York in 1837 to become secretary of the American Anti-Slavery Society, and turned over the *Philanthropist* to Gamaliel Bailey, who had been his assistant. In 1840 and 1844, he was the presidential candidate of the Liberty Party, the first political party to favor immediate emancipation.

Riots against the Abolitionists

The influence of the Lane Debates and the *Philanthropist* had drawn more whites in Cincinnati into the Underground Railroad. Backlash from this was made apparent in June 1841, during a confrontation at the residence of white abolitionist and confectioner Cornelius Burnett, when Burnett attempted to prevent a policeman and a slaveholder from apprehending a fugitive slave who was staying with Burnett. Nevertheless, the slave was taken into custody by the authorities and returned to slavery in Kentucky, and Burnett was arrested and put in jail.

The incident soon became public knowledge and a mob gathered around the Burnett residence on Fifth Street between Vine and Walnut and vandalized it.

However, things cooled until September of that year when a major riot occurred that resulted in the death of several individuals and serious injuries to another 20 or 30. One of the businesses wrecked during the melee was Burnett's. Also ransacked were the *Philanthropist* and the printing company of W. T. Truman, who was an officer in the city's antislavery society. A major gun battle occurred on MacAllister Street when the mob demanded that an alleged fugitive slave be released from the Dumas House, a boarding house with a black proprietor. The violence continued for days and the police were unable to control the mob, which primarily consisted of citizens from Kentucky, where rallies and bonfires were occurring nightly across the river. In an effort to protect the black citizens, nearly 300 black men were put into jail to prevent their being harmed. Nevertheless, mobs continued to attack the black community, and it was only after the governor came to the city that the violence ended and about 40 proslavery individuals arrested. The aftermath of this rioting was that a citizens' police force was organized to prevent future riots.

Despite the opposition, antislavery sentiment continued to grow in Cincinnati. Even across the river in Covington, Kentucky an Underground Railroad station was located in the Thomas Carneal house at 405 E. Second Street. According to legend it had a secret tunnel leading from the cellar to the Licking River that was large enough to hide dozens of refugees. The fugitive slaves used the passage to get down to the river and cross into Ohio. Also, black Underground Railroad agent William Casey sometimes brought fugitive slaves across from Covington.

One fugitive slave whom Casey helped to freedom was a young woman named Jane. Her master treated her well but he died, and she became the property of his son who decided to sell her and her child south. In desperation, she appealed to an English couple who went to Casey for help. He made a plan and the Englishman relayed it to Jane. At the appointed time, she and her child met him in an alley and he escorted them to the river, where Casey was waiting in a boat. He took them to Levi Coffin, where they stayed until he felt it was safe, and then he entrusted her to William Beard who brought her to Indiana and sent her along the Underground Railroad, and eventually to Canada.

Levi Coffin

Coffin had moved to Cincinnati in 1847 from Indiana, and had reorganized the city's Underground Railroad. He had, by his own count, aided an estimated 2,000 fugitive slaves in Indiana, and assumed that he would retire from his activities in the Underground Railroad after moving. "My wife and I," he wrote, "hoped to find in Cincinnati enough active workers to relieve us from further service, but we soon found that we would have more to do than ever" (Coffin 297). While very active, the city's Underground Railroad was poorly managed, and management of the Underground Railroad was a skill he had in abundance.

He purchased a building at 6th and Elm streets and opened a free produce store—a grocery that sold only goods made with non-slave labor. Its attic connected to adjacent buildings, as did tunnels leading from its cellar. His wife Catherine, or "Aunt Katy" as she was known to many, led the Antislavery Sewing Society that met at the Coffin home on Ninth and Walnut Street every week, sewing and gathering clothes for fugitive slaves.

Among the Coffins' coworkers in the Underground Railroad were: Reverend William Henry Brisbane; Zion Baptist members Hatfield and William Casey; black entrepreneur, Henry Boyd; confectioners, Cornelius and Thomas Burnett, and Edward Harwood; attorneys, Samuel Lewis, Salmon P. Chase, Rutherford B. Hayes, and John Joliffe; philanthropist Nicholas Longworth; local pork producer, George Davis; black minister, Green; and black community leaders, Thomas and Kitty Doram.

By now tunnels in the downtown area were being used to move fugitive slaves, including a major tunnel beneath the Franklin and Lafayette Bank building built in 1840, opposite 127 E. Third Street. The tunnel originally was built to transport money from ships along the waterfront to the banks. Other downtown locations known to harbor fugitive slaves, in addition to those already mentioned were Davis's pork house at 113 Sycamore Street; Hayes's law office at the address opposite the bank; and until 1847, when he moved to Washington, D.C., to take over the *National Era*, Bailey's residence at Sixth and College streets.

Laura Haviland

Another devoted Underground Railroad worker who came to Cincinnati and became part of its operation was Laura Haviland. From Adrian, Michigan, she already had been aiding fugitive slaves for many years and she took a room at the Coffin residence, where she stayed for nearly four years. While in Cincinnati, she took a position at the Zion Baptist Church teaching young black girls. Coincidentally, her classes took place in the church's basement, where it harbored fugitive slaves.

On more than one occasion, Haviland went into Kentucky to bring out slaves. Sometimes she traveled with them to Canada in wagons or boats on the Miami and Erie Canal that led to Toledo. One particular case involved the cleaning lady for the Zion Baptist Church. Mary French was a slave from Kentucky whose master allowed her to work on her own. She had nine children, but her oldest daughter recently had fled to Canada because her master was going to sell her south. When he planned to sell another of her children, Mary decided she would have to find a way to free her entire family. As she often crossed the river, both to work her job at the church and to sell produce for her master, he trusted her. She went to Haviland for advice. She suggested that she hide her family in the wagon her master let her use to sell his produce and directed her to three safehouses: Levi Coffin's on the corner of Ninth and Walnut streets; the

Reverend Jonathan Hall on McAllister Street; or to John Hatfield of Zion Baptist. Haviland left on a trip back to Michigan; when she returned, she found French and some of her family members with the Coffins, the rest having been placed in other safehouses. Eventually they all were forwarded to Canada.

Use of the Legal System

One of the Underground Railroad's most useful tools was its use of the court system, and Cincinnati's legal community was one of the strongest defenders of fugitive slaves. Hayes, who would become the nineteenth U.S. president, was an assistant district attorney in Cincinnati during the 1850s. Years later, he said that for every fugitive slave case he publicly represented, there were 10 not made public. "There was a period there when I never went to bed without expecting to be called out by Levi Coffin," he said (President Rutherford B. Hayes, interview by Wilbur Siebert, January 10–11, 1893). He also said that local justice officials were sympathetic to fugitive slaves, including Justice of the Peace, David Fisher; County Prosecuting Attorney, Joseph Cox; and Prosecuting Attorney of the Police Court, William Dickson.

Salmon Chase, Cincinnati's most prominent attorney, rose up the ranks through his defense of fugitive slaves, whom he represented pro bono, and was called "the Attorney General for Negroes" by proslavery citizens. Chase eventually became governor, a U.S. senator, and chief justice of the U.S. Supreme Court. His most important abolitionist case involved John Van Zandt, which was tried before the U.S. Supreme Court, the first case before the high court to question the constitutionality of the Fugitive Slave Law.

John Van Zandt

Van Zandt, who had moved from Fleming County, Kentucky to Ohio just north of Cincinnati after emancipating his slaves, was caught transporting nine fugitive slaves in April 1842. Van Zandt had rendezvoused with them at Lane Seminary. In broad daylight, Van Zandt took the slaves into his wagon, allowing one of them named Andrew to act as the driver. However, about 15 miles north of Cincinnati, they were confronted by two men who apprehended them, though not without a scuffle, which allowed two of the fugitive slaves to escape.

The trial went before Justice McLean of the U.S. Supreme Court, at Cincinnati, in July 1842. The defense did not deny the facts as stated, but further stated that there was no case of unlawful harboring or concealment of fugitives because Van Zandt did not know that the group had escaped from Kentucky. The case went to a jury and Van Zandt was found guilty. Chase's motion for a new trial was granted and Van Zandt was released on bail. Despite that his church barred him and some of his friends avoided him, he resumed his activity in the Underground Railroad.

Four years later the case went before the Supreme Court. By this time, Van Zandt had gone bankrupt paying his fines and legal bills, and the stress of the litigation had broken his health. When the Supreme Court rejected Chase's appeal in 1847, Van Zandt was near death. When asked if he regretted helping the fugitive slaves that led to his problems, he said that saving a person from slavery was worth any sacrifice. He is buried in Wesleyan Cemetery in Cincinnati.

Margaret Garner

Probably the most famous defense of a fugitive slave in Cincinnati was the case involving Margaret Garner, whose attorney was Joliffe. A Kentucky slave, Garner had four children, three of whom it was believed were those of her master, who some historians believe was raping her. She was 22 years old when on a cold January night in 1856, she and her slave husband, Robert, his parents, and her four children, rode a sleigh 20 miles to the frozen Ohio River, which they were able to cross on foot to Cincinnati and their destination—the home of her cousin. Before long, however, they were tracked down by slavecatchers who battered down the door. Garner then grabbed a butcher knife and slit the throat of one of her daughters. She went after her other children but was stopped by the slavecatchers.

Joliffe made an able defense, pleading insanity, but she was convicted of murder. Instead of being sent to prison she was returned to slavery and sold to a slave trader, who took her into the Deep South, where she died two years later of tuberculosis.

Another case involved a slave named Lewis who had escaped from Fleming County, Kentucky. He was captured in Columbus, Ohio and taken to Cincinnati for trial, where he was defended by attorneys Joliffe and Hayes. Judge Carpenter, who tried the case, was sympathetic to the abolitionist cause and this might have played a role in what happened. The courtroom was overflowing with supporters, including Coffin, and Carpenter was extremely deliberate in his conduct of the proceedings. Gradually Lewis was moved back into the crowd and suddenly vanished from view. Led out of the courtroom by supporters, he was placed in hiding in a local church, where he remained for several weeks. When the commotion had died down, he was disguised as a woman and led out of Cincinnati in the carriage of a Presbyterian minister and his wife who had been visiting. They put him on the Underground Railroad and he escaped through Sandusky to Canada.

John Hatfield and John Fairfield

John Hatfield, who later moved to Amherstburg, Canada because of the oppressive laws in Ohio, described several incidents in which he helped fugitive slaves during an interview for the 1855 book, *Northside View of Slavery.* He said he personally had harbored as many as 27 in a single year. He was best known, however, for helping Levi Coffin arrange a mock funeral from Wesleyan Cemetery to the village of College Hill as cover for 28 escaping slaves being led by his friend, the infamous slave rescuer, John Fairfield.

College Hill, a community eight miles north of Cincinnati, was heavily involved in the Underground Railroad up through the early 1850s. In fact, it had become so notorious that its operations came nearly to a standstill in the latter half of that decade because it was being watched so closely. To get to College Hill, fugitive slaves hiked along the Mill Creek through a bucolic ravine with steep hillsides that today remains largely undeveloped. On the west side of the ravine is the present day Hamilton Avenue, where a number of the community's safe houses still exist.

Harriet Wilson, whose two brothers and sister were involved in the community's Underground Railroad, wrote a lengthy letter to Wilbur Siebert in 1892 describing its participation, "fugitives had begun coming," she wrote, "they were cared for and sent on their way rejoicing, others followed and thus the work continued to grow until it became quite a heavy financial burden on the few who so long carried on the work" (College Hill, Cincinnati, Ohio, April 14, 1892).

College Hill

Though Wilson was unsure of how aid to fugitive slaves began in College Hill, it may have been due to a black couple who lived there during the 1830s. Amy Clark was a fugitive slave who escaped to Cincinnati in 1832 and found a job in College Hill. Before long she married Joseph Barber, who was conducting fugitive slaves in his wagon to Lebanon, about 35 miles north. The couple finally moved to Windsor, Canada in 1837.

Among those who participated were Zebulon Strong, whose house remains today on Hamilton Avenue and is now the Six Acres Bed and Breakfast. At night Strong would take fugitive slaves in his wagon to the next stop, which was located at the junction of Colerain and Springdale roads. Isaac Skillman, Strong's neighbor, who had a grocery store also participated. Freeman Cary, Strong's half-brother who lived across the street, was another agent. A later excavation revealed a tunnel that led from the ravine to Cary's house. Freeman's brother Samuel Cary and their father, William, also were active.

But the best documented family operating in College Hill was that of Samuel Wilson and his wife, Sally Nesmith, the parents of Harriet Wilson. The Wilsons moved to College Hill in 1848, and were friends of the Beechers and the Stowes. They harbored fugitive slaves in their basement; their sons, David and Joseph, were active in forwarding fugitive slaves, and their daughter, M. G. Pyle, harbored them. According to Harriet Wilson, they and others in College Hill worked with William Beard, from Billingsville, Indiana, who picked up former

Samuel Wilson house, College Hill (Cincinnati), Ohio; home of a family of abolitionists who aided fugitive slaves. (Courtesy of Tom Calarco)

slaves at Lane Seminary and College Hill and led them to the eastern trunk of the Underground Railroad in Indiana.

Among the incidents Harriet described was the one involving the mock funeral that brought Fairfield and those 28 fugitive slaves through College Hill. They were gathered in the house of the college janitor, she wrote, "scared and trembling, waiting for the wagons to take them across the Ohio boundary into the safer Quaker settlements in Indiana. . . . Some daring students . . . had with others made all the necessary arrangements . . . to see them off" (ibid.). It was one of several journeys Fairfield made with fugitive slaves through College Hill.

As late as the 1930s, the O'Neil family who next occupied the Wilson house had strangers come to visit, asking permission to see the basement where their parents and great-grandparents had been hidden.

Beyond College Hill, the next stop was Mt. Healthy. There, too, agents were ready to help fugitive slaves. One of them was Charles Cheny, who raised mulberry trees to feed his silk worms in a fledgling silk industry venture. Hiding the escapees in his wagon, he would transport them to the next station. Nearby Farmers' College also was involved, including its president Rev. Dr. Bishop and a professor, a Dr. Scott, who built a brick building in downtown Mt. Healthy and whose basement had tunnels and hidden rooms. The building remains at 7601 Hamilton Avenue where a plaque identifies it.

John Hatfield Recalls Outwitting Slavecatchers in Cincinnati

By 1855, former Cincinnati resident John Hatfield had moved to Canada because of Ohio's oppressive laws against blacks. Interviewed for the book *Northside View of Slavery* by Benjamin Drew, this was one of the incidents he described about his experiences in the Underground Railroad:

> I never felt better pleased with anything I ever did in my life, than in getting a slave woman clear ... She came on board a steamboat to Cincinnati. She had got to a friend's house in the city. Word came to my ear that too many knew where she was. ... about dark [the friend] came to me ... told me they had been there ... to the back door—he wrapped her in a blanket, took her out of a front window ... across the street ... I took a young man's clothes ... and dressed her in them—we came out at a gate ... crossed over the street—there were five or six persons then coming towards us—all I could say was, "walk heavy!". ... They walked with us half a square—I was scared only for her. They stopped a little—we got fifty yards ahead of them. I then told her, "they are coming again—hold your head up, and walk straight and heavy!" ... they walked with us a whole square, looking right in her face ... We came to where there was a light opposite—I did not want to have her come to the light—I turned the corner and said, "Come this way, Jim." She understood, and followed me. Upon this, they turned and walked away ... (Drew 364–365).

Source: Drew, Benjamin. *A North-Side View of Slavery. The Refugee: Or the Narratives of Fugitive Slaves in Canada. Related by Themselves, with an Account of the History and Condition of the Colored Population of Upper Canada.* Boston: John P. Jewett And Company, 1856, pp. 364–365.

Spread Eagle Tavern

A major Underground Railroad stop was the Spread Eagle Tavern across the Hamilton County line in Butler County on U.S. 42. Fairfield said he often stayed in Cincinnati with a Mrs. Layman; during that period, the mistress of the Spread Eagle Tavern was Anna Layman Conrey. Located equidistant between Cincinnati and Lebanon at the top of Mount Pisgah, it was customary to exchange horses there. John Conrey operated the Lebanon stagecoach and his brother James owned the inn. The Sharonville to Springboro route was one of the busiest in transporting fugitive slaves and stagecoaches were often used. From the Spread Eagle, fugitive slaves also were sent to Oxford and Hamilton along the Cincinnati-Dayton Road about a mile away.

Diverse routes went northward from Cincinnati, into Indiana or continuing on through Ohio, seeking safe houses in Hamilton, Eaton, Springboro, and northward to the Lake Erie ports of Toledo, Sandusky, Huron, or Cleveland. In later years, the development of the railroads helped fugitive slaves move more easily through Ohio to Lake Erie. The Little Miami Railroad and the Mad River Railroad connected Cincinnati to Columbus and Sandusky. This occurred just before the passing of the Fugitive Slave Law in 1850. In several incidents, Levi Coffin described sending fugitive slaves to the train depot with Rev. Green.

In 1856, Coffin sold his store and leased a large building with more than 30 rooms at the southeast corner of Franklin and Broadway, just south of the current Liberty Street. In addition to making it his residence, he also used it as a boarding house for local educators and clergy, as well as a meeting place for personal friends and Quakers who came to Cincinnati on business. As would be expected, it also functioned as "a very suitable depot of the Underground Railroad" (Coffin 576). During this time, Coffin had a wagon made specifically for the purpose of transporting runaways. It had a passenger compartment with curtains and seats for six passengers. Friends called it "the Underground Railroad car" and Coffin's horse, "the locomotive."

The increasing antislavery sentiment in the city was evident with the installation of Rev. Nathaniel Colver, an abolitionist minister of national stature, as pastor of the First Baptist Church in 1856. Colver's sermons continually attacked the Fugitive Slave Law. But perhaps nothing was more illustrative of the city's increased support for antislavery than the incident involving Cincinnati *Commercial* reporter James Connelly, who was caught harboring two fugitive slaves in his office in 1858. Connelly was convicted and sentenced to spend 20 days in jail. There he was visited daily by supporters. On his release he was celebrated as a hero with a parade through the city's main streets, complete with a marching band, which was followed by Connelly giving a speech explaining his antislavery principles.

—Cynthia Vogel, Betty Ann Smiddy, and Tom Calarco

Further Reading

Levi Coffin, *The Reminiscences of Levi Coffin* (Cincinnati: Robert Clark & Co., 1880).

Benjamin Drew, *A North-Side View of Slavery* (Boston: John P. Jewett and Company, 1855).

"Ex-Pres. Rutherford B. Hayes Tells of Severe Winters When Many Slaves Crossed the Ohio River; also of Operators in Cincinnati," interview with Wilbur Siebert, January 10–11, 1893.

"Inventory of the Erasmus Gest Papers, 1834–1885," Ohio Historical Society, Columbus, Ohio.

"Letter from H. N. Wilson to Wilbur Siebert," College Hill, Cincinnati, April 14, 1892.

Calvin Fairbank, *Rev. Calvin Fairbank during Slavery Times* (Chicago: Patriotic Publishing, Co., 1890).

Keith P. Griffler, *Front Line of Freedom: African Americans and the Forging of the Underground Railroad in the Ohio Valley* (Lexington: University Press of Kentucky, 2004).

Wilbur H. Siebert, *The Mysteries of Ohio's Underground Railroads* (Columbus, OH: Long's College Book Company, 1951).

Wilbur Siebert, "The Underground Railroad in Ohio," *Ohio History*, 4 (1896): 44–63.

Betty Ann Smiddy, *A Little Bit of Paradise . . . College Hill, Ohio*, 2 ed., 2008, www.samuelhannaford.info.

Harriet Beecher Stowe, *The Key to Uncle Tom's Cabin* (London: Clarke, Beeton, and Co., 1853).

Nikki Taylor, *Frontiers of Freedom: Cincinnati's Black Community, 1802–1868* (Athens: Ohio University Press, 2005).

Cynthia Vogel, *Civil War Women: They Made a Difference* (Fletcher, OH: Cam-Tech Publishing, 2007).

Mark S. Weiner, *Black Trials*, "Silent Witness," Chapter Six (New York: Knopf, 2004).

Mary Ann Yannessa, *Levi Coffin, Quaker: Breaking the Bonds of Slavery in Ohio and Indiana* (Richmond, IN: Friends United Press, 2006).

CLERMONT COUNTY, OHIO (BETHEL, MOSCOW, NEW RICHMOND, FELICITY, WILLIAMSBURG)

Clermont County began harboring fugitive slaves at least as early as the 1820s and was among the nation's most active Underground Railroad crossover points. It occupies 21 miles of shoreline along the Ohio River, across from which are the formerly slaveholding counties of Campbell, Pendleton, and Bracken, Kentucky. But it was not solely its geographic location that made it important but also its residents, who were among the nation's most ardent abolitionists.

No one community can be singled out. At least five villages in this rural county had significant involvement. All had strong evangelical influence and their churches were often the center of Underground Railroad activity.

The major routes moving up from the Ohio River started at the river ports of New Palestine, New Richmond, and Moscow. These led to two major roads, which are now the present-day State Route 132 leading directly from New Richmond and Route 133 that followed a buffalo trace and Indian trail out of which was constructed a road in 1807 and which passed through Felicity, Bethel, Williamsburg, and eventually all the way to Xenia and points north. This road was used by soldiers during the War of 1812 to get to points north on the way to Canada; it was during this war, as a result of slaves accompanying their masters, that slaves began to learn about Canada as a destination where they could be free. Both 132 and 133 crossed the present-day 125, which was a road that led directly to Cincinnati and which fugitive slaves coming from Ripley in neighboring Brown County often used.

Bethel

Bethel was the home of the nation's first U.S. senator to publicly profess his support for immediate emancipation. Thomas Morris, a long-time state legislator, was appointed to the U.S. Senate in 1833 and began speaking out against slavery in 1836. This led to confrontations with one of the Senate's most powerful, senior members, the South's foremost apologist for slavery, John C. Calhoun from South Carolina. Nevertheless, Morris was not intimidated. He was the first to point out the overrepresentation of the South in key positions of power in the federal government, which led to the development of the theory of the slave power. This theory maintained that the South had hijacked the U.S. Constitution in the name of slavery, abrogating first amendment rights, including the right of petition, and fourth amendment rights, in acts of search and seizure, of those who opposed slavery.

Finally, because of his continued opposition to slavery in the Senate, Morris was dismissed from his Senate seat at the end of his term in 1838. Morris then became involved in the Liberty Party, serving as its vice-presidential nominee for the 1844 election, and later joined the Free Soil Party before his sudden death in 1847.

Bethel also occupied a key link in the Underground Railroad network of the county, and fugitive slaves came there from New Richmond, Moscow, and Felicity. The center of its Underground Railroad activities was the Sugar Tree Wesleyan-Methodist Church, and its leader was Isaac Holmes Brown. Brown became involved in the Underground Railroad around 1835 and transported fugitive slaves in his wagon from Felicity to Williamsburg, a distance of about 15 miles, to Charles Huber's house. Benjamin Rice, another church member, assisted Brown. Written testimony claims that Rice aided the escape of as many as 100 fugitive slaves from one plantation in Kentucky alone. Another Bethel resident, Dr. William E. Thompson, who lived to the age of 105, signed an affidavit at the age of 95, testifying to his participation in the Underground Railroad, which he said he began when he was 14. Thompson was known to have kept surveillance on the presence of slavecatchers and to frustrate their searches would shoot their tracking dogs, sometimes called "Negro dogs" or "Nigger hounds."

Moscow

Moscow may have been the earliest location in the county where there were organized efforts to aid fugitive slaves. As early as 1816, a ferry operated there, bringing passengers across the river. By the 1820s, it is alleged that the ferry's operator, Thomas Fee, Sr., was aiding fugitive slaves. It is not surprising then that Fee's son, Robert, was chosen to undertake a mission to return the family of Vincent Wigglesworth, a free black man, which had been kidnapped by six slavecatchers one October night in 1842. After a lengthy search led him to Missouri in 1845, and armed with warrants for their extradition, Fee found that the family suddenly had disappeared.

The experience radicalized Fee and he became extremely active in the Underground Railroad. His large federal-style house sat atop a hill overlooking the Ohio River, not far from the ferry that was operated by his brother, Thomas, and he kept lighted candles that could be seen from across the river. Slavecatchers often came to the house at night and the Fees kept loaded guns nearby as a precaution.

Robert Fee became involved in another dramatic case in 1852 when he was accused of abducting slaves from a Kentucky family with whom he was friends. Fee also knew the slaves because one of them had worked for him as a domestic.

Thomas Fee house, Moscow, Ohio, Clermont County; home on the banks of the Ohio River of the ferry operator who was believed to have harbored fugitive slaves. (Courtesy of Tom Calarco)

What happened was his friend who was their owner wanted to emancipate them but her son had conspired against this and was planning to sell them instead. When he learned of this, Fee took them to safety in Ohio. He was later indicted but was never brought to trial and the case was eventually dropped.

Thomas Fee, Jr. also is alleged to have been involved in the Underground Railroad. His house sat at the foot of the ferry landing and also was alleged to have had a candle burning nightly in one of its windows to signal fugitive slaves that it was a safe house.

New Richmond

New Richmond is 20 miles east and upstream from Cincinnati. It was a thriving community during the antebellum period with a tannery, distillery, and a boat-building industry, and its First Presbyterian Church was the center of its abolitionism. Such luminaries of the Gospel as the Reverends John Rankin, John Gregg Fee, and George Beecher, the brother of Harriet Beecher Stowe, sermonized against slavery there. The village was about as staunch an antislavery community as you might find on the border with the South.

The noted abolitionist from Kentucky, James Birney, started publishing his antislavery newspaper, *The Philanthropist*, in New Richmond. He had wanted to publish it in his hometown of Danville but was literally driven out of Kentucky by threats on his life after announcing his intention of starting an antislavery newspaper there. His first choice after that was Cincinnati, where he had moved, but when he found the climate hostile there as well, he accepted the invitation of Thomas Donaldson to publish in New Richmond. The first issue came out on January 1, 1836.

Although the community of New Richmond was very supportive, there were threats from slaveholders in Kentucky just across the river. As a result a vigilance committee was formed to protect the office of the newspaper. Despite its relatively safe location, Birney moved it to Cincinnati after only three months and the paper was attacked there several times by a mob, forcing him to move briefly again, this time to Springboro. After things calmed down, he moved back to Cincinnati. Not long after, however, he left Ohio and the paper was taken over by the more conciliatory Gamaliel Bailey and the attacks ended.

Among those who stood guard at the *Philanthropist*'s offices in New Richmond was Dr. John Rogers, whose wife was the daughter of Thomas Morris. Rogers later would be an active member of both the Liberty and Free-Soil parties. Donaldson, a temperance Baptist and successful businessman, was involved in several enterprises. Some of antislavery's most prominent activists stayed with him during visits to Ohio, including New Englanders William Lloyd Garrison and Parker Pillsbury. He was also well acquainted with Gamaliel Bailey and abolitionist U.S. Senator Joshua Giddings.

The village also practiced what it preached and was active in the Underground Railroad. One incident involved two Louisville slaves, Jim and Joe. Jim's master was very lenient and this allowed him to get a crate and box Joe up like Henry "Box" Brown and ship him aboard a steamboat to New Richmond, where Jim's free parents lived nearby. Joe remained in the box for 36 hours but he survived and gained his freedom. Jim was then sent to Levi Coffin in Cincinnati, who put him on the Underground Railroad to Sandusky where he took a boat to Canada. A few months later, Jim and his wife went by the same route and joined Joe in Canada.

Among the village's Underground Railroad agents, Caleb Walker was a member of the New Richmond Methodist Church and a circuit rider and temperance advocate. He was elected president of the New Richmond Anti-Slavery Society in 1837. It is believed that he used six houses he had built for former slaves in New Richmond as safe houses.

New Richmond's black community was the largest in Clermont County. From 1850 to 1860, it grew from 225 to 574. Records indicate a large migration from Southern states during this period, including 42 from Mississippi. This occurred because of strict laws hindering emancipation there. As a result, slaveholders who wished to emancipate their slaves came to Ohio where the laws made emancipation easier. The large number of blacks in New Richmond also was a reflection of its tolerance, which made it a desirable destination for fugitive slaves. Nevertheless, it was still illegal to help fugitive slaves no matter where you lived, and one free black man, William Green, was caught attempting to move two slave women and two children to New Richmond in 1859 and was sent to prison.

How customary it had become to help fugitive slaves in the New Richmond area was conveyed in the 1888 memoir, *Reminiscences of Slavery Times*, by John Henry Tibbets, recalling the year 1838 when he was a young man there. He describes an incident helping a fugitive slave with his friend Thomas Coombs. He was very matter of fact, explaining that when he and his friend, both teenagers, met a fugitive slave for the first time, they knew exactly what to do: they took him on horseback to a house in Brownstown, Ohio about 15 miles away in the middle of the night.

Such savviness is not surprising, considering the Coombs family were close friends of John Rankin and that Andrew Coombs, Thomas's father, was a preacher at the Baptist Church in nearby Lindale and the recording secretary of the Mt. Gilead Anti-Slavery Society. The Coombs house in fact was a link between John Rankin in Ripley and Levi Coffin in Cincinnati, and the Coombs are reputed to have hidden slaves in the back rooms and lower parts of his house, as well as in a store that he opened.

Another location near New Richmond that was important to the county Underground Railroad was New Palestine, where Jacob Ebersole lived along the river with a "fleet" of skiffs ready for use. At night lanterns on the Kentucky side would signal that passengers were awaiting transport across the river. Ebersole, whose wife was the niece of U.S. Senator Thomas Morris, then took them north in wagons 18 miles to Williamsburg and the home of Charles Huber.

Felicity

The second most populous village in Clermont County in 1857 with about 1,500 residents, Felicity may have been the county's most active Underground Railroad site. The Presbyterian and Methodist churches were shapers of local opinion, and the noted abolitionist and Underground Railroad conductor, John Rankin of Ripley, was pastor of the Presbyterian Church there for a year.

During the 1840s, both churches were fractured by the issue of slavery. A new Methodist Church was formed in 1847, aligning itself to the Wesleyan-Methodists, a denomination that had broken away from the parent Methodist denomination on account of their opposition to slavery and maintaining fellowship with those who held slaves. The Felicity Wesleyan-Methodist Church grew quickly and became a frequently used stop along the Underground Railroad. Church member John O'Neill wrote to the denomination's organ, *True Wesleyan*, that hundreds of fugitive slaves passed through Felicity during the winter of 1856.

In 1857, the noted Underground Railroad conductor, Rev. Luther Lee, who for three years aided hundreds of fugitive slaves in Syracuse and one of the leaders of the schism that formed the Wesleyan-Methodist Church, took over as pastor in Felicity. In his autobiography, Rev. Lee confesses to doing a "little Underground Railroad work" while there.

Oliver Perry Spencer Fee, a shopkeeper in Felicity, was widely known for his outspoken criticisms of abolitionists and "conductors." Because of this, Kentucky slave hunters often turned to Fee for help in capturing their lost property. Fee's denunciations were only a ruse, however, to gain the slaveowners' confidence. When the slavers asked Fee for his help, he sent them in the opposite direction. Fee also supplied food and clothing to the fugitives from his store. Among those in the village who assisted Fee were storeowner Lewis Miller; businessman Andrew Powell who transported fugitive slaves from the river to Felicity in an elegant carriage; James Abbott who had moved from Covington where he had been participating in the Underground Railroad; Arthur Fee, a cousin of Oliver; and Salathiel Burrows, a former slaveowner, who had a house on the road between Felicity and Bethel. A number of blacks from the village also were active, including Isaac Rumsey, Alexander Jefferson, Benjamin Logan, and Will Sleets.

In 1858, Sleets, a local blacksmith, crossed into Kentucky to aid a family of 10 slaves in their flight to freedom. They crossed the river in two small boats and were taken directly to Sleets's house. The group included six children and two adult women. One of the men was Peter Stokes, who, in 1895 while living in Canada, told the story during an interview with historian Wilbur Siebert.

Slavecatchers were in pursuit, so they were put in hiding in a barn on the banks of the Ohio River for two weeks. They were then moved farther north and stayed for three days with Eliza Woods, the sister of their master's wife. They continued to be moved up the line until they were put into the baggage of a train bound for Cleveland, where they took the boat, *Morning Star*. It took them to Detroit from where they crossed into Windsor, Canada.

Another interesting story involving a Kentucky slave who came to Felicity did not turn out so well. Julett Miles, a Bracken County slave owned by John Fee, the father of courageous Kentucky abolitionist, Rev. John Gregg Fee, had her freedom purchased by the younger Fee. Thereafter, she moved to Felicity. However, she left behind her two sons, three daughters, and four grandchildren. During an attempt to bring them out of slavery, she was captured and convicted of slave stealing and sent to prison. Her family was sold away, and she eventually died in prison, never to see them again.

Williamsburg

Charles "Boss" Huber was the center of Underground Railroad activity in Williamsburg. Not only did he work secretly to transport and assist fugitive slaves, as many as 500, according to some estimates, but he was an ardent and very public abolitionist crusader, who would get up on a soapbox in the middle of town and harangue against slavery and slaveholders. He was a leader in the Clermont County Anti-Slavery Society and ran for state office several times as an abolitionist candidate. Numerous sources testify to his participation in the Underground Railroad. One of them reports an occasion when he brought 12 fugitive slaves to the home of Dr. Isaac Beck in Brown County, which borders Clermont County. Another time, he brought food to a party of 17 fugitive slaves. Huber hid fugitive slaves both at his home in Williamsburg and also at his farm, which was located outside the village. Among those who assisted him were Samuel Peterson, who sometimes forwarded fugitive slaves from Huber's locations to Isaac Brown in Bethel; Marcus Simms, an employee of Huber, who was known to have driven fugitive slaves to Martinsville in Clinton County and Sardinia in Brown County; and Huber's neighbor, Dr. Leavitt Pease, who took over as stationmaster of Williamsburg after Huber's death in 1854.

—Tom Calarco

Further Reading

Gary L. Knepp, *Freedom's Struggle: A Response to Slavery from the Ohio Borderlands* (Milford, OH: Little Miami Publishing Co., 2008).

CLEVELAND, OHIO

Cleveland, on Lake Erie in Cuyahoga County, was considered the "North Star" for many fugitive slaves. The first antislavery society formed here in 1810, and as early as 1815, fugitive slaves arrived at Western Reserve ports on their way to Canada. Reaching Cleveland meant being one step from freedom. Many slaves could not read and had no maps for their journey north. Looking to the skies and following the North Star was their way of seeking freedom. When fugitive slaves reached Cleveland, they could cross the lake to Port Stanley, Ontario, a distance of about 85 miles.

The Junction of Many Routes

Cleveland became the junction of many routes in Ohio for fugitive slaves. One ran from Norwalk through Wakeman to Oberlin, then northward through Lakewood to Cleveland. A second route extended northeast through Medina to Berea, then to Lakewood and east to Cleveland. From New Philadelphia, a third route ran to Massillon and Cuyahoga Falls, northeast to Brecksville and on to Cleveland. Sometimes fugitive slaves went through Salem or Hudson before using this route. After the Erie and Ohio Canal was completed in 1832, fugitive slaves could cross the Ohio River at Portsmouth, Ohio and using canal boats or the towpath, travel all the way to Cleveland. The Cleveland, Columbus & Cincinnati Railroad, completed in March 1851, carried fugitive slaves on night trains from Cincinnati to Cleveland. The Cleveland & Western Railroad, as well as the Cincinnati & Springfield Railroad aided in transporting fugitive slaves across Ohio to Cleveland.

Some Conductors

A conductor on the Massillon route was Zebedes Stout, a Yankee farmer who lived a few miles south of Akron and transported fugitive slaves about 35 miles to the Cuyahoga Port. Other conductors to Cleveland were Dr. Joseph Cole of Akron, Dr. Amos Wright of Talmadge Township, and John Hall of Springfield Township near Akron. Another station was at Brechsville, at the home of Carey Oakes on the Massillon route. Quakers who lived in Summit and Stark counties would guide fugitive slaves into the dense woods along the shore east of Cleveland to wait for a "friendly" vessel that took them to Canada.

Cyrus Ford, who had moved from Massillon to a farm on Buffalo Road in East Cleveland in 1841, was frequently sent a closed carriage full of Canada-bound fugitive slaves from associates in Massillon. Also on the Buffalo Road, fugitive slaves could be hidden in freedman John Bell's barbershop, the last stop before boarding a boat to Canada.

Another site alleged to have been a stop was the Wade House, a tavern kept by Edward Wade at the corner of Pearl and Columbus streets. Built in 1846, St. John's African Methodist Episcopal Church, located on East Fortieth Street, earned its reputation as "Station Hope" on the Underground Railroad. Fugitive slaves hid in the bell tower, watching for a signal that a boat was ready to take them across Lake Erie to Canada.

The Cozad-Bates House, an example of Italianate architecture, built in 1853, also is believed to have been a station. It is the only pre-Civil War structure still standing in the University Circle area of Cleveland. The house was neglected and stood empty for many years, but was finally renovated and has been listed in the National Register of Historic Places since 1974. The Cozad and Ford families, prominent members in the antislavery effort, owned much of the land now known as University Circle. The Cleveland Restoration Society and the City of Cleveland Landmarks Commission hopes to transform the Cozad-Bates House into a teaching center celebrating Cleveland's Underground Railroad history.

West of Cleveland, in Lakewood, Philander Winchester had a home where he kept fugitive slaves in his cellar. They were transported to Lakewood at night from the villages of Lodi and Seville in Medina County. From this port, row-boats were launched to carry the fugitive slaves out to sailing vessels or steam-boats anchored in the harbor awaiting their cargo to bring to Canada.

The Role of Women

Women, both black and white, had always been a part of the Underground Railroad, primarily with the work of feeding, sheltering, clothing, and nursing fugitive slaves when they arrived at a safe house. In Cleveland, four of the nine members of the city's very active, all-black Vigilance Committee (sometimes called the Committee of Nine) were women. This committee oversaw the Underground Railroad work and planned and strategized the forwarding of 275 fugitive slaves to Canada in less than one year, from mid-1854 to early 1855.

William Wells Brown

William Wells Brown, a former slave, was employed on one of the ships that sailed on Lake Erie from Cleveland harbor. He gained a reputation for taking fugitive slaves aboard his ships and delivering them to Canada at no cost to the passengers from 1836 to at least 1842 (though based in Buffalo after 1836, his ship likely made stops in Cleveland during this period). Very few voyages to Canada were made without first taking on a group of men and women from the wharf on the Cuyahoga River. He gave safe passage on his boat to 69 fugitive slaves during one 7-month period in 1842.

Ashtabula County

Just east of Cuyahoga County and about halfway between Cleveland, Ohio and Erie, Pennsylvania, Ashtabula County boasted more than 30 stations along the Underground Railroad, several of which remain today. Hubbard & Company, shipping merchants of Ashtabula, would hide fugitive slaves in their warehouses and ship them across to Port Burwell during the night. Captain Austin Shepard, resident of Ashtabula, ran the steamer *Cleveland* from Cleveland to Port Stanley and other ports on the Canadian side of Lake Erie, carrying freight to all points. Along with the freight were often hidden fugitive slaves. The ship's mate, John Kimburgh, also helped in hiding and transporting them.

The Hubbard House in the Ashtabula Harbor was the home of Colonel William and Catherine Hubbard and their six children. Located at 1093 Walnut Boulevard, it was known on the Underground Railroad as "Mother Hubbard's Cupboard." Conductors brought fugitive slaves to this home where they stayed in the cellar or hayloft. The main house had a barn in the back with a trap door leading to the beach. This may have been an escape route to the bay so that row-boats could take the fugitive slaves out to waiting vessels. Joseph D. Hulburt, a partner of Colonel Hubbard, hid fugitive slaves in the Little Yellow Warehouse or behind stacks of lumber until he could put them on departing vessels. Hulburt knew which lake captains could be trusted with these passengers. He also was the owner and supervisor of sailing vessels for these fleeing passengers.

Today the Hubbard House is the site of the Hubbard House Underground Railroad Museum. The first floor is furnished as the Hubbard house of the mid-1880s; the second floor has an Underground Railroad exhibit; and the Civil War and Americana exhibit area is in the basement. The museum presents information on more than 30 other Underground Railroad sites in Ashtabula, none of which are open to the public.

Another Ashtabula stop was the First Presbyterian Church on Park Avenue. The Reverend August Pomroy of the church was jailed for helping fugitive slaves. In the 1840s and 1850s, members of the church were active in the Underground Railroad. As with many other churches, there were people on both sides of the issue, creating much controversy as to whether slavery was something that should be tolerated. In 1860, about one-third of the congregation left the church and formed the First Congregational Church just across the street. One reported reason for the split was that members said the pastor of the church was not strong enough against slavery.

Several other stops in Ashtabula included the home of Amos Fisk, who established the first abolitionist society in Ashtabula in 1833 and founded the First Baptist Church on Park Avenue. The society was the first civic organization in Ashtabula. On Austinburg Road was the site of Mathew Hubbard's Grist Mill, which was on a waterway that joined the Ashtabula River. Fugitive slaves could easily hide at the mill and use the Ashtabula River as an escape route.

Another alleged safe house in Ashtabula was Park Haven owned by Nehemiah Hubbard, the son of Mathew Hubbard. Built in 1847, the home housed an underground tunnel that once ran all the way to Main Avenue. Through this large tunnel several hidden rooms could be accessed, which are believed to have harbored fugitive slaves.

Located on West Avenue in Ashtabula was the McDonald House. Deacon Jesse McDonald painted the house white with black trim around the top, which legend suggests symbolized a safe house. McDonald hid fugitive slaves in the barn behind his house and was jailed for assisting them. On Lake Avenue was the J. I. B. Nellis House. Nellis was among those who left the Presbyterian Church to join the Congregational church because of his abolitionist views. The basement of the Nellis House, which still stands, has many hiding places.

In Jefferson lived Joshua R. Giddings, the renowned antislavery leader in the U.S. Congress who regularly harbored fugitive slaves at his home. Giddings persuaded the fugitive slave, Charles A. Garlick, who was only 16 years old when he escaped, to settle in Jefferson and work for him. Later, Giddings sent Garlick to Oberlin College, where he became part of the "Liberty Hall" class of 60 or 70 "colored" boys in 1847. Garlick eventually became a successful businessman.

Fairport Harbor, located between Cleveland and Ashtabula, was another point of departure for fugitive slaves. Fugitive slaves reached there after coming through Painesville, and before that Concord, where several Underground Railroad routes converged. These routes came north from Akron or Ravenna or Warren. Conductors from Painesville were Joseph H. Pepoon, a farmer and millwright, who hid fugitive slaves in his hayloft before moving them to Fairport; James H. Paine, a lawyer, who aided fugitive slaves at every opportunity; Seth Marshall, who owned a hardware store on Main Street; and Eber D. Howe and Frank Rogers.

Samuel Butler, the lighthouse keeper at Fairport Harbor, hid fugitive slaves in the garret of his tavern. Both he and Phineas Root hid some in the warehouses near the harbor. Butler himself sometimes transported groups of fugitive slaves across the lake to Canada in his scow.

During the early 1800s, in Huron County, west of Cleveland, Jabez Wright purchased a large tract of lakeside land on the north side of what is now Cleveland Road. Wright, an early Huron County judge, built a large farmhouse with eight rooms that later served as a station on the Underground Railroad. Fugitive slaves could reach Lake Erie through a 16-foot-wide and 90-foot-long tunnel that was dug out beneath Wright's farmhouse. Entrance into the tunnel was through a trap door in the basement and fugitive slaves could exit the tunnel into a corncrib located only 100 feet from Lake Erie. At this point, the fugitive slaves could wait for the arrival of rowboats that transported them to larger vessels heading north to Canada.

Lake Erie Ports

Every port on the Ohio shore of Lake Erie could be a final stop of the Underground Railroad. At least eight among them have been identified as significant terminals in Underground Railroad history: Conneaut was the end of one route that led from eastern Ohio and the Western Reserve area; Painesville, the final stop of three routes; Ashtabula, of four routes; Cleveland, of four or five routes; Toledo, of four or five routes; Sandusky, of four routes; and Lorain and Huron, one each.

—Cynthia Vogel

Further Reading

Joseph Henderson Bausman, *History of Beaver County, Pennsylvania* (New York: Knickerbocker Press, 1904).

Levi Coffin, *The Reminiscences of Levi Coffin* (Cincinnati: Robert Clark & Co., 1880).

B. L. Higgins and S. Pearsall, *Next Stop, Freedom!: A Resource Guide on the Underground Railroad through Ohio and across the Great Lakes* (Vermilion, OH: Great Lakes Historical Society, 1998).

Wilbur H. Siebert, *The Underground Railroad from Slavery to Freedom* (1898; reprint, New York: Arno Press and *The New York Times*, 1968).

Wilbur H. Siebert, *The Mysteries of Ohio's Underground Railroads* (Columbus, OH: Long's College Book Company, 1951).

COLUMBUS, OHIO

Columbus, Ohio, located near the center of the state, has served as the capital since 1816. This city, along with the nearby towns of Westerville, Worthington, Clintonville, and Reynoldsburg, provided safe houses for many fugitive slaves beginning in the 1820s. Some fugitive slaves that went through Columbus on their way to freedom had crossed the Ohio River at Marietta, then traveled through Chillicothe to Circleville, Columbus, Worthington, and Westerville, and then north to Lake Erie and on to Canada. Others crossed the Ohio River at Ripley, proceeding north through Hillsboro or Washington Court House. A third line that went through Columbus began at Portsmouth on the Ohio River. Fugitive slaves traveled north along the Scioto River to Columbus.

Some Conductors

Samuel Patterson, a farmer who lived northeast of Columbus, began harboring runaways in the early 1820s. By the 1840s, he was organized to the point that he had fugitives working on his farm and people who lived in the area watching for slavecatchers.

James Westwater, an antislavery Democrat, hid runaways in Columbus as early as 1840. They were hidden in a smokehouse near his home, located on Chestnut Street near Fourth Street. Drivers took the fugitive slaves hidden in wagons up High Street to Clintonville, a section in Columbus today that is located in center of the city, where Jason and Alonzo Bull were active conductors.

Blacks also had active roles in the Columbus Underground Railroad. In 1846, a free black man, Jerry Finney, was kidnapped. The people of Columbus came to his aid and raised money for his release, but he died shortly afterward. In 1847, Rev. James Preston Poindexter, pastor of the Second Baptist Church and an avid abolitionist, led a friendly split of the church and formed the Anti-Slavery Baptist Church. The latter group was involved in the Underground Railroad; but in 1858, the two reunited, apparently because the other groups now supported the more radical abolitionist doctrine.

Another local important black leader was Charles Henry Langston, a free black man originally from Louisa County, Virginia, who settled in Ohio during the mid-1830s. In 1836, he established a school for black children in Chillicothe, Ohio, 40 miles south of Columbus. In 1842 and 1843, he attended Oberlin College. During that period he joined the Liberty Party, and in 1843 he moved to Columbus to edit the antislavery newspaper, *The Palladium of Liberty*, from 1843 to 1844. In 1856 he was appointed principal of the Columbus Colored School, and two years later he took a leadership role in the Oberlin-Wellington rescue of the fugitive slave, John Price, for which he was the only person convicted.

Blacks who aided fugitive slaves in addition to Poindexter and Langston were John T. Ward, a self-employed wagon hauler, and David Jenkins, another editor of *The Palladium of Liberty*, and also John Bookel, William B. Ferguson, Jeremiah Freeland, James Hawkins, Lewis Washington, and William Washington.

The Kelton House, built in 1852, was one of several safe houses on East Town Street in Columbus. At that time, it was surrounded by pastureland. Columbus was a divided town with strong supporters of slavery and those who were adamant that slavery was wrong. Fernando Kelton was steadfast against slavery. He and his wife Sophia did all they could to aid fugitive slaves, disregarding the danger and the consequences that would result if they were caught by the state and federal laws prohibiting this. Fugitive slaves could have found safety in the servants' quarters of the home or in the 300-gallon cistern in the yard. The Keltons were progressive in their view of the fugitive slaves. In 1854 two former slave girls were found hiding in the shrubbery at their home. Sophia invited the girls in and let them stay in the house. One of the girls, Martha, was too ill to move on to the next safe house when her sister, Pearl, continued her trip northward. Martha stayed in the family home for the next 10 years, being raised and educated as one of the family. She married a free black carpenter, Thomas Lawrence, who worked for Fernando Kelton. Their oldest son, Arthur Kelton Lawrence, became a pharmacist and physician, practicing medicine in Columbus for 33 years.

Dr. James H. Coulter was a homeopathic doctor in Columbus whose Underground Railroad activities began in 1849. The attic of his large house, located on the east side of Third Street between Gay and Long Streets, provided safe refuge for fugitive slaves. A barn behind the house also served as a safe place. From the Coulter residence, fugitive slaves were sent to Westerville or Alum Creek.

The Hanbys

William Hanby was a minister with strong abolitionist sympathies whose home in Westerville was a station. One night in 1842, a fugitive slave came to the house of Doctor Simon Hyde, who lived in Rushville, where Hanby lived before moving to Westerville. The man, Joseph Selby, was suffering from pneumonia and was seeking shelter with Hanby. Hyde summoned Hanby, but Selby was too sick and had to stay in the doctor's office for treatment. Selby told the story of how he ran away hoping to earn enough money in Canada to buy the freedom of his sweetheart, a slave named Nelly Gray. Selby was deathly ill and sadly, within a few days, he died. During his last hours, he revealed the story of his beloved Nelly Gray who had been sold and sent south the day before they were to be married. William Hanby repeated this story to his children as they grew up. In 1856, Hanby's son Benjamin, inspired by the Joseph Selby story, wrote the song, *Darling Nelly Gray*. The tune was very popular in the North before and during the Civil War. It inspired other slaves to take a chance at escaping to freedom.

Beginning in 1853, when the Hanbys moved to Westerville, the Hanby family's participation in the Underground Railroad was quite active. They lived next door to Otterbein College President Lewis Day, who had been a conductor since the college opened in 1847. A barn behind their house, which served as Hanby's saddle and harness shop, was another place where the fugitive slaves were hidden. The fugitives would have dinner in the house with the Hanby family, and it was young Ben's job to cover the windows to prevent them from

William Hanby house in Westerville section of Columbus, Ohio; Ben, the son, not only helped his father aid fugitive slaves but was the composer of the Civil War ballad, "My Darling Nellie Gray," and the Christmas children's class, "Up on the Rooftop." (Courtesy of Tom Calarco)

being seen. It was also his job to lead the fugitive slaves out of the barn during the night to the false bottom wagon of toolmaker Thomas Alexander. They were then safely transported to other safe houses in Alum Creek or Delaware, on their way to Sandusky or Cleveland.

The Hanby House remains today in Westerville on the campus of Otterbein College and is a museum operated by the Westerville Historical Society.

Joseph Morris

At the Shaw Creek Friends' Settlement, about 30 miles north of Columbus, was a house owned by Joseph Morris. This house was used as an emergency line out of Columbus when other lines were thought to be too dangerous. The Morris House was an unpretentious, two-story frame dwelling with gable ends and a portico. Morris was a well-known Quaker philanthropist and abolitionist.

The house had a low attic and in the cellar he had built false partitions to provide secret chambers for the fugitive slaves. Dozens of fugitives could hide in these secret chambers. The rooms were hidden behind large cupboards. From the cellar two tunnels led out, one to the barn and the other to a corn crib. These tunnels provided a safe escape when slave hunters surrounded the house. This house, which still stands, was probably the safest retreat for fugitives in northern Ohio. It received numerous passengers from Alum Creek Quaker Settlement, but also from the Olentangy River, a tributary of the Scioto River that runs along the east side of Columbus and continues about 60 miles north, as well as fugitives from Cincinnati. From the Morris home, fugitives went to the Friends' Settlement at Adrian, Michigan, or to Detroit, and then to Windsor, Ontario.

Several additional stations or safe houses are listed for Columbus and the surrounding area. They include the Kappa Sigma Sigma House (Henry Neil Mansion) and the Caroline Brown House in Columbus; the Livingston House and the David and Nancy Graham House in Reynoldsburg; the Henry and Dolley Turk House, the Ozem Gardner House, and the Ansel Matoon House in Worthington; and the Southwick-Good Funeral Home (Clintonville Methodist Church) and the residences of Reverend Jason Bull and Alonzo Bull in Clintonville. Alexander Livingston of Reynoldsburg had a huge covered wagon called "the ark" that he used to transport fugitive slaves as far as Mt. Vernon, where the members of the First Congregational Church (originally Free Presbyterian Church) received the fugitive slaves.

Because of Columbus's central location in Ohio, many Underground Railroad routes that zigzagged across the state eventually went through this area, connecting numerous communities along the Ohio River with numerous ports on Lake Erie.

The Fugitive Law of 1850 stimulated a rush to Canada by both slaves and free blacks, who no longer felt safe even in the northern states. About this same time, a new means of transportation became readily available to the fugitive slaves: the rail system that connected Cincinnati, Dayton, and Columbus to Sandusky and Cleveland. When fugitives traveled by wagon, they depended on stations that were located about 15 miles apart and they depended on conductors to drive these wagons. With the development of the railroads through Ohio, including the Little Miami Railroad from the south of Columbus and the Mad River Railroad to the north, fugitive slaves could board a train in Cincinnati, Dayton, or Columbus, exit the train in Cleveland or Sandusky, and then take a boat to freedom in Canada.

—Cynthia Vogel

Further Reading

Levi Coffin, *The Reminiscences of Levi Coffin* (Cincinnati: Robert Clark & Co., 1880).

E. Delorus Preston, Jr., "The Underground Railroad in Northwest Ohio," *Journal of Negro History*, 17, No. 4 (October 1932).

Wilbur Siebert, "A Quaker Section of the Underground Railroad in Northern Ohio," *Ohio History*, 39, No. 3 (July 1930).

Wilbur H. Siebert, *The Mysteries of Ohio's Underground Railroads* (Columbus, OH: Long's College Book Company, 1951).

Wilbur H. Siebert, *The Underground Railroad from Slavery to Freedom* (1898; reprint, New York: Arno Press and *The New York Times*, 1968).

Ralph M. Watts, "History of the Underground Railroad in Mechanicsburg," *Ohio History*, 34 (1934).

CONCORD, MASSACHUSETTS

Concord was one of a number of small Underground Railroad stops on routes leading from Boston that included such locations as Andover, Amesbury, Danvers, Fitchburg, Framingham, Groton, Leominster, Lynn, Medford, Newburyport, Salem, and Worcester, Massachusetts. Its leading influence was its female antislavery society, which was closely associated with William Lloyd Garrison, and it was home to at least one member of the vaunted all-male Boston Vigilance Committee. It also boasted two of the nation's foremost philosophers, both of whom were outspoken abolitionists—Ralph Waldo Emerson and Henry David Thoreau.

Concord Female Anti-Slavery Society

The village's primary significance to the Underground Railroad and the abolitionist movement was the promulgation of the concept of civil disobedience, which was passed on through the famous essay written by Thoreau and which is one of the greatest legacies of the Underground Railroad. Thoreau's ideas were strongly influenced by Concord's female abolitionists, who founded the Concord Female Anti-Slavery Society in 1837. Not only were Thoreau's mother, Cynthia, sisters, Helen and Sophia, and four of his aunts active members, but its founding president, Mary Wilder and her husband, boarded with the Thoreau family for a time.

It also was a fairly active Underground Railroad stop. In an 1892 interview, Ann Bigelow, who harbored the well known fugitive slave, Shadrach Minkins, claimed that fugitive slaves were hidden in Concord "nearly every week" during the 1850s. Although this seems to be an exaggeration, it might not be so surprising to have occurred during the first few years of the decade when the Boston Vigilance Committee alone reported aiding 230 fugitive slaves during the four years following the passage of the second Fugitive Slave Law. This also doesn't take into account the estimated 600 fugitive slaves living in Boston at the time of the law's passage, many of whom fled the city after the enforcement of the law there in the rendition of Thomas Sims in 1851.

The most influential members of the society were Mary Brooks, its secretary, who persuaded William Lloyd Garrison to come to the village on a number of occasions to speak; Abby Alcott, sister of the noted abolitionist Samuel J. May, whose husband Bronson was a member of the Boston Vigilance Committee, a connection that brought fugitive slaves to Concord with regularity; and Bigelow. Another dedicated member was Mary Rice, a spinster who harbored fugitive slaves and who collected the signatures of 350 Concord children on a petition requesting Lincoln to free all slave children. Among the society's most important activities was its fundraising to support the Massachusetts Anti-Slavery Society. Each year they supplied goods and staffed the annual Boston Anti-Slavery Bazaar, the nation's largest abolition fundraiser, and annually led the region in its charitable donations to the cause.

Shadrach Minkins

As for the Underground Railroad, more than oral tradition testifies to its operation there. The celebrated fugitive slave, Shadrach Minkins, the most noteworthy beneficiary of the village's defiance of the law, was brought in a horse and buggy by Boston Vigilance Committee member, Lewis Hayden, to the home of Ann and Francis Bigelow at 3 a.m., on February 16, 1851. Visiting the Bigelows that night were Mary and Nathan Brooks; the next day when Shadrach left Concord for the home of Jonathan Drake in Leominster in a wagon driven by Francis Bigelow, he sported a silk hat given to him by Brooks.

Accounts from the diaries of both Abby and Bronson Alcott recount their harboring of fugitive slaves in December 1846 and February 1847. In an undated journal entry for December 1846, Abby records: "The arrival of a Slave named for the present John—an intimate in my family until some place where work can be provided—An amiable intelligent man Just 7 weeks from the 'House of Bondage.'" The following February 2, Bronson writes, "there arrives from the Maryland plantations a fugitive to sit at my table and fireside." A week later, his entry discloses that "our friend the fugitive, who has shared now a week's hospitality with us, sawing and piling my wood, feels this new taste of freedom yet unsafe here in New England, and so has left us for Canada" (Petrulonis 401–402).

Another documented instance of Underground Railroad activity in Concord comes from the 1854 rescue of a fugitive slave aboard the ship, *William*, in Boston harbor by members of the Boston Vigilance Committee, which apparently brought the runaway to the Brooks home.

Thoreau

Henry David Thoreau was one of the village's most active participants in the Underground Railroad. Ann Bigelow said that "Henry Thoreau went as escort [with fugitive slaves] probably more often than any other man [in Concord]" (Emerson, Dr. Edward W., "Notes on the Underground Railway in Concord and the Concord Station." Allen French Papers, Concord Free Public Library, Concord, Massachusetts). At a July 4 rally in Framingham in 1851, he said, "The judges and lawyers, and all men of expediency consider not whether the Fugitive Slave Law is right, but whether it is what they call constitutional. They try the merits of the case by a very low and incompetent standard. Pray, is virtue constitutional, or vice." (Thoreau, Henry David, *Walden and Other Writings*, Barnes & Noble, 1992: 315).

Thoreau himself recorded the following entry in his journal on October 1, 1851 about a fugitive slave sent to the Thoreau family by Garrison:

> Just put a fugitive slave who has taken the name of Henry Williams into the cars for Canada. He escaped from Stafford County Virginia to Boston last October, has been in Shadracks place at the Cornhill Coffee-house-had been corresponding through an agent with his master who is his father about buying-himself . . . heard that there were writs out for two Williamses fugitives—and was informed by fellow servants & employers that . . . the police had called for him. . . . Accordingly fled to Concord last night on foot-bringing a letter to our family from Mr. Lovejoy of Cambridge—& another which Garrison had formerly given him. . . .
>
> He lodged with us & waited in the house till funds were collected with which to forward him. Intended to dispatch him at noon through to Burlington—but when I went to buy his ticket saw one at the Depot who looked & behaved so much like a Boston policeman, that I did not venture that time. . . .
>
> The slave said he could guide himself by many other stars than the north star whose rising & setting he knew—They steered for the north star even when it had got round and appeared to them to be in the south. They frequently followed the telegraph when there was no railroad. The slaves bring many superstitions from Africa. The fugitives sometimes superstitiously carry a turf in their hats thinking that their success depends on it. (*A Year in Thoreau's Journal: 1851*, with an introduction by Henry Peck, New York: Penguin Books, 1993: 247)

Another occasion that recalled the arrival of a fugitive slave was when Moncure D. Conway, a native of Virginia who had moved to the North and Concord on account of his abolitionism, went one morning to the Thoreau house. He found that the family was excited about the arrival of a slave, who had to be assured that Conway was a friend.

Emerson

Ralph Waldo Emerson, whose wife, Lydia was a member of the female antislavery society, also was a devoted abolitionist. In 1844, he spoke at a meeting of the society on the emancipation of slaves in British West Indies that had occurred 11 years earlier. He also spoke out after the passage of the second Fugitive Slave Law, made contributions to the Boston Vigilance Committee, and in July 1854, he and Lydia participated in a meeting of Concord abolitionists in which they pledged to aid any fugitive who came seeking their assistance.

Emerson and Thoreau were admirers and supporters of John Brown who first came to Concord in 1857, as the guest of Franklin Sanborn, who operated a school in Concord and who was one of Brown's famed "Secret Six" of financial supporters. Both philosophers spent time with Brown, the Thoreaus having him over for dinner. Later, on May 8, 1859, Brown spoke at the Concord Town Hall. He told the audience that the two most important documents were the Bible and Declaration of Independence, and that it was "better that a whole generation of men, women and children should pass away by a violent death than that a word of either should violated" (Renehan, Edward J., *The Secret Six: The True Tale of the Men Who Conspired with John Brown*, New York: Crown Publishers, 1995: 118). Seven months later, on the morning of Brown's execution, Thoreau spoke at a church in Concord and offered a plea for Captain John Brown: "Some eighteen hundred years ago, Christ was crucified," Thoreau said. "This morning, perchance, Captain Brown was hung. . . . He is not Old Brown any longer; he is an angel of light" (Thoreau, Henry David, *Walden and Other Writings*, Boston: Elibron Classics Series, 2006: 772).

Mary Brown

Further evidence of Concord's militant abolitionism was the arrival of Mary Brown and her daughters in Concord following Brown's execution. They came with the widow of Brown's son, Watson, who died at Harpers Ferry and were the guests of the Emersons. Later, they boarded with the Alcotts during which time Mary Brown enrolled her younger children at Sanborn's school.

While Concord was overtly militant, the entire region was no less supportive and equally ready to be part of the Underground Railroad. Wilbur Siebert accounted for five routes radiating from Boston, as well as a route coming from Rhode Island that skirted east of Boston through Concord. In Natick, about 12 miles south of Concord, the wealthy Edward Walcott welcomed fugitive slaves who came by way of the Boston and Albany Railroad. It is believed that Walcott forwarded them to Israel How Brown, a black grocery peddler, who hid fugitive slaves in his false bottom market wagon. According to Siebert, Brown aided more than 100 fugitive slaves.

—Tom Calarco

Further Reading

Sandra Harbert Petrulonis, "Swelling That Great Tide of Humanity: The Concord, Massachusetts, Female Anti-Slavery Society," *The New England Quarterly*, 74, No. 3 (September 2001).

Wilbur H. Siebert, *The Underground Railroad in Massachusetts* (Worcester: American Antiquarian Society, 1936).

D

DETROIT, MICHIGAN

With its proximity to Canada, the river port of Detroit, Michigan, became an early destination for fugitive slaves and, with the influence of many free blacks who settled there, soon grew to be a major stop on the Underground Railroad. It also became the headquarters for a separate, black organization, known as the Negro Secret Order, which worked hand-in-hand with more visible, white abolitionists toward the same goal.

Many of the Underground Railroad routes through western Ohio, Indiana, and Illinois converged on Detroit, though some led to Port Huron, Michigan, and others ran to lakeshore towns in Wisconsin. To reach Detroit, some runaways needed to cross Lake Michigan or Lake Huron. Boats along Lake Erie also carried fugitive slaves to Detroit from Cleveland and Sandusky, Ohio. Others traveled along routes in western Ohio through Toledo and Adrian, then on to either Ann Arbor or Ypsilanti and finally Detroit.

Routes Leading to Detroit

Three lines from Kentucky led through Indiana to Cassopolis in southwestern Michigan, but a fourth line led some Kentucky slaves along the eastern side of Indiana to Coldwater, Michigan, where it divided into several routes, all going to Detroit. Missouri slaves might have passed through Illinois by one of six or seven different lines, and many of them continued on to Detroit as well. In the 1840s, in what is today the Midwest but was then considered the West, one route ran from Quincy, Illinois, through Galesburg, Princeton, Chicago, and southern Michigan, ending in Detroit. By 1854, the route extended across Iowa, and some fugitives came to Detroit by way of St. Louis, and Alton, Illinois. From Detroit runaways crossed the Detroit River to enter Canada and freedom.

The Gateway

The Detroit River, which is a borderline between the United States and Canada, connects Lake St. Clair to Lake Erie and separates Detroit from Windsor, Ontario. It is possible to stand on one shore and see the other in the distance, less than one and a half miles away, a sight that must have inspired hope in many fugitive slaves. Today, the 7,500-foot Ambassador Bridge spans the river; but in Underground Railroad days, there was no bridge, and fugitives relied on ferries and row boats, as well as their own ingenuity.

Nothing was going to stop William "Bush" Johnson from reaching Canada— and freedom—one cold January day in 1852. He had already put his life at risk by virtue of leaving his Kentucky master, Axem Skinner, after Skinner threatened to ship him where the dogs wouldn't bite. To Johnson that meant the cotton and rice fields down south, where it was rumored the slaves grew so thin, they didn't have enough meat on their bones to tempt a dog.

Johnson made his way to the Ohio River and then crossed it in a skiff, using two stolen boards from a lumberyard as paddles. Somewhere along his journey, Johnson paired up with another slave, and the two became traveling companions. They rode the Underground Railroad to Detroit. As a slave, Johnson had been told that the Detroit River was 3,500 miles wide. Until reaching Detroit, he had no way of knowing that it was a lie meant to dissuade slaves from attempting to escape. They soon boarded a ferry and should have reached Canada that day in comfort, but the Detroit River had frozen, and the boat could not cut a path through the ice. The other man returned to Detroit, but Johnson jumped from the ferry and walked across, though the ice began wavering beneath his feet.

Despite that slavery was banned in the Michigan territory by the Northwest Ordinance of 1787, some individuals resisted it and there were still 32 slaves in the Michigan territory in 1830—five years before it became a state and permanently prohibited it. Nevertheless, runaway slaves and free blacks flocked to Detroit as early as the 1820s. Whether they settled in the city or crossed the river to what was then called Sandwich, Ontario, later renamed Windsor, many of them played active roles in the Underground Railroad, particularly in the highly ritualized Negro Secret Order.

DeBaptiste and Lambert

Two of the foremost conductors of the Negro Secret Order on the Underground Railroad were prominent residents of Detroit: George DeBaptiste, who acted as manager of the Detroit office, and William Lambert, who filled the role of secretary. Both men were born free on or about the year 1815. Lambert was born in Trenton, New Jersey, and DeBaptiste was born near Fredericksburg, Virginia. Lambert's father had purchased his own freedom, but his mother had always been free. Both of DeBaptiste's parents had been slaves, but somehow managed to become free before he was born. The similarities did not end there. Both men arrived in Detroit with useful trades: Lambert was a tailor; and DeBaptiste, a barber.

Lambert visited Detroit in 1838 at the age of 23 and moved there in 1840, perhaps drawn to the city, in part, by news of black uprisings, such as the June 1833 Blackburn incident. After their escape from slavery in Kentucky, Thornton and Lucie/Ruth Blackburn resided in Detroit, until the day their master arrived to claim them. Then the couple was arrested, jailed, and decreed the legal property of the slave owner. The black community of Detroit was enraged and took matters into their own hands.

The rescue of Mrs. Blackburn was a genteel affair carried out by two unidentified women who visited her in jail. The names of married women from this time period are not always easy to find. In this case, one source gives Mrs. Blackburn's name as Ruth (*Michigan and the Fugitive Slave Acts* 4) and the other as Lucie (*I Came as a Stranger* 88). "One of the women exchanged clothes with the prisoner, who then walked out with her face covered, pretending to be weeping. By the time the ruse was discovered, Lucie [or Ruth] was safely in the hands of friends" (ibid.).

In contrast, men rescued Thornton Blackburn by force. A mob attacked the sheriff with stones and clubs and then transported the Blackburns across the river to Canada. The violence had a chilling effect and frightened the white community on both sides of the border. The secretary of war sent federal troops to Detroit, and city authorities arrested 30 black men. In Sandwich, the Canadians first imprisoned the couple, then refused to extradite them, citing that self-theft was not a crime under their law. Soon the pair was released, and the Blackburns went on to become wealthy citizens of Toronto. Sheriff John Wilson, who sustained a skull fracture and lost several teeth in the raid, never recovered from his injuries and died within the year.

Before becoming involved in the Underground Railroad, DeBaptiste had traveled in high circles. He served as manservant to William Henry Harrison, during Harrison's campaign for president and while he was in the White House. However, a month into his term, President Harrison died of pneumonia and pleurisy in 1841, and DeBaptiste returned to Madison, Indiana, a community with an active Underground Railroad, where he had been living. From Madison, the Underground Railroad passed through Ohio to White Pigeon, Michigan, and on to Detroit. DeBaptiste ran the Madison station from his home along the Ohio River. There, he loaned his certificate of freedom to fugitives who fit his physical description: five feet seven and a half inches tall, mulatto, in his twenties. "Even so, it is said he used his certificate thirty-three times to aid slaves to escape; and during his eight years as an agent in Madison, he started one hundred and eight fugitives on the way to Canada in his own wagon" (Lumpkin 69).

DeBaptiste relocated to Detroit in 1846 when he was in his early thirties and became part owner in several businesses, including a barbershop, a bakery, and a Lake Erie steamship line that ran from Detroit to Sandusky, until settling down with a catering business.

Both DeBaptiste and Lambert were established in Detroit by the late 1840s, when Robert Cromwell needed their help. Cromwell had escaped from slavery in Arkansas, settling first in Indiana, and then moving to Flint, Michigan, where he opened a barbershop. A few years passed, and he began to feel safe. He wrote to his former master, John Dun, asking to buy his sister for $100. Although he dated the letter from Montreal to mislead his former master, the Flint, Michigan postmark gave away his true location, and Dun set off to recapture him.

Meanwhile, Cromwell realized his error, and he sought Lambert's help. Hoping to evade capture, he left another man in charge of his barbershop and moved to Detroit, where he opened a restaurant. But Dun traced him there and tricked him into entering the courthouse. Federal law would have forced the U.S. district judge to order that Dun could take Cromwell back, so when Judge Ross Wilkins, who sympathized with the former slave, heard the commotion on the floor below him, he hid, apparently in the attic.

Cromwell tried to escape out the window, while the court clerk, George Ball, warned Cromwell against coming upstairs. Lambert and DeBaptiste arrived with a lawyer named George Rogers, but they could not get in the building until Ball tossed a key from the window. They entered with a score of others and rescued Cromwell from the courthouse. While a crowd, including some Irishmen, who taunted Dun as a mansteler, blocked Dun from taking chase, others put Cromwell on a skiff and took him to Canada.

Lambert and DeBaptiste hired lawyers, who charged Dun on a state law that made it an offense to entice or kidnap a fugitive slave to return to slavery. No one denied that Dun had enticed Cromwell to the courthouse, and it could be said he had attempted to kidnap him, but there was no proof that he did so to return Cromwell to slavery. As Lambert remarked, "Our law point was bad, but we were many in number, and resolute" (Lumpkin 68). Out of fear of the mob, Dun spent nine months in jail on postponements, but when he came to trial, he went free.

Cromwell was not the only former slave to inadvertently give away his position by writing home. A railway worker and fugitive slave, who went by the names William Anderson and William Jones, ran into trouble after the interception of two letters he had written home to Missouri, one to his wife and another to a blacksmith friend. Laura Haviland, of Adrian, received a letter claiming that his family had come to Detroit and wished to meet him there. Haviland asked DeBaptiste to help, and the fugitive passed through Detroit on his way to Windsor and the Refugee Home Society run by Henry Bibb.

Although Lambert earned his living in Detroit as a tailor, and also ran a dry cleaning business, he made time for many volunteer activities. He led the Detroit Vigilance Committee, served his church as a deacon, lobbied for public education for black children in Detroit, and played a key role in the Negro Secret Order.

The Detroit Vigilance Committee, run by Lambert, raised funds to help more than 1,500 fugitives during its peak years in the mid-1850s, providing food, clothing, transportation, and whatever else a runaway slave might need, including medical care. Like other abolitionist vigilance committees, the group also alerted members when slave catchers arrived. Vigilance committees also existed in the South, but there the vigilance was exercised in the opposite direction, protecting slave-holding interests.

The Negro Secret Order

The Negro Secret Order went by more than one name, including African-American Mysteries, Order of the Men of Oppression, Order of Emigration, and, in one book, the League of Freedom. It was formed by free blacks to help those who remained in bondage move to free territory. The order operated for a decade or more under a large membership and played a role in John Brown's final plans. Lambert himself was a friend of John Brown and participated in the meeting at Chatham, Canada West, which preceded the Harper Ferry raid.

In 1886, a reporter from the *Detroit Tribune* interviewed Lambert about his Underground Railroad activities, and during the interview he showed the reporter two sheep-bound books that he kept in a desk along with a copy of *Walker's Appeal to Freedom*, and letters from John Brown, William Lloyd Garrison, Wendell Phillips, and Lucretia Mott. The books also held Lambert's handwritten records of the rituals, degrees, test words, grips, emblems, and lessons of the Negro Secret Order.

There were three degrees of membership: the Captives, the Redeemed, and the Chosen. Within the first degree, Captive, there was a special step called Confidence, designed for agents of the Underground Railroad. Within the third degree, there were five progressively difficult stages: rulers, judges and princes, chevaliers of Ethiopia, sterling black knight, and knight of St. Domingo.

There is no evidence of women in the organization, and logic suggests that membership was for males only. Whites, however, could join if they passed certain loyalty tests, but their numbers were small and they belonged to their own chapter, with restricted access. One of the few white men to be admitted to one of the highest degrees of the Negro Secret Order was Richard Realf, a friend of John Brown, revered for his antislavery poetry. The Grand Lodge of the Order was located in Detroit on Jefferson Avenue, between Bates and Randolph.

Caroline Quarrelles

When Caroline Quarrelles was just 15 or 16 years old, she became the first passenger on the Underground Railroad to arrive in Detroit from Wisconsin in 1842. Quarrelles had been a house slave in St. Louis, Missouri, where her duties included waiting on her mistress and completing the household's fine sewing and embroidery. She had been looking for the opportune time to run when, in a fit of anger, her mistress cut off her long, beautiful hair.

This gave Quarrelles the excuse she needed to risk escape. She boarded a Mississippi River steamboat, and then rode a stagecoach to Milwaukee. During her flight, she was hidden in a hogshead, typically a 63-gallon barrel, on a city sidewalk; another time she hid in the bottom of a buggy under a buffalo robe. The danger was real. Her owner had enlisted the steamboat company to help recapture her by holding them liable for negligence in his loss because the crew failed to deny her passage.

Despite the steamboat clerk's frantic efforts to recapture her, Quarrelles reached Mr. and Mrs. Ambler's house in Detroit, in about three weeks, and the steamboat company was compelled to pay $800 plus costs to Quarrelles' owner. Along the way, many helped her, including Lyman Goodnow from Waukesha, Wisconsin. Crossing the Detroit River turned out to be a harrowing experience, not because of the weather, or because of pursuit, but because Quarrelles mistook the river for the Mississippi and feared she had been tricked into going back to St. Louis. Until she landed in Sandwich, Ontario, and knew that she was safe, Quarrelles was inconsolable.

In 1895, Solon Goodell talked about his father, Jotham Goodell, and his role in the Underground Railroad. Jotham had raised a family of 11 in Superior, Michigan, two miles north and three miles east of Ypsilanti, and though he did not belong to any church, Solon described him as an enthusiastic abolitionist. Solon thought the fugitives probably came to his father from Adrian, about 30 miles to the south. They hid in the loft of the Goodell barn, located 30 rods (almost 500 feet) from the road, until his father had to go to Detroit to sell his produce. Then the fugitives rode in the produce wagon to the River Rouge Hotel, about eight miles from Detroit, where another agent took over.

Rev. Jacob Cummings

The escape of the Reverend Jacob Cummings from slavery near Chattanooga, Tennessee, took him on a four- or five-year journey along the Underground Railroad through Milton, Cabin Creek, Fort Wayne and Goshen, Indiana, then on to Cassopolis, Battle Creek, Royal Oak, and Detroit, Michigan. Cummings, whose name was Jacob Smith when he was in slavery, ran off in July 1839, when he was about 23 years old.

He had been tied up, put in the stocks, whipped 150 strokes, and salted over the wounds for the minor infraction of being seen in a nearby town on a Sunday. Another time, Cummings's master knocked him unconscious with a slab of wood. Mr. Leonard, a white man in Chattanooga, heard about the cruelty and decided to help. He showed Cummings maps of Ohio, Indiana, and Lake Erie, and took him out one night to show him the North Star, instructing him how to follow it and what to do on cloudy nights. After one last visit with his mother, Cummings paid a man to write credentials showing him to be free, then swam, walked, and boated toward Detroit but not without being captured and escaping four times.

At the time, an abolition steamboat called the *Arrow* ran from Sandusky, Ohio to Detroit. There was also a ferry, called *Little Jim*, that ran from Detroit to Windsor, but when Cummings wanted to cross, there were too many people aboard to risk traveling on it. Instead, two boys rowed Cummings across the Detroit River to Windsor, Canada. On the Canadian riverfront, he found his way to a supply store owned by Henry Bibb.

George W. Clark, the Liberty Singer, described Bibb as an almost-white fugitive from slavery in Tennessee, who had come through Detroit in 1842, only one or two years before Cummings. Bibb became a public speaker for his race through the Liberty Association, and he established the antislavery newspaper called *The Voice of the Fugitive*. In addition, Bibb supplied slaves with free boots, hats, bedding, and other goods, and he helped new arrivals, including Jacob Cummings, find a place to stay. Like many fugitives, Cummings repaid the help given to him by helping others. From Windsor, he traveled to Amherstburg, then the Dawn settlement, and finally took residence in the Depuce settlement, 14 miles northeast of Detroit. There he became an agent for the Underground Railroad. In his role as agent, he collected goods for fugitives and shipped them to Detroit.

Seymour Finney

When Seymour Finney, a Baptist businessman, gave an Underground Railroad agent the key to his barn on the corner of Griswold and State Streets, it became the passenger depot for many years at the north end of the line, and today a plaque marks the spot where his barn once stood. George Dolarson, the black janitor of the Old Capitol School of Detroit, kept the key to the Griswold Street door of Finney's barn. It was said that agents on the Underground Railroad knew where to find that key without him—if necessary.

Finney had built the barn shortly after opening the Temperance Hotel on the corner of Gratiot Street and Woodward Avenue in Detroit in the spring of 1851. Finney kept a couple of pigs and fed them with refuse carted from the hotel to the barn in a wheelbarrow. Sometimes a tin pail of food was sent over, too. That was for the fugitives. On at least three occasions, the hotel guests, who dined not 20 feet away from the barn, were there hunting the very slaves hidden in Finney's barn. Fugitives would arrive in country wagons between one in the morning and dawn and hide in the loft behind six to ten tons of hay during the day. When safe, someone would guide them to the river for crossing.

As a 16-year-old boy from New York, Finney had been bound out to learn the trade of a tailor. Four years later, he came west with his father, who settled on a farm in Redford, about 15 miles west of Detroit. By 1838 his health was too frail for tailoring, and he became a clerk in a succession of hotels, before opening his own. In 1852, Finney left the Democratic Party to join the Free Soil movement;

in 1854, he used his influence at the Jackson convention to persuade the Whigs to accept the Free Soil candidate for governor. This was among several developments in northern states that led to the formation of the Republican Party.

J. G. Reynolds

Another important figure in Detroit's Underground Railroad was J. G. Reynolds, a black agent sent to the city by Levi Coffin. The Reynolds home was one of the rendezvous points for the Negro Secret Order, and fugitives often stayed there before departing for Canada. Reynolds is mentioned in a May 1858 diary entry by George R. Gill, a member of John Brown's company. Gill wrote that under a pledge of secrecy, Reynolds showed him a fine collection of arms kept by the Negro Secret Order in Sandusky, Ohio, another residence of Reynolds, and told him that members of the order were waiting for Brown, or someone else, to make the initial move before setting their forces in motion.

Other Fugitive Slaves

Many times members of the Underground Railroad and those they helped crossed paths in unexpected ways. In 1836, Levi Coffin helped a former slave known as Aunt Rachel, one of the best cooks he had ever known, make her escape to Canada. When he visited Detroit in 1844, he found she had moved there with her husband and was doing well, except for the pain that bothered her ankle, caused by the chain she once wore.

By the time John Reed was interviewed about his travels on the Underground Railroad, he had been living in Canada for 41 years. A Kentucky slave trained as a carpenter, Reed married at the age of 30, and when he and his wife had a son, he decided he couldn't let the boy grow up a slave. They left Maysville, Kentucky in the spring and went down the river in a small boat to Ripley, Ohio. They arrived in Cleveland after a month on the run, where they remained for two months before taking a night packet to Detroit, arriving early the next morning. They stayed the night at a colored tavern called Gordon's, located near the Central Depot, then crossed the river three months after leaving Maysville and made Windsor their home. Three months after arriving in Canada, they received their belongings in a shipment sent by John Rankin in Ripley, Ohio.

When 57-year-old Edward Walker talked about his escape from slavery in 1858 at the age of 21, he owned a grocery store, a hotel, and a farm, and had become one of the wealthiest men in Windsor. Walker was born 10 miles from Covington, Kentucky, on the Hayden Nelson plantation. At the age of four he was doing small chores. When he was 10, he had to work in the cornfield with the adults. Even as a child, he resented being a slave; by the time he turned 15, he began looking for ways to escape.

When he was 18 and about to run away, his uncle's family escaped from a neighboring plantation and this made his master more cautious. To avoid being sold to a trader, he pretended to be happy and carefree. As a result, he waited three more years before trying his luck. He and his brother, Moses, escaped with a friend and his brother's wife and child, who lived on another plantation four miles away. The friend was a slave who traveled to different planters for work, and he was able to make arrangements with a white agent of the Underground Railroad to have a rowboat at the Ohio River near Covington.

In preparation, their friend bought a horse and the Walker brothers stole two more from their master. The child rode with Edward, and Moses and his wife shared a horse. They left the horses behind when they neared the river. To reach the river, they had to cross a 12-foot span of quicksand. None of them knew what it was. Walker stood in it, and passed the child and his brother's wife over. His brother crossed next followed by their friend; but when he tried to follow, he started to sink.

Calling out for help was not an option; the area was patrolled by guards looking for runaways. Fortunately, Walker's brother noticed his absence, retraced his steps, and pulled him out. After staying a week in Cincinnati, the group rode by buggy to Bellefontaine, Ohio, about 100 miles north, then took a train to Sandusky. From Sandusky they boarded a boat for Detroit, and then hopped the ferry to land in Canada on April 20.

The only education Walker had was two weeks of instruction in letters from his first master's grandson, who was close to his age. He picked up numbers by himself and learned to add, multiply, divide, and work with fractions, and no doubt this helped him succeed in business. But demonstrating his intelligence while he was a slave only caused him trouble. He was called a "long-headed nigger" and kept under close watch. Slave owners knew from experience that the smarter the slave, the more likely he would run off.

Today there are a number of Underground Railroad sites available for tours in Detroit, including the Second Baptist Church at 441 Monroe Street. The church, founded in 1836 by 13 former slaves, was the first all-black congregation in the city. Among those who came there to worship were Sojourner Truth, John Brown, and Frederick Douglass.

The First Congregational Church also aided fugitive slaves at its original location at Fort and Wayne streets. Now located at Woodward Avenue, it helps visitors participate in a condensed reenactment of the year-long journey of a slave who escaped on foot from Louisiana. Visitors may also tour the Historic Elmwood Cemetery, located at 1200 Elmwood, across from Martin Luther King High School. Several Michigan founders of the Underground Railroad are buried in the cemetery, including Dr. Joseph Fergusson, George DeBaptiste, William Lambert, and William Webb. Former Detroit mayor Jacob Howard, who wrote the Thirteenth Amendment that emancipated the slaves at President Lincoln's request, is also buried there.

—Rae Hallstrom

Further Reading

Charles L. Blockson, "The Underground Railroad," *National Geographic*, July 1984.

Tom Calarco, *People of the Underground Railroad* (Westport, CT: Greenwood Press, 2008).

David G. Chardavoyne, "Michigan and the Fugitive Slave Acts, the Court Legacy," 12, No. 3, The Historical Society for the United States District Court for the Eastern District of Michigan (November 2004).

An Epic of Heroism: The Underground Railroad in Michigan 1837–1870, a Study Guide and Resource Booklet (Museum of African American History, May 1988).

"Freedom's Railway," *Detroit Sunday News Tribune*, January 17, 1887: 2.

Honorable J. W. Finney, Interview with Wilbur Siebert, July 27, 1895, Detroit, Michigan.

"Stories of Runaway Slaves," *Journal*, Louisville, Kentucky, August 12, 1894.

Evelyn Leasher, "William Lambert, an African American Leader of Detroit's Anti-Slavery Movement," http://clarke.cmich.edu/undergroundrailroad/freedomsrailway.htm.

Katherine DuPre Lumpkin, "The General Plan Was Freedom, a Negro Secret Order on the Underground Railroad," *Phylon*, 28, No. 1 (1967): 63–77.

Bryan Prince, *I Came as a Stranger* (Toronto, Canada: Tundra Books, 2004).

Wilbur H. Siebert, "The Underground Railroad in Michigan," *Detroit Historical Monthly*, Detroit Historical Society, 1, No. 1, March 1923.

Robin W. Winks, *The Blacks in Canada, a History* (New Haven: Yale University Press, 1971).

E

ELEUTHERIAN COLLEGE/LANCASTER, INDIANA

Eleutherian College was one of the nation's first schools to open its doors to blacks, and was perhaps the first destination where fugitive slaves could get an education. It was located in Lancaster, Indiana, a small hamlet seven miles northwest of Madison, Indiana, a major entry point of the well-traveled trunk through eastern Indiana already in place when famed conductor Levi Coffin moved to Newport, Indiana, in 1826.

As early as the 1820s, free blacks, many of whom were liberated slaves from Virginia and Kentucky, were aiding fugitive slaves in Madison, and Lancaster became part of that route. Its benevolent character, which made it a hospitable stop for fugitive slaves, was molded by evangelical Christians from New England. The first family to put down stakes was the Nelsons. Brothers James and Daniel, veterans of the War of 1812, came from Vermont in 1820. They were followed in 1834 by Lyman Hoyt, also from Vermont, whose wife Lucy was the sister of James Nelson's wife. Hoyt brought with him his brothers, one of whom married Daniel Nelson's daughter, Harriet. The final piece of what evolved into an Underground Railroad clan came when members of the Tibbets family, originally from Maine, began to settle in Lancaster in the mid-1830s. They had immigrated first to Clermont County, Ohio, where the family patriarch, Dr. Samuel Tibbets, had become engaged in the Underground Railroad and worked with the famed conductor and abolitionist, John Rankin of Ripley, Ohio.

Neil's Creek Anti-Slavery Society

It was in these households that the Neil's Creek Anti-Slavery Society was born in 1839, with Lyman Hoyt emerging as their leader.

An 1883 history of southern Indiana by William Wesley Woollen testifies to their activities: "The abolition sentiment in Lancaster was considered a plague-spot on the body politic. The Hoyts, the Nelsons, and the Tibbetses of that

Lyman Hoyt house, Lancaster, Indiana; home of the leader of the Neil's Creek Anti-Slavery Society. (Courtesy of Tom Calarco)

neighborhood, although honorable and peaceable men, were tabooed because they believed in the equality of all men before the law. The Eleutherian school at College Hill received the maledictions of the people because in it the fountain of knowledge was as free to the negro as to the white man" (Woollen 534).

John Henry Tibbets

John Henry Tibbets, the son of Samuel, described the participation of Lancaster in the Underground Railroad in a series of reminiscences written in 1888.

"My first adventure after I moved to Indiana was in the August of 1845," Tibbets wrote. "I received word from George Debaptist [DeBaptiste] of Madison Indiana, that there would be a lot of ten to leave Hunter's Bottom on Sunday night and he wished me to make arrangements to transport them on the underground road that I was acquainted with."

DeBaptiste, a free black barber who had moved to Indiana from Virginia and who for a short time was the valet of President William Henry Harrison until Harrison's untimely death one month after taking office in 1841, was at the time one of the leaders of the Underground Railroad in Madison.

Tibbets continued: "About five o'clock in the evening my wife and myself got into my big covered wagon and started for my wife's uncle, Lyman Hoyt. He lived about three miles from where we lived on the road to Madison. After dark I drove to the place agreed upon to meet in a piece of woods one mile from the town of Wirt (a short distance from Lancaster). I had been at the appointed place but a very short time when Mr. Debaptist sang out, 'Here is $10,000 from Hunter's Bottom tonight.' A good negro at that time would fetch from $1,000.00 up [at least $20,000 in today's currency]. We loaded them in, drew down the curtains and started with the cargo of human charges towards the North Star. We always made good time and close connection. At a given point my wife's brother, James Joseph Nelson and Leonidas Cushman and nephew of mine were in waiting with a fresh team to put to the wagon and drive as far as possible before (daylight). They drove to Albert Allies beyond where they took breakfast, rested and the next day to James Hamilton's, seven miles from Greensburgh on Sand Creek" (Tibbetts "Reminiscences").

DeBaptiste later said in an 1870 interview in the *Detroit Post* that he brought a total of 108 fugitive slaves through the Lancaster terminal.

Tibbets' memoir reveals a number of additional incidents that outline a network of Underground Railroad conductors who worked together from Madison to Greensburg, Indiana. Notable among them were the Hicklin brothers, who were Methodist ministers in San Jacinto, a hamlet about 10 miles north of Lancaster, and Elijah Anderson, the important black leader in Madison, who later coordinated Underground Railroad activities in southern and western Ohio after a riot by a proslavery mob in Madison persuaded him to leave there.

Eleutherian College

Eleutherian College, founded in Lancaster in 1848, was one of the nation's first schools to open its doors to blacks, and was perhaps the first destination where fugitive slave slaves knew they could get an education. It was the idea of Rev. Thomas Craven of Oxford, Ohio, who initially came to Lancaster as a guest preacher at the Neil's Creek Anti-Slavery Baptist Church.

It was Craven's idea to start a school that accepted both whites and blacks, and men and women together. He bought 80 acres of land in the town of Lancaster and donated 8 acres to the college. He took the name for the college from the Greek word "eleutherous" meaning freedom or equality.

Virginia and Leddy Harris from Memphis, Tennessee, were the school's first black students and lived with the Hoyt family. In 1852, dormitories were completed and classes were held in a local meeting house until the college was ready in 1854. The entire structure was not completed until 1857, with the installation of the bell tower.

Among other black students was Moses Broyles, who attended from 1853 to 1856. Broyles was born in slavery in Maryland but then sold to a slave owner in Paducah, Kentucky. He was able to purchase his freedom, however, and came directly to the college, though no one knows how he knew about the school. In 1856 there were 18 African American students, 10 of whom were born slaves; and in 1860, the hey-day of the college, there were 200 students enrolled, 50 of them African American. Among its students were two black grandchildren of Thomas Jefferson.

When the Civil War began, most of Eleutherian College's male students, both black and white, joined the Union forces. The Indiana 6th Regiment used the college grounds for training before leaving for active duty, and many of the college's students were either killed or wounded.

Eleutherian College declined after the war, and there were few black students thereafter. John Gill Craven, the school's first teacher and the son of Thomas Craven, tried to revive the college but failed and sold it. It was finally shutdown after the 1887–1888 school year, and sold again and turned into a grade school for which it served another 50 years.

It was abandoned for more than 50 more years and near collapse when Jae Breitweiser and Dottie Reindolar purchased it in 1990. Today, through their hard work, the college is now completely restored and a National Historic Landmark. It is being turned into a museum that is a tribute to freedom, equality, and the Underground Railroad. For more information go to http://www.eleutherian.us/.

—Tom Calarco

Further Reading

Jae Breitweiser, Interview with Tom Calarco, September 29, 2006.

Peggy Sailors, "Bringing Secret History to Light." *Indiana Preservationist* (January/February 2005).

John Henry Tibbetts, "Reminiscences of Slavery Times." Unpublished memoir written in 1888.

William Wesley Woollen, *Biographical and Historical Sketches of Early Indiana* (Indianapolis: Hammond and Co., 1883).

ELMIRA, NEW YORK

A major connection linking Philadelphia and other Underground Railroad locations in eastern and central Pennsylvania to Canada, Elmira was aiding fugitive slaves at least as early as 1840. The development of transportation avenues like the Chemung Canal that connected the city with Seneca Lake in central New York, and the completion during the 1850s of railroad lines to Niagara Falls, however, made it much more frequented. The Chemung River, a tributary of the Susquehanna River that wound its way from Chesapeake Bay through Maryland and Pennsylvania to New York and that was used as a means of travel by many fugitive slaves, also passed through the city. In addition, during the 1830s, the settlement there of a number of upright religious individuals who abhorred slavery factored into making Elmira an important stop on the Underground Railroad. In 1837, the first recorded abolition meeting in the city was organized by Thomas Day and drew 200 individuals. During this period the

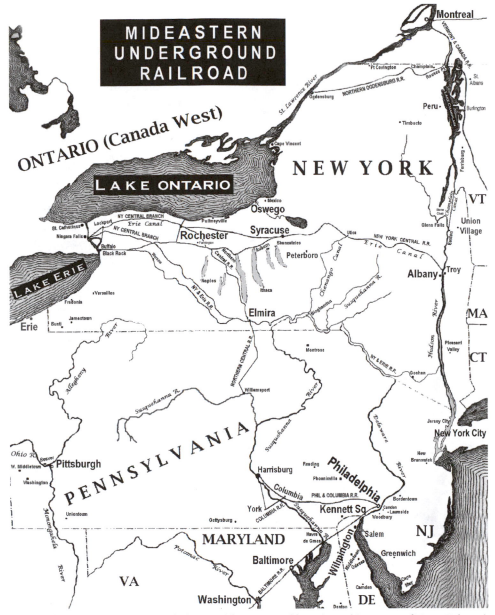

The Mideastern entries covered along with associated locations. (Courtesy of Tom Calarco)

city's most prominent white abolitionist, Jervis Langdon, moved here. The future father-in-law of author Mark Twain, Langdon was a successful merchant and devout member of the First Presbyterian Church. In 1845, he was among the leaders of the split from the parent church in which 41 members formed a new antislavery church, the Park Church. It included John Selover, Sylvester G. Andrus, Ira Gould, Silas Billings, Joshua Cleeves, and Grandison A. Gridley.

Jervis Langdon

By this time, Langdon and others had been actively aiding fugitive slaves. Among them was hardware merchant Riggs Watrous. A member of the First Baptist Church, he hid fugitive slaves in the upstairs rooms of his house on Lake Street. A letter written to the *Elmira Star* at the turn of the nineteenth century stated: "My father, Charles G. Manley was the man to whom the runaway slaves were sent from Williamsport. From Alba, father sent them here to Elmira to Riggs Watrous. I did not know Riggs Watrous, but I do know that many a poor black man and woman can thank him and my father and others for their freedom" (Ramsdell).

Another letter, from 1876, written by Augustus Holt described an incident in which he, Langdon, and Ed Messer aided 39 fugitive slaves who were being pursued by slavecatchers out of Elmira toward Canada. Holt said that an unnamed black preacher and Messer were leading two parties of fugitive slaves coming toward each other from different directions. There they met Langdon and Holt, who came in a carriage filled with supplies at a prearranged destination about nine miles outside Elmira. They distributed food, clothing, and gave them each $5 to help them along their way. Before they departed, Langdon led them in a prayer, asking God for their protection. They eventually arrived in Oswego, where a schooner chartered by Underground Railroad agents took them to Canada.

On another occasion in 1845, according to a letter written to Wilbur Siebert in 1896 by Susan Crane, Langdon's daughter, she stated that her father was called into the office of a judge who informed him that two slaveholders along with Southern law enforcement officers were on their way to Elmira. They had a warrant for 12 fugitive slaves who were living in the town. At once Langdon's business partner, Sylvester Andrus, went on horseback to warn the men who were working on farms outside the city. He arrived only 15 minutes before the slave owners, but it was enough time for them to go into hiding. When it was safe, they moved on to Canada.

John W. Jones

It was about this time that one of the many fugitive slaves who came to Elmira decided to stay rather than move on to Canada. John W. Jones was first aided by Dr. Nathaniel Smith and his wife in 1844. They gave him and his two brothers food and shelter in their barn outside the city. After about a week Jones went to the city to seek work. With the help of a local judge who took a special interest in him, Jones became educated and worked his way up to a position as a caretaker for the First Baptist Church. By 1850, Jones had become allied with the city's abolitionists and began to work closely with Jervis Langdon. For a time, Jones resided with Langdon and on one occasion when slavecatchers were passing through, Langdon had to put him in hiding in another part of town.

When the Second Fugitive Slave Law was passed, Jones helped organize an antislavery society of black citizens. In an article to *The Liberator*, he reported that the society resolved:

> That we, the colored citizens of Elmira, do hereby form ourselves into a society for the purpose of protecting ourselves against those persons, [slave-catchers] prowling through different parts of this and other States since the passing of the diabolical act of Sept. 18th, 1850, which consigns freemen of other States to that awful state of brutality which the fiendish slaveholders of the Southern States think desirable for their colored brethren, but are not willing to try it themselves. (*The Liberator*, November 15, 1850)

Jones hid as many as 30 fugitive slaves at one time in his home. In 1854 when the Northern Railroad from Williamsport to Elmira was completed, Jones obtained permission from railroad workers to hide fugitive slaves in the baggage cars that took them directly to Niagara Falls via Watkins Glen and Canandaigua.

Further testifying to his participation is a letter written by Jones to William Still on June 6, 1860. It said in part: "All six came safe to this place. The two men came last night, about twelve o'clock; the man and woman stopped at the depot, and went east on the next train, about eighteen miles" (Still 530).

Jones wasn't the only fugitive slave who settled in Elmira and worked for the Underground Railroad. In 1852, Thomas Stewart escaped through the swamps of Virginia and after six weeks of flight reached a Quaker settlement in Bellefonte, Pennsylvania. He stayed there for the winter before coming to Elmira where he settled.

Stewart married a local girl, Ann Johnson, and worked for the Elmira Female College, as well as serving as caretaker of the Trinity Episcopal Church for more than 30 years.

Other Elmira residents who aided the operation of the Underground Railroad were Rev. Thomas Kennicut Beecher, the brother of Harriet Beecher Stowe. Pastor of the antislavery Park Church from 1854 to 1900, Beecher was always be ready to contribute to the aid fugitive slaves. Another was jeweler, William P. Yates, a member of Trinity Church where Stewart was caretaker, and yet another, Mrs. John Culp, the first person who employed John Jones when he came to Elmira.

In later years Jones, who it is claimed aided as many as 860 fugitive slaves, gave all the credit to Langdon. "He was all of it," Jones said, "giving me at one [time] his last dollar, when he did not know where another would come from" (Ramsdell).

Jones's comment is a reflection of the true operation of the Underground Railroad, an integrated network that brought out the best efforts of diverse individuals working together.

—Tom Calarco

Further Reading

Michael P. Gray, "Elmira, a City on a Prison-Camp Contract," *Civil War History*, 45, No. 4 (1999).

Tendai Mutunhu, "John W. Jones: Underground Railroad Station-Master," *Negro History Bulletin* (March–April 1978).

Barbara S. Ramsdell, "A History of John W. Jones," Crooked Lake Review, ammondsport, New York (Winter 2003).

William Still, *The Underground Railroad* (Philadelphia: Porter and Coates, 1872).

Abner C. Wright, "Underground Railroad Activities in Elmira," Chemung County Historian, 1945.

ERIE, PENNSYLVANIA

Erie, a port on Lake Erie, is located in the northwestern corner of Pennsylvania in Erie County. It was the last stop for fugitive slaves before leaving the United States and crossing the lake to Port Royal, Ontario, Canada, and freedom. This crossing was shorter than any of the crossings that began with Ohio ports on Lake Erie. The area that stretches from Erie eastward to Cleveland, Ohio, had many points of departure for fugitive slaves who boarded sailboats, steamers, and schooners for Canada. Towns between these two large cities that saw intense activity on the Underground Railroad include the Ohio communities of Conneaut, Ashtabula, Geneva, Madison, Painesville, and Kirtland. On some of the older highways of northwest Pennsylvania and northeast Ohio, there are still buildings that served as stations on the Underground Railroad; for example, the Hubbard House in Ashtabula and the Hiram Lake house in Conneaut.

Conductors

Conductors Henry Frank, Dr. Hudson, Jeheil Towner, James and Jeb Reeder, William Gray, Stephen C. Lee, William Himrod, and Hamlin Russell led the operation of the Underground Railroad through this area. The fugitive slaves were relatively safe in Erie and were provided with food, shelter, and money, until there was an opportunity to send them to Canada.

The major Underground Railroad stations in Erie were the recently restored Perry Memorial House (also known as Dickson Tavern) at Second and French streets; the home of Captain Daniel Porter Dobbins, at Third and State streets; the William Himrod house at the foot of French Street; and the Josiah Kellogg house, east of French Street on East Second Street overlooking the harbor. In 1824 Himrod founded the French Street School for Colored Children at the Himrod Mission, and it is believed to have become a stop on the Underground Railroad. Himrod also is believed to have purchased a large tract of land in 1827 just outside of the city of Erie, which became known as Jerusalem, and was used for the benefit of blacks and destitute whites. He later joined the Erie County Anti-Slavery Society in 1836.

An indication of the fugitive slave traffic occurring at the Lake Erie ports was the frequency of advertisements in local newspapers offering rewards for fugitive slaves. As early as 1805, slave owners began advertising rewards for their missing slaves in Pennsylvania newspapers. Rewards varied from only a few cents to hundreds of dollars, depending on the "value" of the slave. The advertisements described the fugitive slave in detail, including name, age, height, and languages spoken.

Was Tunnel Part of the Underground Railroad?

As recently as 1979, Erie city repair workers digging about 12 feet below the surface of South Park Row unearthed a tunnel thought to be part of the Underground Railroad leading from the old Park Presbyterian Church to the bay. Local historians claim that a wide network of tunnels existed beneath the north side of Erie in the central city area that were used to move fugitive slaves to the waterfront.

Other Underground Railroad stations in Erie County were in the towns of North East, Cory, and Girard. In the northeast corner of Erie County, Sixteen Mile Creek emptied into Lake Erie through the town of North East. At the mouth of this creek lived the abolitionist farmer James Crawford, who along with his neighbor, John Glass, a foundry owner, forwarded fugitive slaves at night. Federal agents were often stationed around this waterfront to watch for fugitive slaves.

Wesleyville Methodist Church, located on Buffalo Road east of Erie, harbored fugitive slaves in the belfry of the church, though many church members were opposed to this involvement in the Underground Railroad.

Routes to Erie

Almost all fugitive slaves who passed through Erie County came by way of one of three routes. The first route brought fugitives through eastern Pennsylvania by way of the towns of Bellefonte, Brookville, Franklin, Meadville, and into Corry or Waterford. From there, the fugitive slaves were moved to Erie and then across the lake. A second route brought fugitive slaves north from Virginia to Pittsburgh, Beaver Falls, New Castle, Mercer, Meadville, Waterford, and Erie. A third major route brought fugitive slaves through Coopertown, Townville, Meadville, and then to Erie.

Noted in these routes is the town of Meadville, located in Crawford County. This was a community with a free black population that moved into the area in the early 1800s. Since blacks lived in Meadville, it provided a cover for fugitive slaves. The Henderson house was a safe house located in Meadville. Richard Henderson, born a slave in Maryland, escaped to Meadville in 1824 where he became a barber. His home on Arch Street is estimated to have harbored

500 fugitive slaves prior to the Civil War. Henderson also helped to form Meadville's Bethel African Methodist Episcopal Church in 1849 and served as an early trustee. Many members and trustees of this church were active in the Underground Railroad.

Miles Barnette, a cousin of John Brown who lived in Richmond, 10 miles east of Meadville, from 1826 to 1836, operated an Underground Railroad station in Waterford, between Meadville and Erie. Brown who harbored fugitive slaves while there, sometimes accompanied Barnette to Erie.

The first antislavery society in the county, which was also one of the earliest in the Pennsylvania, was formed in 1836. Col. J. M. Moorhead was chosen president and William Gray, secretary. The principal members were Philetus Glass, Dr. S. Smedley, and Truman Tuttle, of North East; Col. Moorhead, Mr. Jessup, and Samuel Low of Harbor Creek; William Himrod, Alex Mehaffey, and Aaron Kellogg of Erie; Giles and Hamlin Russell of Mill Creek; Stephen C. Lee of Summit; Rev. T. H. Burroughs of Concord; and William Gray of Wayne. Another society was formed in North East about the same time, with Truman Tuttle as president, James Duncan as vice president, Dr. E. Smedley as secretary, and R. L. Loomis as treasurer.

Frederick Douglass spoke at the AME Church in Erie in April 1856. Henry Catlin, editor of the *True American*, the first outspoken abolition paper in the city, invited him, welcomed him when he arrived, and bravely transported him to the places where he spoke. Though the city was active on the Underground Railroad, many locals did not approve of a black man speaking there.

Conneaut, Ohio, located just across the Ohio-Pennsylvania border, was another escape route for fugitive slaves. This route went from Youngstown, through Trumbull County, to Kinsman, and north to Conneaut. The home of Hiram Lake, which still stands on Main Street, had a secret cellar under the kitchen where fugitive slaves could hide. This was the beginning of a tunnel, no longer existing, which reached the banks of Conneaut Creek, about 500 feet away. The Reverend Charles L. Shipman, a circuit preacher associated with the Universalist Church, was an organizer and manager of a 40-mile Underground Railroad route from Andover, Ohio to Conneaut.

The steam packet ship, *Sultana*, made frequent round trips between Buffalo, New York, and Chicago, Illinois, making stops at Conneaut and other Ohio ports. Under the command of Captain C. W. Appleby, one of the noted steamboat captains on the lakes, this ship often carried fugitive slaves from several ports on Lake Erie to Canada, usually landing them at Fort Malden, Ontario.

—Cynthia Vogel

Further Reading

Joseph Henderson Bausman, *History of Beaver County, Pennsylvania* (New York: Knickerbocker Press, 1904).

Charles Blockson, *The Underground Railroad in Pennsylvania* (Jacksonville, NC: Flame International, 1981).

Levi Coffin, *The Reminiscences of Levi Coffin* (Cincinnati: Robert Clark & Co., 1880).

Wilbur H. Siebert, *The Mysteries of Ohio's Underground Railroads* (Columbus, OH: Long's College Book Company, 1951).

Wilbur H. Siebert, *The Underground Railroad from Slavery to Freedom* (1898; reprint, New York: Arno Press and *The New York Times*, 1968).

William J. Switala, *Underground Railroad in Pennsylvania* (Mechanicsburg, PA: Stackpole Books, 2001).

F

FARMINGTON, CONNECTICUT

The crossroads of the Underground Railroad in Connecticut was most certainly Farmington. Centrally located in the state, it received fugitive slaves both from the east, moving laterally after journeying part way up the Hudson River from New York City, or from the south, mainly from New Haven but also coming up the Connecticut River. Many of the latter came by way of the sea on boats from New York City or the Southern states.

Early Accounts of Fugitive Slaves

Residents of Connecticut, which instituted a gradual emancipation law in 1797, were helping fugitive slaves there at least as early as 1790 when a number of persons in Norfolk, in the northeastern part of Connecticut, harbored the Mars family, whose owners were planning to move them to Virginia. Another early incident involved the fugitive slave, William Grimes, who escaped to Connecticut in 1808 after stowing away aboard a ship out of Savannah, which landed him in New York City. From there, he proceeded on foot to Connecticut, where he worked as a barber in New Haven before marrying and settling in Litchfield. In 1823 his whereabouts were discovered by his former owner, but thanks to the generosity of his neighbors, his freedom was purchased. Another fugitive slave, Daniel Fisher, later known as Uncle Billy Winters, escaped from South Carolina in 1828 and, after an epic journey, received aid in Philadelphia, from where he was forwarded to New York, whose agents sent him to Deep River, Connecticut. There, a former slave provided him with a new identity and advice on his new life. Another account from 1838 tells of a fugitive slave, James Lindsey Smith, who escaped from Virginia to Philadelphia, where he entered the Underground Railroad, receiving help from a shoemaker named Simpson, who in turn sent him to David Ruggles in New York City and then moved to Connecticut and finally to Dr. Samuel Osgood in Springfield, Massachusetts, where he found work as a shoemaker. He eventually settled in Norwich, Connecticut. Another fugitive slave, William Green, followed the same route from Ruggles to Osgood, around the same period, and also settled in New England.

Farmington was linked with Hartford and New Haven by a system of turnpikes, as well as the Farmington Canal. Chartered in 1822 and opened for service in 1828, it linked the Long Island Sound at New Haven with Northampton, Massachusetts, which was near the residence of Rev. Osgood and a cadre of Underground Railroad conductors in nearby Florence. A stronghold of abolitionism, Farmington had both male and female antislavery societies, with 70 members in the former and 40 in the latter. It also had a relatively substantial black population of about 120 residents out of a total population of 2,000.

First Documented Underground Railroad Incident

The first documented Underground Railroad incident in Farmington took place in 1838. It was written down in 1840 by John T. Norton, one of the participants, and involved a fugitive slave named Charles, who had settled in Hartford and found a job working for an abolitionist known only as "Mr. B." One day to his astonishment, Charles saw his former master arrive in town with another individual. It could mean only one thing: his master had traced his whereabouts. Immediately, Mr. B contacted his associates in Farmington and placed Charles in hiding there. At least five Farmington residents, one of them black, took part, and two different houses sheltered Charles during the several days he was in town. Finally, he was placed in a secure location 40 miles to the north. Negotiations for the purchase of Charles's freedom were attempted with the slaveholder, but they failed and Charles was sent to Canada.

The Amistad Refugees

While New Haven also was a major destination, with such notable abolitionists as the Reverends Amos Beman and Simeon Jocelyn, and Hartford also had a strong abolitionist presence, Farmington figures more prominently in great part for its role in hosting the Amistad refugees from the Mendi tribe of Sierra Leone in West Africa for eight months in 1841. In all they numbered 38: 34 men, 3 girls, and a boy.

The Amistad refugees had been kidnapped in Africa, brought to Cuba, and sold in 1839. While slavery was legal in Cuba, the importation of slaves was not. Nevertheless, such trade was commonly practiced. The new owners then sought to resell them in nearby Haiti, but on the voyage there, the Mendi revolted and took over the ship, killing several of their captors. However, unschooled in navigation, they wandered the seas for two months in an attempt to return to Africa and landed off the coast of Long Island, where they went ashore to seek food and assistance. It was during this time that they were spotted by a U.S. Navy ship and taken into custody.

The Mendi were charged with piracy and murder and placed in the New Haven jail, and a committee of U.S. abolitionists under the leadership of Lewis Tappan, Joshua Leavitt, and Jocelyn formed to organize their defense. A two-year legal battle followed that involved the countries of Spain, England, and the United States. The case eventually reached the U.S. Supreme Court before whom former U.S. President John Quincy Adams spoke on behalf of the Mendi. The Court ruled that the Mendis should be set free. However, no provisions were made for their return to Africa. So, they were sent to Farmington while arrangements were made by the committee of abolitionists to prepare a voyage to return them to their homeland.

Austin Williams and Samuel Deming were the leaders of the group in Farmington that offered to house the Amistad refugees in the interim. Williams had a dormitory built for them and tutors were hired to teach them English and other subjects; the three girls were housed in private residences. They also were given jobs and made members of the village's Congregational Church.

On November 27, 1841, the Mendi left the port of New York for their homeland in Sierra Leone. However, one of the girls, Margru returned and was sent to school at Oberlin College. She graduated and returned to Sierra Leone, where

Samuel Deming house, Farmington, Connecticut; leader of the movement to bring the Amistad refugees to Farmington. (Courtesy of Tom Calarco)

she opened a school and maintained communications with Farmington throughout her life.

The experience with the Mendi strengthened Farmington's resolve to aid fugitive slaves. In addition to Williams and Deming, other Underground agents included Horace Cowles, William McKee, Levi Dunning, Lyman and George Hurlburt, and Elijah Lewis, as well as a black man whose name was never recorded and who made his home with George Hurlburt. The black man had contacts with the Underground who alerted him to incoming fugitive slaves. When this occurred, he went to Elijah Lewis and the two would meet the fugitive slaves and provide them with assistance.

On one occasion, Lewis sold land to a fugitive slave, who planned to settle there. Unfortunately, the fugitive slave's master came to town, and he quickly fled, never to return. Another fugitive slave who had settled in town learned from another who had followed him that his mother had been beaten by his master. The man whose name was Henry decided to return to the South and rescue his mother. Not only did he rescue her, but eight other slaves, all of whom he took to Canada, except for one young pregnant woman who died along the way.

Routes to and from Farmington

Most of the fugitive slave traffic in Connecticut moved through the western part of the state. Among those involved in the western route was William Wakefield of Wilton who took fugitive slaves in his wagon to the home of Rev. Joel Blakeslee, the pastor of the Congregational Church in Plymouth, a distance of about 40 miles. After a stay with Bakeslee, he would bring them to Farmington. Another minister, Rev. Samuel Dutton, pastor of the North Church in New Haven, also took fugitive slaves to Farmington. Another active station near Farmington was the house of U.S. Senator Francis Gillette in Bloomfield. In 1853, Gillette purchased a farm outside Hartford that also was used to harbor fugitive slaves. Just to the north, the home of Phineas Gabriel in Avon was a stop. Fugitive slaves are also believed to have found shelter at the Chaffee house in Windsor and in Granby and Suffield. Across the state line was Hiram Hull's farm in Westfield. As many as 20 fugitive slaves at one time are alleged to have been sheltered by Hull and his older brother Liverus. From Westfield, the route would follow to the Springfield area where Rev. Osgood was the coordinator. He could send them north to J. P. Williston in Northampton or to one of the many dedicated agents in Florence.

Fugitive slaves also came by way of the ports of New London and Old Saybrook and took steamers and other boats up the Connecticut River. Jesse G. Baldwin of Middletown owned two schooners that are believed to have transported fugitive slaves. To a much lesser extent fugitive slaves came up the eastern part of the state. Some of these fugitive slaves came from Rhode Island and such individuals as Charles Perry in Westerly, Elizabeth Buffum Chace in

Reverend Amos Beman Reports Aiding Fugitive Slaves, 1851

Reverend Amos G. Beman, first Negro minister of the Temple Street Church, came to New Haven, Connecticut, in 1838. Joining the New Haven Vigilance Committee, he became an agent of the Underground Railroad. In a series of letters Rev. Beman wrote to Henry Bibb's *The Voice of the Fugitive*, he discussed some of his Underground Railroad activities. The following is taken from the May 18, 1851 issue (OurOntario.ca Community Newspapers Collection, http://knowledge.library .utoronto.ca/newspapers/):

On the sixth instant [January 1851], we had the pleasure of receiving and sending on her way an interesting passenger from the land of chains and whips by the underground railroad notwithstanding it was said by one of the orators in the Union Meeting that "we have made some underground railroads and permitted it to be done it is our duty to prevent their establishment." But who will blot out the North Star?

Valley Falls, and Nathaniel Borden in Fall River. One of the earliest stations in eastern Connecticut was kept by Rev. Samuel May, who began aiding fugitive slaves in Brooklyn in 1834 and collaborated with Effingham L. Capron at Uxbridge, Massachusetts. In later years with the development of the upperground railroad, fugitive slaves were sometimes sent via the Norwich and Worcester Railroad to Worcester and the Providence-Worcester Railroad to Boston.

—Tom Calarco

Further Reading

Wilbur H. Siebert, *The Underground Railroad in Massachusetts* (Worcester, MA: American Antiquarian Society, 1936).

Horatio Strother, *The Underground Railroad in Connecticut* (Middletown, CT: Wesleyan University Press, 1962).

FLORENCE, MASSACHUSETTS

Florence, Massachusetts, is an unincorporated village in the town of Northampton. Sparsely settled until the 1830s, the village became a key center of abolitionist sentiment in Massachusetts and, given its small size, home to a surprising number of fugitive slaves.

Northampton Association of Education and Industry

The town's principal attraction to blacks generally was the Northampton Association of Education and Industry (NAEI), founded in 1842. The association was one of three Utopian communitarian groups organized in antebellum Massachusetts and one of 119 communal societies established in the United States in the first six decades of the nineteenth century. Like other such groups, NAEI aimed to develop functioning economic and social systems devoid of the perceived corruptions of the prevailing order. It was atypical, however, in its commitment to racial equality (Clark 46, 184). Many utopian communities evinced some measure of commitment to abolitionism and equal rights, but only the NAEI articulated those commitments as one of its seven constitutional principles: the association, its founders declared, was dedicated to the principle that "the rights of all are equal without distinction of sex, color, or condition, sect or religion." "It was a place to extinguish all aristocratic pretensions," Frederick Douglass noted after a visit to Florence in the early 1840s. "There was no high, no low, no masters, no servants, no white, no black" (Sheffeld 130).

Seven of the eleven founders of NAEI were abolitionists, and seven were from northeastern Connecticut, an early hotbed of abolitionist sentiment. Chief among them was George W. Benson (1808–1879), whose brother-in-law was William Lloyd Garrison. Another was Samuel Lapham Hill, who had founded the male antislavery society in Willimantic, Connecticut, and was a textile mill overseer. They and the other NAEI founders chose to set their community in Florence, in the fertile Connecticut River Valley, because it had been a center of silk manufacture since 1835. The antebellum interest in silk is often tied to antislavery: unlike cotton, silk was a fabric produced by free, not enslaved, labor, and some abolitionists customarily wore silk and linen as a protest of the South's slave-based economy. Three years after silk production began, the abolitionist David Lee Child moved to Northampton to begin the cultivation of beets as an avowed alternative to slave-produced cotton; he and his wife, Lydia Maria Child, editor of the *National Anti-Slavery Standard*, lived in Florence through the early 1840s.

Lydia Maria Child and David Ruggles

The Childs are credited with having brought New York conductor David Ruggles to Florence after Lydia had learned of the abolitionist's financial and medical difficulties while at the *Standard*. Until 1839 Ruggles had been the secretary of the New York Vigilance Committee, and numerous accounts of fugitive slaves cite his assistance. In 1842 David Lee Child asked the NAEI to invite Ruggles to become a member, which he did shortly after moving to the village. Ruggles began a water cure facility, believed to be the nation's first hydropathic hospital, in one of the Florence buildings NAEI rented, and in 1845 several abolitionists helped him finance the expansion of the facility. The Florence water cure was widely known and patronized by many Boston-area abolitionists, including Garrison.

Ruggles clearly knew something about abolitionism in the Connecticut Valley of Massachusetts before the NAEI invited him to settle in Florence. In 1836, with the aid of New York abolitionist Joshua Leavitt, a native of Charlemont, Massachusetts, Ruggles directed the fugitive slave Basil Dorsey and his family to the valley. The Dorseys were briefly in Northampton and then moved to Charlemont, the native place of Leavitt. After his wife died in 1844 Dorsey moved to Florence and worked as a cotton mill teamster for Northampton abolitionist James Payson Williston (Smedley 356–362; Hampshire Gazette,

April 2, 1867). In 1838 Ruggles sent the fugitive slave James Lindsay Smith on the same route up the Connecticut Valley to Springfield and in 1839 or 1840 sent Maryland fugitive slave William Green by that route. The extent of Ruggles's association with Florence before moving there is unknown; by the time of his move he was nearly blind and otherwise in poor health, and he died in Florence in 1849.

Sojourner Truth

Also drawn to the NAEI was Sojourner Truth, who had fled slavery in New York's Hudson Valley in 1826. In 1843 Truth visited the association and moved to the village after having become convinced of its commitment to equality. She joined the NAEI, whose members helped her find work and buy a home. Truth lived in Florence until she moved to Battle Creek, Michigan, in 1857. Another among the better-known fugitive slaves to have lived in Florence was Thomas H. Jones (1809–1890), who had escaped from Wilmington, North Carolina, in 1849 after having arranged for his free wife and their enslaved children to move to the North. Jones, who wrote several narratives recounting his escape, was an active antislavery lecturer. His wife, Mary, acquired the former Basil Dorsey house in 1854 and lived there with her children, and intermittently with her husband, through 1859.

Northampton proper was not known for its abolitionist sentiment. A summer resort for Southerners, it exhibited a "lofty slave-holding spirit," Lydia Child once noted, but a small group of abolitionists were active there. Perhaps most prominent among them was Williston, who assisted Dorsey as well as other fugitive slaves by housing them, moving them farther north, and employing them. Still, Florence was home to a disproportionate number of Northampton's people of color. Almost 37 percent of Northampton's black population lived in Florence, whose population was only 17 percent of the total population of Northampton. People of color were 9.6 percent of the village's total population, compared to 1.9 percent of Northampton's. One NAEI member noted that because the village was "a house of refuge for the ill-treated wanderer whether from Southern slavery or Northern barbarity," many people of color settled in Florence "and were fraternally greeted and guarded" (Hill). Sixteen fugitive slaves, fourteen by name, have so far been identified as living in the village in the 1840s and 1850s; in one 1843 letter NAEI schoolteacher Sophia Foord wrote, "This is becoming or has already become quite a depot for fugitives—one left here on Thursday & another arrived the day following who will probably tarry a short time." In October 1850 five Florence fugitive slaves, openly identifying themselves as such, signed a call for a meeting to protest the passage of the Fugitive Slave Act. That the population of people of color dropped from 56 in 1850 to 22 in 1860 further suggests that a good number of them had escaped slavery.

Samuel Hill's son, Arthur Gaylord Hill, born in Florence in 1841, recalled his father's participation in the Underground Railroad to have been extensive. "A good many passengers stopped 'five minutes for refreshments' at my father's, and conductors were often changed here," he wrote in the 1890s. "On a few trips I was either conductor or assistant conductor. Quite a number of the through passengers temporarily took up their abode in Florence, the balmy anti-slavery climate here proving very attractive to them" (ibid.). About the same time Hill told Underground Railroad historian Wilbur Siebert, "Our station was on the line from Hartford going North, though sometimes we had passengers who would come up part way through the Hudson River Valley or diagonally across from the Pennsylvania line" (Hill to Siebert). By 1857 Hill's farm had been sold to NAEI member Austin Ross, who is also asserted to have assisted fugitive slaves. The Dorsey-Jones house, the Truth house, and the farm of Samuel Hill and Austin Ross are all extant.

—Kathryn Grover

Further Reading

Christopher Clark, *The Communitarian Moment: The Radical Challenge of the Northampton Association* (Ithaca and London: Cornell University Press, 1995).

Frederick Douglass, "What I Found at the Northampton Association," in Charles Sheffield, *The History of Florence, Massachusetts, Including a Complete Account of the Northampton Association of Education and Industry* (Florence, MA: by the editor, 1895).

Sophia Foord, Northampton, to Robert Adams, May 8, 1843, private collection.

A. G. Hill, "Florence the Sanctuary of the Colored Race" (Arthur G. Hill Papers, Forbes Library, Northampton, Massachusetts).

Arthur G. Hill, Boston, July 18, 1896, to Wilbur H. Siebert, Massachusetts volume, Siebert Notebooks, Houghton Library, Harvard University.

Milton Meltzer and Patricia G. Holland, eds., *Lydia Maria Child: Selected Letters, 1817–1880* (Amherst: University of Massachusetts Press, 1982).

R. C. Smedley, *History of the Underground Railroad in Chester and the Neighboring Counties of Pennsylvania* (Lancaster, PA: Office of the Journal, 1883).

James Lindsay Smith, *Autobiography of James L. Smith* (Norwich, CT: Bulletin, 1881).

FLORIDA

As early as the 1680s, African slaves fled from what is now Georgia to Spanish Florida seeking freedom. Some of them formed small, isolated communities now known as Maroons, while others took refuge with Native tribes. At the time, Spain was involved in a protracted conflict with England, France, and other European nations over the possession of territory in the New World. In an effort to weaken the English, the Spanish King Charles II promised freedom in 1693 to English slaves who came to Florida. This was contingent on their conversion to the Catholic faith and their military service in support of

Spain. Before long it became known that the Spanish settlement of St. Augustine in northern Florida welcomed fugitive slaves.

As a result, fugitive slaves began regularly escaping from South Carolina, which also comprised the territory occupied by Georgia until they became separate colonies in 1732. The escape of slaves became so common that English colonists alleged that blacks and Indians from Florida were conducting raids and stealing their slaves. Finally, the situation led to a series of slave uprisings in South Carolina that culminated in a major revolt in Stono in September 1739 that drew as many as 80 slave combatants.

Fort Mose

In 1738, the Spanish established Fort Mose, a community of ex-slaves, just north of St. Augustine that served to warn and protect the city from invaders. It is believed to be the first free black town in North America. In 1740, their black militia repulsed an attack by the British on St. Augustine and several more during the next two decades. But in 1763, Spain ceded Florida to the English after the Seven Years War, and its free black citizens in St. Augustine were shipped by the Spanish to Cuba.

The Seminoles

This also brought slavery to Florida and a decrease of fugitive slave traffic. However, a dispute had occurred among the tribes of the Creek nation in Georgia, causing a large number of them to move to Florida. Along with other indigenous tribes in Florida, these Creek exiles formed a group that became known as the Seminoles. When the Revolutionary War began, not only were the English able to recruit the Seminoles, but they also offered freedom to slaves who would serve in their army against the American colonists. An alliance between the Seminoles and the emancipated blacks developed, which likely had its roots in earlier relationships fugitive slaves had developed with the earlier indigenous Florida tribes.

The defeat of the British resulted in the return of Florida to Spain, a concession made in acknowledgment of Spain's neutrality during the war. Naturally, it brought a resumption of fugitive slave traffic. Meanwhile the relationship between the Seminoles and blacks deepened. Though Seminoles called their black allies, slaves, it was in name only as blacks lived in separate locations and were in complete control of their lives, aside from obligations of military aid and small tributes of crops and livestock. A unique culture was developed by them that was a mix of Native American, African, and Spanish traditions.

The increasing numbers of fugitive slaves joining the Seminoles compelled the United States to intercede with the Creeks in Georgia in assisting the return of fugitive slaves. The treaties of New York and Colerain in 1790 and 1796 were made for this purpose. But they only engendered the animosity of the Seminoles.

By 1810 the number of slaves who had escaped to Florida numbered in the thousands, according to Georgians. In secret, the following year, the U.S. Congress secretly voted to attempt to seize Florida from Spain in effort to slow this exodus and commissioned the Georgia militia to attack St. Augustine, a stronghold of the Black Seminoles. This invasion led to the so-called Patriot War, which the United States alleged was the result of individuals from Georgia acting independently to foment revolution in Florida.

During the attacks on St. Augustine, the Spanish refused to fight and left their defense to the black militia of Mose.

"Indeed, the principal strength of the garrison at St. Augustine consists of negroes," wrote the governor of Georgia to Secretary of State Monroe (*State Papers* VIII).

Although the Patriot War turned out to be a complete failure, the United States was fighting another very public war against the British, who were being aided by the Native tribes and blacks in Georgia and Florida. A phase of this war was a campaign against the Creeks and the leader of the American forces was Andrew Jackson, who would become one of America's most implacable foes of Native and Black Americans.

The Negro Fort

After defeating the Creeks at Horseshoe Bend in southern Georgia, Jackson targeted Spanish Florida. He was well aware of the fugitive slave situation and considered the blacks in Florida to be lawless criminals who needed to be returned to slavery. Of particular concern was the "Negro Fort" on the Apalachicola River in western Florida that emptied into the Gulf of Mexico. It had allegedly drawn more than 1,000 fugitive slaves, who lived mainly in the surrounding fields. By 1816, they were cultivating land as far as 45 miles up from the mouth of the river.

An American force under General Edmund Gaines was sent there with an attachment of Creek warriors under William McIntosh. They hoped to draw the fort into a confrontation and then destroy it. The excuse for entering Spanish territory was to rendezvous with supply ships coming from New Orleans that were using the Apalachicola River. On June 17, 1816, Colonel Duncan Clinch was sent with 100 American soldiers and 150 Creek warriors down the river to meet the boats coming up the river near the site of the Negro Fort. Jackson surmised that if those in the fort initiated fire, it would provide justification for the Americans to attack and destroy it. The plan worked perfectly; when the American ships came into view, they were fired upon by the fort. Accompanying the supply ships were gunboats. They retaliated with fire. In an astonishing turn of fate, one of the hot cannon balls fired by the Americans landed in the fort's gunpowder storeroom, causing an explosion so massive, that was said to have been heard 100 miles away.

More than 250 black and Indian warriors and family members died, and many were wounded and captured, and later sold into slavery. This hostile act had been carried out on Spanish soil, but the Spanish refused to act. The survivors moved to communities in east and central Florida, and the Seminoles prepared to retaliate in what became the first of three Seminole Wars. In a series of battles that followed, Jackson's army routed them, the last one in 1818 along the Suwannee River that drove the black Seminoles farther south, where they joined a small maroon community along the Manatee River, near present-day Bradenton, called Angola.

The inability of the Spanish to defend Florida from the incursions of the Americans left them little recourse but to cede Florida to the United States. In 1821 it took possession, making Jackson its first governor.

Florida Ceded to the United States

Once again slavery was the rule in Florida. However, the large expanse of land provided many opportunities for slaves to escape. To maintain control, the first territorial legislature established a strict legal system to minimize slave unrest and adopted a severe slave code that included a system of local slave patrols and a policy of discouraging the contact of free blacks with slaves.

Jackson remained committed to eliminating the territory's fugitive slaves and before he left as governor, two of his Creek allies made a surprise attack on Angola, capturing 300 blacks, plundering their farms, and scattering the survivors, many of whom fled to the Bahamas before eventually settling on the nearby Andros Island.

Nevertheless, an estimated 800 Black Seminoles still remained in Florida. Though no longer governor, Jackson continued to use his influence in the government to push for their removal. He urged the federal government to merge the Seminole tribe with the Creeks in Alabama, who believed in the practice of slavery, and warned that if fugitive slaves were not removed from Florida that it would result in continued bloodshed.

Instead the federal government drew up a treaty that moved the Seminoles, who now comprised about 5,000 persons, to a reservation. Under the terms of the Treaty of Moultrie Creek, the Seminoles were required to renounce all claims to lands in Florida, in exchange for a reservation of about four million acres in the center on Florida. The United States was obligated to protect the Seminoles as long as they remained peaceful and law-abiding. It also was supposed to compensate them for relocation, supply food for a year, and distribute farm implements and livestock. The government was also supposed to pay the tribe $5,000 per year for 20 years and provide an interpreter, a school, and a blacksmith. In turn, the Seminoles were required to allow roads to be built through the reservation and to apprehend and return fugitive slaves.

It was not an ideal situation, however. The farmland on the reservation was poor and there was no access to the coastline, which hindered their ability to fish. In addition, slave raiders from Georgia and the Carolinas increased their attempts to kidnap Black Seminoles. Nevertheless, the Seminoles spent a period of relative peace there, from 1826 to 1830. The latter year saw the passage of the Indian Removal Act pushed through Congress by Jackson who was now president.

Seminole War

The Seminoles had no desire to move despite the less-than-ideal conditions of their reservation. In 1832, a delegation of Seminole leaders was persuaded to visit the lands in Oklahoma that had been selected for them. Unfortunately, these lands were under the control of the Creek nation from which they had split to move to Florida and which had been allies of the Americans during the war against them, including the horrible destruction of the Negro Fort. Furthermore, the Creeks were not on friendly terms with the Black Seminoles and would have no reluctance to enslave them. The Seminole chiefs also were not satisfied with the colder climate there. Nevertheless, the chiefs signed the Treaty of Fort Gibson, which stipulated their move to the western lands.

When their tribal members learned this, however, they vehemently rejected it. A meeting was set up with the government representative, Wiley Thompson, in 1834. At this meeting, a new Seminole leader emerged. Osceola made a demonstrative show of protest by plunging his knife into the paper on which the treaty was printed and declaring, "The only treaty I will ever execute is with this!" (Howard 57).

A confrontation was inevitable, and the Seminoles began preparations. Part of their plan was to recruit slaves from the plantations to join them.

Finally, in November 1834, Osceola struck the first blow, killing a Seminole chief who had been friendly to the Americans and who had been preparing to move west. Then a week before Christmas, the Seminoles launched the first of three offenses that would shock the Americans. It was coordinated by the black warrior, John Caesar, and the Seminole Chief King Philip whose men ransacked five large plantations outside of St. Augustine. They wrecked mills, burned homes, confiscated livestock and corn, and recruited slaves to their cause. Nearly 300 joined them. Another battle followed with the St. Augustine guards at a plantation, which the Seminoles decisively won.

Meanwhile, Osceola carried out the second phase of the plan. In the bushes outside of Fort King, he and six of his men ambushed and murdered Wiley Thompson. A shootout followed killing six more soldiers. At almost the same time, 100 miles away, a band of 180 Seminole warriors were about to execute the third and most dramatic phase of the plan.

Five days earlier, 108 U.S. soldiers had left Fort Brooke under the command of Major Francis L. Dade. They marched along a dirt road through pinewoods and savannah, guided by a local slave, Louis Pacheco. Little did they realize that Pacheco was leading them into an ambush. Half the U.S. officers fell at the first volley of shots by the Seminoles. The Americans soldiers used artillery to keep the Indians at bay, but when their ammunition ran out, they had no chance. Only three American soldiers survived, while the Seminoles lost only three warriors. Pacheco, who was not killed, later denied foreknowledge of the ambush.

The next morning after celebrating, the Seminoles met a contingent of 750 U.S. soldiers under General Clinch in a skirmish during which they forced the soldiers to retreat with four killed and many more wounded.

The early victories buoyed the confidence of the Seminoles. By February 1836, less than two months into the war, the Seminoles had destroyed 21 plantations and another major victory was won in March. By April, nearly 400 slaves had joined their ranks. However, they needed many more slaves to join them if they expected to defeat the American army with its almost limitless resources.

President Jackson was furious. He had sent five different generals to manage the war and all of them had been defeated, including the illustrious Winfield Scott. He finally turned to General Thomas Jesup, who took command in December 1836. Jesup had a different idea about how to win this war.

"This," he said, "is a negro, not an Indian war; and if it be not speedily put down, the south will feel the effects of it on their slave population before the end of the next season" (Granade 29).

His plan was to divide the Blacks and the Indians. To do this, he organized hit-and-run operations to burn crops, confiscate food, horses, and livestock, and capture Black Seminoles. In one raid, his men seized 90 head of cattle; in another they destroyed Osceola's headquarters and captured 52 blacks. After two months in Florida, Jesup had captured 150 Seminoles, mostly women and children. But they would prove to be extremely effective weapons as hostages. He then arranged negotiations with the spokesman for the blacks, Abraham.

They agreed to meet at Fort Dade, which had been erected near the site of the Seminoles' victory over Major Dade and his company, only a little more than a year before. It is not known what was said, only that Jesup had convinced Abraham to ask the Seminole chiefs to stop the fighting and meet with him to discuss a peace agreement. On March 6, the meeting was held and the chiefs signed an agreement to cease hostilities and emigrate west by June. A major provision of the agreement was that the Seminoles would be allowed to keep blacks who had become their slaves and not send them back to slaveholders who had claimed them. Of course, slavery among the Seminoles was more of a hierarchical status than actual slavery.

The agreement outraged Florida slaveholders. Slavecatchers soon sabotaged the plans for peace. They swarmed the Seminole camps, searching for blacks they could claim against Jesup's orders. Being pressured by politicians, both local and national, Jesup entered into a secret agreement with one of the Seminole chiefs. On behalf of the tribe, he agreed to turn over all slaves who had escaped during the war. However, differentiating between fugitive slaves who had escaped during the war and those who had escaped before the war was not so easy.

Tribal leaders were equally outraged when they learned of this agreement. At the time, General Jesup was still hopeful for peace. He had gathered 700 Seminoles near Fort Brooke, near present-day Tampa Bay, preparing to board ships in the harbor to take them west. But Seminole leaders John Horse, Osceola, and Sam Jones came to the fort and led them away to a new, secret location in the Everglades.

Angered, Jesup decided to try another approach. He allowed his soldiers to confiscate possessions of the Seminoles for their own personal gain. "There is no obligation to spare the property of the Indians," he wrote. "Their negroes, cattle, and horses . . . will belong to the corps by which they are captured" (Giddings 158).

In addition to Creek allies who had aided him in the war, he also tried to recruit more militant tribes like the Delaware, Shawnee, and Sioux.

Jesup also had an important bargaining chip: two hundred Seminole hostages, including the Black Seminole spokesman, Abraham. In September 1837, one of Jesup's hostages led him to the camp of King Philip, the chief who had coordinated the attacks on the plantations in the St. Augustine area. Taking King Philip hostage enabled Jesup to arrange a parley with Philip's son, Coacoochee, one of the Seminoles most able warriors, and another separate meeting with Osceola and John Horse, two other important leaders. In both situations, despite that the Seminole leaders came under a flag of truce, they were seized and taken into custody.

The Seminole leaders were taken to El Castillo de San Marcos, the fort built by the Spanish in St. Augustine, and now called Fort Marion. Escape from the dungeon at Fort Marion was believed to be almost impossible. Having the Seminole leaders in custody, it seemed that Jesup had finally put an end to the war. In addition, many of the slaves who had left the plantations were turning themselves in because of the harsh conditions they were enduring in avoiding recapture. But on November 29, 1837, John Horse and Coacoochee managed to escape, leaving behind the much older Osceola and King Phillip. They quickly headed to the Everglades camp of Sam Jones.

Nevertheless, Jesup continued to resort to duplicity and under the guise of peaceful mission captured the Seminole's top chief, Micanopy and 81 tribe members, and quickly shipped them off on boats to the West. In another discouraging development, the Seminole leader, Osceola died in prison.

But the Seminoles would not give up, though they had not yet learned of Osceola's death. They were ready when a force of about 1,000 soldiers under then Colonel Zachary Taylor left Fort Gardner in central Florida for Lake Okeechobee in search of them. The Seminole warriors chose the location for the battle and prepared their position carefully in a swampy area. They notched gun rests in the trees and cleared grass in precise locations to expose the enemy to their fire. The American soldiers reached the location at noon on Christmas day. They spotted the Seminoles camp with hundreds of cattle and ponies in the distance but no sign of Seminoles. After some discussion, Taylor ordered a frontal assault.

Though the American force outnumbered the Seminoles by three-to-one, the Seminoles dropped dozens of soldiers in the first volley. The fight lasted until 3 p.m., when the Seminoles finally retreated. Taylor could not give chase, because his own forces had been severely damaged with 26 dead and 112 wounded. This compared to 11 dead and 14 wounded for the Seminoles. It was only a pyrrhic victory for the Seminoles. They realized they could not resist the American army indefinitely, and Osceola's death was discouraging.

Most of the Seminoles had been deported and Jesup recommended that a truce be arranged to end the war. However, the federal government rejected the peace plan. After another seizure of Seminoles, Jesup took an even more aggressive approach in his dealings with the Black Seminoles. He offered them freedom: "that all Negroes the property of the Seminole . . . who . . . delivered themselves up to the Commanding Officer of the Troops should be free" (Porter 78).

The surrender of the Black Seminoles, including their leading warriors, John Horse and Cooachee, who migrated to the West, significantly weakened the resistance. Though there were skirmishes with the remaining Seminole holdouts, there were no more major battles. The second Seminole War finally ended in 1842. Only those still living on the reservation were allowed to stay. The remainder were deported to the West.

The Branded Hand

In 1844, the year before Florida was made a state, a very controversial and widely publicized incident occurred involving fugitive slaves. The center of the incident was a 45-year-old white abolitionist and mariner from New England who originally had come to Pensacola, Florida, in 1837 to work for a railroad company there. Jonathan Walker had left in 1842, but had returned in his 25-foot whaleboat this summer to do some salvaging from a recent wreck. He had hired some slaves to help him in his preparations and during their work either he or they brought up the subject of their freedom. Whichever, he agreed to help them escape. Getting to the North and freedom was a long journey, and getting there on land was almost impossible. Their best option he said would be to take them to the Bahamas, a British colony where slavery had been abolished. It too was a long journey, about 750 miles, and not without hazards, notably being spotted, but it certainly was achievable.

Originally, the plan was for Walker to take four slaves but on the night of their departure, there were seven. He had loaded the ship with enough food and water for five, but he wasn't about to refuse the new arrivals. The weather was bad the first few days at sea and Walker was feeling ill, but turning back was not an option. After 18 days they had gone 700 miles and were at the tip of the mainland of Florida when they were spotted by a salvage vessel that pulled alongside. The ship's captain was suspicious and Walker, unable to talk his way out, confessed to his illegal activity.

They took him ashore where he was treated brutally, and was chained to the wall in his cell, which did not have a bed. During his trial he pleaded not guilty on his belief that helping men to freedom was not a crime. He was found guilty and sentenced to one year in jail, one hour in public pillory, and, the final indignity, to be branded on the hand with the initials, "S. S.," for slave stealer. Walker also was sued civilly for damages of $106,000, toward which he relinquished his boat, a charge that was later dropped. After his release, however, "The Man with the Branded Hand" became a celebrity of the abolitionist circuit in the North and the subject of a famous poem by John Greenleaf Whittier.

The Walker incident inflamed the passions of Florida's proslavery citizens whose suspicions of abolitionists approached paranoia. Following his case, the territory's legislature made slave

Texas-Mexico

Slavery was abolished in Mexico in 1829 by President Guadalupe Victoria. As a result, Mexico became a haven for fugitive slaves, to a lesser degree like Canada.

In 1834, Colonel Juan N. Almonte, acting as an agent of the government, promised the abolitionist journalist, Benjamin Lundy, that he could colonize ex-slaves in Tamaulipas in northeastern Mexico. Lundy made a number of trips into Mexico with fugitive slaves from 1829 to 1835, as part of a plan to establish fugitive slave colonies there.

Mexican authorities reaffirmed Almonte's commitment in 1836 when they refused to allow H. W. Karnes and Henry Teal, Texas colonial army captains, to reclaim fugitive slaves in Mexico.

An important abolitionist during the colonial days of Texas was Stephen Pearl Andrews, son of a Massachusetts Baptist minister. In 1839 he urged England to intervene to end slavery in Texas and later went there to personally advocate this.

Among the slaves who claimed their freedom in Mexico was John Horse, also known as *Juan Caballo* and *Gopher John*. A leader of the Afro-Seminole soldiers who fought American troops during the Seminole Wars of the 1830s, he became a scout for the United States Army and led a number of Black Seminoles to Mexico, where he died. "The Mexicans," he said, "spread out their arms to us" (Tyler, Ronnie C., "Fugitive Slaves in Mexico," *The Journal of Negro History*, 57, No. 1. [January, 1972]: 2).

The escape of slaves destabilized Texas's plantation system. Both the state and private individuals launched expeditions to recover them, but they were hampered by the Mexican government. One in October, 1855 led by James Hughes Callahan, included a force of 111 men. Large plots by slaves in Texas to escape to Mexico were common and the number of fugitive slaves who fled to Mexico may have been in the thousands.

stealing a crime punishable by death, stating that: "It is no longer as mere larceny, but a species of treason against the State—a direct assault upon the very existence of our institutions" (Bordewich 291). While many in Florida believed he was part of some larger Northern conspiracy, the truth was the Walker was a merely a good man helping others gain their freedom.

Aside from Native Americans, the only real resistance to slavery in Florida was made by the slaves themselves.

—Tom Calarco

Further Reading

Herbert Aptheker, *American Negro Slave Revolts* (New York: International Publishers, 1993).

Fergus Bordewich, *Bound for Canaan* (New York: Harper-Collins, 2005).

Joshua R. Giddings, *The Exiles of Florida* (Columbus, OH: Follett, Foster and Company, 1858).

Ray Granade, "Slave Unrest in Florida," *Florida Historical Quarterly*, (55), 1, July 1976: 18–36.

Major-General O. O. Howard, "Famous Indian Chiefs," *St. Nicholas Magazine*, 35, 1907: 56–58.

Kenneth W. Porter, *The Black Seminoles: History of a Freedom-Seeking People* (Gainesville: University Press of Florida, 1996). *Rebellion: John Horse and the Black Seminoles, First Black Rebels to Beat American Slavery*, http://www.johnhorse.com/trail/index.htm.

Eugene Portlette Southall, "Negroes in Florida Prior to the Civil War," *Journal of Negro History*, 19, No. 1, January 1934: 77–86.

State Papers and Publick Documents of the United States, from the Accession of George Washington to the Presidency, Exhibiting a Complete View of Our Foreign Relations since That Time, 9 (Boston: T. B. Wait and Sons, 1817).

FORT WAYNE, INDIANA

Fort Wayne was on several of the busiest Underground Railroad routes in eastern Indiana. Oral tradition claims that the first fugitive slaves passed through here in 1829. Its location in Allen County, at the confluence of three rivers, the St. Joseph, the St. Marys, and the Maumee, made it a natural destination. Huntertown, a small community also in Allen County, about 10 miles north, led the way because of its politically progressive Universalist Church whose creed professed belief in equality among races and genders.

Allen County had many "staunch Republicans," people who belonged to certain churches, who had an association with known abolitionists in the area, and who, of course, supported Abraham Lincoln.

Routes to and from Fort Wayne

Fugitive slaves who fled through eastern Indiana crossed the Ohio River at various locations, including Madison and Evansville, Indiana, and Cincinnati, were transported at night in wagons. The travel was usually in increments of about 10 miles per day. Many fugitives gave up their flight and established homes in the friendly Quaker communities between Richmond and Fort Wayne. But more continued their flight to Fort Wayne and then eastward along the Maumee River toward Toledo, Ohio; Detroit, Michigan; and finally to Canada and freedom.

Another route called the Wabash Line went through Fort Wayne, following the towpath of the Wabash and Erie Canal. It began near the confluence of the Wabash River with the Ohio River in western Indiana. After 1853, this water route could be followed all the way from the Ohio River to Toledo, where many free blacks and whites provided the way north to Detroit or across Lake Erie to Canada.

A third line from the Fort Wayne area went west around Chicago into Wisconsin.

Abolitionists in the Fort Wayne area

Many Fort Wayne houses, including Frederick Nirdlinger's house in the 200 block of West Main Street, became stations on the Underground Railroad.

Between Richmond and Fort Wayne, located in Jay County, was the Quaker community of Pennville. Lindley Ninde and his wife, Beulah Puckett Ninde (a niece of Levi Coffin), first lived in Pennville and moved to Fort Wayne in 1850. Their large homestead was located on the present-day Fairfield Avenue. Ninde, an attorney, frequently represented black citizens of Fort Wayne when they were unfairly treated under the harsh laws of the period and harbored fugitive slaves during the early 1850s.

The Nindes also owned property in Aboite Township. This community, known as Aboite Devil's Hollow, was a major Underground Railroad station. This area consisted of large ravines and rugged terrain. The Nindes, along with Dr. Mary Frame Myers Thomas, served as conductors from this station. Lindley's sister, Rhoda Ninde Swayne, also assisted the fugitives in this area. A house in the town that was likely an Underground Railroad stop that still remains is the Jesse Vermilyea House, near the old Wabash and Erie towpath.

Other abolitionists in the Fort Wayne area were Daniel W. Burroughs, a Baptist preacher, and Alexander Rankin, the younger brother of John Rankin of Ripley and pastor of the Second Presbyterian Church. Burroughs was the publisher of a newspaper, *The Fort Wayne Standard*, the community's first abolitionist paper. His residence and the location of his bookstore and newspaper office were speculated to be hiding places for the fugitive slaves. Rankin was a founding member of both the Ohio Anti-Slavery Society (1834) and the Indiana Anti-Slavery Society (1837). His home, built in 1841 on Lafayette Street, still stands. Research cannot verify that it was an Underground Railroad station, but its basement with a concealed area would have been a good hiding place. Reverend Rankin has a connection with the Huntertown area. In 1834, he held the first-ever religious service in a log cabin in that location. Three local families in this community, the Duntens, the Parkers, and the Woods, were later among the charter members of the Huntertown Universalist Church. The Universalists were known as abolitionists as early as the eighteenth century and openly argued against slavery. In the nineteenth century, they took a leading role in the progressive causes of abolition, temperance, and women's suffrage. The church built in 1851 and located on Old Route 3, just south of Cedar Canyons Road, still stands.

Another minister, Charles Beecher, a brother of Harriet Beecher Stowe, succeeded Rankin and was the pastor at the Second Presbyterian Church from 1844 to 1850. Oral tradition claims that he too was involved with helping the fugitives through Fort Wayne.

The stations and conductors mentioned previously in this article were white, and verification of their involvement in the Underground Railroad comes from printed materials such as documents and letters. However, in Fort Wayne, prior to the Fugitive Act of 1850, free blacks also assisted many fugitive slaves. Less documentation exists regarding their participation.

Black Agents

Free black settlers in Fort Wayne during the 1840s and 1850s were a diverse group—socially, educationally, and economically. They were blacksmiths, laborers, and small business owners. Those who have been verified as assisting fugitive slaves include Henry Cannady, whose home was located next to the Presbyterian Church on East Berry Street; and Nelson Black, a blacksmith and minister of the Fort Wayne African Methodist Episcopal Church. Others mentioned in oral tradition are George Fisher, the William Willis Elliot family, the Griffins, the Lynches, and the McClanahans.

—Cynthia Vogel

Further Reading

Levi Coffin, *The Reminiscences of Levi Coffin* (Cincinnati: Robert Clark & Co., 1880).
T. B. Helm, *History of Allen County, Indiana* (1880).
Angela M. Quinn, *The Underground Railroad and the Antislavery Movement in Fort Wayne and Allen County, Indiana* (Fort Wayne, IN: ARCH, Inc., 2001).
Wilbur H. Siebert, *The Underground Railroad from Slavery to Freedom* (1898; reprint, New York: Arno Press and *The New York Times*, 1968).

G

GALESBURG, ILLINOIS

Perhaps the most active Underground Railroad location in the state of Illinois, aside from Chicago, Galesburg was founded by George Washington Gale, also the founder of the Oneida Institute in central New York, which was a haven for fugitive slaves and one of the first schools to offer higher education to blacks. Galesburg's early settlers included Presbyterians and Congregationalists, who joined together to form the First Church of Galesburg, whose members formed the backbone of the village's Underground Railroad. Among them were Nehemiah West, George Davis, Abram Neely, George Blanchard, and Samuel Hitchcock.

Most of the fugitive slaves who came to Galesburg were from Missouri, and most had stopped at the Quaker settlements of Salem and Denmark in southeastern Iowa, where Friends would then bring them to Galesburg.

Among antislavery contacts in the area was Rev. Jeremiah Porter of Peoria. After a visit to Galesburg, Porter wrote a letter to the *Peoria Register and Northwestern Gazetteer* describing the business of assisting colored people to escape slavery. Several houses, as well as barns, located at the edges of Galesburg, were used to harbor runaways. Accounts claim that the Old First Church belfry was used as a hideout for fugitive slaves, one of them from George Churchill in an 1896 letter to Wilbur Siebert.

The Black Laws

A great obstacle to those in the Underground Railroad were the Illinois "Black Laws."

Among the provisions of these laws were that anyone aiding a fugitive slave would be fined $100, and if any black was found within 10 miles from his master's dwelling, without a pass or some type of written permission, he or she could be striped with up to 35 lashes. Dancing or celebrations for slaves or servants of color, at any time, were prohibited and subject to a $20 fine. All coroners, sheriffs, judges, and justices of the peace were obliged to publicly whip every slave committing these acts with 39 stripes on his or her bare back.

Rev. John Cross

Around 1840 Rev. John Cross moved to Elba in Knox County, about 15 miles from Galesburg. He later would establish a line of the Underground Railroad across Illinois and southern Michigan. During a chance meeting with a local justice of the peace, Jacob Kightlinger, Cross openly threatened to violate the state's Black Laws by aiding fugitive slaves. Not surprisingly, Kightlinger found six fugitive slaves hiding on the property of Cross. One of them was Susan Richardson, later known as Aunt Sukey. An indentured servant of Andrew Borders, which made her a virtual slave until the age of 32, she had escaped with her three sons and another female slave after she learned that Borders's wife had planned to beat her.

Kightlander had the runaways committed to jail, while Cross went to a judge and had him issue a warrant against Kightlander for kidnapping. The judge fined Kightlinger $100, but he appealed the decision and the case was thrown out. Cross, however, was indicted and found guilty of stealing Negroes and sent to jail. However, his case also was thrown out.

Richardson was allowed to go free, but her sons were sold down South and she never saw them again. She settled in Galesburg, where she became known as Aunt Sukey and became involved in the Underground Railroad. Late one Saturday night, a fugitive slave named Bill Casey showed up at her door. He was hungry and his bare feet were severely swollen. He needed shoes if he were to continue his journey to freedom. Local abolitionists were alerted and they fitted him with shoes after several trips to the store to find the right size. After everything was fully arranged, Casey was conveyed to the next station. In a year or two he returned to Galesburg and was working as a lumberjack when two Southern bounty hunters arrived and set their sights on him. Charley Love, a black boy who later owned a barbershop in Galesburg, warned Casey and he was able to escape before they could find him.

By the late 1840s the attitudes of the citizenry in Galesburg toward runaways progressively became more open and tolerant. At the same time, the business of kidnapping blacks and returning them into servitude in the South increased. Blacks continually warned their children about the possibility of being captured by the "manstealers," and black ministers continually reminded their congregations of this threat. In 1849 there were 16 blacks living in the village, some of them fugitive slaves, including Louis A. Carter, a fugitive slave who later wrote about Galesburg and its early black population. By the start of the Civil War the black population was approaching 100.

Some Conductors

Those aiding fugitive slaves included William Mead who hid them in the hay mows of his old barn, known as the largest in the county. He would place the runaways under straw in a box-wagon and send them on to the next station, often Princeton, which was northeasterly from Galesburg.

The most active depot near Galesburg was the home of Samuel Hitchcock, three miles to the northwest, just south of Henderson Grove. He and his wife, Catharine, and their three children lived in a strategically advantageous location, where numerous hiding places existed in a thick section of woods.

To the northwest about seven miles north was the Ontario residence of C. F. Camp. He collaborated with Hod Powell, who conducted fugitive slaves to the next station. Fugitive slaves were usually brought to Camp by Galesburg resident, Abram Neely. Another destination north of Ontario was in Altona and Dr. R. C. Edgerton. In one incident in 1844, slavecatchers came to his residence after he had harbored some Missouri runaways. With the help of abolitionists from Galesburg, who outnumbered the slavecatchers, they were able to persuade them to leave the area.

Other routes north included Andover and Cambridge in Henry County, and farther north to Geneseo. Another route east toward the Knox County/Stark County line led to a lookout point called "Pilot Knob," which was an excellent hiding place because of the visibility it provided of approaching slavecatchers.

Fugitive slaves were forwarded to Stark County, where they were welcomed by Nehemiah Wycoff, Rev. Samuel G. Wright, and W. W. Webster. The People of Illinois brought an indictment against Wright and Webster, and Owen Lovejoy of Princeton for the crime of harboring 10 Negro fugitives in 1843, the same year an indictment was brought against Rev. Cross. But they too avoided conviction.

Wright Diary

A diary written by Rev. Wright described his participation in the Underground Railroad. Three typical entries read as follows:

> February 6, 1843—Friday, another fugitive from slavery came along, which makes 21 that have been through this Settlement on their way to Canada.
>
> January 5, 1847—Arrived home Friday evening and learned that two fugitives had been along—pursuers had gotten a search warrant . . . they searched our premises in vain, however, for the birds had flown.
>
> June 6, 1848—Friday carried a fugitive to Osceola and preached at half-past four.

Chicago, Burlington, and Quincy Railroad

In December 1854, the Chicago, Burlington, and Quincy Railroad connected Galesburg to Chicago. By March 1855, the railroad extended to Burlington, Iowa, on the Mississippi, and on September 1, 1959 to Ottumwa, Iowa, on the Des Moines River. The 280-mile journey to Chicago then could be traveled in approximately 15 hours.

Galesburg agents made good use of the railroad in forwarding fugitive slaves to freedom, hiding them in freight trains or the baggage cars of passenger trains.

Samuel G. Wright Diary

Samuel G. Wright was a graduate of Lane Seminary in Cincinnati. He came to Illinois in the early 1840s on a mission for the Knox Presbytery that was chaired by George Washington Gale. In 1843 he was prosecuted for aiding fugitive slaves, but the case was dismissed. He kept a diary up through the end of the antebellum period, which is now in the collection of the Knox College Library. Among other things, he recorded his antislavery activities and his aid to fugitive slaves. Three more entries, in addition to those already listed, are the following:

August 22, 1842—There is an effort to destroy the influence of this church by reporting that we are abolitionists, and have formed lines for helping runaways. Hence we are as bad as horse thieves (Owen Muelder, *The Underground Railroad in Western Illinois*, Jefferson, NC: McFarland and Company, 2009: 124).

December 27, 1842—In the providence of God several fugitive slaves, at different times, had found their way into our neighborhood, and although the laws of our state are exceedingly severe rendering one liable to a fine of $500 who shall feed or harbor a colored man who does not give undoubted evidence of his freedom, yet our brethren felt that the statutes of Heaven were to be regarded before those of men and did not hesitate to "feed the hungry" (125).

July 24, 1854—Last week I assisted some in the harvest field and prepared one sermon. On Friday 5 fugitives came here who had escaped from their master in labor in Fremont County, Iowa as he was taking them through from Mississippi to Salt Lake. I carried them up to Esq. Autin's in the daytime. They were intelligent for men who could not read. One of them said he would not be taken back alive, for he had determined on liberty, or death with him. . . . (130).

When a train came into Galesburg, a lamp was placed in a location that was a signal for the engineers to slow nearly to a stop and enable the fugitive slaves to jump aboard. Among railroad employees from Galesburg who made the upper-ground railroad part of the Underground Railroad was a black resident, Solom Kimball. Another was William Patch, a member of the Congregational Church and a good friend of the Reverend Edward Beecher, who had become pastor there in 1855. On one occasion Patch hid two fugitives on the train who had been hiding at Beecher's house.

—Melissa Waddy-Thibodeaux and Tom Calarco

Further Reading

Charles C. Chapman & Co., *The History of Knox County, Illinois*, Chapter VIII, "The Underground Railroad," Chicago, 1878: 201–215.

Owen Muelder, *The Underground Railroad in Western Illinois* (Jefferson, NC: McFarland and Company, 2007).

H

HARRISBURG, PENNSYLVANIA

Harrisburg, the county seat of Dauphin County and the capital of Pennsylvania, was the hub of the central route of the Underground Railroad in Pennsylvania. Because of geography, the state played a pivotal role in the Underground Railroad: a 200-mile-long border with Maryland and easy access to the Potomac and Susquehanna rivers and the jumble of waterways and railways that connected the state to Virginia, Maryland, New York, New Jersey, and the Chesapeake Region.

Susquehanna River

Fugitive slaves often were transported on the Susquehanna River from Maryland to Harrisburg, a distance of about 50 miles. Overland trails entered Pennsylvania from Maryland near Gettysburg, Rouzerville, or Mercersburg, then went north and northeast, passing through a variety of towns, splitting into numerous sub-routes, most of which converged in Harrisburg. Another route came from Lancaster County through Lebanon County to Harrisburg.

Harrisburg Agents

Harrisburg was a hub for two main reasons: it had a large black population, and because many possible escape routes existed leading into and out of the city with a variety of alternatives, by road, rail, or water. Fugitive slaves found a safe haven in an area known as Tanner's Alley, near today's Capitol Park and Walnut and Fourth streets. Fugitive slaves hid at the homes of Joseph Bustill and Dr. William "Pap" Jones and were cared for at Wesley Union A. M. E. Zion Church.

Dr. Jones and his wife were members of the Wesley Union Church, founded in 1829. He practiced medicine in his home, a frame building on River Avenue near Barbara Avenue. He had acquired a thorough knowledge of the routes leading northward and was always prepared to furnish competent guides to help fugitive slaves travel out of Harrisburg. He often transported fugitive slaves in his large covered wagon, posing as a rag merchant, to Wilkes-Barre or Pottsville.

Rudolf F. Kelker, hardware store merchant and son of a prominent Harrisburg family, was a well-known abolitionist. His home at 9 South Front Street, now the site of the present-day Dauphin County Courthouse, was often used to hide the fugitive slaves. At night he would take them to his barn that stood on the corner of River and Barbara streets. Dr. William Wilson Rutherford, who lived next door, helped convey many slaves to safety. He would transport them to Samuel S. Rutherford (known by his friends as Little Sam), at Paxtang, where they were hidden in the old barn that stood by the spring near the present Paxtang Park. Dr. Rutherford was a vice president of the Harrisburg Antislavery Society. In 1847, he arranged for William Lloyd Garrison and Frederick Douglass to speak in Harrisburg at the Wesley Union A. M. E. Zion Church.

Other nearby stations included Carlisle, 15 miles west of Harrisburg, where known conductors were barber John Peck, who was influential in converting the noted conductor, J. Miller McKim, to abolitionism, and John McClintock, a professor at Dickinson College. Other stops were Quincy, Caledonia Furnace, Pine Grove Furnace, and Boiling Springs, where fugitive slaves stayed at the Bucher Hill Mansion. Here fugitive slaves hid in a secret chamber above a large closet in the main bedroom of the home. Daniel Kaufman, the founder of Boiling Springs, 15 miles southwest of Harrisburg, was only 17 when he became an agent on the Underground Railroad in 1835. Kaufman hid slaves in his barn, as well as in a dense thicket known as Island Grove, near Boiling Springs. Kaufman claimed to have helped at least 60 fleeing slaves from 1835 to 1848.

Two other men associated with the Harrisburg Underground Railroad were black abolitionists, Thomas Morris Chester, who worked for the *Philadelphia Press* and the only black journalist at a major American daily during the Civil War; and William Howard Day, a former New Yorker who spent 30 years in Harrisburg and helped establish fugitive slave settlements in Canada. Their work extended beyond Harrisburg and continued after the Civil War.

From Harrisburg, there were many routes through which fugitive slaves could take to Canada, including along the Susquehanna River to Sunbury, where it divides, one branch flowing northeast and the other west. Fugitive slaves could go northeast to Elmira, Canandaigua, Rochester, Buffalo, or Niagara Falls, New York, or west to Pittsburgh and onward to Erie. From these locations, they could find passage to Canada. Other overland routes from Harrisburg went to Hollidaysburg, Bellefonte, Reading, Williamsport, Canton, and Montrose, Pennsylvania; then on to Binghamton, Elmira, Ithaca, Auburn, Syracuse, and Oswego, New York, and other stations that connected to Canada.

—Cynthia Vogel

Further Reading

Charles Blockson, *The Underground Railroad in Pennsylvania* (Jacksonville, NC: Flame International, 1981).

Ronald V. Di Ninni. *History of Rutherford, Pennsylvania* (Baltimore: Gateway Press Inc., 1979).

"Proceedings of the Harrisburg antislavery Society," January 14, 1836, MG 12, Harrisburg Antislavery Society, Dauphin County Historical Society.

Wilbert H. Siebert. *The Underground Railroad from Slavery to Freedom* (1898; reprint, New York: Arno Press, 1968).

R. C. Smedley, *History of the Underground Railroad in Chester and the Neighboring Counties of Pennsylvania* (1883; reprint, Lancaster, PA: Stackpole Books, 2005).

William J. Switala. *Underground Railroad in Pennsylvania* (Mechanicsburg, PA: Stackpole Books, 2001).

Underground Railroad in Pennsylvania (Wesley Union AME Zion Church. Souvenir Program of the 150th Anniversary and Dedication of Wesley Union AME Zion Church Harrisburg: Wesley Union AME Zion Church, 1966).

HUDSON, OHIO

Hudson, a village in Summit County, was the boyhood home of John Brown. His father, Owen Brown, was one of its earliest settlers and a friend of the village's founder, David Hudson. Both were Connecticut natives and vehemently opposed to slavery, and it was David Hudson who influenced the elder Brown's settlement there.

John Brown's Family

Aid to fugitive slaves in Hudson began at least as early as 1820. Both Hudson and Owen Brown were staunch antislavery supporters, and Owen Brown taught these principles to John from his earliest age. John Brown's oldest son, John, Jr., son recalled his father aiding fugitive slaves while living in Hudson:

> When I was four or five years old, and probably no later than 1825, there came one night a fugitive slave and his wife to father's door. . . . Mother gave the poor creatures some supper; but they thought themselves pursued, and were uneasy.
>
> Presently father heard the trampling of horses crossing a bridge on one of the main roads, half a mile off; so he took his guests out the back door and down into the swamp near the brook, to hide, giving them arms to defend themselves. . . . It proved a false alarm. . . . Father then . . . brought them into the house again, sheltered them awhile, and sent them on their way. (Du Bois, W. E. B., *John Brown*, Philadelphia: George Jacobs & Company, 1909: 84)

In 1826, David Hudson's son wrote in his diary on January 25 of that year that "Two men came this evening in a sleigh, bringing a Negro woman, a runaway slave, and her two children" (Caccamo 21).

Western Reserve College

Western Reserve College also was an antislavery stronghold. It was the site of a controversy over antislavery that resulted in two professors, Elizur Wright and Beriah Green, who were in favor of immediate emancipation and opposed to the American Colonization Society, leaving the college. The school's trustees favored colonization. On November 11, 1834, John Buss wrote in his diary that a fugitive slave and his wife and child sought refuge at the college, where students collected five dollars to help transport them to Cleveland.

Another Underground Railroad agent in Hudson was Brown's boyhood friend, Lora Case, who hid fugitive slaves in a wooded lot behind his house, and with whom Brown kept in contact throughout his life.

The entire Brown family was ready to aid fugitive slaves, including Owen Brown's other sons who lived in Hudson: Oliver, Frederick, and Jeremiah, who allegedly hid fugitive slaves in a dry cistern beneath his farmhouse. It was at Jeremiah's home where John Brown is believed to have stored guns that were to be used for his slave rebellion. Brown's sisters Marion and Florella also were abolitionists. The latter went to Kansas with her husband, Samuel Adair, to support those fighting to make Kansas a free state. John Brown stayed with them for a month during his last visit to Kansas after becoming ill. The extent of Owen Brown's leadership can be gauged from his founding in 1842 of the Free Congregational Church, which was devoted to antislavery.

Secret Location Outside Hudson

A Hudson resident, F. C. Waite, claimed in 1908, that a group of cabins was set aside for fugitive slaves. He said sometimes there were enough to fill a boat to Canada. The procedure was to send word ahead to the port of Willoughby on Lake Erie where a boat was made ready while wagons were loaded with the fugitive slaves who were hidden under hay and taken there. Lora Case, the city's stationmaster from 1856, stated that during the late 1850s fugitive slave traffic had slowed considerably, though he did report aiding seven fugitive slaves on one occasion in 1859 and identified John Markillie as his most frequent collaborator.

Waite also identified Jesse Dickinson and Asahel Kilbourne as active participants. Kilbourne, a member of the Free Congregational Church, attended the organizational meeting of the state antislavery society in 1835.

Fugitive slaves came to Hudson from Akron and Canton, and from the Portage County villages of Ravenna, home of the *Ohio Star* abolitionist newspaper, whose editor was Lyman Hall, a Hudson native, and Randolph. From Hudson, they were sent to Cleveland, Brecksville, Bedford, and Chagrin Falls. Two canals, which were common thoroughfares for runaways, passed through this region were the Ohio and Erie that led from the Ohio River all the way to Cleveland, and the Pennsylvania and Ohio Canal that led to abolitionist centers in Pittsburgh and western Pennsylvania. In later years, the Cleveland and Western Railroad was commonly used and tickets were supplied by Newton Peirce of Alliance. Another thoroughfare was the Painesville-Chillicothe Road that connected Akron, Cuyahoga Falls, and Hudson.

In 1846, a slave couple, John and Harriet, escaped from their owner, William Stedman, after they had been brought to Randolph from Parkersburg, Virginia. Slavecatchers came to town the next year and attempted a rendition of the couple, but abolitionists led by Dr. Joseph Price rescued the couple and forwarded them to Canada.

Local Network

Hudson was literally surrounded by communities contributing to the Underground Railroad. For example, the strength of regional antislavery sentiment is reflected by an 1848 petition in protest of slavery, demanding that Ohio withdraw from the Union made in Randolph by 39 residents of Portage, Stark, and Summit counties. Just to the southwest, among very active Underground Railroad operators were Ezra Garrett of Savannah, Ohio, Ashland County, who allegedly harbored an estimated 400 fugitive slaves and Hiram B. Miller in Hinckley, Medina County, who helped more than 1,000. These estimates are based on oral and family tradition like the following from a Haines family member in Alliance to the east of Hudson. According to a Haines descendant, Erma Grant Pluchel, "Many a fugitive slave was assisted to escape by Ridgeway Haines. . . . Many a night he stood guard gun in hand, taking care of the poor slaves he was harboring in the little attic room over his kitchen. His son, John C. or 'Tump' as he was known, a boy of twelve also stood guard and helped to drive the slaves to the next station under cover of darkness" (Pluchel to Carnegie Free Library, Alliance, Ohio). The Haines farmhouse was along a route that led to Randolph and that continued on to Hudson. The farm also was the site of abolitionist meetings in 1859 and 1860 when the prominent Underground Railroad leaders, William Whipper and Jermaine Loguen, were the featured speakers.

It's not surprising that in Hudson during a church service commemorating the slain abolitionist Elijah Lovejoy in 1837 that John Brown vowed to sacrifice his life to end slavery: "Here, before God, in the presence of these witnesses, from this time, I consecrate my life to the destruction of slavery!" (Oates, Stephen B, *The Approaching Fury*, New York: HarperCollins, 1997: 172).

—Tom Calarco

Further Reading

James F. Caccamo, *Hudson, Ohio, and the Underground Railroad* (Hudson, OH: Friends of the Hudson Library, Inc., 1992).

I

INDIANAPOLIS, INDIANA

Located in the center of Indiana in Marion County is the state capital of Indianapolis. Many fugitive slaves traveled through this city on their way to freedom, and many free blacks lived in Indianapolis, starting in the 1830s. A notable case occurred in 1834 when Jermaine Loguen, who would become one of the most prominent black leaders of the antebellum era, and another fugitive slave, escaped from Tennessee and received aid from a free black Indianapolis resident, James Overrals. Described by Loguen as an educated man respected by both blacks and whites, Overrals advised the men not to conceal that they were slaves unless they were encountering those thought to be slavecatchers, because he said that slaves were treated better in Indiana than free blacks. With that advice, he forwarded them 40 miles north to a community of Quakers.

Indiana Routes

Underground Railroad activity occurred in every county of Indiana with three main routes leading north through the state. One trail went roughly through the center of the state, leading from the Ohio River at two main locations at Louisville, Kentucky, into New Albany and Jeffersonville, Indiana, and about 40 miles up the river at Madison, Indiana. Once the fugitive slaves crossed the Ohio River, they were not only in free territory, but they had placed that river between themselves and their pursuers. Most important, however, was that they could find citizens who were eager to help. From these river ports, they proceeded north through Salem, Columbus, Bloomington, Mooresville, Indianapolis, and Westfield. From Westfield, fugitive slaves were transported on to New London, Logansport, Plymouth, and South Bend, Indiana, then to Niles, Battle Creek, and Detroit, Michigan, and Canada. Another route from Indianapolis went northwest through Crawfordsville or Rensselaer, sometimes on the way to Portage County, where Ben Cristman and Norman Tanner occasionally used their homes as stations. From Rensselaer, they continued into

Michigan, then to Detroit and Lake Erie or perhaps to Port Huron on Lake Huron and then into Canada.

The Bethel African Methodist Episcopal Church was the first AME church in Indianapolis and occupies a unique place in the history of the Underground Railroad. Originally founded in 1836 by William Paul Quinn and Augustus Turner, this church has played an important role in the city's black community for over 170 years. Known today as "Indianapolis Station" because of its ties to the Underground Railroad, it originally was only a small congregation that met in Turner's log cabin. In 1841 a small house of worship was constructed on Georgia Street, and by 1848 the church with its 100 members had become active in the antislavery movement, often harboring fugitive slaves on their way to Canada. In 1857, a new location was selected for the church and a new house was built. However, some locals did not approve of the church's activities in the Underground Railroad, and on July 9, 1864, the church was burned to the ground. Arson was suspected. This did not stop the congregation and they rebuilt the church in 1867—the same church that stands today at 414 West Vermont Street.

Westfield

In Hamilton County, just to the north, is the village of Westfield, a hub of the Underground Railroad more active than Indianapolis Fugitive slaves traveling north from Mooresville, Indianapolis, Lafayette, Darlington, and various places in Henry County and farther south found refuge here. Many Quakers in this village were abolitionists. Most of the settlers in this region came from North Carolina, South Carolina, and Virginia to escape what they considered the "curse" of slavery. One of Westfield's founders, Asa Bales, owned a home and a large frame barn with a cellar beneath it. These buildings provided refuge for many fugitive slaves from 1834 when the town was founded. While excavating on these properties, tunnels were found connecting the home and the location of the barn. The Bales home on Union Street and the Aaron Lindley House north of Westfield, another safe house for fugitive slaves, still stand. Lindley helped establish a monthly meeting here of antislavery Friends on March 4, 1843. Bales donated the land for the meetinghouse and cemetery.

One of the reasons Westfield acquired the reputation that a fugitive slave was safe once he reached Westfield was its proverbial "dismal swamp," perhaps taking its name from the much larger and more renown Dismal Swamp that covered hundreds of miles in Virginia and North Carolina. This natural swamp area with trees, shallow water, and areas of quicksand became a refuge for fleeing slaves and a death trap for slavecatchers. Locals who assisted the fugitive slaves knew the swamp and could lead them safely across the area to other safe houses. Slavecatchers unfamiliar with the area often did not survive if they entered it.

The Roberts Settlement

The Roberts Settlement, a colony of several free black families founded by Elijah Roberts, was located north of Westfield and near the dismal swamp. Fugitive slaves could stay there or with black families in Westfield.

Riley Moon, the son of Simon Moon of the Society of Friends, grew up in an antislavery atmosphere in Washington Township (later the town of Westfield). His father and two brothers, William and Simon, Jr., made their homes Underground Railroad stations where fugitive slaves were hidden during the day. At night they were taken from hideout to hideout, being hauled over back roads in wagons, carriages, or on horseback. The local Society of Friends disowned Riley and Susannah Moon in 1844 because of their Underground Railroad activity. The original farmhouse built by Riley Moon still stands and is located two miles north of Westfield on Flippins Road, near the former site of the dismal swamp. The upper story of the house was a single room. At the top of an enclosed stairway a small inconspicuous door near the floor opened into a tiny room, where fugitive slaves were hidden.

Nathan Hunt, a staunch antislavery supporter sometimes appeared to assist slavecatchers, but would turn on them with a large stick if the fugitive slaves were truly threatened. Apparently this threat often caused the slavecatcher to do as he was advised and leave the village. Many fugitive slaves "saved" by Hunt were liberated and money was collected from the community to pay the slave owner for the loss of his property. Other Westfield Quakers who provided shelter, food, and transportation for fugitive slaves included J. Roberts, James L. Hiatt, O. C. Lindley, Robert Tomlinson, the Brays, Stanleys, Stouts, Talberts, and Baldwins.

John and Lewann Rhodes and their children lived in Hamilton County on an 80-acre farm six miles north of Westfield. The family had escaped enslavement in Missouri in 1837. In 1844, a former owner, Singleton Vaughn, had hunted them down and captured them on their farm. Local Quaker residents from Westfield and the surrounding area rioted and helped the Rhodes family escape. Court documents provide details of how the Quakers defended the Rhodes family, winning a judgment against Vaughn, who wanted to take the Rhodes family back to Missouri. Vaughn sued some people who were in the crowd, for interfering with his right to reclaim slaves. In *Vaughn v. Williams*, in 1845, the jury found the defendants not guilty, learning that the Rhodes family had been freed when a previous owner moved them to Illinois, a free state. Rhodes and his family continued to live in Hamilton County for many more years.

Effect of the Fugitive Slave Law of 1850

The Fugitive Slave Law of 1850 brought about great changes in how blacks were treated in Indiana. This law made it more dangerous to assist fugitives, and many documents regarding the activities of the Underground Railroad were intentionally destroyed, as both blacks and whites feared prosecution for assisting fugitive slaves. Under this unfair law, slavecatchers could simply swear before a judge that their captives were fugitives, and the captive was not allowed to give testimony to the contrary.

Closely following the passage of the federal Fugitive Law of 1850 was the passage of Indiana's new state constitution in 1851. Article 13 of this new constitution banned "Negro" migration into the state, and made it illegal for any black or biracial person to settle in the state. It was also illegal for citizens of Indiana to employ blacks or make contracts with them, or in any way encourage them to remain in the state. Any persons, black or white, found committing such activities were to be fined between $10 to more than $500. Blacks had to register with the county of their residence to receive a certificate allowing them to remain in the state. At first these laws were only occasionally enforced across the state of Indiana, but they caused the Underground Railroad activities to become more secret and made Underground Railroad activities thereafter even more difficult to substantiate.

One well-documented case exists in Indianapolis where an attempt was made to kidnap a free black and sell him into slavery. John Freeman had lived in Indianapolis since 1844 and had become a wealthy entrepreneur. In 1853, a man came to Indianapolis and claimed that Freeman was his slave "Sam" who had escaped in 1836. Freeman was arrested, placed in the Marion County jail, and the case went to court. Since Freeman was an established and respected member of the community, he was able to hire an attorney. At great financial expense ($6,000 worth of property), Freeman had his freedom proven.

Many blacks chose to leave Indiana after state voters approved Article 13 (1851) and sought refuge in Michigan, Canada, or states and territories farther west.

—Cynthia Vogel

Further Reading

Levi Coffin, *The Reminiscences of Levi Coffin* (Cincinnati: Robert Clark & Co., 1880).

Gwendolyn J. Crenshaw, *Bury Me in a Free Land; the Abolitionist Movement in Indiana, 1861–1865* (Indiana Historical Bureau, 1986).

Logan Esary, *A History of Indiana from 1850 to 1920* (Bloomington: Indiana University Bookstore, 1935).

Emma Lou Thornbrough, *The Negro in Indiana before 1900* (Indiana Historical Bureau, 1957).

K

KENNETT SQUARE, PENNSYLVANIA

Kennett Square in Chester County was the hub of a large and tightly connected Underground Railroad in southeastern Pennsylvania. Less than three miles from the Delaware border, it had a close relationship with Thomas Garrett in Wilmington, Delaware, about 10 miles away. Among its foremost conductors were John and Hannah Cox; Isaac and Dinah Mendenhall; the Barnard brothers, Simon and Eusebius; and Dr. Bartholomew Fussell. All were Quakers and part of that region's huge Quaker network that collaborated with a smaller but also fairly large number of free black conductors. Recent scholarship has identified 132 known Underground Railroad agents in Chester County alone that included 82 Quakers and 31 blacks.

The Mendenhalls' home was the closest stop to the Delaware border that aided fugitive slaves. Generally, the runaways were sent by Thomas Garrett, who began collaborating with them around 1831 and whose wife was their relative. To assure the Mendenhalls that the individuals were not imposters, Garrett would write "I send you . . . bales of black wool" (Smedley 249).

Beginnings of Underground Railroad

But the custom of aiding fugitive slaves had begun in the region more than 30 years earlier. Jacob Lindley of Avondale, four miles west of Kennett Square, was receiving fugitive slaves as early as the year 1801 along a line established by Baltimore abolitionist, Elisha Tyson. Another important and early member of the regional network was Daniel Gibbons, who lived in Lancaster County, six miles east of Columbia, Pennsylvania, and about thirty miles west of Kennett Square. Gibbons, whose father was a staunch abolitionist, is said to have begun aiding fugitive slaves as early as 1797 and continued the practice until his death in 1853, aiding upward of a 1,000. His most frequent collaborators were Thomas Bonsall, Lindsey Coates, Thomas Whitson, who lived in the western part of Chester County, and Dr. J. K. Eshleman, who worked closely with Eusebius Barnard.

The region's avowed Quaker leadership substantiates the traditional belief that Quakers were in the forefront of the Underground Railroad, as they were in such Underground Railroad strongholds as New Bedford, Massachusetts, the New Garden Meeting in Indiana, the Alum Creek Settlement in Ohio, and the Cass County section of Michigan, among others. While the Hicksite-Orthodox split in 1827 later gave rise to a revisionist theory that Quakers were not as active in the Underground Railroad as traditionally believed, the reverse is actually true because many of those who sided with the Hicksites, which was a substantial number, were among the most dedicated participants in the Underground Railroad. And it was primarily Quakers, who in 1853 formed the Hicksite Longwood Meeting in Kennett Square, who comprised the bulk of the community's Underground Railroad.

Hannah and John Cox

Hannah Cox and her husband John were among Kennett Square's most active participants in the Underground Railroad and founding members of the Longwood Meeting, donating the land on which its meeting house was built. Their involvement in abolition increased around 1835 when the noted antislavery lecturer Charles Burleigh came to Kennett Square and gave a series of lectures. The Kennett Anti-Slavery Society was founded shortly after and John Cox was

Hannah and John Cox house, Kennett Square, Pennsylvania; home of Quaker abolitionists and founders of the Longwood Meeting who sheltered hundreds of fugitive slaves. (Courtesy of Tom Calarco)

made president. In 1838, the society resolved that whoever "aids in the restoration of the fugitive to his master . . . is guilty of a crime against humanity and religion" (http://undergroundrr.kennett.net/densmorelongwoodprint.html). Along a major thoroughfare, their home, also known as Longwood, became a regular stop for fugitive slaves coming from Thomas Garrett. Fugitive slaves often were brought to their house by a black man named Jackson from Wilmington. If women and children, they were brought in a Dearborn (a four-wheeled carriage with curtains); if it were only men, they would be brought on horseback or on foot. Jackson would signal with three raps on their fence and call out, "friends." He would then dispatch the fugitive slaves and leave immediately. The Coxes either hid the fugitive slaves in an unfinished attic or in a cellar where they had bins furnished with cots. The Coxes' son, Will, frequently forwarded fugitive slaves, often to Isaac Meredith, a neighbor, rapping at the door with the greeting, "Will Cox, got a wagon load." As many as eighteen fugitive slaves came to the house at one time.

Mendenhalls and Barnards

Isaac Mendenhall was treasurer of the Chester County Anti-Slavery Society from its inception at Coatesville in May 1838 until its demise in 1865. For 34 years, Mendenhall and his wife, Dinah, opened their home to fugitive slaves, assisting several hundred according to one estimate. The largest number at one time was 14, with the women hidden in the Mendenhall's spring house and the men in the barn. Among their collaborators were neighbors, Josiah and Mary Wilson. Often Josiah would accompany Isaac in piloting fugitive slaves to John Jackson in Darby, a distance of about 25 miles. On one occasion, a fugitive slave named Mary stayed with the Mendenhalls for three months, working as a house servant. Fugitive slaves also were taken to John Vickers, and William and Simon Barnard. Another collaborator was James Pugh of Pennsbury, who often went to Philadelphia and made arrangements with the vigilance committee there to meet Mendenhall somewhere outside Philadelphia.

Simon Barnard, from Newlin about four miles due north of the village of Kennett Square, aided hundreds of fugitive slaves, according to Smedley, and kept a large, two-horse, close-covered wagon called "Black Maria," hanging a quilt behind where he sat, in which he could conceal as many as a dozen fugitive slaves. He took runaways to Marshallton, Downington, and West Chester. Sometimes he collaborated with Isaac and Thomazine Meredith, who also lived in Newlin, directing fugitive slaves to their home, providing them with a paper of introduction. On one occasion, 13 fugitive slaves were taken by him to Nathan Evans in Willistown, about 10 miles from his home. On another occasion while being pursued by slavecatchers, he led a wagonload of fugitive slaves through Marshallton to John Vickers in Lionville, also a distance of about 10 miles. Barnard moved to West Chester in 1852, where he entered the lumber and house-construction business; he also had business interests in Philadelphia, in real estate, and in making bricks.

Eusebius Barnard, of Pocopsin, about five miles from Kennett Square, and three miles from his brother, Simon, aided fugitive slaves sent by Garrett, Mendenhall, and Bartholomew Fussell. Fugitive slaves often came in the middle of the night and, if not given shelter in the kitchen where mattresses were provided on the floor, were piloted by Eusebius. If in no immediate danger, they were put to work for a few days to earn some money. If there were no children, they were sent on foot to the home of William Sugar, a distance of about six miles. On one occasion, 17 fugitive slaves arrived on foot when only the Barnard children were home. His son, then barely able to ride a horse, at once went to the home of his uncle, William, to obtain his help. On many occasions in later years, Eusebius's oldest son, Eusebius R., took fugitive slaves in their Dearborn to Dr. Eshleman in Downingtown, who was a frequent collaborator.

Bartholomew Fussell

According to Robert Smedley, Bartholomew Fussell may have assisted as many as 2,000 fugitive slaves. In 1831, he established a medical practice in Kennett Square after marrying Lydia Morris. Having earlier established a friendship with Thomas Garrett, Fussell made his home near Kennett Square, known as "the Pines," one of Kennett's earliest refuges for fugitive slaves. His son Joshua recalled that a free black named Davy, who peddled fish and fruit, was the agent who brought fugitive slaves from Garrett to the Fussell household. Frequently, among the fugitive slaves Fussell sheltered, were students whom he had taught at his Sunday school in Maryland.

During the late 1830s, the Fussells moved to a farm adjoining that of his older sister, Esther Lewis, and her daughters in West Vincent, Pennsylvania, about 20 miles north of Kennett Square. Lydia died in 1840 and Fussell married Rebecca Hewes in 1841. They moved to York, Pennsylvania, while his brother William, and later his nephew Edwin, also a physician, took up residence on the farm adjoining the Lewises, continuing the Lewis-Fussell Underground Railroad collaboration in West Vincent. In the latter part of the 1850s Fussell moved back to Chester County. He continued to collaborate with conductors in the region up through the Civil War.

Black churches in the region served as the hub for Underground Railroad connections among free blacks. Prominent among them was Hosanna in Upper Oxford Township (Chester County), whose Underground Railroad collaborators were Samuel Glasgow, Thomas Amos, and William and George Walls. The church itself also was a stop, going west to Christiana in Lancaster County. In West Chester, there was the Bethel AME Church, among whose conductors were Thomas Brown, John Smith, and Benjamin Freeman. In Kennett Square, a free black, James Walker, who lived at 233 South Union Street, was a collaborator of Garrett's. Walker forwarded fugitive slaves to Zebulon Thomas in Downington. A notably prominent black conductor was the West Chester black agent, Abraham Shadd, the father of abolitionist journalist Mary Ann Shadd, and one of six blacks who were founding members in 1833 of the American Anti-Slavery Society. Shadd received fugitive slaves from a white Presbyterian minister, William Everhart of West Chester.

Some of the most prolific conductors in the region were also among the most discreet. Daniel Gibbons always gave this advice to the fugitive slaves he forwarded: "be civil to all, and answer no questions of strangers who seem too eager to get information" (Smedley 69).

Two conductors who often received fugitive slaves from Gibbons also followed this advice.

Thomas Bonsall, whose father Abraham Bonsall hired fugitive slaves as early as 1805, lived in Wagontown and later, Christiana. He was active for 33 years but kept no records and regularly hid fugitive slaves in the granary of his double-decker barn. The majority of them he forwarded to John Vickers, using a free black man John Price to transport them. Price is believed to have aided as many as 300 fugitive slaves.

Thomas Whitson, who lived in Bart, Lancaster County, was another discreet conductor. He became active about 1841. An excellent speaker and debater, who participated regularly in antislavery meetings, he was very low key about Underground work, though it is believed he aided hundreds, many of them from Gibbons, whose typical procedure was to send fugitive slaves to him with an introduction written on a piece of paper. Whitson often found work for fugitive slaves. He was widely respected, and though it is likely that suspicions arose about his activities, his home was never searched.

The stories of a number of memorable incidences have been preserved. One of them involved Simon Barnard, sometime after the passage of the second Fugitive Slave Law. Two fugitive slaves came to his home one night in a wagon that belonged to their owner, who was in hot pursuit with a posse of slavecatchers. At once Barnard led the men to the home of neighbor, Isaac Meredith, and the four of them sped to the home of John Vickers, who lived in Lionville about 10 miles north. Later, they would learn that on their journey they actually passed the house where the slaves' owner and his posse were spending the night. Vickers moved them to the house of a black couple named Robinson, who lived a mile up the road, and told them to leave their owner's wagon with him.

The next day, after Barnard and Meredith had returned home, the slavecatchers were able to track the fugitive slaves to the Vickers' farm. When they arrived, however, only Vickers' daughter-in-law was at the house. She was well aware of the situation involving the fugitive slaves, and when the slavecatchers asked about them, she said they would have to talk to her husband, Paxson, who was in the fields and for whom she would send word to come to the house. On hearing of the slavecatchers arrival, he immediately sent word to Robinson to move the fugitive slaves. When he returned to the house, Paxson told the slavecatchers that two men had come in the night and had left behind a wagon. He offered to help the slavecatchers search his farm to see if they were hiding there. As was a common tactic in the Underground Railroad, Paxson did a thorough and methodical search of his father's farm with the slavecatchers in order to give the fugitive slaves as much time as possible to get away. After being satisfied that the slaves were not on the Vickers' farm, the slavecatchers took their wagon and returned home.

Another memorable incident involved a couple with five children, who arrived at the home of Eusebius Barnard on October 27, 1855. They had been forwarded by Thomas Garrett, who had occupied the slavecatchers pursuing them by pretending to help the slavecatchers search locations in Wilmington where they might be hiding. Barnard's son, Eusebius R., was entrusted with the task of bringing them to Zebulon Thomas in Downingtown, where it was decided to divide the group, splitting up the couple and their children, some being sent to John Vickers, some to Graceanna Lewis, and some to Elijah Pennypacker, who forwarded his group to another conductor in Norristown. The Philadephia Vigilance also was involved in the coordinating the itineraries. In the end the fugitive slaves were sent by train, reunited along the way, and successfully transported to St. Catharines in Canada.

Slavecatchers

Slavecatchers were often bold in their attempt to recapture their fleeing slaves, and with the Kennett Square area being so close to slave territory, it made them even bolder. One of their tactics was to send decoys or spies posing as runaways to the houses of those suspected of aiding fugitive slaves. They had no scruples about breaking the law to achieve their ends.

On the night of April 19, 1848, while everyone in the household was asleep, slavecatchers broke into the home of Zebulon Thomas, and took a fugitive slave and her child, despite the efforts of Thomas to fight them off. As early as 1820, John Reed, a fugitive slave living in Kennett Square, fought off his old master and overseer who had come to capture him, killing them both. Another noteworthy incident occurred in 1849. Thomas Mitchell, a former slave who had been living in Unionville, Chester County for 12 years, was abducted on August 21 from his home at midnight. Mitchell's Quaker employer, George Martin, along with Samuel Pennock and others pursued the abductors to Baltimore, also enlisting the help of Thomas Garrett. But it was to no avail as Martin was prosecuted for aiding fugitive slaves and Mitchell was taken to a slave trader and sold into the Deep South. It was one of many such kidnappings in the region by slavecatchers, whose boldness increased after the passage of the second Fugitive Slave Law in 1850. A third noteworthy case occurred in January 1852, when Joseph C. Miller, of West Nottingham, Chester County, was lynched in Maryland after he had gone there with others to try to obtain the freedom of a black woman who had been kidnapped from his home.

But these confrontations are not surprising considering the proximity of Kennett Square with slave territory, and the overt intentions of abolitionists in the region not only to aid fugitive slaves but to abolish slavery, like a statement made on October 15–16, 1851, when the Pennsylvania Anti-Slavery Society met at West Chester and resolved:

> That while we rejoice in the escape of every fugitive from Slavery, and in the opportunity to give assistance, shelter, and protection to all such fugitives, our chief and all important work is,—not to aid the escape of individual slaves, nor to prevent the extension of Slavery but the immediate and total abolition of Slavery wherever it may exist. (*Pennsylvania Freeman* October 24, 1851)

—Tom Calarco

Further Reading

William C. Kashatus, *Just over the Line* (West Chester, PA: Chester County Historical Society, 2002).

James A. McGowan, *Station Master on the Underground Railroad: The Life and Letters of Thomas Garrett* (Jefferson, NC: McFarland, revised edition, 2004).

R. C. Smedley, *History of the Underground Railroad in Chester and Neighboring Counties of Pennsylvania* (Lancaster, PA, 1883).

William Still, *The Underground Railroad* (Philadelphia: Porter and Coates, 1872).

William J. Switala, *The Underground Railroad in Pennsylvania* (Mechanicsburg, PA: Stackpole Books, 2001).

L

LICK CREEK, INDIANA

Lick Creek is one of many communities settled by blacks in the Midwest, but what made it different was that it became racially integrated long before the Civil War. Twenty miles north of Leavenworth on the Ohio River, it was settled by free blacks and Quakers sometime after 1810. They came to Indiana together from North Carolina and settled in the hills of southeastern Orange County, Indiana. Though a free state, Indiana had many laws that discriminated against blacks, and despite this, the settlers of Lick Creek lived and worked side-by-side as equals and at peace.

The first blacks to buy land in the area were William Constant and Charles Goin in 1817; but by 1820, there were 63 African Americans living in Orange County and by 1830, there were 112. Records indicate that Lick Creek was for a time a boomtown and landholdings in the 1840s increased tremendously. The number of black residents doubled to a total of 260 by 1860.

Some question whether those who settled Lick Creek helped fugitive slaves. Although Quakers had a well-deserved reputation for abolitionist activity and involvement in the Underground Railroad, harboring runaways in the settlement invited trouble from proslavery residents in the area, and Kentucky slave hunters, who crossed the river in search of runaways, sometimes kidnapped free blacks and took them south. Some folks with long family ties to the area, however, say that stories handed down claim otherwise.

Likelihood of Underground Railroad Participation

But there is little doubt that Lick Creek played a role in the Underground Railroad. Fugitive slaves crossing the river were often assisted by free blacks and sought out or were directed to African American settlements. Especially early in their journey, fugitive slaves not only trusted other blacks more but were able to blend in more easily into their communities and go undetected. The support that Quakers and other white abolitionists gave them has long been documented, and while much about the role of free blacks in the freedom movement is unknown, research is ongoing.

Quaker landowners have been identified in the Lick Creek area from as early as the War of 1812. They welcomed blacks and any others who faced discrimination, and shared the land and allowed them to build their homes. For the next several years, this small, integrated community remained a rarity. It is difficult to say exactly how integrated it was because the land records show who owned land next to whom, but not who lived next to whom. Some landowners may not have lived on their land but rented it out to tenant farmers who paid rent in cash or crops. This was considered "sharecropping," which many blacks were forced to do after being freed. Along with the black codes established in states like Indiana, Illinois, and Ohio, it also was a system designed to prevent the African American family from progressing financially.

Free blacks who settled in Lick Creek and surrounding areas of Indiana, likely remained in the area mainly to assist others obtain their freedom. An examination of black settlements in Indiana reveals that in nearly every case, these settlements were located on one of the routes of the Underground Railroad. This tells us that escaped enslaved people tended to seek out members of their own race because they lived in relatively isolated rural farmsteads.

Constant efforts to put limits on the freedom of free blacks plagued them because they were constituted as a threat, acting as leaders and allies in the overthrow of slavery. Free blacks were known to live in communities such as Lick Creek that were not "towns" per se, but rather a loose-knit system of farmsteads spread over the rural landscape. An especially important component of these rural black settlements was their churches.

Bishop William Paul Quinn

Bishop William Paul Quinn, who was a founding member of the African Methodist Episcopal (AME) Church in Philadelphia in 1816, was remembered by historians of the AME as a "militant soldier of the cross" who left a legacy of radical activism (LaRoche 76). He defied slavery and organized AME churches in communities in the East and Midwest, including St. Louis, Missouri and Louisville, Kentucky, and ordained ministers in New Orleans a decade before the Civil War. He came to New Albany, Floyd County, Indiana, as a circuit preacher during the 1830s and the Quinn Chapel AME across the river in Louisville, Kentucky, was named after him. This chapel was known as the abolitionist church. Of seven antebellum black churches in Louisville, Quinn Chapel was probably more than any of the others, "part of the network associated with Underground Railroad activity in north central Kentucky" (Hudson 109). And "from Bethel AME church in Woodbury, New Jersey through Pennsylvania, Ohio, Indiana, Illinois, and Kentucky, Bishop Quinn's name is consistently linked to Underground Railroad sites" (LaRoche 78).

Blacks, who aided fugitive slaves near the Ohio River on the border with slave territory, did not consider their actions related to an organized Underground Railroad. To them it was simply an extension of their community values, and they viewed the Underground Railroad as an organization of whites or blacks who lived elsewhere, which generally was much farther north. In 1836, Quinn established an AME Church in New Albany. He also established churches in Jeffersonville, also in Floyd County, and in Salem and Paoli in Washington County, and at his home in Richmond in Wayne County, Indiana. The establishment of AME churches in Greenville, Snow Hill, and Cabin Creek in Randolph County also were likely influenced by him. These churches were a vital link to the eastern branch of the Underground Railroad, north of Wayne. In 1840, Quinn was put in charge of the Brooklyn, Illinois, circuit and was given oversight of all the circuits of the Indiana Conference, which included the Lick Creek settlement.

During the 1830s and early 1840s, Quinn led several hundred Midwestern free people of color into the AME church. He also had strong ties to Quakerism and would have been at home among them in Lick Creek. He had learned about the sect from an English Quakeress and was befriended by Elias Hicks, the leader of the Separation of 1827–1828 that resulted in formation of the Hicksite Friends, who were noted for their activist role in the antislavery movement. Hicks, a staunch and uncompromising abolitionist, led a campaign against the use of slave-made products. Abolitionist writer Lydia Maria Child reported that Hicks was so opposed to slavery and the use of slave-made products that his dying concern was that no cotton blanket should touch his skin.

In 1850 and 1851, back-to-back laws were passed—one national and one local—that created a very hostile atmosphere for blacks in Lick Creek and elsewhere. Politically, Indiana had never been receptive to having African Americans within its borders. The Great Compromise of 1850 passed by the U.S. Congress created the Fugitive Slave Law. It allowed slave owners, or slave "catchers" hired by the slave owners, to travel into any state of the union to retrieve an escaped slave. It obliged residents to become de facto slave catchers themselves, which most in the North disagreed with. In 1851, Indiana adopted a new state constitution that prohibited the future settlement of black people in Indiana and required those who lived there to post a large cash bond that guaranteed their good behavior.

Throughout the turbulent 1850s and the events leading up to the Civil War, Lick Creek adapted to changes and somehow managed to thrive. Something terrible happened though, in the year of 1862, when there was an exodus from Lick Creek in the month of September when seven residents sold over 500 acres of land and left the area. One man sold all of his land and possessions for half the value. In 1870, there were only 75 black residents residing in Lick Creek. Most had gone farther north and several relocated outside of the United States in Canada. Unlike most settlers, blacks at Lick Creek and other predominantly

Oakland City, Indiana

Oakland City, the site of the home of James W. Cockrum, an active participant in the Underground Railroad, is about 30 miles north of the Ohio River in western Indiana. Today, the campus of the small Baptist-affiliated college, Oakland City University, is located on the site of the Cockrum homestead. Cockrum's son, William, also participated in a number of incidents as a teenager, and in his old age wrote a history of the area's Underground Railroad, *History of the Underground Railroad: as it Was Conducted by the Anti-Slavery League*. It described a secret network of abolitionist spies that were funded by important abolitionists in the East and whose Indiana supervisor was an enigmatic figure allegedly named John Hanson, but who later identified himself in a letter to James Cockrum written near the close of the Civil War as John Hanover.

Cockrum's book reads more like folklore than actual history, and its veracity has been questioned by modern historians, especially because no mention of the Anti-Slavery League has been found anywhere except in his book. However, his description of methods used by the Underground Railroad and the actions characteristic of slavecatchers, whose activities in southern Indiana are well documented, conform to accepted beliefs. In addition, the Cockrums were men of unimpeachable integrity and highly respected in their community. More scrutiny of Cockrum's claims is needed before we can rule out their authenticity.

There is no doubt, however, that individuals like John Posey, Ira Caswell, John Dole, and Hanson/Hanover were real. For example, Dole, who is described as a native of Maine, actually can be documented to have participated in antislavery organizations in Maine, prior to the time he allegedly came to Indiana.

Diamond Island, Indiana, on the Ohio River, was the site of activities of the Anti-Slavery League described by William M. Cockrum of Oakland City, Indiana. (Courtesy of Tom Calarco)

black communities in the state of Indiana faced more obstacles than their white neighbors realized. The discrimination, repressive laws, and race hatred created untold problems for blacks in Indiana. The same was true throughout much of the nation as laws prevented blacks from voting, serving on a jury, testifying in a court of law, and attending public schools.

Exodus from Lick Creek

Some historians believe that the reason for this mass movement out of the Lick Creek area was because many local residents harbored Southern sympathies. The number of violent incidents toward blacks increased statewide during the Civil War. Although there is no evidence of racial strife in Orange County, hostility grew in the nearby towns of Paoli and Chambersburg, where black residents would have needed to go to trade and purchase items. After the war, many moved out of the area for industrial jobs in urban areas such as Indianapolis and Chicago. By 1890, there was only one black resident still working the land in Lick Creek, and all that remains there today is a small, humble cemetery.

Bishop Quinn died on February 3, 1873, at the age of 83 in Richmond, Indiana, where he had settled and is buried in the cemetery at Earlham College, a Quaker institution in Richmond. Today his home is listed in the National Register of Historic Places in recognition of the significant role he played in the organization of Bethel AME in Richmond and his efforts in the Underground Railroad.

—Melissa Waddy-Thibodeaux

Further Reading

J. Blaine Hudson, *Fugitive Slaves and the Underground Railroad in the Kentucky Borderlands* (Jefferson, NC: McFarland and Company, 2001).

Cheryl Janifer LaRoche, "On the Edge of Freedom: Free Black Communities, Archaeology, and the Underground Railroad," (Ph.D. Diss., University of Maryland, College Park, 2004).

LOUISVILLE, KENTUCKY

Louisville was the first European settlement in Kentucky and founded on Corn Island in 1778 by George Rogers Clark, the noted Revolutionary War military leader. Located along the Ohio River, it was named after King Louis XVI of France, whose soldiers assisted American soldiers in the Revolutionary War. Much of its initial growth can be attributed to having been a center of the domestic slave trade. The high level of slave-trade activity naturally presented numerous opportunities for slaves to escape, as well as the city's location on the border between slavery and freedom.

Black Churches

As in most urban areas with substantial free black populations, the black churches were ready to help slaves who sought their freedom. In Louisville, the most prominent was the Quinn African Methodist Episcopal Church, founded by Rev. William Paul Quinn. Considered by many in Louisville as the abolition church, Quinn Chapel was financially supported by Quakers in Indiana, so slaveholders forbid their slaves from visiting it.

Crossover Locations

There were three major crossing points for slaves fleeing from Louisville: Brandenburg, Kentucky, north to Corydon, Indiana; Louisville, north to New Albany and Jeffersonville, Indiana; and Charleston Landing, Indiana. The most heavily traveled route north of Louisville passed through the Indiana border counties of Crawford, Harrison, Floyd, and Clark. Among the most notable early escapes involved the couple, Thornton and Lucie Blackburn. They fled on July 3, 1831, only about a year after moving to Louisville from Maysville, Kentucky.

They crossed into Jeffersonville, posing as free blacks, and took passage on the steamboat *Versailles* to Cincinnati. They took a stagecoach to Sandusky and reached Detroit, where they settled. Their entire journey took them 15 days. Two years later they were discovered by slavecatchers, who took them into custody.

However, Detroit's free black community came to their rescue. First, the wives of two black Baptist ministers, Mrs. George French and Mrs. Madison Mason, paid a visit to Lucie in jail. They brought with them a change of clothes and a disguise and somehow managed to bring Lucie out surreptitiously and snuck her on a boat to Canada. As for Thornton, 400 men stormed the jail where he was locked up and freed him. During the melee, the Sheriff was beaten so badly that he eventually died of his injuries. Thornton joined his wife in Canada where they lived the rest of their live in freedom and prosperity.

The most important crossing point from Louisville was located in Portland, going directly to New Albany, Indiana. Many accounts dealing with fugitive slaves report the use of ferries. As early as 1821, five ferries were already in use in the Louisville area, including one in Portland. In 1857, an average of 1,200 passengers per day was reported to have used the ferry between Portland and New Albany.

Systematic use of the Portland area as an exodus for fugitive slaves dates from at least 1850 when free blacks from Louisville, New Albany, and Cincinnati met in Louisville to discuss the formation of a Masonic Lodge. The group decided to locate the lodge in New Albany and received its charter from the Grand Lodge of Ohio as Mount Moriah Lodge No. 1 on June 12, 1850. For three

Looking at the Ohio River from the Portland section of Louisville, which was a regular crossover location for fugitive slaves. (Courtesy of Tom Calarco)

years they remained at New Albany but "labored under many disadvantages, such as crossing the river in skiffs at midnight . . . at the risk of their lives, and then walking five miles up to the city" (Hudson, 2002, 113). As a result, they moved to Portland.

A 1930s interview with Henry Webb of New Albany whose father was a slave in Louisville confirmed that a major fugitive slave route ran through Louisville and New Albany:

> runaway Negroes used to come across the Ohio River from Portland [and that] Plans for escapes were hatched in a colored Masonic Lodge, located in Portland. The Negroes would cross the river in a skiff, manned by [individuals posing as] fishermen and if the coast was not clear on this side they would go up the river for a short distance. . . . Many that crossed hid with friends in the hills back of New Albany and then after all danger was past made their way north by way of Salem. (Ibid.)

William Tatum

William Tatum, alias John Jones, was one of those who used the Portland ferry. In 1858, he was indicted for aiding a fugitive slave named Hugh. Tatum is probably the "Jones" referred to by Levi Coffin, who aided 27 fugitive slaves one year from Louisville.

Coffin described his mode of operation. Jones would reserve a couple of berths in a packet going from Louisville to Cincinnati. On some occasions, Jones would accompany the slaves in the second berth, and on others he would arrange to make it look like they were servants and leave a key in the room. When he did not accompany the slave, he would telegraph Coffin who would send a black agent to meet the slaves at the wharf and bring them to Coffin.

Suspicions arose about Jones and he was framed by the authorities and put in jail. After two trials in which he was convicted, his attorney was able to find illegalities, and a third trial was scheduled. The judge set an extremely high bail and he was forced to wait in jail where his health deteriorated. An appeal was made to Coffin to raise the funds, and with the help of friends in Philadelphia, he obtained it. Jones then went to Cincinnati where he forfeited bail and remained in hiding with Coffin before he and his wife moved to Iowa. After the Civil War, Jones and his wife returned to Cincinnati where he attended medical school and became a physician.

Washington Spradling

Among the more important individuals in Louisville who helped slaves obtain their freedom was Washington Spradling, a former slave, who became a barber. He was the first freed slave to obtain significant wealth in Kentucky, which he obtained mainly through real estate. This provided an opportunity for him to help slaves become free through legal means. He did this by loaning the money to the slave to purchase his freedom with the agreement that the money would be repaid. He freed 33 slaves this way, though some of them did not repay him.

Though Spradling's involvement in aiding slaves through the illegal operation of the Underground Railroad is not clear, his close association with Shelton Morris, another former slave who was a barber and his brother-in-law, suggests this. Freed in 1820, Morris initially moved to Harrison County, Indiana. He also acquired wealth through real estate investment in Louisville. However, he moved to Cincinnati in 1841 and later, to Xenia, Ohio. It is significant to note that Wilbur Siebert included Shelton in a list of "efficient" Underground Railroad operators in Cincinnati.

Another notable Louisville citizen who assisted fugitive slaves was the musician, James Cunningham. Under suspicion of the authorities, he was arrested in 1855. Not only was he found in possession of letters from Calvin Fairbank but also with clothing of slaves who had escaped. He also had been implicated by Shadrach Henderson, who was arrested in Louisville for aiding fugitive slaves with Moses Bard in an incident that involved the river crossing at Portland. However, this circumstantial evidence was not enough to convict him, and he was released on bail.

Interracial cooperation, like most localities involved in the Underground Railroad, occurred in Louisville. Clothing and a daguerreotype of slaves who had attempted to escape from Louisville were found among the possessions of William Lewis, a local white man who operated a boarding house. They belonged to fugitive slaves who had been apprehended at the home of a free black man, Dick Buckner. Both were arrested. Additional incriminating evidence was found at Buckner's home, including a letter from a fugitive slave originally from Shelby County, Kentucky, who was living in Chatham, Canada West. Lewis was placed in jail in lieu of failing to pay bail, and Buckner was sentenced to two years in prison.

Collaboration with New Albany

Louisville's Underground Railroad agents had a close relationship with those in New Albany, and sometimes moved their residences back and forth between the two cities. In 1854, for instance, Sarah Lucas, a free black woman who shifted her residences between Louisville and New Albany, was arrested for aiding a slave whom she was attempting to pass off as free. Also having this connection were three Louisville blacks who collaborated with New Albany Underground Railroad agent, William Harding: William H. Gibson, Jesse Merriweather, and James R. Cunningham. All three men were subscribers of *Frederick Douglass' Paper* and had their newspapers sent to Harding's address. Cunningham also helped Rev. Calvin Fairbank with the escape of the slave, Tamar, from Louisville, which led to Fairbank's arrest and return to prison.

The numerous opportunities available for escape to slaves in the Louisville area because of its busy boat traffic prompted them to use various means. Rachel was aided by a Louisville grocer, Edward Cope, who had fallen in love with her. His plan was to join her in Canada, but it was foiled when Rachel's master visited her in Canada, and she gave him letters that proved Cope's involvement in her escape. In actuality, Rachel used Cope to get to Canada to join William Gilchrist, already known by both her and Cope. Though the letters incriminated Cope and he was tried for violating the Fugitive Slave Law, a hung jury prevented his conviction.

Isaac Throgmorton escaped from Louisville Kentucky in 1853 simply by accompanying a free black man on the ferry. His friend, who produced emancipation papers, said that Throgmorton had forgotten his papers, and they were both allowed to board the ferry, where they crossed over and came back that evening. Throgmorton returned the next day alone and was granted admission because he was known from the previous day. Throgmorton then headed straight to Canada.

Some of those who operated ferries were sympathetic to fugitive slaves. The Brandenburg ferry, 30 miles downriver from Louisville, was one of those means of escape. It was operated by Charlie Bell and his son, Daniel, who lived south of

Corydon, Indiana. Their involvement became known when they aided a fugitive slave named Charles Woodruff in 1857, who successfully reached Canada. They were arrested and while awaiting trial, two of the Bell brothers came from California and broke their father and brother out of jail.

Jeffersonville

Connections also existed between the Underground Railroad agents in Louisville and Jeffersonville, Indiana. It was while in Jeffersonville, that Calvin Fairbank was asked to rescue Tamar, who was about to be sold at auction in Louisville. Though he had some problems getting Tamar out, he was successful in bringing her to Salem, Indiana, where she was placed on the Underground Railroad, and eventually arrived in Canada. Fairbank, on the other hand, was kidnapped in Jeffersonville a week after the rescue by a group of Kentuckians led by Tamar's owner and placed in a Louisville jail.

In September 1858, Miles Wilson, a free black man was arrested for aiding a fugitive slave whom he accompanied on the Jeffersonville ferry boat. Wilson implicated John Lancisco, a white coffeehouse owner in Jeffersonville.

Another abolitionist from Jeffersonville was Dr. Nathaniel Field, a former slaveowner, who had freed his slaves. Born in Jefferson County, Kentucky, he went to medical school in Lexington, Kentucky, and moved to Jeffersonville in 1829. He organized the city government of Jeffersonville under a charter that he drafted and that was passed by the legislature in 1830. He also was the founder of the first Christian Church of that city and, in 1847, the Second Advent Christian Church.

Dr. Field assisted fugitive slaves and encouraged their quest for freedom. His wife worked in the community and was charitable to the poor. One time she was returning on the ferry boat from Louisville and sat in a section where a Negro man was also sitting. The guard ordered him to the back of the boat and immediately began to assault him. Upon her return to Jeffersonville, Mrs. Field filed a warrant against the guard.

Just up the river from Jeffersonville, oral tradition claims that the Charlestown Landing was another crossing point, and just east, on Bull Creek, lived three cousins named Adams, who were said to harbor fugitive slaves.

—Sharron L Pope and Tom Calarco

Further Reading

Levi Coffin, *The Reminiscences of Levi Coffin* (Cincinnati: Robert Clark & Co., 1880).

J. Blaine Hudson, *Fugitive Slaves and the Underground Railroad in the Kentucky Borderlands* (Jefferson, NC: McFarland and Company, Inc., 2002).

Pamela R. Peters, *The Underground Railroad in Floyd County, Indiana* (Jefferson, NC: McFarland and Company, 2001).

$\sim$ M

MADISON, INDIANA

Madison, Indiana, was a major center of the Underground Railroad in southern Indiana. Like Cincinnati, 50 miles to the east, its location along the Ohio River made it a commercial hub for southern markets and a frequent destination of slaveholders. And like Cincinnati many of its free black citizens were former slaves who had family still in slavery, which also made it a likely destination of fugitive slaves.

Beginnings of Abolitionism

Abolitionist sentiment in the Madison area began in 1809 when Benjamin Whitson, a Methodist minister from the South, moved there and expressed open opposition to slavery. This sentiment grew with the arrival of a number of Presbyterian abolitionist ministers in the region and attracted free blacks who began settling here. It was these settlers who established the area as a refuge for fugitive slaves.

Englishman E. S. Abdy visited the United States from 1833 to 1834 to observe the conditions of free blacks and slaves and published an account of his travels entitled *Journal of a Residence and Tour in the United States of North America*. During his visit to Madison he reported a farming community of 129 blacks on the city's outskirts where the Underground Railroad was active. Among these early black Underground Railroad conductors was George Evans, who took slaves from the community of Hanover on the west side of Madison to Decatur County. Another early black conductor was the grocer John Carter, who lived in the Georgetown neighborhood of Madison, and who continued to aid fugitive slaves throughout the antebellum period.

Black Agents

During the 1830s, three blacks originally from Virginia moved to the Georgetown section of Madison and became instrumental in increasing local involvement in the Underground Railroad. The first was William Anderson, who had been born free but had been sold into slavery as a boy. In 1836, he escaped from an Ohio River steamboat near Louisville and found his way to Madison, where he became a businessman and minister. The following year saw the arrival of Elijah Anderson and George DeBaptiste. Anderson set up a blacksmith shop and DeBaptiste became a merchant who traveled frequently on the steamboats between Madison and Cincinnati. During one of DeBaptiste's business trips he met General William Henry Harrison and became the General's valet until Harrison's untimely death a month after he took office as the U.S. president in 1841. Thereafter, DeBaptiste returned to Madison and opened a barbershop and began his participation in the Underground Railroad.

William Anderson claimed to have aided more than 100 fugitive slaves while in Madison, and in his 1857 autobiography he stated that, "My two wagons, and carriage, and five horses were always at the command of the liberty-seeking fugitive. . . . I have carried them away in broad daylight, and in the grim shades of night" (Anderson 38–39).

DeBaptiste was known to have worked with the Underground Railroad community in Lancaster, Indiana, and sometimes escorted fugitive slaves the full seven miles to Lancaster, a steep hilly trek, on foot during the night and return in the morning to open his barbershop. He claimed to have personally aided 108 fugitive slaves during his time in Madison.

Elijah Anderson, who was light-skinned enough to pass for white, was known to travel into Kentucky to take slaves to freedom and was said to have penetrated as far south as Frankfort, about 50 miles from Madison. He was the most active of the three during this time. Other prominent black Underground Railroad agents in Madison during this period were a former slave from Virginia, Griffith Booth, and David Lott, who was Elijah Anderson's neighbor.

Riot against Black Agents

However, continual harassment and a riot by proslavery whites about the year 1846 forced many of Madison's black Underground Railroad agents to leave town, including Elijah Anderson, George DeBaptiste, and Griffiths Booth. During this riot, Booth was nearly drowned. An incident related to the riot involved Elijah Anderson and Chapman Harris, another blacksmith, in the beating of a Madison black, John Simmons, whom Underground Railroad agents believed was sabotaging their operations. Both Anderson and Harris were prosecuted by Simmons and forced to pay heavy fines.

The fallout from the 1846 riot led to the emigration from Madison of a number of important black Underground Railroad operatives, including DeBaptiste, Booth, and Elijah Anderson. DeBaptiste moved to Detroit, Booth to Canada, and Anderson up river, first to Lawrenceburg, Indiana, and finally to Gallia County, Ohio, where both expanded their Underground Railroad activities. William Anderson was forced to resign from the Colored Methodist Episcopal Church, for whom he built their first church because of his Underground Railroad activities. As a result, he organized a new church, the African Methodist Episcopal Church, in 1849, for which he became the minister.

Chapman Harris

Though Underground Railroad operations in Georgetown continued, they diminished and the center of its activity moved outside the city, mainly on the east side up through the Eagle Hollow ravine where Harris lived. An emergency situation called Harris into the service of the Underground Railroad. Following the riot, there was a shortage of Underground Railroad agents and he was approached by John Carter, who had been his neighbor in Georgetown before he moved to Eagle Hollow. It led to his becoming Madison's stationmaster and also involved the participation of his sons, who met fugitive slaves crossing the river at the foot of the ravine. He also established a communication system, whereby he would hammer an iron plate that he had embedded into a gigantic sycamore whose trunk he had hollowed out, to alert fugitive slaves crossing over that it was safe.

During this period, Chapman collaborated with white abolitionists and black agent John Carr, who lived at the top of Eagle Hollow on Rykers Ridge, to forward his passengers. He also worked with a Kentucky slave, Freeman Anderson, who would bring fugitive slaves to Madison during trips he made on business for his master.

Nevertheless, on the west side of Madison, black farmers continued their Underground Railroad that had begun in the 1820s. A white abolitionist Lyman Lathrop, moved to that area from upstate New York during the early 1840s, and collaborated with Rev. John Todd (not to be confused with the Iowa abolitionist), one of the early Presbyterian ministers who had come to the area and had fomented abolitionist sentiment. What made the west side especially inviting to fugitive slaves was a sandbar along the river that sometimes made it possible, when the river was low, to actually walk across it. Also on the west side was the Clifty Falls section, a rocky area with many caves where fugitive slaves could hide. Use of the latter became more frequent after the capture of 15 runaways by pro-slavery whites who were members of the racist organization, Knights of the Golden Circle, which was active throughout southern Indiana.

Collaboration with Lancaster

By the mid-1840s, collaborations between abolitionists in the Madison area and Lancaster, and further north with the Hicklin settlement and the Hicklin family of ministers, was common. Though we have no evidence to support the continuation of DeBaptiste and Elijah Anderson in the Underground Railroad of Madison following their departure around 1846, it is reasonable that their former connection was useful both to those in Madison and to their new fields of operation. For example, Anderson was regularly traveling between the Ohio River ports and Sandusky, Ohio, accompanying fugitive slaves by train, whose service was connected to the river around 1850, and DeBaptiste had established a steamboat service between Sandusky and Detroit, with stopovers in Canada. Anderson claimed to personally have aided more than 800 fugitive slaves after the Fugitive Slave Law of 1850 and DeBaptiste's vigilance committee in Detroit, of which he was one of the two leading members, was aiding upward of 1,500 fugitive slaves a year by 1855. Also, another of their collaborators in Madison, John Lott, had moved to Sandusky and was involved there in the Underground Railroad.

Delia Webster

During the early 1850s, the Underground Railroad in Madison was confronted with a new distraction. Whether it had an impact on its activities is not known, but it surely brought attention to them. This distraction came in the person of the notorious Delia Webster, the infamous slave stealer, who had been convicted of assisting fugitive slaves in Lexington, Kentucky, in 1844 and had served time in prison as a result.

A Vermont native, Webster came to Madison in 1849. It is not clear what her true intentions were, but she was installed by her former warden and alleged lover Newton Craig and his wife, Lucy, as a teacher for their children there. She also set up a school for black children. In 1852, Webster bought a farm across the river from Madison in Trimble County, Kentucky, in union with a Vermont abolitionist minister, Norris Day. Her dream was to establish a school for blacks on the model of Oberlin College, which she had briefly attended around 1842 before moving to Lexington.

Their public intentions at the time, however, were to use the location as an experiment in using free labor; but in 1853, they began helping local slaves to escape on the Underground Railroad. Both were brought to trial on these charges in 1854 and acquitted. Day fled the area after his acquittal, but Webster hung on despite threats on her life and destruction of her property while away on trips to visit family in the East. For the next 15 years, she would try various schemes to make use of it: offering the land to be used for a college; bringing 30 families from Massachusetts to live there and open a shoe factory; offering it as a site for a memorial to Lincoln after the assassination.

During the latter part of the 1850s, Elijah Anderson, William Anderson, and Chapman Harris all were arrested on charges of aiding fugitives. Only Elijah was convicted. He was sentenced to prison in Frankfort, Kentucky, where he was found dead in his cell on the day of his scheduled release in 1861, likely the result of a homicide. Harris became increasingly militant and always was heavily armed when traveling. A reported meeting with John Brown at Eagles Hollow in 1859 indicated that Harris and his associates were planning a slave insurrection at plantations near the Kentucky border that Brown asked them to delay until he completed his mission at Harpers Ferry. Whether or not Brown's failure had a bearing on their decision to abort their plans is not known.

Remnants of the Underground Railroad Today

Today, the remnants of the Underground Railroad remain in the Georgetown neighborhood of Madison. Researchers have identified eight structures associated with the Underground Railroad. Among them are:

1. The Walnut Street Methodist Church (originally the Colored Methodist Episcopal Church built by William Anderson), 711 Walnut Street
2. The first home of William Anderson, 713 Walnut Street
3. The home of Elijah Anderson, 626 Walnut Street
4. The home of David Lott, 624 Walnut Street
5. The second home of William Anderson, 313 East Fifth Street
6. The African Methodist Episcopal Church (founded by William Anderson), 309 East Fifth Street, built 1849

The full story of the Underground Railroad in Madison is yet to be told. What is known testifies to the fact that it was a major crossover point for fugitive slaves and that its many area resident abolitionists, both black and white, aided hundreds of fugitive slaves obtain their freedom.

—Tom Calarco

Further Reading

William Anderson, *Life and Narrative of William J. Anderson* (Chicago: Daily Tribune Book and Job Printing Office, 1857).

Tom Calarco, *People of the Underground Railroad* (Westport, CT: Greenwood Press, 2008).

Diane Perrine Coon, "Southeastern Indiana's Underground Railroad Routes and Operations" (A Project of the State of Indiana, Dept. of Natural Resources, Division of Historic Preservation and Archaeology and the U.S. Dept. of the Interior, NPS, April 2001).

J. Blaine Hudson, *Fugitive Slaves and the Underground Railroad in the Kentucky Borderlands* (Jefferson, NC: McFarland and Company, 2001).

MARIETTA, OHIO

Marietta is located at the confluence of the Ohio and Muskingum rivers in Washington County, which borders over 65 miles of the Ohio River. Many Underground Railroad safe houses and more than 16 Underground Railroad stations were located in Marietta and Washington County. Fugitive slaves came to Marietta and Harmar, Ohio, crossing the Ohio River during the night in skiffs and flatboats.

Agents

Among the most prominent Underground Railroad workers in the region was Ephraim Cutler. He came to Marietta in 1795, where he was appointed as a territorial judge. During the next 10 years he lived in Waterford, along the Muskingum River, and in Ames Township. He was one of the three delegates elected to represent Washington County at the Ohio Constitutional Convention held at Chillicothe in November 1802. In 1806, he moved to Warren Township, midway between Marietta and Belpre where he founded the community of Constitution and established a profitable stone quarry. His experience as a territorial judge, statehood convention delegate, state legislator, and founding Trustee at Ohio University, provided him with contacts throughout the state. Along with other abolitionists in Ohio, he helped formulate secret plans to circumvent the Fugitive Slave Law of 1793, and Constitution became an early Underground Railroad station. Jules Deming and Dyar Burgesses were among those who helped him operate the Constitution Station.

Marietta's premier abolitionist and Underground Railroad conductor was David Putnam Jr., who operated a mercantile business in Harmar, now part of Marietta. The Historic Harmar District was where the first African American was born in the Northwest Territory. Putnam's home was located on Maple Street on two acres behind the Harmar Congregational Church. Putnam became a strong abolitionist while growing up across the Ohio River from Wood County, Virginia, where slavery was legitimate and very profitable. As a young man, he became acquainted with some of the slaves, listened to their stories, and even witnessed slaves being sold "down the river" to plantations in the Deep South. By the time he was a teenager, he had decided that he would fight slavery and took on an active role as an abolitionist. A Virginia plantation owner, George Washington Henderson, once brought a lawsuit against Putnam for the loss of nine slaves. Henderson claimed that Putnam had helped them to escape, somehow influencing them to become fugitives. The suit was filed in the U.S. District Court in Columbus, with Salmon P. Chase as Putnam's attorney. The plaintiff filed two suits for compensation for lost property: one for $5,000 for the value of the slaves; and the other for $10,000, for compensation due to breach of contract, lost labor, and legal fees. On October 12, 1852, the case was dismissed on a legal technicality.

Other abolitionists were free blacks Jerry Jones, Daniel Strawther, and Tom Jerry. Many others in Marietta, who assisted fugitive slaves, were members of the Washington County Anti-Slavery Society. Many were prosperous farmers or prominent business professionals, who discreetly used their positions and influence to assist fugitive slaves. Theodore D. Weld came to Marietta for several weeks during the summer of 1835, and spent afternoons lecturing in the town library. Many Marietta College students and citizens attended these lectures and formed an antislavery society and are believed to have helped in the Underground Railroad. The Marietta Anti-Slavery Society existed for many years, with members often being chased from their meetings by proslavery activists.

A slave with the code name of Josephus lived across the Ohio River from Marietta, in Williamstown, Virginia. Each month, for many years, Josephus delivered two or three fugitive slaves to the mouth of Duck Creek, near where the present-day Interstate 77 Highway Bridge crosses the Ohio River. This highway closely follows the former route of the Underground Railroad that went from Marietta to Cleveland.

Area Network

Belpre, located directly across the river from Parkersburg, Virginia, about 10 miles south of Marietta, also was a favorite place for slaves to cross because Virginia had a road from Alexandria to Parkersburg. The road was well-traveled by stagecoaches and freight wagons in which fugitives could hide. Belpre had a long river frontage and was near Vienna Island that was used as a steppingstone from Virginia. Several of Belpre's pioneers were practicing abolitionists, including Daniel Goss, Perley Howe, Jonathan Stone, Colonel John Stone, T. T. Hebbard, and Joseph Smith.

Jonathan Stone, who was a friend of Judge Ephraim Cutler, and his son Colonel John Stone ran the Belpre Station, now called the John Stone House at 110 Stone Road in Belpre, and frequently hid fugitive slaves in a large cornfield on their farm. Colonel Stone, who spent his entire life in Belpre, became an abolitionist at a young age when he witnessed the capture of a slave near the Ohio River. The Stone farm was located near the Ohio River's confluence with the Kanawha River, a river commonly used by fugitive slaves coming from (West) Virginia. Stone worked closely with "Aunt Jenny," a free black woman who lived in Parkersburg, Virginia. As a signal, Aunt Jenny blew a horn from the Virginia banks, announcing to Stone that a fugitive slave would be crossing the Ohio River on a boat. Stone returned her signal with owl calls to indicate when it was safe to cross.

Washington County had many other Underground Railroad stations. In the extreme southeast corner was the Curtis-Sawyer House, called the Little Hocking Station, built in 1798. It harbored fugitive slaves as early as 1820. In the western part of Washington County, from around 1825 until 1861, James and Margaret Smith, and their five sons, operated an Underground Railroad Station from their farm located two miles south of Cutler, Ohio. Another stop, the Barlow Station was also located in the western part of the county. This house, located about 12 miles north of the Ohio River and 12 miles west of Marietta, was built by abolitionist James Lawton, Sr. in 1819. During the 1850s, several abolitionists brought passengers to Barlow, including Church Tuttle from Monroe County, Ohio, and James Lawton Sr. Also in the western part of Washington County was the hamlet of Bartlett, whose conductors Uriah Bailey, William Hale, and others transported fugitive slaves 12 miles north to the Quaker Community at Chester Hill, in Morgan County.

Just west of Marietta a free black man known as Logan operated the Tunnel Station. It was used only in emergencies when bounty hunters were close to catching fugitive slaves.

About four miles north of Marietta, the Hoyt Family owned a big farm on the Little Muskingum River. Beginning in 1835, fugitive slaves traveled to this station and then on to the Jewett Palmer Station in Liberty Township. Located 10 miles north of Marietta along the Muskingum River where the Rainbow Creek flows into the Muskingum was the Rainbow Station. Here Thomas Ridgeway, a staunch abolitionist, helped approximately 100 fugitive slaves escape to freedom. From here, the route divided, one branch running northeast 15 miles to Middleburgh in Noble County, and the other, 15 miles northwest, where it connected with an easterly route to Summerfield.

Another Washington County Underground Railroad station was the Waterford Station, about 12 miles north of Barlow on the Muskingum River. A slave called Micah "Cajoe" Phillips started this station. Among a number of other stations was Vincent in Decatur Township. The Vickers family was active there, receiving fugitive slaves from Belpre and transporting them to the Barlow or Cutler Stations.

From Washington County, fugitive slaves were transported north along the Muskingum River to Zanesville and then on to Cleveland. They might also be transported northwest through Lancaster, reaching Sandusky, Huron, or Lorain as their ports of exit. Other northern routes went northeast through Quaker City, Salem, and to various ports on Lake Erie east of Cleveland.

—Cynthia Vogel

Further Reading

Charles L. Blockson, *Hippocrene Guide to the Underground Railroad* (New York: Hippocrene Books, 1994).

Charles L. Blockson, *The Underground Railroad: Dramatic Firsthand Accounts of Daring Escapes to Freedom* (New York: Berkley Books, 1994).

Minnie Kendall Lowther, *Ritchie County in History and Romance* (Parsons, WV: McClain Printing Company, 1990).

Wilbur H. Siebert, *The Underground Railroad from Slavery to Freedom* (1898; reprint, New York: Arno Press and *The New York Times*, 1968).

Wilbur H. Siebert, *The Mysteries of Ohio's Underground Railroads* (Columbus, OH: Long's College Book Company, 1951).

MAYSVILLE/AUGUSTA, KENTUCKY

Maysville, in Mason County, and Augusta, in Bracken County, were important gateways on the Underground Railroad. Bordering the Ohio River, they included a small number of residents, both black and white, who were sympathetic to slaves and helped them cross the river into freedom. Less than 20 miles apart, these communities were almost equidistant from Ripley, Ohio, the famed Underground Railroad center, located on the other side of the river.

Lexington-Maysville Turnpike

An important development that facilitated fugitive slave traffic through the area was the opening of the Lexington-Maysville Turnpike in 1835, the state's first macadamized highway, a state-of-the-art process at the time with 13 toll booths and 6 covered bridges. It was along this 64-mile stretch of road that Calvin Fairbank and Delia Webster took Lewis Hayden and family from Lexington to eventual freedom in 1844, and led to their publicized imprisonment.

Even before this highway, which made the promise of freedom more accessible for Kentucky slaves, fugitive slave traffic was a problem in Maysville. As early as 1827, an association of slaveholders had formed in the area to undertake measures to stem the number of slaves escaping (*Maysville Eagle*, 11, July 25, 1827). Just 10 miles west across the river was Ripley, Ohio, where Southerners who hated slavery had begun migrating more than 20 years earlier. According to some sources, about 1,000 fugitive slaves had passed through Ripley by 1820.

Thome and Fee

Among the most fervent abolitionists in Kentucky were two men from Bracken County: James Armstrong Thome and John Gregg Fee.

Thome was the son of Arthur and Eliza Thome of Augusta. Arthur was a successful businessman, and Eliza was the sister of one of the founders of Augusta College, the first Methodist college and according to tradition a refuge for fugitive slaves. In an 1839 article published in *The Colored American*, edited in New York by Charles Ray, a slave named Robert claimed that Arthur often aided fugitive slaves, hosting them in the middle of the night and giving them food, money, and clothing.

It's not surprising then that James Thome would become one of Kentucky's most outspoken abolitionists whose public declaration of aid to a fugitive slave forced him to flee to New York. One of the famed Lane Rebels and a close friend of Theodore Weld, Thome matriculated to Oberlin College following the noted Lane debates and became one of Weld's famed original 70 antislavery lecturers for the American Anti-Slavery Society. In 1838, he went on assignment to the West Indies for the Concord, New Hampshire, antislavery newspaper, *Herald of Freedom* to study the results of emancipation in Antigua, Barbados, and Jamaica. This led to the publication of his book, *Emancipation in the West Indies*. The following year, while at Oberlin, Thome revealed that he had aided the escape of a slave of the Chalfont family in Augusta. The story was printed in a college circular and the news quickly traveled to Augusta. Fearing retaliation, he fled to New York.

One of the antebellum era's most courageous preachers came from the Augusta-Maysville area. Rev. John Gregg Fee was born in Bracken County in 1816, the son of a slaveholder and a Quaker mother. His desire to enter the ministry was inspired by a Methodist minister, Joseph Corlis, who, for a time, boarded with the Fees. He graduated from Lane Seminary, where he said his lifelong devotion to the cause of antislavery and civil rights originated. After attempting to convert his father to abolitionism without success, he began his ministry, joining the antislavery New School Presbyterian sect in 1844, after refusing the pastorate of several churches whose offers were contingent on avoiding the issue of slavery. His first congregation was in Lewis County, Kentucky, where he began preaching antislavery but was censured by his synod and assaulted. It would not be the last time he would be assaulted. Many times his life was threatened, one of his churches was burned down, and once he was nearly hung. As he said in his autobiography, "I was . . . shot at, clubbed, stoned; by force kept out of church houses; and . . . been in the hands of six regularly organized mobs of violent men" (Fee 55). It was a miracle he survived to establish Berea College, Kentucky's first school of higher education to admit blacks.

Julett Miles

Among the tragic episodes in his life involved the purchase of Julett Miles, one of his father's slaves. Fee was close to Julett because she cared for him when he was a child, and when his father decided to send her away in 1847, he demanded that he be allowed to purchase her so that she would not be separated from her husband and children. His father finally agreed and Fee borrowed the money from his uncle to complete the transaction. However, the elder Fee wasn't pleased when his son decided to immediately emancipate Julett. He didn't want her on his land and threatened to sell her before his son could complete the necessary emancipation papers. They came to a compromise and the elder Fee agreed to provide a cabin for Julett and her husband, Add, though it was not without consequences for John as his father left him out of his inheritance.

Julett and Add remained in the cabin for seven years before they finally moved to Felicity, Ohio, about 10 miles from Augusta, with their four free children. But Julett still had nine or ten children and grandchildren enslaved on the Fee plantation; four years later, she learned the elder Fee had plans to sell them south. One night, she took a boat across the Ohio River, went to the Fee plantation, and gathered her children and grandchildren. But when they reached the river at Rock Springs, there was no boat waiting. Instead, they were captured by slave patrollers. Julett was taken to jail and her children and grandchildren were sold to a slave trader. John G. Fee, who was on a trip east for the American

Missionary Association, which had been sponsoring his ministry, learned the news while on his way home during a stop in Cincinnati from Levi Coffin.

Shortly after, Julett was tried and convicted of stealing her own children from slavery and sentenced to three years in the state prison, where she died not long after a visit from Fee and his family, never again seeing her children.

Eliza

The Augusta/Maysville area is rich with stories about escapes to freedom. In fact, one of the most famous in the entire lore of the Underground Railroad occurred in Mason County in 1838. A slave owned by John G. Bacon of Dover, made a dash one winter night across the floating ice cakes of the Ohio River with a baby in her arms and a slave patrol with bloodhounds in close pursuit. Not only was she helped by the Rankins in Ripley but was sent north where she also stayed with Levi Coffin when he was still living in Indiana. She was later immortalized as the character, Eliza, in *Uncle Tom's Cabin* by Harriet Beecher Stowe, who was told of her story by John Rankin.

John Price

Another slave also from the Dover plantation of Bacon was John Price, who was the subject of the famed Oberlin-Wellington rescue in 1858 that made national headlines. Price escaped around 1856 and joined a community of fugitive slaves living in Oberlin. His arrest by a federal marshal touched off a near riot in Wellington about 10 miles south of Oberlin, where the marshal had stopped with Price while on their way to Kentucky and where a mob of hundreds of Oberlinites rescued Price.

Abolitionist Sentiment

By 1850, fugitive slave escapes from Kentucky and Maysville, one of the primary gateways, were an everyday occurrence. Citizens in Maysville for instance had become rather apathetic in regards to their support for the institution of slavery. For example, on February 12, 1849, 523 citizens of Maysville met and called for a gradual end to slavery that would culminate in colonization, concluding that "we are utterly opposed to any system which will not result in the final removal of the Black race from Kentucky" ("Emancipation in Indiana," *Indiana Whig*, February 24, 1849). So, while they held racist opinions, they nevertheless believed that slavery was immoral. One assessment of newspaper accounts of the day, which is based only on what was accessible, showed more than 800 escapes reported publicly during the decade from 1850 to 1860 (Purtee 77). Another report from 1852 concluded that of all escapes attempted by fugitive slaves in Kentucky, 95 percent of them met with success, though it should be noted that renditions of slaves who made attempts on their own were not always reported.

A typical example was that of Ed Mofford, the slave of Theodore Hamilton, the brother-in-law of John Fee Gregg's mother-in-law. Hamilton had died and they were going to sell Mofford, who fled to the house of Gregg's mother-in-law, Betsy Hamilton, after learning this. Her husband was away and she hid Mofford in her cellar until she could make arrangements to send him on safely. A boarder, William Lincoln, then conducted him to a rendezvous at the river's edge at night and he was brought across to Ohio and then put on the Underground Railroad.

Slave Stampede

But there were noteworthy successes by proslavery forces. For example, a fugitive slave stampede led by Edward James "Patrick" Doyle, a young Irish immigrant and student at Centre College in Danville in 1848 that began in Lexington and ended in Bracken County, 15 miles from the Ohio River, was prevented by the authorities. The stampede that began with 44 armed fugitive slaves and whose numbers swelled to as many as 100, according to some accounts, led to the arrest of 40 slaves and the hanging of three of them. Doyle was sentenced to the Kentucky penitentiary where he died three years later.

Fairfield

In Augusta, the notorious slave rescuer, John Fairfield, spent time in jail during the early 1850s before somehow escaping or being released. Also in Augusta, a 76-year-old slave known for his herbal cures, Doctor Perkins, was sentenced to prison where he died for aiding fugitive slaves. In all, at least 44 men and women of both races are known to have been convicted and sent to the Kentucky penitentiary for aiding fugitive slaves, eight of them who died there, according to a study of prison records. More recent scholarship has identified 20 free blacks being prosecuted for enticing slaves to escape in Bracken County, and three from Mason County.

Some Reported Escapes

Among newspaper account reporting escapes through Maysville were the following: in December 1855, seven slaves escaped, but their boat capsized, killing three women and a child; in September 1856, eight slaves escaped from plantation of B. Million of Maysville, which led to prosecution of David Waite of Rome, Ohio for harboring them; on September 20, 1857, 17 slaves escaped. In 1858, Horace Washington escaped with his nephews from nearby Washington, Kentucky. He told the story of his escape to Wilbur Siebert in 1895, saying that they were helped across the river by a white Irishman from Maysville who had helped "hundreds" of fugitive slaves.

Although many were apathetic in the Maysville area, there were others who used fugitive slaves for their own profit. For example in the early 1830s, John A. Murrell who claimed to be a man of the cloth enticed slaves to escape so that he could capture them and obtain the rewards offered. Similarly during the 1850s, Ben Ball of Maysville, did the same, but his scheme was finally exposed and he was arrested for it in 1858.

Another of the famous incidents that occurred in Bracken County was the rescue of a slave couple and their baby during the latter days of the antebellum period by the noted slave rescuer from Ripley, John Parker. Modern historians have identified the plantation where the rescue took place as that of S. L. Sroufe, and that the home of his incredible incident still exists. The story was told in detail in Parker's autobiography. He had made arrangements to help a slave couple, but on the night of the intended rescue, their master being suspicious of their intentions, took their baby into his bedroom to discourage their flight. When Parker arrived and learned of this, he stealthily entered the Sroufe house, tiptoed up the stairs to the bedroom and while Sroufe and his wife slept somehow grabbed the baby before Sroufe could awaken and dashed out of the house, running to his waiting boat and passengers while Sroufe fired futile shots at him in the dark.

Arnold Gragston

Another notable slave rescuer in Mason County was Arnold Gragston, a slave on the plantation of Jack Tabb, and who by his own count rowed about 100 slaves across the Ohio River to freedom before finally making his own escape sometime around 1863. His typical run included three or four refugees, and he would meet them in a house or in a field at night. Because he normally did not know his passengers, they had to give him the password "Menare," which he had been told came from the Bible, though he did not know its meaning, which comes from the Italian, to lead someone on a journey. One personal recollection of Mr. Gragston's experience was as follows:

It was in 1863, when one night I carried across about twelve on the same night. Somebody must have seen us, because they set out after me as soon as I stepped out of the boat back on the Kentucky side. From that time on they were after me. Sometimes they would almost catch me. I had to run away from Mr. Tabb's plantation and live in the fields and in the woods. I didn't know what a bed was from one week to another. I would sleep in a cornfield tonight, up in the branches of a tree tomorrow night, and buried in a haypile the next night. The river, where I had carried so many across myself, was no good to me; it was watched too close.

Finally, I saw that I could never do any more good in Mason County, so I decided to take my freedom, too. I had a wife by this time, and one night we quietly slipped across and headed for Mr. Rankins' bell and light. It looked like we had to go almost to China. I didn't stay in Ripley, though. I wasn't taking no

Sroufe house, Bracken County, Kentucky near Augusta, where John Parker rescued a slave baby from the master's bedroom while the master and his wife were sleeping. (Courtesy of Tom Calarco)

chances. I went on to Detroit and still live there with most of my ten children and thirty-one grandchildren. (*Bullwhip Days*, 268–269)

—Sharron L Pope and Tom Calarco

Further Reading

John Gregg Fee, *Autobiography of John G. Fee, Berea, Kentucky* (Chicago: National Christian Association, 1891).

J. M. McElroy to Wilbur Siebert, Ottumwa, IA, September 17, 1896.

James Mellon (ed.), *Bullwhip Days* (New York: Weidenfeld & Nicholson, 1988): 263–269.

Caroline Miller, *Grapevine Dispatch: The Voice of Antislavery Messages* (South Maysville, KY: Bracken County Historical Society, 2009).

James M. Prichard, "Into the Fiery Furnace: Anti-Slavery Prisoners in the Kentucky State Penitentiary 1844–1870," http://www.ket.org/underground/research/prichard.htm.

Edward O. Purtee, "The Underground Railroad in Southwestern Ohio," (Ph.D. diss., Ohio State University, 1932), 47, 75–81, 113, 128, 161–162.

Horace Washington, Interview with Wilbur Siebert, Windsor, Ontario, August 2, 1895.

The Midwest entries covered along with associated locations. (Courtesy of Tom Calarco)

MECHANICSBURG, OHIO

Mechanicsburg in Champaign County, Ohio, was a strategically important stop for fugitive slaves. The inhabitants of Mechanicsburg were well known for their abhorrence of slavery. Fugitive slaves often stayed in Mechanicsburg until safe passage was secured to points in northern Ohio, notably Sandusky and Cleveland, and eventually Canada.

The routes through Mechanicsburg were established in the 1840s, when earlier routes through nearby Springfield and Urbana became well known and were so frequently watched that they had to be abandoned.

Routes to Mechanicsburg

Most of the fugitive slaves that fled through Mechanicsburg crossed the Ohio River near Ripley, Ohio. They went from this station to William Miner's station, six miles north of Ripley. From this station they traveled to a station near Russellville, conducted by a stationkeeper named Patton. There were actually two distinct routes that started in Ripley: one through Hillsboro, Wilmington, and Xenia; and the other through Washington Court House and London, Ohio. Both of these routes eventually merged in Mechanicsburg.

Udney Hyde

Underground Railroad activity in Mechanicsburg became heaviest after 1851 when local farmer Udney Hyde began personally escorting fugitive slaves. Charles P. Morse, then living near Marysville sometimes aided him. From his home, Mr. Morse usually took his cargo immediately to Delaware, Ohio. But in the event that he could not make arrangements for immediate transport, the slaves were hidden in a loft in a barn in back of his house.

On Hyde's first trip in 1851, he transported seven fleeing slaves, four from South Charleston and three from Urbana, by horse and wagon to his cabin near Mechanicsburg where they stayed the night. Over the next six years, he became extremely active, transporting most of his slaves directly to the Alum Creek Quaker Settlement.

Over the years, Hyde aided 517 fugitive slaves by his own count, none of whom were ever recaptured. The largest number he ever carried in one load were 11 men, 11 women, and 2 children. When Mr. Hyde moved from his cabin into Mechanicsburg, he continued his activities in a small frame house on School Street. He concealed the escaping slaves in a cellar, access to which was obtained through a trap door in the bedroom. Here was born the first black child in the town of Mechanicsburg.

While in Mechanicsburg, Hyde sometimes used a large swamp near the town, called Gaddus Lands, as a hiding place for slaves. These wetlands were infested with snakes and other vermin, so it was used during the day. At night the fugitives would hide in the Hyde home, in the old Joiner livery stable, or in a well near Hyde's livery barn next to his home on School Street. The well was six or seven feet in diameter and had a platform built in it.

Addison White

In May 1857, a fugitive slave named Addison White, bearing the surname of his Kentucky master, came to town and began working on Hyde's farm. He had worked about six months, earning money to send for his wife and children. His master tracked him down and obtained a warrant for his arrest at the U.S. Court in Cincinnati. On May 15, three federal marshals and five slavecatchers entered Hyde's home, where White was staying. Guns were fired, apparently from both White, who had fled into the attic, and the slavecatchers. When a crowd of neighbors gathered, the slavecatchers left. Twelve days later, 10 federal marshals returned to learn that White and Hyde had gone into hiding. They arrested several people in the neighborhood on the charge of aiding a fugitive slave and took custody of them to face the charges in Kentucky.

The group traveled through Clark and Greene Counties, and was encountered by abolitionists in Springfield and had the slavecatchers arrested for assault, and they were put into the Springfield jail overnight. The next day, the slavecatchers returned to Cincinnati. During the debate over whether or not the Ohio residents had violated the Fugitive Slave Act, or the marshals were guilty of assaulting the residents, Ohio Governor Salmon P. Chase conferred with President James Buchanan and Secretary of State, General Lewis Cass. The legal haggling over this case took nearly a year. The result was that the U.S. district attorney at Cincinnati was instructed to drop all suits against citizens of the state for aiding a fugitive slave, with the understanding that the charges against the U.S. marshals be dropped.

The Addison White/Udney Hyde incident became a test case against the Fugitive Slave Laws. People who did not realize the horror of the condition of slavery were influenced by the determined "fight" of the fleeing slave and his supporters and rescuers. As a result, Addison White was purchased from his master for $950 by the citizens of Mechanicsburg.

White later served in the Union Army with Company E, 54th Massachusetts Infantry for two years. He then remarried and eventually returned to Mechanicsburg where he continued to live until his death in January 1885.

"Jakie" Ware

Others in Mechanicsburg were active in the Underground Railroad, notably Joseph "Jakie" Ware, who had a basement that was arranged with crevices, hidden rooms, and dungeons, sometimes called the "catacombs," and who got started in the Underground Railroad before Hyde. Like Hyde, Ware concealed his passengers under hay in his wagon. On one trip, in order to avert suspicion, Ware allowed his daughter, Mrs. Anna Sabine, to drive the wagon. One of the places that Ware frequently took fugitives was a farm operated by Pearl Howard, called "Lazy Man's Rest." Here the slaves were kept in a false-walled vault in the cellar, a hiding place at the end of a long tunnel.

Other stations in the area were northeast of the town in Woodstock and North Lewisburg. Operators from this locality were Erastus Martin, Ephraim Cranston, Ott Howard, Johnnie MacDonald, John R. Wilson, and the Winder boys. The Winder brothers, Thomas, Edward, and Joshua owned large farms with large houses that became famous as safe houses. These stations served many fugitives on their route from Mechanicsburg to Alum Creek and places farther north.

Another house in Mechanicsburg that would have been of great interest to the present generation was owned and operated by Levi Rathbun on East Sandusky Street. It was destroyed in the late 1990s. The upper story of this house was a maze of small rooms and closets tucked snugly into suspicious-looking compartments protected by hip roofs, and accessible only by means of small, inconspicuous doors. For over 100 years after the Civil War, it stood as a landmark in the history of Mechanicsburg, a silent reminder of the struggles of men whose convictions were such that danger, time, and money could not defeat them in their struggle to rid their country of a shameful institution.

—Cynthia Vogel

Further Reading

Wilbur H. Siebert, *The Mysteries of Ohio's Underground Railroads* (Columbus, OH: Long's College Book Company, 1951).

Wilbur H. Siebert, *The Underground Railroad from Slavery to Freedom* (1898; reprint, New York: Arno Press and *The New York Times*, 1968).

Ralph M. Watts, *History of the Underground Railroad in Mechanicsburg* (Columbus, OH: The F. J. Heer Printing Co., 1934).

MONTPELIER-BURLINGTON-ST. ALBANS, VERMONT

Vermont was an alternate route of the Underground Railroad. There is some question about how widely traveled it was, but there is no doubt about its widespread antislavery sentiment. The first statewide antislavery organization in the nation was formed in Vermont in 1834. By 1837, more than 4,700 individuals had joined one of the state's 89 antislavery societies, making it fertile ground for the Underground Railroad. In addition, its location bordering Canada and the accessible getaway provided by Lake Champlain along its western border made it a likely destination.

While a study from 1998 could account for only 47 fugitive slaves being assisted in the state, various accounts and reports suggest that 10 times that number likely passed through the state with most of them receiving assistance from the Underground Railroad. Two main trunks made up the Vermont line: one leading up the western part of the state through Burlington, and the other along the eastern border and up the center of the state through Montpelier.

Joseph Poland

According to Joseph Poland of Montpelier, editor of the *Green Mountain Freeman* from 1843 to 1849 and among the state's most active conductors, "Every large town had one or more reliable men to whom the fugitive could be consigned with perfect safety" (Letter to Wilbur Siebert, Montpelier, Vermont, April 7, 1897). He also stated that the greatest traffic through the state occurred from 1840 to 1850, and that hundreds came. The question of when the largest number of fugitive slaves passed through the state is debatable. Another spike of traffic likely occurred during the two or three years following the passage of the second Fugitive Slave Law in September 1850. More than 600 fugitive slaves were estimated to be living in Boston when the law was passed. But after the attempted rendition there of fugitive slave Shadrach Minkins in April 1851, most of them left the city and fled to Canada, according to Lewis Hayden, whose comments were recounted in the memoir, "Cheerful Yesterdays," by Boston Vigilance Committee member, Thomas Wentworth Higginson. One pathway was through Vermont, which Minkins had used as his escape route during his well-publicized flight.

Rowland T. Robinson

Many letters and reports from the period testify to Underground Railroad activities in Vermont. One of the earliest was an 1837 letter from Oliver Johnson, a Vermont native who was on an antislavery lecture tour in Pennsylvania. Johnson's letter was addressed to the Quaker, Rowland T. Robinson, who lived near the hamlet of Ferrisburgh, Vermont, part of the western trunk of the route. He wrote on behalf of a fugitive slave named Simon, who had "intended going to Canada in the spring, but says he would prefer to stay in the U.S. if he could be safe. . . . I could not help thinking he would be a good man for you to hire. . . . he is very trustworthy, of a kind disposition, and knows how to do almost all kinds of farm work" (Oliver Johnson to Rowland T. Robinson, Jenner Township, Somerset County, Pennsylvania, January 27, 1837).

It was not the last such letter that has come down to us from Robinson, who hired fugitive slaves to work on his farm called Rokeby, which was in a remote area and relatively safe from slavecatchers. Another the following year from newspaper editor and politician Chauncey Knapp to Mason Anthony, a Saratoga, New York Quaker, relates that Knapp had successfully rendezvoused at Rokeby with a fugitive slave, whom Anthony had brought there.

> I write to inform you that the lad who is indebted to you and your father's great kindness for a safe arrival at my friend R. T. Robinson's, is now sitting in my office in the State House. . . . Providentially, I arrived at friend Robinson's only an hour after your departure; and on Saturday last took the lad (now Charles) and brought him on to Montpelier, a distance of 43 miles. By my friend Robinson's earnest request I have assumed the office of guardian to Charles. Having no family myself, I have found a home for him for the present in an excellent family a mile from this village, when, I doubt not, he will be received as becometh abolitionists. (Letter from C. L. Knapp to Mason Anthony, Montpelier, August 20, 1838)

Vermont Network

Another Quaker, Samuel Keese, who lived in Peru, New York, near the western shore of Lake Champlain across from Vermont, is mentioned in a diary as possibly receiving fugitive slaves from the Robinson connection. And in an 1887 interview during which he gave an account of his own activities aiding fugitive slaves, Keese's nephew, Stephen Keese Smith, also from Peru, said that Robinson aided "scores."

Two letters from members of the Eastern New York Anti-Slavery Society document traffic using this western trunk during this earlier period. In a letter dated November 24, 1840 that accompanied two fugitive slaves being sent to Charles Hicks of Bennington County, Vermont, Troy conductor Rev. Fayette Shipherd wrote: "As the canal [the Champlain the canal that connected Troy with Lake Champlain] has closed I shall send my Southern friends along your road & patronize your house. We had a fine run of business during the season. . . . We had 22 in two weeks 13 in the city at one time."

Another letter dated June 9, 1842, accompanied a fugitive slave sent by Albany conductor, Rev. Abel Brown to Hicks. It said in part, "Please receive the Bearer as a friend who needs your aid and direct him on his way if you cannot give him work he come to us well recommended was a slave a few weeks since."

This western line that started at Bennington traversed north through to Manchester, Wallingford, Castleton, Fair Haven. Some of the operators along this route were Daniel Roberts in Manchester, D. E. Nicholson in Wallingford, Erastus and Harley Higley in Castleton, and Zena C. Ellis in Fair Haven, who sent fugitive slaves from Whitehall at the inlet to Lake Champlain in a canal boat with barges to bring back lumber from Canada. A significant number of fugitive slaves also were forwarded along this line through Brandon, the home of Rodney Marsh and Orson Murray, on the way to Burlington.

Montpelier, in the center of the state and its capital, was one of its Underground Railroad hubs. It received fugitive slaves from both the western and eastern routes. In addition to Poland, the editor of the *Green Mountain Freeman*, and Knapp, a powerbroker in Vermont state politics and the editor of the *State Journal*, Montpelier boasted another important figure in the Vermont Underground Railroad in Colonel Jonathan Miller. A state legislator for three years and a freedom fighter in Greece, Miller had arranged for local stagecoaches to pick up any suspected fugitive slaves along the road and bring them to his house. Poland also harbored fugitive slaves at his newspaper office.

Fugitive slaves traveling the state's eastern trunk that hugged the New Hampshire border, came either from Rhode Island and eastern Massachusetts, or up from Connecticut along the Connecticut River.

Accounts from letters, diaries, and genealogies suggest a fair number of fugitive slaves passing through the vicinity of Norwich, Vermont, and Lyme, New Hampshire, on the way to Montpelier. One genealogy from the family of Stephen Carver Boardman of Norwich claims that Boardman aided 600 fugitive slaves, an impressive but rather high number based on what we know at this point. The genealogy also includes a story told by Boardman's son Charles about a fugitive slave couple with a small child who came with slavecatchers and bloodhounds in hot pursuit. The Boardmans moistened the fugitives' feet with spirits of camphor to throw the dogs off their scent, and then hid them in a location beneath the ground in the middle of their cornfield. Boardman demanded a warrant from the slavecatchers. While they went to retrieve it, Charles, then 13, led the fugitive slaves through the fields about a mile or so, where they later rendezvoused with his father. He took them in a wagon to a location where they boarded a Central Vermont Railroad freight train for Canada.

Those who came up from Connecticut traversed a route that took them through Brattleboro and northward to Townshend, Chester, Windsor, Woodstock, and Montpelier. Fugitive slaves were aided by Willard Frost in Brattleboro, W. R. and Oscar Shafter in Townshend, and Oscamel Hutchinson in Chester.

From Montpelier, fugitive slaves could go to Burlington, St. Albans, and Hardwick. One metaphorical description of fugitive slave traffic comes from a letter written by Rev. Kiah Bailey of Hardwick to the Emancipator in 1843: "I have seen in the Emancipator an account of a Bale of Cotton moving off from New Haven. . . . This Bale, after moving from place to place for about three weeks, rolled into my house last evening, and this morning started for the dominion of Victoria, where it is now safely stowed away."

Bigelow, Young and Converse

Burlington was possibly the most frequently traveled destination of fugitive slaves in the state. It bordered Lake Champlain and provided easy access by boat to Canada and had a fairly large number of persons ready to assist fugitive slaves. The most active conductor there was Lucius Bigelow. Described by collaborators as a man of means, he lived in a large, three-story stone colonial

Rev. Joshua Young house, Burlington, Vermont; home of an active conductor who also performed the services for John Brown's funeral in North Elba. (Courtesy of Tom Calarco)

house. Fugitive slaves generally came to his residence at night, and he would harbor, feed, and clothe them. Rev. Joshua Young, a Boston minister, who aided fugitive slaves there, said in an 1852 letter to Wilbur Siebert that he collaborated with Bigelow after moving to Burlington. For a brief period, he wrote Siebert, fugitive slaves arrived daily in Burlington. Along with Simon Wires, they would forward them by boat or train to Montreal. However, as time went on, Bigelow was put under close scrutiny, and he and Wires were forced to drive fugitive slaves by carriage to St. Albans, about 20 miles to the north.

Another active conductor in Burlington area was the Rev. John Converse, pastor of the First Congregational "White" Church from 1832 to 1846. In 1834 he helped establish the Burlington Female Seminary for which he became principal, a position he held for many years. He also was secretary of the state chapter of the American Colonization Society for 43 years, and pastor of the Colchester Congregational Church from 1850 to 1855. Multiple sources said he aided fugitive slaves and, according to one widely believed story, there was a tunnel that led from Converse's residence to the seminary where he sometimes hid them.

Lawrence Brainerd

In St. Albans lived Lawrence Brainerd, probably the most prominent individual involved in the Underground Railroad in Vermont. He began coordinating the movement of fugitive slaves there before 1840. An entrepreneur, he operated a boat line along Lake Champlain and played a leadership role in the establishment of the Vermont and Canada Railroad, which was completed in 1851. Heavily involved in state politics, he was elected to the state assembly in 1834 and later to the U.S. Senate in 1854. He both harbored fugitive slaves and personally forwarded them, either in his own carriage to Missisquoi Bay, 18 miles north, or by boat to St. Johns, Quebec. A fugitive slave from Richmond, Virginia, Jeremiah Boggs, was sent to Vermont in 1843 by the Eastern New York Anti-Slavery Society and remained to work for Brainerd. But after a year, he was discovered by a man who knew his owner, forcing Boggs to flee and go to Liberia under the sponsorship of the Colonization Society.

Considering that there were only about 700 free blacks in the state out of a total population of more than 300,000 during the period from 1840 to 1860, only a handful of blacks participated in the Underground Railroad here. Among them were William Davis, a barber in St. Albans; Tony Anthony, a cook who worked in the Burlington hotels and on the steamboats; as well as the famed abductee, Solomon Northup, and Taylor Groce, a fugitive slave. The latter two men were alleged to have assisted "Lame" John Smith, a Methodist minister, who lived in Hartland in the western part of Vermont. Before assisting Smith, it was said that Groce had rescued two members of his family from the South.

Lawrence Brainerd house, St. Albans, Vermont; home of a U.S. senator who was one of Vermont's most active conductors. (Courtesy of Tom Calarco)

Question about Slavecatchers

Some contemporary historians contend that once a fugitive slave reached Vermont, there was no danger of recapture because slavecatchers never came to the state. They point to the relative safety in which fugitive slaves who came to Rokeby were able to work on the Robinson farm. However, they fail to explain why, if there were no threats from slavecatchers, Samuel Barker was appointed to be a lookout for slavecatchers, as reported by Robinson's son. Also, numerous stories have come down regarding attempts to recapture slaves, one even from the Robinson family, which was described in a letter by Rowland T. Robinson's grandson to Wilbur Siebert in 1935. Others already cited come from Lawrence Brainerd and Stephen Boardman. Another is described in the following account from Lucius Bigelow.

A fugitive slave had settled in Burlington with his wife and children. He had a job as a waiter at the Lake House, a hotel near the city's railroad station. One day when he went into the dining room, he saw his master seated at a table. He immediately left the hotel and went to Bigelow who drove the man out of town and then put him on a train to Canada. After this, Bigelow brought the man's family to his home

Letter from Rev. Joshua Young, Re: Burlington, Vermont

Rev. Joshua Young, a New England Congregational minister, became notorious in some circles when he officiated at the funeral services for John Brown in North Elba, New York. Because of this, he was dismissed from his position as pastor of his church in Burlington, Vermont. Previous to this, Young had regularly been aiding fugitive slaves on their flight to Canada, whose border was only 40 miles to the north of Burlington. On April 21, 1893, he revealed his participation in a letter to Wilbur Siebert (Wilbur H. Siebert Collection, Ohio Historical Society).

About ten years before the breaking of the Civil War I was pastor of the Unitarian church in Burlington, Vermont which may be called one of the termini of the U.G.R.R. as that city then town is only about fifty to sixty miles from the Canada Line. During my residence there together with my friend and parishioner L. G. Bigelow, a noble man now gone to heaven for he loved his fellow man; did considerable business. How many tales of cruelty I listened to, how many backs scared by the slave driver's lash and some not healed, I looked upon, how many poor scared creatures I secreted in cellars or garrets until the danger was past I cannot tell, only this I did again and again, both while living in Boston and in Burlington, until with all the rest of the employers of the road I was dismissed by the guns of Fort Sumter which I may say I heard standing in a telegraph office.

while he arranged to have them join him in Montreal. Following this, Bigelow conducted the sale of his house and property, sending the man the proceeds.

That fugitive slaves were threatened, even in Vermont, is not surprising. The passage of the second Fugitive Slave Law in 1850 brought a surge of slaveholders to the North, emboldened by the favorable provisions of the new law. An account that appeared in the August 8, 1857 issue of the *National Anti-Slavery Standard* reported that Charlotte, a fugitive slave from Baltimore, was pursued to Maine by slave-catchers before finally eluding them and making her escape through St. Albans.

—Tom Calarco

Further Reading

Tom Calarco, *The Underground Railroad in the Adirondack Region* (Jefferson, NC: McFarland and Company, 2004).

Wilbur H. Siebert Collection, Correspondence dating from 1892 to 1951, and miscellaneous selections dating from 1840 to 1954, Columbus, OH: Ohio Historical Center.

Wilbur H. Siebert, *Vermont's Anti-Slavery and Underground Railroad Record* (1937; reprint, New York: Negro Universities Press, 1969).

Raymond Paul Zirblis, "Friends of Freedom" (Vermont Division of Historic Preservation: Montpelier, 1996).

MONTREAL, CANADA

By the mid-1850s, Montreal was the most important Underground Railroad terminal in Canada East. New York City and Boston were the primary centers of Underground Railroad activity in the Eastern United States, and they were linked to Montreal by an extensive transportation network. The Champlain

Line was the principle Underground Railroad passageway to Montreal. It was the last link in a system of waterways that began at the mouth of the Hudson River in New York City, proceeded north to Albany and Troy, and terminated at the northern end of Lake Champlain at Rouses Point, a lakeside village strategically located one mile south of the international border. Fugitives were forwarded to Rouses Point from Troy. They were sent across Lake Champlain from Burlington and St. Albans, Vermont. Some had come from Massachusetts on the "Vermont Road."

Routes to Montreal

At Rouses Point, fugitives could board westward bound trains for Ogdensburg where steamboats took them to the Canadian side of the St. Lawrence River or up river. Runaways could also board trains at Rouses Point for Montreal. Others arrived in Montreal on the Boston-Portland Railroad, which connected Canada East to Vermont, New Hampshire, Maine, and Massachusetts.

Although most of the fugitives who went to Canada settled in refugee communities in Canada West (in present day Ontario between Windsor and Toronto), members of Montreal's small and closely knit refugee community were frequently in the news, especially after Congress passed the controversial Fugitive Slave Bill of 1850. A woman who was the daughter of her Maryland master escaped to Montreal by way of Massachusetts and the Portland railroad in the summer of 1850. In Saratoga Springs in the fall of 1851, slave catchers pursued Lucretia Van Pelt who had escaped from her Georgia master in 1846 while he was visiting New York. Mrs. Van Pelt gave birth to a son in Montreal in 1852, but by 1855, her husband, John, had taken the family back to New York. Shadrach Minkins fled through Vermont to Montreal in the winter of 1851 after a group of black men led by fugitive slave Lewis Hayden rescued him from the Boston Court House. Before Clarence F. Sheldon went to Montreal, he spoke on the subject of liberty at an 1857 meeting in Troy. Edwin Moore escaped from his Virginia master in 1843 and settled with his wife and three children in Manchester, New Hampshire, where he made a good living as a barber until he was tracked down by slavecatchers in the summer of 1854. Moore fled to Montreal and took up his trade on St. James Street. In 1855, the *Montreal Gazette* published a letter that "police officer and constable" John H. Pope of Frederick, Maryland, had sent to the city's Chief of Police. Pope offered "large rewards" to "an efficient person" who would capture fugitive slaves and return them to the United States. In the winter of 1861, Lavinia Bell escaped to Montreal from Texas. Several newspapers published an account of her life and a doctor's description of the horrible wounds and scars that her brutal master had inflicted on her body.

Such stories secured Montreal's reputation as the most important terminal station on the Underground Railroad in Canada East. The city's legacy has been proudly preserved by Larry Hall, a great-great grandson of Charles

Williams who escaped to Montreal from Boston in 1851, and by Bud Jones, who loves to share the story of how his great-great grandfather's brother, George Edward Jones, took Lavinia Bell from Rouses Point on a train bound for Montreal.

Number of Fugitive Slaves

How many fugitive slaves actually fled to Montreal is difficult to determine. According to the 1861 census, there were 228 blacks living there. Gary Collison, who did extensive research on the black population in Montreal of this period for his book on Shadrach Minkins, believed the figure was closer to 400 as estimated by the *Montreal Gazette* at that time. In addition, Collison's research found that most of those who admitted U.S. ancestry were born in Southern states, an indication that most were likely fugitive slaves.

—Don Papson

Further Reading

"A Fugitive Slave," *National Anti-Slavery Standard*, August 30, 1850.
"Another Fugitive Slave Case," *Glens Falls Free Press*, September 17, 1851.
Gary L. Collison, *Shadrach Minkins: From Fugitive Slave to Citizen* (Boston: Harvard University Press, 1977).
"Fugitive Slaves in Canada," *National Anti-Slavery Standard*, January 20, 1855.
"Mr. Pope, The Slave-Catcher," *National Anti-Slavery Standard*, February 10, 1855.
"Narrative of the Escape of a Poor Negro Woman from Slavery," *Montreal Gazette*, January 30, 1861.
"Rev. and Dear Sir . . .," *The Colored American*, October 21, 1837.
"Safe from the Bloodhounds," *The Liberator*, July 7, 1854.

MONTROSE, PENNSYLVANIA

Located in Susquehanna County in northeastern Pennsylvania, Montrose is just 12 miles south of the New York border. Fugitive slaves passed through Montrose heading north from various Underground Railroad sites in New Jersey, Delaware, and southeastern Pennsylvania. The location of Susquehanna County and surrounding counties on a network of rivers, canals, Indian paths, and railroads provided fugitive slaves easier access to travel north and freedom.

Routes to Montrose

An important route leading to Montrose originated in the towns of Quakertown, about 35 miles north of Philadelphia, and Bethlehem, about 12 miles farther north, just east of Allentown, following the Lehigh River to Palmertown.

Continuing to follow the Lehigh River northward, fugitive slaves could use the Lehigh Indian Path, which would take them directly into Wilkes-Barre. From Wilkes-Barre, conductors such as William Gildersleeve, Charles Bailey, Leonard Batchelor, and John Fell guided them northward to Waverly, Montrose, Towanda, and Friendsville, and eventually into upstate New York, where they often head straight to the Lake Ontario port of Oswego, New York.

Another major escape route for the fugitives began in Stroudsburg, about 30 miles northeast of Bethlehem, and zigzagged its way northeastward to Dunmore and Waverly and then following the shores of the Susquehanna River to Towanda and into New York.

These escape routes were close to the railroads and canals of the Lehigh Coal and Navigation Company, and the Delaware and Hudson Railroad, which passed through Carbon, Luzerne, Susquehanna, Wayne, and Wyoming counties. The fugitives could also use these canals and railroads as an avenue through which to escape.

Composition of Underground Railroad

In northeastern Pennsylvania, the African Methodist Episcopal (AME) Church was the center of the Underground Railroad. Quakers, while not predominant in the northeastern counties as in southeastern Pennsylvania, did settle in Monroe and Susquehanna counties, so they likely helped build the Underground Railroad here as well. Abolitionists in the area also came from the Presbyterian, Baptist, Universalist, Methodist, and Moravian churches. Although religious conviction strongly motivated many individuals to help former slaves achieve their freedom, the various denominations varied as to how this should be accomplished. All believed that slavery should be abolished, but not all participated in the Underground Railroad.

Albert L. Post, Horace Brewster, Samuel Bard, Isaac Post, Ben R. Lyon, and William J. Turrell ran the Underground Railroad stations in Montrose. A colony of black farmers, established by Dr. Robert Rose in 1836, was located in Silver Lake Township between Montrose and the New York border. William Smith, a black man who escaped from slavery, stayed in Montrose, where he built a home. Others followed Smith and built their own homes.

Local Agents

Albert L. Post, born in Montrose in 1809, was well educated and studied law. In June 1836, he established the *Spectator and Freeman's Journal* in Montrose. The *Spectator* was a Whig paper devoted to free speech and the freedom of blacks, and became the press for abolitionists.

Post's co-editor, Oliver N. Wordon, was the son of the Montrose Baptist Church minister. Both Post and Wordon supported the Republican Party and antislavery efforts. Post and his family worked with a black conductor, named

David Nelson, in relocating three fugitives, John Booey, Charles Hammond, and William Smith to nearby communities.

Nearby, in the borough of Friendsville, Caleb Carmalt sent fugitives directly into New York from his home. Carmalt was a Quaker who had moved from Philadelphia to Friendsville, located in the northwest corner of Susquehanna County. Friendsville was named for the colony of Quakers who settled there.

In 1816, Dr. Robert Rose, a philanthropist and owner of 100,000 acres in the Silver Lake area, built the Silver Lake Bank, the first bank in Susquehanna County. In 1829 the bank closed and for a time housed the Presbyterian Church. In 1840, Montrose merchant and abolitionist Frances Blake Chandler purchased the former bank, and from 1840 to 1865 was involved in the Underground Railroad. The building still stands and is one of Montrose's oldest buildings.

Another route through northeast Pennsylvania came north from Reading. Fugitive slaves could continue north to Pottsville, then Shenandoah, and then on to Wilkes-Barre where some would meet with Reverend William C. Gildersleeve, a Presbyterian stationmaster who was an active member of the Pennsylvania Anti-Slavery Society. Reverend Gildersleeve, one of the region's most radical abolitionists, sheltered fugitives in his home and store located near Ross Street in Wilkes-Barre. Two of his employees, Lucy Washburn, a maid, and Jacob Welcome, a laborer, conducted fugitives between his home and other stations in the area. Because his abolitionist views were unpopular in the area, Gildersleeve often faced threats to his safety. Nevertheless, he transported fugitives from the Wilkes-Barre area to Montrose. When they reached Montrose they were assisted by Benjamin R. Lyon, who brought them to David or Isaac Post, two brothers who were sympathetic to fugitive slaves, allowing them to live and work on their land in Montrose.

Influence of Free Blacks

A factor that makes northeastern Pennsylvania unique in its Underground Railroad history is that during the time when most fugitive slaves were escaping to Canada, many free blacks already lived in this area. About 4,000 Africans who were made slaves in Pennsylvania had arrived by 1730. Pennsylvania's Gradual Abolition Act of 1780, the first of its kind in the United States, emancipated many of them. The Act required all slaveholders in the state to register their slaves and provide for the emancipation of those born after March 1, 1780, when they reached 28 years of age. Because of this act, Pennsylvania became a primary destination for fugitives from Delaware, Maryland, and Virginia.

In Bradford County, just west of Susquehanna County, was the town of Towanda. Free blacks Henry Butler, Douglas Wilson, John Carter, Sam Berry, Soloman Cooper, and Abner McCloe lived in Towanda and helped hide and transport fugitive slaves through the area. In Wilkes-Barre, Luzerne County, were hotels, farms, and a new anthracite industry that provided employment to fugitive slaves James Phillips, William Thomas, and Lewis Tucker. They were invited to worship at the Bethel AME and Zion African Methodist churches located in the town. In Waverly, located in Lackawanna County, members of the AME Church helped fugitives George Keyes and Lot Norris settle in the community of free blacks living along Carbondale Road. Norris's master followed him there, intending to take him back to the South. However, church members and neighbors with pitchforks convinced the slaveholder to return home without him.

Free black communities in Susquehanna County also welcomed fugitive slaves. In 1792, Brooklyn Township was home to Printz Perkins, a former Connecticut slave. By 1811, a small free black community had been established. Perkins' descendants, as well as those of the Dennis family, another founding family from Connecticut, welcomed other fugitives to this region. Because of its well-known resistance to slavery and its close proximity to the colony of black farmers at Silver Lake Township, Montrose became an active station on the Underground Railroad and was home to fugitives such as William Smith, who became a preacher at the Berry Street A. M. E. Zion Church, and Edward and Lewis Williams.

Northeast Pennsylvania served as a passageway to freedom in Canada, but it was also where former slaves settled permanently and successfully took up jobs in farming and a variety of businesses, including the anthracite and lumber industries.

Both whites and free blacks were active in the abolition movement in this area, regularly working together, and they came from a variety of religious backgrounds. Blacks, however, were often more aggressive in providing safe houses and transportation for the fugitive slaves, especially after 1850. Both helped former slaves find jobs that enabled many of them to settle there.

—Cynthia Vogel

Further Reading

Charles Blockson, *The Underground Railroad in Pennsylvania* (Jacksonville, NC: Flame International, 1981).

Edward H. Magill, "When Men Were Sold, Reminiscences of the Underground Railroad in Bucks County and Its Managers," *A Collection of Papers Read before the Bucks County Historical Society*, 1909.

Matthew Pinsker, *Vigilance in Pennsylvania: Underground Railroad Activities in the Keystone State 1837–1861* (PHMC, Division of History, 2000).

Wilbur H. Siebert, *The Underground Railroad from Slavery to Freedom* (1898; reprint, New York: Arno Press and *The New York Times*, 1968).

Rhamanthus M. Stocker, *Centennial History of Susquehanna County* (Philadelphia: R.T. Peck, 1887).

William J. Switala, *Underground Railroad in Pennsylvania* (Mechanicsburg, PA: Stackpole Books, 2001).

MOUNT PLEASANT, OHIO

Mount Pleasant, Ohio, was not only a frequent stop along the Underground Railroad but an influential center of abolitionism. The first newspaper advocating immediate emancipation, *The Philanthropist*, was published there in 1817 by Charles Osborn, and it also was an early residence of Benjamin Lundy, perhaps the most influential antislavery advocate prior to 1830.

Geographic Location

A small village in southeastern Ohio, its abolitionist sentiments and its location less than 10 miles from the Ohio River made it a destination for fugitive slaves. Most runaways who came here crossed the river at Wheeling, Virginia (today West Virginia), but they also came from the Licking River (near Cincinnati), the Muskingum River (near Marietta), or other ports along the river like Portsmouth, fleeing from Kentucky. Aid also was provided to them in Steubenville, 20 miles north. From Mount Pleasant, the 100-mile route to Lake Erie ports like Cleveland or Ashtabula and boats that transported them to Canada also led through stops like Salem and numerous other locations with safe houses and conductors.

Quaker Roots

Mount Pleasant was founded in 1803 by Quakers, who were part of the great migration of Friends from North Carolina to the Northwest Territory that began in 1800 and lasted into the mid-1820s. As many as 8,000 Quakers migrated to Ohio, Indiana, and Illinois during that period after a law was passed in North Carolina stipulating that any slaves who were freed could immediately be re-enslaved. After the Revolution, Quaker meetings nationwide had proscribed the ownership of slaves. To circumvent the law in North Carolina, Quakers had been sending their freed slaves north of the Mason-Dixon Line or put them into the custody of their Yearly Meeting, which supervised their emancipation and relocation. But the hostility they faced and their aversion to slavery caused them to seek new homes.

"Jesse-Bob Town" was what they called Mount Pleasant during its early years, taking its name after Robert Carothers and Jesse Thomas, the men who laid out the village. By 1814 there were a reported 1,693 Quaker families in Ohio, and Mount Pleasant was chosen to be the site of the Ohio Yearly Meeting's first annual convention. A large plain two-story brick building with an A-frame roof that accommodated 2,000 people was built and it remains today as the village's most significant historic building.

Osborn and Lundy

The first annual convention of the Ohio Yearly Meeting in 1815 was a festive affair. The featured speaker was Osborn, a Quaker from Tennessee, who the previous year had formed the nation's first society calling for the immediate end to slavery.

Also in attendance was a young man whose name would become synonymous with the antislavery movement, Benjamin Lundy. He had moved to Mount Pleasant in 1811, got a job working as a saddle maker for Jesse Thomas, and had recently married a girl from nearby Short Creek. Originally from New Jersey, Lundy had moved to Wheeling, West Virginia, just across the Ohio River, less than 10 miles from Mount Pleasant where he learned his trade. It was in Wheeling, which lay between the slave-breeding centers of Maryland and Virginia, and the new developing plantations in need of slaves in Kentucky and Missouri, where he saw the chain gangs, called coffles with as many as 100 slaves shackled to each other on their way to their new masters. It moved Lundy to write in his diary that his "heart was deeply grieved at the gross abomination; I heard the wail of the captive; I felt his pang of distress, and the iron entered my soul" (Wilson, Henry, *History of the Rise and Fall of the Slave Power in America*, Boston: James R. Osgood And Company, 1873: 167).

Circumstances soon drove Lundy into a lifelong mission to end slavery.

It was the strong antislavery sentiment in the region that persuaded Osborn to move to Mount Pleasant and publish *The Philanthropist*. Lundy, who had moved to nearby St. Clairsville, had formed an antislavery society and had written a circular expressing his opposition to slavery. Enthusiastic about the paper, he began submitting articles under the name, "Philo Justitia." Osborn sold *The Philanthropist* in 1819, and in 1821 Lundy moved back to Mount Pleasant and began publishing his own antislavery paper, *The Genius of Emancipation*. The house where Lundy lived during his second residence in Mount Pleasant remains today and is a National Historic Landmark and on the National Register of Historic Places.

Lundy lived in Mount Pleasant for only about another year before moving to Tennessee and beginning his one-man crusade to end slavery. He died in 1839 in Illinois, never seeing the fruits of his efforts.

Local Agents

Mount Pleasant is believed to have begun aiding fugitive slaves around the time of the War of 1812. It was during the war when slaves serving the American army became aware of the freedom that awaited them in Ohio and other places north of the Mason-Dixon Line. On occasion, it is said that David and Benjamin Stanton, members of one of Mount Pleasant's earliest pioneer families, visited the marketplace in Wheeling and took fugitive slaves to Ohio, concealed in their wagons, by way of Martins Ferry. With the antislavery publications coming out of Mount Pleasant, word spread that the village was a haven for fugitive slaves. Michigan Underground Railroad conductor, Nathan Thomas, who claimed to have aided about 1,000 fugitive slaves, grew up in Mount Pleasant and left during the 1820s. He wrote in his autobiography that "many a panting fugitive from slavery" passed through the village. Thomas described two specific incidents: one in which a fugitive slave was rescued by a former slave who lived in Mount Pleasant, and another incident in which a fugitive slave who had been settled in Mount Pleasant for three years was apprehended by his former master but managed to escape and was forwarded to a place of safety in northern Ohio.

Adding circumstantial evidence to the claims of Underground Railroad activity was the substantial number of free blacks in the area. In close proximity were at least two black settlements, one of about 40 families, who mainly comprised the slaves of Virginian Thomas Beaufort, who were manumitted in 1825 and provided with a 200-acre tract near Smithfield, which was known as the McIntyre settlement. Another small settlement called New Trenton was located just south about a mile west of Short Creek. And one of the village's earliest settlers, Abigail Stanton, the grandmother of Edwin Stanton, Lincoln's secretary of war, came from Virginia specifically to free her husband's slaves as instructed in his will. She provided the slaves with plots in the village. In fact, by 1860, nearly 15 percent of the town's population was black, a significantly higher percentage than most towns in Ohio. Black settlements are known to have been magnets for fugitive slaves.

Among others who were active in the area's Underground Railroad in Mount Pleasant was Borden Stanton, who built the Hanes Mill outside the village along the Colerain Pike in 1801. According to tradition, a tunnel under the mill was used to hide fugitive slaves. Two Presbyterian ministers, Reverend Benjamin Mitchell, Presbyterian, and Reverend John Walker, of the Seceder sect, some of whom settled in Mount Pleasant, also were prominent in helping fugitive slaves. Among homes in Mount Pleasant that served as hiding places that remain today as private residences was the home of George Jenkins on Quaker Hill; the Jonathan Binns house located on the highest spot in the entire county, where fugitive slaves were hidden in a captain's walk that had a lantern lit that could be seen from the Ohio River, five miles away; the John Hogg mansion, a large opulent structure built in 1813 that had a passage from a well that led to vats for tanning hides where fugitive slaves were hidden; the David Updegraff house, which also had a captain's walk that was used as a lookout place for fugitive slaves; the home of the aforementioned Benjamin Stanton; and the homes of George and Samaria Clark and William and Jane Robinson in nearby Emerson about mile to the west of the village, the latter of which had a spacious tunnel leading from its basement that some claim was used to hide fugitive slaves.

A significant antislavery development in Mount Pleasant was the establishment in 1848 of a free labor store, which did not sell goods produced with slave labor. Their merchandise ranged from groceries to dry goods. Rice, for example, was made by Quakers, and cotton was made by German immigrants, but nothing in the store was produced, manufactured, or transported with the toil of slaves. Similar stores were established in other places in the North, most of them operated by Quakers. In 1857 the stockholders voted to dissolve the company. The closing of the Free Produce Company after nine years was not caused by any lessening of antislavery sentiment in Mount Pleasant. The activities of the

Underground Railroad would continue until the Emancipation Proclamation in 1863.

Further testimony to the area's high level of fugitive slave traffic comes from a report by the noted New York Underground Railroad conductor, Charles Ray, who made a trip in 1839 along the Ohio River in behalf of his newspaper, *The Colored American.*

> At five o'clock this day, we arrived at Wheeling in Virginia. . . . I saw a number of colored men whose appearance did not indicate them to be slaves. . . . After tea, I walked up into, and about the City in company with an Abolitionist, and an English gentleman. We called into a barber shop. . . . we began by asking him how many slaves there were in the place, when to our surprise we were informed, that there were not to his knowledge, 20 in the City, in a population of 12,000 people. This place has become nearly free by voluntary elopement. . . . as soon as they are sufficiently old, to be of any service to their masters . . . they are off to provide for themselves. . . . The best of all was that none have recently been overtaken who have exercised this inalienable right. Our informant told us, he had known slaves to be missing, and in fifteen minutes a strict search set on foot, to no possible purpose, and they never heard of unless by intelligence from Canada. ("A Trip Down the Ohio River," *The Colored American*, September 28, 1839)

—Cynthia Vogel and Tom Calarco

The Peripatetic Abolitionist

Born in New Jersey to Quaker parents in 1789, Benjamin Lundy moved to Wheeling, Virginia, at the age of 19. The sight of a coffle gang there inspired his crusade against slavery.

Lundy was always on the move: from Wheeling to Mount Pleasant, Ohio, then to St. Clairsville, Ohio, and Jonesborough, Tennessee. He traveled twice to St. Louis from 1819 to 1821, becoming engrossed in the debate over slavery in Missouri. After returning to Ohio on foot, more than 500 miles, he published *The Genius of Universal Emancipation*. He produced eight issues, walking 20 miles each way to have it printed.

He moved to Baltimore in 1824 and by 1826 had helped organize 81 antislavery societies, 73 in slaveholding states. He also traveled outside the United States to colonize emancipated slaves, first in Haiti, and later Mexico and Canada. On his return from Haiti, he found his wife had died, so he sent his five children to live with friends. By 1830, he had traveled 25,000 miles, 5,000 on foot, promoting abolition.

In 1828, he met William Lloyd Garrison at a boarding house in Boston. Later, he walked 600 miles to ask Garrison to join him at *The Genius*. Their partnership was short-lived but it inspired Garrison to launch *The Liberator* in 1831.

Lundy carried a trunk in which he kept his printing tools and issued *The Genius* wherever his travels took him. In 1836, he founded the *National Enquirer and Constitutional Advocate of Universal Liberty*, later the *Pennsylvania Freeman*, in Philadelphia. After two years he turned it over to John Greenleaf Whittier and stored his possessions in the newly built Pennsylvania Hall. The great fire that destroyed the building also destroyed them.

He reunited with his children in Illinois, where he died in 1839 after printing the last issues of *The Genius*.

Further Reading

Donald E. Bensch and James L. Burke, "Mount Pleasant and the Early Quakers of Ohio," *Ohio History*, 83, 1974: 220–255.

Thomas Earle and Benjamin Lundy, *The Life, Travels and Opinions of Benjamin Lundy*, (Philadelphia: James Parrish, 1847).

Wilbur H. Siebert, *The Underground Railroad from Slavery to Freedom* (1989; reprint, New York: Arno Press, 1968).

Wilbur H. Siebert, *The Mysteries of Ohio's Underground Railroads* (Columbus, OH: Long's College Book Company, 1951).

N

NEW ALBANY, INDIANA

New Albany in Floyd County, which borders the Ohio River, became an important destination for fugitive slaves not only because of its location but also because of the New Albany-Salem Railroad, whose proprietors were abolitionists and which as early as 1853 extended all the way to Lake Michigan.

New Albany was founded in 1813 when the Scribner brothers from Albany, New York—Joel, Abner, and Nathaniel—moved to the area and named it after their hometown. It was incorporated as a town in 1817 as a part of Clark County; in 1819, after Indiana was admitted as a state, New Albany became the seat of government for Floyd County.

Major Entry Point

Numerous fugitive slaves attempted to flee through Floyd County and its approximately 13 miles of riverfront, and it became a major entry point for the state's central Underground Railroad that led through the counties of Harrison, Crawford, Floyd, and Clark. Playing a significant role in New Albany's Underground Railroad were free blacks whose work took them back and forth between Kentucky and Indiana. In tandem with them were evangelical white Christians who made up the former Second Presbyterian Church and those in charge of the Presbyterian Theological Seminary, as well as German immigrants, who lived near the predominantly black West Union section of New Albany.

Early Account

An account that has come down from as early as 1822 suggests that aid to fugitives had already been commonplace in New Albany. One of the best documented reports dates from 1839. Rev. Jacob Cummings, interviewed by Wilbur Siebert, related his escape from Chattanooga, Tennessee, that year to

Former Second Presbyterian Church, New Albany, Indiana. (Courtesy of Tom Calarco)

New Albany where he met three black abolitionists, Uncle Charley Lacey, William Finney, and Uncle Zeke Goins. They gave him work and then sent him to Charleston in southeastern Clark County where he was arrested. But he was released by the judge and then put on the Underground Railroad, which forwarded him to Canada.

Numerous newspaper accounts of the day also testify to the continuous movement of fugitive slaves from Louisville to New Albany, which is directly across the Ohio River. One case in 1857 reported the arrest of a white New Albany resident, William Hosea, the driver of an omnibus, a kind of urban stagecoach, for transporting fugitive slaves. It stated that Hosea was seen "for about two hours, dodging about, evidently looking for someone" (Hudson 62), and talking with a slave named Ralph who authorities also suspected of aiding fugitive slaves. But without any concrete evidence, and supported by testimony of individuals who vouched for his good character, he was released from custody.

Black Community

Research strongly indicates that organized efforts to aid fugitive slaves existed in the "Near Northeast Neighborhood" of New Albany, the residence of relatively prosperous blacks. More than a dozen blacks, who lived in this area, have been identified as being part of the network. Most prominent among them were William Harding and George Washington Carter.

A steward on riverboats, Harding was also known as Harden. He resided in Louisville before moving to New Albany in 1848, where he lived for a time on Main Street between East Fifth and Sixth streets. During the 1850s he moved to the east side of East Sixth Street where it is believed he helped Carter and Carter's family members in the Underground Railroad. In fact, their backyards faced each other. Just across the street from Carter lived the aforementioned Hosea.

Carter was a barber and retailer of tobacco supplies well known in New Albany as "Uncle Wash." He owned substantial real estate, including a livery stable and a vineyard. A native of Virginia, he came to New Albany during the mid-1820s, also living in southern Ohio where he met his wife. They returned to New Albany in 1832 and during the 1830s moved for a time to Canada. Several of his sons were educated at the fugitive slave community at Buxton from 1846 to 1856, and family history claims that he made many trips to Canada as part of his involvement in the Underground Railroad.

Others who lived in the neighborhood who may have been part of the New Albany Underground Railroad network were blacksmith Henry Clay, who worked on the steamer *New York* and for the New Albany–Salem Railroad; the riverboat stewards, Washington Johnson, James Porter, and John W. Sanders; boatman, Peter Findley; barbers, James Carter and John Hill, both relatives of George Washington Carver; and rope-maker, Henson McIntosh, whose work associated him with the shipping industry. What is significant about the employment of these men is that most were involved in the transportation industry through which they were able to forward fugitive slaves.

A descendant of a fugitive slave, Sarah Merrill, related a story about fugitive slaves who crossed over the Ohio River at Portland that involved her uncle, Lewis Barnet. Merrill said he came to New Albany with twelve other fugitive slaves and found refuge with a black family by the name of Bailey. However, after the Baileys harbored them for two days, they turned them over to the authorities for a reward.

Second Presbyterian Church

In the white community the foremost players in the Underground Railroad were the members of the Second Presbyterian Church. The church formed after severing relations with the First Presbyterian Church in 1837 as a result of the split between the Old and New School groups over the issue of slavery. The differences between the Old and the New School were addressed in a letter written by Second Presbyterian pastor, Rev. Samuel K Sneed, to the American Home Missionary Society that expresses his unhappiness with the Old School's resistance to abolitionism. In his New Albany church, antislavery views were openly made known.

Members of the church were among the organizers of the New Albany and Salem Railroad in 1847. They included elder James Brooks, its first president; elder James Haines, the New Albany conductor during the antebellum years, and John R. Nunemacher who printed the railroad tickets. The railroad's freight commissioner, R. H. Campbell, was a neighbor of the church's pastor, Rev. John G. Atterbury, only a block away from the church.

Brooks wrote in an 1849 pamphlet, showing the need for the railroad, that an average of 200 wagons per day passed each way on the road from New Albany to Salem. These wagons carried an estimated one ton of freight going to the river and one-quarter of a ton going out daily. The large number of blacks involved in this transportation is another compelling explanation for the operation of the Underground Railroad in New Albany, and the development of the railroad made it more effective. By 1853, the railroad connected all the way to Lake Michigan.

In 1855 Haines was accused of assisting a fugitive slave. According to the account in the *Louisville Courier,* a black man was arrested in New Albany and confessed to being a fugitive slave. However, two abolitionists rescued him and then secreted him in one of the passenger cars. Apparently, Haines and some others forcefully prevented the authorities from entering the train to apprehend the fugitive slave and it left New Albany with the fugitive slave on board. The account also alleged that the New Albany train depot was aiding fugitive slaves and stated that "We are advised that, on an average, at least one slave for every day effects his escape on the cars of the New Albany and Salem road" (Peters 95). It is difficult to assess the accuracy of this statement, but it does show that this railroad was heavily involved in the Underground Railroad. Another interesting historical detail is the claim of a contemporary historian that the railroad lost a huge amount of revenue because of the many free passes given out by Brooks. Although the historian is referring to passes given to local farmers, it is not too much of a stretch to speculate that some of these passes were given to fugitive slaves. The fact that the railroad passed through the Near Northeast Neighborhood at a very slow speed as it made its way out of New Albany also suggests the ease of fugitive slaves being harbored to hop aboard.

Other accounts in the contemporary newspaper report fugitive slaves using the railroad, a notable one in April, 1860, that described that apprehension of a fugitive slave who had been shipped in a box from Nashville, Tennessee. The box was being shipped to Mrs. Margaret M. Thompson in care of Levi Coffin in Cincinnati, Ohio, on the railroad leading through Madison.

Participation of Germans

According to oral tradition in New Albany's black community, support for the Underground Railroad there is also believed to have come from German immigrants, Otto Knoefel and Louis Hartman, who lived in the West Union section of town. Both were members of the Methodist Church: Knoefel, being a druggist who owned a hotel that employed blacks, and Hartman, who came to New Albany in 1854 from Germany at the age of 15, being a civic leader and supporter of blacks throughout his life.

Henson McIntosh

Probably the most mysterious individual who was part of the Underground Railroad in New Albany was a black rope-maker named Henson McIntosh, who also used the aliases Henry McIntosh and Henson Fremont. Indiana Underground Railroad historian, Pamela Peters, has suggested that McIntosh may have been a member of the Anti-Slavery League described by William Cockrum. A native of Maryland, he came to New Albany around 1850 with his wife and four children. Near the end of the decade, he and his family moved next door to riverboat steward, John Sanders. Around this time, he began spending considerable time in Louisville and listed addresses both in New Albany and Louisville.

On July 3, 1859, he was with two slaves, "Frank" and "Betty," who belonged to Samuel K. Richardson of Louisville aboard the Ohio and Mississippi on a train headed for Cincinnati when they were arrested by the authorities. They had taken the ferry from Portland to New Albany where they obtained a horse and buggy and rode to Salem, where they caught the New Albany & Salem train to Mitchell. There they transferred to the Ohio and Mississippi railroad line. McIntosh had supplied them with forged freedom papers and with money to pay for their tickets and other expenses. But he was not arrested at that time. However, he was put under surveillance.

On February 12, 1861, he was arrested and charged with two offenses—one, of migrating into the state of Kentucky illegally, and second, of aiding the slaves of Richardson. He was sentenced to prison in Frankfort, Kentucky, for five years. He did manage to escape on one occasion but was quickly apprehended and he was not released until May 20, 1868. His wife, by that time, had remarried and had four children with her second husband. A legal agreement was reached in which his wife chose to remain with her second husband after which Henson left town.

Henson's use of aliases, his twin residences—one of them in the heart of New Albany's Underground Railroad community—and his ability to fund the escape of fugitive slaves despite being a mere rope-maker make one suspect that he was working with an organization providing him with funding, possibly the legendary Anti-Slavery League (ASL). Henry Webb, quoted earlier, described a scenario similar to Cockrum's claim that the ASL had operatives posing as fishermen all along the Ohio River.

On August 1, 1860, an incident occurred in New Albany that suggests the connection of New Albany's black community to the Underground Railroad. At an anniversary celebration in New Albany commemorating Haitian Independence, Rev. Kelly, a black abolitionist preacher from Louisville, gave a militant sermon that referred to the local Underground Railroad, openly mentioning sixteen fugitive slaves who had been helped a week earlier. Two days later, George Washington Carter sent a letter to the *New Albany Daily Ledger* repudiating Kelly's speech, signed also by Harding and others in the Near Northeast Neighborhood. Obviously, it was an attempt to divert attention away from them and cover their tracks.

Remnants of Underground Railroad Today

Possible remnants of New Albany's Underground Railroad still exist in two blocked off tunnels under Main Street leading from the basement of the Second Presbyterian Church, now the city's Second Baptist Church. Although there is no documentation that the tunnel was used to hide fugitive slaves, oral history maintains this. Other alleged sites include a home at 1401 State Street, believed to have a basement below its basement and the Sloan/Bicknell house at East Main Street, which was built in 1852 and that is reported to have a tunnel that leads from the basement to the Ohio River. All this, however, is still purely speculative.

—Tom Calarco

Further Reading

Blaine K. Hudson, *Fugitive Slaves and the Underground Railroad in the Kentucky Borderlands* (Jefferson, NC: McFarland, 2001).

"The Invisible Road to Freedom through Indiana," as recorded by the Works Progress Administration Writers Project, compiled by Hurley C. Goodall (Muncie, IN: H. C. Goodall, 2000).

Pamela R. Peters, *The Underground Railroad in Floyd County, Indiana* (Jefferson, NC: McFarland and Company, 2001).

NEW BEDFORD, MASSACHUSETTS

The whaling capital of the world by the mid-nineteenth century, New Bedford, Massachusetts was also a major center of fugitive slave settlement, fugitive slave assistance, and abolitionist activity. It became so through a confluence of circumstances—its highly active port, efficient and relatively quick waterborne connections to Southern ports, the presence of a historically Quaker population, the accessibility of the maritime industry to people of color, and the whaling industry's persistent need of labor. Research has documented the presence of some 200 fugitive slaves living in or passing through New Bedford, and contemporary estimates placed the number living in the town at from 300 to 600. Even at the more conservative estimate, fugitive slaves would then have made up nearly one-third of the local population of color.

Early Involvement

New Bedford, and coastal Massachusetts more generally, harbored fugitive slaves from an early point because the commonwealth had deemed slavery unconstitutional in 1783 and was virtually encircled by jurisdictions in which slavery persisted. In 1790 the federal census recorded no enslaved persons in Massachusetts, Maine, and Vermont (where slavery was also unconstitutional) but 3,874 in other New England states and 21,193 in New York; as late as 1830 enslaved people were still counted in states bordering Massachusetts. New Bedford was also a key Quaker enclave, one in which Friends led commercial activity for many decades after the town's settlement about 1760. A group of early New Bedford Quakers was spurred to fugitive assistance by their ideology as well as by the punitive Fugitive Slave Law of 1793.

The documented presence of and aid to fugitive slaves in New Bedford dates at least as early as 1787, some five years before the Fugitive Slave Law was enacted. Friend William Rotch Sr., then the town's leading whaling merchant, worked to secure the freedom of a man enslaved in Rhode Island who had escaped to Nantucket and was working for Rotch's son-in-law, Samuel Rodman. In 1792 Rotch's son and namesake was among those who assisted the flight of a fugitive and his family who had come to New Bedford the year before and had been working in the family of Rotch's brother Thomas. Rotch relative Thomas Hazzard sent the man on to abolitionist Moses Brown in Providence with a letter stating in part, "We think considering all circumstances, it will be best for them to leave this place in the most private manner, that no person here may know where they have gone, so that when the person who is in pursuit of them arrives, he may not be able to follow them." In a letter to his uncle in 1792 William Rotch Jr. stated that he was "almost daily concerned in protected the injured Africans and promising their liberation where any pretence can be found to avoid the law," and, though instances of his later aid to fugitive slaves have not so far been documented, Rotch remained an active abolitionist until he died in 1851 (Grover 69).

From the early 1790s notices in New Bedford newspapers document the landing of fugitive slaves in the town, both by sea captains who knowingly carried them and those who claimed to be unaware of their presence on board. Up to that decade most whaling vessels ranged through the Atlantic as far south as Brazil and sometimes traded with Southern ports in the offseason, but as voyages to whaling grounds in the Pacific grew common, whaling vessels no longer stopped in these places. Most fugitive slaves probably came to New Bedford in trading vessels, not in whalers. By 1845 New Bedford was the fourth most active port in the United States, due not only to whaling but to its robust coastwise trade as well. Numerous fugitive slave narratives establish the use of trading vessels in escapes, and, as historian Gary Collison noted, New Bedford was only five hundred miles by water from Norfolk, Virginia—about a four-day sail in cooperative weather. No doubt this waterborne commerce was responsible for the fact that a remarkably large number of New Bedford's people of color were from Norfolk and Portsmouth, the city across the Elizabeth River from Norfolk; smaller but still substantial numbers were from the District of Columbia, Alexandria, and coastal Maryland and North Carolina. Indeed, in 1850 nearly 30 percent of all people of color in New Bedford told census takers that they had been born in a Southern state, nearly double the proportion that claimed Southern birthplaces in Boston and New York.

Openness to Fugitive Slaves

New Bedford was not only relatively easy to reach but also offered employment, both in the shoreside work that supported whaling and shipping, and at sea. By the mid-1850s, New Bedford's whaling fleet comprised more than 300 vessels, with anywhere from 60 to 135 fitting out and sailing in any given year. That activity translated into a great deal of work, from wharf labor to sailmaking and ship carpentry, and historically the maritime trades had been more hospitable than most others to the participation of people of color. In addition, filling out a crew grew increasingly difficult as the idea of whaling as a romantic adventure gave way to the reality that it was dangerous, dirty, risky, and poorly compensated. A crew member's pay depended on his station on board and the success of any given voyage. An inexperienced foremast hand could be entitled to as little as one two-hundredth of a voyage's net profit, and many men returned to shore after years at sea with little or no money or in debt to vessel owners. Whaling merchants were increasingly in search of crews who would accept such conditions. And at least some fugitive slaves would. In 1842, once at sea on the whaling bark *Milwood*, the Maryland fugitive slave John Thompson told his captain, "I am a fugitive slave from Maryland, and have a family in Philadelphia; but fearing to remain there any longer, I thought I would go on a whaling voyage, as being the place where I stood least chance of being arrested by slave hunters" (ibid. 195). Thompson was away for two years, but at that time many whaling voyages lasted from three to six years, and all of them traveled well beyond the reach of pursuers. The reasons that impelled Thompson to join a whaling crew were surely shared by many fugitive slaves who came to New Bedford, though it has been difficult to document with certainty more than a handful among whaling crews.

Still, men of color were a key part of whaling crews to about midcentury, and they lived however briefly among a large black population both in raw numbers and in proportion to the size of the city. Between 1820 and 1860 people of color were between 5 and nearly 9 percent of New Bedford's total population—at most if not all times a greater proportion than prevailed in any Northern city, including Philadelphia. At the end of 1853, New Bedford's population of 18,000 included 1,600 people of color, or 8.8 percent of the total; 2,500 people of color lived in Boston, a city nearly eight times its size, and formed only 1.8 percent of the total. Moreover, whaling brought people of many races and nationalities into the city and fostered a high degree of transience. Thus it was probably relatively easy for a fugitive slave to live in New Bedford, being a face in a largely nameless crowd.

New Bedford Network

According to their extant records, both the Philadelphia and New York vigilance committees sent more fugitive slaves to New Bedford than to any other New England place, including Boston. Certainly the best known of those fugitive slaves was Frederick Douglass, who escaped Maryland in 1838 by way of New York City. From there, New York Committee secretary David Ruggles, reasoning that Douglass might apply his skills as a caulker in New Bedford, sent

Nathan Johnson house, New Bedford, Massachusetts; home of a black couple who were leading citizens in New Bedford's black community and who lodged Frederick Douglass and his wife when they first came to live in New Bedford. (Courtesy of Tom Calarco)

him with a letter of introduction to Nathan Johnson, one of its foremost black abolitionists. Johnson gave Douglass the surname by which he would ever after be known. It was Douglass's address to fellow congregants at the town's African Methodist Episcopal Zion church in 1841 that effectively launched his career as a spokesman for equal rights: after hearing him there, New Bedford abolitionist William Coffin invited Douglass to speak before the Massachusetts Anti-Slavery Society meeting in Nantucket. Douglass is believed to have been the first fugitive slave ever to have lectured on the antislavery circuit.

Other Fugitive Slaves

Other fugitive slaves who are now well known lived in New Bedford for a time, including John S. Jacobs, the brother of fugitive slave author Harriet Jacobs, who came in search of her and went to sea on the whaling ship *Francis Henrietta* in 1839, and Henry "Box" Brown, whose escape in a wooden crate from Richmond, Virginia, to Philadelphia in 1849 gained almost instant notoriety.

Brown's escape is one of the best documented in Underground Railroad history. Sent by a Richmond, Virginia, shopkeeper to James Miller McKim in Philadelphia, Brown was sent by McKim to New Bedford oil manufacturer Joseph Ricketson, one of the most active white abolitionists in the city. Upon Brown's arrival Ricketson wrote to McKim that he had "received your very valuable consignment of 200 pounds of Humanity last evening," that Brown's sister was already in New Bedford "at service," and that "he has many friends here who former[ly] lived in Richmond" (ibid 202). Other accounts of fugitive slaves in New Bedford mention the presence of kin and friends from their native towns, a factor that clearly increased the appeal of the place among Southern-born people of color both free and fugitive.

Jacobs and Brown became important members of the antislavery lecture circuit, as did Alexander Duval, who escaped from slavery in Baltimore in 1848, settled in New Bedford, and worked as a cooper. Three years later, having seen his owner in New Bedford, Duval escaped to Liverpool with the aid of the Boston Vigilance Committee. Duval spoke often at antislavery events in London. Of greater renown was the fugitive William H. Carney, whose father had earlier escaped from Norfolk to New Bedford in the late 1850s. During the war Carney joined the 54th Regiment of the Massachusetts Volunteer Infantry and later earned the first Congressional Medal of Honor ever given to a person of color for his bravery at the doomed assault on Fort Wagner.

Most fugitive slaves in New Bedford were, however, a good deal more obscure. Clarissa Davis's story is known through Philadelphia Vigilance Committee secretary William Still, who wrote of her escape in his 1871 *Underground Railroad*. She had tried but failed to escape with her brothers from Norfolk in late 1853 and was compelled to hide in what Still described as a "miserable coop" for 75 days. The steward of the steamboat *City of Richmond* then hid her on board his vessel, which brought her to Philadelphia and the office of Still, who forwarded her to New Bedford. There she found her brothers and a sister as well as her father, who had escaped while she was in hiding. She lived in New Bedford as Clarissa Armstead. Her sister Ann married in Norfolk to a man who later fled to New Bedford. Her father, her sister, and her brothers William and Charles (who worked as a caulker) all died in New Bedford between 1857 and 1917, but how or where Clarissa ended up is as yet unknown. Another relatively unheralded fugitive slave was William Ferguson, who escaped from Norfolk with his wife Nancy in 1847. Local poor relief records identified them at the time as "runaway slaves," and in 1910, nine years before he died, he told a New Bedford reporter the story of his escape on the coal schooner *Pornony* to Boston. Whether he had been generally known to be a fugitive slave before that time is not known.

In addition to Rotch, Johnson, and Ricketson, those whose work in assisting fugitive slaves in New Bedford is best documented include the Quaker John Bailey (1787–1883), the merchant and onetime Quaker Andrew Robeson, and the African Americans William Jackson (1818–1900) and William Bush (1798–1866). Bailey worked in New Bedford producing watches and chronometers, the latter used in whaling. And as a frequent *Liberator* contributor, he was probably the most vocal fugitive slave assistant in the town. According to his daughter, their home was frequently visited by both antislavery lecturers and fugitive slaves. Underscoring the fact that abolitionism was always a minority reform movement, Bailey's house and family were repeatedly assaulted, and New Bedford merchants fearful of the growing political power of local people of color withdrew their business from him. Financially ruined, Bailey and his family moved to Lynn in 1837. More successful in both business and local abolitionism was Andrew Robeson, a wealthy whaling merchant who housed and employed the fugitive David Wright Ruggles (who took his name from Ruggles in New York, who helped him escape), who provided substantial financial support to the *Liberator* and William Lloyd Garrison and is documented to have played a major role in assisting several fugitive slaves after the passage of the 1850 Fugitive Slave Act.

William Jackson, later the chaplain of the 55th Massachusetts, was a free man from Norfolk who had become a Baptist minister. He came to New Bedford as a visiting preacher in 1852 and permanently in 1855. Jackson had been arrested in Philadelphia for leading the efforts to rescue an apprehended fugitive slave shortly after the Fugitive Slave Act passed and knew and worked with William Still. And his Second and Salem Baptist churches may rightly be viewed as the equivalent of Leonard Grimes' Twelfth Baptist Church in Boston, which was known at the time as the "church of the fugitive slaves." Records of admissions, baptisms, and vital statistics that Jackson kept include the names of many fugitive slaves; in some instances the presence of certain fugitive slaves in New Bedford is documented in no other known source.

William Bush and his family came to New Bedford in 1849 from Washington, D.C., and housed fugitive slaves in one of his several boardinghouses. When the fugitive slave George Teamoh came to New Bedford in late 1853 or early 1854 from Norfolk, he stayed with Bush. "Quite a large number of fugitive slaves for a time stayed at his house and received the same hospitalities as did his regular boarders, notwithstanding the former were not able to pay their way," Teamoh wrote. "If any reliance may be placed in the statement of many of the older citizens of N.B.[,] Deacon Bush . . . has been one of the most zealous, hard working and liberal friends the fugitive ever found" (ibid. 236).

Connection with Outside Agents

In addition to its own abolitionists, New Bedford attracted others whose aid to fugitive slaves effectively transformed them into martyrs for the cause. Jonathan Walker, whose 1844 attempt to carry enslaved people from Pensacola, Florida, ended in his arrest and his "branded hand"—seared with the initials "S. S." for "slave stealer"—was a Cape Cod native working as a mariner in New Bedford before his move to Florida. And Daniel Drayton, whose efforts to remove 77 enslaved people from the District of Columbia aboard the schooner *Pearl* in

1848 was similarly ill fated, took his life in a New Bedford hotel in 1857 after visiting his "old friend" William Bush; Bush's wife, Lucinda, is believed to have helped escapees reach Drayton's vessel, and a year after the Pearl episode they moved with their family to New Bedford. Drayton is buried in New Bedford's Rural Cemetery.

Fugitive slave assistance was probably not solely the work of documented individuals but of the black community at large as well. In *My Bondage and My Freedom* (1855) Frederick Douglass had noted that the "spirit of the colored people of New Bedford," is that they "are educated up to the point of fighting for their freedom, as well as speaking for it." He added, "A slave could not be taken from that town 17 years ago, any more than he could be so taken away now" (Douglass 348). Indeed, none of the renditions known to have been attempted in New Bedford succeeded. People of color had their own antislavery society, were members of antislavery societies formed by whites, and had formed their own Vigilant Aid Society "which has for its object the fundamental principles of the Gospel, and aids the poor panting fugitive out of the clutches of wicked human bloodhounds, and gives him a crust of bread and a cup of cold water, and bids him God speed on his way from the prison-house of bondage" (Grover 256). Abolitionists of both races cooperated on numerous civil rights challenges and on resisting attempts to return fugitive slaves to slavery. In March 1851, New Bedford abolitionists learned that a federal marshal in Boston planned the wholesale "seizure and carrying way of fugitive slaves from New Bedford" (ibid. 222) to prove, in the wake of the failure to take Shadrach Minkins from Boston a month earlier, that the Fugitive Slave Act could be enforced. White and black abolitionists quickly mobilized to defend local fugitive slaves, though the raid never materialized.

The rumored raid and numerous other sources make clear that New Bedford's reputation as a fugitive depot was well known in the North, and it was also a matter of consternation among Southerners. To the Norfolk, Virginia, *American Beacon*, New Bedford was "that den of negro thieves and fugitive protectors," a "rank stew of fanatics and outlaws" (ibid. 14). The newspaper estimated that Norfolk and its surrounding area had lost more than $30,000 worth of slaves "by the aid of abolitionists" in 1854 alone. "We would ask if New Bedford, Boston, or any other community of abolitionists were losers in any kind of property, would they sit so quietly and not call for redress from the 'powers that be.' It is time that the South should take some action" (ibid. 242). The Petersburg, Virginia, *Express*, advocated that all Southern ports cease purchasing New Bedford whale oils, but no measurable effort to cripple the city's commerce or forestall the flight of fugitive slaves there appears to have been made. Indeed, the population of color in the city continued to grow. Although other northern cities lost black population after the passage of the Fugitive Slave Act, New Bedford gained on this measure, increasing from 1,008 persons in 1850 to 1527 in 1855.

—Kathryn Grover

Further Reading

Jeffrey Bolster, *Blackjacks: African-American Seamen in the Age of Sail* (Cambridge: Harvard University Press, 1997).

Kathryn Grover, *The Fugitive's Gibraltar* (Amherst: University of Massachusetts Press, 2001).

Wilbur H. Siebert, *The Underground Railroad in Massachusetts* (Worcester: American Antiquarian Society, 1936).

NEW PHILADELPHIA, ILLINOIS

This tiny free Pike County black settlement in southern Illinois, not far from the Mississippi River, aided fugitive slaves from the time it was founded in 1835 by "Free Frank" McWorter. A slave for 42 years, McWorter was born in 1777 in Union Colony near the Pacolet River in South Carolina and purchased his freedom. Eventually, he also purchased the freedom of most of his family.

Free Frank

After his master moved to Kentucky, Free Frank saved the extra money he accumulated while hiring out himself and started a saltpeter business in Danville, Kentucky. Saltpeter was used in the production of gunpowder. Despite being a slave, he became a very successful businessman. He was able to pay for his wife Lucy's freedom in 1817 and two years later, he was able to purchase his own freedom. His hardest decision was which of his family members to purchase first. However, he continued to provide funds to purchase family members throughout his life and even after his death, in 1854, as he had made such arrangements in his will.

Frank and his wife, Lucy, and four of their children left Kentucky in the spring of 1831 after obtaining their freedom. By then, they already were familiar with Canada as a destination for fugitive slaves because their oldest son, Frank Jr., had fled to Canada in 1826 for fear, it is speculated, of being sold away from the family. Free Frank sold his saltpeter business to purchase the freedom of his oldest son, and thereafter family tradition claims that the McWorters were active in the Underground Railroad.

It is believed that Free Frank chose the location of his own cabin in Illinois with deliberate intentions of helping fugitive slaves. It set on a hill in the midst of trees outside the town proper of New Philadelphia and had a panoramic view of the area. When he built it, he selected a site with a deposit of granite that he used as the walls for his cellar. An opening in the walls led to a room that was used to hide fugitive slaves. The thick granite prevented detection by Negro dogs that slavecatchers used.

Though Illinois was a free state, it was hostile to blacks. The laws there at that time included black codes that restricted their freedom and denied them access to legal recourse. The state did not welcome them and the threat of violence loomed over blacks and those who sympathized with them. Only 50 miles away in Alton, Illinois, the abolitionist Elijah P. Lovejoy was murdered in 1837. Not only did they have to contend with legal restrictions and racial hostility, but this section of Illinois was known to be frequented by slavecatchers who often resorted to kidnapping free blacks and selling them into slavery.

Free Frank did not immediately found the town. It began in 1835 as an 80-acre tract purchased from the federal government for a total amount of $100. Jonathan Piper, the local justice of the peace, granted Frank's claim and his plat of a new town named "Philadelphia" on September 16, 1836. This was the beginning of the township of New Philadelphia, which Free Frank decided to name after the "City of Brotherly Love."

Location

New Philadelphia was located on a relatively flat section of land in the midst of rolling hills. Although the black church maintained a prominent position in the lives of the inhabitants of most black settlement, this was not the case in New Philadelphia, and though Frank did attempt to build a school and a church, they were never completed.

Of all the historical black settlements in the country at that time, New Philadelphia was different in that it held legal status due to Frank's incorporation of the town. This differentiated it from black communities like Lick Creek in Indiana, Rocky Fork and Miller Grove in Illinois, and Poke Patch in Ohio, which were all unincorporated settlements either named or recognized for the founder or the landscape features. Also, unlike black settlements across the country with historical legacies such as Weeksville in Brooklyn, New York, New Philadelphia was the only one with legal status.

At New Philadelphia, "The McWorter family not only gave the fugitives specific instructions on how to get to Canada, but in many instances Free Frank's sons accompanied the fugitives to Canada to insure that they would get there safely" (LaRoche 126).

The McWorters were knowledgeable about the settlements in Canada, probably because of the oldest son's early escape there, and many of their grandchildren were born there. For example, their grandson, Squire, was born in Chatham, Ontario, in 1846. One McWorter descendant stated that their son Solomon assisted many slaves on their way to freedom in Canada, and that his brothers Squire and Commodore traveled to Canada for the purpose of aiding fugitive slaves.

Number of Fugitive Slaves

It is not likely that great numbers of fugitive slaves passed through New Philadelphia despite its disposition to aiding them. The major line of the Underground Railroad in western Illinois began in Quincy, which was about

25 miles northwest of New Philadelphia and continued in a northeasterly direction. However, Benjamin Henderson, another free black man, was a known conductor in Jacksonville, about 40 miles due east of New Philadelphia. He forwarded fugitive slaves to Springfield, and may have collaborated with the McWorters. This suggests that further research is needed to determine how many fugitive slaves were aided in New Philadelphia and what routes they used from New Philadelphia on their way to Canada.

Interestingly, though a small settlement of only 58 persons, New Philadelphia had two shoemakers. This has led some to believe that the McWorters may have provided shoes to fugitive slaves, as Thomas Garrett did in Delaware.

In helping others obtain their freedom, Free Frank used whatever means necessary, but for his family he took the legal route, and over a 40-year period, Frank was able to purchase the freedom of 16 members of his family, as well as his own, at a total cost of $14,000. He was able to do this, in part, because he maintained good relations with his former owner, Obediah Denham, in Kentucky. As long as his enslaved family members were not sold "down South," there was still the possibility of Frank purchasing their freedom, and Denham continued to hold his family members as slaves.

Free Frank's Legacy

His dream was that he would purchase the freedom of all of his family before he died, but due to Denham's refusal to release his granddaughter, Charlotte, Frank never saw his dream come true. His son, Solomon, due to the lifelong financial legacy Frank set in place during his lifetime, was able to complete the four generation quest and purchased the freedom of Charlotte and all her children in 1859. This was possible by selling family farmland and town lots he owned in New Philadelphia.

The site of the town of New Philadelphia is located approximately three miles east of Barry, Illinois, and all that is left today is an archaeological resource now under investigation by an interdisciplinary team. The project was initiated and is supported by the New Philadelphia Association as part of a cooperative effort linking the University of Maryland, University of Illinois, Urbana-Champaign, Illinois State Museum, the New Philadelphia Association, and the University of Central Florida.

—Melissa Waddy-Thibodeaux

Further Reading

Cheryl Janifer LaRoche, "On the Edge of Freedom: Free Black Communities, Archaeology, and the Underground Railroad" (Ph.D. Diss., University of Maryland, College Park, 2004).

Juliet E. K. Walker, " 'Free' Frank and New Philadelphia: Slave and Freedman, Frontiersman and Town Founder" (Ph.D. diss., The University of Chicago, 1976).

NEWPORT (FOUNTAIN CITY), INDIANA

One of best-known stations on the Underground Railroad was an eight-room Federal style brick home in Newport (Fountain City), Indiana. To thousands of fugitive slaves this was a safe haven on their journey to freedom. It was the home of Levi and Catharine Coffin, Quakers who moved from North Carolina because they opposed slavery. During the 20 years they lived in Newport (1826–1847), the Coffins helped an estimated 2,000 fugitive slaves safely reach freedom. Levi Coffin was often referred to as the "President of the Underground Railroad," and their house in Newport as the "Grand Central Station."

Newport is located about eight miles north of Richmond, Indiana, in Wayne County and 15 miles south of Cabin Creek in Randolph County, a very active area for free blacks and for Underground Railroad safe houses and conductors. Levi Coffin first visited Indiana in 1823 and he and his wife moved there in 1826. They settled in Newport where he operated a general store, supplying groceries, dry goods, and hardware. In 1836 he began manufacturing linseed oil as part of his business operations.

Coffins Begin to Aid Fugitive Slaves

The Coffins aided their first fugitive slave in Newport during the winter of 1826, and encouraged other Quakers in the area to do the same. Fugitive slaves who went through Newport crossed the Ohio River at Jeffersonville and Madison, Indiana, and Cincinnati, Ohio. Occasionally some were transported from Ripley, Ohio. Two stations in Jefferson County, Indiana, (Madison) were homes of free blacks, Chapman Harris and Elijah Anderson. Even though the authorities knew their cabins were well-known stopping places for fugitive slaves, they were successful in hiding fugitive slaves soon after they crossed the Ohio River and helped transport them north to Union County. Many traveled through Union County in two-horse wagons and were helped by conductor William Beard from Billingsville, Indiana, 30 miles south of Newport. Beard drove a market wagon, a large covered wagon that could hold a large number of fugitive slaves. Beard's Underground Railroad activities were far-reaching, covering a geographical area that included southwestern Ohio and southeastern Indiana.

The Coffins not only housed fugitives in their home, they also provided shelter, food, and transportation, and even shoes and clothing for the fugitives. The young ladies in the neighborhood organized a sewing society and made clothes for the fugitives. Catharine (Aunt Katie) was an excellent cook and housekeeper and would feed the runaways any time of the day or night. Another house in Newport that served as an Underground Railroad station was the home of William "Billy" Hough. This home had a large attic above the kitchen that was accessed via a closet under the stairway.

Many times fugitive slaves required medical assistance and would stay and work before moving on. Dr. Henry H. Way was a friend of Levi Coffin and of the fugitive slaves. As a coworker on the Underground Railroad in Newport, he was often called on to attend to the sick fugitive slaves. Many fugitives benefited from his attention and medical care, receiving remedies for malnutrition, frost-bite, or disease.

Slavecatchers

Newport and the surrounding communities were often visited by slavecatchers. Levi Coffin usually intimidated them, threatened to have them arrested for tres-passing, and because of his business influence and acquaintances was never prosecuted. Often fugitive slaves were hidden in the homes of neighbors and mingled among the many customers in his store. Coffin claimed that not one fugitive that went through his station was ever captured.

Several lines merged in Newport from the South and lines leading north from Newport ran in different directions—north to Cabin Creek and Winchester and on to several lines north from there, east to Greenville and eventually to Sandusky, and even northwest to Marion County, Indiana, and on into Michigan.

Aunt Rachel and Eliza

The story of the fugitive slave Aunt Rachel mixes tragedy with success. She and her family were slaves in Lexington, Kentucky. She was separated from her husband when he was sold to another master. Two years later she was sold to a cotton plantation owner in Mississippi while her children remained with owners in Lexington. Life on the plantation proved too difficult for Aunt Rachel, as she was not used to hard physical labor and was severely punished for not doing the work. She escaped and fled back to Lexington, a journey of 500 miles. She was caught, put into jail, and shackled with ball and chain. With remarkable determination she managed to escape again and, aided by a free black family, freed herself from the shackles.

She eventually found her way to Madison, Indiana, where she stayed through the winter at a black settlement. When another fugitive slave was captured in the settlement, she was sent to Newport to stay with Levi and Catharine Coffin. She stayed with the Coffins for six months on her way to Canada. She was wel-comed into the household, especially since she was a good cook and house-keeper. She lingered as long as possible, waiting to hear from her children. After six months, she continued on toward Canada fearing slavecatchers would find her. The Coffins provided her with a trunk full of clothes and she was sent north dressed like a Quaker woman.

Levi and Catharine also helped Eliza Harris of *Uncle Tom's Cabin* fame escape to Canada. When Eliza came to the Coffins, she had only a first name, and Aunt Katie Coffin gave her the last name of Harris. After leaving Newport, she moved successfully to Canada.

Beginning in 1844, William Beard approached Coffin, requesting that the two men take a short trip to Canada to check on the welfare of the fugitives who had passed through their stations. On their first trip to Canada, Beard and Coffin stopped in Detroit and were spotted by Aunt Rachel who was living in Detroit and was married to a prosperous black man. They made several trips over the next 10 years. The Coffins also were reunited with Eliza Harris in Canada in 1854.

Newport Network

People from Newport were important in the formation of anti-slavery societies, beginning in 1838. Anti-slavery Society lecturers who visited Newport included Arnold Buffum, Frederick Douglass, and Charles Burleigh. Others who worked on the Underground Railroad in Newport, in addition to Dr. Way and Hough, were Benjamin Thomas, William "Billy" Bush (a former fugitive slave), Harvey Davis, Robert Green, Samuel Clark, Harmon Clark, William R. Williams, and Robert Bailey.

Other communities in Wayne County were also active in the Underground Railroad. Many Quaker families had come to this part of Indiana from North Carolina when slavery in that state became unbearable for them. The communities of Economy, Lynn, and Williamsburg, in Wayne County, and Cherry Grove, Cabin Creek, and Spartansburg in Randolph County, provided safe houses and transportation for fugitive slaves. Many fugitives could hide in Cabin Creek as they "blended in" with other free blacks in this settlement. The sheriff and deputies from Richmond, the county seat of Wayne County, often visited the Levi Coffin house and store, accompanied by slavecatchers and masters from Southern states. However, Richmond had many antislavery people who would warn Coffin that slavecatchers were in the area. So the fugitives could be transported or hidden in other safe houses.

A visit to the cemeteries in Fountain City, the modern name for Newport, further reveals its importance as an Underground Railroad station and the remarkable black history of the community. In the mid-1800s most cemeteries had two sections, a black section and a white section. In the Quaker communities of eastern Indiana, from Wayne County extending north through several counties, that distinction was not made. The Willow Grove Cemetery and the New Garden Cemetery (Quaker), here, have both black and white people buried on the grounds without any distinction of race. According to family oral history, a fugitive slave named William, who intended to seek freedom in Canada, was shipped in a box from Cincinnati to Levi Coffin's home in Newport. When the box was opened and he emerged from the box, his hair and beard were "like a bush." Noting the friendliness and helpfulness of the community, William stayed in Newport and took the name of William Bush. For many years, he harbored fugitive slaves in the houses where he lived. He and many of his descendants are buried in the Willow Grove Cemetery.

The Levi Coffin House still stands in Fountain City, and is a National Historic Landmark, maintained as an Underground Railroad Museum. Tours of the house include the hidden garret behind the upstairs bedroom, the indoors deep well in the basement, and a trip to the large barn that still shelters a false bottom wagon that was used to transport fugitives.

—Cynthia Vogel

Further Reading

Levi Coffin, *The Reminiscences of Levi Coffin* (Cincinnati: Robert Clark & Co., 1880).
Randolph County, Indiana, 1818–1990 (Randolph County Historical Society, 1990).
Wilbur H. Siebert, *The Underground Railroad from Slavery to Freedom* (1898; reprint, New York: Arno Press and *The New York Times*, 1968).
Ebenezer Tucker, *History of Randolph County, Indiana* (reprinted by the Randolph County Historical Society, Paducah, KY: Turner Publishing Co., 2008).
Cynthia Vogel, *Civil War Women: They Made a Difference* (Fletcher, OH: Cam-Tech Publishing, 2007).

NEW YORK, NEW YORK

New York City had the second largest population of blacks in the North during the antebellum period, second only to Philadelphia. Its black community had been actively creating churches and self-help organizations since the mid-1790s; before the Irish immigration, it offered many opportunities as domestics, in the maritime and service industries, and in other sorts of occupations. Evidence suggests, however, that New York City was more important as a stop on the path to freedom than it was as a place of settlement for fugitive slaves.

Abolitionism was a minority movement everywhere, but it may have been especially so in New York City. For one thing, its legacy of slavery was recent. Emancipation of the state's enslaved people was not legally universal until 1827, though the federal census listed 75 slaves living in New York City three years after the emancipation. Southerners traveling to and from summer resorts farther North were frequently in the city, and its business community was intimately tied to the South as well. Samuel Ringgold Ward, whose family had escaped from Maryland to New York City in 1826, stated in his 1855 autobiography that New Yorkers owned "a large amount of slaveholding property" and castigated "the truckling of the mercantile and political classes to the slave system" (Ward 26).

Proslavery Sentiment

A notable example of the general absence of abolitionist sentiment among leading New Yorkers was offered by Syracuse abolitionist Samuel J. May in *The Fugitive Slave Law and Its Victims* (1861). In November 1852 Jonathan Lemmon of Norfolk, Virginia, brought eight enslaved people with him to New York en route to Texas. On the grounds that they had been brought by their enslaver into a free state, a judge declared the so-called "Lemmon slaves" free after abolitionists interceded. "The merchants and others of New York subscribed and paid Mr. Lemmon the sum of $5,280, for loss of his slaves" (May, 1861, 24), May wrote, but when the same men were asked to contribute money to alleviate the destitution of the eight enslaved people they offered only two dollars. Much of the New York press was notably unsympathetic to abolitionism as well. The *New York Journal of Commerce* led the campaign to compensate Lemmon, and Ward declared the *New York Herald* "the most persevering pro-slavery paper" in the nation (Ward 257). May claimed that the New York newspapers' "halfway condemnation" of the mob that broke up the founding meeting of the American Anti-Slavery Society in 1833 "virtually justified" antiabolition riots in New York City afterward.

New York City was notorious for the presence not only of vacationing Southerners but those bent on returning fugitives to slavery. Recalling the time he escaped to New York from Maryland in 1828, the Rev. J. W. C. Pennington wrote, "In the city it was a daily occurrence for slaveholders from the southern states to catch their slaves, and by certificate from Recorder Riker take them back" (Pennington 51). The city's first Committee of Vigilance, organized by African Americans in 1835, stated that the city was "infested with slavecatchers" in December 1836. When Frederick Douglass reached New York two years later, a fugitive he knew as Allender's Jake in Baltimore (but as William Dixon in New York City) told him "that the city was now full of southerners, returning from the springs; that the black people in New York were not to be trusted; that there were hired men on the lookout for fugitives from slavery, and who, for a few dollars, would betray me into the hands of the slave-catchers; that I must trust no man with my secret; that I must not think of going either on the wharves to work, or to a boarding-house to board" (Douglass 338). Douglass wrote in *My Bondage and My Freedom* in 1855, "New York, seventeen years ago, was less a place of safety for a runaway slave than now, and all know how unsafe it now is, under the new fugitive slave bill" (ibid. 339). In 1837 the abolitionist newspaper *Emancipator* asserted that some New Yorkers had in fact formed an "organization of slavecatchers."

Fugitive Slaves in New York

The *Emancipator* estimated that 5,000 fugitive slaves then lived in the city. If that figure was accurate, it would have accounted for a third of New York's black population, which, in view of the danger they faced, seems unlikely. In any event, most of the New York City blacks who actively aided fugitive slaves had been born free, and much evidence exists documenting the arrival and speedy removal from the city of escaping slaves.

As a way station, New York City offered many advantages. It was the nexus of a burgeoning road network, of coastwise passenger and freight trade, and of railroads reaching into the North and West, and it was the starting point of the New York State canal system by way of the Hudson River. Although Sydney Howard Gay's mid-1850s "Record of Fugitives" aided in New York City documents their use of all these modes, fugitive slaves appear most likely to have reached the city by vessel. In 1834 the fugitive slave Moses Roper escaped Savannah, Georgia, aboard a New York City packet. "When I arrived in the city of New York," Roper later wrote, "I thought I was free; but learned I was not, and could be taken there" (Roper 77). Unable to find work outside New York City, Roper returned and boarded the same packet, then bound to go up the Hudson to Poughkeepsie. "After a time," he wrote, "I went up the western canal (Erie Canal) as steward in one of the boats. When I had gone about 350 miles up the canal, I found I was going too much towards the slave States, in consequence of which, I returned to Albany, and went up the northern canal, into one of the New England States—Vermont" (ibid. 79). Black abolitionist and editor Charles B. Ray once described having moved 28 fugitive slaves "of all ages, from the old grandmother to a child of five years," to Canada by way of the upstate town of Oswego. "I secured passage for them in a barge, and Mr. [Theodore Sedgewick] Wright and myself spent the day in providing food, and personally saw them on the barge" (Ray 35). As they traveled up the Hudson, Ray himself took "the regular passenger boat" to Albany and in that area raised the funds necessary to move the party from Albany to Toronto.

Fugitive Assistants

New York City also had what historian Benjamin Quarles has termed a "small but persistent" group of fugitive assistants. Many of these abolitionists lived or did business in lower Manhattan, south of Canal and Delancey Streets, close to the wharves and the Chambers Street station of the Hudson River Railroad, chartered in 1846. Among them were whites, Lewis Tappan, the Quaker Isaac T. Hopper, Gay, and blacks, David Ruggles, Ray, Wright, George T. Downing, James McCune Smith, Louis Napoleon, William P. Powell, and Pennington. Before any formal organization dedicated to assisting fugitives was founded in the city, Hopper may have been the most active. A fugitive assistant since his teenage years, Hopper came to New York City from Philadelphia in 1829 and operated a Quaker bookstore on Pearl Street where he is said to have sheltered fugitives. He once stated, "So long as my life is spared, I will always assist anyone who is trying to escape from slavery, be the laws what they may" (Child 457). Hopper was named president of New York City's second vigilance committee at its founding in 1847.

The African American grocer, printer, and journalist David Ruggles also was among the earliest involved in aiding fugitive slaves. Born free in Norwich,

Connecticut, Ruggles moved to New York in 1827; in November 1835, he was made the secretary of the city's first Vigilance Committee, formed by blacks to confront kidnappers of free blacks and slavecatchers, and to supply victims with legal and other assistance. Ruggles claimed to have aided 400 fugitive slaves during the 1830s. A contemporary account, in the July 1838, issue of the vigilance committee's newspaper *Mirror of Liberty*, stated that the committee under Ruggles's leadership had helped 522 free blacks and fugitive slaves maintain their freedom between its founding and July 1838. Numerous fugitive slave narratives document Ruggles's assistance, including those of Frederick Douglass, whom Ruggles sheltered and directed onward in September 1838.

When Ruggles left his vigilance committee post in 1839 he was replaced by Charles B. Ray, an African American journalist born free in Falmouth, Massachusetts, who had moved to New York in 1832. Ray had been among the organizers of the city's first vigilance committee and from 1837 to 1842 was editor of the African American newspaper *Colored American*. Ray once wrote that his "principles and nature" inspired him to work in particular for fugitive slaves, "whose arrival during those times was almost of daily occurrence; and many a midnight hour have I, with others, walked the streets, their leader and guide; and my home was an almost daily receptacle for numbers of them at a time" (Ray 24). From the time of its founding until it disbanded in 1846, the first vigilance committee assisted between 1,300 and 1,700 fugitives. Ray continued as secretary of the second vigilance committee until 1853. In that time the committee assisted 166 fugitives in its first six months of existence (to May 1848), 200 in 1848–1849, 151 in 1849–1850, and 686 between January 1851 and April 1853 (compiled from reports of the *New York Evangelist, North Star*, and the 1853 Report of the New York State Vigilance Committee).

In his autobiography Ray wrote that the Underground Railroad "had its regular lines all the way from Washington, between Washington and Baltimore a kind of branch" and that New York City was "a kind of receiving depot, whence we forwarded to Albany, Troy, sometimes to New Bedford and Boston, and occasionally we dropped a few on Long Island, when we considered it safe so to do. When we had parties to forward from here, we would alternate in sending between Albany and Troy. And when we had a large party we would divide between the two cities" (Ray 35). Much the same pattern appears to have existed over the life of the second organization, the New York State Vigilance Committee, formed in 1847. Abolitionist Sydney Howard Gay, editor of the *National Anti-Slavery Standard* from 1844 to 1858 and clearly connected with the vigilance committee, kept a "Record of Fugitives" he encountered and helped between 1855 and 1858. During 1855 and 1856, Gay and the committee assisted 158 fugitive slaves, and for 133 of them Gay noted the places to which they were sent from New York. Fifty-six were moved along to Syracuse, forty-two to Albany, five to "Syracuse & Canada," four to "Albany & Syracuse," nine to New Bedford, eight to Boston, and nine to Canada. Many of these fugitives had been sent to New York by William Still, secretary of the Philadelphia Vigilance Committee.

Gay's record and other contemporary accounts document the Underground Railroad involvement of New Yorkers somewhat less well known. Gay worked closely with Louis Napoleon, a black porter born in New York, who often met fugitives who had been concealed or concealed themselves on vessels then docked at city wharves and sent them on to Gay. At the end of 1855, Gay paid Napoleon $20.37 for "assistance" in the efforts to help 48 fugitive men, women, and children that year. Historian Charles Blockson has stated that "many stories" describe the activities of George T. Downing, a free African American from Providence, Rhode Island. Downing operated the Oyster House restaurant at Broad and Wall Streets between 1822 and 1866, often serving fugitive slaves in his restaurant's cellar. Lewis Tappan, the wealthy merchant who helped create the New York and American Anti-Slavery Societies, concealed fugitives in the offices of the American Missionary Association, which he founded in 1846, and was frequently involved in other forms of assistance. He once wrote, "I used to say that I was the owner of *half-a-horse* that was in active service, near the Susquehanna River. This horse I owned jointly with another friend of the slave, dedicating the animal to the service of the Underground Railroad" (Wyatt-Brown, 343). William Peter Powell, the proprietor of the Colored Seamen's Home in New York from 1839 to 1851, is said to have concealed fugitives among his boarders; an engraving of the famed fugitive Crispus Attucks hung in the home's dining room. Albro and Mary Marshall Lyons, Powell's successors at the Seamen's Home, assisted "about a thousand" fugitive slaves between 1851 and 1862, according to their daughter, Maritcha.

Use of Churches

New York City may have been notable in the degree to which churches were used to conceal and otherwise assist fugitives. Vigilance committee meetings were held at the African Methodist Episcopal Zion church at Leonard and Church Streets, the oldest African American church in the city. Probably the most deeply involved was the First Colored (later Shiloh) Presbyterian Church. Theodore S. Wright, pastor there from the early 1830s until he died in 1847, is said to have used the church as a "fugitive sanctuary"; his successor, the fugitive slave, J. W. C. Pennington, was also involved in fugitive assistance and raised money among his congregation to help purchase the freedom of Mary Jane and Emily Edmundson, two of the slaves retaken in the infamous *Pearl* episode, in 1848. Henry Highland Garnet, also a fugitive slave, was pastor at this church from 1855 to 1864. In 1859 he wrote in the *Weekly Anglo-African* that he had sheltered 150 fugitives "under my roof, and I have never asked or received a penny for what I gave them, but divided with them my last crust." It seems likely that he may have used the church building as well. Bethesda Congregational Church, which Charles B. Ray served as pastor for two decades, may also have sheltered fugitive slaves. Abolitionist cleric Henry Ward Beecher

Theodore Wright house, New York City; home of the president of the New York Committee of Vigilance. (Courtesy of Tom Calarco)

is believed to have hidden fugitives in the basement of his Plymouth Church of the Pilgrims in Brooklyn, and within the sanctuary he also staged mock "slave auctions" to purchase the freedom of fugitives, including the Edmundson sisters, who sought his aid.

Fugitive Slave Law of 1850

After the Fugitive Slave Act became law in 1850, New York City was the locus of at least eight attempts to enforce it. Of these cases, documented by Samuel J. May, five resulted in the return of fugitives to slavery; in Boston, by comparison, only two fugitive slaves, Thomas Sims and Anthony Burns, were returned to slavery after 1850. The first attempt to enforce the law occurred on September 26 in New York City, only eight days it was signed into law. The fugitive slave James Hamlet was returned to an agent representing his Baltimore enslaver, though abolitionists later purchased his freedom. In December of the same year a Virginia fugitive slave named Henry Long was seized and brought before a series of New York courts; Long was returned and sold at auction in Richmond.

In May 1854, at almost the same time that Burns was taken in Boston, Maryland slave owners found Pennington's brother Stephen Pembroke and his two sons in a "retreat in Thompson Street" and seized them at night. Before their arrest was generally known, a judge had granted a warrant to the owners. While the three fugitive slaves were held in a locked room at the courthouse, abolitionist lawyers learned of their situation and sought to represent them, but before any action could be taken on their behalf the men were returned to Maryland. Abolitionists purchased Pembroke's freedom, but his sons were sold.

Friends of the fugitive slave did see some success in this bleak decade, as Gay's accounts and other sources attest. Yet the population of people of African descent in New York City shrunk significantly between 1840 and 1860—from 16,358 to 12,574—while their numbers grew in such other cities as Boston. That decline may well speak to the generally inhospitable circumstances that confronted African Americans, both free and fugitive, in the nation's largest city.

—Kathryn Grover

Further Reading

Charles L. Blockson, *The Underground Railroad* (New York: Berkley Books, 1987).

Lydia Maria Child, *Isaac T. Hopper: A True Life* (Boston: John P Jewett and Company, 1853).

Sydney Howard Gay, "Record of Fugitives [Slaves], 1855–58," Columbia University Library, unpublished.

Samuel J. May, *The Fugitive Slave Law and Its Victims* (New York: American Anti-Slavery Society, 1861).

Samuel J. May, *Some Recollections of Our Anti-Slavery Conflict* (Boston: Fields, Osgood and Co., 1869).

James W. C. Pennington, *The Fugitive Blacksmith* (London: Charles Gilpin, 1849).

Benjamin Quarles, *Black Abolitionists* (New York: Oxford University Press, 1969).

Florence T. Ray, *Sketch of the Life of Rev. Charles B. Ray* (New York: Press of J. J. Little & Co., 1887).

Henrietta Cordelia Ray and Florence Ray, *Sketches of the Life of the Rev. Charles B. Ray* (1887).

Moses Roper, *A Narrative of the Adventures and Escape of Moses Roper from American Slavery* (Philadelphia: Merrihew & Gunn, 1838).

William Still, *The Underground Railroad* (1872; reprint, Chicago: Johnson Brothers, 1971).

Samuel Ringgold Ward, *Autobiography of a Fugitive Negro: His Anti-Slavery Labours in the United States, Canada, & England* (London: John Snow, 1855).

M. N. Work, "The Life of Charles B. Ray," *Journal of Negro History* 4 (1919): 361–371.

Bertram Wyatt-Brown, *Lewis Tappan and the Evangelical War against Slavery* (Cleveland: Case Western Reserve University Press, 1969).

NIAGARA FALLS, NEW YORK/ONTARIO

By 1830, the Niagara region had become a mecca for fugitive slaves and disgruntled free blacks seeking to start a new life in Canada. Niagara County, which includes the city Niagara Falls, is separated from Canada by the Niagara River, and straddles the famous waterfall, with one leg in the United States and the other in Canada. With such proximity to the British Commonwealth, Niagara Falls became a natural crossover point for fugitive slaves and, as would be expected, attracted Southern slavecatchers.

Bertie Hall

About 1830, William Forsyth, Sr., built a safe-house in Fort Erie, Ontario, that he named Bertie Hall. Bertie Hall, which was directly across from Black Rock, operated at one end of what is known today as the Niagara Freedom Trail, which ran from Fort Erie to St. Catharines and passed through the Canadian town of Niagara Falls. According to legend, slaves entered the house through a secret, underground tunnel, escaping detection by American bounty hunters. The tunnel would have been at risk of flooding, since it connected the basement of Bertie Hall to the riverbank. But the riverbank entrance also was its main appeal. After entering the tunnel, runaways seemed to vanish on Canadian soil.

Escape by Boat

Many fugitive slaves took the ferry that operated from Black Rock. One of the more violent incidents occurred there about 1837 when a band of free blacks, among them William Wells Brown, recovered a family that had been kidnapped from St. Catharines by slavecatchers. They headed straight to the ferry and managed to send the family back to Canada but only after a furious fight with law enforcement officers, whose help the slavecatchers had enlisted.

Waterways were an important thoroughfare throughout the Underground Railroad and many fugitive slaves reached Canada by steamboats crossing Lake Erie. It was on such a steamboat that Wells Brown worked for a number of years, including 1842 when he said he brought 69 fugitive slaves across on his boat. Another boatman, a Mr. Chapman, who operated a commercial boat running between Cleveland and Buffalo, told a story of how a fugitive slave became so excited upon landing in Canada that he actually ate some of the dirt. At Black Rock, where the river narrowed, some used rowboats or even swam across. Versailles, New York, conductor Eber Pettit noted that Black Rock was a common destination of Underground Railroad agents in western New York. The Niagara River must have seen considerable fugitive slave traffic, for oral tradition claims that one boatman concocted some sort of crate with a false bottom where slaves were hidden that could be hauled across the river or pushed if the river were frozen.

Churches Provide Asylum

By the mid-1830s, aid to fugitive slaves was being provided on both sides of the river. In Niagara Falls, Ontario, the British Methodist Episcopal Church, today Dett Memorial Chapel, was active in caring for the needs of the newly arrived refugees. By 1836, more than 400 blacks resided in the section that was known as Negro Town. That year, a fugitive slave named Moseby came there from Kentucky. He used one of his master's horses to make his escape, and after a time his whereabouts were traced to Niagara Falls, and a warrant for his arrest on the charge of horse stealing was issued by Kentucky authorities. As a result, Canadian authorities took custody of him and placed him in jail to await a further decision by the Canadian governor, Sir Francis Bond Head. A group of blacks rallied to Moseby's support and pleaded with the authorities not to extradite Moseby; they pledged to raise the money for the loss of his master's horse as compensation. Nevertheless, the order was given for his release into the custody of Kentucky slavecatchers. But upon his release from jail a mob of his supporters attacked the officers. At least one and, according to another account, possibly two blacks were killed in the melee during which Moseby escaped. Another similar case occurred the next year, upon which Head finally ruled that the Canadian government could not be responsible for the actions of men who escaped from a system that they recognized as unlawful and that they would under no circumstances extradite fugitive slaves who came to Canada.

Abolitionist Sentiment

In Niagara County, New York, there also were many sympathetic souls ready to help. Among the county's early settlers were many Quakers. A report from 1823 notes that two Kentucky slave hunters seized Joseph Pickard, a black barber from Lockport, about five miles from the Falls and brought him before the justice of the peace. It was a Quaker, Darius Comstock, who came to Pickard's defense. But before justice could be served, Pickard jumped out a window. In a short time, so many canal workers had assembled in the street that he could not escape. With drawn pistols, the Kentuckians dragged him before the justice, who nevertheless set Pickard free for lack of evidence. In other circumstances, the Kentuckians might have tried to skirt the law. But local sentiment, backed by an angry mob, favored Pickard. As Friend Darius said, "the prisoner could never be taken away from Lockport" (Merrill 101).

In 1836 Niagara formed a county Anti-Slavery Society, naming Lyman Spaulding, another Quaker, president. Spaulding and Moses Richardson, the editor of the *Lockport Daily Journal,* used the newspaper offices as a holding station for fugitive slaves. In a letter to Wilbur Siebert, Thomas Birnmore wrote that while working there during the years of 1856 and 1857, he was asked to forward several fugitive slaves. "We were much afraid of certain people who would have informed against us," he wrote (Letter to Wilbur Siebert, Montreal, Canada, April 27, 1896). Several times he said he had to give up his bedroom while he worried about eluding the slavecatchers, because those that came to the *Journal* usually had been diverted there because slavecatchers were watching the crossing points in Niagara Falls and Lewiston. Usually, these fugitive slaves were taken to Youngstown, at the northern tip of the river, where a farmer took them across the river in a rowboat.

By 1837, 10 antislavery societies had formed in Niagara County and just to the south in Erie County, the location of Black Rock, there were 21 antislavery societies. The black community in Buffalo was very proactive in their aid to fugitive slaves and one of Buffalo's most frequented stations was the Michigan Avenue Baptist Church. In 1839 it was founded by 33 blacks, who had been members of Buffalo's first black congregation. The church, still standing at 511 Michigan Avenue, hid fugitive slaves in its basement. There were whites who helped as well. For instance, Edward Orton recalled to Wilbur Siebert how his father took in a party of fugitive slaves that came to their home in two sleighs in 1838.

Lockport was an especially active location with fugitive slaves sometimes coming by way of the Erie Canal and being transported along one of several small canals that fed it. Among Lockport's best remembered Underground Railroad conductors was Thomas Root, who lived on a farm east of the city. His obituary in 1903 said that every winter he and his neighbor, Marvin Robinson, brought a "sleigh load of provisions" to fugitive slaves at St. Catharines, Ontario, and that fugitive slaves often sat at his dinner table and were treated just as if they were the most wealthy or cultured persons.

A noteworthy case in Lockport involved a black known as "Gentleman George" Groins. He had escaped from North Carolina by creating fraudulent emancipation papers, and ended up in Wisconsin where abolitionists purchased his freedom for $500. Around 1852 he came to Lockport and became a coachman for the Tremont House hotel. George had come from a large family and was saving his money to purchase their freedom. But a fire burned down the Tremont House and he lost his job and his savings in the process. When this came to the public's attention, a benefit was held for him that raised $1,070. To enable the release of his mother and brother, Judge Jonathan L. Wood was sent to Carolina.

One of the more famous Underground stations in the Niagara area was a massive stone house on a hill overlooking the Niagara River about one-half mile north of Lewiston owned by Amos Tryon. He had settled in Lewiston about 1815 and became quite prosperous. However, after he built this mansion, his wife preferred to stay at their old house in the village. As a result, Amos and his brother, Rev. Josiah Tryon, pastor of the Lewiston Presbyterian Church, used it to hide fugitive slaves. The house had four levels below the main floor that formed a sort of terrace that gradually descended to the river. From his house it was a short rowboat ride to Canada.

Suspension Bridge

When the second Fugitive Slave Law was passed in 1850, Niagara Falls and its vicinity already had become a major destination for fugitive slaves. A suspension bridge had been built in 1848 making it an easy stroll to freedom, though the first such bridge was a bit unsteady and often swayed under the weight of those crossing it. Accounts from prolific conductors like William Still in Philadelphia and John Jones in Elmira, New York, mention it frequently.

With so many fugitive slaves arriving there, it also became a destination for slavecatchers. A typical case of the period occurred in 1851, when a Kentucky slave Daniel Davis, who had been hired out as a steward on a steamship packet running from Louisville to Cincinnati, used the opportunity to escape to Buffalo, New York, about 20 miles south of Niagara Falls. Although caught there, he was set free by a sympathetic judge who dismissed the slave owner's claim. Davis wasted no time heading for Canada. It is likely that Davis came to Buffalo by train hidden in the baggage care by black porters and baggage men.

The Cataract House, a hotel on the American side of Niagara Falls, also bustled with Underground Railroad activity. Black waiters and stewards employed by the Cataract House often served as agents on the Underground Railroad. Among them was a waiter and fugitive slave, Patrick Snead. After dinner one Sunday during the summer of 1853, a constable tried to trick Snead by calling him by his slave name, Watson, and flicking a quarter for a tip to the floor. Snead protested, saying he had not waited on the man and did not want another waiter's money, but the constable grabbed him by the collar. He had brought four more constables with him, and the five of them tried to drag him out the door, but Snead held onto the door, even when they twisted the silk cravat around his neck causing him to gag.

By then, the other waiters had pushed through a crowd of three hundred diners to come to his aid. Two waiters, Smith and Grave, caught hold of Snead's hands, and with the other waiters helping, they pulled Snead from the officers by force, dragging him over chairs, outside, and down to the ferry. As the ferry left, the constables called Snead a murderer, hoping to enlist help. It worked. Snead was 50 feet from the Canadian shore, when another boatman ordered the first to row back. Snead's supporters blocked the hotel landing, but the ferry landed at Suspension Bridge, and the constables snagged him there.

They transported Snead to Buffalo, where they thought he would be at a disadvantage, without contacts or friends. To their surprise, Snead engaged one of the best lawyers in town. Eleven days later, after a two-day trial, Snead was acquitted. He was just freed when a telegram from a Savannah judge arrived, identifying Snead as a fugitive slave. Before a new warrant could be issued, Snead was in a carriage and on his way into Canada.

Slavecatcher Incident

Another case, from the pages of Eber Pettit's *Sketches of the Underground Railroad*, involved a female fugitive slave named Cassey. She had escaped from Baltimore during the mid-1850s, and after a series of dramatic incidents had rescued her son, leaving him in the custody of trusted friends in New Jersey before fleeing to Lundy's Lane, near Niagara Falls, Ontario, where she lived without incident for a few years.

After a while, she found employment on the American side of Niagara Falls, with a wealthy man identified as Colonel P by Pettit (possibly Colonel Peter A. Porter), who offered her better wages. As a result she frequently began crossing over on the Suspension Bridge and also began attending a church on the American side.

But a slavecatcher named Cathcart, who knew Cassey because of his attempt to recapture her before she came to Canada, had since stationed himself in the Niagara region to hunt fugitive slaves. One of his practices was to wait outside black churches and look for persons whose descriptions fit known fugitive slaves. It was during one of these occasions that he spotted Cassey and she him. However, she managed to elude him.

Shortly after, a free black, Ben Jackson, who worked at the hotel, convinced Cathcart to post men at all the bridges crossing over to Canada. He then informed Colonel P of this, and the Colonel then sent Cassey to another agent named Dennis. In the meantime, Cathcart learned that Cassey worked for Colonel P and went to the Colonel's residence with a federal marshal and the local Fugitive Slave Law commissioner. The Colonel was waiting and upon seeing the approach of the slavecatchers, sped off in a carriage, leading the slavecatchers on a wild goose chase to divert them from the trail of Cassey. When the slavecatchers finally discovered that no one was in the carriage with Colonel P, they were at a loss of where to proceed. Meanwhile, Cassey remained safely hidden with an individual in a remote area where Cassey was brought by the Underground Railroad agent. Shortly after, the Civil War began and she returned to New Jersey and reunited with her son.

Despite that the nation was on the brink of Civil War in 1861, slavecatchers continued to be active. Another case around that time concerned a free black man Chancellor Livingstone, who was working for another Underground Railroad agent, Francis Hichens of Lockport. Hichens was the owner of a glass factory and a contractor for the Erie Canal; his house, which set alongside the canal, was used to hide fugitive slaves. Livingstone accepted work on a farm in Kentucky assuming that because he was a free man, he had nothing to fear. However, once he arrived there, his employer immediately declared him a slave.

Suspension Bridge, Niagara Falls

There are many suspension bridges, but in Underground Railroad circles when you talk about the Suspension Bridge, you are referring to the one that crossed the Niagara River into Canada, just north of the falls. The first such bridge was constructed in 1848. It was about 762-feet long and supported by two 80-foot wooden towers on each side; its oak plank roadway was suspended 220 feet above the river. It often swayed or dipped under a heavy load or a strong wind. In 1855, it was replaced by a double-decker bridge that was a railroad crossing on one of the decks.

Hundreds of fugitive slaves undoubtedly crossed the bridge to freedom, and it is referred to in William Still's book and in many other accounts about the Underground Railroad, most notably those of Harriet Tubman. One of her anecdotes from crossing the bridge involved a Maryland lumberman, Joe Bailey, who was being led by Tubman with three fugitive slaves. During their long journey, slavecatchers were hot on their trail and he was worried about being caught. Tubman stopped them before crossing the bridge to look at the scenic view of the falls. But Joe would not look. When they reached the other side, Tubman shouted out, "Joe, you're free!" He shouted with joy and praised God, and said the next trip he was taking was to heaven, to which Tubman replied, "You might have looked at the falls first" (Kate Clifford Larson, *Bound for the Promised Land*, New York: Ballantine Books, 2003: 137).

Fugitive slaves arriving by way of Suspension Bridge could find help in either Niagara Falls at the British Methodist Episcopal Church or at the BME Church in St. Catherines, 25 miles to the northwest, where Tubman lived with her parents for a time just a short walk away from the church.

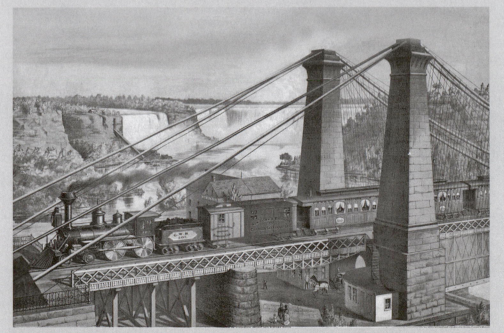

Suspension Bridge that crossed the Niagara River near Niagara Falls into Canada and over which many fugitive slaves, including the parties of Harriet Tubman, crossed into freedom. (Library of Congress)

Black Rock, New York

Black Rock was a community along the Niagara River border with Canada. Originally known for shipbuilding, it was the site of the building of the first steamboat on Lake Erie. It also had a ferry commonly used by fugitive slaves. In 1850, it had a population of about 2,000, and today Broderick Park in Buffalo marks the site of the ferry.

Among Underground Railroad conductors who brought fugitive slaves to Black Rock were Eber Pettit of Versailles, New York. In some instances, when slavecatchers were in the area, rowboats were used. The crossing is less than a half-mile, so it was an easy ride to the Promised Land.

Another story is told by Samuel R. Ward about a fugitive slave on the ferry shoving off for Canada when his master approached brandishing a pistol, threatening to shoot the ferryman if he did not bring the ferry back. In a panic, the fugitive slave found a spike and also threatened him. The ferryman responded that because he could only die once, he might as well go out doing right and the ferry proceeded on its way to Canada.

When the ferry reached the dock on the Canadian side, the fugitive slave leaped onto shore and gave three cheers to the King of England.

Bertie Hall, Fort Erie, Ontario, first refuge for many fugitive slaves, across the Niagara River from Black Rock. (Courtesy of Tom Calarco)

> The passage of the second Fugitive Slave Law in 1850 spurred a mass migration of blacks to Canada. Shortly after, one party of 51 crossed into Canada using the Black Rock ferry led by a B. G. Sampson. "They were all armed to the teeth," said a newspaper report, "and. . . . When they landed on the British side, they paraded on the beach and again swung their hats and gave shouts of joy mingled with song" ("Slave Emigration," *Glens Falls Clarion*, October 8, 1850).

Word got back to Hichens and he not only managed to have Livingstone returned to New York but had the Kentucky slaveholder arrested for kidnapping.

—Tom Calarco

Further Reading

Benjamin Drew, *North Side View of Slavery* (Boston: John Jewett and Company, 1856).

Frederick Douglass, *Life and Times of Frederick Douglass: His Early Life as a Slave, His Escape from Bondage, and His Complete History to the Present Time* (Hartford, CT: Park Publishing Co., 1881).

Arch Merrill, *The Underground, Freedom's Road and Other Upstate Tales* (New York: American Book–Stratford Press, 1963).

Eber M. Pettit, *Sketches in the History of the Underground* Railroad (Fredonia, NY: W. McKinstry & Son, 1879).

Bryan Prince, *I Came as a Stranger* (Toronto: Tundra Books, 2004).

Frank Severance, *Old Trails in the Niagara Frontier* (Cleveland: Burrows Bros, 1903).

Austin Steward, *Twenty-Two Years a Slave, and Forty Years a Freeman; Embracing a Correspondence of Several Years, while President of Wilberforce Colony, London, Canada West* (Rochester, NY: William Alling, 1857).

Robin W. Winks, *The Blacks in Canada, a History* (New Haven and London: Yale University Press, 1971).

O

OBERLIN, OHIO

Oberlin, centrally located in Lorain County, is equidistant from Cleveland and Sandusky, the two most active Underground Railroad ports on Lake Erie, and 10 miles from Lorain, another Lake Erie Underground Railroad port located at the mouth of the Black River. It was a key stop along the Underground Railroad. With a population of only 2,000, some estimate that Oberlin gave aid to as many as 3,000 fugitive slaves before the Civil War, many of whom came up from Ashland and Wayne counties in Ohio.

Lane Seminarians Matriculate to Oberlin

The year 1835 was a milestone in Oberlin's history. That was the year of the defection from Lane Seminary that brought many of its antislavery rebels to Oberlin. It began a tradition at the school in the training of abolitionists and Underground Railroad activity. Among noted abolitionists and Underground Railroad conductors who attended Oberlin College were Calvin Fairbank, Delia Webster, John Todd, Hiram Wilson, and the famous fugitive slave, Anthony Burns, who was a student there after he was emancipated. Many lesser known men and women attended the school during the antebellum period and later became involved in the Underground Railroad.

Settlement of Fugitive Slaves

Many escaped slaves and free blacks resided in Oberlin. For instance, an anti-slavery meeting there on January 1, 1859, was attended by 312 free blacks and 28 fugitive slaves. They worshipped in the same churches as whites, owned businesses, sent their children to public schools, and attended Oberlin College. Among local abolitionists was Congregational minister and missionary, Reverend John Bardwell. Under the eaves of his home were sliding panels hidden behind closet walls. They opened into wide passageways where he hid fugitive slaves. Bardwell was away doing missionary work during most of the decade preceding the Civil War, so the majority of the Underground Railroad work at the house was done by Mrs. Bardwell. In 1866, after the Emancipation Proclamation and the end of the Civil War, John Bardwell was seized and beaten in Mississippi by a former slave owner and a local mob.

But it was mainly Oberlin students and free blacks who were the backbone of its Underground Railroad efforts. For instance, in the fall of 1836, Hiram Wilson, who was setting out for Canada and a life during which he devoted himself to the ministry of fugitive slaves, brought a fugitive slave from Virginia with him. In fact, fugitive slaves were already being aided there on a regular basis. A report written for a legislator in 1840 by David L. Parker, who attended Oberlin in 1835 and 1836, told of an incident when four Kentucky fugitive slaves were brought from Cincinnati by Martin L. Brooks, another Oberlin student. After meeting with college president Asa Mahan, they were sent in a double wagon to Lake Erie under the leadership of student William Sheffield and a couple other armed men. On another occasion, Parker wrote that a fugitive slave who was running off slaves in Virginia, visited Oberlin. He had nearly been caught and had lost his wagon and horses, and was seeking financial assistance, He had with him a letter of introduction from Beriah Green, and funds were raised for his activities. Another report of activity comes from a letter in 1840 from John Jay Shipherd, founder of the college, to his brother Fayette, a conductor in Troy, New York, stating that "not a few" fugitive slaves were being aided and forwarded in Oberlin.

The year 1841, however, was a year of major activity. That spring, Charles Stearns, later one of John Brown's Secret Six, and an Oberlin student, wrote a letter to *The Liberator*, reporting that: "Quite a number of fugitives have passed into Canada already this season, many of them having remained at Oberlin through the winter." The summer was no different, as Milton Clarke described it in his fugitive slave narrative, published in 1846: "During the summer of 1841, the emigration to Canada through Oberlin was very large." Also, that year, Hiram Wilson visited Oberlin and brought a fugitive slave back with him to Canada. The fugitive had come from Cincinnati with a former Lane Seminary student, Hiram Gilmore. And in the fall, a party of seven was reported to have come from Kentucky and stayed in private homes for a period until the arrival of slavecatchers forced them to go to Canada.

Slavecatchers

Slavecatchers were frequent visitors to Oberlin and on more than one occasion, they threatened to burn the town down. A major incident involving slavecatchers occurred in 1841, though largely forgotten, having been overshadowed by the noted events of 1858.

In late February 1841, three slaveholders, led by John Whitford, and accompanied by an Ohio constable, came to Oberlin in search of two fugitive slaves, a man named Jefferson and a woman named Jane. They learned where the slaves were being harbored and forced their way into the home, threatening the owner, Leonard Page, and taking custody of the slaves. However, they did not get very far before they were confronted by a huge armed mob of students and free blacks, estimated to have numbered as many as 500. A local resident intervened to save the slaveholders from violence, and they stayed the night at a tavern.

A warrant was served the next day by an attorney from Elyria, E. S. Hamlin, and all were taken to the local jail. The judge ruled that the slaveholders did not have sufficient evidence to take custody of Jefferson and Jane, but they were allowed time to obtain it and the case was adjourned for a month. After the slaveholders left, Jefferson and Jane broke out of jail with the help of other prisoners and residents of Oberlin and were sped on to Canada. However, an investigation did not charge anyone with being an accessory to their escape.

The next year a posse of slavecatchers came in pursuit of nine fugitive slaves, offering a $1,000 reward for help with their arrest. It was one of many similar incidents occurring in Oberlin, as a correspondent of the *Emancipator* wrote that year: "The people of this part of the country are kept in a lively state of feeling by being called to witness almost daily the fugitive slave fleeing from his bondage to the land of freedom beyond the lake" (*Emancipator and Free American*, October 6, 1842).

Though only sporadic reports continued up through 1855, it is likely that heavy traffic continued based on accounts of the movement of fugitive slaves through Ohio during that period. For instance, in 1848 and 1853, Hiram Wilson wrote about fugitive slaves coming to Canada from Oberlin; in 1851, a report from Oberlin in the *True Democrat* of Cleveland stated that "Six fugitives passed through this palace for the other side of Lake Erie" (November 8, 1851); in 1853, a slave from Kentucky with her seven children and a five-year-old entrusted to her care came to Oberlin. She left the five-year-old in Oberlin because she was ill and the girl died there; and in 1855, the Oberlin Female Anti-Slavery Society reported it was collecting money for a fugitive slave mother and her children who had settled in Oberlin.

Oberlin-Wellington Rescue

In 1858, the controversial Oberlin-Wellington Rescue, involving both students and faculty, received national attention. It illustrated the division in the state of Ohio over slavery. On September 13, John Price, fugitive slave from Kentucky, was arrested by a federal marshal in Oberlin. Price had escaped on horseback during the winter. He had lived in Oberlin without incident for a couple of years before two slavecatchers and two federal marshals caught up with him on September 13, 1858. They tricked him by saying that they had a job for him picking potatoes at a local farm.

The Fugitive Slave Law of 1850 made it mandatory that the federal government assist slaveholders in reclaiming their runaway slaves. Many Oberlin residents were known to be committed to abolitionism. Therefore, to avoid conflict with local people, the marshals took Price to nearby Wellington. Oberlin residents soon heard of the arrest and joined other abolition-minded residents of the Wellington community outside the hotel where the marshals had Price in custody. More than 500 individuals surrounded the Wadsworth Hotel. Peaceful negotiations failed, so the mob forced their way inside and found Price in the attic. They immediately returned him to Oberlin, where his rescuers hid him at the home of James Fairchild, Oberlin College's president. A short time later, they took Price to Canada. Sadly, he died shortly after.

Thirty-seven of the people who participated in freeing Price were indicted by a federal grand jury. They all refused bail and spent three months in jail awaiting their trials. Ohio authorities responded by arresting the federal marshal, his deputies, and others involved in the capture and detention of John Price. Following negotiations between state and federal officials, the arresting officers were freed, as were 35 of those arrested under the federal charges. Only two of those indicted went to trial: Simeon Bushnell, a white man, and Charles Langston, a black man. Both were found guilty in federal court in April 1859. Bushnell was sentenced to 60 days, and Langston, 20 days in jail.

A writ of *habeas corpus* was filed by Bushnell and Langston with the Ohio Supreme Court. The basis of their writ was that the Fugitive Slave Law of 1850 was unconstitutional, and therefore the federal government did not have the authority to arrest or to try them. The Ohio Supreme Court upheld the constitutionality of the law by a three to two ruling. This ruling angered abolitionists in Ohio, and more than 10,000 participated in a rally in Cleveland to oppose it. Supporting this decision was costly to Ohio Chief Justice Joseph Swan, who subsequently failed to win reelection to the court.

Among the rescuers of John Price, who were welcomed home after their release from jail, were James Fitch, Henry Peck, John A. Copeland, Lewis Sheridan Leary, Richard Winsor, John H. Scott, and Jacob Shipherd.

Fitch, whose home had several secret rooms to hide fugitive slaves, drove John Price to the home of John Fairchild. Peck acted as the spokesman for the rescuers during the court trial in Cleveland and also picked up fugitive slaves from Medina for transport to Oberlin. Copeland, a free black carpenter, was very active in the Oberlin Anti-Slavery Society. Some sources state that he was the person who escorted John Price to Canada. He later participated in the raid on Harper's Ferry with John Brown and was caught and hanged—his last words that he would rather die for freedom than be a slave.

Lewis Sheridan Leary was a free black harness maker, as was his father. He was another of the Oberlin citizens who joined Brown in the raid at Harper's Ferry; wounded in the attack, he died the next day.

Richard Winsor was the person who physically rescued John Price from the hotel in Wellington. John H. Scott, a former slave who had become a harness and trunk maker in Oberlin, was with Winsor. The last rescuer mentioned, Jacob Shipherd, was the nephew of the college's founder and the son of the Troy, New York, conductor, Fayette Shipherd, who had by this time moved to

Oberlin. The younger Shipherd later became a Congregational minister like his father and wrote a book about his experience, *The History of the Oberlin-Wellington Rescue in 1859.*

Oberlin College Legacy

Oberlin College was associated with progressive causes from its inception. Its founders were Presbyterian ministers, Philo P. Stewart and Shipherd. Along with the school's second president, evangelist Charles Finney, they were responsible for Oberlin's progressive mandate, which included making Oberlin the first college in the United States to admit black students in the same classroom as whites in 1835. By admitting four women in 1837, and allowing them to attend the same classes in the same classrooms as male students, Oberlin became the oldest continuously operating coeducational institution. Women also were in the forefront of abolition at Oberlin, and they formed two abolitionist societies, the Female and the Young Ladies Anti-Slavery Societies, totaling 134 members.

Oberlin's pioneering efforts in interracial education reached across the nation. Harvey Haviland, the brother of the important Underground Railroad conductor, Laura Haviland, attended Oberlin College, and Haviland said her interracial school, the Raisin Institute in Adrian, Michigan, owed much to her brother's experience at Oberlin. Other schools with abolitionist creeds, especially in the Midwest, looked to the Oberlin model. But not only was Oberlin a pioneer in the higher education of blacks, it also had public schools that educated white and black children side by side at a time when the state of Ohio did not offer public schools for blacks, much less integrated classrooms. Esther Wattles, a black woman who lived in Oberlin, sent her three daughters to public school. She also harbored fugitive slaves in her home.

Owen Brown, the father of John Brown, was a trustee of Oberlin College, and Brown's younger brothers and a sister were students at Oberlin. John Brown had surveyed lands belonging to the college in West Virginia. He also was associated with the Oberlin men who fought in Kansas, but his raid at Harper's Ferry came as a total surprise to the majority of the people of Oberlin.

The First Church built on the Oberlin College campus in 1842 hosted the Oberlin Anti-Slavery Society. It also sheltered fugitive slaves and was the site of several funerals associated with the fight against slavery, including a memorial service for John Copeland, Lewis Leary, and Shields Green, another of the Oberlin men who died as a result of serving in John Brown's army.

—Cynthia Vogel and Tom Calarco

Further Reading

Nat Brandt, *The Town That Started the Civil War* (Syracuse: Syracuse University Press, 1990).

Levi Coffin, *The Reminiscences of Levi Coffin* (Cincinnati: Robert Clark & Co., 1880).

Clayton Sumner Ellsworth, "Oberlin and the Antislavery Movement up to the Civil War" (Ph.D. Dissertation, Cornell University, 1930).

Robert Fletcher, *History of Oberlin College from Its Foundation through the Civil War*, 2 vols. (Oberlin: Oberlin College, 1943), quoting a letter by Nancy Prudden.

Wilbur H. Siebert, *The Mysteries of Ohio's Underground Railroads* (Columbus, OH: Long's College Book Company, 1951).

Wilbur H. Siebert, *The Underground Railroad from Slavery to Freedom* (1898; reprint, NewYork: Arno Press and *The New York Times*, 1968).

OSWEGO, NEW YORK

To portray the role of the Lake Ontario port of Oswego in the Underground Railroad, it is necessary to broaden the scope beyond the city's border to include Oswego County, New York. Small towns, such as Mexico, funneled fugitives to Oswego. This occurred in the famous rescue of William "Jerry" Henry, which succeeded because of help from the greater Oswego community. The county included many abolitionists, such as Asa Sylvester Wing, Edwin W. Clarke, John B. Edwards, Daniel and Miriam Pease, and John Bishop. In addition, Oswego County hosted the 1850 convention of the National Liberty Party that nominated a former slave, the Rev. Samuel Ringgold Ward, for Vice President, and the abolitionist, Gerrit Smith, for President of the United States.

John Edwards

Edwards was Gerrit Smith's business agent, and the two often corresponded about the Underground Railroad. Edwards had moved to the town of Oswego in 1834 to manage the construction of a hydraulic canal. Later, he built and maintained Oswego's docks and piers. By 1831, he was also managing the harbor and real estate investments of Smith, whose ownership of the Oswego Hydraulic Canal and the Pier and Dock Company proved useful in arranging lake crossings for fugitive slaves.

In a July 17, 1847 letter, Edwards told Smith: "Nine poor fugitives from slavery's prison left this port last evening for Canada . . . in much fear that pursuers were after them. They said that they left in a company of 100 and that about 60 of their number were captured before they got out of the slave states."

On April 29, 1852, he wrote Smith that: "the Fugitive Slave Dorsey came to me today with your letter. I have put him aboard of a vessel bound for Canada and gave him a $1.00."

A March 19, 1860 letter from Edwards to Smith shows the longevity of their mutual commitment to the cause of freedom: "the young colored man that was at your house last week arrived at my house last evening. I shall keep him a few days to recuperate."

Earlier, in October, 1851, Gerrit Smith had enlisted support in what became known as the Jerry Rescue. The rescue of William Henry, who went by the first name of Jerry, was a bold message of defiance for the Fugitive Slave Law. The lawbreakers secreted Henry by covered wagon from Syracuse to the Oswego County village of Mexico and the home of Orson Ames, then to Sidney Clarke's home in the port of Oswego, where he crossed Lake Ontario to Canada. Henry, a barrel maker by trade, had been named after his father, a Missouri slave owner. But his mother was a slave, and by the rule of slavery, so was he. Two years after Henry ran away in 1843, his father sold him to another man, and that man, John McReynolds, had been trying to make good on his claim for six long years. Twenty-six men, fourteen white and twelve black, were indicted in the rescue of William "Jerry" Henry, but only one of them, a black man named Enoch Reed, was convicted. Reed died while awaiting his appeal.

Edwin W. Clarke

Sidney Clarke's brother, Edwin W. Clarke, an Oswego attorney, served as president of the Oswego County Anti-Slavery Society and helped raise funds for anti-slavery groups. In 1840, Edwin Clarke campaigned for the release of James Seward, a free black man from Oswego County, who had been kidnapped and transported to Louisiana, where he was enslaved. Although the law was lax toward slavery, Southerners often operated outside the law, and the capture and subsequent enslavement of freemen plagued the Northern states.

There was no room for common ground between opposing sides on the subject of human bondage, the hot-button issue of the day. In a letter to the local

A view of the port of antebellum Oswego where the Oswego Canal met Lake Ontario and fugitive slaves were forwarded to Canada. (Library of Congress)

newspaper, the *Oswego Palladium*, Clarke bayoneted the prospect of compromise: "the principles of slavery and liberty are never dormant, never stand still. They are at constant war, each striving for its own life, and conscious that it can exist only by the annihilation of the other" (Oswego Palladium, April 29, 1840).

Yet, falsehoods spread by slaveholders caused slaves to distrust abolitionists. In 1837, a former slave named George arrived in Mexico, New York, fearing those who championed his cause. He'd been told they were cannibals, numbering in the thousands, always on the lookout for runaways to scalp for a wealthy tanner in the state of New York. The tanner was supposed to make overshoes out of Negro scalps by "turning the woolly part in" (*Emancipator* December 28, 1837). Tall tales like these kept many slaves immobilized or too frightened to ask for help.

Black Agents in Oswego

In spite of the risk of recapture, not all escaped slaves crossed into Canada. By 1855, more than 300 blacks lived in Oswego County, some of whom were fugitive slaves. Many devoted time and resources to help others on the Underground Railroad, such as Nathan and Clarissa Green, who lived on West Eighth Street in Oswego in a home purchased from Gerrit Smith. Nathan was a cook on a steamboat, a useful position for helping runaways. Other Underground Railroad activists included two former South Carolina slaves, John McKenzie, a cartman, and his wife, who lived next door to the Greens.

Tudor E. Grant and Charles Smith, former Maryland slaves, served the Underground Railroad while operating a barber shop at the "black striped pole" in West Oswego. In a June 2, 1835 advertisement, Grant promoted the addition of "a first rate Hair Dresser from Boston" to the staff, so that "ladies can have their hair made into curls, or puffs, or ringlets, and old curls dressed over, at short notice." He also advertised "a full supply of stocks, collars and bosoms of the first quality."

And of course, there were many whites involved in the antislavery movement in Oswego and its surroundings. In 1832, Starr Clark moved from Utica, New York, to the town of Mexico in Oswego County with his wife, Harriet Loomis Clark, and their family. There he set up shop as a stove dealer and tin manufacturer. For almost 30 years, he and his family operated a station on the Underground Railroad, hiding fugitives in the Tin Shop, in their home, and in the homes of other antislavery families. In the 1840s, the Mexico Presbyterian Church barred Starr Clark for advocating the ideal of Christian union, that is, all Christians joining together in one church.

The home of Daniel and Miriam Pease on Cemetery Road in the city of Oswego became a stop on the Underground Railroad, and many of their family members signed antislavery petitions. With the help of his brother-in-law, John Bishop, who lived on a farm about a mile away, Daniel Pease conducted fugitive slaves across the fields, often half a dozen at a time, to the port of Oswego in the middle of the night.

William M. Clarke Letter

William M. Clarke of Syracuse wrote the following letter to his cousin, Edwin Clarke, a business partner of Gerrit Smith, who was extremely active in the Underground Railroad in Oswego (Onondaga Historical Society, Syracuse, New York). It is not certain whether or not "Frisbie" is the real name of the fugitive slave or one that was contrived.

May 31, 1841

Dear Coz,

There were three fugitives shipped on board the old line of packets this morning for Oswego and amid the hurry and bustle, they were not furnished with a "pass," They are Mr. Frisbie and wife from Baltimore and another women from near Baltimore. We commend them to your care

Yours etc

W. M. Clarke

P.S. Another is on his way and you may expect him in a day or two.

Asa Sylvester Wing

At the age of 22, Asa Sylvester Wing was already helping fugitive slaves find freedom. In nine years, by the mid-1840s, he promoted equal rights on a lecture tour through New England. With the passage of the Fugitive Slave Law, Wing increased his efforts. In October 1850 he attended the political convention in Oswego, where Smith and Ward received the Liberty Party's nominations. Earlier, Wing had welcomed his friend, Ward, as a guest at his home.

Married with two children, Wing and his wife, Caroline, routinely hid fugitive slaves in their cellar, accessed through a trap door concealed by a rug. That's likely how they hid Mr. Thompson, his wife, and their five daughters, who were being pursued by slavecatchers, on Christmas Eve, 1850. Several days later, the Thompson family attempted to cross Lake Ontario in a sleigh and was not heard from again.

When Asa Wing died of tuberculosis in the spring of 1854, he was only 38 years old. His friend, perhaps the most famous black man of his day, Frederick Douglass, delivered the eulogy. The following year, abolitionists erected a monument in the Mexico Cemetery in Wing's honor. Three thousand people, including Frederick Douglass, converged on the small town for the dedication.

At the port of Oswego, fugitive slaves might have boarded a steamship, and like the woman seen on the deck of the *William IV* in 1837, might have waved a handkerchief in farewell to a life of bondage. Some refugees traveled in smaller craft, one brave soul floating across Lake Ontario on a wooden gate. Fugitive slaves coming from Oswego landed at Kingston, Cobourg, or Toronto, but no matter where they made their new homes, they could thank the freedom fighters of Oswego for helping them complete the journey.

—Rae Hallstrom

Further Reading

Tom Calarco, *The Underground Railroad in the Adirondack Region* (Jefferson, NC: McFarland and Company, Inc., 2004).

John Jackson Clarke, "Memories of the Anti-Slavery Movement and the Underground Railway." December 19, 1931. Clarke Papers. Oswego County Historical Society.

Mary Ann Gionta, "John B. Edwards." Papers Special Collections, Penfield Library, Oswego, New York.

Letters from John Edwards to Gerrit Smith, Oswego, July 17, 1847, April 29, 1852, March 19, 1860.

Arch Merrill, *The Underground: Freedom's Road, and Other Upstate Tales* (New York: American Book-Stratford Press, 1963).

Judith Wellman, "Asa Wing," discussion from application to National Register of Historic Places of Asa and Caroline Wing property, Mexico, Oswego County, New York, 2000.

Judith Wellman, *Grass Roots Reform in the Burned-Over District in Upstate New York: Religion, Abolitionism, and Democracy* (New York: Garland, 2000).

P

PARKERSBURG, (WEST) VIRGINIA

Parkersburg, an Ohio River port located in Wood County, was a center of transportation for northwestern Virginia. Two major turnpikes converged in Parkersburg: the old Northwestern Virginia Turnpike, later U.S. Route 50, completed in 1838; and the Staunton-Parkersburg Turnpike completed in 1847. The Northwestern Virginia Turnpike crossed the Ohio River at Parkersburg and continued westward through southern Ohio, making it a convenient route for fugitive slaves heading to Ohio and on to Canada. The Staunton-Parkersburg Turnpike, which was 180 miles long and connected Parkersburg with Staunton, Virginia, was taken by many fugitive slaves after they escaped from their masters in southern and central Virginia.

The Northwestern Virginia Turnpike passed through the counties of Wood, Ritchie, and Doddridge on the way to Parkersburg. Numerous inns along the turnpikes in these counties were said to be Underground Railroad stations. A Wood County innkeeper, Parkinson Reed of Williamstown, wrote a biography identifying himself as a conductor. In 1884, he submitted the biography for *Hardesty's History of Wood County.*

Area Abolitionists

An abolitionist colony existed at Valley Mills in Wood County. One of its founders, William Erskine Stevenson, later became the governor of West Virginia. He had been a member of the Pennsylvania legislature until 1857 when he resigned his seat and moved to Valley Mills. Stevenson was once indicted by a Wood County grand jury for circulating an abolitionist book.

The Levi Nutter farm along the Northwestern Virginia Turnpike in Ritchie County was also a station. Another Ritchie County farmer, John Wass, was allegedly assassinated in 1863, for aiding fugitive slaves, and four of Levi Nutter's sons were murdered separately from 1852 to 1862, also likely for aiding fugitive slaves. Such murders showed how dangerous it was to be involved in the Underground Railroad south of the Mason Dixon Line.

Another Ritchie County station was the Harris Inn at Burnt House on the Staunton-Parkersburg Turnpike. The road north from there led to the farmhouse of Wass.

Doddridge County, just east of Ritchie County, was apparently a hotbed of Underground Railroad activity led by clergymen. Reverend Luke Jaco, a Methodist minister, operated a station at Jaco Inn, along the Northwestern Virginia Turnpike just west of West Union, the county seat. Jaco hid fugitive slaves in a cave on Jaco Hill. Two Seventh Day Baptists were also involved there. The Bee Hive was the name of a station on the Underground Railroad operated by Ephraim Bee, and south of West Union, Jepthah Fitz Randolph operated a station on his farm at New Milton. His brick house had four separate basement chambers, which were accessed from hidden trap doors on the first floor of the house.

In Wirt County, south of Wood County, on the Staunton-Parkersburg Turnpike, was a station on the Underground Railroad called the California House. The innkeepers are reported to have owned slaves. Apparently the slaves at this inn carried on Underground Railroad work without their owner suspecting.

In Parkersburg, a black woman named Aunt Jenny is said to have worked with the Underground Railroad. The Point in Parkersburg has a West Virginia historical marker about Aunt Jenny. Another historical marker on Avery Street celebrates the escape of Jane and other slaves from the Harness plantation. An elderly black man called Josephus ferried fugitive slaves from Parkersburg to Ohio when the water level of the Ohio River was high.

Routes from Parkersburg

Once fugitive slaves had crossed the river into Ohio, there were numerous routes that could be taken to Canada. A major port that was a few miles upstream was Marietta. Routes led through a series of stations to Cleveland. Fugitive slaves also could travel down the Ohio River to many Underground Railroad ports in southern Ohio, where conductors would help them get to Canada.

At Point Pleasant, Virginia, about 70 miles downstream from Parkersburg on the Ohio River, the Kanawha River empties into the Ohio. A large concentration of slave labor worked at the Kanawha Salines, which was what they called the saltworks. Slaves mined coal and manned the kettles that boiled salt brine down to produce salt at the Salines. In 1850, there were 3,140 slaves in Kanawha County. This large-scale industry began in the late 1700s. There are many accounts of slaves who escaped to freedom from the Salines.

From Virginia, fugitive slaves also could cross the Ohio River from Point Pleasant, to Gallipolis, Ohio. From here they followed the trail into Jackson County, then into Ross County, and then northeast of Chillicothe through Springfield Township and finally through Pickaway County at Dresbach Station to stations east of Columbus. They would then travel to points north where they

1

were helped by the Wards, Shepherds, Westwaters, and Keltons among others in the Columbus area.

Most Underground Railroad activities were located in "free" states; but in the case of Virginia, many people and places in the northwestern part of the state also were involved in helping fugitive slaves. The land that became West Virginia differed in both surroundings and people. The Allegheny Mountains geographically separated Virginia into two sections. The northwestern portion bordering Ohio and Pennsylvania was settled by pioneering individuals and mountaineers, for whom slavery was disagreeable. Many came here by way of Pennsylvania and included Germans, Protestant Scots, and settlers from the northern states. Westerners, often considered "folks beyond the mountains," wanted to separate from Virginia as far back as 1769, but were unsuccessful. Unlike many of their fellow Virginians in the Tidewater region, they believed in equal opportunity, political liberty, and brotherly love.

—Cynthia Vogel

Further Reading

Charles L. Blockson, *Hippocrene Guide to the Underground Railroad* (New York: Hippocrene Books, 1994).

Hardesty's Historical and Geographical Encyclopedia (New York: H.H. Hardesty & Co., 1884).

Minnie Kendall Lowther, *Ritchie County in History and Romance* (Parsons, WV: McClain Printing Company, 1990).

Wilbur H. Siebert, *The Mysteries of Ohio's Underground Railroads* (Columbus, OH: Long's College Book Company, 1951).

Wilbur H. Siebert, *The Underground Railroad from Slavery to Freedom* (1898; reprint, NewYork: Arno Press and *The New York Times*, 1968).

PERU, CLINTON COUNTY, NEW YORK

Peru became an active stop on northern New York State's Underground Railroad because of its proximity to Canada and its strong Quaker influence. No one knows precisely how many fugitive slaves came through its area, but the antislavery movement there was vigorous. Two of the most significant conductors in its area were Samuel Keese in Peru, Clinton County's southernmost town, and Noadiah Moore, who lived in Champlain, only a couple of miles from the Canadian border.

Quaker Influence

By the end of the American Revolution, almost all American Quakers had liberated their slaves. In Peru and vicinity, Quakers played a vital role in hosting Underground Railroad stops. One dedicated Quaker preacher, Samuel Keese, inspired by his religious teachings, stalwartly condemned slavery. His grandfather John Keese II was one of the founders of the Union, the name given to the Quaker community in Peru.

In 1835 and 1836, Samuel Keese attended the New York Yearly Meeting of the Friends and worked to promote immediate emancipation. In an 1836 letter, he wrote, "We shall encourage the labor of free men over that of slaves . . . we will do all that in us lies consistently with the Declaration [of Independence] to overthrow this most execrable system" (*The Liberator*, July 9, 1836).

A report of a meeting in 1835 opposing the abolitionists indicates the existence of an antislavery society in Clinton County at least by that time. And an account by Peru lawyer Thomas B. Watson, who toured the Adirondacks for the American AntiSlavery Society in the late 1830s, revealed a list of names from organized societies in Peru, Keeseville, Plattsburgh, Beekmantown, Chazy, Champlain, and Moorestown whose total was in the hundreds.

It also is certain that the women of Peru had formed an anti-slavery society by the end of 1835. Though there are no known accounts of the Peru Female Anti-Slavery Society's initial meetings, there is an account of its third annual meeting in 1837 with 200 females attending. Their discussion included a protest of the denial of the right of trial by jury for fugitive slaves that was part of the first Fugitive Slave Law; the oppressive "Gag Rule" that prevented the discussion of slavery in Congress; the abolition of slavery in the District of Columbia; and opposition to the annexation of Texas.

Stephen Keese Smith

The female antislavery society in Peru had two male counterparts: one at the Union, and the other, the West Peru Anti-Slavery Society. In a memoir dictated to D. S. Kellogg in 1887, Stephen Keese Smith, a Quaker and the nephew of Samuel Keese, recalled the formation of the Clinton County Anti-Slavery Society on April 25, 1837:

> [The] delegations (from the town societies at Champlain, Beekmantown, Schuyler Falls, and Peru, with more than a half-dozen wagonloads comprising the Peru delegation) were to meet in the courthouse in Plattsburgh and organize a county anti-slavery society. When our procession of delegates came into Plattsburgh, we were egged and hooted and otherwise mobbed . . . we adjourned to the Stone Church in Beekmantown . . .
>
> Samuel Keese was the head of the depot in Peru. His son, John Keese, myself, and Wendell Lansing [publisher of *The Essex County Republican* and later *The Northern Standard* at Keeseville] were actors. I had large buildings and concealed the Negroes [sic] in them. I kept them, fed them. Often gave them shoes and clothing. I presume I have spent a thousand dollars for them in one way and another. (*Recollections* 59–60)

The Underground Railroad was an intricate mesh of scattered routes. Keese Smith recollected that "There were stations at Albany, Troy, Glens Falls and in

Peru . . . The Negroes would come through the woods and be nearly famished. We kept them and fed them for one or two days and then ran them along to Noadiah Moore's in Champlain" (ibid. 57).

According to Clinton County historian Addie Shields, the route into the county began in Keeseville. There according to oral tradition, Asahel Arthur, who signed the petition calling for the formation of the Clinton County Anti-Slavery Society in 1837 and who was a member of the abolitionist Congregational Church next door, kept a station. The house, which later became a nursing home, extends down a steep rocky slope that overlooks the Ausable River.

To the west of Keeseville were the homes of Stephen Keese Smith and Samuel Keese, only one-half of a mile from each other. Smith's farmhouse, just a short distance from Route 22 on Union Road, was the beginning of a line of stations that led to Moore and the Canadian border.

A house that may have been part of a secondary route and that may have housed fugitive slaves was the John Townsend Addoms homestead in Plattsburgh, just south of Beekmantown. Addoms's name did not appear on any anti-slavery meeting lists, but he signed a petition that called for an antislavery society organization. He also was a member of the Wesleyan-Methodist Church that broke off in 1843 from the parent denomination on account of its opposition to slavery, and we have the testimonies of several individuals claiming his participation that have come down to us.

There are about another dozen other possible stops on the Underground Railroad in the area, among them: the Peter Weaver House and the Weston House in Schuyler Falls, the Barber Homestead on Barber Road in Beekmantown, and the Ransom Tavern and Julius Hubbell home in Chazy. Another alleged station in Keeseville was the Dr. H. O. Tallmadge house on Front Street, which was kitty-corner to the Methodist Episcopal Church, whose minister ironically opposed the abolitionists. Wilbur H. Siebert also claimed that an Underground Railroad station operated in Rouses Point about 37 miles north of Peru, based on the testimony of Troy attorney Martin Townsend who wrote in 1896 that fugitive slaves were sent there by train from Troy.

An insight to the Underground Railroad network in the Adirondacks of northern New York comes from Liberty Party leader Gerrit Smith's journal during his antislavery speaking tour through the region from May 27 to June 15, 1845. Smith's first stop was Saratoga, where he found the abolitionist outreach "unfavorable." Of Glens Falls, he said. "I have never been in a village, which promises better . . . for the anti-slavery cause." Warrensburg, about 15 miles to the north, was just the opposite, but Chester, another 15 miles farther north, drew Smith's praise. Following what was old Route 9 north, Smith's next stops were Schroon Lake, Elizabethtown, and Keeseville. In Plattsburgh, he found few abolitionists but discovered help in the surrounding communities including "that wise and steadfast friend of the slave, Noadiah Moore." Clinton County, Smith wrote, "will probably be the first . . . in our state to throw off its political shackles and stand forth for the slave" ("Gerrit Smith Anti-Slavery Tour," *Albany Patriot*, June 25, 1845).

Champlain Canal

The Champlain Canal was a major factor in the development of fugitive slave traffic in the county. Built in 1823, it linked the Hudson River ports of Albany and Troy with the port of Whitehall, whose steamboats delivered passengers to northern New York, Vermont, and Canada.

An 1837 report that appeared in *Friend of Man* and the *New York Evangelist* reveals that fugitive slaves were already using the Champlain Canal to get to Clinton County. "A slave of middle age, of noble size, six feet high, had made his escape from the southern States, and passed up the Champlain canal," wrote abolitionist Alvan Stewart, "and from Clinton county, passed through Franklin county, into the north part of St. Lawrence county, with intent to go to Ogdensburgh, and cross over [the St. Lawrence River] into Canada" ("Story of a slave whose journey..." *National Enquirer, and Constitutional Advocate of Universal Liberty*, September 21, 1837: 8).

Noadiah Moore

Making the greatest use of the Champlain Canal was the vast lumber industry that had developed in the Adirondacks. It is significant that Clinton County's leading conductor Noadiah Moore was in the lumber trade.

Moore also inspired the Peru operation, just 25 miles south. According to Keese Smith's memoir, "Noadiah Moore... first came to The Union and stirred us up to work in the anti-slavery cause. His place was a station in the Underground Railroad in Champlain, about seven miles from Canada. He went with the Negroes to Canada and looked out for places for them to work" (*Recollections* 57).

It is likely that Moore provided employment to the fugitives at the foundry, lumber mill, wagon shop, or general store that he owned in La Colle, Quebec, five miles north of the Canadian border.

It is not known how many fugitive slaves Moore helped, but his father's biographer said it is likely he spent as much on them as Stephen Keese Smith, which as referred to earlier was about $1,000. In terms of antebellum dollars, this would probably put the number of slaves he aided at about 200.

The strength of Moore's leadership showed in the county's overwhelming support of the Liberty Party initiative to gain voting rights for free blacks in 1846. The county supported the referendum with highest plurality in the state at 72.8 percent. Overall, however, the state initiative failed by a vote of nearly 3 to 1.

Timbucto, Adirondack Region, New York

Frustrated by the failure of the 1846 New York State referendum to gain unrestricted voting rights for black males, Gerrit Smith decided to take matters in his own hands. He set aside 120,000 acres of his own land, primarily in the Adirondacks, to be parceled into 40-acre homesteads for needy, temperate black men between the ages of 21 and 60. This would qualify them to vote under the state property qualification for black men.

One section in the town of North Elba, Essex County, in the midst of the highest peaks of the Adirondacks, evolved into a small community that became known as "Timbucto." Here John Brown moved in 1849 after meeting in Peterboro with Smith, who agreed upon an arrangement in which Brown would assist the black farmers.

Unfortunately, Timbucto disappeared because of the harsh climate and difficulty in farming there. Although Brown left the Adirondacks in 1852, he returned with his family in 1855, but only remained there for short periods thereafter.

Questions remain as to whether Brown ever participated in the Underground Railroad here or whether any fugitive slaves accepted offers for Smith's lands.

At least one fugitive slave, John Thomas, received and settled on Gerrit Smith's land in Franklin Falls in Franklin County, New York. However, he lived there only briefly. Based on other reports, it would not be surprising if there were other fugitive slaves among the 200 blacks who actually tried their hands at farming them.

The evidence also suggests that Brown participated in the Underground Railroad, including a comment from Lyman Epps, who came to Timbucto from Troy with his family and was five when Brown moved to North Elba: "After John Brown come," he said, "they got him to help 'em into Canada," and added that Brown transported his passengers in an ox-cart.

Tom Calarco

The most prominent local, private Underground Railroad site that still exists in Clinton County today is the former home of Stephen Keese Smith. Located on Union Road in Peru, New York, it was originally owned by John Haff, a slaveholder. Haff's son, Abram, a minister and founding member of the Clinton Country Anti-Slavery Society, eventually sold the property to Smith.

—Tom Calarco

Further Reading

Tom Calarco, *The Underground Railroad in the Adirondack Region* (Jefferson, NC: McFarland and Company, Inc., 2004).
Allan S. Everest (ed.), *Recollections* (Clinton County Historical Association: Plattsburgh, 1964).

PHILADELPHIA, PENNSYLVANIA

No city in the eastern United States was more centrally positioned in the Underground Railroad than Philadelphia. As the southernmost major eastern city above the Mason-Dixon Line, Philadelphia was also a major transportation hub, one of the largest ports in the nation, and the nexus of numerous rail and packet lines. Like most major port cities Philadelphia had a historically large population of African Americans, a notable number of them owned and later freed by the city's many Quaker merchants. The existence of this population base coupled with the city's prosperity to draw a steady stream of free black and fugitive people from rural areas, border states, many of them coming on the numerous vessels visiting Philadelphia from both North and South. In addition, historian Fergus Bordewich has noted, Quakers who had plantations in the West Indies sent people they had freed "by the hundreds" to the city, and a large number of enslaved people brought by their masters from Santo Domingo after its 1791 slave rebellion, were freed by the courts. By 1850 Philadelphia's black population was the largest in the free states. At midcentury, when Philadelphia's population was less than a quarter of New York's, nearly six thousand more African Americans lived in Philadelphia.

Racial Unrest

Like New York and Boston, Philadelphia was beset by racial violence from the late 1820s through the 1840s; according to historian Sam Bass Warner, between 1829 and 1850 six major anti-black mob actions took place there (Hershberg 370). The city's extensive commercial ties to the South and proximity to slaveholding states enhanced proslavery sentiment and hostility. In 1841, the antislavery newspaper *Pennsylvania Freeman* stated that Philadelphia was at that time "infested with kidnappers" (Blockson 10). Nevertheless, from 1790 through at least 1820, Philadelphia's black population grew far more rapidly than the black populations of Boston and New York; from the 1780s, it developed a significantly greater number of schools, churches, and benevolent societies. Black, white, and mixed-race organizations dedicated to abolishing slavery were founded from 1775 forward, and Philadelphia was home to the first free colored people's convention in 1830 and the first annual meeting of the American Anti-Slavery Society in 1833.

Early Fugitive Assistance

Philadelphians had been involved in fugitive assistance from at least 1787, when the 16-year-old Quaker Isaac Tatem Hopper sent an escaped slave sailor identified only as Joe to the Bucks County, Pennsylvania, home of John Stapler with directions and a letter of introduction (Child 33–35). Hopper's involvement in the movement both in Philadelphia and in New York (where he moved in 1829) involved not only aiding escapes but also, despite his lack of legal education, extensive work in the courts. Author, editor, and reformer Lydia Maria Child termed his knowledge of slavery law "proverbial" and added, "Friend Hopper's quickness in slipping through loop-holes, and dodging round corners, rendered him exceedingly troublesome and provoking to slaveholders. He often kept cases pending in court three or four years, till the claimants were completely wearied out, and ready to settle on any terms" (Child 202–203). Her 1853 biography of Hopper, published the year after his death, describes 33 instances of Hopper's Underground Railroad work between 1787 and 1827. "Many more narratives of similar character might be added," Child pointed out, "for I think he estimated at more than one thousand the number of cases in which he had been employed for fugitives, in one way or another, during his 40 years' residence in Philadelphia" (Child 201–202).

Richard Allen

From an early point, too, Richard Allen (1780–1831) is said to have sheltered fugitives at "Mother" Bethel Church, which was erected in 1805. Historian Charles Blockson has noted that speakers at the first colored people's convention in 1831, held at this church, "encouraged the use of churches as sanctuaries for runaway slaves, an idea which would be carried out by nearly all black churches in Pennsylvania and elsewhere" (13). The church's online history states that some modern-day members of the congregation descended from fugitives who were assisted by earlier members.

Vigilance Organizations

Underground Railroad agents, Hopper and Allen worked without the benefit of any formal fugitive-assistance organization, but the system they developed no doubt served as a model for such associations in Philadelphia, if not elsewhere. Like Boston and New York, Philadelphia had two successive vigilance committees, one formed in 1837 and the other in 1852. Historian Joseph Borome has suggested that the creation of the first, formally the Vigilant Association of Philadelphia, was stimulated by the case of the fugitive Dorsey brothers. In the summer of 1836, Basil, Charles, Thomas, and William Dorsey escaped from a Frederick County, Maryland, plantation and made their way to Reading, Pennsylvania. No evidence has surfaced to date that the Dorseys' escape from Maryland was assisted, but their route suggests reliance on places of known Underground Railroad activity. Robert Purvis, a leader in Philadelphia's African American community, learned of the brothers' escape and brought them to Philadelphia; Thomas preferred to remain in the city, but Purvis brought the other brothers to his farm in the Bucks County town of Bristol. Basil Dorsey worked for Purvis, who found work for Charles and William on nearby farms. The arrival of Basil Dorsey's free wife in Bristol shortly afterward triggered his owner's attempt to reclaim him when her brother-in-law revealed their location. While plowing one of Purvis's fields, Basil Dorsey was taken and jailed in Bristol. Purvis secured legal counsel for him, helped Charles and William escape, and organized the local African American community to attend Basil's forthcoming trial; and if the court determined to return him to slavery, planned to engineer his escape. The local court dismissed the case against Dorsey on a technicality, however, whereupon Purvis took Dorsey to his mother's Philadelphia home. He then brought him to abolitionist editor Joshua Leavitt in New York, who sent him along to his father's farm in Charlemont, Massachusetts. Dorsey later moved to Florence, Massachusetts, home of the utopian and antislavery Northampton Association for Education and Industry, where he remained until he died.

Purvis suggested forming Philadelphia's first vigilance committee in the same month that the court released Basil Dorsey. Created to raise funds "to aid colored persons in distress," the Vigilant Association's first officers were African American men. Less than a year later African American women founded the Female Vigilant Association to work with and raise funds for the men's group. The group's records, kept by barber and association secretary Jacob C. White from early June 1839, document its activity. Transcribed by Borome, the "Minute Book" documents the group's aid to 46 fugitives in its first six months. Of these, the association sent thirteen to New York, twelve to Canada, another five to interim locations but bound for Canada, and nine to towns in Bucks and Montgomery counties to the north. In three months in 1842 it handled 117 cases, either assisting escapes or dealing with fugitives' legal issues. In December 1843 the association was reorganized and renamed the Vigilance Committee of Philadelphia, because "the number of toil-worn fugitives from southern injustice & slaveholding cruelty has increased to such an extent" that the committee must "adopt more liberal & systematic measures to add them in their efforts to escape" (Minute Book quoted in Borome 348).

Robert Purvis

Born in 1810 in South Carolina, Purvis moved with his family to Philadelphia in 1819, and he was elected president of the Vigilant Committee in 1839. According to his 1898 *New York Times* obituary, Purvis once estimated that he helped an average of one fugitive a day between 1831 and 1861 and had thus assisted more than 9,000 over the course of his life. In a letter to historian Robert C. Smedley written at some point before 1883, he described how part of the Philadelphia Underground Railroad system worked. Vessels carrying Southern lumber north, he wrote, often brought fugitives to the Vigilance Committee, which "distributed" some among committee members. "But most of them," Purvis stated, "were received at my house in Philadelphia, where by the ingenuity of a carpenter, I caused a place to be constructed underneath a room, which could only be entered by a trap door in the floor" (Smedley 355–356).

Purvis also described one aspect of the connection between Philadelphia to Baltimore. "The most efficient helpers, or agents we had, were two market women, who lived in Baltimore, one of whom was white, the other 'colored.' By some means, they obtained a number of genuine certificates of freedom or passports, which they gave to slaves who wished to escape. These passports were afterwards returned to them, and used again by other fugitives. The generally received opinion, that 'all negroes look alike,' prevented too close a scrutiny by the officials" (Smedley 355–356). In his final autobiography Frederick Douglass described this exact subterfuge, which he used to effect his own escape in 1838.

Purvis was clearly regarded as a leader in the Philadelphia black community, not only by African Americans but by whites as well. This made him the target of a mob that attacked his house during a race riot triggered by the 1842 Supreme Court decision in *Prigg v. Pennsylvania*, which had overruled a state law banning the removal by force of any Pennsylvanian with the intent of selling or enslaving them. Purvis armed himself in defense and shortly afterward brought property in the Bucks County town of Byberry, by which action he effectively removed himself from the center of the vigilance committee.

James Miller McKim

James Miller McKim was involved in the Vigilant Committee at least from its 1843 reorganization and remained among the most active Underground Railroad agents in Philadelphia. An antislavery lecturer since 1836, McKim was hired as publishing agent of the Pennsylvania Anti-Slavery Society and editor of its newspaper *Pennsylvania Freeman* in 1840; he later became the society's corresponding secretary and general agent. Though McKim may have been more heavily involved in legal matters confronting fugitives, he played a central role in the escape of Henry "Box" Brown from Richmond, Virginia, in 1849. One the most well-publicized escapes of the antebellum period, it is also one of the best documented. In December 1848, four months after his wife and children were sold to a planter in North Carolina, Brown developed a plan to ship himself as freight to the free states. He shared his idea with white shopkeeper Samuel A. Smith, who visited McKim in March 1849 to seek his advice and assistance. McKim wrote to a friend that Smith "was very desirous as to secure the escape of a man in that city who was held as a slave. He proposed to ship him by overland express in a box to this city." McKim thought the plan too dangerous, but Smith "satisfied me that the plan was feasible, said as a merchant he frequently shipped large boxes in that way &c &c. All he wanted he said was a man in Phila who would engage to receive the box" (Ruggles 29). Though he feared that Brown could not survive the ordeal, McKim ultimately agreed to be the recipient and declined to accept the $100 Brown had saved for that purpose.

With the aid of Brown's friend, James Caesar Anthony Smith (to whose name "Boxer" was later added), Brown put himself in a box barely large enough to hold him and carried a supply of water and biscuits, and a gimlet to bore a hole in the box for air should he need it. McKim wrote at the time that Brown was in the box for 27 hours on both steamship and rail, which shifted six times, and "set down with his back, shoulders, & head downwards" three times. Edward M. Davis, the son-in-law of James and Lucretia Mott, arranged for a driver to deliver the box to the antislavery society's office. "The express wagon had left & I entered the office alone dreading lest I should find the man inside dead," McKim wrote. "You can better imagine than I can describe my feelings when tapping on the box & calling out, 'all right,' the prompt reply came from within, 'all right sir.' I never felt happier in my life hardly" (*National Anti-Slavery Standard*, June 7, 1849).

McKim took Brown to the Motts' house, and James Mott then brought him to the home of black activist William Still, where he spent several days. Afterward Brown was sent on to Sydney Howard Gay of the New York Vigilance Committee and then to abolitionist Joseph Ricketson in New Bedford. The story of Brown's escape was an immediate sensation both in and outside the abolitionist movement, and he spent many years recounting it as a speaker on the antislavery lecture circuit and later as an entertainer in England, where he moved in 1851.

William Still

William Still was among those present when Brown's box was opened at the antislavery office, and he and McKim were the principal players in the formation and operation of the 1852 Vigilance Committee of Philadelphia. Born in Burlington County, New Jersey, in 1821, the son of a free father and fugitive mother, Still had come to Philadelphia in 1844. In 1847 he met McKim and soon afterward was hired as a clerk at the antislavery society's office. When the new vigilance group was formed Still was appointed the head of an "acting committee" to deal directly with fugitive cases, while McKim was named the committee's president and Purvis the chair of its general committee. At the organizing meeting McKim stated the 1837 vigilant association had become "disorganized and scattered" and that over the past few years the job of fugitive assistance had fallen to individuals, "sometimes in a very irregular manner." A new committee was in order, he said, because "the friends of the fugitive slave had been for some years past, embarrassed, for the want of a properly constructed active, Vigilance Committee" (*Pennsylvania Freeman* quoted in Still 635). McKim, Purvis, White, and James J. G. Bias were among members of the first committee who also belonged to the 1852 committee.

Although Purvis was the only African American on the state antislavery society's executive committee at the time, thirteen of the nineteen members of the General Vigilance Committee were African American, two others probably were, and three of the four members of the acting committee were black. That fact distinguishes the Philadelphia committee from the 1850s Boston Vigilance Committee, which was overwhelmingly white, and underscores the key position blacks occupied in fugitive assistance in Pennsylvania and elsewhere. Blockson asserted, "It is safe to say that the operation of the Underground Railroad in Philadelphia was carried out predominantly by black conductors after 1840" and that the African American neighborhood of Paschall's Alley at Fifth and Coates streets "aided and sheltered more fugitives slaves than any other section of the city until the Civil War" (17) though he cited no evidence for the claim.

According to historian James O. Horton, William Still "was one of Philadelphia's most effective and most widely known abolitionists and Underground

Railroad leaders. . . . Reputedly, he knew almost everything and everyone of significance in the Eastern underground movement." He further asserted that Still was "one of the UGRR's most significant historians," having recorded in great detail the stories of the 649 fugitives who received the vigilance committee's assistance between 1852 and the Civil War (Horton 177–178). Numbers of the fugitive slaves aided by Still vary slightly among various accounts. For instance, a report in the Wilbur Siebert collection that breaks them down by year and state of origin, totaled 664, and this number did not include the years from 1850 to 1852, so the total number is likely above 800 as some other accounts estimate.

In 1872 Still compiled most of these accounts, along with letters from fugitives and those who aided their escapes, in *The Underground Railroad: A Record of Facts, Authentic Narratives, Letters, &c., Narrating the Hardships Hair-breadth Escapes and Death Struggles of the Slaves in Their Efforts for Freedom, as Related by Themselves and Others, or Witnessed by the Author*, which remains the most authoritative text on the movement.

Before the second Vigilance Committee was created, Still was involved in the escape of William and Ellen Craft, who, disguised respectively as a manservant and a white master, escaped from Georgia in 1848 and came through Philadelphia en route to Boston. In August 1850 he also handled the case of Peter Friedman (or Freedman), of whom Still made the shocking discovery was his own lost brother. When Still's mother first escaped from Maryland with four of her children (including Peter) they were retaken, but on her second successful escape in 1807 she took only her two youngest daughters. Peter and his brother Levin were soldto a slave trader who sold them to a Kentucky slaveholder. They later were moved to Alabama, where Peter was able to purchase his own freedom. By questioning the man about his parents and early history, William Still was able to determine that Friedman was his brother and promptly reunited him with his mother and siblings. Peter returned to Alabama to attempt to purchase the freedom of his wife and three children, but the state's legal restrictions on the practice discouraged him, and he returned to Philadelphia.

Peter Still and Seth Concklin

In the meantime, white abolitionist Seth Concklin, who had read about the Stills' reunion and Peter's wish to redeem his wife and children, volunteered to help them escape. Concklin managed to get the family to Vincennes, Indiana, only to be arrested there and jailed. Concklin also was subsequently arrested, and was the victim of a suspicious drowning in the Ohio River while being brought back to Alabama with the Still family to stand trial.

Peter was not about to give up, however, and his brother arranged a tour for him to tell his story on the antislavery lecture circuit so that he could earn $5,000, the amount for which his family's owner had agreed to sell them. In October 1854, his family reached the free states and moved to Burlington, New Jersey, where Peter died in 1868.

Jane Johnson

Perhaps the most notorious case in which Still was involved after the formation of the 1852 committee was that of Jane Johnson, who had been purchased with her two sons in 1853 by John Hill Wheeler, then a North Carolina state legislator. Appointed U.S. minister to Nicaragua by President Franklin Pierce in 1854, Wheeler and the family were en route to Nicaragua when their steamer stopped in Philadelphia. While Wheeler went to dinner at a nearby hotel, Johnson later stated:

> I saw a colored woman and told her I was a slave woman, that my master had told me not to speak to colored people, and that if any of them spoke to me to say that I was free; but I am not free; but I want to be free; she said: "poor thing, I pity you;" after that I saw a colored man and said the same thing to him, he said he would telegraph to New York, and two men would meet me at 9 o'clock and take me with them. (Still 94)

The man and woman to whom Johnson spoke sent a message to Still. Accompanied by vigilance committee member Passmore Williamson, Still went to the steamboat wharf with a description of Johnson and her sons. Finding her with Wheeler on the steamer's second deck, Still told her that Pennsylvania law

Samuel Johnson house in Germantown section of Philadelphia, Pennsylvania; home of Quaker abolitionist family who aided fugitive slaves. (Courtesy of Tom Calarco)

stipulated that any enslaved person brought to a free state by an owner was automatically free. Still and Williamson managed to take Johnson and her children from the vessel while two men of color, later jailed for a week, kept Wheeler at bay. Johnson was taken out of Philadelphia quickly, and Williamson, who refused to reveal their destination—and may not have known it— was jailed for contempt of court. Still wrote that Johnson and her children went to Canada, but they were in fact sent to the New York Vigilance Committee, whose records document her arrival and her later passage to Boston. In several letters, one to Williamson, the Boston African American abolitionist William C. Nell stated that he had escorted Johnson from the Boston rail depot and helped her find a job and a place to stay. Boston Vigilance Committee records show that the committee gave her money for clothes and furniture and reimbursed the black boardinghouse keeper William Manix for housing her and her sons upon their arrival. The genealogist Katherine E. Flynn found that Johnson married in Boston, where she died in 1872, and has argued that she was the probable author of *The Bondwoman's Narrative*, now believed to be the first novel written by a once-enslaved black woman.

Other Agents

Still and others cite the work of many other Philadelphians in the Underground Railroad. Jacob C. White, who once accompanied a family of fugitives to Canada, is said to have sheltered "hundreds" of escapees in his Old York Road home. African American confectioner Mary Myers once concealed a woman in her cake shop who had, like Henry Box Brown, come to Philadelphia in a crate; the black chimney sweep John Lewton is believed to have put fugitives to work in his own business until he could safely move them north. The assistance extended to fugitives by African American ministers Stephen H. Gloucester and James John Gould Bias is documented in the minute book of the city's first vigilance committee. Philadelphian Samuel D. Burr is, born, probably free, in Delaware in 1808, worked with Wilmington abolitionist Thomas Garrett and others as he traveled into the slave states to encourage and assist escapes. Burris was arrested and jailed in Dover, Delaware, and sentenced to be sold as an indentured servant, but McKim and other Philadelphians hired the white abolitionist Isaac S. Flint to buy Burris at auction in 1851; he was thus free and moved to California the next year. Among the numerous white fugitive assistants was the Quaker Esther Moore. Still wrote of her:

> No woman, white or colored, living in Philadelphia for the same number of years, left her home oftener, especially to seek out and aid the weary travelers escaping from bondage, than did this philanthropist. It is hardly too much to say that with her own hand she administered to hundreds. She begged of the Committee, as a special favor, that she might be duly notified of every fugitive reaching

Philadelphia, and actually felt hurt if from any cause whatever this request was not complied with. (637)

As in any other place, the extent of fugitive traffic to and through Philadelphia is impossible to gauge. While Purvis and Hopper reported having helped thousands and others were credited with hundreds of acts of assistance, the vigilance committee's documented aid to 649 persons seems a surprisingly small number. But Still himself pointed out that "others besides the Committee were deeply interested in The Road; indeed, the little aid actually rendered by the Committee, was comparatively insignificant, compared with the aid rendered by some who were not nominally members" (635). The degree of fugitive presence in the city, to say nothing of those who, like Frederick Douglass, came and quickly moved on, is suggested by federal census figures: between 1850, the year the Fugitive Slave Act became law, and 1860 Philadelphia's black population fell by more than 25 percent, from 19,587 to 14,420 persons over that decade.

—Kathryn Grover

Origin of the Term, Underground Railroad

No one knows for certain where the name Underground Railroad came from. There have been several stories circulated over the years. The most often-told story came from Ripley, Ohio, about a fugitive slave named Tice Davids fleeing from Kentucky, who swam across the Ohio River in 1831. His master was in hot pursuit and saw Davids plunge into the river. But while searching for a boat to cross, he lost sight of him. Davids's master carefully searched the area but without luck, and it supposedly caused him to reply in exasperation, "He must have gone on an underground road."

According to Eber Pettit, a legendary conductor from western New York, the term was first used in a Washington, D.C., newspaper sometime after 1839, referring to a fugitive slave who had escaped to Albany. Another source claims its use in 1842 in an obscure newspaper, the *New York Semi-Weekly Express*: "We passed 26 prime slaves to the land of freedom last week. . . . All went by 'the underground railroad.'"

Whatever the case, the name caught on. It had a magical ring, using the metaphor of the railroad, the technological marvel of the age, and gave an aura of power and secrecy to it that was far greater than its reality. In actuality, it was simply a network of mostly selfless people breaking an unjust law to help people escape from slavery, and the means they used to get it done was any conveyance available that could slip by unnoticed.

Further Reading

Charles L. Blockson, *The Underground Railroad in Pennsylvania* (Jacksonville, NC: Flame International, 1981).

Joseph A. Borome, "The Vigilant Committee of Philadelphia," *Pennsylvania Magazine of History and Biography* 92, 3 (July 1968): 320–351.

L. Maria Child, *Isaac T. Hopper: A True Life* (Boston: John P. Jewett and Co.; Cleveland: Jewett, Proctor and Worthington; London: Low and Co., 1853).

Katherine E. Flynn, "Jane Johnson, Found! But Is She 'Hannah Crafts'? The Search for the Author of *The Bondwoman's Narrative*," *National Genealogical Society Quarterly* 90, 3 (September 2002), reprinted in *In Search of Hannah Crafts: Critical Essays on the Bondwoman's Narrative*, eds. Henry Louis Gates and Hollis Robbins (New York: Basic Civitas Books, 2004).

James Oliver Horton, "A Crusade for Freedom: William Still and the Real Underground Railroad," in *Passages to Freedom: The Underground Railroad in History and Memory*, ed. David W. Blight (Washington, D.C.: Smithsonian Books, 2004), 175–193.

Jeffrey Ruggles, *The Unboxing of Henry Brown* (Richmond: The Library of Virginia, 2003).

Dr. Robert C. Smedley, *History of the Underground Railroad in Chester and the Neighboring Counties of Pennsylvania* (Lancaster, PA: The Journal, 1883; reprint, Mechanicsburg, PA: Stackpole Books, 2005).

William Still, *The Underground Railroad* (1872; reprint, Chicago: Johnson Publishing Co., 1970).

PITTSBURGH, PENNSYLVANIA

Pittsburgh was a hub of activity for the Underground Railroad because of its location in western Pennsylvania near the slave state of Virginia and its substantial black population. The confluence at Pittsburgh of three major rivers, the Allegheny, the Monongahela, and the Ohio, played a critical role in its Underground Railroad. Fugitive slaves came north on the Ohio River from Kentucky and Virginia in riverboats, while others traveled along the shoreline of the Monongahela River from Morgantown in Virginia.

Routes to and from Pittsburgh

In addition, three overland routes reached Pittsburgh: the first one originating in Wheeling, Virginia; the second from the town of Washington, to the south of Pittsburgh; and the third from Uniontown in southern Pennsylvania. While these routes brought fugitive slaves to Pittsburgh, three other routes took them out of the city. One went a few miles west down the Ohio River to Beaver County. From here the travelers could head north over a well-organized network to Erie, Pennsylvania. A second exit route went up the Allegheny River to the town of Franklin, a stopping place before going on to Erie. The third route took the fugitive slaves overland directly north to Franklin and Erie. From Erie, they boarded boats and crossed the lake to Port Royal, Ontario, Canada, and freedom. Fugitive slaves entering western Pennsylvania might pass through Pittsburgh under the care of Philanthropic Society members, then typically headed toward Erie. Some stayed with a community of free blacks in Mercer County known as Freedom Road. Another route that went northwest to Pittsburgh from eastern Virginia involved rail and overland travel. John Fairfield, originally from Virginia, orchestrated a number of escapes through Pittsburgh for fugitive slaves coming from Maryland and the Philadelphia area. Fairfield used disguises as his main device for getting the fugitive slaves to safety. He dressed them in wigs and makeup to look like white Southerners and bought them tickets on the Baltimore & Ohio train to Pittsburgh. This method was successful, however, only with light-complexioned blacks that could pass as whites.

Black Agents

Blacks were instrumental in the success of the Underground Railroad network in Pittsburgh because of their leadership, which was crucial for many successful escapes. While several whites helped and the general attitude was supportive of the cause, it was primarily blacks who made the Underground Railroad work there.

Among the leaders in the Pittsburgh Underground Railroad network were Charles Avery, Martin R. Delany, John B. Vashon, Reverend Lewis Woodson, and John C. Peck. The only white person in the group was Avery. He came to Pittsburgh in 1812 from Westchester County in New York and, because of his successful business endeavors, quickly became one of the wealthiest people in the city. Avery, a devout Methodist minister and an ardent abolitionist, was convinced that education was the key by which blacks could advance in society. In March 1849 he founded the Allegheny Institute and Mission Church for young blacks living in and around the city. The church was reported to have a tunnel that led to a canal on the Allegheny River. The school, later known as Avery College, was built at Nash and Avery streets in Allegheny City across the Allegheny River from Pittsburgh. Soon after the school opened, Avery hid fugitive slaves in the building. According to legend, Avery sometimes disguised himself as a coachman and took the fugitive slaves to safety hidden in a carriage he drove or sent them up the Allegheny River in boats.

Martin R. Delany was the most famous of the four black leaders of the Underground Railroad in Pittsburgh. Born in Charleston, Virginia, on May 6, 1812, his family relocated in Kerrstown, Pennsylvania, a small free black community near the town of Chambersburg. When he turned 19, he decided to cross the Allegheny Mountains on foot to Pittsburgh. When he arrived, he met prominent black civic leader, John B. Vashon, who convinced him to further his education. He enrolled in the school run by the Bethel African Methodist Episcopal Church. Showing great promise as a student, and wanting to become a doctor, he began to study medicine in 1832 and eventually was accepted by the Harvard University School of Medicine. Because of the bigotry he faced from his fellow students, he stayed at Harvard for only one year and then returned to Arthursville, a black community in Pittsburgh. He opened an office on Smithfield Street where he provided black patients with various medical assistances. Delany then began to publish a newspaper called *The Mystery*, the first newspaper in Pittsburgh owned by a black. He also briefly co-edited the *North Star* with Frederick Douglass.

Delany helped to found the Philanthropic Society in Pittsburgh, a group that aided fugitive slaves, and is reported to have helped 269 fugitive slaves escape in one year alone. One of the most famous examples of Delany's involvement in Underground Railroad activities occurred in 1853. A Southern slavecatcher, Thomas J. Adams of Nashville, Tennessee, tricked Alexander Hendrickure, a free black man from Kingston, Canada, to come to the United States. Delany received a telegram from Philadelphia saying that Adams and Hendrickure had arrived and that they were going to take the train to Pittsburgh. The telegram also stated that Adams had tricked Hendrickure and planned to enslave him when he arrived at Pittsburgh. Delany and several other abolitionists were waiting at the station when the train arrived. They took Hendrickure, despite Adams' protests, saying that the young black boy belonged to Delany. A policeman named John Fox took Hendrickure and Adams to the St. Clair Hotel at the corner of St. Clair and Penn streets where they were held until a local magistrate could settle the issue. Delany then contacted the Honorable Judge Williams, a Justice of the Bench of the District Court for the Western District of Pennsylvania. The judge issued a writ and Hendrickure was given to Delany. Adams was ordered to appear before the judge on the charge of kidnapping, but he fled and Hendrickure was set free.

John B. Vashon was a free black man who came to Pittsburgh in 1829 to help the black community. He and Reverend Lewis Woodson were instrumental in founding the Pittsburgh African Education Society in 1832. He served as the society's first president. The following year he helped organize the Pittsburgh Anti-Slavery Society, a group that devoted a great deal of effort to helping fugitive slaves. Vashon opened two businesses in 1833, a barbershop situated at 59 Third Street, in the downtown area of Pittsburgh, and a bathhouse called the City Baths, located next to his barbershop. Both locations gathered useful information for the Underground Railroad agents. White Southern slave owners traveling through Pittsburgh often stopped at these establishments and would talk freely about any slaves they might have with them and where they were staying in the city.

In 1850, a fugitive slave, named George White, had reached Pittsburgh and Vashon provided him with a place to stay and hired him in his barbershop. Unfortunately, two years later, White's former master, Mr. Rose from Wellsburg in western Virginia, came to the shop and immediately recognized White. To avoid any legal action, Rose agreed to accept the payment of $200 from Vashon for the purchase of White.

The Reverend Lewis Woodson came to the city in 1815 and, a few years later, helped to establish the Bethel African Methodist Episcopal Church (AME) at the corner of Water and Smithfield streets in the downtown area. It was the first AME Church west of the Allegheny Mountains. Under his leadership the church filled a role as spiritual, educational, and cultural center for the black community in Pittsburgh. The church also provided assistance to fugitive slaves.

John C. Peck was born in Hagerstown, Maryland, in 1802. In 1821 he moved to Carlisle, Pennsylvania, where he became very active in the African Methodist Episcopal Church, serving as a deacon. In 1837 Peck moved to Pittsburgh and became a successful businessman, opening a barbershop, a wig making shop, a clothing store, and a restaurant, called The Oyster House. He joined the Underground Railroad and gathered information on Southern masters and their slaves, when the masters stopped by his restaurant or barbershop.

Two predominantly black sections of Pittsburgh were Arthursville and Hayti, located not far from the downtown section. In the early 1800s, Arthursville was a hub of the Underground Railroad and the center of the black community. In Arthursville, the black working class and black business elite were united through religion, temperance societies, and educational efforts. Fugitive slaves were often hidden here, helped by agents and conductors, including Reverend Woodson, Samuel Bruce, George Gardner, and AME Bishop Benjamin Tucker Tanner. Blacks staffed the hotels in Pittsburgh and also worked as domestics in the homes of many wealthy citizens in the area. One of those homes belonged to Thomas Bingham, a leading attorney and journalist in Pittsburgh. He had a home in the Mt. Washington district of the city and, apparently with his approval, his free black staff used it as an Underground Railroad station.

A prominent hotel in downtown Pittsburgh, the Monongahela House, employed over 300 blacks. They often aided fugitive slaves who accompanied their visiting masters prior to the 1847 law that made it illegal for slaveowners to bring their slaves into the state. Thomas Brown, a former slave from Maryland, worked with the Monongahela House where he became associated with Lewis Woodson and Martin Delany in the Underground Railroad. Brown also worked on the boats along the river traveling between Pittsburgh and Cincinnati.

Other Agents

Jane Grey Cannon, born in Pittsburgh on December 6, 1815, became a schoolteacher at a very young age, and married James Swisshelm when she was 21. The couple moved to Louisville, Kentucky, where they lived on a farm. In Kentucky, Jane witnessed the horrors of slavery firsthand and became a devoted abolitionist. For a short period of time she worked on the Underground Railroad, but she was well known for her sharp, witty lectures and publications against slavery and for women's rights as well as civil rights for blacks. In 1848 she established her own antislavery newspaper, the *Pittsburgh Saturday Visiter.*

The people in Pittsburgh who helped fugitive slaves were greatly diversified; they were black, white, rich, poor, male, and female. Many were important contributors to the abolitionist movement and the activities of the Underground Railroad.

—Cynthia Vogel

Further Reading

Joseph Henderson Bausman, *History of Beaver County, Pennsylvania* (New York: Knickerbocker Press, 1904).

Charles Blockson, *The Underground Railroad in Pennsylvania* (Jacksonville, NC: Flame International, 1981).

Larry Gara, *The Liberty Line: The Legend of the Underground Railroad* (Lexington, KY: University of Kentucky Press, 1967).

Wilbur H. Siebert, *The Underground Railroad from Slavery to Freedom* (1898; reprint, New York: Arno Press and *The New York Times*, 1968.

William J. Switala, *Underground Railroad in Pennsylvania* (Mechanicsburg, PA: Stackpole Books, 2001).

POKE PATCH, OHIO

Located in the western "notch" of Gallia County, adjacent to Lawrence County, the southernmost county in Ohio, Poke Patch was founded in the 1820s as a predominantly black community. Both free blacks and former slaves found employment as farmers or in the area's booming iron industry. Due to the dangerous working conditions in the iron foundries, many whites refused employment, allowing blacks to secure jobs there.

Poke Patch had a population of less than 100 people. The John J. Stewart family, Peter Coker and his sons, and Benjamin Holly were among the early settlers. It harbored fugitive slaves until the end of the Civil War. Here they hid in the settlement, which was a system of farmsteads spread over a hilly five-mile radius, and which included some whites and Native Americans. At least as many as 200 escaped slaves are believed to have passed through this community.

Poke Patch Network

Another nearby black community and important gateway for fugitive slaves was Burlington, located in Lawrence County on the Ohio River, south of Poke Patch. It had been populated by slaves who had been emancipated and settled in Lawrence County by the masters. Because these blacks were securely provided for, they could purchase land and not have to struggle as many freed slaves did. In 1849, James Twyman came to Ohio with a group of 32 freed slaves and settled just east of Burlington on a 640-acre farm of hills and bottom land, with one large frame house and several small tenant houses. Several such migrant groups came to Burlington and other communities of Lawrence County where they formed the nucleus of a strong self-reliant black community.

Burlington was opposite the mouth of present-day West Virginia's Big Sandy River, providing "easy" access from Virginia and other Southern states to the Ohio River. Fugitives who crossed at Burlington were helped by several agents, including free black Philip Wilson who took them to the Mount Vernon and Olive Furnaces, from which they went to Poke Patch. Reverend Beaman and

Dr. Cornelius Ball, Presbyterians, and Stephen Wilson, a Methodist, also transported fugitive slaves. John Dicher, a black man known as a fearless conductor, transported fugitive slaves from Proctorville, located nine miles east of Burlington, following the railroad tracks before going through a wooded section to the Poke Patch Settlement. Dicher and another black, Gabe Johnson, were active in the Underground Railroad over a 65 mile distance along the Ohio River, from Portsmouth to Proctorville. Between Burlington and Huntington, Virginia, was a sandbar located between Twelve Pole Creek and Four Pole Creek, which allowed fugitive slaves to cross the Ohio River on foot. Further east, along the Ohio side of the river were Quaker Bottom, Proctorville, and Red Hill, all active stations on the Underground Railroad.

Another busy Underground Railroad route that followed north to Poke Patch came from the port of Ironton. As fugitive slaves continued north from the ports in Lawrence County, they passed through the Hanging Rock Iron Region, a 31 iron ore belt that included the Ohio counties of Jackson, Vinton, Lawrence, and Scioto and a portion of Kentucky. Slave owner John Means of South Carolina came to Lawrence County with his slaves in 1819. He was an early leader in the Hanging Rock iron industry, establishing the Union Furnace, a charcoal-fired, cold blast furnace in 1826. Other communities in Lawrence County on the route to Poke Patch were Mount Savage, Monroe, Bucklin, Mount Vernon and Olive furnaces, names depicting the iron industry of the area. Research indicates that profits from the prosperous iron furnace industry in the Hanging Rock Iron Region were used to subsidize the Underground Railroad in that area, supplying horses, saddles, and wagons. Both black workers and white owners were instrumental in helping fugitive slaves in this region.

John Campbell, an iron master and a follower of John Rankin, was one of Ohio's most notable abolitionists. Campbell founded and named Ironton in 1840, naming the streets after the furnaces in the region. Many other ironmasters were abolitionists who supported the Underground Railroad, both financially and by providing transportation routes for fugitive slaves from one furnace to another. Campbell, John Peters, and others were responsible for the construction of the Mount Vernon Furnace and the Olive Furnace in Gallia County.

Many of the small black settlements along the routes to and from Poke Patch had black Baptist churches active in the Underground Railroad activities. In Macedonia, a black settlement near Burlington, was the Macedonia Baptist Church. Organized in 1807 and established in 1813, it was built on Charley Creek Hill two miles north of Burlington, and was reached by means of a trail that led up the hill. Many fugitive slaves running for freedom sought this church on the trail to Canada. It also was the first recorded African American Church in Ohio, and known as the "Mother Church" from which many Baptist churches were established, including the Union Baptist Church at Black Fort and the Big Rock Baptist Church. Other churches in the area that were active in helping fugitive slaves were the African Methodist Episcopal Church in

Gallipolis and the Paint Creek Baptist Church. Together these congregations founded the Providence Anti-Slavery Missionary Baptist Association in 1831 and the black settlements they served became recognized as stations on the Underground Railroad from Burlington to Poke Patch.

Fugitive slaves also found refuge in nearby Morgan township in north Gallia County before coming to Poke Patch. Free blacks in Morgan township, Howell James, Caliph James, John Chavis, and William P. Ellison, were agents for the Underground Railroad. From Poke Patch, most fugitives went north through Jackson and Chillicothe and from there several routes led to Lake Erie.

Other Gallia County stops on the Underground Railroad included Rio Grande, Porter, Vinton, Thurman, and the Ohio River port of Gallipolis. Fugitive slaves from Rio Grande could travel southwest to Poke Patch before heading north. From the other stops, most fugitive slaves would travel north through Athens and then take various routes to Lake Erie. Porter Underground Railroad agents included the notorious and prolific conductor, Elijah Anderson, who moved here from Indiana, as well as Dr. Julius A. Bingham, George J. Payne, Daniel Clark, William Clark, John D. Marshall, Dr. N. B. Sisson, and Summer Porter. Fugitive slaves crossing the Ohio River at Gallipolis along the Kanawha River found refuge at the John Gee African Methodist Episcopal Church. They then traveled along a system of routes through Porter, Rio Grande, and either to Poke Patch or on to Thurman. A free black named Noah Brooks would transport them 15 miles to Berlin Cross Roads in Jackson County, another settlement populated primarily by former slaves and free blacks. Several of the Woodson families, the Nookes, Cassell and Leach families operated stops on the Underground Railroad there. Two of the Woodson men, John and Thomas Jr., were beaten to death because of their work on the Underground Railroad.

Elijah Anderson

Anderson had been a blacksmith and Underground Railroad conductor in Madison, Indiana, before moving to Gallia County sometime after 1846. Reports have him living in other locations during this period, including Cleveland and Lawrenceburg, Indiana. By his own count, he had aided more than 1,000 fugitive slaves by the mid-1850s. In Gallia County, he began earning his living as a Baptist preacher. But in December 1856, after being tricked by a group of proslavery men, he was arrested near Louisville, Kentucky, and charged with "enticing" slaves to run away. Once arrested, authorities transported Anderson to Frankfort, Kentucky, where he was jailed. Accounts differ about what happened to him thereafter. Some originating from Gallia County say that friends went to the prison to negotiate his release but returned only to find that he had been murdered. Another report claims on the day he was scheduled to be released he was found dead in his cell. Prison reports say he died in prison of a heart attack.

The growing opposition to slavery in Ohio did not mean the people of the state were open to granting free blacks equal rights. As a result, they often formed their own communities like Poke Patch in which they could rely on themselves and make a good life with less of the rampant prejudice that existed at the time.

The Poke Patch Settlement continued until the early 1900s. Today, little exists of this community, and it is now part of the Wayne National Forest.

—Cynthia Vogel

Further Reading

Henry Howe, *Historical Collections of Ohio in Two Volumes*, Vol. II (Cincinnati, OH: C. J. Krehbiel & Co., Printers and Binders, 1902).

George Knepper, *Ohio and Its People* (Kent, OH: Kent State University Press, 2003).

Cheryl Janifer LaRoche, *On the Edge of Freedom: Free Black Communities, Archaeology, and the Underground Railroad* (Ph.D. diss., University of Maryland, College Park, 2004).

Wilbur H. Siebert, *The Mysteries of Ohio's Underground Railroads* (Columbus, OH: Long's College Book Company, 1951).

PRINCETON, ILLINOIS

Bureau County, Illinois, the location of Princeton, was a stronghold of abolitionism that stirred up central Illinois. Those who assisted slaves to escape were regarded as violators of the law and thought to be bad citizens. However, these individuals acted out of great moral integrity and believed that they were doing their duty.

Local Agents

The following were among those actively engaged in assisting runaways in the Princeton area: Owen Lovejoy; John Walters; Caleb Cook; Lazarus Reeve; Seth C. Clapp; Charles Phelps; John Howard Bryant, and his brothers, Cyrus, and Arthur; Elijah Smith; John T. Holbrook; E. E. Norton; and John, Robert, and William Leeper.

At least two general routes led to Princeton from Galesburg, one coming from a more westerly direction through Cambridge in Henry County, and the other from a more southwesterly direction through Tiskilwa in lower Bureau County. The latter likely used the often mentioned stations in Osceola and Toulon.

An 1896 letter to Siebert from Harriet Hall Blair, whose father was involved in the route between Galesburg and Princeton described a farming community about 20 miles north of Galesburg called "Nigger Point," where three staunch conductors lived: W. W. Webster, Jonathan Pratts, and Rev. Samuel G. Wright. The latter kept a diary that mentioned some of his activities aiding fugitives and in one described taking a fugitive slave to Osceola.

Blair also mentioned Agustus Dunn, the Wycoff family, and Hugh Rhodes, the latter who brought fugitive slaves to her father, Dr. Hall, who in turn brought them to Liberty Stone and William Hall, possibly a relative, in Osceola. From Osceola, she said they were taken to Daniel Clark and James Pilkerton in the Bureau County communities of Boyds Grove and Providence.

Early Account

Perhaps the earliest account of aid to fugitive slaves in this section of Illinois, which was yet a wilderness, occurred in December 1835. A slavecatcher named Harris took lodging with two fugitive slave girls he had captured in Wisconsin at the home of Elijah Smith, which also served as a public house. Smith and his wife had abolitionist beliefs as did another lodger, James Ross. They heard the slaves' story of attempted escape and made a plan to help them. Ross feigned sickness and pretended to go to his room, but instead hitched up horses to Smith's wagon and snuck the slave girls out of the house. They were gone several hours before the slavecatcher discovered this, and after a thorough search of the house along with Smith, he accused Smith and his wife of helping them escape. But whatever Smith told him after his threats was to no avail, and Harris never saw them again.

Owen Lovejoy

The Underground Railroad in Bureau County, however, dates its true origin with the arrival in Princeton of Rev. Owen Lovejoy in 1838. The brother of the martyr, Elijah Lovejoy, whose murder the year before had invigorated the antislavery movement nationwide, Owen had just finished co-authoring the biography of his late brother with another brother Joseph. Through the assistance of Rev. Edward Beecher, an older brother of Harriet Beecher Stowe, and a rabid abolitionist and friend of Elijah, he had been assigned as pastor of the Hampshire Colony Congregational Church.

Princeton was then a tiny village of about 200 people, and not everyone there was as yet amenable to abolitionism. But Lovejoy, who had been at his brother's side when he died, had vowed to continue his brother's crusade against slavery and did not hesitate to preach antislavery sermons. At first some members of his congregation walked out, but he would shout after them, "I shall preach this doctrine until you like it and then I will preach it because you like it!" They soon did like it, and he remained as pastor for the next 16 years.

H. D. Hickok, whose father in Troy Grove collaborated with Lovejoy, related two incidents involving the two in a 1914 letter to Siebert. In both, Lovejoy brought them to his father in a wagon, and in one he was being hotly pursued by slavecatchers and his father had to intercept him and warn him that slavecatchers were up ahead.

One of the better known stories involving Lovejoy concerned the attempted abduction of a black man named John who was working on the farm of John Holbrook in Lamoille, Illinois, about 12 miles northeast of Princeton. They were claiming him as a fugitive slave and had tied him up. Immediately, local abolitionist summoned the authorities and John was placed in jail awaiting a trial. However, during the proceedings, the abolitionists who filled the courtroom managed to engineer John's escape and he was provided with a horse and sent to Lovejoy's home. The slavecatchers followed in pursuit but Lovejoy refused to allow them to search his property without a warrant. In midst of the commotion, a man was seen getting on a horse outside the barn behind Lovejoy's home. He took off and the slavecatchers followed in pursuit. When they caught him, however, they found he was not John but another black man, and when they returned, they learned that a woman had been driven off from the Lovejoy residence in a carriage. That woman was John in disguise.

Leeper Account

H. B. Leeper, whose father and brothers were actively involved, said as many as 31 fugitive slaves were harbored at his father's home during one six-week period. He gave a description of the Underground Railroad in the Princeton area to Wilbur Siebert:

> These negroes when they left the Slave States Crossed into Southern Illinois did not all of them at first find the road but traveled on foot & alone at night living on wild fruit & such things as they could gather up until they reached some Christian home of humanity. Then they were carried on after night in waggons, often concealed under hay or straw. Often they were stowed away in garretts and cellars until their pursuers had left of pursuit. This mode of operation was continued up to about 1852 or 3 when in the north part of the state they could be taken safely by day light, as publick sentiment began to change rapidly about that time. (Letter to Wilbur Siebert, Princeton, IL)

John Cross

From Princeton, fugitive slaves were sent to Lamoille where John Cross, the organizer of the western Underground Railroad, lived from 1843 to about 1850 when he moved to Lee County. This was the general mode of operation until about 1855 when the Chicago, Burlington and Quincy Railroad was completed from Chicago to Galesburg. Then fugitive slaves were commonly sent north on the train, which had several Underground Railroad accomplices working for it. Another agent in Lamoille was Roderick Frary, and farther north was John Weldon, who described taking fugitive slaves in a wagon to Dr. Charles Dyer in Chicago in an 1896 letter to Siebert. Weldon claimed that about 20 fugitive slaves per month were being sent by the Underground Railroad to Chicago after the passage of the second Fugitive Slave Law. A particularly active

The Western entries covered along with associated locations. (Courtesy of Tom Calarco)

period was in 1854, when the *Western Citizen* reported in December 16, 1854, that 300 fugitive slaves had passed through Chicago in the preceding six months.

In 1860, Owen Lovejoy, then a U.S. Congressman, gave one of his memorable speeches during which he proclaimed his participation in the Underground Railroad. He described a woman who had fled to escape the advances of her overseer:

> She escaped into the swamps. Bloodhounds were set on her trail. She boarded a little steamboat which plied on a small river which emptied into the great Father of waters. In the fullness of time she landed at the first station in Illinois . . . and proceeded from station to station. Finally, she arrived in Princeton . . . She came to my house hungry and told me her story . . . So from station to station, she crossed the Northland far from baying dogs on her trail, and out from under

the shadow of the flag we love and venerate, into Canada. Today, she lives there a free and happy woman. (Muelder 146–147)

—Melissa Waddy-Thibodeaux

Further Reading

N. Matson, *Reminiscences of Bureau County (IL)* (Princeton, IL: Republican Book & Job Office, 1872).

Owen Muelder, *The Underground Railroad in Western Illinois* (Jefferson, NC: McFarland and Company, Inc., 2007).

Q

QUINCY, ILLINOIS

Quincy, Illinois, was like Ripley and Cincinnati, Ohio, and Madison, Indiana, a major terminal on the borderline between slavery and freedom.

Founded about 1825 on the banks of the Mississippi River, it was named after the newly elected President John Quincy Adams. During this time, the largest concentration of slaves in the state of Missouri lived in the region just to the west of Quincy. In some of these Missouri counties, slaves comprised as much as 50 percent of the total population.

Origin of Abolitionism

Quincy's antislavery sentiment originated with its settlement by New Englanders, including Rev. Asa Turner and Dr. Richard Eells, both graduates of Yale University. In 1835, Eells and Turner helped organize the Adams County Anti-Slavery Society. That same year the Reverend David Nelson, the president of Marion College, a missionary college near Palmyra, Missouri, about 10 miles southwest of Quincy was inspired by an abolitionist lecture of Theodore Weld in Pittsburgh. He returned to Missouri afire with the fervor of abolition and began preaching it at his church and promoting it at his school. Several incidents occurred. The final one resulted in a scuffle during a revival meeting between a supporter of Nelson and a slaveholder that nearly caused the latter's death. The people of Palmyra were furious and Nelson was forced to flee to Quincy.

Temptation for Slaves Who Wanted to be Free

The knowledge that friends who would help slaves lived just across the river was a great temptation for them to escape, and the Underground Railroad developed from this. The early gathering place for the local abolitionists and refuge for fugitive slaves was Turner's church, on the west side of Fourth Street, which became known as "the Lord's Barn." During this period Nelson and other abolitionists inspired with evangelical zeal would incite the public with powerful

Richard Eells house, Quincy, Illinois; home of the leading abolitionist and trustee of the Mission Institute. (Courtesy of Tom Calarco)

lectures about slavery and its horrors, describing scenes of floggings and other more cruel punishments. The public at this time was very much divided and proslavery forces confronted the abolitionists, resulting in riots that occurred in 1837. An 1866 history of Quincy stated that the Lord's Barn "was prepared for defense, and beneath the platform of the rough pulpit, were hidden the arms of every sort, including hickory clubs, ready for instant use if needed."

In 1838 the Van Dorn brothers, John and James, purchased a sawmill along the riverfront between Delaware and Ohio streets in Quincy. It became the first stop on the road to freedom for fugitive slaves coming from Missouri, and it is alleged that the Van Dorns aided as many as 300 fugitive slaves during the ante-bellum period.

The Mission Institute

Nelson, Eells, and Turner also formed the Mission Institute, a missionary school similar to Marion College, in 1838. Though not explicitly stated in its handbook, it was zealously devoted to the antislavery principles of its founders. That year, the Institute was joined by an eccentric and learned reformer from upstate New York, Moses Hunter, whose long hair and robes similar to those worn by men of Biblical times, called attention to him. The Institute quickly developed a reputation as being on the fringe of society and it was not reticent about its intentions to aid fugitive slaves.

A former Mission Institute student, N. A. Hunt, explained in an 1891 letter to Underground Railroad historian Wilbur Siebert that Nelson who was the school's president came to him one day about the year of 1840 and asked him to go with another student across the Mississippi River to patrol the shore opposite Quincy and tap stones together. This was a signal to slaves who might desire to escape. From there they would be taken to a red barn, 16 miles east of Quincy. This was likely near Mendon and the home of Jireh Platt, another emigrant from Connecticut, whose sons were Mission Institute students and also active in the Underground Railroad. Hunt added that these patrols were regularly carried out on Sunday nights, which was usually the slaves' day off.

In 1841, two Mission Institute students and an antislavery activist attached to the school achieved a measure of historical notoriety after being captured by a Missouri mob while attempting to bring two slaves to freedom. James Burr, George Thompson, and Alanson Work were betrayed by the very slaves they were attempting to help. They were convicted of slave stealing and sentenced to 12 years in prison. All were pardoned within five years, and Thompson wrote a book about their ordeal, *Prison Life and Reflections*, which was published in 1849, three years after his release.

The case created a national furor and focused greater attention on Underground Railroad operations in Quincy. On the night of August 21, 1842, a free black, Berryman Barnet, was patrolling the river bank for the local Underground Railroad, watching for fugitive slaves. He spotted a man swimming across the river. It was a fugitive slave named Charley, and Barnet took him at once to Eells's house. Eells gave him a change of dry clothes and took him in his buggy led by his horse, White Lightning, who had developed a reputation as the fastest horse in the region. They headed for a safe house at the Mission Institute, but Charley's master, Chauncey Durkee, was in hot pursuit with a posse and they spotted Eells's buggy. Apparently knowing of his association with the Mission Institute, they headed him off farther up the road. Eells drove through their roadblock and managed to drop off Charley in a cemetery and double back home, but Charley was captured hiding in a stable the next day.

An indictment was brought against Eells, who spent the rest of his life in a legal battle. At one point, while awaiting trial, an order to extradite him to Missouri to face charges was issued by Governor Ford of Illinois. An extradition to Missouri put Eells in jeopardy of being lynched by a mob there, and he went into hiding. During this time it was believed he went to Chicago and was able to get the assistance of influential friends who convinced the governor to rescind the extradition order. In April 1843, Circuit Court judge Stephen A. Douglas, the future senator of national fame, fined him $400 for harboring a slave. The case eventually was brought before the U.S. Supreme Court in 1852, six years after Eells's death, with Salmon P. Chase arguing unsuccessfully that the Illinois law against harboring fugitive slaves was unconstitutional.

These activities in Quincy induced slaveholders in Missouri to organize slave patrols that would carefully watch the movements of slaves along and near the border and even interrogate white strangers passing through. These patrols also destroyed unattended boats and rafts. It was one such group of vigilantes that came to Quincy on the night of March 16, 1843, and burned down the chapel at the Mission Institute.

These confrontations took a toll on the health of Eells and Nelson, who died the following year after a stroke at the age of 51. Eells, nevertheless, continued his active role in the cause of abolition until his death. He was elected president of the state antislavery society in 1843 and was a candidate for Congress under the banner of the abolitionist Liberty Party in 1844. He also continued to aid fugitive slaves at 415 Jersey Street and in all it is believed he aided upward of 200. But his health continually worsened despite a trip to the West Indies in 1845 in the hope of restoring it. He died of pneumonia on an Ohio River steamboat at the age of 46 in 1846.

Eells's horse, White Lightning, also died in the service of the Underground Railroad. One night the horse and buggy were taken out by conductor Rasselas Sartle to scout ahead of a wagon carrying nine fugitive slaves. Unfortunately, they were confronted by a dozen slavecatchers who shot and killed the horse. Fortunately, the fugitive slaves were able to escape.

The Underground Railroad Continues Despite Opposition

By 1850 the Mission Institute had closed, but the Underground Railroad continued through Quincy. One story from the 1850s published in the *Galesburg Evening Mail* on June 19, 1909, described what happened when a fugitive slave was captured by Quincy police:

> On the evening of his capture, three women of that city, Mrs. Dr. Foote, wife of the Rev. Dr. Foote, for many years a trustee of Knox college and at one time a pastor of the first church in this city; Mrs. Willard Turner, and the wife of Dr. Eels, called at the police station and requested that they be admitted to bring the slave his supper. The jailer was a kind-hearted old man, knew the women well, and he granted their request. He allowed them to enter the cell and then he withdrew to the end of the corridor. After a while the women announced they were ready to go, and the jailer escorted three women from the jail and locked the cell. The next morning when he went to the cell to feed his prisoner he was greeted by a bright and cheery "Good morning!" by one of the women who met him at the cell door. In reply to his questioning she told him that he had locked her in the cell the night before, and that she was ready to get out. He could not or would not detain her, and by that time the negro was well on his way.

Letter from Jeremiah Platt, Mendon, Illinois

Nearby Mendon, Illinois, was the first stop from Quincy for fugitive slaves. Deacon Jireh Platt kept a station there. On March 28, 1896, Jeremiah Platt sent a lengthy letter to Wilbur Siebert, as his brother H. D. had done only a week earlier, describing the participation of his family and others in his area. The following is an excerpt (The Wilbur H. Siebert Collection, Ohio Historical Society):

Runaways crossing the river near Quincy somehow found friends, who would escort them to some of the Conductors, of which there were several, A Mr. Van Dorn being a prominent one, and Mission Institute two miles east of Quincy was full of them. Some of those Conductors would lead them in almost every conceivable way, usually in the night to my Fathers who by some member of the family, or a neighbor, would escort them to Plymouth the following night. Sometimes a carriage would drive into my Fathers barn in the day time with a colored man dressed up in fine clothes, and a Stove pipe hat, for a driver, with the conductor on the back seat. Sometimes a person with a lady's cloak, hood and veil on would alight from the back seat of a carriage, with the conductor driving. Fathers barn or the haymow used to be the place for refreshment and retiring. In the summer time, the hazel thicket in the pasture was used for the same purpose.

During this period, fugitive slaves were being sent to Quincy from the Quaker village of Salem, Iowa, and the Congregational Church of Asa Turner, who had moved to Denmark Iowa. From Quincy, the route continued through Mendon where the Platt family, and Levi and Henry Stillman were among the foremost conductors. They took their passengers to Plymouth whose conductors included Marcus Cook, and from there to Augusta and the home of Strong Austin. Farther on, they were passed to the Ellison family in Macomb, and on to Farmington, Galesburg, Princeton, and eventually to Chicago where they were dispatched on steamers to Canada or, in later years, by railroad to Michigan.

H. D. Platt, who attended the Mission Institute from 1841 to 1847, provided a detailed description of Underground Railroad operations during the 1840s and 1850s in Adams County in an 1896 letter to Siebert. The son of the aforementioned Jireh Platt, H. D. was one of four brothers, three of whom became Congregational ministers. How many fugitives slaves passed through the gateway of freedom at Quincy probably will never be known, but the number certainly was substantial.

—Tom Calarco

Further Reading

Henry Asbury, *Reminiscences of Quincy, Illinois* (Quincy, IL: D. Wilcox and Sons, 1882).

Tom Calarco, *People of the Underground Railroad* (Westbrook, CT: Greenwood Press, 2008).

Terrell Dempsey, *Searching for Jim* (Columbia, MO: University of Missouri Press, 2005).

Helen C. Frazier, *Runaway and Freed Missouri Slaves* (Jefferson, NC: McFarland and Company, Inc., 2004).

"Friends of the Dr. Richard Eells House," a paper prepared for the Quincy Historical Symposium, November 6, 1999.

Owen Muelder, *The Underground Railroad in Western Illinois* (Jefferson, NC: McFarland and Company, 2008).

H. D. Platt and J. E. Platt letters (Wilbur Siebert Collection, Ohio Historical Society, 1896).

George Thompson, *Prison Life and Reflections* (Hartford: Work, 1849).

R

RIPLEY, OHIO

One of the most celebrated stops in Underground Railroad history, Ripley in Brown County is synonymous with the exploits of the Rankin family, whose house still sits atop that high hill overlooking the Ohio River, and whose 30-foot, candletopped pole outside their home was a beacon of liberty for slaves in northern Kentucky.

Early Involvement

The Underground Railroad in Ripley involved many more individuals than the Rankins. Hundreds of locals participated and even before Rankin family patriarch, Rev. John Rankin, moved to Ripley in 1822, it is believed that more than 1,000 fugitive slaves had been aided there.

The village's origins date from 1804, when Colonel James Poage, a Virginian, acquired the land on the banks of the Ohio River through a 1,000-acre land grant for his service in the Revolutionary War. In 1812, he laid out the town and called it Staunton, which was changed four years later to Ripley, in honor of General Eleazer Wheelock Ripley who was an American commander in the War of 1812.

The Ripley of this period was a community with continuous fights and shoot-outs, and saloons were a common business, as John Rankin recalled when he set-tled here in 1822, calling it "exceedingly immoral" with infidelity and heavy drinking commonplace (Bordewich 191–192). However, he also found that it was actively involved in the Underground Railroad, and having been a staunch abolitionist since 1815, which led to his emigration from his native Tennessee and early pastorate in Kentucky, it was a fitting location for him to settle.

Rankin's *Letters on American Slavery*

In Ripley, many were open to Rankin's antislavery message, but he found a wider audience through the publication of a series of letters explaining the evils of

John Rankin house, Ripley, Ohio; home of the famed abolitionist and conductor, whose involvement in the Underground Railroad was truly a family affair. (Courtesy of Tom Calarco)

slavery. They began in response to a letter he received from one of his brothers, informing him of his purchase of slaves. Instead of sending them to his brother, he had them published in the *Castigator*, a local paper. These letters were widely circulated and eventually collected in a book, *Letters on American Slavery*, published by the American Anti-Slavery Society after their serialization in *The Liberator*. The book was very influential and went through 18 editions.

Rankin was already a nationally known abolitionist when the Ripley and Ohio Anti-Slavery societies were formed in 1835. By this time, he also had moved from his first residence along the river's edge to the hilltop home that would become an icon in Underground Railroad lore. The entire family—wife, Jean, and children—helped care for the needs and provided transport for the fugitive slaves. As many as 12 fugitive slaves were harbored on one occasion, and in the barn behind the house, there was a hidden room under barn floor. At least one of Rankin's sons (there were nine in all, though some were born in the late 1830s, so they wouldn't have been involved until the last years of the Underground Railroad) was expected to be on call to quickly move fugitive slaves to their next destination. Traveling was sometimes on foot or horseback and other times by wagon, and the route was dictated by the circumstances.

In 1836, he joined the American Anti-Slavery Society's band of lecturers at the request of Theodore Weld and undertook a successful campaign through the southwestern counties, establishing numerous antislavery societies. However, he also endured more than 20 attacks, and the stress of constantly encountering angry mobs took its toll. After six months, he decided that he could be more useful fighting slavery at home in Ripley.

Eliza

In 1838, he aided the escape of a fugitive slave whose story was immortalized by Harriet Beecher Stowe in *Uncle Tom's Cabin*. It was from Rankin that Stowe learned of the story of Eliza, a Dover, Kentucky slave, who had crossed the partially frozen Ohio River, jumping across the ice cakes and nearly drowning while being pursued by slavecatchers and bloodhounds. Fortunately, a Ripley resident, Chauncey Shaw, known to be an informant for slavecatchers, but taking pity on her, helped her ashore.

He brought her to the Rankins, who generally left their door open and a fire burning in case fugitive slaves arrived. John and Jean Rankin awakened on hearing Eliza enter. They gave her food and a change of clothes, and entrusted her to Calvin and John who took her to Rev. James Gilliland in Red Oak. From Rev. Gilliland's home Eliza was taken to Decatur, then Sardinia, and as a precaution, northwest into Indiana, where she was led to the home of Levi Coffin, who corroborated the story of Eliza in his book of *Reminiscences*.

Composition of Ripley's Network

The Underground Railroad in the Ripley area had three interlocking components. The first were Presbyterian ministers, most of whom were Southerners, who had begun around the year 1800 to come north to escape the horrific climate of slavery. Later, united through an administrative body known as the Chillicothe Presbytery, they formed an established web of relationships that linked Ripley to Red Oak, Sardinia, Russellville, and other towns in southern Ohio.

The second component included activist abolitionists. The Ripley Anti-Slavery Society, which held its organizational meeting in Red Oak at the Presbyterian church of Rev. James Gilliland, enlisted 337 members in its first year, an exceptionally large number by comparison with other community antislavery societies. They elected Alexander Campbell, president; Gilliland, vice-president; and Rankin, secretary. Five years later, John Mahan of Sardinia led a small group in Brown County who supported the Liberty Party. Rankin did not join them until 1843, though his son Lowry was one of the original Liberty Party men in Ripley.

The third component was a sizable population of free blacks and a small number of courageous slaves who lived across the river in Kentucky in Mason and Bracken counties. Most of the free blacks were members of the two Gist settlements, just north of Ripley, which were comprised mainly of slaves and their ancestors from Virginia, who had been emancipated after the death of their master, Samuel Gist, in 1819.

Alexander Campbell

Among Ripley's most important abolitionists was Dr. Alexander Campbell. Born in Virginia in 1769, he started his medical practice in Cynthiana, Kentucky, and served as a representative to the Kentucky General Assembly, where he supported a constitution abolishing slavery. Campbell moved with his family to Ripley in 1803. He had slaves at the time and emancipated them. From 1809 to 1813, he served as a U.S. senator. Although there are no accounts of actual assistance to fugitive slaves by Campbell, he figured strongly in the planning and operation of Ripley's Underground Railroad; in 1838, a reward of $2,500 was offered in Kentucky for the abduction or assassination of Campbell and Rankin of Ripley, and Mahan and Dr. Isaac Beck of nearby Sardinia.

The Collins Family

The Collins family is mentioned in numerous Underground Railroad incidents that occurred in Ripley. Nathaniel Collins owned a home along the river almost directly in line with the Rankin homestead, but it was mainly his sons, Theodore and Thomas, who conducted fugitive slaves, often working with Rankin's sons. Theodore owned property behind the Rankins' hilltop property, which would serve as a stop on the way to Red Oak. Theodore, who had manufactured coffins in a workshop behind his house, often would transport fugitive slaves in them.

The Collins collaborated with the Rankins when Eliza returned in 1841 to seek help in rescuing her adult daughter and seven grandchildren from slavery. She had come to the Rankins accompanied by a French Canadian, who had agreed to help her for a price. Her daughter's owner, Thomas Davis, owned a farm near Dover. John Rankin warned her not to go but he offered to help nevertheless.

While the Canadian went to Kentucky to get a job and prepare for the escape, Eliza was sent to Red Oak to work for Anthony Hopkins. When the night was set for the escape, Eliza was brought on horseback to Ripley dressed as a man by two of the Rankin boys, John, Jr., and Calvin, still teenagers. They met the Canadian and Tom Collins at the river. While Collins took care of their horses, the Rankin boys took Eliza and the Canadian across the river.

The plan was for them to escape the next night, but they were delayed because of all the baggage Eliza's family wanted to take. As a result, the Canadian fearing discovery devised a plan to fool the slaveholders. He took a skiff across the river and left it in plain view while Eliza and her family hid in the woods. It worked to perfection as the slaveholders thought they had already made their escape and scoured the Ripley area the next day. Unable to find them, they gave up their search, and in the wee hours of the following night, the Canadian brought them across the river to Ripley.

Tom Collins and Robert Patton, another Ripley agent, were waiting for them and took them by prearrangement to the residence of Thomas McCague, the wealthiest man in Ripley. He and his wife harbored them until it was safe to bring them to the Rankins. They were then escorted by John Jr. and two of his classmates, Hugh Wiley and John Newton, to the home of John Hopkins in Red Oak.

Rev. James Gilliland

In Red Oak, about five miles north of Ripley, one of the most active Underground Railroad agents was Rev. Gilliland. He and his wife and five children left North Carolina in the early 1800s. He was among the earliest abolitionists, and his entire congregation was devoted to the work of aiding fugitive slaves. He worked closely with Robert and William Huggins, who often rode halfway between Ripley and Sardinia to meet Lowry Rankin to pick up fugitive slaves. Higgins would then hide the fugitive slaves beneath hay or fodder piled high on their wagons. On Robert's farm, a cabin was built with a false hearth that could be raised to uncover a space large enough for fugitive slaves to hide if slavecatchers were near.

The McCagues

Thomas and Catherine "Kitty" McCague, who harbored Eliza's family in 1841, were active supporters and occasional participants. McCague owned the largest pork packing house and the largest flour mill on the Ohio River. Not only was he the source of Ripley's prosperity, but he also helped to fund the local Underground Railroad. However, the McCagues were careful to keep a low profile because of their business contacts, and few knew of their participation. It was Kitty who personally took Eliza's smallest grandchild on horseback to Red Oak.

Isaac Beck and John Hudson

Another frequent destination for fugitive slaves being forwarded from Ripley was Sardinia, about 20 miles north, though it may have been used with less regularity after the passage of the second Fugitive Slave Law of 1850. As Dr. Isaac Beck, one of the principal agents in Sardinia, reported in an 1892 letter to Wilbur Siebert: "After the passage of the Fugitive Slave Law, I enquired but little what my friends were doing. . . . If they wanted help, I gave it. . . . I judge others did the same, for in case of a prosecution . . . 'ignorance was bliss' " (Letter to Wilbur Siebert, Sardinia, Ohio, December 26, 1892).

Beck was born in Bethel, Ohio, Clermont County, and one of the founders of Sardinia. His uncle was Thomas Morris, the first antislavery U.S. senator and later Liberty Party vice-presidential candidate. Among those he worked with were the Pettijohns, a clan of twelve households, all of whom were Presbyterian and active in the Underground Railroad, and the families of Robert and William Huggins, who had settled first in Ripley then moved to Red Oak. The latter's sons often rendezvoused with the Rankin sons to move fugitive slaves farther north. Beck also worked closely with John Mahan and John Hudson.

Hudson, a black man who was one of Gist's emancipated slaves from Virginia, lived near Sardinia. Hudson began helping fugitive slaves in the 1820s. He was paid 25 cents each, from Beck, Mahan, and the Pettijohn brothers for transporting fugitive slaves. Both Beck and Mahan said Hudson guided more fugitive slaves than anyone they worked with. Fearless in confronting slavecatchers, of an imposing physique, and literate, which was uncommon for newly emancipated slaves, Hudson could be depended on to run off slavecatchers or harbor fugitive slaves.

John Mahan

Sardinia had been an important stop since the early 1820s, primarily because of Mahan. A Methodist minister, he was born in Kentucky in 1801. His parents, Jacob Mahan and Martha Bennington abhorred slavery and in 1804 moved their family from Kentucky to Bethel in Clermont County, Ohio. In 1820 his father became a member of the United Brethren Church, which was known for its abolitionist beliefs. Mahan opened the first tavern in Sardinia and had rooms for overnight guests, as well as a pub-like eatery that did not serve alcohol. It was soon known as a safe stop for fugitive slaves. He also built a sawmill, purchased other pieces of property, and began plans to open a dry-goods store. All of his properties were used to harbor fugitive slaves.

Like Rankin, Mahan gave antislavery lectures and was Brown County's first vocal supporter of the Liberty Party. Like Rankin, he also knew and worked with Levi Coffin. Rankin's son, Lowry, also developed a close relationship with Coffin in their Underground Railroad work and was an early supporter of his Liberty Party advocacy, prior to his father. Mahan frequently worked with Beck, John Nelson in Highland County, the Pettijohns, the Huggins, and most often with Hudson.

In September 1838, Mahan was arrested on a charge of aiding the slaves of Mason County slaveholder, William Greathouse. Armed with a warrant from Governor Vance of Ohio, which was based on false evidence, Mahan was taken to Washington, Kentucky, where he spent eight weeks awaiting trial and enduring intolerable conditions that led to him developing tuberculosis. In the end he was found innocent, but the experience took a great toll on his health. It also led to a successful civil suit brought by Greathouse against Mahan that put him into debt and caused him further stress. In December 1843, after extensive lecturing for the Liberty Party and the unexpected death of his daughter, Mahan died of tuberculosis.

Attack on the Rankins

One of the most violent episodes in Ripley involved the storming of the Rankin home by a posse of slavecatchers in 1841, shortly after the riot against abolitionists that had occurred in Cincinnati. On the evening of September 12, Calvin and his cousin, John P. Rankin, who was staying over that night, heard a whistle at about 2:30 a.m. They woke up Lowry, the oldest son, and the two boys armed themselves with pistols and slipped out the back door. Calvin went around the front and encountered a man. When he demanded to know his reason for being there, the man fired a shot that barely missed him. At the rear of the house, another man shot at John but missed. He then began to run and exposed himself, and John fired and hit him. The man would later die.

More shots followed, and Jean Rankin bolted the door inside. She and John figured the boys had been murdered, and they didn't want any more family members to die. But Lowry and Sam went out one of the windows. They saw that the attackers had set a fire by the barn. As Calvin, John, and Samuel engaged in a gun battle, Lowry ran to the barn with a pail of water and put out the fire. At this point John Rankin allowed the rest of his boys out, and the Rankin clan effectively warded off the attackers, who beat a hasty retreat as a mob of Ripley citizens stormed up the hill.

That week, Rankin published a warning in the *Ripley Bee*. He announced that from this time on, any strangers found on his property after bedtime came at their own risk. The warning put an end to intruders, and the Rankins continued their Underground Railroad work, never losing a passenger.

An interesting but not widely published account was described by Rankin's son, Richard, in an 1892 letter to Wilbur Siebert. It concerned 11 slaves owned by slaveholders Schultz and Bradley of Washington, Kentucky, who escaped in December 1844, led by the husband of one of them, a free black, Peter Dent. A reward of $2,200 was being offered for them and an intensive search was made throughout Ripley and the surrounding area. So tight was the surveillance that it was impossible for anyone to go beyond Red Oak without scrutiny. Rankin was with them the entire time they were in Brown County and was forced to constantly move them to different hiding places. His description provides an insight to the many little known agents who lived in the Ripley area.

> We were compelled to run them from William Minnow's to Aunt Mary Pogue's. When the pursuers came to Pogue's, we would run them to Washington Campbell's, from there to James McCoy's, and from James's to William McCoy's, thence to Kirby Bill Baird's, and thence back to Aunt Mary Pogue's, thence to Minnow's and across the woods to Campbell's, and so on. (Letter from R. C. Rankin to Wilbur Siebert, April 8, 1892)

This constant movement continued for several days until James Henry, who was actually feeding many of the bounty hunters and who had never aided a fugitive slave, offered to hide them at his place deep in the woods, suggesting that no one would suspect him.

The slaves were hidden upstairs and Rankin stayed for dinner, which he shared with a couple of the bounty hunters. In the morning, Rankin, accompanied with a band of armed men, accompanied the slaves along a roundabout route that took them to a Colonel William McIntire's near North Liberty in Adams County. From there, they were taken up into Highland County. Ebenezer McElroy picked up their trail in an 1896 letter to Siebert, writing that Dent and six others—his wife, children, and wife's sister and brother-in-law stayed at his father's home in Greenfield for the next month, when slavecatchers caught up with them again. They were then placed in two, curtained carriages driven by armed guards and taken on a circuitous route that landed them in Twin Hills, only 10 miles away. They stayed there another 10 days before finally being sent north to Canada.

Overlooking the Ohio River Valley from the John Rankin house in Ripley. (Courtesy of Tom Calarco)

John Parker

Probably the most daring of all the Ripley Underground Railroad operators was the free black entrepreneur, John P. Parker, who moved to Ripley in 1849, and opened a foundry that was very successful. However, Parker's greatest success was in running slaves to freedom.

Parker was born a slave in Virginia in 1827. He was sold several times and as he grew into adolescence he made several attempts to flee. Finally, he made an agreement with an owner who allowed him to work his way out of slavery with money he made working in foundries. Once he obtained his Certificate of Freedom he moved to Cincinnati, where he met and married Miranda Boulden. It was after his help was requested in the escape of two slave girls from Maysville, while still living in Cincinnati, that he began his work in the Underground Railroad and shortly after moved to Ripley.

Parker found work in a foundry owned by Thomas McCague, who became a friend, and soon was able to save enough money to purchase his own foundry and other properties in Ripley. Parker did his daring work at night, when he would wait on the Ohio side of the river, for a signal that there were fugitive slaves waiting to cross to freedom. Once across the river, fugitive slaves were taken to the homes of conductors in Ripley.

At one time, there was a bounty of $2,000 posted for Parker's capture, dead or alive. He seemed to get a thrill out of this dangerous work as well as the satisfaction that he was weakening slavery and helping those who had been slaves like he had been. The first two years in Ripley, Parker had kept a diary with the names, dates, and circumstances of the people he had helped, but destroyed it after the Fugitive Slave Law was passed for fear of jeopardizing his business and his family. In this short period, he already had aided 315 fugitive slaves.

Rescue at the Sroufe House

His most memorable rescue involved the slaves of Thomas Sroufe in Mason County. Sroufe's son worked at Parker's foundry and wagered that Parker couldn't take a slave from his father's plantation. Parker carefully planned the escape of a young slave couple who had a baby. Sroufe was suspicious of their intentions and began to take their baby each night to sleep in the bedroom of him and his wife. Parker had no idea that this was occurring and on the night of the rescue learned of the recent action taken by Sroufe. He was not deterred, however, and taking off his shoes, he slipped into the house and boldly crept up the stairs into Sroufe's bedroom where the slavemaster and his wife were sleeping with the baby in its cradle at the foot of the bed. Ever so carefully he grabbed the cradle and raced down the stairs before Sroufe realized what had happened. Making a futile effort, the groggy Sroufe fired some passing shots at the fleeing Parker but to no avail.

Parker knew and collaborated with John Rankin and his sons and on one occasion saved the life of one of the Rankin boys.

Another conductor that assisted fugitive slaves to Ripley was the slave, Arnold Gragston, who lived on the Jack Tabb farm in Mason County, seven miles from the Ohio River. For four years he conducted slaves in his small boat, rowing them across the river. In his memoir, he described a lighthouse that could be seen for miles at the top of the hill overlooking Ripley and that he watched every night while on the river. It came from a lantern atop a 30-foot pole erected outside the Rankin home, and he said that slaves knew it as a symbol of freedom.

It is not possible to determine how many slaves passed through Ripley to freedom. One of the Rankin boys said his family aided about 2,000, and John Parker estimated he aided another 440. It is probably safe to say that thousands were helped to freedom in Ripley by a large group of individuals who devoted their lives to helping the oppressed become free.

—Sharron L Pope and Tom Calarco

Further Reading

Fergus Bordewich, *Bound for Canaan* (New York: Harper-Collins, 2005).

Paul Grim, "The Rev. John Rankin, Early Abolitionist," *Ohio History*, 46 (1937).

Ann Hagedorn, *Beyond the River* (New York: Simon & Schuster, 2002).

John Parker, *His Promised Land*, Stuart Seely Sprague, editor (New York: W. W. Norton and Co., 1996).

Andrew Ritchie, *The Soldier, the Battle, and the Victory: Being a Brief Account of the Work of Rev. John Rankin in the Anti-Slavery Cause* (Cincinnati: Western Tract and Book Society, 1868).

ROCHESTER, NEW YORK

Many persons fleeing bondage spent a final night before their dash to Canada in the Genesee Country, a region of New York State that today encompasses several contiguous counties centered on the Genesee River. Significantly, that river flows out of western Pennsylvania, northward, through the heart of Rochester into Lake Ontario, a body of water New York State shares with Canada. Frederick Douglass, Isaac and Amy Post, Samuel Porter, and William Bloss were well-known here for the care they rendered and for launching the freedom seekers on their final leg to freedom. It was estimated that during the 1850s that Rochester's conductors annually assisted 150 fugitive slaves en route to Canada. Douglass recalled an occurrence in which 11 freedom seekers found shelter under his roof. Still, he likened the system to attempting to "bail out the ocean with a teaspoon" (Douglass 272).

The character of the Underground Railroad in Genesee Country is to a significant degree indebted to settlement of a post-Revolutionary War dispute in which both Massachusetts and New York claimed the same frontier territories that lay essentially west of Albany, New York. Eventually, Massachusetts was persuaded to allow New York's claim to those territories. New England Yankees and Atlantic Coast Southerners were drawn to the frontier. Among the latter were Colonel Nathaniel Rochester, Fitzhugh Carroll, and Captain William Helm.

After passage of the Fugitive Slave Act in 1850, escape routes to Canada through and around Rochester became more frequently traveled. Stationmasters in the Genesee Country had regular contact with agents in other states. Douglass had a close connection with Philadelphia Vigilance Committee secretary, William Still, and his home was often visited by Harriet Tubman. She also was aided by Isaac and Amy Post, and others, and sometimes quartered her charges in the Rochester office of the African Methodist Episcopal (A. M. E.) Zion Church, of which she was a member.

Jermaine Wesley Loguen, who became an A. M. E. Zion minister as his freedom matured, took leave of Tennessee slavery around 1831. Escaping to Canada, he soon returned stateside, and for a time was employed as a porter at a Rochester hotel. After attending the Oneida Institute, he eventually made his home in Syracuse where he became known as the "King of the Underground Railroad" and a bishop in the A. M. E. Zion Church. The Loguen and Douglass families were united in the movement. Moreover, Loguen's daughter, Amelia, married Lewis Henry Douglass, the oldest of three Douglass sons.

Founding Father of Afro-Rochester

Rochester's anti-slavery posture was also fostered by one who preceded Colonel Rochester's residency in the village. Austin Steward was born in Prince William County, Virginia, into one of several families owned by Captain William Helm. Steward's path from slavery to freedom was framed in Bath, Steuben County, New York, to which Helm had relocated around 1805. Fleeing Bath in 1814, Austin found sanctuary in Ontario County, with Town of Farmington founding father and Quaker, Otis Comstock. When Helm came demanding his property, Comstock argued that based on a clause in the state's "gradual" emancipation act, Helm had forfeited his claim to Austin. Helm left, determined to rally political support to sustain his claim. The rally was still-born, for Helm soon died.

Comstock treated Steward humanely and paid him for the work he performed, including transporting and selling his produce. En route to Hartland, roughly 100 miles west of Farmington, Steward passed through the hamlet of Rochesterville, which he described as "a very small, forbidding place at first sight, with few inhabitants, and surrounded by a dense forest" (Steward 124). Yet, in that year of 1817, Steward settled in that area on the west bank of the river that ran through the Genesee Country. He established a store in rented quarters just west of the river. White men objecting to his action sought to intimidate him and drive him back into the status of a slave. Edwin Scrantom, a distinguished journalist, and elder in an early Rochester church, witnessed Steward's "commencement in business, and the outrage and indignity offered you in Rochester by white competitors on no other grounds than that of color. . . . I remember your unsullied character, and your prosperity, and when your word or endorsement was equal to that of any other citizen" (Steward 7–8).

Steward's capacity to meet such challenges stemmed in part from the fact that he grew up during the era of New York's "gradual withdrawal" from its identity as a slaveholding state. Steward's autobiography, *Twenty-Two Years a Slave, and Forty Years a Freeman*, provides insights into other freedom seekers' efforts to settle in the Genesee Country. He reported that in 1822 a fugitive slave named Ellen, who had escaped from bondage in Virginia to live with her husband, a barber in Rochester, was hunted down and arrested. A magistrate determined that she be returned to Virginia on claim of a "Mr. D.," to whom she owed service.

Details of the same incident, attributed to another "self-emancipator," states that about 20 of Rochester's tiny African American population overpowered the officers who guarded Ellen. But the rescuers were pursued and were themselves overpowered. In desperation, Ellen committed suicide, choosing death over separation from her husband and nine-month-old baby.

Born a slave in Canajoharie, 50 miles west of Albany, New York, in 1804, a slave named Tom fled in 1821, before the state's universal emancipation in 1827, following the unfinished Erie Canal route all the way to Ontario, Canada. Within months, he was back in New York State. In Rochester, he found employment at a warehouse servicing the newly opened Erie Canal. Other workers called him, Jim. Simultaneously, he took on the challenge of learning to read and write, and during the process answered a call to the ministry. Thus, he became the Reverend Thomas James and started Rochester's African Methodist Episcopal Zion Church (AMEZ), which soon become an Underground Railroad station.

Later, Rev. James was installed as pastor of the Second Street AMEZ Church in New Bedford, Massachusetts, where he encountered 20-year-old Frederick Douglass, also new to the community. In 1838, Douglass had been assigned the role of "exhorter" in the church. James recalled that the younger man:

> was, so to speak, right out of slavery, but had already begun to talk in public, though not before white people. . . . [S]ometime afterwards I licensed him to preach. . . . On one occasion, after I had addressed a white audience on the slavery question, I called upon Fred Douglass, whom I saw among the auditors, to relate his story. He did so, and in a year from that time he was in the lecture field with Parker Pillsbury and other leading abolitionist orators. (James 8)

While Douglass was only a Maryland toddler, a man named Davis underwent a travail strikingly similar to that of the aforementioned, Ellen. When enslaved in Kentucky, Davis assisted his master with his duties as a physician. Davis escaped and settled in Rochester. Over the years, applying what he had learned from his master, he came to be regarded as a healer. The title, "Doctor," was bestowed on him by people of color who sought him for treatment.

At length, agents of Davis's former owner, tracked him to Rochester, and in short order, had him in shackles. During the court proceedings at which he was to be remanded to agents that would take him back to Kentucky, several black men surrounded him and somehow managed to dress him in a disguise that enabled him to leave the court room undetected.

Days later, while the agents circulated handbills offering a reward, Davis was dispatched to Buffalo. The handbills were effective, and he was soon in custody again. Unable to accept re-enslavement, Davis produced a razor with which he cut his throat. Dreading the burden of having a "dead negro" on their hands, his captors fled. Fortunately, friends "doctored" the doctor, who recovered and relocated to Canada.

John Jenkins, who resided in Rochester for about 16 years, is listed in the 1844 City Directory as a Rochester grocer. However, he exhibited skill in the use of herbs and in blood-letting, and in giving accurate responses to those seeking relief from various ailments. Moreover, in 1847, William Cowles studied under Jenkins in order to learn the medical practitioner's trade. All of this supported the increasing frequency with which he was referred to as "Dr. Jenkins."

While practicing the medical arts in Rochester, Jenkins increased his efforts to raise funds for the purchase of his two daughters still enslaved in Virginia from which he had fled. However, after learning that his former owner had issued a claim for him and sobered by the threat of the toughened Fugitive Slave Act, he fled to Canada. There, his faith unshaken, he worked, planned, and persevered. In 1856, a 24-year search ended when he located his brother, who put him on the trail of his youngest daughter and her free husband. Finally, he purchased his older daughter from the former governor of Florida for $400 and his family circle was whole again.

Freedom for some slaves was purchased by friends and relatives who raised money on the lecture circuit: Emily Edmundson raised $60 at a lecture in Rochester's Corinthian Hall toward the purchase of her brother; a Rev. Cross raised $32 to buy his brother; Melinda Noll collected money to free her son; Lewis Smith of Ohio raised money from four Rochester churches to pay the final installment on his children.

The antislavery movement presented a mixed picture; and in the view of various twentieth-century writers, whites in Rochester felt little love for black descendants of slavery. Their numbers were few and they were largely marginalized. Nevertheless, a small, dedicated antislavery group took shape in Rochester.

By 1840 fugitive slaves were finding their way to the home of William Bloss, who is said to have acquired his hatred of slavery during an experience as a school teacher in Maryland and South Carolina in the years prior to establishing his tavern in Brighton, a neighboring town of Rochester, in 1823.

The barn of Samuel Porter also was said to be a "safe house" for those in flight. The close relationship between Porter and Douglass is well documented. Not only was he an abolitionist and Underground Railroad stationmaster, but he also was active in local politics and regularly ran for mayor of Rochester, despite that he rarely received more than thirty votes.

"Frederick the Great," as Frederick Douglass is sometimes called, is regarded as the central figure in the freedom movement that unfolded in Genesee Country, and arguably, the entire nation. Yet, Douglass as an Underground Railroad figure stands on the shoulders of others. Scholars are generally mute on the matter, but it was surely Anna Murray Douglass—wife, mother, and benefactress, who had more "hands on" experience with freedom seekers than did her husband. It was Fred Bailey who relied on Anna to help him escape from Maryland slavery, and she continued to persist, sheltering at her hearth, many freedom seekers passing through "Genesee Country."

Other Places and Spaces

In 1851, under the leadership of Hiram Sibley, a group of men organized the New York and Mississippi Valley Printing Telegraph Company in Rochester's Reynolds Arcade. At that time, sending a telegram was awkward and costly, because so many entities, using the limited technology, were trying to "do their thing." The Sibley group used friendly persuasion to organize the struggling companies into what became the Western Union Telegraph Company. Thereafter, messages could be sent across many miles, with greater efficiency.

One very vital message came in October 1859, following John Brown's capture at Harpers Ferry. From Frederick Douglass, then in Philadelphia and a confidant of Brown, it read in part: "Tell Lewis to secure all the important papers in my high desk" (Douglass 313). If found by lawmen bearing warrants for Douglass's arrest, the "important papers," could have been used as evidence to convict him of conspiring with John Brown to raid the federal arsenal at Harpers Ferry, Virginia. Fortunately, the telegrapher, B. F. Blackall, was able to convey the coded message to Frederick Douglass's eldest son, Lewis, who did "secure" the papers. A few days later, Douglass was himself dispatched to Canada by fellow members of Rochester's Underground Railroad network.

A few yards from the Reynolds Arcade, E. C. Williams hid fugitives in the sail loft of his chandler shop, a business that offered supplies for sailing ships. Williams handled some of the traffic forwarded from Douglass's home on South Avenue, or from the *North Star* offices across the street in the Talman Block.

The Talman Block

In the 1800s, waters of the Erie Canal washed against the rear of three connecting buildings that comprised the Talman Block. The southwest corner of the block housed Quaker, Isaac Post's pharmacy, a likely "safe house" for freedom seekers. About 600 yards to the west Isaac and wife Amy made their home—the most-frequented station in the county. Number 25 in the block, east of

Post's apothecary, is the entrance to the suite at which Frederick Douglass published the *North Star*, and other antislavery periodicals. It was said that freedom seekers, as stowaways, or in the guise of canal boat passengers, exited at night and camped on the *North Star* doorstep to await the arrival of Douglass.

During 1849–1850, Harriet A. Jacobs and her brother, John, operated an antislavery reading room in the same building as Douglass's office. John and Harriet had escaped separately from Edenton, North Carolina. Whereas John became known as an antislavery speaker, Harriet tended the reading room, which was also a meeting place for the Rochester Ladies Anti-Slavery Society. Amy Post, wife of Isaac, was a member of the society, and was Harriet's confidant. Her support gave Jacobs the courage to find a publisher for her autobiography, *Incidents in the Life of a Slave Girl*.

A. M. E. Zion Church

Frederick Douglass's relocation to Rochester was an act that reaffirmed his independence. He needed to put distance between himself and William Lloyd Garrison, who had mentored his transition from New Bedford, Massachusetts, refugee to New England Anti-Slavery Society "lecturer." Early in 1848, Douglass was readying the first edition of his own antislavery newspaper, the *North Star*. It was printed in the basement of the Rochester church organized under the Reverend Thomas James. On occasion, the church also sheltered Harriet Tubman's passengers.

The founding pastor, Reverend James, had purchased the lot in 1830 and erected a small building in which to worship. Over time the congregation would erect a second, then a third edifice. But it was in that first modest structure that the first edition of the *North Star* was printed.

Douglass Home Site

In 1852, the Douglasses moved from Alexander Street, to a farm, south of the city, in part to shield Underground Railroad operations from prying eyes. It was a well-used station; often Harriet Tubman rested there with her passengers before proceeding west to Canada. Early in 1858, for about a month, the Douglass home also housed John Brown for about month, while his plan to seize the federal arsenal at Harpers Ferry, Virginia, percolated. During his stay, Brown met Shields Green, assisting in the operation of the "safe house," though Green was himself a fugitive from South Carolina slavery. Green later joined him at Harpers Ferry.

Kelsey's Landing

After passing through one or more of the Rochester area stations, a freedom seeker might well have been slipped aboard a Canada-bound cargo boat, moored at Kelsey's Landing, a commercial port on the west bank of the Genesee River, north of Driving Park Bridge. Once aboard a Canadian vessel, the fugitive was as good as free.

Conclusion

In the years between 1789 and 1865, descendants of Africans forced to become property in the land that was becoming the United States of America, made up a fraction of the population that settled in the Genesee Country. A larger number passed through the territory, bound for "safe[r] harbor" in Canada. Commentary by Austin Steward and Thomas James provide insights into the determination of kinsmen to be free, and to the resistance mounted on behalf of those slated for return to Southern slavery. Yet, such accounts from those who had been enslaved are all too few.

During the era of the Underground Railroad the voice of the person of color is, save for Douglass, James, and Steward, nearly mute. The Rochester-Monroe County Freedom Trail Commission has advanced the term, Afro-Rochester, in hopes of mounting a sustained effort to recover more of the presence of those people of color that did settle in the Genesee Country, and in whatever quiet way contributed to development of the region and its Underground Railroad.

—David A. Anderson

Further Reading

Howard Coles, *The Cradle of Freedom: A History of the Negro in Rochester, Western New York and Canada* (New York: Oxford Press, 1943).

Amy Hanmer-Croughton, "Anti-Slavery Days in Rochester," 14, Rochester Historical Society, (1936).

Frederick Douglass, *Life and Times of Frederick Douglass* (Hartford, CT: Park Publishing Co., 1881).

Thomas James, "The Autobiography of Rev. Thomas James," *Rochester History*, 27, No. 4 (October, 1975).

Lee McCanne, "A Path to Freedom: One Underground Railroad Route in Monroe County," Monroe County History Office (1964) .

Arch Merrill, *The Underground, Freedom's Road, and Other Upstate Tales* (New York: American Book-Stafford, 1963).

Milton Sernett, *North Star Country: Upstate New York and the Crusade for African American Freedom* (Syracuse, NY: Syracuse University Press, 2002).

Rochester/Monroe County Freedom Trail Commission, "Network to Freedom: A Guide-Book," Rochester (2004).

Wilbur Siebert, *The Underground Railroad from Slavery to Freedom* (1898; reprint, New York: Arno Press, 1968).

Austin Steward, *Twenty-Two Years a Slave, and Forty Years a Freeman . . .* (Rochester, NY: William Alling, 1857).

ROCKY FORK (ALTON), ILLINOIS

Rocky Fork, located near Rocky Fork Creek, is among a number of little known black Underground Railroad communities. Located in a densely wooded and secluded area near Godfrey, Madison County, Illinois, it is approximately three miles west of Alton, Illinois, the legendary location where Elijah P. Lovejoy was murdered by a violent proslavery mob. The Rocky Fork Creek flows into the Big Piasa River, which connected the community and the land to the Mississippi River.

"Rocky Fork" describes its landscape of rocky outcroppings where an old road made a fork and ran downhill to the west of the present-day New Bethel African Methodist Episcopal (AME) Church rather than the east as it presently does now. It led to Rocky Fork Creek at the bottom of the hill. Huge glacial boulders made it difficult to farm, but locals nevertheless cultivated all the usable acreage. Surrounding waterways and intersecting creeks made Rocky Fork accessible by water for fugitive slaves.

Origin of Rocky Fork

The history of Rocky Fork can be traced through the New Bethel Church formerly called Rocky Fork and family stories that were passed down. Founding members of the church, Eurastus Green and George Hindman, served in the Civil War and resumed leadership roles when they returned to Rocky Fork. Settlement of the area by blacks also was encouraged by white residents like A. W. Hawley, a cattle farmer, who gave them an opportunity to work and allowed them to purchase 40-acre parcels of land. Rocky Fork was the first stop heading north for runaways fleeing Kentucky, or those coming from the slave state of Missouri. Many oral testimonies about local Underground Railroad efforts are available. According to tradition, fugitive slaves made their way up the Mississippi River to Piasa Creek, which they followed to the Rocky Fork Creek. Rocky Fork was deep in the woods and this helped discourage slavecatchers, who often abandoned their search before reaching the settlement. Fugitive slaves rested and recuperated in Rocky Fork before moving north to avoid slavecatchers who were in pursuit. However, some stayed and were among those who organized the Rocky Fork (AME) Church.

According to local resident Charlotte Johnson, Frank Hogg was the first person of color to arrive in Rocky Fork. After arriving there between 1805 and 1807, he started a sawmill that he later sold. Hogg also owned parcels of land in and around the Rocky Fork area. Research into census records tells us that fugitive slaves passed through the area as early as 1816. The 1845 Census shows that there were 2,607 residents total living in the Alton area, of which 187 were black. In 1855, there were 97 blacks listed in the Rocky Fork community, in the Township of Godfrey, out of a total population of 247. Of that number, 52 of those African Americans lived in close proximity to a white man named Don

Rocky Fork African Methodist Episcopal Church, near Alton, Illinois. (Courtesy of Tom Calarco)

Alonzo Spaulding. He allowed them to work for him, clearing his land, and some of them eventually obtained ownership of the land.

Development of Rocky Fork

According to Joseph Hindman, grandson of A. J. Hindman, "the Spaulding and Hawley families set up a system of selling land to the one-time slaves, who availed themselves of the offer." Johnson added that, "when the escaped slaves came over [Spaulding and Hawley] gave them the ability to work and as they worked for them they could move on or they could stay there and build their homes and buy property" (LaRoche 149).

There also was a large group of black women from Virginia who became landowners in the area. One of them, Ann Maria Bell, was among the founders of Rocky Fork.

Bishop Quinn

Oral accounts identify William Paul Quinn, later a Bishop of the AME Church, as the founder of the Rocky Fork congregation sometime before 1840. He also had organized the AME Church in nearby Brooklyn, Illinois, with the help of John and Priscilla Baltimore prior to 1837. Recent research suggests that wherever Bishop Quinn established a church, it also became a haven for fugitive slaves.

Rocky Fork Network

Brooklyn was located directly across from St. Louis, south of Rocky Fork. Priscilla Baltimore, who purchased her freedom, and her husband, John, led eleven families, including fugitive slaves and freemen, to Brooklyn. Paralleling the actions of Free Frank in New Philadelphia, Illinois, the Baltimores purchased land on which the settlement was founded. From Brooklyn, fugitive slaves were led north through the forest into Alton, which was populated by free blacks at least as early as the 1820s.

One of the three major escape routes for fugitive slaves along the Mississippi River led from Alton, just north of St. Louis, Missouri (the others, Quincy and Cairo, Illinois). Siebert dates the rise of the Underground Railroad in Alton to 1831 and centers its establishment with the Presbyterian Church. Located on steep hills overlooking the Mississippi River, the city was strategically situated between Rocky Fork to the west and Brooklyn to the south in St. Clair County, and near the mouth of the Illinois River that led north through Illinois almost all the way to Chicago.

Alton was one of several towns near Rocky Fork with free black communities. Others included Hunterstown, Rocky Fork, and Wood Station absorbed runaways. Charles Hunter was one of Alton's conductors. The Hunterstown area, which he developed in the 1830s, had many free blacks residents, some of whom were fugitive slaves. It was in this area that Elijah Lovejoy lived when he moved to Alton.

Alton had a thriving black population that supported the Union Baptist Church and Campbell Chapel AME Church, which are among the oldest black churches in Illinois. Most free blacks worked in the river trade or at the brick works; it is believed that some of them conducted an Underground Railroad network running the length of the Mississippi River. One alleged conductor, James P. Thomas, lived in Alton on Belle Street, the site of the current Post Office. Another, Isaac Kelly, lived near Sixth and George streets.

Within a seven-block radius in upper Alton, there are five documented Underground Railroad stations. Situated across from St. Louis, Alton was reached by runaways either from the Missouri or the Illinois side of the River. According to Wilbur Siebert, once the runaways were near Alton "they met friends who were generally expecting them" (ibid. 160).

After a series of group escapes in 1845, a St. Louis paper speculated that perhaps the runaways had been enticed by abolitionists who had helped them along " 'the great under-ground railway' through Alton and Chicago to Canada." According to Mary Ann Clark, her great-grandmother swam across the Mississippi River, through a tunnel to Alton where she was sheltered overnight before moving on to Rocky Fork. Like William Wells Brown, who made several escape attempts before succeeding, slaves often escaped in anticipation of an impending sale or while being taken to auction in St. Louis. On one of Brown's unsuccessful escape attempts that began in St. Louis, he used a board to row a skiff across the Mississippi River. Landing south of Alton, he then headed on the main road toward Alton, hiding in the woods during the day.

In 1854, a black man drove through Madison County with fifteen men, women, and children concealed in his covered wagon. The conductor was a free black living in Alton who had brought his passengers from eastern Missouri where they crossed the river in skiffs. He eventually sent them on to Chicago.

From the Rocky Fork area, blacks moved along a route that converged in Springfield with possible refuges in White Plains, Jerseyville, Waverley, Quincy, and Jacksonville along the Illinois River. It led through LaSalle and Ottawa, and on to Chicago, where among the city's most prominent Underground Railroad conductors were former Alton resident, John Jones, and his activist wife, Mary Richardson.

The proximity of Rocky Fork to Alton, its geographic and religious relationship with Brooklyn, its accessibility to the Mississippi River and the Rocky Fork Creek, its location among sympathetic whites, and the historical record of the AME church's aid to fugitive slaves, all provide compelling evidence that Rocky Fort was an active stop on the Underground Railroad.

—Melissa Waddy-Thibodeaux

S

SALEM, IOWA

Perhaps the most active Underground Railroad community in Iowa, Salem also was probably the first to become actively engaged in aiding fugitive slaves.

Quaker Influence

The village was founded by Quakers who maintained strong connections to the New Garden Meeting in Wayne County, Indiana, the home of the prominent conductor, Levi Coffin, though there is no record of direct collaboration with him. Nine Quaker families moved from there to Salem in 1837, two years after Isaac Pidgeon established his pioneering homestead on Little Cedar Creek, just south of what became the village.

These settlers included the Frazier family, from which three members, Thomas, Elihu, and John would become part of the Underground Railroad. Their migration, however, was only a tiny part of a large move by Quakers in the east to Iowa; by 1840 Henry County, whose population was mainly accounted for by Salem, had a total of 3,772 residents.

Salem was 25 miles from the Missouri border and the friendly Quaker disposition toward fugitive slaves soon became known to Missouri slaves. In fact, Elihu Frazier once visited Missouri to make this known to slaves and was captured by slave patrollers who were suspicious of his activities. In an effort to make him confess, they threatened to hang him, but he still refused to admit this and they finally released and allowed him to return to Salem.

In 1843, a number of the Salem Quakers became part of the Indiana Yearly Meeting of Anti-Slavery Friends, which grew to nearly 2,000 members. Among those from Salem to join were the Fraziers, Elwood Osborn, Henry Lewelling, Marmaduke Jay, James Comer, Eli Jessup, Nathan Hammer, Jonathan Cook, and Aaron Street, Jr., son of one of the village's founders, who laid out the streets of the village. Interestingly, Aaron Street, Sr., was a native of Salem, New Jersey, which had been an Underground Railroad stop before 1820 and which continued to be an active station up through the Civil War.

Joel Garretson

Perhaps Salem's most prominent conductor was not a Quaker. Joel Garretson did, however, work closely with Quakers. A native of Virginia, Garretson became an ardent foe of slavery from the time he observed a passing coffle gang as a teenager. In 1837, he moved to Iowa and became involved in the antislavery movement, later becoming an organizer of the Free Soil Party in Iowa. But his most significant contribution was his participation in the Underground Railroad.

Garretson's home was five miles southeast of Salem. A story told by his son recalled a time when a fugitive slave was protected by his mother when his father was away. Learning that slavecatchers were in pursuit, Mrs. Garretson directed him to hide in the cover of tall grass and shrubbery in their peach orchard. The slavecatchers soon arrived and searched the Garretson farm but failed to find the fugitive slave. When Mr. Garretson returned, he brought the fugitive slave to a hiding place on the farm of Quaker Joseph Hoag, whose land was adjacent to the Garretsons. Hoag, who built a secret room to harbor fugitive slaves under a staircase in his house, helped care for the runaway until his wife and children were found. After the fugitive slave family was reunited, they were taken to Nathan Kellum of New Garden, Iowa, who forwarded them to Denmark, another community of Quakers active in the Underground Railroad, about 20 miles southeast of Salem.

Other Agents

Important Underground Railroad stations in Salem were the homes of Dr. Theodore Shriner and Quaker Henry Lewelling. The latter's home had a concealed trap door in the kitchen floor that opened to a crawl space under the house. Also, groups of fugitive slaves were reported to have been fed in an open lot behind the John Garretson home and the Congregational Church of abolitionist preacher, Rev. Hemmenway. An indication of the numbers aided was the large kettle used to prepare food for them. Among others in Salem who assisted fugitive slaves were Duvall Henderson and Quaker Peter Hobson, as evidenced by an incident when Hobson in his buggy rendezvoused with a fugitive slave disguised as a woman outside of Henderson's large two-story brick house that was used to board travelers. Henderson also piloted fugitive slaves at times in his wagon.

The residents of Salem took care to conceal their aid to fugitive slaves. No one, especially the children, were permitted to speak about it and no notes of it were ever recorded in the minutes of the Monthly Meetings of the Quakers. This contributed to their success but this also led to an inevitable confrontation with slaveholders in Missouri.

Ruel Daggs's Slaves

In July 1848, nine slaves owned by Ruel Daggs of Clark County, Missouri, escaped into Iowa. Unfortunately, they were caught hiding in the bushes just a mile or so south of Salem by two slavecatchers, Slaughter and McClure, after abandoning a wagon with horses owned by a Salem Quaker, John Pickering, who had been driving it. They were being led back to bondage in Missouri when Elihu and Thomas Frazier and William Johnson confronted them and demanded that the fugitive slaves be taken to Salem before their justice of the peace to determine if they were indeed slaves.

The case was heard at the Friends Meeting House, and when the slavecatchers were unable to prove their claims on the fugitive slaves, the justice of the peace, Nelson Gibbs, dismissed the case. At once the Salem Underground Railroad took steps to move the fugitive slaves to safety. One local who made a public demonstration of his antislavery beliefs was a hard-boiled old abolitionist, Paul Way, who shouted and created a commotion as he galloped away on his horse after the trial with a fugitive slave and his child in pursuit on another horse.

Outraged, the slavecatchers returned a few days later with a band of marauders, estimated to number as many as 300. They demanded to search every "nigger-stealing house" or burn down the entire town. Surrounding the town and blocking the streets, they sent men to search the houses of local abolitionists. Among those targeted was Elihu Frazier, who had been harboring fugitive slaves and who had hurried them out into the woods. The vigilantes found nothing but Frazier and his family calmly eating dinner. Others like Theodore Shriner threatened to shoot anyone who entered his home, and Paul Way did likewise, except that he boldly stated that he was harboring fugitives at that very moment. The alleged ringleaders of the Salem Underground Railroad, whom the slaveholders had put a $500 price on their heads, Eli Jessup and Joel Garretson, went into hiding.

Finally, word of the invasion reached abolitionists in Denmark. They immediately organized an armed posse and came to assist their neighbors. The slaveholders offered no resistance and quietly left Salem. But it was not to be the end of Daggs's effort to seek his justice. A case was brought in federal court in 1850. The jury found Elihu Frazier, Thomas Clarkson Frazier, John Comer, Paul Way, John Pickering, and William Johnson guilty, and Daggs was awarded $2,900 in compensation.

Despite the case, the work of the Underground Railroad in Salem continued without interruption up through the Civil War. Fugitive slaves passing through generally were taken east to Denmark, where Congregational minister, Rev. Asa Turner, was the leader. They also sometimes stopped in New Garden, which was midway between the two communities, and from Denmark were taken to Burlington, which bordered the Mississippi River. They also were sent in the direction of Crawfordsville about 20 miles due north.

—Melissa Waddy-Thibodeaux and Tom Calarco

SALEM/GREENWICH, NEW JERSEY

Both of these small communities in southern New Jersey lay along tributaries of the Delaware River and were populated primarily by Quakers and blacks. Near the village of Greenwich in Cumberland County were the black communities of

Springtown and Othello, and near Salem in Salem County were the black communities of Moore's Corner, Claysville, and Marshalltown. Both communities were among the earliest sites of the emerging African Methodist Episcopal Church (AME) founded in 1816 by Richard Allen in Philadelphia, and both had dedicated Quaker abolitionists who were ready to offer aid and protection to fugitive slaves and free blacks who were in need.

Early Involvement

This tandem of Quakers and blacks developed close relations with organized abolitionists and religious leaders in Philadelphia. For instance, oral tradition claims that southern New Jersey was the first area in which Allen ministered after leaving Delaware, sometime around 1783, and that fugitive slaves already were regularly being aided in the region.

Fugitive slaves primarily entered the state from Delaware, crossing the Delaware River from Wilmington to Salem, and the Delaware Bay farther south from Smyrna and Dover to Greenwich. Others came from Maryland in boats to Cape May. One such escape was recorded by William Still.

Thomas and Mary Ann Sipple, Henry and Elizabeth Burkett, John Purnell, and Hale Burton were slaves in Munkletown, Worcester County, which borders the Atlantic Ocean. They had been anticipating an escape in a boat for a long time and had saved up what bits of money they could for the journey. Part of this went to the purchase of the boat. As they rowed up the coast of Delaware, they were approached by a boat with five white men near Kitt's Hammock who attempted to seize them and their boat. A brief struggle with each of them using their oars followed. The aggressiveness of the blacks surprised the whites who retreated, then took out their pistols, firing and hitting all four of the men, though none seriously.

The fugitive slaves continued until they came to an island near Cape May, where they rested during the night. There, they met the captain of an oyster boat who agreed to take them to Philadelphia for $25, which was all the money they had. In Philadelphia, they were led to the vigilance committee office and William Still, and on to John Jones in Elmira, New York, who forwarded them to Canada.

Springtown

Springtown, where most of the blacks in Greenwich lived, became an asylum for fugitive slaves. In his autobiography, Samuel Ringgold Ward told of his family escape in 1820 from Maryland when he was three and said they had intentionally chosen Cumberland County because of its reputation:

> To reach a Free State, and to live among Quakers, were among the highest ideas
> of these fugitives; accordingly, obtaining the best directions they could, they set
> out for Cumberland County, in the State of New Jersey, where they had learned

slavery did not exist—Quakers lived in numbers, who would afford the escaped any and every protection consistent with their peculiar tenets—and where a number of blacks lived, who in cases of emergency could and would make common cause with and for each other. Then these attractions of Cumberland were sufficient to determine their course. . . .

They found, as they had been told, that at Springtown, and Bridgetown, and other places, there were numerous coloured people. . . . [And that] in deed and truth . . . when slave-catchers came prowling about the Quakers threw all manner of peaceful obstacles in their way, while the Negroes made it a little too hot for their comfort. (Ward 22–23, 25)

Rev. Thomas C. Oliver, who was born about 15 miles from Greenwich in Salem and worked in the Underground Railroad from the time he "was big enough to drive a horse," claimed as many as 600 fugitive slaves settled in the Greenwich area (Thomas Oliver, Interview with Wilbur Siebert, August 2, 1895). Their settlement he said was encouraged by Quakers like Thomas and J. R. Sheppard, who owned a mill, a store, and a ferry business that employed many blacks.

Abigail Goodwin

Salem, site of the first AME Church, Mount Pisgah, in New Jersey, and the beginning of the first circuit established in 1822 by the AME Church in New Jersey, was the home of stalwart Quaker abolitionist, Abigail Goodwin, who along with her sister, Elizabeth, lived and worked together to aid fugitive slaves, which included fashioning new clothes for them. They also maintained close contact with abolitionist leaders in Philadelphia.

Esther Moore, the first president of the Philadelphia Female Anti-Slavery Society, wrote of Goodwin that "New Jersey contained a few well-tried friends, both within and without the Society of Friends, to which Miss Goodwin belonged; but among them all none was found to manifest, at least in the Underground Rail Road of Philadelphia, such an abiding interest as a co-worker in the cause, as did Abigail Goodwin" (Still 617). According to William Still: "It was so characteristic of her [Goodwin] to take an interest in everything that pertained to the Underground Rail Road, that even the deliverance of a little nameless boy was not beneath her notice. To her mind, his freedom was just as dear to him as if he had been the son of the President of the United States" (619).

Goodwin had frequent correspondence with Still during the 1850s and often enclosed money to support the vigilance committee. In the following letter, she is inquiring of fugitive slaves she had sent to Still and of another she was about to send:

I presume the Carolina freed people have arrived by now. I hope they will meet many friends, and be well provided for. Mary Davis will be then paid—her cousins have sent her twenty-four dollars, as it was not wanted for the purchase money—it was to be kept for them when they arrive. I am glad thee did keep the ten for the fugitives. . . .

Samuel Nixon is now here, just come—a smart young man—they will be after him soon. I advise him to hurry on to Canada; he will leave here to-morrow, but don't say that he will go straight to the city. I would send this by him if he did. I am afraid he will loiter about and be taken. . . . He said they will go on tomorrow in the stage—he took down the number and street of the Anti-slavery office—you will be on your guard against imposition—he kept the letter thee sent from Norfolk. (Still 216–217)

In a letter to another Philadelphia abolitionist, Mary Grew, Goodwin described her role in the Underground Railroad as follows: "I am truly willing to take upon myself the superintendence of Salem County. I have acquaintances in different townships who will assist me . . . but you must not expect a very long list of names. We are poor here in the abolitionist faith." (Robert Harper, "South Jersey's Angel to Runaway Slaves," *Sunday Press*, June 15, 1975: 4).

However, white abolitionists like Goodwin could not have carried out their work without the assistance of the many free blacks who lived nearby, most of whom were ministers and mariners, whose occupations required travel and provided them with access to fugitive slaves and contacts to aid them. In Cape May, for instance, more than half of the black population was involved in the seafaring industry. And the AME Church had established three additional circuits that covered the eastern, central, and northern sections of the state by 1843.

Black Agents

Some black agents like Ezekiel Cooper, the namesake of a prominent white Methodist minister of the time and who was both a minister and mariner, were ubiquitous individuals. He was one of the early ministers at Springtown's AME Church, then moved to Port Elizabeth along the Maurice River tributary of Delaware Bay and worked in the seafaring industry. Making him even more elusive was that three generations of black Ezekiel Coopers lived in southern New Jersey during the antebellum period, and all of them participated in the Underground Railroad.

Others like Edward Turner, whose farm near Cold Spring, Cape May County was a primary station, had relatives who were both ministers and mariners. Turner personally forwarded fugitive slaves in his wagon to the village of Snow Hill, today the city of Lawnside, where there was a settlement of free blacks known as Free Haven. There he could have placed them in the care of Peter Mott, pastor of the Mt. Pisgah AME Church, or driven them farther on as oral tradition claims to Haddonfield and other points north.

Rev. Thomas C. Oliver Account

Rev. Oliver provided significant information about the Underground Railroad in New Jersey in two interviews with Wilbur Siebert in 1895 at Windsor,

Canada, where he had settled. Born in Salem, he moved with his family to Philadelphia and later settled in Camden, New Jersey, just across the river. It was there he helped his father and members of the Philadelphia Vigilance Committee like James J. G. Bias in transporting fugitive slaves through north-central New Jersey. He also affiliated with the AME Church before eventually becoming a Presbyterian minister. His intimate knowledge of the struggle over slavery went back as far as when he was seven years old and observed a riot involving slaveholders, fugitive slaves, and free blacks during a revival preached by Rev. Richard Allen in Salem County. This gave him a broad perspective of the Underground Railroad in the state.

From Salem, fugitive slaves were transported by wagon or stage through Swedesboro, where the black community of Woolwich worshipped at the Mount Zion AME Church, then moved on to Woodbury, Snow Hill, Evesham Mount (today Mount Laurel), Mount Holly, and Bordentown.

From Greenwich, where they often were harbored at the homes of blacks in Springtown and Othello, they followed a route that took them through Bridgeton, Vineland, Swedesboro, and then on, as the route from Salem. Oliver said those in Greenwich worked closely with agents in Port Elizabeth, among whom was his uncle, apparently the eldest Ezekiel Cooper, whom we know from census records was still alive in 1840. A rendezvous near the shore in the vicinity of Greenwich sometimes was made at night with boats transporting fugitive slaves that used yellow and blue lanterns as identification.

Trusty Accounts

Another interesting story based on oral tradition reveals the role of Native Americans, most significantly in their assistance to black mariners. Emma Marie Trusty, whose family traditions claim several generations and family lines of Underground Railroad work in southern New Jersey and from whom Henry Highland Garnet was descended, identified two Natives who had important roles.

Nathaniel Murry was among a nucleus of agents in Greenwich that also included Levin Bond, Thomas Brown, Jacob Bryant, the eldest Ezekiel Cooper, and Alges and Julia Stanford, all members of the Bethel AME that formed there in 1817. The role of the other Native, David Boley, is more speculative. However, he fit the description of the legend that claims a Native American brought fugitive slaves from Delaware and used smoke signals to alert agents in Cumberland and Cape May counties that they were coming. Boley regularly traveled to Delaware to sell the baskets he weaved.

Native Americans, who had a presence in the area for centuries, also are believed to have taught local black mariners how to better navigate the tricky currents of Delaware Bay. This was important because fugitive slaves who tried to cross the Delaware Bay unaided often met with disaster, and it was common for their bodies to wash up in Stow Creek, which flowed north of Greenwich and Bridgeton.

Other important Underground Railroad agents in southern New Jersey were members of the large Trusty family from three generations. Among them were David Mapes Trusty, who married Caturrah Seagraves in 1853 and moved to Lower Cape May where he was a mariner. He took fugitive slaves in his wagon to Port Elizabeth and Mays Landing, from where his cousin James brought them to Mullica Hill. In Atlantic County, Joseph Trusty was the superintendent and was joined by his brothers, Alexander and Job. Fugitive slaves were also brought from Cape May to Port Norris, Port Elizabeth, and Springtown.

While the railroads were sometimes used to transport fugitive slaves in New Jersey, it was generally only for short distances. Thomas Oliver referred to their use as "poison," apparently owing to problems of surveillance. According to Trusty family stories, fugitive slaves sometimes jumped off the trains before reaching the train station in Bordentown, where Thomas and Mary Ann Trusty offered assistance. Nevertheless, accounts mention use of the West Jersey, and Camden & Atlantic City railroads, and one railroad porter, Benjamin Jackson, a member of the Bethlehem AME Church in Mount Laurel, is said to have aided fugitive slaves on his trains.

A northern route described by Thomas Oliver, included a "Philadelphia Line," which started in Philadelphia and took fugitive slaves across the river to Camden and Rev. Oliver. He then took them to Perth Amboy by wagon following the course of the river to Burlington, Bordentown, Princeton, and New Brunswick, usually changing horses several times. He was able to do this without difficulty, he explained, because he possessed the keys to numerous stables where horses were made available. In New Brunswick, where he had to cross the Raritan River, he sometimes was forced to take an alternate route because of surveillance.

Other Routes

Robert Purvis described another route from Philadelphia that turned north through Bucks County in Pennsylvania. Near Morrisville, conductors led fugitive slaves across the Delaware River and into Trenton. From there they proceeded to Newtown and New Brunswick. At this point, they made their way to New York.

In the center of the state, Enoch Middleton operated an important station in Crosswicks, following his retirement and move from Philadelphia. Middleton kept close contact with Lucretia Mott and William Still, and either he or his son, Rudolph, would transport the runaways at night as far as New Brunswick.

At other times fugitive slaves used the Delaware & Raritan Canal, which opened in 1834, to move across the state. It connected the Delaware River in Bordentown with the Raritan River in New Brunswick. The Raritan emptied into Lower New York Bay at Perth Amboy. They also would go from New Brunswick to Jersey City, or Newark. It was a short distance from either to New York City and passage on a train or Hudson River boat.

—Tom Calarco

Further Reading

Wilbur Siebert, *The Underground Railroad: From Slavery to Freedom* (New York: Macmillan, 1898).

William Still, *The Underground Railroad* (Philadelphia: Porter and Coates, 1872).

William J. Switala, *The Underground Railroad in New Jersey and New York* (Mechanicsburg, PA: Stackpole Books, 2006).

Emma Marie Trusty, *The Underground Railroad Ties That Bound Unveiled* (Amed Literary, 1999).

Samuel Ringgold Ward, *Autobiography of a Fugitive Negro: His Anti-Slavery Labours in the United States, Canada, and England* (London: John Snow, 1855).

SALTWATER UNDERGROUND RAILROAD

Along the Atlantic coast, it is very likely that escape from slavery by ocean-going vessels of various sorts was more common than escape overland. Moving freight and passengers from Boston, New York, Philadelphia, and other Northern areas to the South, where coastal inlets and swamps impeded movement, was far more efficient over water than by rail or road. It was only natural that fugitives should recognize these facts in their efforts to escape to the free states.

Commerce between the North and the South

Waterborne commerce between North and South was robust throughout the 1800s. Northern merchants sent manufactured goods to the factory-poor South: shoes, harness, ceramics, wool and felt hats, lighting and machine oils, and cloth—including "negro cloth" to be made into slave clothing—very often traveled by schooner to such ports as Washington, Baltimore, Norfolk/Portsmouth and Richmond in Virginia, and Wilmington, Edenton, and New Bern in North Carolina. These vessels returned with foodstuffs—flour, barreled beef and pork, corn, rice—as well as the lumber and naval stores such as tar, turpentine, and pitch upon which northern shipbuilding depended. In addition they often carried the two chief products of slave labor, tobacco and cotton, the latter essential to the North's textile economy.

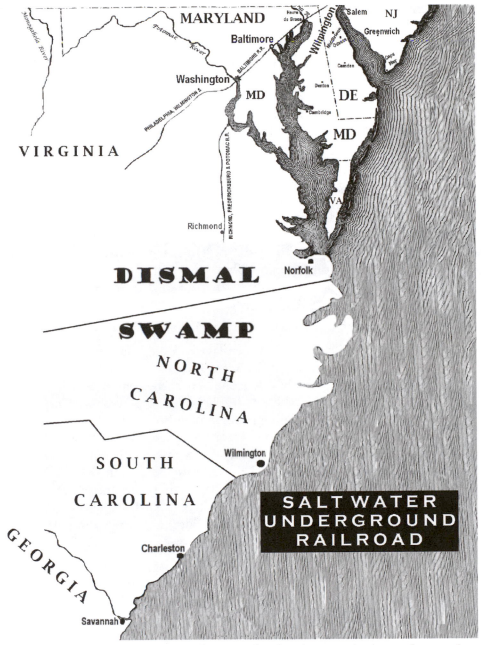

The geography of the Saltwater Underground and major ports in the southern region. (Courtesy of Tom Calarco)

Coupled with this prolific coastwise trade was the fact that seaports and vessels in the North and South were heavily populated by people of African descent. As historian Ira Berlin has observed of Southern ports, "Probably nothing arrived or left these cities without some black handling it" (62).

Historian John Michael Vlach has stated, "In any harbor a runaway encountered black fishermen, stevedores, carpenters, caulkers, sailmakers, blacksmiths, chandlers, hucksters, roustabouts, and ferrymen, in addition to sailors, pilots and even a few ship's captains" (104). By 1850, fully two-thirds of all employed men of color in Baltimore's second ward, which embraced the Fell's Point shipyards, were working on vessels, on the docks, and in ropewalks and other maritime industries. Men of color were always well represented in crews of coastwise and trans-Atlantic trading vessels and were often from slave states as well. Crew lists and seamen's protection papers, which every mariner was to carry to verify citizenship, document that nearly half of all Philadelphia crews were born below the Mason-Dixon Line in the 1810s, and between 1830 and 1850 at least one of every three Philadelphia black seamen identified Delaware, Maryland, and Virginia as their places of birth. It was therefore possible for fugitives to blend in along the waterfront and within crews, with or without the knowledge of vessel captains. One planter called Wilmington, North Carolina, "an asylum for Runaways" both because it was an active port and its population was then 40 percent African American (Vlach 104).

Advertisements Indicate Seafaring Vessels Used by Fugitive Slaves

The widespread expectation that enslaved people would escape by vessel is demonstrated in virtually countless notices offering rewards for their return. Notices placed in newspapers published along or near the coast routinely stated that any vessel captain or crew member who sheltered, employed, or transported a fugitive was subject to fine or imprisonment, or both. The Negro Seamen's Acts of many Southern states, which in theory confined sailors of color to their vessels while in port, were put in place mainly because Southerners believed Northern black mariners encouraged and aided slaves' escapes. In 1823 Charleston slaveholders bemoaned the fact that vessels arriving from the North almost always had at least two men of color employed on board. "Abolition Societies in the North," they charged, would no doubt "intrigue, through this class of persons, with our slave population," who would surely be "seduced" from the service of their masters in great numbers (Bolster 191).

Slave Narratives Support Use of Seafaring Vessels

Fugitive narratives, correspondence among Underground Railroad agents, and other sources offer considerable evidence supporting slaveholders' suspicion. Most dramatic was the response in the South to *Walker's Appeal . . . to the Colored Citizens of the World* (Boston, 1829), which urged enslaved people to overthrow the slaveowning class. Author David Walker, a free North Carolinian who moved to Boston about 1825, had the treatise sewn into the lining of black mariners' jackets so that they might distribute it among literate free and enslaved blacks, who would then read it or otherwise convey its message to the masses of illiterate slaves. Coastal Southern towns as well as states enacted laws mandating severe penalties for anyone found to be circulating *Walker's Appeal,* and after Nat Turner's insurrection of 1831, the *Appeal* and abolitionist newspapers were taken from some town post offices and burned. When fugitive escapes intensified in the 1850s, Virginia legislators passed a law requiring that all Northern vessels be inspected for fugitives before leaving its ports (Kneebone 76). Information about waterborne escapes appears not to have been inhibited, however. Abolitionist mariner Daniel Drayton, who attempted to remove 77 slaves from the District of Columbia on the schooner *Pearl* in 1848, noted the phenomenon:

> My trading up and down the bay ... of course brought me a good deal into contact with the slave population. No sooner, indeed, does a vessel, known to be from the north, anchor in any of these waters—and the slaves are pretty adroit in ascertaining from what state a vessel comes—than she is boarded, if she remains any length of time, and especially over night, by more or less of them, in hopes of obtaining a passage in her to a land of freedom. (*Personal Memoir of Daniel Drayton* 20)

The overall success of escape by vessel depended on the willingness of vessel masters or crew to violate various Southern strictures designed to stifle contact with enslaved people. Of the undoubtedly many captains and crew who knowingly aided fugitives, some few have been identified. William Still's 1872 *Underground Railroad* attests that Alfred Fountain, who for some years commanded the packet steamer *City of Richmond,* carried at least 60 fugitives from Richmond to Philadelphia, and the volume of such traffic borne on his steamer was almost certainly higher. A steward whom Still identified only as Minkins was instrumental in numerous escapes aboard this vessel. In November 1855 Fountain brought 21 fugitives north, perhaps the largest number he ever carried at one time. Fountain was never arrested, but William D. Baylis, who like Fountain was paid by fugitives or their families for his services and carried fugitives on his schooner *Keziah,* was not so fortunate. Baylis "would bring any kind of freight that would pay the most." Still wrote. "Quite a number of passengers at different times availed themselves of his accommodations and thus succeeded in reaching Canada" (60). But in June 1858, a search of Baylis's schooner revealed five fugitives and prompted his arrest. Baylis served seven years—until the fall of Richmond—of a 40-year sentence.

Assistance along the Shore

Many shoreside African Americans also assisted in escapes by vessel, and in their case as well, only a handful have been identified. Henry Lewey, who used the nickname Blue Beard in correspondence with abolitionists, aided such significant numbers of fugitives that he excited the suspicion of slaveholders and ultimately escaped to Canada. Betty, a friend of famed fugitive Harriet Jacobs, gave her "a suit of sailor's clothes" and told her to "put her hands in her pockets

The Great Dismal Swamp

The Great Dismal Swamp, located primarily in North Carolina, extends into southern Virginia. It occupies approximately 1,200 square miles, but was even larger during the antebellum period, and is a forbidding place, filled with alligators and poisonous snakes. It was a good sanctuary for fugitive slaves, and they established as many as 50 self-sufficient communities called Maroons up through the Civil War.

Despite the inhospitable environment, Maroons survived in situations that were preferable to slavery. Besides hunting, fishing, and farming, they traded with farmers on the edge of the swamp. They sometimes engaged in looting nearby plantations. They also incited slaves on the plantations to revolt. Such outbreaks in the regional vicinity of the Swamp occurred in Chesterfield and Charles City counties, Virginia, in 1792, in Elizabeth City, North Carolina, in 1802, in Princess Anne County, Virginia, 1818; and in North Carolina near the ports of Elizabeth City, New Bern, and Wilmington from September through January, 1831, less than a year before the Nat Turner rebellion.

The Swamp also served as a stopover for fugitive slaves seeking to go North. There they could find work cutting lumber or slicing bark for shingles, a prosperous enterprise in the Swamp, or working in the naval stores industry, extracting pine sap used for materials in the building of boats. Many of them were headed to nearby ports like Norfolk, where many ships were headed North, and they often needed money to pay sailors on the ships to hide them and bring them food. The use of fugitive slaves in the Swamp's industries was so rampant that the North Carolina General Assembly took steps to regulate their hiring practices in 1847. Captain Alfred Fountain who collaborated with Thomas Garrett is alleged to have transported fugitive slaves from the Swamp.

and walk rickety, like de sailors" in order to escape from Edenton in 1842 (Jacobs, Harriet M., *Incidents in the Life of a Slave Girl*, edited by L. M. Child, Boston, 1861: 170).

—Kathryn Grover

Further Reading

Ira Berlin, "Time, Space, and the Evolution of Afro-American Society on British Mainland North America," *American Historical Review* 85, 1 (February 1980).

Jeffrey Bolster, *Black Jacks: African American Seamen in the Age of Sail* (Cambridge: Harvard University Press, 1998).

David S. Cecelski, *The Waterman's Song: Slavery and Freedom in Maritime North Carolina* (Chapel Hill: University of North Carolina Press, 2001).

John T. Kneebone, "A Break Down on the Underground Railroad: Captain B. and the Capture of the Keziah, 1858," *Virginia Cavalcade* 48, 2 (Spring 1999): 74–83.

Philip D. Morgan, "Colonial South Carolina Runaways: Their Significance for Slave Culture," *Slavery and Abolition* 6 (December 1985): 57–78.

Gerald W. Mullin, *Flight and Rebellion: Slave Resistance in Eighteenth-Century Virginia* (London, Oxford, New York: Oxford University Press, 1972).

John Michael Vlach, "Above Ground on the Underground Railroad: Places of Flight and Refuge," in *Passages to Freedom: The Underground Railroad in History and Memory*, ed. David W. Blight (Washington, DC: Smithsonian Books, 2004): 95–115.

SANDUSKY, OHIO

Sandusky was one of the most important Underground Railroad terminals along Lake Erie. How many fugitive slaves escaped to freedom on one of the many steamboats that visited its port is not known, but numbers increased substantially after 1850 when railroad connections were completed to it from several sections of the Ohio River.

What made it even more compelling as a destination for fugitive slaves was that it was close to a series of islands on the way to Canada that provided easy access to the Promised Land. Among them was Pelee Island, which was Canadian soil and only 20 miles away.

Lake Erie Terminals

Sandusky was one of a ring of Lake Erie Underground Railroad terminals in Ohio that also included Conneaut, Ashtabula, Painesville, Cleveland, Lorain, Huron, and Toledo, and accounts of its participation dates as early as 1820.

The story of its beginnings involved the Parker family, who were farmers near Peru, about 20 miles south of Sandusky. They aided a fugitive slave whose owner was in hot pursuit, forwarding him to a black hostler, John Dunker, who worked at Marsh's Tavern in Sandusky. The tavern also was the residence of Captain P. Shepard, who then took the fugitive slaves in his sailing vessel to Fort Malden.

Integrated Effort Came Later

For the most part, it was an integrated effort of blacks and whites, but the latter's sustained contributions did not begin until sometime after 1837. In fact, one of the city's most ardent white abolitionists, Attorney Francis D. Parish, had actually prosecuted a local black conductor for harboring fugitive slaves in 1834, only later to have a change of heart. Nevertheless, fugitive slave traffic remained sporadic here until about 1845.

Before 1850, the common mode of travel for fugitive slaves to the Lake Erie ports was the frequently cited passage by wagon, 15 miles at a time or sometimes more, by individual conductors. After that, when the connection by railroad between Cincinnati and the Lake Erie ports was completed with the extension of the Little Miami from the south and Mad River Railroad from the north, the upperground railroad often was used. This made Sandusky even more active because only Cleveland and Sandusky were terminals of the upperground railroad.

Henry F. Paden, a conductor on the Mad River Railroad, related an incident that occurred a short time after John Brown's execution. He had hidden nine fugitive slaves, all men, in a railroad car. After their arrival in Sandusky when the passengers disembarked at what was the end of the road, he left them in the car. Later that night, he took them to the home of black conductor, George

Reynolds, who lived on Madison Street. Reynolds forwarded them to Canada. The men had fled despite that five of them had left behind wives and children.

Attorneys Were Important Contributors

Among Sandusky's leaders in helping fugitive slaves were attorneys Lucas Beecher, Francis Parish, Joseph Root, and Rush Sloane; master builders, Henry Merry, and the Irvine brothers, John and Samuel; and Padin, who was later the city's mayor. They collaborated with leading members of the black community, who included Rev. Thomas Boston, Grant Ritchie, John Lott, and Reynolds, a former slave and founding member of the black Second Baptist Church. Originally the Zion Baptist Church when it was founded in 1849 by a group that included seven former slaves, it changed its name to the First Regular

Rush R. Sloane house, Sandusky, Ohio; home of a leading citizen and entrepreneur who played a prominent role in the Underground Railroad in northwestern Ohio. (Courtesy of Tom Calarco)

Anti-Slavery Baptist Church. This made its intentions quite clear to fugitive slaves or slavecatchers who came to town. And there were many of the latter.

Two significant legal confrontations with slavecatchers involved Parish and his protégé, Rush Sloane, who became the city's most visible conductor. The first occurred shortly after Lucas Beecher and Parish had successfully defended two boys in court who were fugitive slaves, enabling their release and escape to Canada. A mother with her four children were seen entering Parish's home by the same slavecatchers who had filed a claim against the boys. They were fugitive slaves, and the slavecatchers, one of whom claimed to be the son of the owner of the slave family, filed a suit. This second prosecution was successful and Parish was fined $500 for hindering and obstructing the arrest of the fugitive slaves. With court expenses, it cost him a total of $1,500.

The Sloane case occurred in 1852 when two men, two women, and three children were arrested and taken from a steamboat just about to leave for Detroit. The fugitive slaves were brought before Mayor F. M. Follett by a man who claimed to be their owner, and Sloane, then a young fledgling attorney, was enlisted to represent them. Because no one claimed custody of them, Sloane suggested that there was no reason to detain them. At once, the crowd led by John Lott, John Irvine, and S. E. Hitchcock hurried the fugitive slaves out the door. Despite the protests of a man who shouted that he was the owner, the crowd brought them to the boat of Captain James Nugent for transport to Canada. The owner held Sloane responsible and two court cases followed that resulted in Sloane being found at fault and fined $3,000, in addition to paying more than an additional $1,000 in legal fees.

Boats That Transported Fugitive Slaves

The ready access to boats traveling to Canada made Sandusky an obvious destination for fugitive slaves. Among notable fugitive slaves who made their escape through Sandusky were Josiah Henson, Lewis Hayden, Lewis Clark (the model for George Harris in *Uncle Tom's Cabin*), and the real person on whom the fictional character Eliza in *Uncle Tom's Cabin* was based. There were a number of boats and boatmen ready to transport them. In addition to Nugent, there were Captain Thomas McGee of Sandusky; Captain George Swiegel, who worked with Sloane; Captain J. W. Keith and Captain Atwood of the *Arrow*. Some of the noted ships used in addition to the *Arrow* were the *Bay City*, the *Mayflower*, and the *United States*. On one occasion, the latter was transporting 20 fugitive slaves when it was boarded by the fugitive slaves' owners. However, they couldn't serve legal claims because it was on a Sunday, so they told the Captain they would pay the Captain $50 if he didn't land in Fort Malden, Ontario before reaching Detroit. Nevertheless, the Captain outsmarted them by lowering a boat with the fugitive slaves near the shore of Fort Malden, thereby abiding with the agreement of not landing until he got to Detroit and enabling the fugitive slaves to escape to freedom.

Routes to Sandusky

An important Underground Railroad connection to Sandusky was the Ohio River port of Madison, Indiana. Sloane identified it as the origin of one of the two major lines that ran to Sandusky, the other coming from the east and Ohio River port of Gallipolis, Ohio. Local conductor John Lott fled from Madison around 1846 after a riot there against blacks involved in the Underground Railroad by a proslavery group. Two other conductors, Elijah Anderson and George DeBaptiste, who worked with Lott there also fled from Madison about the same time. They increased their Underground Railroad activities in their new locations and worked frequently with the Sandusky terminal. Anderson set up operations first in Lawrenceburg, Indiana, and then Gallia County, Ohio, often forwarding fugitive slaves by train to Sandusky and Cleveland. DeBaptiste moved to Detroit where for a time he operated the commercial steamboat *T. Whitney* on Lake Erie that also brought fugitive slaves from Sandusky to Canada.

An especially interesting case in 1855 concerned a fugitive slave whose whereabouts had been tracked to Shelby, Ohio, 40 miles south of Sandusky, and feared he would be caught if he left. He had good reason to be careful, as a member of a ring of slavecatchers lived in the village. This group consisted of as many as 20 slavecatchers and also had members in Shelby, and the counties of Lucas, Wood, and Erie. Their operations ranged as far south as the Ohio River crossover point at Gallipolis.

His host, however, conceived of a plan along the lines of Henry "Box" Brown, and had him forwarded by train in a coffin, which it was claimed contained the remains of a man to be buried in Sandusky. This information was forwarded to Samuel Irvine in Sandusky. Though it was only a two-hour trip by rail, the fugitive slave nearly died from the ordeal. Nevertheless, he recovered sufficiently in a few days to make the trip to Canada.

Today in Sandusky, locals commemorate the Underground Railroad with a tour of the homes still extant that were used to harbor fugitive slaves. Among them was the Oran Follett home, which is now a museum, where Follett's wife, Eliza, was said to have fed fugitive slaves to the displeasure of her husband, who was opposed to breaking the law.

Rush R. Sloane

Another site is the Victorian mansion of Rush Sloane at the corner of E. Adams and Franklin Street, which the present owner is making efforts at historic preservation. Claims have been made that a tunnel led from his cellar to the lake, but aside from a cistern in it, there is no evidence of one. Local historians also are dubious because the city is constructed atop a bed of limestone, making such a tunnel highly unlikely.

In a speech Sloane delivered in 1888, he gave the names of 81 fugitive slaves that were aided in Sandusky after 1850, but added they were a "very small proportion of the whole number." He said, echoing to a degree some of the critics who scoff at the legends that depict the Underground Railroad as a complex web of intrigue and surreptitious organization, that his story was "a plain and unvarnished story of events . . . of the escape and kidnapping of fugitives which even now, but much more in the time to come, will seem like a fairy tale" (*The Firelands Pioneer* 59).

—Tom Calarco

Further Reading

The Firelands Pioneer, Firelands Historical Society, Norwalk, Ohio: The Chronicle Publishing Company, V (July 1888).

Freedom Seekers: Ohio and the Underground Railroad (Columbus, OH: The Friends of Freedom Society/Ohio Underground Railroad Association, 2004).

J. Blaine Hudson, *Fugitive Slaves and the Underground Railroad in the Kentucky Borderlands* (Jefferson, NC: McFarland and Company, 2001).

Reverend W. W. Mitchell, *The Underground Railroad* (London: William Tweedie, 1860).

Wilbur Siebert, *The Mysteries of Ohio's Underground Railroads* (Columbus, OH: Long's College Book Company, 1951).

SOUTHEASTERN PENNSYLVANIA

The counties of York, Lancaster, Chester, and Delaware in southeastern Pennsylvania hold a unique place in Underground Railroad history. A collision

Looking at the Susquehanna River from Columbia, Pennsylvania, at the site of the original bridge that was a landmark for fugitive slaves. (Courtesy of Tom Calarco)

of circumstances—a large black population, a large activist Quaker population, and the proximity of the area to slaveholding states—made the area the primary battleground between fugitive slaves and those who assisted them on the one hand, and slave owners and their agents on the other. Fugitives who believed that they had reached freedom upon crossing into these counties were often quickly discouraged. In an 1866 memoir the fugitive William Parker, who stood at the center of the 1851 Christiana riot, stated that he learned soon after his escape from Maryland to Columbia, Lancaster County, that in order "to preserve my stolen liberty I must pay, unremittingly, an almost sleepless vigilance" (Slaughter 48). The area also is unusual because African American resistance to pursuers was often forcible, in contrast to other northern areas where violent confrontations between blacks and whites were rare.

Smedley

The preservation of the Underground Railroad history of the area is greatly indebted to Dr. Robert C. Smedley's *History of the Underground Railroad in Chester and the Neighboring Counties of Pennsylvania* (1883). Smedley's history was based on interviews with surviving Underground Railroad participants and on correspondence with them and their children. According to historian and archivist Christopher Densmore (Smedley, introduction, ix), Smedley was influenced by William Still's 1871 history of the Underground Railroad, which was based on his own interviews with fugitives as secretary of the Philadelphia Vigilance Committee, contemporary correspondence from them and those who aided them, and his own relationships with Underground Railroad assistants throughout the Northeast. Densmore has pointed out that Smedley paid short shrift to African American participation in the Underground Railroad and made no use of newspapers, court records, and fugitive narratives published up to that time, but his history is, like Still's, a seminal and essentially primary account even though, like Still's, it was written after the Civil War. However incomplete, Smedley's account documents widespread Underground Railroad activity in the region and hints at how complex the movement probably was in other places. Still's book also extensively documents fugitive assistance in this area. However, few of the active Underground Railroad workers in the area kept records of their encounters with fugitives, and those who did—most notably Daniel Gibbons, whom Still credited with having assisted about 900 fugitives between the late 1790s and his death in 1853—often destroyed them (Smedley 57; Still 669).

Proximity to Mason-Dixon Line

Some towns in these southeastern Pennsylvania counties were scarcely 10 miles from the slave states of Maryland and Delaware. The Wilmington, Delaware, home of Underground Railroad activist Thomas Garrett, who allegedly assisted more than 2,700 slaves, was only eight miles from the home of Underground

Railroad workers Diana and Isaac Mendenhall in Kennett Square, Pennsylvania, which was home to numerous other fugitive assistants as well. The Adams County town of Gettysburg, where the Underground Railroad was also active, was no more than eight miles from the Mason-Dixon Line; the town of Columbia in Lancaster County, a well-known fugitive destination, was less than thirty miles from the Maryland border. As historian Stanley Campbell has observed, the cost accruing to a slave claimant for returning a fugitive to slavery was high enough to discourage a great number of rendition attempts in areas farther north, but traveling to southeastern Pennsylvania was a relatively inexpensive proposition. As Smedley noted (114), "So frequently did colored men go to work in the fields and never return, and were colored girls snatched from the homes of their employers, or whole families carried off in the night and never again heard from, that it was an almost daily question with them, 'Whose turn will come next?' "

York County was the site of one of the most notorious renditions before the passage of the Fugitive Slave Act. In 1837 slave agent Edward Prigg seized the fugitive Margaret Morgan, who had escaped to York County from Maryland five years earlier. Prigg was convicted under an 1826 state law that made the forcible removal of any resident to another state to sell or enslave them a felony; but in 1842 the U.S. Supreme Court, in *Prigg v. Pennsylvania*, overturned the conviction. The case incensed abolitionists and effectively gave greater license to slave owners and their agents. One white Lancaster resident recalled that after the 1850 passage of the Fugitive Slave Act, "every peaceful valley, as well as populous town, was infested with prowling kidnappers. . . . Quiet homes and peaceful communities were constantly threatened with midnight incursions of manhunters, with their treacheries, stratagems, their ruffian outrages and bloody violence, and menacing the defenseless people of color with a 'reign of terror' " (Slaughter 45).

Attraction to African Americans

Nevertheless, the area was attractive to African Americans, both enslaved and free, because it had a large black population and an active network of fugitive assistance. The proportion of blacks in the population of Chester County was more than double that of Philadelphia and four times that of Pennsylvania as a whole, and in some towns, the proportion was much greater. In the Lancaster County town of Columbia, there were 873 persons of African descent out of a total population of 4,140 in 1850, 21 percent of the population. An 1871 letter from Columbia black abolitionist William Whipper to William Still suggested that a large number of its black residents were fugitives from slavery when it stated that the black population of the town was cut nearly in half between 1850 and 1855, when almost 500 left for Canada (Still 766).

According to abolitionist Edwin Fussell, a large number of fugitives who arrived in Chester County "found friends and a home," lived there "undisturbed," and remained for decades (Smedley 184). William Whipper noted that some fugitives, "induced by high wages, and the feeling that they were safe in

Columbia, worked in the lumber and coal yards of that place. I always persuaded them to go to Canada, as I had no faith in their being able to elude the grasp of the slave-hunters" (Still 764). Long-term settlement was possible in large part because black and white abolitionists had developed an intricate network of safe places to and from which fugitives might travel. Although on the whole Quakers were perhaps no more active in the Underground Railroad than members of other denominations, the participation of Quakers in southeastern Pennsylvania's operation was overwhelming. Densmore has pointed out that of 132 Chester County fugitive assistants recently identified by historian William Kashatus, 83 of the 107 whose religious affiliation is known were Quaker. Though only slightly more than 5 percent of the county's population, Quakers accounted for nearly 78 percent of its identified Underground Railroad participants.

Quaker Influence

And fugitive-assisting Quakers were in many instances knitted together by marriage. William Wright of Columbia, for example, married Phebe Wierman of Adams County, whose parents were Underground Railroad activists, and her sister Hannah married Daniel Gibbons, one of the most active fugitive slave assistants in the region. William Wright's sister was the mother of abolitionist Samuel Mifflin, who married Wright's daughter Hannah. Underground Railroad agent John Lewis married Esther Fussell, the sister of agent Bartholomew Fussell, and the Lewis's daughter Rebecca married Fussell's nephew Edwin. Esther Lewis, and her daughters Mariann, Grace Anna, and Elizabeth were extremely active in fugitive assistance as well. Furthermore, these family relations connected southeastern Pennsylvania fugitive assistants with those in other regions. Charles Calistus Burleigh, active in the Underground Railroad in both Massachusetts and this region, married Gertrude Kimber, the daughter of Chester County Underground Railroad activist Emmor Kimber; Philadelphia Vigilance Committee member James Miller McKim married Sarah A. Speakman, the daughter of agents Micajah and Phebe Speakman of the Chester County town of Warren; and agent Isaac Mendenhall was cousin to Thomas Garrett's second wife Rachel.

Black Agents

African American Underground Railroad agents in southeastern Pennsylvania are far less fully documented, but Smedley's account—which cites at least 26 black participants, most by name—hints at the possibility that they were numerous as well as regularly involved. According to him, William C. Goodrich (or Goodridge) of York was routinely notified when " 'baggage' was on the road" and the day before their expected arrival arranged for Cato Jourdan to pick them up with his team and bring them across the Susquehanna River to Columbia. Jourdan took them to "another trusty colored man" in Columbia who sheltered them overnight, at which point the black lumber merchants William Whipper and Stephen Smith carried them in the "false end of a box car" they owned to an agent in Philadelphia (46–47). Whipper told Still in 1871 that from one to seventeen fugitives stayed in his home on any given night and that, though he kept no records, he "passed hundreds to the land of freedom" between 1847 and 1850 (Still 736). Smedley described Robert Loney, born about 1814 in Maryland, as a "well known colored man . . . who ferried fugitives across the river in the night at various places below Columbia, and gave them into the hands of William Wright, who distributed them to other agents"; at one time Loney also brought 13 fugitives across the river to agent Samuel Mifflin and at another carried a family to the home of Jeremiah Moore at Christiana, southeast of Columbia (Smedley 29, 51, 78). A diary kept by David Evans, who with his father aided fugitives at their home in Willistown, Chester County, reveals that he worked with an African American man named Henry Lee at least twice over two months in 1842; at one point an agent sent 35 fugitives at once to the Evanses, who passed half of them to the African American John Wright, who brought them to another, unnamed, safe place. Smedley also described a practice among some Lancaster County farmers that probably typifies how information about escapes was diffused among enslaved people generally:

> Many of the farmers in Drumore township went to Baltimore market with loads of produce, taking with them their colored drivers. The slaves sought opportunity to talk with these teamsters and to ask them many questions, as to where they came from, whom they lived with, and what kind of work they did, how they were treated, etc., etc. These colored teamsters gave them all the information they could, which was liberally conveyed to others, and especially to the slaves who accompanied their masters from the planting states to Baltimore on business. These would tell it to other slaves on their return. (228–229)

Considerable Fugitive Slave Traffic

The extent of fugitive traffic through southeastern Pennsylvania is impossible to determine accurately, but Smedley and Still provide evidence to suggest its extent. Between August 19, and November 15, 1842, according to David Evans's diary, fugitives came to his home 11 times in groups ranging from 2 to 25 people. Over those three months Evans and his father assisted 69 fugitives. In a November 1857 letter to Still, Elijah Pennypacker of Phoenixville wrote, "We have within the past two months, passed forty-three through our hands, transported most of them to Norristown, in our own conveyance" (Smedley 365). Groups of from 20 to 30 fugitives, while probably uncommon, sometimes arrived at the homes of individual assistants; at one point, the Esther Lewis family sent 40 from their home to the next safe place. In 1857 Thomas Garrett wrote Still to notify him of a group of 27 then on the road between Centerville and Kennett Square. Eighteen of the group were somehow directed to the home of John and Hannah Cox in that town, while the other nine—an entire family who had been among 15 enslaved people to escape from a single owner—went to Pennypacker. And although most abolitionists disapproved of Underground Railroad agents who went into the South to encourage escapes, Benjamin Kent of Penn Township once went with others into Maryland to bring a group of 35 fugitives, all armed to put down any effort to take them, into southeastern Pennsylvania (Smedley 309–310).

In addition to Smedley and Still, other contemporary sources offered detailed accounts of the workings of the Underground Railroad in this region and of individual fugitives themselves. William Wright figured critically in the life of James W. C. Pennington, the Congregational minister, abolitionist, and writer whose 1841 *Origin and History of the Colored People* is considered the first history of African Americans ever written. Born in Washington County, Maryland, in 1809, Pennington (then Jim Pembroke) came from Hagerstown, Maryland, to the home of Wright in the fall of 1828. En route he had been jailed once and had escaped; when he reached Pennsylvania, a tollkeeper directed him to Wright's home. He remained in the household until March or April 1829, during which time Wright paid him for his labor, worked with him to develop a strategy to thwart potential slave agents, taught him to read and write, and told him of "coloured persons, of whom I had not heard before, and who had distinguished themselves for learning, such as Bannicker [Banneker], Wheatley, and Francis Williams" (Pennington 44). Wright sent Pennington either to Daniel Gibbons or directly to Philadelphia, and from there he went to New Haven, Connecticut. Smedley related the story of an unidentified fugitive who, believing he had seen his master, jumped from a train near Wilmington, Delaware, that then crushed his foot. He was brought to the Chester County home of Esther Lewis to recuperate, remained there through the winter, and was then sent to Still, who directed him to Boston; there, Smedley wrote, the man's leg was amputated and replaced with an artificial one (178). The records of the Boston Vigilance Committee round out the story. An August 19, 1858, entry into the committee's records identifies the man as Johnson H. Walker, "who in his flight from Slavery in Maryland had his food crushed by the car wheels at the Railroad station in Wilmington, Delaware." The records show that the committee paid $100 to "Palmer & Co." for an "artificial leg"; Palmer donated half the cost, while 18 Boston abolitionists supplied the rest in donations of from 50 cents to $5. The Kennett Square Underground Railroad Web site states that the injured fugitive was brought to the home of James Walker, who lived in Kennett Square, and was "hidden for many weeks" in a space over Walker's kitchen; the fugitive took the name Johnson Hayes Walker in honor of the three Kennett Square people who helped him (http://www.undergroundrr.kennett.net/).

Christiana Riot

Southeastern Pennsylvania is perhaps best known in Underground Railroad history for the riot that took place in the Lancaster County town of Christiana on

September 11, 1851. The incident was only one in a series of armed encounters with slavecatchers; Smedley cited at least six incidents in which African Americans in the area assaulted and attacked pursuers or assembled to confront them with all manner of weapons, including farm tools. William Parker stated in his memoir that he had "beaten and driven" kidnappers "out of the neighborhood" and had once struck a slave agent with a pair of tongs, knocking him out.

The encounter at Christiana arose in 1849 when Edward Gorsuch, whose slaves numbered among the largest in the state of Maryland, discovered that four of the people he enslaved were stealing grain and reselling it; in that year they escaped into Pennsylvania. Empowered by the passage of the Fugitive Slave Act, Gorsuch, his son Dickinson, and six others, including a federal marshal, went to Christiana, where an informant had told them three of the four were living. Two were said to be living in the home of William Parker. Parker had been warned of their intentions, and with six others, waited inside his house for their arrival. When they demanded to enter, Parker threatened them and his wife, Eliza, ran to the garret of the house and blew a horn, a signal to blacks in the neighborhood of impending danger and a call to assemble. Historian Thomas Slaughter has stated that from 75 to 150 black men and women, 50 of them armed, came to Parker's house to confront Gorsuch and his party. When Dickinson Gorsuch moved to shoot Parker, Parker knocked the gun from his hand, and a general riot ensued. In the end Gorsuch was killed and his son wounded. Parker fled along with his brother-in-law, Alexander Pinckney, and his fugitive boarder, Abraham Johnson. Within two days they reached Rochester, New York, where Frederick Douglass put them on a Canada-bound steamer. At least three of the area's white Underground Railroad workers sheltered other African Americans who had taken part in the riot and moved them along. The Christiana Riot was immediately notorious, and historians cite it as the first violent response to the Fugitive Slave Act of 1850. Southern newspapers viewed it as an outrageous affront to their region; the *Baltimore Clipper* called for "prompt retributive justice upon the heads of the wretches who have instigated and committed the bloody deed." In the end the 35 blacks and 2 whites who were arrested after the riot were acquitted, but the Christiana incident heightened the already high level of violence and tension surrounding southeastern Pennsylvania's Underground Railroad.

—Kathryn Grover

Further Reading

William Parker, "The Freedman's Story," *Atlantic Monthly* 17 (February–March 1866).

James W. C. Pennington, *The Fugitive Blacksmith; or, Events in the History of James W. C. Pennington, Pastor of a Presbyterian Church, New York, Formerly a Slave in the State of Maryland, United States* (London: Charles Gilpin, 1849).

Thomas P. Slaughter, *Bloody Dawn: The Christiana Riot and Racial Violence in the Antebellum North* (New York and Oxford: Oxford University Press, 1991).

Dr. Robert C. Smedley, *History of the Underground Railroad in Chester and the Neighboring Counties of Pennsylvania* (Lancaster, PA: The Journal, 1883; reprint, Mechanicsburg, PA: Stackpole Books, 2005).

William Still, *The Underground Railroad* (1872; reprint, Chicago: Johnson Publishing Co., 1970).

SPRINGBORO, OHIO

Founded by Quakers from Pennsylvania, Springboro is located about 35 miles north of Cincinnati and was one of the primary destinations of fugitive slaves coming from that city. One of the Quakers, Jonathan Wright, set aside a portion of land that he had purchased to form the village, surveying and plotting it out in 1815, and naming it "Springsborough," for the numerous springs found in the area.

Wright was born in 1782 in Pipe Creek Maryland. He became a surveyor and miller in Menallen, Pennsylvania, but when his father decided to make his home in Ohio's Miami Valley, Jonathan sold his business and moved with him.

Quaker Influence

Springboro's involvement with the Underground Railroad was greatly influenced by the Quakers' hatred of slavery. Also, it was situated between the Great and Little Miami rivers, only a two-night trip by wagon north of the Ohio River. Even though aiding fugitive slaves was against the law, Springboro's residents, both Quaker and non-Quaker, were always ready to assist them.

Ohio became a destination for many fugitive slaves. The entire Ohio River was a borderline to freedom stretching nearly 1,000 miles. There were numerous paths to freedom crossing the Ohio River from bordering communities in Kentucky and West Virginia, and fugitive slaves came to Springboro along many of these paths.

In addition to Wright, who also was a farmer, businessman, and philanthropist, there were numerous others who assisted fugitive slaves in Springboro. Among them were Achilles Pugh, who for a time published the abolitionist newspaper, the *Philanthropist*, after he was driven out of Cincinnati; Alfred Thomas, the village librarian; Warner Bateman, who would later become a U.S. district judge; Jeremiah Stansel, whose father was a close friend of Daniel Boone; James Stanton, the nephew of Lincoln's secretary of state, Edwin Stanton; Simon Kenton, a frontier military officer who was also a friend of Daniel Boone and George Rogers Clark; Jonah Thomas; Mahlon Wright; James Janney; James Farr; and Napoleon Johnson.

Means of Travel

Many fugitive slaves fled on foot but the bolder individuals expropriated their masters' horses or mules. Travel generally occurred at night, and often they were forced to hide in places for days and sometimes weeks. Many stopped at farms and stole food to take on their journey. They had to be resourceful and think of ways to survive and prevent themselves from being detected, and had to always be on the lookout for slavecatchers, who would track them using the advertisements with their descriptions published in the Southern newspapers.

Among the unusual stories passed down through Springboro residents was one about a slave who put a pig in a wheelbarrow and walked from Kentucky to Canada. When he was stopped, he answered that he was pushing the pig to the next farm for his master. But most fugitive slaves needed the help of the Underground Railroad.

Napoleon Johnson

Both whites and blacks were Underground Railroad conductors, and there were even some slaves who participated. Napoleon Johnson was a plasterer in Springboro for 33 years. He was born in 1820. His parents, Embra and Polly, were slaves on the same plantation. They had ten children of which five died, and three were sold to other slaveowners. Napoleon's parents finally died, and Napoleon was the only family member left when a new master emancipated all 39 of his slaves on their plantation in 1847. Napoleon left, looking for a place to settle. Once he found a place, he promised to return for Celia Anderson, another slave who had been freed. His journey ended when he found Springboro. In 1849, they married and settled in Springboro with her mother, and the cabin he built soon became a part of the Underground Railroad.

Many Homes Used Still Exist

Many of the homes used to harbor fugitive slaves in Springboro still exist and can be viewed today. There were hiding places in barn lofts, concealed closets, hidden rooms, crawl spaces, and tunnels. In the front closet of Jonathan Wright's home on 80 State Street, now a bed and breakfast, boards removed from the floor reveal a long three-foot by three-foot tunnel. It was connected to the homes of Jonah Thomas and Mahlon Wright on South Main by a five-foot high tunnel, as was the Bateman tanneries on South Main Street. There also was said to have been a 700-foot-long tunnel that stretched from Mahlon Wright's home to Little Creek, allowing fugitive slaves the opportunity to get to water and make their getaway in boats to get to freedom. The Wilson home on Lytle-5 Point Road had a hole big enough for three men that was cut into an area behind a chimney. The Hormel home on East Mill had an irregularly shaped attic, and behind one wall, which followed the contour of the house, was a narrow room. Some homes had more than one owner during the antebellum period and all of them were involved in the Underground Railroad. An example of this was the Joseph Thomas house originally owned by James

Janney, who bought the house in 1835 and sold it to James Farr in 1838. Joseph Thomas finally bought it in 1866.

In all, there are 27 confirmed Underground Railroad depots in Springboro, 18 in the village, and 9 in the surrounding township, as well as 9 alleged tunnels. Whether or not any of the tunnels or hiding spaces were actually used on the Underground Railroad is difficult to determine, but considering the location of Springboro, there is a strong likelihood that hiding places were needed for the fugitive slaves harbored there.

—Sharron L Pope

Further Reading

Wilbur H. Siebert, *The Mysteries of Ohio's Underground Railroads* (Columbus, OH: Long's College Book Company, 1951).

ST. CATHARINES, ONTARIO

Several notables of the antislavery struggle are associated with St. Catharines, including the reverends Hiram Wilson, Anthony Burns, and Alexander Hemsley; Harriet Tubman, known as the Black Moses for leading her people to safety; and John Brown of Harper's Ferry fame, whose connection with St. Catharines as a major terminal on the Underground Railroad, may have been the most fleeting.

About a month before holding his 1858 convention in Chatham, John Brown solicited support from the blacks of St. Catharines, a community regarded as a beacon of hope for the fugitive slave. But he was unable to recruit any former slaves in Canada to participate in his raid on Harpers Ferry, perhaps because they would have risked capture in the United States.

Harriet Tubman

In an 1868 letter to Harriet Tubman, who lived in St. Catharines with her parents for a time, Frederick Douglass praised her for the perils and hardships she encountered in service to their enslaved people. Knowing full well the danger, Tubman usually carried a pistol for self-defense. It is believed she quieted crying babies with a bit of opium, a fairly common cure of the day. And she returned to the South not once, but 13 times to bring slaves to the North, conducting more than 70 refugees along the Underground Railroad and bringing many to St. Catharines. She moved there herself in 1851, staying periodically during a 10-year period and attending the British Methodist Episcopal Church, earlier known as the African Methodist Episcopal Church. The name had been changed by former slaves to reflect loyalty to the British Empire. Regarding her thoughts on slavery, Tubman told Benjamin Drew:

I grew up like a neglected weed—ignorant of liberty, having no experience of it . . . every time I saw a white man I was afraid of being carried away. I had two sisters carried away in a chain-gang—one of them left two children. We were always uneasy. Now I've been free, I know what a dreadful condition slavery is. I have seen hundreds of escaped slaves, but I never saw one who was willing to go back and be a slave. (Drew 30)

Alexander Hemsley

By the age of 60, Alexander Hemsley had served the people in the provinces in and around St. Catharines for 20 years as a Methodist minister. He escaped from slavery in Maryland at the age of 23, but did not cross into Canada at the time. Instead, he took a job in Northampton, Massachusetts, where he lived without incident until October, 1836, when Southern speculators caught up to him. As he recalled, four or five men had bought him running from the executor of his late master's estate. To buy a slave running, meant to purchase a legal title at low cost for a slave who had run away. This was a high-risk investment that could result in great profit, provided the slave could be recaptured. Before committing their money, the southern speculators took the time to locate Hemsley, and "pretended to be gunning" while they observed him and his children, "appraising their value in case they could get them" (ibid. 34). Later, Hemsley learned that they had promised his oldest son as payment to a lawyer, in exchange for trying the case.

It seemed Hemsley was doomed to a life in chains, when a last minute writ of habeas corpus by one of his counsel spared him from a proslavery judge, and a second trial before a different judge resulted in a declaration of freedom. As good as the outcome was, it was only a stopgap measure. The law in Massachusetts could not prevent underhanded tactics, and it was rumored that his pursuers would attempt to smuggle him to a slave state, where he would lose his rights. To preserve his freedom, Hemsley left the country without delay, and years later, harbored no regrets about leaving:

When I reached English territory . . . a man was a man by law . . . in a few days, I left for St. Catharines, where I have ever since remained . . . salt and potatoes in Canada, were better than pound cake and chickens in a state of suspense and anxiety in the United States . . . there, [in the U.S.], I would be afraid of the ghost of a white man after he was dead. (ibid. 38)

Anthony Burns

Anthony Burns, born a slave in Virginia, escaped to Boston in 1854, but had the poor fortune to be the last fugitive slave to be returned to slavery by the state of Massachusetts, under the second Fugitive Slave Law, passed by Congress under President Millard Fillmore in the fall of 1850. After the Rev. Leonard Grimes of Boston negotiated his freedom after a trip to the South, Burns became a student at Oberlin College in Ohio. He did not move to Canada until 1860, when he became a pastor with the Zion Baptist Church of St. Catharines and where he died only two years later.

Rev. Hiram Wilson

Reverend Hiram Wilson, a selfless philanthropist who would share his last crumbs with refugees, arrived in St. Catharines in 1849, leaving the settlement of Dawn that he had helped to establish with Josiah Henson. During the remainder of his life, which he spent in St. Catharines (he died in 1864), he engaged in his most active efforts in support of the Underground Railroad, setting up a Mission House and Sabbath school there, and providing room and board for newly arriving fugitive slaves. He wrote a number of letters to American abolitionist newspapers, commenting on the "refugee" situation in Canada West, and once did surveys that provided estimates of the numbers of fugitive slaves who were living there. In this excerpt from a letter sent to one of his benefactors, Miss Hannah Gray of New Haven, Connecticut, he describes his activities in St. Catharines:

> We are doing all we can for the comfort & elevation of the colored people in this glorious land especially for the numerous strangers who are constantly thronging our shores; at the same time I am serving the cause of philanthropy among the sailors on the Welland Canal. Am kept as busy as a bee every day in the week. I may say every hour of every day and the Sabbath is with me emphatically a day of labour, not of rest as I have more exercise than any other day in the week.
>
> Our cause is prospering – Sabbath school very interesting & we are all in good spirits. (Letter to Miss Hannah Gray, St. Catharines, June 15, 1853)

Although St. Catharines served as a place of refuge for the persecuted, it would be a mistake to assume that refugees enjoyed life without discrimination. By the turn of the twentieth century, only certain jobs were available to blacks, and wages for those occupations were low. Women cleaned houses. Men cleaned furnaces and yards. And they often worked at the hotel as porters, waiters, cooks, masseurs, and masseuses. While they could vote, they could not hold office. Worship was limited to the black church.

Yet, before the U.S. Civil War, when freedom was a matter of life and death, the whites of St. Catharines treated black refugees more warmly than most. And for all the barriers that remained, St. Catharines offered former slaves a place to sleep easy at night, for perhaps the first time in their lives.

—Rae Hallstrom

Further Reading

Benjamin Drew, *A North Side View of Slavery* (Boston: John Jewett and Company, 1856).
Ross Frances, "The Blue-Blooded Blacks of St. Catharines," *What's Up Niagara*, 1, No. 3 (1982).
Bryan Prince, *I Came as a Stranger* (Toronto: Tundra Books, 2004).

Benjamin Quarles, *Black Abolitionists* (New York: Oxford University Press, 1969).
Robin W. Winks, *The Blacks in Canada, a History* (New Haven and London: Yale University Press, 1971).

SYRACUSE, NEW YORK

Among the nation's most abolitionized communities, Syracuse in Onondaga County, New York, aided several thousand fugitive slaves during the antebellum period. It also was the site of the Jerry Rescue, one of the most celebrated incidents of defiance against the Fugitive Slave Law.

Heart of the Burned-Over District

Syracuse's location in the heart of the so-called "Burned-over District," which became inflamed with the second Great Awakening and its message of doing good deeds to attain salvation, made it fertile ground for the Underground Railroad. Slavery was never widespread in this region. For instance in 1820, there were only 59 slaves in Onondaga County and 195 free black persons. In 1837, black New York City abolitionist Charles Ray made a visit and reported in the *Colored American* that it was "a very pleasant little place, [where blacks] will undoubtedly receive encouragement from the whites." And in 1842, its first black congregation, The First African Methodist Episcopal Church of the Village of Syracuse, was founded on July 4, 1842, installing a former fugitive slave, Thomas James, as pastor.Other churches involved in local abolitionism included the First Congregational Church founded in 1838 by comeouter members of the First Presbyterian Church. So devout were its antislavery sentiments that it wasn't deterred after a cannon was fired outside the church to disrupt its services. The church later formed another Congregational Church in a wooden chapel in 1855, and named it "Plymouth" after Henry Ward Beecher's famous antislavery church in Brooklyn. The Unitarian Church of the Messiah, another important abolitionist congregation, was led by the one of the nation's most important abolitionists, Rev. Samuel J. May, who came to Syracuse in 1845, from Connecticut, where he had been aiding fugitive slaves during the previous decade. He remained as pastor until after the Civil War. Last to be formed among the city's antislavery churches was the Wesleyan Methodist, completed in 1847. It was part of a new denomination founded only four years earlier in Utica on account of its antislavery doctrine and the refusal of the parent Methodist Church to disavow members who were slaveowners. It too was served, from 1852 to 1855, by another of the nation's leading abolitionist clergymen, Rev. Luther Lee.

Antislavery Societies

Numerous antislavery societies formed in the region during the mid-1830s, including a county society. The organization of the state society occurred in nearby Utica in 1835 and abolitionist strongholds like the Oneida Institute, a manual labor school in Whitesboro, just west of Utica, and the Peterboro estate of one of the nation's most influential abolitionists, Gerrit Smith, fortified its abolitionism. The state society newspaper, *Friend of Man*, also was published in Utica and printed by the Oneida Institute. Among other important regional centers of the Underground Railroad were Oswego, where Smith had business interests, and Skaneateles, the home of influential Quaker and conductor, James Canning Fuller.

Early Rescue

The first major documented incident related to the Underground Railroad in the area came from Utica and was reported by *Friend of Man* in 1837 when two fugitive slaves from Virginia, Harry Bird and George, who had been apprehended by a slavecatcher, were rescued by an organized group armed with clubs who broke into the jail and freed them.

Another well-documented incident involved the rescue of Harriet Powell in 1839, whose master was visiting Syracuse that year. This was before the 1841 law that prohibited slaveholders from bringing slaves into the state, on the penalty that they automatically would become free. Powell was staying with her master and his family in a Syracuse hotel. Black employees, learning of her desire to be free, contacted local abolitionists, and a plan was hatched to rescue her. The plan was adroitly executed, and by the time her master realized she was missing, she was under the protection of operatives of the Underground Railroad. She was moved around to several locations until finally being kept at Gerrit Smith's mansion until the situation was favorable for her removal to Canada.

May, one of the founding members of the American Anti-Slavery Society in 1833, began aiding fugitive slaves soon after his arrival in Syracuse. In his book, *Some Reflections of our Anti-Slavery Conflict*, he related an incident about a local black man, Sanford, who he had assumed was a free man but came to learn was a fugitive slave. The man requested May's help in purchasing his mother who was still held in bondage. An apt illustration of how the Underground Railroad operated and the extent of its influence is what May did next. He contacted John Needles, a Baltimore Quaker, who contacted a fellow Virginia Quaker who lived near the plantation of Sanford's mother, to make an offer for her purchase. However, her owner refused to sell her. As May wrote, "It was better to him than money to punish the runaway slave through his disappointed affections, now that he could not do it by lacerating his back or putting him in irons" (May 284).

Vigilance Committee of 13

By 1850, Syracuse had become one of the most notorious Underground Railroad centers in the nation. When the second Fugitive Slave Law was passed, a public meeting was held on October 4, with the full approval of the city's mayor, to protest the law and to resolve to disobey it. They denounced Daniel Webster, then secretary of state, and President Fillmore for approving it, and formed a Vigilance Committee of 13 to protect individuals who might be deprived of their liberty by it. Those members were the following: Charles A. Wheaton, a local hardware store owner and founding member of the come-outer First Congregational Church; Abner Bates, another retail merchant and First Congregational member; John Wilkinson, a proprietor of the Syracuse branch of the New York Central Railroad; Rev. Jermaine Loguen, the noted black activist; Captain Hiram Putnam, a founding member of Church of Messiah; Charles B. Sedgwick, later a member of Congress; E. W. Levenworth, a local lawyer; Patrick H. Agan, a local printer; George Barnes, a local bookkeeper; Baptist minister, Rev. R. R. Raymond; Dr. Lyman Clary; V. W. Smith; and John Thomas, who later would be the ghost writer for Loguen's autobiography.

Samuel May wrote that a larger association of supporters formed eight days later, among whom he was a member. Their mode of operation was that if any member of the association learned that someone was in danger of capture by slavecatchers that they go to the nearest church and toll its bell. An emergency meeting place also was established. Members changed over the years, and other antislavery notables among its membership included the aforementioned Lee, black activist Samuel R. Ward; and Erie Canal merchant and publisher of the *National Era*, Linnaeus P. Noble.

In June 1851, Daniel Webster, then U.S. secretary of state, visited the city and threatened the abolitionists.

"Those persons in this city who mean to oppose the execution of the Fugitive Slave Law are traitors!" Webster declared. "This law ought to be obeyed, and it will be enforced—yes . . . in the city of Syracuse it shall be enforced, and . . . in the midst of the next anti-slavery Convention, if then there shall be any occasion to enforce it" (May 373–374).

Jerry Rescue

Webster's prediction came true in October 1, 1851, when federal marshals arrested William "Jerry" Henry, a fugitive slave from Missouri who had settled in Syracuse, New York, and was working in a cooper shop making barrels. Just as Webster had said, the arrest came on the day an antislavery convention was taking place. Vigilance committee member, Charles Wheaton, interrupted the proceedings with the news of the arrest while other members tolled church bells throughout the city. En masse, the abolitionists went immediately to the city courthouse, which was soon overflowing. During the confusion, Jerry briefly escaped and the judge called for an adjournment. This gave the vigilance committee, under the leadership of Gerrit Smith, time to plan Jerry's rescue.

With the plan in place, the hearing resumed but before the matter could be settled, a stone crashed through a window. Another adjournment was called and the sheriff and four federal marshals who had arrested Jerry were left to prevent the abolitionists from taking Jerry. They took him to a holding cell in the rear of the building and bolted the door, but the abolitionists armed with clubs and axes finally broke down the door with a large plank. By this time it was dark and the abolitionists had turned off the gas that lit the lamps inside the building. The police fired a few aimless shots in the dark, but it did not deter the abolitionists. They freed Jerry, and two black men, Peter Hollinbeck and William Gray, took him on a circuitous route to a house where they cut off his shackles and dressed him in women's clothing before taking him to the home of Caleb Davis, who had formerly been a pro-slavery advocate. There Jerry remained in hiding for five days. He was moved to two more locations before finally being sent on a boat from Oswego to Canada.

Twenty-six indictments were made against 14 white and 12 black men in the Jerry Rescue. Smith, May, and Wheaton, three of the ringleaders were never indicted despite public declarations of their involvement, and only one participant, Enoch Reed, was actually convicted. But he died while his case was on appeal. An interesting sidelight to the incident is that vigilance committee flaunted its success by sending President Millard Fillmore the shackles that had been put on Jerry after his arrest. Thereafter, October first was commemorated in Syracuse for the rest of the decade with major celebrations while it continued to defy the Fugitive Slave Law.

Other Incidents

Among the many incidents involving aid to fugitive slaves in Syracuse, May recounted several involving himself in his book on the antislavery movement. He wrote that fugitive slaves came to him from Maryland, Virginia, Kentucky, Tennessee, and Louisiana, at all hours of the day and night. One man, he wrote, was so dirty, he had to throw away his clothing; another was dressed elegantly and well educated. The latter said he had an easy master, but explained that he decided to run away when he learned he was to be sold. May offered to find him a good job in Syracuse but he declined, fearing that his master would send slavecatchers after him and, in fact, had already advertised him as a fugitive slave. Another time, he was approached by a woman who had come from New Orleans aboard a boat that took her to New York, and then had come by way of Lewis Tappan in New York and Stephen Myers in Albany. Her master had been her father, and she too fled after learning she was about to be sold.

In 1852, Rev. Luther Lee moved to Syracuse to become pastor of the Wesleyan Methodist Church. In the past, he had briefly been a pastor of the local Methodist Church there before the split. Lee was an outspoken opponent of the Fugitive Slave Law, and continually preached the refrain of abolitionist clergy, that "disobedience of the Fugitive Slave Law was obedience to God." He admitted to helping as many as 30 fugitive slaves in a month in his autobiography. In 1896, Joseph A. Allen, a member of the vigilance committee, claimed in a letter to historian Wilbur Siebert that during one of the years Lee was in Syracuse he aided 365 fugitive slaves. Oral tradition says the fugitive slaves were hidden in the cellar of the church. Many believe that seven clay faces found in the church basement in later years were made by fugitive slaves, though this has not been confirmed.

Lee later wrote that: "My name, the name of my street [39 Onondaga Street], and the number of my residence, came to be known as far south as Baltimore, and I did a large business." He also described the functioning of the Underground Railroad in Syracuse as a community-wide effort:

Wesleyan-Methodist Church, Rev. Luther Lee pastor (1852–1855), Syracuse, New York. (Courtesy of Tom Calarco)

Precaution was taken against any surprise by slave-catching officers. A signal was arranged. A particular ring of a very far-sounding bell in the Congregational church told the people for four and five miles that help was wanted for a fugitive slave, and they would come rushing down from Onondaga Hills in a manner that meant business. (Lee 334)

Lee also explained the city's attraction to fugitive slaves.

[It] was a convenient shipping-point. I could put them in a car and tell them to keep their seats until they crossed the suspension bridge, and then they would be in Canada. . . . [And] it cost nothing to ship fugitive slaves from Syracuse to Canada. From all other points their fare had to be paid; if they could get to Syracuse they went free the rest of the way. The fact was, I had friends, or the slave had, connected with the railroad at Syracuse, of whom I never failed to get a free pass in this form: "Pass this poor colored man," or "poor colored woman," or "poor colored family," as the case might be. The conductors on the route understood these passes, and they were never challenged. (332)

The friend Lee was talking about was likely either John Wilkinson, one of the original vigilance committee members, or Horace White, a director of the New York Central Railroad, who lived in Syracuse. White's son, Andrew, wrote Wilbur Siebert in 1897, that people often rattled the windows of their house as a signal that passes were needed for fugitive slaves, and that his father readily supplied them. Another member of the vigilance committee, Charles Merrick, also identified White as the individual who supplied passes to ride the train.

Radical Abolitionist Party

In June 1855 as tensions grew in Kansas over whether it would become a free or slave state, a three-day convention was held by the Radical Abolitionist Party, organized under the leadership of Gerrit Smith. Among those participating were Loguen, May, Frederick Douglass, Lewis Tappan, John Brown, abolitionist editor, William Goodell, and James McCune Smith, long-time member of the New York Committee of Vigilance, who was appointed chairman. An outgrowth of the Liberty Party, it advocated the use of force to end slavery and justified this in its belief that slavery was against the laws of nature and God.

During the mid-1850s, there was continuous traffic of fugitives through Syracuse and its neighboring communities. Fugitive slaves were coming both from Albany, where Stephen Myers was forwarding hundreds annually, and from Philadelphia up through Elmira, New York, and other lower New York communities. In some instances, daring abolitionists went into the South to rescue slaves. Eber Pettit told of a certain "Mr. Barbour of Onondaga County" in his *Sketches of the Underground Railroad,* who went into Virginia and rescued a woman named Statie and her daughter Lila. He said he hid them under straw in his wagon and stopped at taverns or farmhouses. When asked what was in the wagon, he said he was peddling clocks. No one ever questioned him further (Pettit 53).

Another much more celebrated slave rescuer sometimes passed through Syracuse. William E. Abbot, treasurer of Syracuse's Fugitive Aid Society, wrote to Samuel Porter in Rochester, on November 29, 1856, about Harriet Tubman, "an escaped bondwoman" who he was forwarding with "the second company that she has brought forth out of the land of servitude."

Rev. Jermaine Loguen, Stationmaster

Earlier that year, to accommodate the growing numbers of fugitive slaves coming there, the Syracuse Fugitive Aid Society was formed to raise funds. An arrangement was made with Loguen to lodge fugitive slaves at his residence at 293 East Genesee Street. By 1857, Loguen became the Society's general agent, and advertisements began appearing in newspapers requesting "that all fugitives from slavery coming this way may be directed to the care of Rev. J. W. Loguen; also, that all moneys subscribed or contributed or subscribed be paid directly to him as UGRR conductor; and that all clothing or provisions contributed may be sent to his house, or such places as he may designate" (*National Anti-Slavery Standard,* October 3, 1857).

In the advertisement, Loguen said that he would report his activities, including money received and runaways aided, to *Frederick Douglass's Paper* and the *Syracuse Standard and Journal,* and that his account book was open to public inspection.

That year, Frederick Douglass had occasion to stop in Syracuse. While getting off the train, he encountered a group of nine fugitives who wanted to know where Mr. Loguen resided. Douglass took them there, and wrote that, "We had scarcely struck the door when the manly voice of Loguen reached our ear. He knew the meaning of the rap, and sung out 'hold on.' A light was struck in a moment, the door opened and the whole company, the writer included, were invited in. Candles were lighted in different parts of the house, fires kindled, and the whole company made perfectly at home" (Syracuse *Post Standard*, November 28, 1857).

"We have so much to do in the night that some nights we get little or no sleep," Loguen wrote about this period. "They often come sick, and must be cared for forthwith" (*Douglass' Monthly*, May 1859).

By this time, following a number of other community-wide efforts to resist the Fugitive Slave Law in Boston, Oberlin and Mechanicsburg, Ohio, and Christiana, Pennsylvania, as well as numerous pledges to resist the law in other communities in the North, many fugitive slaves were remaining in the United States. Loguen would help them find jobs. In 1859, 30 fugitive slaves for whom he had found jobs made a contribution to the Fugitive Aid Society and added personal gifts for the Loguen family.

Heaven and Peterboro

Peterboro, New York, a tiny hamlet in Madison County, located between Utica and Syracuse was the home of Gerrit Smith. Here fugitives were always welcome, and many of the nation's most important abolitionists met regularly not only to discuss strategies on how to end slavery but to request funding for their various schemes and activities, for Gerrit Smith was one of the most generous philanthropists in U.S. history.

Certainly, Smith's wealth and prominence—he was for a time a U.S. congressman—provided some insulation from slavecatchers, as did his benevolent character, as he was among the most dedicated evangelists who often recited passages from Scripture in the many public speeches he gave. He applied this Christian spirit to his daily life; according to one estimate, he donated, based on today's figures, $650 million.

Fugitive slaves were constantly moving in and out of Peterboro. As many as 50 were harbored at the Smith mansion at a single time. "On such occasions," wrote Elizabeth Cady Stanton, Smith's cousin, "the barn and the kitchen floor were utilized as chambers" (Stanton, *Eighty Years and More ...1898: 51*). Henry Highland Garnet said of Peterboro that, "There are yet two places where slaveholders cannot come, Heaven and Peterboro" (*The North Star*, December 8, 1848: 1). Garnet, Samuel Ward, and Jermaine Loguen, all prominent black abolitionists, were deeded land in Peterboro and resided there for short periods. John Brown also made a number of visits, discussing his plans for the raid on Harpers Ferry that Smith helped fund. Abolitionist luminaries who were guests included James Birney, William Lloyd Garrison, Lucretia Mott, and Frederick Douglass.

Describing Peterboro and Smith's hospitality, Stanton wrote, "To go anywhere else, after a visit there, was like coming down from the divine heights into the valley of humiliation" (ibid. 53).

In all, Loguen's autobiography claims he aided upward of 1,500 runaways from 1851 to 1859.

—Tom Calarco

The Oneida Institute

The Oneida Institute, a devoutly antislavery manual labor school, was among the first institutions of higher learning to admit black students. Located in Whitesboro, New York, just west of Utica, it was founded in 1827 by evangelical minister, George Washington Gale, the mentor of Charles Finney. Among Gale's first students was Theodore Weld, who spent three years there. Here Weld drew the attention of the Tappans of New York City. With their support, the manual labor school idea gained popularity. Its rationale was for students to cast off elitism, engage in the egalitarian exercise of physical labor, and devoutly follow the equalizing tenets of Christianity.

In 1833, Gale moved to Galesburg, Illinois. Appointed in his place as president was Beriah Green, another evangelist and rabid abolitionist who had left Western Reserve College in Hudson, Ohio, when his outspoken opposition to the American Colonization Society brought disapproval from the school's trustees. One of his stipulations on acceptance was the admittance of black students.

The school became so popular that it had to turn away students in its early years. Among prominent black students were Henry Highland Garnet, Alexander Crummell, Jermaine Loguen, and William G. Allen. Another noted white abolitionist who attended was fugitive slave missionary, Hiram Wilson.

Being close to the Erie Canal, the Institute had its share of visits from fugitive slaves. Green openly declared that the school would not turn them away; in 1838, an attempt by slavecatchers to take a fugitive slave hidden there was foiled by students and staff.

The school also received support from Gerrit Smith, but ran into financial difficulty during the Panic of 1837. It never recovered, especially as Green's prickly personality alienated supporters. In 1844 the school was purchased by the Freewill Baptists and closed the following year.

Further Reading

Carol M. Hunter, *To Set the Captives Free* (New York: Garland, 1993).

Luther Lee, *Autobiography of Luther Lee* (New York: Phillips & Hunt, 1882).

J. W. Loguen, *The Rev. J. W. Loguen as a Slave and as a Freeman* (New York: Negro Universities Press, 1968, originally published in 1859).

Samuel J. May, *Some Recollections of Our Anti-Slavery Conflict* (Boston: Fields, Osgood & Co., 1869).

Eber M. Pettit, *Sketches in the History of the Underground Railroad* (1879; reprint, Westfield, N Y: Chautauqua Region Press, 1999).

Milton Sernett, *North Star Country: Upstate New York and the Crusade for African American Freedom* (Syracuse: Syracuse University Press, January 2002).

T

TABOR, IOWA

A small settlement, 23 miles north of the Missouri border and 60 miles east of the Kansas border, Tabor was founded by abolitionists in 1852 and soon became the main station for the Underground Railroad in southwestern Iowa. Among the settlement's founders were the Reverend John Todd, a Congregationalist minister and graduate of Oberlin College in Ohio, and G. B. Gaston, a native of Oberlin.

The people of Tabor had a true commitment to assisting those people of color who were fleeing to freedom. Their operation of conducting slaves was very similar to those of Salem, Iowa. Reverend Edwin S. Hill, G. B. Gaston, and Reverend John Todd were conductors in this area. Many fugitive slaves were hidden in the basement of the home of Reverend Todd, which had a tunnel that led to the Gaston home, two blocks away. Typically, Tabor's conductors would dress both men and women fugitives as Quaker women, with a veil and gloves, and sometimes would sit them beside the drivers of the wagons transporting them to the next station.

First Reported Episode

The first reported episode involving the escape of fugitive slaves in Tabor happened on July 4, 1854. A Mormon family stopped in Tabor with six slaves: two men, one of whom had a wife and two children, and a second woman. They camped along Main Street, and a couple of the slaves were sent to fetch water at the local well. They spoke to locals and told them they wanted to be free. At once the word was passed, and with many of Tabor's residents being natives of Ohio where the Underground Railroad already had been active for more than 30 years, they quickly made arrangements.

Gaston made arrangements for their hiding place at the home of Mr. C. W. Tolles, outside, and Jesse West, S. H. Adams, John Hallom, Joshua K. Gaston, and Irish Henry were chosen to escort the slaves there during the night while their master slept.

When the Mormon master awoke, he found the slaves missing. Unable to find anyone in Tabor to help them conduct a search, he found others nearby who agreed to help him. One of them, however, was an abolitionist who knew where the slaves were hidden. He deceived the Mormon into thinking that he had searched that area and did not find them. The Mormon finally gave up and continued westward with his family with one of his slaves, who had refused to leave him.

When it was certain the Mormon was gone, the Tabor conductors took the slaves to the Nishnabotna River near Randolph, Iowa. There they met two other conductors, Cephas Case and William L. Clark, who guided them to Lewis, Iowa, in Cass County, Iowa. From there, they traveled to a station in Injun Town, Iowa, and then on across the Des Moines River near Oskaloosa, Iowa. From there, they went to Peoria, Illinois, and then all the way to Detroit, Michigan, where they crossed into Canada.

Other Slave Escapes

Tabor had many tales of slave escapes. Two fugitive slaves had been captured in Missouri and put in the Linden jail. They requested hot coals to keep them warm during this harshly cold night. They later used the hot coals to burn a hole in the floor big enough to escape through. They became separated from each other in a terrible blizzard while crossing the Missouri River. One of them arrived in Tabor and stayed with Gaston, working on his farm, hoping his friend would turn up. Fortunately, he did and they continued their trip to freedom when the other arrived.

Another case involved two slave girls who belonged to S. F. Nuckolls of Nebraska City, Nebraska. They had escaped to Iowa with the help of a free black man, John Williamson, who brought them to the home of Dr. Ira D. Blanchard of Civil Bend, one of Tabor's primary Underground collaborators. Blanchard brought them to Tabor where they were hidden with B. F. Ladd until nightfall. As soon as Nuckolls realized that his slaves were missing, he organized a search party. However, this proved unsuccessful.

Nuckolls then returned to Nebraska City and gathered a posse of vigilantes and stormed into the area surrounding Civil Bend, where he believed his slaves might be hiding. They forced their way into people's homes and searched their premises without a warrant. But they were unable to find his slaves.

Among those whose homes Nuckolls searched was Reuben Williams. He resisted and was bludgeoned on the head. The injury permanently damaged his hearing, and a trial later took place that awarded Williams several thousand dollars in damages.

The Underground Railroad, of which Tabor was a part, ran west from Civil Bend, now known as Percival, about five miles from Nebraska and about

25 miles from the Missouri border. It crossed the Missouri River to Civil Bend, now Percival, and then went to Tabor. The next station was about 45 miles away in Lewis, Iowa, where Rev. George B. Hitchcock was the primary conductor.

Tabor and John Brown

Tabor also was a final stop for free settlers migrating to the neighboring Kansas territory to oppose proslavery forces who had moved there in the hope of making it a slave state. Free staters from the east were working hard to populate the state with antislavery people to outnumber the proslavery people to win the referendum that would determine whether it would be free or slave.

Due to growing tension in Kansas, a Republican Association was organized in Tabor on April 21, 1856, to further the goal of a Free Kansas. R. B. Foster served as president, John Todd as vice-president, and Jonas Jones as secretary. In July of that year, Dr. Samuel G. Howe, superintendent of an institution for the blind in Boston went to Tabor in July, 1856, to help open a route for free-state people to enter Kansas. On July 29, an army of 28 men was formed in Tabor under the command of Gaston. They received arms from the state and were on call at the request of Iowa's governor. This led to its becoming an arsenal for the abolitionist army in Kansas.

Captain John Brown and his army of men met and trained in Tabor, both while fighting in Kansas and, later, fully supported by the abolitionists there. During the years leading up to Harper's Ferry, he visited Tabor many times, and stored guns in Todd's cellar. But on Brown's trip in 1859, following his raid in Missouri during which he rescued eleven slaves, he was repudiated by the community because during the rescue, one of his men was forced to kill a slaveholder. In a carefully worded resolution, they stated that, "while we sympathize with the oppressed, and will do all that we conscientiously can to help them in their efforts for freedom . . . we have no Sympathy with those who go to Slave States, to entice away Slaves, and take property or life when necessary to attain that end" (Smith 76).

Nevertheless, Brown made one last trip to Tabor in the weeks before the Harpers Ferry raid to bid farewell to his friend, Jonas Jones.

—Tom Calarco

Further Reading

Glenn Noble, *John Brown and the Jim Lane Trail* (Broken Bow, NE: Purcells, 1977).

Charles Edward Smith, "The Underground Railroad in Iowa" (Master's Thesis, Northeast Missouri State College, August 1971).

John Todd, *Early Settlement and Growth of Western Iowa or Reminiscences* [with "Biographical Sketch of Rev. John Todd, of Tabor Iowa" by J. E. Todd] (Des Moines: Iowa Historical Department, 1906).

TROY, NEW YORK

Troy was closely associated with Albany in the Underground Railroad. It also was the connecting point of the Erie and Champlain Canals, the latter which was completed in 1823, establishing a continuous water route from New York City to Canada. As a result, it was a stop for fugitive slaves moving between New York, Albany, Vermont, and points farther north.

Black and White Collaboration

But perhaps a more compelling reason for Troy's participation in the Underground Railroad was the network that had developed between blacks in the region through regional "colored" moral improvement societies that were organized during the 1830s, and the association that developed between white evangelical Christians and its black community.

It was the latter that led to the organization of the Liberty Street Negro Presbyterian Church. Organized by a white minister, Rev. Nathan Sidney Beman, and a white Customs House official, Thaddeus Bigelow, it was dedicated in 1834 by New York City Underground Railroad leader Rev. Theodore Wright and used as a Sunday school until 1840. A year later the important black leader Henry Highland Garnet became its pastor.

Rev. Henry Highland Garnet

Born a slave in Maryland, Garnet escaped to freedom with his family when he was only nine years old and settled in New York City. He attended a number of schools and it was as a student that he met Rev. Wright, pastor of the Negro Presbyterian Church in New York City, who became like a second father to him.

During this time, he was very active in the Underground Railroad, working with Rev. Wright and Charles Ray of the New York Committee of Vigilance. Ray specifically indentifies Garnet as an Underground Railroad contact in a journal entry published in Ray's biography, which relates a situation in which barges were used to send fugitive slaves up the Hudson River to Albany and Troy.

An Underground Railroad story involving Garnet took place at his church shortly after he gave his widely publicized "Address to the Slaves" speech in Buffalo in 1843, which had called for slaves to revolt and had disturbed even some abolitionists. He had received a group of runaways at his church. As usual he hid them in the basement, but before they were able to resume their journey, his church was surrounded by an angry mob. It is not known what happened to the fugitive slaves, only that they were driven away and that Garnet was beaten. Perhaps they escaped through some trap door or tunnel as only a couple of blocks away was a legendary stop at 153 Second Street with which there have been stories that claimed tunnels led from its cellar.

Rev. Fayette Shipherd

Another important Underground Railroad agent in Troy was the Rev. Fayette Shipherd, an evangelical Christian minister and follower of Charles Finney. In 1832, Shipherd helped organize the Bethel Church, which ministered to the boatmen of Troy. Not only were many local boatmen, black, but the main thoroughfares of the area's Underground Railroad were waterways like the Hudson River and Champlain Canal.

In a letter, dated November 24, 1840, from Shipherd to Vermont conductor, Charles Hicks of Bennington, Shipherd indicates that the Champlain Canal was regularly used to transport fugitive slaves: "As the canal has closed I shall send my Southern friends along your road & patronize your house. We had a fine run of business during the season. C. G. We had 22 in two weeks 13 in the city at one time."

Both Shipherd and Garnet belonged to the Liberty Party, the radical abolitionist political party, and became members of the executive (vigilance) committee of the Eastern New York Anti-Slavery Society (ENYASS) founded in 1842 by the noted Underground Railroad conductors, Abel Brown and Charles T. Torrey. The ENYASS is known to have assisted hundreds of fugitive slaves during its brief three-year existence. In 1844, Brown moved from Albany to Troy. He also worked with Charles Hicks in Bennington and a letter of introduction for a fugitive slave that Brown sent to Hicks in 1842 exists today in the archives of the Vermont Historical Society. An important agent in this collaboration was Garrett Van Hoosen, a resident of Hoosick, whose home was situated along the road leading to Bennington, Vermont. Van Hoosen was president of the Rensselaer County Liberty Party, and his name was recorded on the Shipherd letter to Hicks.

Other Troy Abolitionists

Several abolitionists held key positions during the 1830s and 1840s at the port of Troy, which connected with the Champlain Canal north, and the Erie Canal west. They likely were involved in moving fugitive slaves along its waterways. There was Bigelow, the city's customs house officer who oversaw the transport of goods in and out of the port, and president of the Troy Anti-Slavery Society; the antislavery society's vice-president Gurdon Grant, a trustee of the Bethel Church and a grain dealer whose offices looked out at the Hudson River on 101 River Street; and the society's treasurer Pliny A. Moore, Grant's partner and a shipping agent. Several accounts, including those of Abel Brown and Stephen Myers, cite the use of the Champlain Canal and Lake Champlain, the earliest in 1837.

In 1843, Shipherd organized his own Free Congregational Church on the east side of Seventh Street between Albany and State streets. When Brown moved to Troy, he gave a series of lectures urging support of the Liberty Party at

Shipherd's church. Another strong supporter of the Liberty Party at that time in Troy and who may have been involved in the Underground Railroad there was Rev. Merrit Bates, pastor of North Second St. Methodist Church 1842–1843, and founder of True Wesleyan Methodist Church in 1844 on Federal St between River and North Second streets.

The lectures by Brown engendered a great deal of hostility and the final one caused a riot and provoked his attack by a mob on the city streets from which he was lucky to escape alive. Brown died shortly after when he came down with meningitis during a trip to Rochester, and his cohort Torrey was imprisoned for aiding fugitive slaves in Baltimore. Among Brown's eulogists were Garnet and Bates. His death was a blow to the ENYASS from which it could not recover, and it disbanded sometime after its annual meeting in May 1845.

Shipherd left Troy in 1846 and Garnet in 1848, but the Underground Railroad continued. About 10 miles southeast of Troy was the radical abolitionist community of Sand Lake, which was home to the Sand Lake Baptist Church that for a time was the congregation of Abel Brown and whose membership included Charles Gregory, a member of the executive committee of the ENYASS. It had close ties with the community of Troy and was the site of the second evangelical Lutheran Church, a member of the Frankean Synod, a radical abolitionist comeouter church that is reputed to have actively aided fugitive slaves and whose leaders were Rev. Nicholas Van Alstyne, Rev. H. L. Dox, and Rev. John D. Lawyer.

William Rich

With the passing of the ENYASS, Troy's Underground Railroad leadership fell about the black community. William Rich, a black barber who had been in a leadership role in Troy's black community as least as early as 1835 when he was a founding trustee of the Liberty Street Church, and a director in the area black improvement societies during that decade, became the stationmaster. He was the primary speaker at an anti-Fugitive Slave Law meeting held in Lansingburgh, Rensselaer County at the African Methodist Episcopal Church following the passage of the law in 1850. Frisby Way, another black leader from the days of the black improvement societies, chaired the meeting. The group resolved that "We welcome to our door everyone who . . . has broken away from the Southern house of bondage. . . . that [if his] Master or his minion presume to enter our dwellings and attempt to rescue any of our brethren who he may call his slaves, we feel prepared to resist his pretension" ("Proceedings of the Colored Citizens of Lansingburgh in relation to the FSL," *Lansingburgh Democrat*, October 1850).

A later report showing the mobilization of the local black community in the Underground Railroad was published in the *Troy Daily Times* in 1857 by the Troy Vigilance Committee. It stated that 55 persons had passed through Troy during the preceding year and gave the names of vigilance committee members, identifying William Rich as its leader. Other members were Rev. Jonathan C. Gibbs, a successor to Garnet as pastor of the Liberty Street Church; Philip Owens, a whitewasher, who lived at 320 Congress Street; William Henry, a furnaceman, at 26 Division Street; Captain Hawkins, who was probably Zebedee Hawkins at 37 Green Street; William E. Bishop, a whitewasher, at Church Street near Ferry; R. Schoonmaker, also a whitewasher at 129 William Street; Southy Bingham, a cook at 146 Third Street; and Charles Hagerman, all black men.

There were nevertheless some whites who continued to play a role, including the wealthy entrepreneur Uri Gilbert and the attorney Martin Townsend. Both were involved in the major abolitionist incident of Troy's antebellum period.

Charles Nalle Rescue

Charles Nalle, of Virginia, had escaped from his master (and half-brother), Blucher W. Hansbrough of Culpeper County, Virginia, in mid-October 1858 and ended up in Sand Lake. In 1860, he moved in with William Henry in Troy to take a job as a coachman for Gilbert. However, his identity was discovered, and on April 27, 1860, a Virginia slavecatcher and a deputy U.S. marshal nabbed him in Troy and arrested him under the jurisdiction of the Fugitive Slave Law. Before he could be sent home, however, a mob numbering several hundred persons, both blacks and whites, surrounded the U.S. commissioner's office. By chance Harriet Tubman was in town visiting her cousin, John Hooper, another reputed Underground Railroad agent. She led a large crowd of persons who battled police when Nalle was being moved out of the jail and freed him.

Despite escaping across the Hudson River, he was recaptured in West Troy. Several hundred enraged citizens stormed the stronghold, braving police gunfire, and Nalle was liberated again. Weeks later, locals purchased his freedom for $650, enabling Nalle to reunite with his already freed wife and children. Townsend, who had been Nalle's attorney, wrote several letters to Wilbur Siebert in 1896, describing the Troy Underground Railroad. He identified Hooper as one of its operatives and stated that fugitive slaves were forwarded either to Rouses Point near the Canadian border in Clinton County or to Suspension Bridge, which crossed over to Canada near Niagara Falls.

Today in Troy, most Underground Railroad landmarks like the Liberty Street Church are gone. For some years before its destruction, the historic church was used as a laundromat, but all that remains is a vacant lot at the corner of a rundown alleyway. Of two houses on actual locations, there is a question as to whether the current structures actually date from the antebellum period. One is the 153 Second Street house that was home to fugitive slave Lewis Washington, an antislavery lecturer and traveling companion of Abel Brown, and afterward to Hooper; the other is the site of Trojan Hardware Company at 137 Fourth Street, where Henry Garnet resided during part of his eight years in Troy.

—Tom Calarco

Further Reading

Tom Calarco (ed.), *Abel Brown Abolitionist* (Jefferson, NC: McFarland, 2006; reprint of C. S. Brown, *Memoir of Rev. Abel Brown*, Worcester, 1849).

Tom Calarco, *The Underground Railroad in the Adirondack Region* (Jefferson, NC: McFarland, 2004).

Scott Christianson, *Freeing Charles: The Struggle to Liberate a Slave on the Eve of the Civil War* (Champaign, IL: Illinois University Press, 2009).

A. H. Gordon, "Henry Highland Garnet," *Journal of Negro History* (January 1928).

Letter from Fayette Shipherd to Charles Hicks, Rensselaer County, NY, November 24, 1840, *Tocsin of Liberty/Albany Patriot*, 1841–1848.

Martin B. Pasternak, *Rise Now and Fly to Arms: The Life of Henry Highland Garnet* (New York: Garland Publishers, 1995).

Fayette Shipherd, "A Legacy for My Beloved Wife, Catherine Shipherd," unpublished memoir. Troy, 1846, and "My Legacy to My Beloved Wife and Children," unpublished memoir, 1870; in the Bragdon Family papers, Rush Rhees Library, University of Rochester, Rare Books & Special Collections.

U

UNION VILLAGE (GREENWICH), WASHINGTON COUNTY, NEW YORK

Greenwich in upstate New York, known during the abolition period as Union Village, was the center of abolition in the Adirondack region and a well-known refuge of fugitive slaves. It got its former name, according to one nineteenth-century historian, "on account of the harmony and goodwill that prevailed among the inhabitants" (Morhous, Henry C., "History of the village of Greenwich, N.Y.," scrapbook, 1878: 1–3). Ironically, this center of abolition owed its growth and prosperity to the profits of a cotton-spinning factory, the nation's second such factory, built by an ambitious young man from Rhode Island named William Mowry.

Hiram Corliss

In 1833, its destiny changed when the fever of abolition struck the village, or at least it struck Dr. Hiram Corliss, perhaps its leading citizen. He led the formation of a county anti-slavery society the following year, and the next year, a schism in the Dutch Reformed Church over the issue of slavery. Joining Corliss in igniting the village with a burning desire to end slavery were William H. Mowry, son of the town founder; Baptist minister Rev. Nathaniel Colver; and abolitionist congressman, Erastus Culver.

Champlain Canal

Accounts of fugitive slaves coming to the village were being reported by 1837, coming to and up through the county by packet boat on the Champlain Canal that connected with the Hudson River in Troy, New York. Also that year a new abolitionist church, the Orthodox Congregational "Free Church," was founded under Corliss's leadership. It comprised most of the village's elite, including Mowry; his sisters, Ann Caroline and Mary; and their husbands, banker Henry Holmes and entrepreneur John T. Masters, who became trustees.

At a major convention in 1839 held at the Free Church and attended by important abolitionists such as Gerrit Smith, Joshua Leavitt, William L. Chaplin, Henry B. Stanton, and Luther Lee, a strong resolution was passed to aid fugitive slaves. And an 1840 letter from Troy abolitionist, Rev. Fayette Shipherd, indicated that the Champlain Canal that passed nearby was being used regularly at that time to forward fugitive slaves.

Eastern New York Anti-Slavery Society

In 1842, the Eastern New York Anti-Slavery Society (ENYASS) was founded by the devoted abolitionist and Underground Railroad conductors, Rev. Abel Brown and Charles T. Torrey, and Corliss and Mowry were made president and vice-president. The ENYASS connected every county along the Hudson River from New York City and publicly advertised its assistance to fugitive slaves in its newspaper, the *Albany Patriot.* Its 1843 annual report stated that the society had helped "hundreds" of fugitive slaves during the previous year.

However, after the tragic deaths of Brown in 1844 and Torrey in 1846, the ENYASS disbanded. Nevertheless, the Free Church continued to grow, and an important abolitionist, Leonard Gibbs, moved to town in 1846. He joined the Free Church and took the place of Mowry, who had died the year before, as Corliss's most important associate.

Reports of Fugitive Slave Living in Union Village

Following the passage of the second Fugitive Slave Law in 1850, the local abolitionist movement was reinvigorated. A "large and enthusiastic" meeting was held in protest of the law. Speaking were Culver, Gibbs, and John Masters. One of their resolutions was that: "In view of the enormities of the present Fugitive Slave Law, its opposition to the spirit of the Constitution framed to establish Justice; and in view of the good character of those in our midst who have escaped from slavery, that we will obey God who commands us to hide the outcast and obey the dictates of the Golden Rule—and *never* whatever pains and penalties we may suffer, assist into remorseless Slavery those who in our midst may be claimed as Fugitives from the Southern prison-house, but defend to the extent of our duty as Christians, citizens and men" ("Spirit of the Washington County Press," *Salem Press*, October 22, 1850: 2).

Easton

A year later Quakers from Easton, a farming community adjacent to the village and nearby Quaker Springs across the Hudson River, formed the Old Saratoga

Anti-Slavery Society. They named Corliss president and Gibbs chairman of its vigilance committee. Important in the operation of the local Underground Railroad during this decade were Easton Quakers Esther and Job Wilbur, who collaborated with Corliss and whose activities aiding fugitive slaves were described in a memoir written by their grandson, Oren B. Wilbur. Among visitors coming to speak to local abolitionists during this decade were Frederick Douglass, William Lloyd Garrison, William Wells Brown, Lucretia Mott, Sojourner Truth, and Charles Burleigh. Also during this period, the Free Church sent funds to Rev. John Fee to assist his efforts in organizing an abolitionist church in Kentucky.

Many of those in Union Village who lived along Park Street, today Church Street, opened their homes to fugitive slaves. On Main Street, at the corner on which it was intersected by Park Street, lived Leonard Gibbs, whose daughters lived well into the twentieth century and for many years recounted stories of the village's aid to fugitive slaves.

A compelling link of the village's Free Church to the Underground Railroad was that among its membership were relatives of fugitive slaves. Listed on the church rolls from 1837 to 1851 was Priscilla Weeks. She and her sister Susan married the well-known fugitive slave brothers, John and Charles Salter. The Salters had fled from Maryland and arrived in Washington County around 1846. Their intention had been to go to Canada, but Hiram Corliss persuaded them to stay, assuring them that the local abolitionists would protect them from slavecatchers. Little did he anticipate that his word would be tested in 1858.

Slavecatcher Incident

That year, the *People's Journal* in Union Village reported that "a number of slave hunters were prowling about the [neighboring] town of Easton," and that a committee of vigilance led by Leonard Gibbs was appointed, pledging themselves to use all means in their power to rescue any fugitive who should be kidnapped. The fugitive slaves they were hunting were the Salter brothers.

"Fortunately," the report continued, "the kidnappers were baffled in their vile attempt and accomplished nothing by their ill-timed and unwise movement, save to awaken the jealousies and arouse the anger of the Quakers" (April 22, 1858).

The village continued to support the effort to end slavery until the Emancipation Proclamation. Hiram Corliss maintained a close relationship with Gerrit Smith throughout the antebellum period and was a guest at the Smith mansion just prior to John Brown's assault on Harpers Ferry. Shortly after, Leonard Gibbs made a fervent plea to Smith to organize a rescue of Brown after he was sentenced to be hung, but little did he know that Smith had suffered a nervous breakdown and had entered a mental health institution. On the day of Brown's execution, a public indignation meeting was held at the Free Church.

The Stone Chair, Kingsbury, New York

In 1837, a report written by Alvan Stewart, one of central New York's leading abolitionists, recounted a story of an escape by a slave during which he used the Champlain Canal as a means of transportation.

It gives credence to the local legend in Washington and neighboring Warren County, New York that claims that the area bordering the canal was part of the Underground Railroad. For as long as their collective memories recall, they have been reminded of this by one of the most curious artifacts anywhere.

This mysterious object is a headstone that was once shaped in the form of a chair with markings chiseled on it that create a picture. How this Stone Chair originated and who created it have been lost to history. But for the last century local historians have subscribed to a theory that the markings are actually a map directing runaway slaves to places of safety.

Though the markings have worn away over time, they can yet be discerned. Still very clear is the emboldened date—1841. Original markings, which were preserved in a 1930s sketch, showed May 23, 1841. They also illustrate what appear to be a fort, a mountain, a smokestack, and a sailboat. According to local interpretation, they are juxtaposed to portray actual locations. The fort represents the village of Fort Ann, about four miles distant and the site of Underground Railroad stations; the mountain, the small range among which is Putnam Mountain; the smokestack, the Mt. Hope Blast Furnace that sets just north of the mountain; and the sailboat in the top right corner above the fort, boats waiting in South Bay, the inlet to Lake Champlain, on which they could take fugitive slaves directly to Canada and freedom.

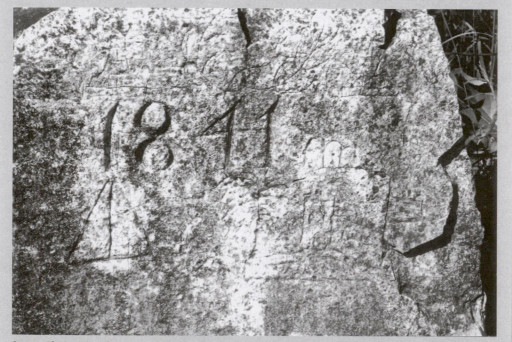

Stone Chair, Kingsbury, New York, was believed to be guidepost leading fugitive slaves north to boats that could take them up Lake Champlain to Canada. (Courtesy of Tom Calarco)

Union Village may have been a remote village in the foothills of the Adirondack Mountains, but its citizens were as ready as any community in the North to assist fugitive slaves and to give as much as their means would allow to support the cause to end slavery.

—Tom Calarco

Further Reading

Tom Calarco, *The Underground Railroad in the Adirondack Region* (Jefferson, NC: McFarland and Company, Inc., 2004).

UPPERGROUND RAILROAD

Around 1850, a surge in railroad building occurred throughout the country, and it led to increasing use of railroads by Underground Railroad agents, who recruited railroad employees into their work. The following railroad lines were used by the Underground Railroad, often with the complicity of those who worked for the railroad.

New York Central

Horace White of Syracuse was not only president of the New York Central Railroad, but a diehard abolitionist. White's son, Andrew, wrote in an 1897 letter to Wilbur Siebert, that people often came to their house in secret to receive passes. Luther Lee, the Wesleyan-Methodist minister, who aided more than 300 fugitive slaves during one of the years while he was in Syracuse, corroborated the use of the New York Central in his autobiography: "[I] had friends . . . connected with the railroad at Syracuse, of whom I never failed to get a free pass. . . . The conductors on the route understood these passes, and they were never challenged" (Lee 327).

New York and Erie Railroad

Free passes were given for fugitive slaves on the New York and Erie Railroad by its director, A. S. Murray of Goshen, New York, which is about 60 miles northwest of Manhattan (King 26). This railroad connected downstate New York with central and western New York.

Northern Railroad

In 1854, the tracks from Williamsport, Pennsylvania, to Elmira, New York, were completed, connecting Elmira with Philadelphia. John W. Jones of Elmira, who traded correspondence with William Still, arranged the travel of fugitive slaves with the Northern Central Railroad during its 4 A.M. stop. They were hidden in the baggage car and then were taken to Canandaigua, where they were transferred to the New York Central Railroad. The last leg of the trip took them to Niagara Falls, where they crossed into Canada over a new, double-decker Suspension Bridge, which started to accommodate rail cars in 1855.

Illinois Central Railroad and Rock Island Railroad

George Burroughs, a free black, born in Canada, became a member of the True Bands, a black improvement organization that promoted black self-reliance and aided newly arrived fugitive slaves. In an 1896 letter to Wilbur Siebert, Burroughs wrote that he moved to Chicago where he met a fellow Canadian, Robert Celany, who asked him to become an Underground Railroad agent and found him employment as a porter with the Illinois Central Railroad that went to Cairo, Illinois, on the Mississippi River. Burroughs's mission was to entice fugitive slaves to escape and hide them on his train. Burroughs described one incident when he encountered a slave girl of about eight years old, whom he was able to hide in a box on the train and safely bring her to Underground Railroad agents in Chicago.

Celany worked for the Rock Island Railroad, which gradually expanded from Illinois into Iowa during the 1850s. During the journey of John Brown and his men from Missouri with 12 fugitive slaves in 1859, the Rock Island took them from West Liberty, Iowa. William Penn Clarke in Iowa City and Josiah Grinnell of Grinnell, Iowa, arranged for their ride on a freight car in West Liberty, Iowa.

Chicago, Burlington and Quincy Railroad

Accounts claim that Galesburg agents hid fugitive slaves in the freight trains or baggage cars of the Chicago, Burlington and Quincy Railroad, which connected it with Chicago in 1854. Galesburg abolitionists who were C B & Q employees were Solom Kimball and William Patch, who was a friend of Reverend Edward Beecher. On one occasion Patch hid two fugitives on a train, who had been harbored at Beecher's. One of the procedures it used was to place lamps alongside the tracks as signals for the engineers to slow down to allow fugitive slaves to board.

Michigan Central Railroad

In Chicago, railway arrangements for John Brown and his party of fugitive slaves during their rescue from Missouri were made by Allan Pinkerton, the Chicago detective, on the Michigan Central Railroad that took them from Chicago to Detroit. Also, Detroit and Sandusky Underground Railroad agent, George Reynolds, was employed for a time by the Michigan Central Railroad.

The account of Richard Daly, a fugitive slave, who lived in Trimble County, Kentucky, states that he used the Michigan Central Railroad during his escape with his family in 1857 or 1858.

Erie-Kalamazoo Railroad

The Erie-Kalamazoo Railroad was completed in 1836, and on one occasion it was used by Laura Haviland to transport five runaways to Adrian.

Ohio Railroad System

By 1845, the Little Miami Railroad reached from Cincinnati to Xenia and by 1848 to Springfield. The rail connection between Cincinnati and the Lake Erie ports, notably Sandusky, was completed around 1850 with the extension of the Little Miami Railroad from the south and the Mad River Railroad from the north. Thereafter, the use of the upperground railroad by the Underground Railroad became more frequent. Sandusky was one of the two terminals of this railroad system, along with Cleveland, and as a result after 1850, fugitive slave traffic there increased considerably. Another rail line, the Cleveland, Columbus & Cincinnati, connected Cincinnati through Columbus to Cleveland. Underground Railroad conductor Rush R. Sloane of Sandusky was active in the development of this rail system. He reported that the conductor, Elijah Anderson, the Indiana and Ohio conductor, often escorted fugitive slaves on rail systems. Another Sandusky resident, Henry Paden, was a conductor on the Sandusky, Mansfield & Newark Railroad. In December 1859, he was informed by a fellow employee, Colonel V. B. Alsdorf that fugitive slaves were being taken aboard in Utica, Ohio. Paden hid the nine fugitives in a freight car and left them inside at the final stop in Sandusky. Later, that night, when all was clear, he removed them from the car and took them to the Sandusky home of George Reynolds, who later took them by sled in the dead of winter to Canada. In eastern Ohio, the Cleveland and Western Railroad was commonly used and tickets were supplied by I. Newton Peirce of Alliance.

New Albany and Salem Railroad (Indiana)

Members of the abolitionist Second Presbyterian Church in New Albany were among the organizers of the New Albany and Salem Railroad in 1847. They included elder James Brooks, its first president; elder James Haines, the New Albany conductor during the antebellum years; and John R. Nunemacher who printed the railroad tickets. They employed a large number of blacks, and by 1853, the railroad connected all the way to Lake Michigan. In 1855 Haines was accused of assisting a fugitive slave. According to the *Louisville Courier*, a fugitive slave was arrested in New Albany. However, two abolitionists rescued him and hid him in a passenger car. Haines and some others prevented the authorities from entering the train and it left New Albany with the fugitive slave. This account alleged that the New Albany train depot was aiding "on an average, at least one slave for every day . . . on the cars of the New Albany and Salem road" (Peters 95).

Philadelphia, Wilmington, and Baltimore Railroad

As early as 1837, the Philadelphia, Wilmington, and Baltimore Railroad connected Baltimore and Philadelphia, and it was on this railroad that Frederick Douglass made his famous escape in 1838, posing as a seaman.

Philadelphia and Columbia Railroad

William Whipper, the noted black activist from the Philadelphia area, purchased a small railroad and moved back to Columbia, Pennsylvania, the town where he grew up about the year 1847. There he became actively involved in the Underground Railroad, often by his own admission sending fugitive slaves in the freight cars of his own railroad from Columbia to Philadelphia:

> My house was at the end of the bridge, and as I kept the station, I was frequently called up in the night to take charge of the passengers. On their arrival they were generally hungry and penniless. I have received hundreds in this condition; fed and sheltered from one to seventeen at a time in a single night. At this point the road forked; some I sent west by boats, to Pittsburgh, and others . . . in our cars to Philadelphia. (Still 736)

Richmond, Fredericksburg, and Potomac Railroad

In 1849, Henry "Box" Brown began his journey in his box on the Richmond, Fredericksburg, and Potomac Railroad, which connected Richmond with Washington, D.C., in 1842. He then traveled on the Baltimore and Ohio Railroad from Washington to Baltimore, and then was transferred to the Philadelphia, Wilmington, and Baltimore Railroad that went to Philadelphia.

The year before, William and Ellen Craft made their celebrated escape from Georgia, traveling much of their journey by upperground railroad and reaching the station in Philadelphia on Christmas day.

New England Railroads

Shadrach Minkins, the noted fugitive slave who was rescued from federal authorities in Boston in 1851, boarded a train of the Fitchburg Railroad in North Ashburnham, Massachusetts, four days after his rescue. It is believed he used the rail system for most of the rest of his journey to Montreal.

Elizabeth Buffum Chace of Central Falls, Rhode Island, said her husband forwarded fugitive slaves on the Providence and Worcester railroad, traveling with them a short distance to arrange their safe passage with the conductor on board and then leave them in his care. They were then transferred to agents at Worcester who forwarded to the Unitarian minister, Joshua Young, who forwarded fugitive slaves, usually by rail, to Canada, though Young and others sometimes needed to convey them to the train station in St. Albans for fear of detection.

Another instance of rail travel use in New England involved members of the Boston Vigilance Committee in 1854. A slave who had been rescued off a ship in Boston Harbor by Austin Bearse was escorted by Samuel May, Jr., on the Boston and Worcester Railroad to Station to Worcester (Siebert 58).

Riding Atop the Upperground Railroad

One of the most daring uses of the upperground railroad was made by the fugitive slave, George Thompson, who rode outside atop a passenger car from Alabama to Virginia, clinging to its roof. Though Thompson was caught and put into custody, he managed to escape again and ended up in the office of William Still, to whom he told of his daring escape attempt.

—Tom Calarco

Further Reading

Tom Calarco, *The Underground Railroad in the Adirondack Region* (Jefferson, NC: McFarland and Company, Inc., 2004).

Elizabeth Buffum Chace, "Anti-Slavery Reminiscences," Central Falls, RI, 1891.

"Richard Daly . . ." *Detroit Sunday News Tribune*, reprinted in *The Journal*, Louisville, KY, August 12, 1894.

The Firelands Pioneer, Norwalk, OH: The Historical Society Society, 1888: 19–27.

Roger A. King, *The Underground Railroad in Orange County* (Monroe, NY: Library Research Associates, Inc., 1999).

Luther Lee, *Autobiography of Luther Lee* (New York: Phillips & Hunt, 1882).

Owen Muelder, *The Underground Railroad in Western Illinois* (Jefferson, NC: McFarland and Company, Inc., 2007).

Pamela R. Peters, *The Underground Railroad in Floyd County, Indiana* (Jefferson, NC: McFarland and Company, 2001).

Wilbur Siebert, *The Underground Railroad in Massachusetts* (Worcester, MA: American Antiquarian Society, 1936).

William Still, *The Underground Railroad* (Philadelphia: Porter and Coates, 1872).

W⚬⟋ ─────────────────────────────────

WASHINGTON COURTHOUSE, OHIO

Washington Court House in Fayette County is a part of Virginia military survey that was reserved in 1783 and granted to Virginia soldiers, who were joined in their settlement by pioneers from Kentucky and Pennsylvania. It was originally laid out on a plot containing 1,200 acres belonging to Benjamin Temple of Logan County, Kentucky. Temple donated another 150 acres to Fayette County on the condition that Washington Court House would be the site of the county seat.

After about 1820, Fayette County became a part of the Underground Railroad. The county was not only a haven for fugitive slaves, but also a significant source of aid while they were on their journey to freedom. Many families were involved in the Underground Railroad and lived relatively close to one another.

Local Church Involvement

There was a strong connection between the Underground Railroad and the churches in Fayette County. Many local churches opposed slavery and joined the movement to abolish it. Even though there were many individuals, groups, and organizations in Fayette County that were associated with the Underground Railroad, the common denominator usually was the churches. Many ministers preached against slavery and were also stationkeepers.

An August 2, 1860, article in the *Washington Herald* speaks of the involvement of an African American church in Washington Court House, likely the Second Baptist formed in 1855. Another church there that opposed slavery was the Presbyterian Church, which had parishes in both Washington Courthouse and nearby Bloomingburg, both of which were served by Rev. William Dickey, a native of South Carolina. He preached for 40 years, often condemning slavery, and was very well liked. He was a delegate to the Ohio Anti-Slavery Society, and the family of his second wife, Ellen Ghormly of Greenfield, were known abolitionists and Underground Railroad operators.

Quakers played a very important part in the Underground Railroad in Fayette County, as the county was one of the destinations for slaves manumitted by the North Carolina manumission societies of the Friends. Many Quakers lived near each other and were related through marriage. The Todhunter family was one of the first Quaker families to move to Fayette County and Isaac Todhunter was a founding member of the county Society of Friends. He moved from Lost Creek, Tennessee, in December 1804.

In April 1833, the Anti-Slavery Society of Paint Valley formed and included Highland, Ross, and Fayette counties. Their meetings were held in Washington Court House, Hillsboro, Bloomingburg, Greenfield, and South Salem. The Fayette County group grew so quickly that it split and formed another branch in Green Township. After the 1840s, however, no records exist of its meeting.

Means of Travel

Many of the stationkeepers were farmers or merchants. The fugitive slaves who came to Fayette County were taken from station to station on horseback, in wagons, carriages, boats, or on foot. They traveled in numbers of from one to twenty or more, and sometimes stole horses from pastures as they traveled. They steered clear of towns and sought less-traveled roads.

For some families in Fayette County, helping slaves escape became a family tradition. Because many of the families who participated in the Underground Railroad lived close to each other, they devised their own ways to communicate with each other.

Some Agents

Rev. John McElroy, a Presbyterian Minister, grew up four or five miles north of Greenfield, Highland County, and about seven miles from Washington Courthouse. The home of his parents was a safehouse, and John recalls being awakened in the night by the barking of dogs, and the "rattling" of a window shutter at the rear of the house. An inquiry would be made "who's there?" and the answer would be "Friends." The door would open and in would come an operator along with several fugitive slaves. The stationkeepers knew the men who brought passengers and knew they could be trusted.

Some other stationkeepers in and around Washington Court House included William A. Ustick, who moved from New York to Fayette County; Minor Cawkins, a minister, who wrote for the *Fayette Democrat*; William Edwards, born in South Carolina; Jeremiah Hopkins, a farmer born in Washington County, Pennsylvania; Jacob Puggsly, born in Virginia; Moses Rawlings, a farmer and a bookkeeper; George Stewart, a farmer, who harbored and transported fugitive slaves; John L. Van Deman, a member of the Washington Court House Presbyterian Church; J. A. Merchant, a member of the Anti-Slavery

Society; Samuel Wilson, a tavern keeper, born in either Virginia or Pennsylvania; and George S. Gillespie, a farmer born in New York.

Mills Gardner, born in Russellville, Brown County, Ohio, was a member of the Washington Court House Presbyterian Church and a state senator, and helped to organize the village's African Methodist Episcopal Church (AME). AME churches were known sanctuaries for fugitive slaves.

The abolitionists, free slaves, and Quakers worked together for the cause of helping fugitive slaves to escape slavery. Many slaves came from the northern Kentucky (Maysville) area. They crossed the Ohio River at or near Ripley, Ohio, and traveled north passing through Fayette County, Ohio. Crossing through Fayette County, they would sometime pass several miles east of Washington Court House. At Rocky Springs, five miles south of Greenfield, Highland County, the prominent conductors were Colonel Thomas Rodgers, John Ripley Strain, and Squire William Wilson.

Many fugitive slaves did not settle in the Fayette County area possibly for fear of being captured and sent back into slavery like John Marshall, who was kidnapped in 1860. Marshall, who had been emancipated as a child, had been working for Judge Daniel Mclean Collins for four years when he was kidnapped by Anderson Jennings and Percival S. Collins. They went to the home of Tommy Keese, a black man with whom Marshall lived, and asked him for a drink of water. When Marshall obliged and brought the water to the carriage, an attempt was made to seize him. He ran back into the house, but he was overcome and taken away. A warrant was issued for the arrest of the perpetrators. But authorities in Kentucky claimed that Marshall was not free, and Collins and Anderson were acquitted of kidnapping charges.

Rev. William M. Mitchell

The Reverend William M. Mitchell, a black minister, worked the Underground Railroad in southern Ohio. His book, *The Under-Ground Railroad*, was written in Canada the year prior to the start of the Civil War.

Mitchell was an orphan born in Guilford County, North Carolina, born of a Native American mother and black father. He was indentured for twelve years, after which he became his employer's overseer for five years. In the latter position, he assisted his employer in the slave trade. He later expressed regret and horror at the role he played in punishing slaves and separating them from their families. When he moved to Ross County, Ohio, in 1843, he atoned for it by dedicating his life to the Underground Railroad.

The first runaway slave incident in which he participated involved a slave from Maryland who had settled in Ohio and had joined the local Methodist Church. To the runaway's shock and dismay, his pastor reported him to claim the $100 reward. Three slavecatchers led the man away with a rope around his neck. They had gone about three miles from town when a posse of about 200 black men, among them Mitchell, surged up behind them. The slavecatchers, fearing for their lives, cut the rope and dashed away before they could be captured. The man, Mitchell said, was never bothered by slavecatchers again.

As noted, slavecatchers were common in southern Ohio, and Mitchell said that an association of them had formed in the Kentucky counties of Mason and Bracken that bordered the Ohio River.

Mitchell said his greatest period of activity in the Underground Railroad occurred after he moved to Washington Courthouse. Here, one of the road's greatest rescuers became a regular visitor to his home. John Mason had escaped to Canada and then took up the profession of slave rescuing. Mitchell said that Mason brought 265 runaway to his home during a 19-month period. Obviously, to undertake such hazardous and lengthy missions, Mason by necessity would have been getting compensated. In all, Mason claimed that he aided as many as 1,300 fugitive slaves. But eventually he was captured. In the process both his arms were broken. Mason was sold to New Orleans. Eighteen months after his capture, however, Mitchell received a letter from him that he was back in Canada.

On one occasion, Mitchell wrote that his house was surrounded by slavecatchers. They were searching for the fugitive slave he was hiding and they demanded to be allowed to enter. Mitchell demanded that they get a warrant. While they did, Mitchell's wife dressed up the fugitive slave as a woman and took him in their wagon to the nearest safe house.

On another occasion, three fugitive slaves came to his locality with slavecatchers trailing close behind. While the slavecatchers searched the area, a wooden box large enough to accommodate two of them was constructed. The local agents transported two of them in the box to a station eight miles away; when the box was returned, they sent the third one in it.

—Sharron L Pope

Further Reading

Rev. William M. Mitchell, *The Under-Ground Railroad* (London: William Tweedie, 1860).

Wilbur H. Siebert, *The Mysteries of Ohio's Underground Railroads* (Columbus, OH: Long's College Book Company, 1951).

WASHINGTON, D.C.

From the early 1830s to the Civil War, the District of Columbia was one of the most active centers for trading and transshipping enslaved people in the nation. The existence of slavery and slave trading in the nation's capital incensed Northern abolitionists, who held that because slavery was a state and not a federal institution, Washington, as a district, could not permit slavery within its borders. Still, the institution persisted there until 1862. Numerous slave-trading firms operated in Washington and in Alexandria (part of the district until 1846) amid repeated petitions calling for Congress to ban slavery in the district. When these efforts finally succeeded in a ban on slave trading in Washington in 1851, according to historian Stanley Harrold, traders simply moved their operations to Alexandria. Despite its centrality in slave trading, however, Washington was a key center of antislavery and Underground Railroad activity, and the well-publicized escapes of people enslaved by U.S. congressmen were high-profile embarrassments much touted by abolitionists.

Created from land ceded by the slave states of Virginia and Maryland, the District of Columbia lay within a large Tidewater region experiencing a lessening demand for enslaved labor. By 1830 wheat, whose cultivation required only part-time labor, had replaced tobacco as the predominant crop, and the need to maintain large pools of slave labor for tobacco culture dissipated. Between 1820 and 1860 the population of slaves in Washington fell by nearly 50 percent while the population of the city more than doubled (Harrold 4); by the time the Civil War began there were five free black people for every one enslaved person in the District (White House Historical Association).

Center of Slave Trading

The decline in Tidewater tobacco culture created a regional surplus of enslaved labor at the same time that the rapidly growing cotton culture in the Deep South opened a market for it. By 1830 the District of Columbia, which then embraced both Georgetown and Alexandria, had replaced Baltimore as the regional center of slave trading. Harrold has asserted that the shift to Washington occurred because the district was "more centrally located in the Chesapeake 'buying market'" (30) and placed fewer legal constraints on slave trading. As the proceedings of the 1834 New England Anti-Slavery Society convention stated, "The District of Columbia is a great market to which human flesh is duly sent for sale from neighboring states, and then sold again to supply the markets of the South" (Laprade 26). Washington attorney and abolitionist Jacob Bigelow called the district "the Man-Market of the Nation" (Harrold 106).

The nation's largest and most notorious slave traders operated in Washington—(Isaac) Franklin and (John) Armfield, (John) Bruin and (Henry) Hill, James H. Burch (later Price, Burch and Company), Benjamin O. Shekels, Bushrod Taylor, and William H. Williams. In 1838 Philadelphia abolitionist James Miller McKim visited Williams's "slave jail," where he found 30 slaves confined to 3 cellar rooms and was told that as many as 139 had been kept there at a time. In a letter to his brother McKim stated, "These are some of the abominations that exist in the District of Columbia! the national domain of the American REPUBLIC! within sight of the Capitol and under the stars and stripes of our national flag!" (*The Colored American*, March 3, 1838). McKim was far from alone in pointing out the galling contradiction between Washington as a slave market and as the capital of a nation professedly committed to equality. "In the District of

Columbia is a vast and diabolical slave trade," journalist and abolitionist David Lee Child wrote in 1834. "The red sign of the auctioneer is stuck up under the flag which waves from the towers of the Capitol" (Laprade 26).

Abolitionist Sentiment Late in Coming

A limited antislavery movement existed in the District from the mid-1790s, when George Drinker and other Quakers formed the Alexandria Society for the Relief and Protection of Those Illegally Held in Bondage. The society, which petitioned for the freedom of manumitted or otherwise freed blacks who were claimed as slaves, was defunct by 1801, and antislavery activity appears then to have been minimal until the late 1820s. In 1827 Drinker and Quaker Samuel M. Janney helped organize the Benevolent Society of Alexandria, dedicated to the same work as the earlier organization; in 1828, Quaker journalist Benjamin Lundy and more than 1,000 residents of the District submitted among the earliest petitions to Congress calling for the abolition of slavery in Washington. Harrold dates the emergence of organized antislavery in the District of Columbia to the 1830s, when "the first cadre of white antislavery northerners" (34) began to assemble there. John Quincy Adams, who began his long service in the U.S. Congress in 1832, was a nominal head of a group of federal legislators dedicated to antislavery, among them Joshua R. Giddings of Ohio, William Slade of Vermont, and Seth Gates of New York. These legislators combined with such lobbyists as Joshua Leavitt and Theodore Weld, journalists such as David Lee Child and Gamaliel Bailey, and African American activists, many of them members of one of the twelve black churches in the District. Adams devoted years attempting to repeal the so-called Gag Rule, enacted by Congress in 1836 to table all antislavery petitions without discussion or debate after they had begun to flood the Capitol, especially after the American Anti-Slavery Society was formed in 1833.

Fugitives in small numbers, chiefly from the Tidewater region, had sought refuge with the black population of Washington since at least the early 1800s, but Underground Railroad traffic probably did not become significant until the 1830s. In 1833 one slaveholder asserted that African Americans in the district hid fugitives "in a labyrinth that has no clue" and paid their passage to Philadelphia (Harrold 52). One notable 1830s attempt to assist fugitives was undertaken by Leonard Grimes, later the African American pastor of the Twelfth Baptist Church in Boston, often called in its time the "fugitive slaves' church."

Leonard Grimes

Born free in Leesburg, Virginia, Grimes moved to Washington as a boy and by the 1830s operated as a hackman with his own carriages and horses.

In October 1839, he went into Virginia to help an enslaved woman identified only as Patty and her six children escape, and in March 1840, a District of Columbia marshal arrested him for his alleged role in the incident. Grimes spent two years in state prison in Richmond, Virginia, and moved to Massachusetts by 1845. According to historian Philip Schwarz, evidence exists to document that Grimes had been involved in assisting fugitives before this incident, and he continued to be an active Underground Railroad agent in Boston until emancipation.

Torrey and Smallwood

About the time Grimes was released from prison, the Congregational minister Charles Turner Torrey and African American shoemaker Thomas Smallwood began to collaborate in fugitive assistance. Smallwood, born in Maryland in 1801 and manumitted when he was 30 years old, called himself "the establisher" of the Underground Railroad in Washington and asserted that he "was as independent of the Abolitionists in my operations as oil is of water, with one or two exceptions" (Smallwood 28). Torrey, born in Massachusetts in 1813, came to Washington in December 1841, as a correspondent for antislavery newspapers and within months was arrested for taking notes at a slaveholders' convention in Baltimore. Learning of his action, Smallwood came to Torrey's Washington boardinghouse after his release to seek his aid in liberating a family of enslaved people owned by George E. Badger of North Carolina, then the secretary of the Navy, who planned to sell them. The family, however, chose to arrange for the purchase of its bound members rather than to leave slavery as fugitives.

The case appears to have prompted Torrey and Smallwood to establish a systematic Underground Railroad venture that, according to some abolitionists, assisted some 400 fugitives between early 1842 and mid-1844. Smallwood described the operation in his 1851 autobiography. He and Torrey, Smallwood wrote, established "two places of deposit" over the 86 miles between Washington and some point over the Pennsylvania line, and paid teamsters as much as fifty dollars to carry a group of fugitives only to the first stop, 37 miles away. Unidentified abolitionists helped fund the enterprise. Smallwood offered more details of their procedure:

> I frequently had lots of slaves concealed about in Washington, who had fled to me for safety when they got wind that their masters were about to sell them to the slave traders. . . . I employed persons and furnished them with the means to purchase food for them until a convenient time should arrive for their departure, and then I would pack them off. . . . I generally went out on the suburbs of the city previous to the night intended for their departure and selected the place at which they were to assemble, never selecting the same place a second time, nor were more than two allowed to come in company to the place selected, and that in different directions, according to the advice of Mr. Torry. (Smallwood 24–25)

Charles Turner Torrey remained in Washington only until the fall of 1842, when he moved to Albany to become editor of the antislavery *Tocsin of Liberty* (later the *Albany Patriot*), but it is clear that he continued to work with Smallwood in fugitive assistance at least until Smallwood himself moved to Canada in October 1843. In a letter to the *Tocsin of Liberty* written under the alias Samuel Weller Jr., Smallwood reported that he had assisted 150 fugitives in their flight between March and November 1842. A collaboration between them to bring two Washington families to the free states in October 1843 failed. Torrey then began to operate from the home of James G. G. Bias in Philadelphia. In December 1843 he helped John Webb and his five children escape from Winchester, Virginia, and in June 1844 he brought three people enslaved by William Heckrotte to the free states. In the latter month he was arrested and imprisoned for his role in both incidents, and he died in the Maryland state penitentiary in May 1846.

After Torrey left Washington, Smallwood stated, "I was the sole proprietor of the so-called underground railroad in that section, it having been started without the assistance of any earthly being save Torry, myself, my wife, and the Lady with whom he boarded" (ibid. 25). Torrey's landlady, identified only as Mrs. Padgett, Elizabeth Smallwood, and others, mainly African American "harborers and agents," had played large roles in effecting the escapes of the four hundred Torrey and Smallwood are said to have assisted, according to Harrold. Padgett hired enslaved people to work in her boardinghouse, some of whom were no doubt fugitives. Smallwood and others cited the participation of John Bush, an African American who concealed carriages and fugitives and was arrested, jailed, and later acquitted for assisting fugitive escapes. Harrold also has provided evidence that congressmen Giddings, Slade, and Gates knew some of the first fugitives whom Smallwood and Torrey helped; Gates directed one enslaved man who had once tended him during an illness to Torrey to learn "how to get off" (Harrold 79, 81, 82, 93).

William L. Chaplin

Harrold has stated that Torrey and Smallwood "made Washington the center of an organized escape route that served the needs of black families and challenged slavery in the Chesapeake" and that the "network" they established "continued to exist in altered form into the Civil War years" (93). Most likely the attorney Jacob Bigelow and the journalist William L. Chapin, both born in Massachusetts, assumed their mantle after 1843–1844. Bigelow came to Washington in 1843, and Chaplin moved to the district in December 1844 to replace Torrey as correspondent for the *Albany Patriot*. Harrold has asserted that Chaplin preferred to purchase enslaved people's freedom (which Torrey and Smallwood, among many others, abhorred as constituting payment to thieves) rather than to help them escape. But Chaplin's assistance to enslaved people in flight is documented, and he played a central role in the single largest escape attempt in the history of the Underground Railroad, the *Pearl* episode of April 1848.

The Pearl

On April 15, 1848, Daniel Drayton, a vessel master who had earlier succeeded in carrying off a family of six from slavery to his native Frenchtown, New Jersey, boarded 77 enslaved people from in and around Washington on the chartered schooner *Pearl*, then docked at the White House Wharf, with the intent of bringing them to the free states. Probably since at least February of that year Chaplin had been working with Daniel Bell, a manumitted man who worked at the Washington Navy Yard, to bring his family out of slavery, and later that month he met with Drayton in Washington to discuss the emerging plan. Three weeks before the rescue attempt Chaplin confided to the New York abolitionist Gerrit Smith that he had chartered a vessel in Philadelphia large enough to carry a substantial number of fugitives. "The number of persons here, who are anxious to immigrate, is increasing on my hands daily," he told Smith. "I believe there are no less than 75 now importunate for a passage" (Harrold 127). Bell and other African Americans guided fugitives to the wharf. After seeing the *Pearl* off on the evening of April 15, Chaplin told Joshua Giddings and the antislavery Hutchinson Family Singers, then staying at the National Hotel while on tour, what he had done.

The rescue effort was undone when a black hackman who had helped bring some of the fugitives to the wharf revealed the plot to several owners. These claimants hired a steamer and overtook the *Pearl*, hampered by a becalmed Chesapeake Bay. Drayton, his two crew members, and the fugitives were bound "two-and-two" and, Drayton wrote, "exhibited to the mob collected on the wharves to get a sight of us" and who "signified their satisfaction by three cheers" (Drayton 39). As the entire party was marched from Steamboat Wharf to Washington jail, a slave trader named Gannon attempted to stab Drayton, and an "immense mob of several thousand persons" formed "with the avowed intention of carrying us up before the capitol, and making an exhibition of us there" (40). A crowd of similar size gathered around the jail and later attempted to destroy the offices of the *National Era*, the antislavery newspaper then edited by Gamaliel Bailey.

Ultimately nearly all of the enslaved people were sold, many on the New Orleans slave market. Among the few whose freedom was purchased were the sisters Mary and Emily Edmundson, who soon became important figures on the antislavery lecture circuit. Drayton was convicted of larceny and transporting stolen property and spent more than four years in Washington Jail, but he never implicated Chaplin or anyone else who helped arrange the escape attempt. Chaplin continued his activity. That fall he brought two fugitives with him to the annual colored people's convention, held that year in Philadelphia, and asked black clergyman Henry Highland Garnet to bring them into western New York. Later that year he wrote Smith about more fugitives, including one in his home, "who ask assistance in attempting to escape from slavery" (Harrold 155). But in August 1850, Chaplin was arrested as he attempted to convey two men enslaved by separate Georgia congressmen to the free states; he was beaten and imprisoned for 19 weeks in first a Washington and then a Maryland jail. Released on bail in mid-December 1850, Chaplin did not return to face trial and resettled in New York, apparently severing his connection with the Washington Underground Railroad.

Jacob Bigelow

After Chaplin's removal, Jacob Bigelow, who regularly served as defense attorney for African Americans in kidnapping and freedom suits, became the district's principal fugitive assistant. In 1854 Bigelow developed a collaboration with Philadelphia Vigilance Committee secretary William Still, whose 1871 *Underground Railroad* documents Bigelow's activity. By that year, Harrold has asserted, Bigelow "organized group escapes on a weekly or biweekly basis" (213). Still termed Bigelow, whom he often cited simply as "J. B.," as a "trusty and capable conductor of the Underground Rail Road in Washington," and Sydney Howard Gay's records of the New York Vigilance Committee's fugitive assistance identified him as a Washington Underground Railroad agent. Bigelow was instrumental in effecting numerous escapes, perhaps most notable that of the 15-year-old Ann Maria Weems in 1855 by removing her from her master's home outside the city, hiding her in Washington for six weeks, and then dressing her as a young male coachman. Weems was met in front of the White House by Dr. Ellwood Harvey of the Pennsylvania Female Medical College, whom Still had recruited to bring her to Philadelphia; she was ultimately sent on to Buxton, one of Ontario's several fugitive settlements.

Just as Smallwood had begun to use an alias when he felt his Underground Railroad work put him in danger, Bigelow began to write to Still under the name "Wm. Penn" by 1855, and he often included false statements about himself in letters to Still to "blind the eyes of the uninitiated" (Still 177); these Still was to recognize by the brackets Bigelow placed around them. And like Torrey, who once proposed to Smallwood that they "should try and obtain a team and proceed to Washington, and bring away as many slaves as we could" (Smallwood 37), Bigelow suggested a more ambitious system of fugitive assistance to Still beginning in October 1854. He wanted, he said, to "find a man . . . who will come to Washington to live, and who will walk out to Penn's, or a part of the way there, once or twice a week" to pick up "parties of say, two, three, five or so, who will pay him at least $5 each, for the privilege of following him, but will never speak to him; but will keep just in sight of him and obey any sign he may give; say, he takes off his hat and scratches his head as a sign for them to go to some barn or wood to rest, &c." In planning his route, Bigelow suggested, such a person should pick several places of safety where the groups might hide during the day. "I think he might make a good living at it," he wrote to Still, "He might then take ten or a dozen at a time, and they are often able and willing to pay $10 a piece" (Still 186). In 1856 he suggested to Still that a man identified only as "powder boy," one of the schooner captains who sometimes took fugitives from Southern ports, be enticed to establish a base south of Annapolis and carry on a regular trade in wood, oysters, and fugitive transport.

Jacob Bigelow Reports Arrangements Made for Fugitive Slaves

Jacob Bigelow was a lawyer who moved to Washington, D.C., in 1843. He lived alone in a tiny room and was extremely private. What people did not realize was that he was deeply involved in the Underground Railroad, often coordinating the escapes of slaves, or when that was not feasible, making arrangements to pay for their freedom. The following letter to William Still, on June 22, 1854, which was published in Still's book, *The Underground Railroad* (41), deals with the movement of three fugitive slaves. Note the euphemisms and the alias used to conceal both the activity and the identity of one of the individuals involved:

> Sir-I have just received a letter from my friend, Wm. Wright, of York Sulphur Springs, Pa., in which he says, that by writing to you, I may get some information about the transportation of some property from this neighborhood to your city or vicinity. A person who signs himself Wm. Penn, lately wrote to Mr. Wright, saying he would pay $300 to have this service performed. It is for the conveyance of only one SMALL package; but it has been discovered since, that the removal cannot be so safely effected without taking two larger packages with it. I understand that the three are to be brought to this city and stored in safety, as soon as the forwarding merchant in Philadelphia shall say he is ready to send on. The storage, etc., here, will cost a trifle, but the $300 will be promptly paid for the whole service. I think Mr. Wright's daughter, Hannah, has also seen you. I am also known to Prof, C. D. Cleveland, of your city. If you answer this promptly, you will soon hear from Wm. Penn himself. Very truly yours, J. BIGELOW

Marvellously Large Business

In 1858 Still noted that the Underground Railroad to Washington "was doing about this time a marvellously large business. 'William Penn' and other friends in Washington were most vigilant, and knew where to find passengers who were daily thirsting for deliverance" (498). Among those working with or at the same time as Bigelow was the journalist Ezra L. Stevens, who was instrumental in arranging to purchase the freedom of several of Weems's brothers who had been sold to owners further south. Others were Myrtilla Miner, who founded a school for African American girls in Washington in 1851; Gamaliel Bailey, who serialized *Uncle Tom's Cabin* in the *National Era*, and Bailey's wife Margaret, who edited an antislavery monthly journal for young people; and Noah C. Hanson, a free man of African descent, who was arrested in 1851 for hiding two people enslaved by the

South Carolina Congressman William F. Colcock under the kitchen floor in his employer's Washington home. Abolitionists were unable to raise funds to pay Hanson's bail, but President Franklin Pierce pardoned him in 1854 (Harrold 156, 160). Others who assisted Smallwood, Torrey, Chaplin, and Bigelow have not yet been identified.

—Kathryn Grover

Further Reading

William T. Laprade, "The Domestic Slave Trade in the District of Columbia," *Journal of Negro History* 11, No. 1 (January 1926): 17–34.

J. C. Lovejoy, *Memoir of Rev. Charles T. Torrey* (Boston: John P. Jewett and Co., 1847; reprint, New York: Negro Universities Press, 1969).

A Narrative of Thomas Smallwood, (Coloured Man:) Giving an Account of His Birth— The Period He Was Held in Slavery—His Release—and Removal to Canada, etc. Together with an Account of the Underground Railroad. Written by Himself (Toronto: James Stephens, 1851).

Stanley Harrold, *Subversives: Antislavery Community in Washington, D.C., 1828–1865* (Baton Rouge: Louisiana State University Press, 2003).

Josephine F. Pacheco, *The Pearl: A Failed Slave Escape on the Potomac* (Chapel Hill: University of North Carolina Press, 2005).

Personal Memoir of Daniel Drayton (Boston: Bela Marsh, 1854).

William Still, *The Underground Railroad: A Record of Facts . . .* (Philadelphia: Porter and Coates, 1872).

WASHINGTON, PENNSYLVANIA

Washington is the county seat of Washington County, located about 25 miles southwest of Pittsburgh, Pennsylvania. Several of its residents were involved in the Underground Railroad, and many more were involved in the antislavery movement.

Abolitionist activity began in Washington County in 1824 with the formation of the Western Abolitionist Society on January 26, 1824, in the courthouse in Washington. Fifty members joined this Society. Abolitionist activity was unpopular at that time and there were still some slaves remaining because the gradual emancipation law that had been passed in 1780 did not apply to those born before that time.

After the era of widespread calls for immediate emancipation began with the launching of *The Liberator* in 1831, the Washington County Anti-Slavery Society was organized on July 4, 1834, with Joseph Henderson elected president. Several ministers were among the organizers of this society. The county abolitionists were bold, openly committing numerous disorderly acts against slavery. Meetings of the anti-slavery society were announced in the newspaper and its opponents often attacked the participants at the meetings. Their meetings became as much as an issue about free speech as ending slavery.

Francis LeMoyne

The LeMoyne House, 49 East Maiden Street, Washington, Pennsylvania, once the home of Dr. Francis J. LeMoyne, was a center of antislavery activity from the 1830s until the end of slavery. In 1834, LeMoyne joined the Washington Anti-Slavery Society and became the organization's president from 1835 until 1837. He also was commissioned by the American Anti-Slavery Society to be its regional agent. LeMoyne, along with his children and wife Madeleine, were active in the Underground Railroad. Stories passed down by family members (and a few documented letters) confirm that they helped fugitive slaves. One story is about Madeleine who successfully hid seven fugitive slaves under their large bed when slave hunters had entered the house in search of the slaves. Mrs. LeMoyne pretended to be deathly ill and the men did not want to disturb the lady.

LeMoyne became one of the most noted abolitionists in Pennsylvania, and was a candidate for governor in 1841, 1844, and 1847. His prominence extended nationwide. For instance, he was nominated for vice president as James G. Birney's running mate at the Liberty Party (Abolition Party) organizational meeting held in Albany, New York, in 1840.

The McKeever Family

Matthew McKeever was well known in Washington County, but few knew that he was the active manager of a line of the Underground Railroad. That is, until notices were posted offering a reward for his capture. He was a conductor for 40 years, driving a spring wagon with a chicken coop on each end and fugitive slaves in the middle, hidden beneath a cover. He was often helped by a free black named John Jordan who took runaways and hid them in the loft of his sheep shed. Often fugitive slaves were hidden on the McKeever farm for weeks at a time, unknown to his family members. One of his earliest ventures was when a group of fugitive slaves was shipped from the home of his brother-in-law, Joseph Bryant, in Wheeling, Virginia, accompanied by conductor William Arnet, and Matthew's son, Campbell McKeever. The person who brought them to Wheeling turned state's evidence, and told their masters that Bryant had fed them and sent them to another safe house. At the request of the masters, the sheriff arrested Bryant and lodged him in jail in Wheeling. He stayed there for 15 days during which a reward of $500 was offered to anyone who would bring in Matthew McKeever, dead or alive. The judge in this case finally decided that they could not punish an accomplice (Bryant) while the principal (McKeever) was at large, and Bryant was sent home.

Matthew McKeever's brother, Thomas, lived on a farm near West Middletown, Washington County. He provided shelter for fugitive slaves in his barn until they could safely be transported toward Washington. Another brother, William McKeever, hid fugitive slaves in his attic, at his house in the town of

Thomas McKeever house, outskirts of Washington, Pennsylvania; home of the abolitionist and friend of John Brown and who was involved in the Underground Railroad. (Courtesy of Tom Calarco)

West Middletown. If none of these places were safe for the fugitive slaves, they could hide in a wooded place called "Penitentiary Woods," about a mile from town on the Washington Road. A cabin in this area provided safe lodging for the fugitives for long periods of time. When it was safe to travel, they were led north to Beaver County by neighboring free black conductors. The McKeever men were personal friends of abolitionist John Brown, who visited Thomas McKeever several times. Generally fugitive slaves coming to Washington went through the home of Bryant in Wheeling, coming there by way of Bethany in Brook County, Virginia. He would send them to Washington, where they were forwarded north to Pittsburgh, Buffalo, or Cleveland. In his book on the history of western Pennsylvania, George Swetnam states that a major escape route operated between Wheeling and the city of Washington, Pennsylvania. The fugitive slaves choosing this route usually traveled over the National Road, which connected the two sites. An alternate route had fugitives going from Wheeling to the town of West Middletown to the north of the city of Washington. From West Middletown, the McKeever family, the leading Underground Railroad agents and conductors in the town, would take them hidden in their poultry wagons to Pittsburgh. Philip Schwarz, author of *Migrants Against Slavery*, cites the work of the many abolitionists in Washington County, Pennsylvania, who helped slaves escape from the Wheeling area in the 1840s.

Another local abolitionist was Joseph Gray who owned a farm near Graysville south of Washington in Greene County that was a station on the Underground

Railroad. Gray hauled fugitive slaves from his farm to the McCoy place in West Alexander, west of Washington, near the Virginia border. They were transported by wagon where they were concealed under hay, grain, or even among pigs. Tar Adams, a free black, aided fugitive slaves. A fast runner, he often used crutches to fool the slavecatchers. He was an effective informer when slaver catchers were in the area. If he spotted someone who was looking for a fugitive, he would drop his crutches and run quickly to a place where fugitive slaves were being hidden. Other free blacks who helped fugitive slaves were Ermine Cain, a janitor from Waynesburg, the county seat of Greene County, and Samuel W. Dorsey who was a barber in Washington.

Washington County was an active part of the Underground Railroad, but perhaps its most notable contribution to the fight against slavery was the establishment of antislavery societies and antislavery meetings that both angered and influenced the people of their region.

—Cynthia Vogel

Further Reading

Joseph Henderson Bausman, *History of Beaver County, Pennsylvania* (New York: Knickerbocker Press, 1904).

Earle Forrest, *History of Washington County*, 1 (Chicago: J. Clarke Co., 1926): 415–428.

Philip J. Schwarz, *Migrants against Slavery* (Charlottesville, VA: University of Virginia Press, 2001).

George Swetnam, *A Guidebook to Historic Western Pennsylvania* (Pittsburgh: University of Pittsburgh Press, 1976).

WATERWAYS

Perhaps the most useful thoroughfares to freedom for fugitive slaves were the waterways: streams, rivers, canals, lakes, and the sea. This entry will explore all of these but the sea, which is described in the entry, Saltwater Underground Railroad.

Ohio River System

The Ohio River, a border between slavery in Kentucky and Virginia, and freedom in Indiana and Ohio, which stretched nearly 700 miles, was undoubtedly the most significant river of freedom. Making it even more attractive to fugitive slaves were the many settlements on the free side settled by whites who had left the South because of opposition to slavery. Some like Ripley and Marietta, Ohio, and Madison, Indiana, became centers of the Underground Railroad. Others like Maysville, Kentucky, and Moscow, Ohio, became gathering places for slavecatchers. Settlements of emancipated slaves like Poke Patch and the Gist communities in Ohio, and Lick Creek in Indiana near the Ohio River, also became havens. Other important crossover points were on the eastern section of the river bordering what is now West Virginia. These included Wheeling, Parkersburg, and Point Pleasant. Crossing the river from Virginia was easier because it was not very deep in this area during the antebellum period before later construction of dams. It was sometimes possible for fugitive slaves to swim or wade across in some areas, and during the winter the shallow river often froze and was easy to walk across. Another notable crossing point on the Ohio was Diamond Island just west of Henderson, Kentucky, which was described in William Cockrum's book.

Along with its tributaries and connecting canals, and its connection to the Mississippi River, the Ohio River provided an avenue of escape from New Orleans to Cleveland. This was accomplished with the completion of the Portland and Louisville Canal around the rapids on the Ohio River in 1830, and the Ohio and Erie Canal through central Ohio in 1832, which connected Cleveland to Portsmouth, Ohio. For example, in Dresden, Ohio, east of Columbus, George and Edward Adams operated a flourmill on the canal. The brothers also owned warehouses, a boat yard, and a cooper shop where they made barrels. They made deliveries of flour by boat to New Orleans; they often returned with fugitive slaves hidden beneath the deck of their ship.

Abolitionists using steamboats on the Mississippi River to transport fugitive slaves to Ohio and points father north may have been widespread by the middle of the 1850s. One of these boats was the *Gladenel*, and among these abolitionists was Henry Roberts, a young blacksmith from Cortsville, Ohio, four miles southeast of Springfield. He left home in 1852 for Louisiana, ostensibly to work on a plantation as an overseer. However, his real purpose was to assist the escape of fugitive slaves on boats going north on the Mississippi. One of his collaborators had the surname Paul and from Cleveland. On his last mission, in 1855, he assisted the escape of 18 fugitive slaves to Cincinnati (Siebert 60).

The Miami and Erie Canal, which also connected the Ohio River with Lake Erie through the western section of Ohio, was completed in 1845. During the late 1840s, the celebrated Underground Railroad conductor, Laura Haviland, escorted seven fugitive slaves on a packet boat on the canal from Cincinnati along the entire length of the canal that led to Toledo, and then arranged a boat ride on Lake Erie on which she took them to Canada.

Another waterway used by fugitive slaves that connected with the Ohio River was the Wabash and Erie Canal. Its construction began in Fort Wayne, Indiana, reached west to Lafayette by 1843, Terre Haute by 1848, and finally to Evansville on the Ohio River in 1853. The canal also connected eastward around 1843 with the Miami and Erie Canal, just south of Defiance, Ohio, where the waterway met the Maumee River that emptied at Toledo into Lake Erie. Among the strongly abolitionized communities along the canal was Lafayette, Indiana, where the leading Underground Railroad agent was the merchant, Lewis Falley.

One of the most daring escape attempts that used the Ohio River was executed by Seth Concklin in 1851, who had traveled from Philadelphia,

Pennsylvania to Tuscambia, Alabama, to rescue the family of Peter Still. Concklin's passengers were Still's wife, 10-year-old daughter and 20- and 22-year-old sons. Concklin obtained a six-oared, flat-bottomed rowboat for the trip. The first leg of the journey took them downstream along the Tennessee River to the Ohio, a distance of about 250 miles. The next leg went from the Ohio upstream to the Wabash River, a journey of about 75 miles, followed by another 44-mile trip up the Wabash. Most of the rowing was handled by Still's sons. However, after leaving their boat and proceeding on foot, they were spotted by a slavecatcher, and Concklin's suspicious behavior led to their arrest and the ultimate tragedy that led to his drowning in the Ohio River at the port of Smithland, Kentucky.

Another Underground Railroad agent who used the Ohio to transport slaves was William Tatum, alias John Jones, who conveyed them from Louisville to Cincinnati. He aided 27 fugitive slaves in 1858 while working with Levi Coffin. According to Coffin, Tatum passed them off as his slaves and transported them to the docks in Cincinnati where they were met by black agents sent by Coffin. However, his operation finally came to an end when he was arrested and tried though not convicted for aiding fugitive slaves. Thereafter, he moved to Iowa.

These are only a few examples of use of the Ohio River system to transport slaves to freedom. Other likely avenues included one of its sources, the Allegheny River in Pennsylvania, which led north to Underground Railroad centers in northeastern Pennsylvania and southwestern New York; the Muskingum River that flowed from the Ohio at Marietta to Columbus; the Scioto River that flowed from the Ohio at Portsmouth to Columbus; the Little Kanawha and Kanawha Rivers that reached the Ohio at Parkersburg, Virginia and Gallipolis, Ohio, both known to have local Underground Railroad agents; and the Little Sandy and Big Sandy Rivers that flow north into the Ohio, just east of Portsmith and the entrance to the Ohio and Erie Canal.

Mississippi River

The Mississippi River was a major crossing point for slaves fleeing from Missouri into Illinois. The most important destination on the river was Quincy, Illinois, founded in 1825 and named after the newly elected President John Quincy Adams. During this time, the largest concentration of slaves in the state of Missouri lived in the region across the river from Quincy. During the 1840s, it became the source of major confrontations between slaveholders and abolitionists from the Mission Institute Seminary led by its president, David Nelson, and one of its trustees, Dr. Richard Eels. On one occasion, a school building was set fire by an angry mob of Missourians. The conflicts led to the conviction of three Mission Institute members, students, James Burr, George Thompson, and Alanson Work, as well as Eels in a separate incident, for aiding the escape of slaves.

A second important crossover point was near Rocky Fork, Illinois, where the Rocky Fork Creek flows into the Big Piasa River. It connected the black community of Rocky Fork to the Mississippi River, approximately three miles west of Alton, where an African Methodist Episcopal Church was established by the abolitionist minister, Rev. Paul Quinn, a known agent of the Underground Railroad. A third was Cairo, Illinois, where the Ohio River empties into the Mississippi. Cairo also was the end of the line of the Illinois Central Railroad, which connected it to Chicago in 1856.

Susquehanna River

The Susquehanna River begins at Otsego Lake, New York, and empties after 444 miles into the Chesapeake Bay. The southern end of the river was more significant as a crossover point. In the years prior to 1840 at Havre de Grace, Maryland, fugitive slaves took a ferry across the river on the way to many havens in the nearby southern Pennsylvania counties of Lancaster and Chester. In later years, when vigilance increased at the ferry, they crossed the river farther north over the bridge to Columbia, Pennsylvania. Founded by Quakers, Columbia was the site of an unsuccessful attempt to kidnap a slave in 1804. Following this incident, a significant black population settled there, and it became a busy Underground Railroad stop with William Whipper becoming its most important agent after 1847. Another important stop on the eastern side of the river across from Columbia was the Mifflin family, well-known conductors who on at least one occasion hosted the notorious slave rescuer, Charles T. Torrey.

From Harrisburg the river was used often, despite travel moving upstream. It split in Sunbury, where it led west to Williamsport. It connected there with the Pennsylvania Canal and lumberman Daniel Hughes who transported fugitive slaves in his lumber barges. Continuing west took it past Underground Railroad stops in Bellefonte and Clearfield, and to southwestern New York and Erie, Pennsylvania. Following it north and east led it to Towanda, where there were several agents, on through Athens, Pennsylvania, and across the border to New York. There it split again, with its tributary, the Chemung River, going west to Elmira, an abolitionized community, and east, to Binghamton, where it met the Chenango Canal. This canal led to the vicinity of Gerrit Smith and many other active Underground Railroad agents in central New York.

Hudson River

By the 1840s, the Hudson River in eastern New York, which flows from its source in the Adirondack Mountains to New York City, had become a major thoroughfare for fugitive slaves heading from New York City. The use of the Hudson River to reach Albany was acknowledged by New York Committee of Vigilance secretary, Charles Ray: "When we had parties to forward from here, we would alternate in sending between Albany and Troy, and when we had a large party we would divide between the two cities" (Ray 35).

In 1856, a broadside published by Albany conductor Stephen Myers indicated that the Albany Vigilance committee had aided 287 fugitive slaves in the prior nine months (Calarco 161). How these runaways may have arrived in Albany is indicated in an 1848 account in the *Albany Patriot*. It told of the *Armenia*, a day-boat from New York to Troy with a "novel design" that included its dining table above deck, as similar boats like it, rather than below where fugitive slaves were likely hidden: "A light, airy saloon, of a hot or a dark day, is altogether more comfortable than a close and dungeon-like place." In identifying the ship steward as Myers, who had begun working on such boats at least as early as 1838, it said that, "Stephen has had a long experience in the culinary department, and can't be beat by white folks" (110).

Associations of the Hudson with the Underground Railroad are further solidified by the organization of the Eastern New York Anti-Slavery Society in 1842 that brought together 100 delegates "all those [counties] bordering the Hudson" (70). The report of its executive committee in September 1843, indicated that it could not estimate how many fugitive slave it had, only that "hundreds" were being aided annually (*Annual Report of the Committee*).

Connecting with the Hudson and leading farther north, was the Champlain Canal, which was completed in 1823 and connected Troy and Albany with Lake Champlain at the port of Whitehall, creating a northwest passage via the Hudson River from New York City to Canada. This canal passed mainly through Washington County, a heavily abolitionized section with a number of documented accounts of aid to fugitive slaves. One related account concerned a member of the ENYASS, Rev. Fayette Shipherd of Troy, notifying Vermont conductor Charles Hicks of the impending arrival of runaways and explained that the customary use of the canal for transportation had to be abandoned because of the weather: "As the canal has closed I shall send my Southern friends along your road and patronize your house. We had a fine run of business during the season. . . . We had 22 in two weeks 13 in the city at one time" (Calarco 59).

St. Lawrence River

The St. Lawrence River, the western border of northern New York with Canada, was an obvious crossing point for fugitive slaves. Two of its major gateways were the ports of Ogdensburg and Cape Vincent, where it emptied into Lake Ontario. An 1838 account tells of the forwarding of a runaway on a St. Lawrence River steamboat, the United States, whose passage was paid by Gerrit Smith. Another fugitive slave, Harriet Powell, who was harbored for a time by Smith in 1839, used the ferry at Cape Vincent to get to Kingston, Canada, where she settled and married. Runaways leaving Oswego, New York, often were taken to Cape Vincent, according to a letter by George C. Bragdon, whose father George Bragdon was among the earliest conductors in Oswego. And Jerry McHenry, the subject of the famous Jerry Rescue in 1851, was forwarded from Oswego by boat to Kingston. Farther up the river is Ogdensburg,

Ogdensburg is mentioned in several accounts, one as early as 1837 in which a runaway traveled up the Champlain Canal in eastern New York then traveled west across the northernmost section of the state into St. Lawrence County. In 1838, the call to organize vigilance committees (to aid runaway slaves) by the New York State Anti-Slavery Society included Ogdensburg (52, 56). An 1859 letter from Erastus Hopkins of Northampton, Massachusetts, to John Brooks Wheeler in Burlington, Vermont, mentions sending a runaway slave named Bill to Ogdensburg.

Erie Canal

Despite indications that fugitive slaves were sent from Albany on the Erie Canal to western New York, there are few documented reports of its use. However, one striking account involves a fugitive slave couple. William and Catherine Harris, and their three-year-old child were riding a packet boat along the Erie Canal nearing Utica. After being told that his master was about to board the boat to apprehend him, possibly in jest, the fugitive slave cut his throat, then jumped off the boat with his wife and child, causing the child to drown.

Another documented report of its use comes from Stephen Myers of Albany, who wrote in the December 8, 1842 issue of his newspaper, the *Northern Star and Freeman's Advocate*, of paying the canalboat passage for a fugitive slave to Oswego.

The canal passed through many sections that were home to Underground Railroad conductors. In Schenectady, the barbershop of Richard P. G. Wright, a known Underground Railroad agent and father of Rev. Theodore Wright, president of the New York Committee of Vigilance, was located along the canal. In Lyons, New York, between Syracuse and Rochester, the home of Columbus Croul, a blacksmith who made horseshoes for Erie Canal tow horses boats, was said to be a station. Three of Rochester's most important agents lived or worked only a short distance from the canal: Isaac and Amy Post, who may have been the city's most active Underground Railroad participants; Frederick Douglass, whose newspaper, *North Star*, was on the same block as Post's pharmacy; and William Bloss, whose antislavery paper, *The Rights of Man* preceded *North Star* and whose home was near the canal in the eastern section of Rochester. Lockport was another city through whose center the canal passed. As early as 1830 canal workmen there rescued a black barber who was seized by slavecatchers, and in 1836 the city abolitionists formed an antislavery society and continued to agitate for the end of slavery up until the Civil War.

Use of the canal by fugitive slaves also may have been facilitated by commercial interests. For example, Linnaeus P. Noble, the owner of a Towboat Line that served the route from New York to Oswego, and E. M. Teall, owner of the Erie Canal Line that operated from New York City to Buffalo, were members of the Albany Anti-Slavery Society. Noble also was an officer in the Eastern New York Anti-Slavery Society and later moved to the Syracuse area, where he was one of the participants in the Jerry Rescue. Not long after that, Noble became publisher of the *National Era* in Washington, D.C., which also had involvement in the Underground Railroad.

Connecticut River

The Connecticut River, which extended from Long Island Sound to near the northern border of New Hampshire, was a thoroughfare for fugitive slaves, moving through New Hampshire and Vermont, as well as Connecticut. Although fugitive slave traffic through the former two states was light and sporadic, fugitive slaves were sometimes brought to Connecticut by seaman and shipbuilders who lived in the ports along the river's southern sections. Ships brought cotton from the South up the river to Connecticut's mills, and from the mid-1820s, steamers ran regularly between New York and Hartford. At least one fugitive slave, James Lindsey Smith, was sent by the New York Committee of Vigilance on one of these steamers.

Hartford was among the most important of these abolitionist river ports, boasting the state's second largest antislavery society and often hosting the state antislavery society's annual meetings. In 1838, after his escape from Virginia, Smith was sent on a steamboat to Henry W. Foster, a black tailor, in Hartford. After spending a few days there and meeting other abolitionists, he was forwarded to Dr. Samuel Osgood in Springfield, Massachusetts, who found him work as a shoemaker and sent him to school. Eventually, he settled in Norwich, Connecticut.

The abolitionism of Middletown was spearheaded by Jesse G. Baldwin, a shipbuilder and merchant, who had traveled through the South while a young man as an itinerant peddler. During this period, he grew to hate slavery. In 1833, he moved to Middletown where he opened a general store and began the manufacture of cotton webbing. The cotton he purchased was grown with free labor from a Quaker settlement in the West Indies. He also was the co-founder of the city's antislavery society and its chief financial backer.

Baldwin later went into shipping, and built two schooners, on which he transported fugitive slaves. He named them, the Jesse G. Baldwin and the W. B. Douglas, the latter after Benjamin Douglas, the other founder of the antislavery society and the city's mayor from 1850 to 1856. According to his grandson, Baldwin harbored slaves at his home after they were brought to Connecticut on one of his ships, then would forward them to Underground Railroad stops by wagon in Hartford and Farmington.

Other Connecticut River seamen who aided fugitive slavers were East Haddam residents, Gideon Higgins, and George E. and William H. Goodspeed. On one occasion, a fugitive slave who was working on the Goodspeed's boat, *The Hero*, was discovered by his master who had booked passage on the boat. North of Connecticut, fugitive slaves traveled up the river, which was the border between New Hampshire and Vermont, and along which a number of locations offered refuge to fugitive slaves who occasionally took this route.

The Great Lakes

Thousands of fugitive slaves took passage to freedom on boats along the Great Lakes. Terminal ports in New York along Lake Ontario included Cape Vincent, the site of Jerry Henry's departure after his rescue in 1851; Pultneyville, the home of conductor, Captain Horatio Throop; Oswego, which had a large and active antislavery community that included John B. Edwards, the business agent for Gerrit Smith, and Smith's Oswego Hydraulic Canal and the Pier and Dock Company; and Rochester, the port from which William Parker and his fellow fugitives were sent after the Christiana Riot in 1851. Along Lake Erie, there were numerous terminal ports: Buffalo, New York, the home port for a number of years of fugitive slave author, William Wells Brown, when he was a boatman aiding fugitive slaves; Erie, Pennsylvania; and the Ohio ports of Conneault, Ashtabula, Painesville, Cleveland, Lorain, Huron, Sandusky and Toledo. Terminal ports on Lake Michigan included Michigan City, Indiana, where the Antislavery League reported by Cockrum docked its surreptitious "Lumber Barge," which hauled fugitive slaves to freedom; Chicago Illinois, the site of many send-offs of fugitive slaves; and Milwaukee and Racine, Wisconsin, the latter from which Joshua Glover disembarked after his rescue in 1854.

Sandusky may have been the most active of all Great Lakes ports. George de Baptiste, the prolific conductor from Detroit, Michigan, operated the T. Whitney, which made regular runs to Sandusky. Numerous accounts mention boats from Sandusky taking fugitive slaves to freedom. Among them were those of Josiah Henson, Lewis Hayden, Lewis Clark, and Eliza Harris, the slave from whom Harriet Beecher Stowe, based her character, Eliza.

—Tom Calarco

Further Reading

Annual Report of the Committee. Albany: Eastern NY A.S. Society & Fugitive Slaves, 1843.

George Bragdon to Wilbur Siebert, August 15, 1896.

Tom Calarco, *The Underground Railroad in the Adirondack Region* (Jefferson, NC: McFarland and Company, Inc., 2004).

William M. Cockrum, *History of the Underground Railroad: As It Was Conducted by the Anti-Slavery League* (Oakland City, IN: J. M. Cockrum Press, 1915).

"Letter to the Editor," Kiah Bayley, *Vermont Freeman,* June 10, 1843.

Levi Coffin, *Reminiscences* (Cincinnati, OH: Robert Clarke & Co, 1880).

Mildred E. Danforth, *A Quaker Pioneer* (New York: Exposition Press, Inc., 1961).

Erastus Hopkins to John Brooks Wheeler, Northampton, Massachusetts, July 11, 1859.

Arch Merrill, *The Underground, Freedom's Road, and Other Upstate Tales* (New York: American Book-Stratford Press, 1963).

Florence T. Ray, *Sketch of the Life of Rev. Charles B. Ray* (New York: Press of J. J. Little & Co., 1887).

Wilbur Siebert, *The Mysteries of Ohio's Underground Railroads* (Columbus, OH: Long's College Book Company, 1951).

Wilbur Siebert, *Vermont's Anti-Slavery and Underground Railroad Record* (1937) (New York: Negro Universities Press, 1969).

Horatio Strother, *The Underground Railroad in Connecticut* (Middletown, CT: Wesleyan University Press, 1962).

WHEELING, (WEST) VIRGINIA

For fugitive slaves during the nineteenth century, crossing the Ohio River at Wheeling had a distinct advantage of being a much shorter trip to Lake Erie and Canada. The direct route from Wheeling to Cleveland was little more than 100 miles. Most other Ohio River ports, such as Cincinnati, Ripley, and Marietta made the trip across Ohio at least twice as long. There were three main points where the Underground Railroad fugitive slaves crossed the Ohio River from western Virginia: Wheeling, Parkersburg, and Point Pleasant. Rather than crossing the river from Virginia, however, fugitive slaves sometimes went north into Pennsylvania.

Crossing the Ohio River from Virginia, however, was usually not difficult because the river was not very deep during the first half of the nineteenth century before the locks and dams were built. Sometimes it was possible for the fugitive slaves to swim or simply wade across the river. And during the winter the river often would be frozen so they could just walk across.

After 1818, when the National Road was completed, Wheeling became a major hub of transportation. It was ranked as the second largest city in Virginia. Prior to the establishment of West Virginia as a separate state in 1863, Virginia was an active slave state. Wheeling was the major river port and a center of slave trading. The phrase "sold down the river" refers to slaves sold for export to the Deep South. Slaves were sold on the auction block in Wheeling at the west end of The Market House built in 1822. They were treated much like animals and prospective buyers could examine their teeth, muscles, and other body parts. Many times entire families were put on the block and sold separately. Witnessing slaves being sold at this auction block inspired abolitionist Benjamin Lundy to later publish his daily newspaper devoted to abolitionism, *The Genius of Universal Emancipation.*

Area Agents

The location of Wheeling, sandwiched between Ohio and Pennsylvania, presented the likelihood that help for fugitive slaves was nearby. Abolitionists sometimes hid the fugitive slaves under sacks of merchandise on their way home from the market in Virginia and rode the ferry back across the river to Martins Ferry, Ohio. Siebert's map has an Underground Railroad route traveling up the Ohio River through Wheeling and Wellsburg. Between these two towns, the route had a branch that went eastward to either the city of Washington or the town of West Middletown in Pennsylvania. According to Siebert, this route was very well traveled and the four counties that made up the panhandle of West Virginia, Brooke, Hancock, Marshall, and Ohio, lost a large number of slaves between 1850 and 1860.

Martins Ferry, Ohio, a couple of miles north of Wheeling, had several stations that aided fleeing slaves. One was the home of Joel Wood on North Third Street, known as Walnut Grove. This home was built on a high bluff overlooking the river, which made it easy to see the Virginia side of the river. Buckeye Hollow, a rural community near Martins Ferry, also provided refuge for fugitive slaves. The log house owned by Tom Pointer, a mulatto slave, had a small garret on the second floor where fleeing slaves could hide.

From Buckeye Hallow fugitive slaves were taken to Joshua Cope's Grist Mill, a large building with many rooms, where they could hide, or to his old log barn where they were hidden under the floor.

On the north end of Martins Ferry lived Richard Naylor and Samuel Cooper, two free black men whose home was a station. "Dick" Naylor, a black abolitionist, is said to have worked on the docks of Wheeling. As an elderly man, he often pretended to be drunk to avoid suspicion of his Underground Railroad activities. He took the fugitive slaves by boat from Wheeling and safely transported them to an abolitionist farmer with a wagon that could conceal the runaways. He also conducted the fugitive slaves over the National Road to the farm of Kenneth McCoy near West Alexander, Pennsylvania. Samuel Cooper's father, Henry, a former slave, also helped transport fugitive slaves to Ohio until he became suspect. The evidence was so strong against him that the authorities were going to arrest him. Fearing that he might be kidnapped and returned to slavery, he left for Canada. There, he was greeted by Samuel, who earlier had moved to Canada. Naylor also left and went to Canada after years of assisting fugitive slaves. Others in Wheeling like Thomas Pointer and Tobe Hance remained, however, and maintained the Underground Railroad.

A prominent Underground Railroad station was the Wheeling House Hotel that stood at the northeast corner of 10th and Market streets. The landlord of the Wheeling House Hotel assisted fugitive slaves by sending them to nearby safe houses. On one occasion, he warned a fugitive slave named Charley that his master had arrived in Wheeling and directed him to a nearby safe house.

The main route from Wheeling went ten miles west to St. Clairsville, Ohio, then northwest to Cambridge and from there to Coshocton. This route was in operation as early as 1820. One of the men who hid fugitive slaves in Coshocton was a respected black man named Prior Foster. Fugitive slaves found refuge in his double shanty, and he accompanied them on the ferryboat across the Muskingum River to Hanging Rock. When it was safe to travel, they went on to New Castle in the northwest corner of Coshocton County. From Coshocton County routes went either to Cleveland or to Sandusky and then across Lake Erie to Canada.

Character of Settlers in Western Virginia

The people of northwestern Virginia often came from northern states and had little in common with wealthy slave owners in eastern Virginia. Historian Charles Ambler once wrote that there were few counties along the Ohio River and in northwestern Virginia that did not have abolitionist colonies. In Wheeling there were active abolitionists and an abolitionist newspaper, *The Wheeling Intelligencer*. In 1856, the 23-year-old abolitionist Archibald Campbell bought the *Intelligencer* and began an antislavery crusade. Young Campbell became a Republican and was a delegate at the GOP convention that nominated Abraham Lincoln for president.

As early as 1830, western Virginians were talking openly of seceding from Virginia because of their abolitionist beliefs. On October 1, 1830, a meeting was held in Wheeling to consider withdrawing from Virginia and affiliating with Maryland. Antislavery sentiment also began to grow in the 1830s. Finally, in 1863, two years after the start of the American Civil War, West Virginia severed all relations with Virginia and became an independent state.

—Cynthia Vogel

Further Reading

Charles L. Blockson, *Hippocrene Guide to the Underground Railroad* (New York: Hippocrene Books, 1994).

Wilbur H. Siebert, *The Underground Railroad from Slavery to Freedom* (1898; reprint, New York: Arno Press and *The New York Times*, 1968).

Wilbur H. Siebert, *The Mysteries of Ohio's Underground Railroads* (Columbus, OH: Long's College Book Company, 1951).

WILMINGTON, DELAWARE

Wilmington was perhaps the most active Underground Railroad station south of the Mason Dixon Line. Its proximity to the Line and to what was probably the most concentrated section of Underground Railroad stations in the nation made this inevitable. Hundreds of agents in Pennsylvania, in Chester and

Lancaster counties, which bordered Delaware, and in Philadelphia, just 25 miles from Wilmington, made this area a mecca for fugitive slaves. Abolition sentiment also had developed early in Wilmington, the first antislavery society being established there in 1789. Another society, The Abolition Society of the State of Delaware, formed in 1802, and reorganized in 1827.

Influence of Geography and Demographics

The geography and demographics of the state of Delaware also were favorable to making it an incomparable location for fugitive slaves to make their escape. Its terrain was very flat and there was a good highway system, leading to Wilmington; there were numerous small rivers, which served as avenues of transportation, both out of the bordering slave state, Maryland, and Delaware into the bay of Delaware; there was strong support from the Quaker, Methodist, and African-Methodist Episcopal denominations; and there was a large population of free blacks—nearly three times as many free blacks as slaves in the state in 1820, more than six times as many in 1850, and more than ten times as many by the time of the Civil War.

Thomas Garrett

These advantages were brought to their ultimate potential by the Quaker, Thomas Garrett. Born in Darby, Pennsylvania, only a short distance from Philadelphia, Garret inherited the disposition to aid fugitive slaves from his father. By the time he moved to Wilmington in 1822, he already was active in antislavery circles and joined abolition groups there. In 1827, he was one of the city's representatives along with John Wales at the National Convention of Abolitionists and by 1830 he was regularly aiding fugitive slaves.

Evidence that fugitive slave traffic through Delaware had become widespread by this time was reflected in the passage of state laws to prevent it that began in 1816, when a fine of $50 per day per individual assisted was levied on anyone found aiding a fugitive slave. A second state law increasing this penalty was passed in 1826. Additional penalties were later added in the years, 1837, 1849, 1852, and 1859.

A successful iron merchant, Garrett also opened a tobacco snuff factory and a shoe factory. Much of the profits of his industries went to support his work to aid fugitive slaves. He harbored them both at his home and at his snuff factory, and also provided those whom he helped with new shoes.

In 1845 he was involved in a famous incident in which he aided a family that included six fugitive slaves, and charges were brought against him and one of his collaborators, John Hunn of Odessa, Delaware. The charges were not brought until the following year, however, and the case went unresolved until 1848. Garrett was fined $5,400 and Hunn, $2,500— well over $100,000 for

Garrett by today's measures. At the close of the case, Garrett made one of the most defiant and famous statements in Underground Railroad history, when he proclaimed in court that despite his conviction he would continue to aid fugitive slaves as his conscience demanded of him. In fact, many friends came to his aid and helped him recoup his finances, and Garrett added a second story to his house, which he used to harbor fugitive slaves.

Wilmington Network

A large network of Underground Railroad agents was active in the Wilmington area, both black and white. Among them were Joseph G. Walker, whom some historians claim was Garrett's chief assistant, and who allegedly assisted 130 fugitive slaves during the fall of one year. Other important agents who have been mentioned in various accounts include Severn Johnson, Harry Craige, Davey Moore, and Samuel Burris, the notorious Delaware slave stealer who often went into Maryland to bring slaves to freedom and who was the conductor in the incident that led to the conviction of Garrett and Hunn. Burris himself was the subject of a notable incident after he was later caught conducting fugitive slaves and nearly sold into slavery, only to be saved by his fellow abolitionists. The African Union Church in Wilmington, which was founded by Rev. Peter Spencer of Wilmington, formerly a founding member of the AME Church, also is believed to have harbored fugitive slaves.

Others who have been mentioned in various listings as Underground Railroad collaborators with those in Wilmington include the Webb family of Benjamin, Thomas, and William, and Isaac S. Flint, a Quaker who operated a school for black children in Wilmington; William and Nat Brinkley, Abraham Gibbs, and Ezekiel Jenkins in Camden; and John Alston, Daniel Corbit, and Hunn of Odessa. William T. Kelley, whose father Jonah was a Delaware abolitionist, wrote the following about Hunn in 1898:

> In my day it has been more to John Hunn's labors and preaching that the Underground Railroad was kept running through Delaware and the Eastern Shore of Maryland than to any other person. After his marriage and settlement on a farm at or near Cantwell's Bridge, [today Odessa], in Delaware, hundreds flocked to him to save them from the galling chains of slavery. (Kelley 4)

Another notable Wilmington abolitionist, who moved to Chester County, Pennsylvania, in 1833, was Abraham Shadd, a shoemaker and the father of the abolitionist journalist Mary Shadd, who published *The Provincial Freeman* in Canada West, from 1853 to 1859. Shadd was one of six black founding members of the American Anti-Slavery Society and president of the National Negro Convention in 1833, and figured prominently in the Underground Railroad in West Chester, Pennsylvania.

A vast and well-connected network of Underground Railroad conductors in neighboring counties of Chester and Lancaster, Pennsylvania, waited just over the line. Among those known to collaborate closely with Garrett were Allen Agnew and his wife, Maria, with Allen sometimes conducting runaways from Garrett's home to Pennsylvania; John and Hannah Cox; Isaac and Dinah Mendenhall; Dr. Bartholomew Fussell; Graceanna Lewis; Elijah Pennypacker; and James Walker. Garrett also could call on his family: his cousins Benjamin Price and Samuel Rhoads; his brother Isaac and half brother Samuel; and his in-laws, the Mendinhalls.

Garrett had numerous options to call upon. He also was closely connected with the Philadelphia Vigilance Committee and numerous letters between him and William Still have survived and many were included in Still's book, *The Underground Railroad*. The following excerpt of one letter discusses the Wilmington agent, Henry Craige, a.k.a. Henry Craig:

Wilmington, 3mo. 23d, 1856 DEAR FRIEND, WILLIAM STILL:—Since I wrote thee this morning informing thee of the safe arrival of the Eight from Norfolk, Harry Craige had informed me, that he had a man from Delaware that he proposes to take along, who arrived since noon. He will take the man, woman and two children from here with him, and the four men will get in at Marcus Hook. Thee may take Harry Craige by the hand as a brother, true to the cause; he is one of our most efficient aids on the Rail Road, and worthy of full confidence. (Still 39)

Another prominent Underground Railroad conductor who took fugitive slaves through Wilmington was Harriet Tubman. She often stopped at Garrett's, and in the following letter, Garrett informs Miller McKim, Still's coworker at the vigilance committee office, that he had forwarded Tubman with seven fugitive slaves to them.

WILMINGTON, 12 mo, 29th, 1854.
ESTEEMED FRIEND, J. MILLER MCKIM: We made arrangements last night, and sent away Harriet Tubman, with six men and one woman to Allen Agnew's, to be forwarded across the country to the city. Harriet, and one of the men had worn their slices off their feet, and I gave them two dollars to help fit them out, and directed a carriage to be lured at my expense, to take them out, but do not yet know the expense. I now have two more from the lowest county in Maryland, on the Peninsula, upwards of one hundred miles. I will try to get one of our trusty colored men to take them to-morrow morning to the Anti-slavery office. (Still 296)

Means of Travel

Fugitive slaves moved to and from Wilmington on foot, in carriages, by boat, or by rail. The fastest way to get from Wilmington to Philadelphia and William Still's vigilance committee office was the train, or the "cars" as they were called. As early as 1838, the Philadelphia, Wilmington, and Baltimore Railroad connected Wilmington with Philadelphia. However, the trains were closely watched for fugitive slaves in Delaware and railroad employees caught helping them or allowing them to board faced severe penalties. So, if no slavecatchers were in close pursuit, Garrett sent fugitive slaves to Pennsylvania train stations in Chester or Marcus Hook. The steamboats that ran up the Delaware River from Wilmington north to Philadelphia also were used.

A number of ship captains brought fugitive slaves through the port of Wilmington. Runaways smuggled on boats to Wilmington were often put ashore at the Old Swedes Church where Garrett would send an agent to meet them. Alfred Fountain was the most prominent. In a four-year period from 1855 to 1859, Garrett mentioned six trips Captain Fountain made to Wilmington, bringing at least 50 fugitive slaves. At least two other seamen from Wilmington were known to be transporting fugitive slaves. William H. Lambdin, who had made a number of successful voyages with fugitive slaves, was caught with five runaways after he was shipwrecked during a hurricane following his departure from Norfolk in 1855. He was tried and sentenced to prison, where he was still lodged in 1858. William B. Baylis, the captain of the schooner *Keziah*, was caught with five fugitive slaves after leaving Petersburg, Virginia, on May 31, 1858. He too was tried and sentenced to prison, where he remained until 1865.

John Hunn's Journal

Interestingly, John Hunn kept a journal of his Underground Railroad activities. But on July 6, 1894, just before he died, he asked his son to destroy it. His son explained his wish as follows: "The issue was closed, and inasmuch as some of the

---

Thomas Garrett Inquires about Fugitive Slaves He Forwarded

This letter was written only a little more than a month after indictments were made against Thomas Garrett and John Hunn for their participation in aiding a party of 13 fugitive slaves in December 1845. There indictments led to their conviction and heavy fines in 1848. In this letter to Quaker Elijah Pennypacker in Phoenixville, Pennsylvania, dated July 5, 1846, which shows how Underground Railroad agents communicated, there is some confusion about who is the husband of the woman mentioned and whether or not she and her children finally reunited with him (James A. McGowan, *Stationmaster of the Underground Railroad*, McFarland and Company, 2005: 185):

Respected Friend, Elijah F. Pennypacker,

Thine of the 2nd, as well as a former letter, came duly to hand, and I at once answered the first letter, which it would appear thee has not receiv'd. I wrote thee, I think, that a few days after the husband left here, a woman with two children came to town and inform'd me that she was the woman that was left by her husband at John Hunn''s, to be forwarded to him as soon as he should get a situation. I then told her I heard nothing of him since he left. Some two or three days after, I received a letter from my brother, Edward, requesting me to have the woman and the children forwarded to Samuel Rhoads, near Waddingtonville. She and the children arrived safe there (the) next evening, one of my sons being there when they arrived. That was some 2 or 3 weeks since. There appears to be some mystery in this business, as I recollect no other man having a wife and children at John Hunn's. If there is any other person, I will make of John Hunn, inquiry—or thee has perhaps better write thyself to him. Direct thy letter to John Hunn, near Middletown, Delaware.

Thine respectfully, Thos. Garrett

---

actors in the affair were yet alive, and might be compromised thereby, he thought it best to cover the whole episode with oblivion" (Conrad, Henry C., *History of the State of Delaware*, Wilmington, Delaware, 1908: 558).

Perhaps a deeper understanding of Hunn's wishes can be derived from a comment he made in a letter to William Still about his Underground Railroad activities: "In this matter the course that I have pursued thus far through life has given me solid satisfaction. I ask no other reward for any efforts made by me in the cause, than to feel that I have been of use to my fellow men" (Still 713).

—Tom Calarco

Further Reading

William C. Kashatus, *Just over the Line* (West Chester, PA: Chester County Historical Society, 2002).

William T. Kelley, "The Underground Railroad in the Eastern Shore of Maryland and Delaware," *The Friends Intelligencer*, 55 (1898).

James A. McGowan, *Station Master on the Underground Railroad: The Life and Letters of Thomas Garrett* (Jefferson, NC: McFarland, revised edition, 2004).

R. C. Smedley, *History of the Underground Railroad in Chester and Neighboring Counties of Pennsylvania* (Lancaster, PA: John A. Hietand, 1883).

William Still, *The Underground Railroad* (Philadelphia: Porter and Coates, 1872).

William J. Switala, *The Underground Railroad in Pennsylvania* (Mechanicsburg, PA: Stackpole Books, 2001).

Z

ZANESVILLE, OHIO

Zanesville is the county seat of Muskingum County, located about 50 miles east of Columbus, Ohio. Its location on the Muskingum River made it an active stop on the Underground Railroad. The Muskingum River begins in Dresden, Ohio, and flows in a southern zigzag pattern, reaching the Ohio River at Marietta. In 1841, the Ohio-Erie Canal was finished from Dresden to Lake Erie, thus providing a continuous waterway from Marietta to Lake Erie, through Zanesville, Coshocton, New Philadelphia, Akron, and Cleveland. It was also located on the National Road west of Wheeling, Virginia, an important escape route for fugitive slaves fleeing from Virginia. At least 25 Muskingum County families risked punishment by operating stations on the Underground Railroad.

Local Agents

Many fugitive slaves crossed the Ohio River near Parkersburg or Point Pleasant and were conducted through Deavertown to Zanesville and westward to New Concord on the way to Bloomfield and Coshocton. The home of Thomas L. Gray, a harness maker in Deavertown was a stop on the Underground Railroad. One of Gray's trusted assistants was Rial Cheadle, teacher, peddler, keelboatman, and maker of pewter buttons. On peddling trips to the South, Cheadle posed as a half-wit and entertained the slaves with eccentric rhymes and songs. The plantation owners, fooled by Cheadle's behavior, saw no connection between his visits and the departure of their slaves. However, Cheadle always had several slaves with him when he returned home to Ohio and knocked at the door of friends and hummed softly, "I'm on my way to Canada, where colored men are free."

The first station one mile north of Deavertown was operated by Affadilla Deaver and his wife. The next stop was at the home of Henry Weller, then the home of Lydia Stokely, the store and tan yard of Andrew Dugan, and the Stokely farm. The safe houses were about two to three miles apart. Then the fugitive slaves found safety at the grist mill of Josephus Powell. Stations between this mill and Putnam were kept at the Five Mile House, and the William Wiley, Cyrus Merriam, and Jenkins homes.

The home of Nelson T. Gant, a former slave, still stands on Main Street in Zanesville. After being freed by the will of his Virginia master, Gant settled in Zanesville and became an active member of the Underground Railroad. Local lore states that Gant hid fugitive slaves in his vegetable wagon while taking them north to secret stops on the Underground Railroad and suggests that he helped free his brothers and sisters by transporting them in his wagon. Gant returned to Virginia and tried unsuccessfully to persuade the master of his wife to free her. When he tried to take Maria back to Zanesville, he was captured. A trial held in Leesburg, Virginia, resulted in his acquittal, with Quakers purchasing Maria's freedom. Gant became a well-respected and wealthy businessman in Zanesville. His house is one of the few homes of former slaves still standing in Muskingum County.

Located across the Muskingum River from Zanesville was the village of Putnam, now called South Zanesville. To understand the events that occurred between Zanesville and Putnam, one must understand their early history. Zanesville was settled by people from Virginia, Pennsylvania, and Maryland who had no objection to slavery. Putnam was settled by New Englanders who hated slavery with a religious zeal. Several buildings in Putnam are located in the Putnam Historic District that had many associations with antislavery activities and the Underground Railroad. One of the oldest churches was the Putnam Presbyterian Church, which still stands at 467 Woodlawn Avenue. The pastor of this church was Reverend William Beecher, brother of famed antislavery preacher Reverend Henry Ward Beecher and world-renowned author Harriet Beecher Stowe. William Beecher served this congregation from 1835 to 1839 and was known for his strong antislavery views.

The Guthrie brothers, Stephen Hand Guthrie, George Guthrie, Julius Guthrie, and Albert Austin Guthrie, were abolitionists who lived in Putnam. All but Julius were well-documented conductors on the Underground Railroad. A. A. Guthrie, the president of the Ohio Anti-Slavery Society in 1836, lived one block from the church on Woodlawn Avenue. Fugitive slaves were frequently hidden in the attic of the house of George Guthrie, also on Woodlawn Avenue. In one recorded incident, George's wife was sitting on her porch and knitting while slavecatchers rode by looking for fugitive slaves hidden in the attic of their home. Both of these houses are still standing.

Local history is preserved at the Putnam Underground Railroad Education (PURE) Center, located in the midst of several sites important to the abolitionist movement. The original house at 522 Woodlawn Avenue in the Putnam Historic District was constructed circa 1838. Prior to the Civil War, the New Englanders in Putnam organized the Muskingum County Abolition Society and this residence was the center of their activity. The house is directly across from the George Guthrie house; next door to the S. H. Guthrie House where abolitionist Stephen Guthrie slept with a pitchfork and two guns at the head of his bed; and diagonally across from the Putnam Presbyterian Church where the Reverend William Beecher preached antislavery sermons.

State Antislavery Conventions

Also located in the Putnam Historic District, on Jefferson Street, is the Stone Academy, one of the oldest and the most historic buildings in Muskingum County. Built in 1809, the Stone Academy was originally constructed to serve as a state house. However, Zanesville, not Putnam, was selected as the Ohio capital from 1810 to 1812. The Stone Academy also was used as a court, various private schools, a meetinghouse, and a church. In April 1835, the first state anti-slavery convention in Ohio was held there. It met with great opposition from local residents. A month before the convention, abolitionist orator Theodore Weld spoke at the Stone Academy. A mob from Zanesville stormed the building and hauled Weld into the street. But Putnam abolitionists rescued Weld and took him to the home of A. A. Guthrie. In anticipation of the convention, the pro-slavery mob burned barns and defaced buildings in Putnam in protest. Nevertheless, the Anti- Slavery Convention went on as scheduled on April 22, 1835.

This building was used again in May 1839 for a second Ohio Anti-Slavery Society Convention. Barns were again burned and the proslavery mob from Zanesville attacked the Stone Academy. In 1840, it became a private residence, and was used as a stop on the Underground Railroad. The Stone Academy is currently operated as a museum by the Pioneer and Historical Society of Muskingum County. The museum's most popular exhibit is a hidden trap door under the staircase leading to a crawl space where fugitive slaves could hide.

Located just north of Dresden, Ohio, in the northwest corner of Muskingum County is Prospect Place. Abolitionist George Willison Adams built this 29-room mansion in 1856. Adams's father, George Beal Adams, and his family (wife and 13 children) had migrated from Virginia to southeastern Ohio in 1808, freed their slaves and settled in Madison Township in Muskingum County. The younger George W. Adams and his brother, Edward, ran an Underground Railroad station from their flourmill that later became known as Adams Mills, Ohio. The brothers operated this flourmill on the Ohio and Erie Canal and owned warehouses, a boat yard, and a cooper shop in Dresden where they made barrels. When men from the Adams flourmill would deliver flour to New Orleans, Louisiana, they would return with fugitive slaves beneath the decks of their boats. After the passage of the Fugitive Slave Law of 1850, the Adams brothers moved their station to George's new home, the Prospect Place Mansion. The mansion still stands in Trinway, Ohio, and is listed on the National Register of Historic Places and the Ohio Underground Railroad Association's list of Underground Railroad sites.

Seven new historic markers have recently been installed to commemorate the Underground Railroad in the Muskingum River corridor that passed through Zanesville and Muskingum County. One of them focuses on the role of the Stone Academy and the Putnam community in the antislavery movement and Underground Railroad.

—Cynthia Vogel

Further Reading

Levi Coffin, *The Reminiscences of Levi Coffin* (Cincinnati: Robert Clark & Co., 1880).

E. Delorus Preston, Jr., "The Underground Railroad in Northwest Ohio." *Journal of Negro History*, 17, No. 4 (October 1932).

Norris Franz Schneider, *Y Bridge City: The Story of Zanesville and Muskingum County, Ohio* (The World Publishing Company, Cleveland and New York, 1950).

Wilbur Siebert, "A Quaker Section of the Underground Railroad in Northern Ohio," *Ohio History*, 39, No. 3 (July 1930).

Wilbur H. Siebert, *The Mysteries of Ohio's Underground Railroads* (Columbus, OH: Long's College Book Company, 1951).

Wilbur H. Siebert, *The Underground Railroad from Slavery to Freedom* (1898; reprint, New York: Arno Press and *The New York Times*, 1968).

J. Hope Sutor, *Past & Present History of the City of Zanesville and Muskingum County, Ohio* (S. J. Clarke Publishing Co., 1909).

SELECTED BIBLIOGRAPHY

General

Contemporary

Blockson, Charles L. *The Underground Railroad: First Person Narratives of Escapes from Slavery*. New York: Prentice Hall, 1987.

Bolster, W. Jeffrey. *Black Jacks: African American Seamen*. Cambridge: Harvard University Press, 1997.

Bordewich, Fergus. *Bound for Canaan*. New York: HarperCollins, 2005.

Calarco, Tom. *People of the Underground Railroad*. Westport, CT: Greenwood Press, 2008.

———. *The Underground Railroad in the Adirondack Region*. Jefferson, NC: McFarland, 2004.

Dempsey, Terrell, *Searching for Jim: Slavery in Sam Clemens' World*. Columbia: University of Missouri Press, 2003.

Gara, Larry. *The Liberty Line: The Legend of the Underground Railroad*. Lexington: University of Kentucky Press, 1967.

Griffler, Keith P. *Front Line of Freedom: African Americans and the Forging of the Underground Railroad in the Ohio Valley*. Lexington: University Press of Kentucky, 2004.

Grover, Kathryn. *The Fugitive's Gibraltar*. Amherst: University of Massachusetts Press, 2001.

Hagedorn, Ann. *Beyond the River*. New York: Simon & Schuster, 2002.

Harrold, Stanley. *Subversives: Antislavery Community in Washington, D.C.* Baton Rouge: Louisiana State University Press, 2003.

Hudson, J. Blaine. *Fugitive Slaves and the Underground Railroad in the Kentucky Borderlands*. Jefferson, NC: McFarland, 2001.

Hunter, Carol M. *To Set the Captives Free: Reverend Jermain Wesley Loguen and the Struggle for Freedom in Central New York, 1835–1872*. New York: Garland, 1993.

Kashatus, William C. *Just over the Line*. West Chester, PA: Chester County Historical Society, 2002.

Knepp, Gary L. *Freedom's Struggle: A Response to Slavery from the Ohio Borderlands*. Milford, OH: Little Miami Publishing Co., 2008.

Lindquist, Charles. *The Antislavery-Underground Railroad Movement: in Lenawee County, Michigan, 1830–1860*. Adrian, MI: Lenawee County Historical Society, 1999.

Merrill, Arch. *The Underground, Freedom's Road, and Other Upstate Tales.* New York: American Book-Stratford Press, 1963.

Muelder, Owen. *The Underground Railroad in Western Illinois.* Jefferson, NC: McFarland and Company, Inc., 2007.

Noble, Glenn. *John Brown and the Jim Lane Trail.* Broken Bow, NE: Purcells, 1977.

Peters, Pamela. *The Underground Railroad in Floyd County.* Jefferson, NC: McFarland, 2001.

Phelan, Helene C. *And Why Not Everyman? An Account of Slavery, the Underground Railroad, and the Road to Freedom in New York's Southern Tier.* Interlaken, NY: Heart of the Lakes Publishing, 1987.

Phillips, Christopher. *Freedom's Port: The African American Community of Baltimore, 1790–1860.* Urbana and Chicago: University of Illinois Press, 1997.

Pirtle, Carol. *Escape betwixt Two Suns: A True Tale of the Underground Railroad in Illinois.* Carbondale: Southern Illinois University Press, 2000.

Prince, Bryan. *I Came as a Stranger.* Toronto: Tundra Books, 2004.

———. *A Shadow on the Household: One Enslaved Family's Incredible Struggle for Freedom.* Toronto: McClellan and Stewart, Ltd. 2009.

Quarles, Benjamin. *Black Abolitionists.* New York: Oxford University Press, 1969.

Ricks, Mary Kay. *Escape on the Pearl.* New York: William Morrow, 2007.

Sernett, Milton. *North Star Country.* Syracuse: Syracuse University Press, 2002.

Siebert, Wilbur. *The Mysteries of Ohio's Underground Railroads.* Columbus, OH: Long's College Book Company, 1951.

———. *The Underground Railroad in Massachusetts.* Worcester: American Antiquarian Society, 1936.

———. *The Underground Railroad from Slavery to Freedom.* New York: Macmillan, 1898.

———. *Vermont's Anti-Slavery and Underground Railroad Record. 1937.* New York: Negro Universities Press, 1969.

Strother, Horatio. *The Underground Railroad in Connecticut.* Middletown, CT: Wesleyan University Press, 1962.

Switala, William J. *The Underground Railroad in Delaware, Maryland and West Virginia.* Mechanicsburg, PA: Stackpole Books, 2004.

———. *The Underground Railroad in New Jersey and New York.* Mechanicsburg, PA: Stackpole Books, 2006.

———. *The Underground Railroad in Pennsylvania.* Mechanicsburg, PA: Stackpole Books, 2001.

Historical

Cockrum, William M. *History of the Underground Railroad: As It Was Conducted by the Anti-Slavery League.* Oakland City, IN: J.M. Cockrum Press, 1915.

Johnson, H. U. *From Dixie to Canada: Romance and Realities in the Underground Railroad.* Buffalo: Charles Wells Moulton, 1894.

Mitchell, Rev. William M. *The Underground Railroad.* London: William Tweedie, 1860.

Northup, Solomon. *Twelve Years a Slave.* Edited by Sue Eakin and Joseph Logsdon. Baton Rouge: LSU Press, 1968 (1853).

Pettit, Eber. *Sketches in the History of the Underground Railroad.* Fredonia, NY: W. McKinstry & Son, 1879.

Smedley, R. C. *History of the Underground Railroad in Chester and Neighboring Counties of Pennsylvania.* Lancaster, PA, 1883.

Still, William. *The Underground Railroad.* Philadelphia: Porter & Coates, 1872.

Stowe, Harriet Beecher. *The Key to Uncle Tom's Cabin.* London: Clarke, Beeton, and Co., 1853.

Biographies

Contemporary

Danforth, Mildred E. *A Quaker Pioneer.* New York: Exposition Press, 1961.

Dann, Norman. *Practical Dreamer: Gerrit Smith and the Crusade for Reform.* Hamilton, NY: Log Cabin Books, 2009.

Hamilton, Virginia. *Anthony Burns: The Defeat and Triumph of a Fugitive Slave.* New York: Random House, 1988.

Harlow, Ralph Volney. *Gerrit Smith: Philanthropist and Reformer.* New York: Henry Holt & Co., 1938.

Hodges, Graham. *David Ruggles: A Radical Black Abolitionist and the Underground Railroad in New York City.* Chapel Hill: University of North Carolina Press, 2010.

McGowan, James A. *Station Master on the Underground Railroad: The Life and Letters of Thomas Garrett.* Rev. ed. Jefferson, NC: McFarland, 2004.

Pasternak, Martin B. *Rise Now and Fly to Arms: The Life of Henry Highland Garnet.* New York: Garland Publishers, 1995.

Ripley, C. Peter, ed. *The Black Abolitionist Papers.* 4 vols. Chapel Hill: University of North Carolina Press, 1991.

Runyon, Randolph Paul. *Delia Webster and the Underground Railroad.* Lexington: University Press of Kentucky, 1996.

Slaughter, Thomas B. *Bloody Dawn: The Christiana Riot and Racial Violence in the Antebellum North.* New York: Oxford University Press, 1991.

Stauffer, John. *The Black Hearts of Men.* Cambridge, MA: Harvard University Press, 2002.

Historical

Benedict, A. L. *Memoir of Richard Dillingham.* Philadelphia: Merrihew & Thompson, 1852.

Birney, William. *James G. Birney and His Times.* New York: D. Appleton and Company, 1890.

Bowditch, Vincent Y. *Life and Correspondence of Henry Ingersoll Bowditch.* Boston: Houghton, Mifflin & Company, 1902.

Brown, C. S. *Abel Brown Abolitionist.* Edited by Tom Calarco. Jefferson, NC: McFarland, 2006 (1849).

Child, L. Maria. *Isaac T. Hopper: A True Life.* Boston: John P. Jewett and Company, 1853.

Coffin, Levi. *Reminiscences of Levi Coffin.* Cincinnati, OH: Western Tract and Supply Co., 1876.

Douglass, Frederick Douglass. *Life and Times of Frederick Douglass.* Hartford, CT: Park Publishing Co., 1881.

————. *My Bondage and My Freedom*. New York: Miller, Orton, & Mulligan, 1855.

Fairbank, Calvin. *Rev. Calvin Fairbank during Slavery Times*. Chicago: Patriotic Publishing Co., 1890.

Frothingham, Octavius Brooks. *Gerrit Smith: A Biography*. New York: G.P. Putnam's Sons, 1878.

Haviland, Laura. *A Woman's Life-Work: Labors and Experiences of Laura S. Haviland*. Cincinnati: Walden & Stowe, 1882.

Hensel, W. U. *The Christiana Riot and the Treason Trials of 1851*. Lancaster, PA: The New Era Printing Co., 1911.

Lee, Luther. *Autobiography of Luther Lee*. New York: Phillips & Hunt, 1882.

Lovejoy, J. C. *Memoir of Rev. Charles T. Torrey, Who Died in the Penitentiary of Maryland, Where He Was Confined for Showing Mercy to the Poor*. Boston: John P. Jewett & Co., 1847.

May, Samuel J. *Some Recollections of Our Anti-slavery Conflict*. Boston: Fields, Osgood & Co., 1869.

Ray, Florence T. *Sketch of the Life of Rev. Charles B. Ray*. New York: Press of J. J. Little & Co., 1887.

Ritchie, Andrew. *The Soldier, the Battle, and the Victory: Being a Brief Account of the Work of Rev. John Rankin in the Anti-slavery Cause*. Cincinnati: Western Tract and Book Society, 1868.

Ross, Alexander Milton. *Memoirs of a Reformer*. Toronto: Hunter, Rose, 1893.

Sprague, Stuart Seely, ed. *His Promised Land: The Autobiography of John Parker*. New York: W.W. Norton and Co., 1996 (1880).

Todd, John. *Early Settlement and Growth of Western Iowa or Reminiscences*. Des Moines: Iowa Historical Department, 1906.

Fugitive Slaves

Contemporary

Brode, Patrick. *The Odyssey of John Anderson*. Toronto: Toronto University Press, 1989.

Christianson, Scott. *Freeing Charles*. Champaign: University of Illinois Press, 2010.

Collison, Gary L. *Shadrach Minkins: From Fugitive Slave to Citizen*. Cambridge: Harvard University Press, 1997.

Hill, Daniel. *The Freedom Seekers*. Toronto: Stoddardt Publishing, 1981.

Ruggles, Jeffrey. *The Unboxing of Henry Brown*. Richmond: Library of Virginia, 2003.

Weisenburger, Steven. *Modern Medea*. New York: Hill and Wang, 1998.

Winks, Robin W. *The Blacks in Canada*. Montreal: McGill-Queen's University Press, 1971.

Historical

Drew, Benjamin. *A North-Side View of Slavery. The Refugee: Or the Narratives of Fugitive Slaves in Canada. Related by Themselves, with an Account of the History and Condition of the Colored Population of Upper Canada*. Boston: John P. Jewett and Company, 1856.

Howe, Samuel G. *The Refugees from Slavery in Canada West: Report to the Freedmen's Inquiry Commission.* Boston: Wright & Potter, 1864.

May, Samuel J. *The Fugitive Slave Law and Its Victims.* New York: American Anti-Slavery Society, 1861.

McDougall, Marion Gleason. *Fugitive Slaves (1619–1865).* Boston: Ginn & Co., 1891.

Pickard, Kate E. R. *The Kidnapped and the Ransomed: Being the Personal Recollections of Peter Still and His Wife "Vina," after Forty Years of Slavery.* New York and Auburn: Miller, Orton and Mulligan, 1856.

Stevens, Charles Emery. *Anthony Burns: A History.* Boston: John P. Jewett & Company, 1856.

Slave Narratives

Anderson, William. *Life and Narrative of William J. Anderson, Twenty-Four Years a Slave; Sold Eight Times! In Jail Sixty Times!! Whipped Three Hundred Times!!! Or the Dark Deeds of American Slavery Revealed . . .* Chicago: Daily Tribune Book and Job Printing Office, 1857.

Bibb, Henry. *Narrative of the Life and Adventures of Henry Bibb, an American Slave.* New York: Published by Author, 1850.

Brown, Henry. *Narrative of Henry Box Brown, Who Escaped from Slavery Enclosed in a Box Three Feet Long, Two Wide, and Two and a Half High.* Boston: Brown & Stearns, 1849.

———. *Narrative of the Life of Henry Box Brown.* Manchester, England: Lee and Glynn, 1851.

Brown, William Wells. *Narrative of William W. Brown, an American Slave.* London: Charles Gilpin, 1849.

Craft, William. *Running a Thousand Miles for Freedom; or, the Escape of William and Ellen Craft from Slavery.* London: William Tweedie, 1860.

Documenting the South, University of North Carolina, http://docsouth.unc.edu/browse/author/. This Web site includes all of the following narratives plus many more—all of which can be downloaded for viewing.

Henson, Josiah. *An Autobiography of the Rev. Josiah Henson ("Uncle Tom"). From 1789 to 1881.* London, Ontario: Schuyler, Smith, & Co., 1881.

Jacobs, Harriet. *Incidents in the Life of a Slave Girl.* Boston, Mineola, New York: Dover Publications, Inc., 2001 (1861).

Loguen, J. W. *The Rev. J. W. Loguen as a Slave and as a Freeman.* New York: Negro Universities Press, 1968 (1859).

Smallwood, Thomas. *A Narrative of Thomas Smallwood, Giving an Account of His Birth—The Period He Was Held in Slavery—His Release—and Removal to Canada, etc. Together with an Account of the Underground Railroad.* Toronto: James Stephens, printer, 1851.

Steward, Austin. *Twenty-Two Years a Slave, and Forty Years a Freeman; Embracing a Correspondence of Several Years, while President of Wilberforce Colony, London, Canada West.* Rochester, NY: William Alling, 1857.

Twelvetrees, Harper, ed. *Story of the Life of John Anderson, the Fugitive Slave.* London: William Tweedie, 1863.

Ward, Samuel Ringgold. *Autobiography of a Fugitive Negro: His Anti-slavery Labours in the United States, Canada, and England.* London: John Snow, 1855.

Slavecatchers

Campbell, Stanley W. *The Slave Catchers 1850–1860.* Chapel Hill: University of North Carolina Press, 1970.
Wilson, Carol. *Freedom at Risk: The Kidnapping of Free Blacks in America—1780–1865.* Lexington: University of Kentucky Press, 1994.

John Brown

Carton, Evan. *Patriotic Treason: John Brown and the Soul of America.* New York: Simon and Schuster, 2006.
DeCaro, Louis A. *"Fire from the Midst of You": A Religious Life of John Brown.* New York: New York University Press, 2002.
———. *John Brown—the Cost of Freedom.* International Publishers, 2007.
———. *John Brown: The Man Who Lived.* Lulu, 2009.
Hearn, Chester G. *Companions in Conspiracy.* Gettysburg, PA: Thomas Publications, 1996.
Hinton, Richard J. *John Brown and His Men with Some Account of the Roads They Traveled to Reach Harper's Ferry.* New York: Funk & Wagnalls, 1894.
Libby, Jean. *John Brown Photo Chronology.* Palo Alto, CA: Allies for Freedom, 2009.
Oates, Stephen B. *To Purge This Land with Blood: A Biography of John Brown.* New York: Harper & Row, 1970.
Redpath, James. *The Public Life of Capt. John Brown.* Boston: Thayer and Eldridge, 1860.
Renehan, Edward J. *The Secret Six: The True Tale of the Men Who Conspired with John Brown.* New York: Crown Publishers, 1995.
Reynolds, David S. *John Brown, Abolitionist: The Man Who Killed Slavery, Sparked the Civil War.* New York: Random House, 2005.
Sanborn, F. B. *The Life and Letters of John Brown; Liberator of Kansas, and Martyr of Virginia.* Concord, MA: F. B. Sanborn, 1885.
Stavis, Barrie. *John Brown: The Sword and the Word.* New York: A. S. Barnes and Company, 1970.
Villard, Oswald Garrison. *John Brown, 1800–1859: A Biography Fifty Years.* Boston: Houghton Mifflin, 1910.

Harriet Tubman

Clinton, Catherine. *The Road to Freedom.* Boston: Little, Brown, 2004.
Humez, Jean McMahon. *Harriet Tubman: The Life and the Life Stories.* Madison: University of Wisconsin Press, 2003.
Larson, Kate Clifford. *Bound for the Promised Land: Portrait of an American Hero.* New York: Ballantine Books, 2004.

Articles

Bailey, William S. "The Underground Railroad in Southern Chautauqua County." *New York History*, New York Historical Society (1935).

Cecelski, David. "The Shores of Freedom: The Maritime Underground Railroad in North Carolina, 1800–1861." *North Carolina Historical Review* 1, no. 2 (April 1994).

Lumpkin, Katherine DuPre, "The General Plan Was Freedom: A Negro Secret Order on the Underground." *Phylon* 28, no. 1 (1967).

Meaders, Daniel. "Kidnapping Blacks in Philadelphia: Isaac Hopper's Tales of Oppression." *Journal of Negro History* 80, no. 2 (Spring 1995).

Ohio History Index. "Abolition Movement" and "Underground Railroad." http://publications.ohiohistory.org/ohstemplate.cfm?action=index.

Okur, Nilgun. "Underground Railroad in Philadelphia, 1830–1860." *Journal of Black Studies* 25 (May 1995).

Preston, Jr., E. Delorus. "The Underground Railroad in Northwest Ohio." *Journal of Negro History*, 17, no. 4 (October 1932).

Pritchard, James M. "Into the Fiery Furnace: Anti-slavery Prisoners in the Kentucky State Penitentiary 1844–1870. http://www.ket.org/underground/research/prichard.htm.

Watts, Ralph M. "History of the Underground Railroad in Mechanicsburg." *Ohio History*, 34 (1934).

Monographs

Contemporary

Coon, Diane Perrine. *Southeastern Indiana's Underground Railroad Routes and Operations*. A Project of the State of Indiana, Dept. of Natural Resources, Division of Historic Preservation and Archaeology and the U.S. Dept. of the Interior, NPS, April 2001.

Crenshaw, Gwendolyn. *Bury Me in a Free Land: The Abolitionist Movement in Indiana*. Indianapolis: Indiana Historical Bureau, 1993.

Grover, Kathryn, and Janine da Silva. *Historic Resource Study: Boston African American National Historic Site*. Boston: National Parks Service, 2002.

Zirblis, Raymond Paul. *Friends of Freedom*. Montpelier, VT: Vermont Division of Historic Preservation, 1996.

Historical

Bearse, Austin. *Reminiscences of Fugitive Slave Days in Boston*. Boston: Warren Richarson, 1880.

Parker, William. "The Freedman's Story." *The Atlantic Monthly*, February–March 1866.

Sloane, Rush R. "The Underground Railroad of the Firelands." *The Firelands Pioneer*. Norwalk, OH: The Historical Society, 1888.

Tibbetts, John Henry. "Reminiscences of Slavery Times." Unpublished memoir written in 1888.

Williams, Harold Parker. *Brookline in the Anti-slavery Movement*. Brookline, MA: Brookline Historical Publication Society, Publication Number 18, 1899.

Indexes

Blassingame, John W., and Mae G. Henderson, eds. *Antislavery Newspapers and Periodicals*. 5 vols. Boston: G.K. Hall, 1980–1984.

Archives

American Antiquarian Society, 185 Salisbury Street, Worcester, MA 01609-1634. www.americanantiquarian.org.

Boston Public Library, 700 Boyleston Street, Boston, MA 02116. www.bpl.org.

Gerrit Smith Papers, Special Collections Research Center, Syracuse University Library, 222 Waverly Avenue, Syracuse, NY 13244-2010. http://scrc.syr.edu.

New York Public Library, Schomburg Center for Research in Black Culture, 515 Malcolm X Boulevard, New York, NY 10037-1801. www.nypl.org/.

Pennsylvania Abolition Society papers, 1748–1979 (includes William Still papers, 1852–1902). Historical Society of Pennsylvania,1300 Locust Street, Philadelphia, PA 1910. www.hsp.org.

Wilbur Henry Siebert Collection, The Ohio Historical Society, 1982 Velma Avenue, Columbus, OH 43211. www.ohiohistory.org.

Wilbur H. Siebert Collection. Houghton Library, Harvard Yard, Harvard University Cambridge, MA 02138. www.hcl.harvard.edu/libraries/houghton/.

Museums and Organizations

Albany, New York Underground Railroad, http://www.ugrworkshop.com/.

Boston African American National Historic Site, http://www.nps.gov/boaf/index.htm

Buxton National Historic Site and Museum, N. Buxton, Ontario, http://www.buxtonmuseum.com/.

Hanby House, http://ohsweb.ohiohistory.org/places/c02/index.shtml.

Historic Eleutherian College, Lancaster, Indiana, http://www.eleutherian.us/.

John P. Parker House, Ripley, Ohio, http://www.johnparkerhouse.org/.

Kennett Underground Railroad Center, Kennett Square, Pennsylvania, http://undergroundrr.kennett.net/.

The LeMoyne House, Washington, Pennsylvania, http://www.wchspa.org/html/house.htm.

Levi Coffin House, Fountain City, Indiana, http://www.waynet.org/levicoffin/default.htm.

Nathaniel Dett Memorial Chapel and Norval Johnson Heritage Center, Niagara Falls, Ontario, http://www.njheritage.ca/.

The National Abolition Hall of Fame and Museum, Peterboro, New York, http://www.abolitionhof.org/index.php.

The North Country Underground Railroad Historical Association, Plattsburgh, New York, http://www.northcountryundergroundrailroad.com/NCUGRHA_Clinton_hp.htm.

Onondaga Historical Association Museum, Syracuse, New York, Permanent Underground Railroad exhibit, "Freedom Bound," http://www.cnyhistory.org/PermExhibits.html.

Owen Lovejoy Homestead, Princeton, Illinois, http://www.lovejoyhomestead.com/.

Pathways to Freedom: Maryland and the Underground Railroad, http://pathways.thinkport.org/aboutsite/.

The Rankin House, Ripley, Ohio, http://www.ripleyohio.net/htm/rankin.htm.

Dr. Richard Eels House, Quincy, Illinois, http://www.nps.gov/history/Nr/travel/underground/il3.htm.

Sandusky Underground Railroad Education Center, Sandusky, Ohio, http://www.sanduskyundergroundrailroad.org/.

The Stowe House, Cincinnati, Ohio, http://ohsweb.ohiohistory.org/places/sw18/index.shtml.

Uncle Tom's Cabin Historic Site, Dresden, Ontario, http://www.uncletomscabin.org/.

Web sites

The Abolitionist Tour, Warsaw, New York, http://warsawhistory.org/tours/tour2.html.

The African American Mosaic, http://www.loc.gov/exhibits/african/intro.html.

The African American Pamphlet Collection, Library of Congress, http://lcweb2.loc.gov/ammem/aapchtml/aapchome.html.

Afrolumensproject, Central Pennsylvania Underground Railroad, http://www.afrolumens.org/ugrr/whoswho/main.html.

American Abolitionism, http://americanabolitionist.liberalarts.iupui.edu/index.htm.

The Black Abolitionist Archive, Collection of the University of Detroit's Mercy Libraries, http://research.udmercy.edu/find/special_collections/digital/baa/.

BlackPast.org, http://www.blackpast.org/.

Connecticut Freedom Trail, http://www.visitconnecticut.com/freedom.html.

Cornell University/*Friend of Man*, New York State Anti-Slavery Society weekly, http://newspapers.library.cornell.edu/collect/FOM/index.php.

Cornell University, the Samuel J. May Collection, http://dlxs.library.cornell.edu/m/mayantislavery/.

Electronic Journals for African American Studies, http://www2.lib.udel.edu/subj/blks/ej.htm.

Flight to Freedom: Emeline's Story, http://history.delaware.gov/freedom/default.shtml.

Gerrit Smith Virtual Museum, http://library.syr.edu/digital/exhibits/g/GerritSmith/, http://www.wvculture.org/history/wvmemory/imlsintro.html.

John Brown and the Valley of the Shadow, http://www2.iath.virginia.edu/jbrown/master.html.

John Brown/Boyd B. Stutler Collection Database, West Virginia State Archives, http://www.wvculture.org/history/wvmemory/imlsintro.html.

The Liberator Files, http://www.theliberatorfiles.com/.

National Parks Service Underground Railroad sites, http://www.nps.gov/history/nr/travel/underground/states.htm.

The Oswego County Underground Railroad, http://www.oswego.edu/ugrr/contents.html.

Primary Research.org, "Selected Articles from Garrison's *The Liberator*," http://www.primaryresearch.org/bh/liberator/vasearch.php?all=%22adelphic%20union%22.

Slavery in America—Directory of Online Resources, http://www.academicinfo.net/africanamslavery.html.

Story of the Black Seminoles, http://www.johnhorse.com/trail/index.htm.

The Underground Railroad Free Press, http://urrfreepress.com/.

The Underground Railroad in Northwest Ohio, http://www.rootsweb.ancestry.com/~ohfulton/UNDERGROUNDRAILROADOFNWOHIO.htm.

The Underground Railroad Living Museum, http://www.the-ugrr.org/index.asp.

Uncovering the Freedom Trail in Syracuse and Onondaga County, http://www.pacny.net/freedom_trail/.

Underground Railroad Research Forum, http://www.afrigeneas.com/forum-ugrr/index.cgi.

World Wide Web Virtual Library, http://vlib.iue.it/history/USA/african-american.html.

INDEX

Note: This index was prepared with the Underground Railroad researcher in mind. It is fuller than the standard index and includes categories that target the interests of researchers: for example, page numbers that identify the Underground Railroad participation of certain church denominations and listings for slaveholders, slavecatchers, court cases involving fugitive slaves, boats used to convey fugitive slaves, fugitive slaves, fugitive slave rescues, and listings by state from which a fugitive slave escaped. Lists of individuals involved in the Underground Railroad in a locality have been collected with the locality listing, following the abbreviation UGRR for Underground Railroad; however, unless the individuals have greater significance, they are not given separate listings. Page numbers in **bold** indicate main entries in the encyclopedia.

Wright, Phoebe Wierman, 312
Wright, RPG, 5, 365
Wright, Samuel G., diary, 133, 134
Wright, Theodore S., 6, 215, 217, 332
Wright, William, 312, 313, 314, 356
Writ of Habeas Corpus, 2, 231, 319

Xenia, OH, 72, 158, 176

York, PA, 313
York County, PA, 309, 311
Young, Rev. Joshua, 181–82, 184, 345

Young's Prairie, MI, 45
Ypsilanti, MI, 96

Zanesville, OH, **376–79**; UGRR: Rial
Cheadle, Affadilla Deaver, Andrew
Dugan, Nelson T. Gant, Thomas L.
Gray, Guthrie family, Jenkins family,
Cyrus Merriam, Josephus Powell,
Lydia Stokely, William Wiley,
376–77
Zion Baptist Church (Cincinnati), 60,
65, 66

About the Authors and Contributors

Lead Author

Tom Calarco is the year 2008 winner of the *Underground Railroad Free Press* award for his contributions to the advancement of knowledge in the field of Underground Railroad history. *Places of the Underground Railroad* is his fifth book on the topic, which also include the reference volume, *People of the Underground Railroad* (2008), and *The Underground Railroad in the Adirondack Region* (2004), which documented the existence of the Underground Railroad in eastern New York, moving it from legend to fact.

Co-Authors

Cynthia Vogel is a retired educator, having taught mathematics in several high schools and a community college in Ohio. She holds degrees from Ohio University (AB in psychology) and Wright State University (M.Ed. in mathematics education). Ms. Vogel has written two non-fiction books, *Civil War Women: They Made a Difference*, and *Civil War Women: They Made a Difference, Book II*. She regularly presents programs on the women of the Civil War period as well as the Underground Railroad activity in Ohio and neighboring states. She recently presented a five-week class at the University of Dayton on "Places of the Underground Railroad."

Kathryn Grover is the author of *The Fugitive's Gibraltar: Escaping Slaves and Abolitionism in New Bedford, Massachusetts* (University of Massachusetts Press, 2001) and *Make a Way Somehow: African American Life in a Northern Community, 1790–1864* (Syracuse University Press, 1994). She is co-author of a National Register of Historic Places context statement on the Underground Railroad in Massachusetts and of numerous National Register and National Historic Landmark nominations for Underground Railroad–associated properties.

Rae Hallstrom is fascinated by the human aspect of Underground Railroad history—the true tales of perseverance, cooperation, and ingenuity in the face of bigotry and greed. She is a freelance writer, engineer, Ameriku®, artist and founder of Ameriku, Ltd., in Ohio. Her trademarked, nature-oriented art may be purchased through her website at http://www.ameriku.com. This is her first book on the Underground Railroad.

Sharron L Pope is a freelance writer and a playwright who lives in Cincinnati, Ohio, with her husband Alfred. She has always had an interest in African-American history and the journeys of the Underground Railroad. Her desire is to follow the path into antiquity and forward to this present-day recognizing the African-American journey.

Melissa Waddy-Thibodeaux is an author, professional actor/historical re-enactor, and CEO of her own production company specializing in history and literacy. She tours extensively throughout the United States and abroad, lecturing to schools, colleges and universities, churches and military bases, educating her audiences about issues pertaining to the Underground Railroad and the life and times of those who assisted fugitive slaves, especially Harriet Ross Tubman Davis, as well as other women who made a difference in American history.

Contributors

David A. Anderson, Ph.D., crafts highly regarded living history programs and Underground Railroad tours conducted by the Rochester, New York–based Akwaaba: the Heritage Associates, Inc., and often takes on the role of Frederick Douglass. He is Chairman of the Rochester-Monroe County Freedom Trail Commission, has served as Visiting Community Scholar at Monroe County Community College since 2007, and was awarded the *Underground Railroad Free Press* Leadership Award in 2008.

Don Papson is president and co-founder of the North Country Underground Railroad Association in New York State. A resident of Plattsburgh, New York, he is an expert on black history in the Adirondack Region and Vermont, and lectures widely on topics related to the Underground Railroad in New York and New England.

Betty Ann Smiddy is an award-winning author of local history, a native Cincinnatian, and graduate of the University of Cincinnati. She has written two books for Arcadia Publications: Cincinnati's Golden Age, Cincinnati's Great Disasters. Her book on the history of the community of College Hill, Ohio, *A Little Piece of Paradise*, including a chapter on the Underground Railroad, is available for free at her website: www.SamuelHannaford.info.

973.7115 Calarco, Tom,
C   1947-

           Places of the
           Underground
           Railroad. MAY 13 2011

DATE			